OUR LEGAL SYSTEM
AND
HOW IT OPERATES

Da Capo Press Reprints in

AMERICAN CONSTITUTIONAL AND LEGAL HISTORY

GENERAL EDITOR: LEONARD W. LEVY

Claremont Graduate School

OUR LEGAL SYSTEM
AND
HOW IT OPERATES

Five Lectures Delivered at the University of Michigan
February 23, 24, 25, 26, and 27, 1948
On the Thomas M. Cooley Lectureship
Enlarged and Revised

By Burke Shartel

DA CAPO PRESS · NEW YORK · 1971

Library of Congress Cataloging in Publication Data

Shartel, Burke, 1889-
    Our legal system and how it operates.
    (Da Capo Press reprints in American constitutional
and legal history)
    Originally published as one of the Michigan
legal studies.
        1. Law — U.S. — Addresses, essays, lectures.
    2. Jurisprudence — Addresses, essays, lectures.
    I. Title. II. Series: Michigan legal studies.
    KF380.S43   1971   340'.0973   73-173666
    ISBN 0-306-70411-0

This Da Capo Press edition of *Our Legal System and How It Operates*
is an unabridged republication of the first edition
published in Ann Arbor, Michigan, in 1951. It is reprinted by
special arrangement with the University of Michigan Law School.

Published by Da Capo Press, Inc.
A Subsidiary of Plenum Publishing Corporation
227 West 17th Street, New York, New York 10011

MICHIGAN LEGAL STUDIES

OUR LEGAL SYSTEM
AND
HOW IT OPERATES

OUR LEGAL SYSTEM
AND
HOW IT OPERATES

Five lectures delivered at the University of Michigan
February 23, 24, 25, 26, and 27, 1948 on
the Thomas M. Cooley Lectureship
enlarged and revised

---

by

BURKE SHARTEL

Ann Arbor
UNIVERSITY OF MICHIGAN LAW SCHOOL
1951

To my Mother

Preface for the Initiated Reader [1]

I. NEED FOR INTRODUCTORY WORK

Throughout the nineteenth century Blackstone's *Commentaries* was used everywhere in the United States as a first book for legal study. Doubtless this work served very well in the period immediately following the Revolution. Blackstone gave an exposition of the English law as it stood right after the middle of the eighteenth century. Our law had its origin in English law, and the prime task of American lawyers and judges was to adapt that law to our conditions. But by the end of the first decade of the twentieth century, almost everyone had come to see that Blackstone was no longer a suitable text for the use of American law students, for two reasons: First, a century and a half of development had so transformed the American scene that the study of Blackstone had become a study of historical antiquities; or perhaps one should say, a study in comparative law—a comparison of English law in the eighteenth century with American law in the twentieth. Second, one of the most characteristic features of American law was our constitutional organization; written constitutions and the judicial power of review over legislation permeated everything that the American lawyer did and must know; Blackstone knew nothing of these institutions. For these and perhaps other reasons the use of Blackstone was everywhere abandoned.

[1] This *Preface* is intended for the information of the person already trained in the law—lawyer, judge, or law teacher. I shall also have occasion now and then in the later chapters to include some side remarks for the ear of the initiated reader. These will be put in special footnotes indicated by an asterisk and introduced with the initials: I.R. The ordinary footnotes, which are intended for the beginning law student and which accompany the text, will be numbered in the usual manner.

Since then, there has been a great deal of talk about the need for some kind of introductory book to fill the place once occupied by Blackstone. But until very recently all this talk was like the common talk of the weather—nobody did anything about it. This was remarkable in view of the fact that in all other important fields of human knowledge such as economics and sociology one finds a plenitude of introductory treatises, and in view of the further fact that in civil law countries of Europe and South America the study of law invariably begins with some kind of introductory course. Indeed, it is always a matter of astonishment to civilian lawyers who come to this country to study American law and who ask to be referred to an elementary text on the subject, to be told that there is no such book.

Of the American student's need for an introduction to the legal system there can be little doubt. For the last several decades the beginning student has been projected into the midst of the law as a person might be thrown into the river, and told to swim. He started reading cases and discussing legal problems without any preliminary explanation of the character or operation or aims of the legal system. If any explanation at all was given, it was furnished quite informally and one-sidedly by individual instructors at the commencement of particular courses such as Contracts, Torts, Crimes, etc. That some students lost heart and failed because of the lack of introductory assistance is not improbable; it is certain that many remained confused and bewildered throughout a large part of their first year's work.[2]

[2] Compare the following from the preface to DOWLING, PATTERSON and POWELL, MATERIALS FOR LEGAL METHOD vii (1946):

"Both teachers and students in American law schools have long regretted the groping and confusion of beginning students when thrown simultaneously into three to five courses presenting, principally through collections of cases, as many different branches of substantive and procedural law. The instructor in each of these courses has heretofore found it necessary either to 'break in' the student by devoting much time to what is here called 'legal method,' or to plunge ahead in his subject with the hope that the student would somehow or other, by the end of the course, acquire a minimum understanding of legal

In the last few years different law schools have attempted to meet the need for some sort of introductory work on law, among them the school to which I am attached. The present volume is the fourth version of my efforts to produce a suitable book of this character. A substantial part of the material was delivered two years ago in a series of public lectures, known as the Cooley Lectures. Revised and enlarged, it is now published as the third volume in the annual series which bears that name.

2. WHAT KIND OF INTRODUCTION

As these materials are not quite like others that I have seen, I feel that it is incumbent on me to refer briefly to possible types of introductory courses which are, or which might be, adopted; and to give the reasons for the particular approach that I have chosen and for the particular materials here offered.

A study of the history of legal institutions may be undertaken by way of introducing the beginner to the study of law. Such historical study is very useful to the lawyer and therefore has a proper place in any legal or prelegal curriculum.[3] In fact I see no objection to the inclusion of

method. Either of these practices is believed to be wasteful of effort and likely to delay unduly the progress made by the great majority of students in the class. The institution of a course on Legal Method and the preparation of this volume as the basis for such a course, are founded on the belief that the job of introducing the student to the study of law can be more efficiently done by concentrating upon it at the outset."

[3] On the subject of historical introductions I can not refrain from referring to Holmes' *Common Law* (1881), a book frequently recommended in bibliographies for prelegal, and legal, reading. I defer to no one in my admiration for this author, and yet I believe this book is equally unsuited for perusal by prelegal students and by beginning law students. The *Common Law* was written seventy years ago. Its good analytical passages are blended with much antiquarian material in a way to make the book confusing and difficult for the beginner. Its use for an introduction to law is to my mind like starting piano lessons with Beethoven's *Appassionata Sonata*. Furthermore, even as legal history the *Common Law* is no longer satisfactory. No legal historian today would express the views, or choose the material for discussion, which Holmes did. All historians recognize that history needs to be rewritten every few decades. Finally, Holmes' views regarding the role of historical study changed

historical study of this sort in the first year of the law course if room can be found for it there. My only question is whether historical study provides the beginning law student with what he needs most. I am convinced that it does not. What is needed at the outset of legal study is a general picture of the legal system, an analytical and functional view of the American "system as is."

The sociology of law, laying special emphasis on the development and social background of the legal system, has also been used to introduce first year students to the study of law. No doubt a knowledge of sociology, like a knowledge of history, is important to the lawyer. The law student will profit immensely from prelegal preparation in sociology. The law teacher should be able and ready to make applications of sociological doctrine to legal materials whenever the opportunity for so doing arises.[4] Furthermore, I believe wholeheartedly in including in the second or third year of the law curriculum a course or seminar which will treat the relations of law and society. But all this does not add up to the conclusion that the legal neophyte needs to begin his work in law with sociological material. Before he can appreciate the sociology of law he ought to have acquired at least a faint general picture of the legal system itself.

Even more questionable than the use of legal history and of sociology of law as ways of introducing the student to legal study, is the use of legal philosophy for this purpose.

radically in the course of his life. At the time when he wrote the *Common Law* he was more or less imbued with an attitude which stressed history for its own sake. Two decades later he looked at the study of history functionally; he could warn of the danger of antiquarianism and declare that legal history is not important except as it gives us light for the conscious and intelligent development of our law. Only so far as man knows nothing better is he bound to adhere to the past; in Holmes' classical phrase (in a speech delivered in 1895), "Historic continuity with the past is not a duty but only a necessity." *Collected Legal Papers* 139 (1920). Certainly we can not blame the illustrious author for the uncritical use which later generations of teachers have made of his early work.

[4] In this sense I have introduced some essential sociological background in the material which follows.

To put legal philosophy at the start of the law course is to put the cart before the horse. While I appreciate the importance of sound theory and careful analysis and while I appreciate that every lawyer will have a philosophy of law whether he knows it or not and will be well advised to make his philosophy explicit, I do not believe that it is advisable for the law student to begin with a consideration of legal philosophy. Philosophy and criticism of legal ideas, so far as they are to be introduced into legal study, belong well along in the student's training rather than at the beginning.[5]

3. The Material Here Presented

What is the nature of the material here presented? How does it differ from the types of introductory material just mentioned?

First, it is descriptive of the American legal system as it now exists, not of past law and not of legal systems in general.

Second, it portrays the legal system as an operating institution. I have made use of two basic ideas: acts and patterns for action, both sufficiently familiar to the beginning student. I have analyzed the operation of the legal system in terms of acts of individuals and officials and in terms of standards intended to control these acts. Too often legal writers of the past have analyzed in terms of high order abstractions which eliminate all elements of human activity and the guidance of human action. Acts and guidance are, to my mind, the most important features of a legal system.

Third, I have given a large place to the discussion of language in relation to law. Language is the lawyer's primary

[5] Like the study of comparative law, which introduces conceptions of other legal systems and presupposes an existing fund of legal conceptions with which to make comparisons, a critical study of general theory presupposes a fund of general ideas to be criticized and analyzed. By the time we reach section 7–45 of this course—where a brief excursion into legal philosophy is made—the student will have acquired such a fund of ideas.

tool. He works with it at every turn. A realistic discussion of the operation of our legal system must be based on an understanding of the communicative processes.

Fourth, I have given a considerable amount of space to a discussion of the ways in which statutes are made and interpreted. This has been dictated partly by what I think is the very real need of every student to achieve an early acquaintance with these processes and partly by the conviction (which many teachers share) that existing curricula put a one-sided emphasis on common law and are calculated to give a distorted notion of the lawyer's field of work.

Fifth, technical ideas and technical terminology have been avoided as far as possible. I have drawn on the notions of common experience wherever I can and have made use of concrete cases to exemplify all major assertions. Illustrations have been drawn mainly from the early part of the student's first year casebooks. The illustrative material has been chosen with an eye to bring out essential connections between this survey course and the rest of the law student's courses. And the arrangement of the material itself has been dictated quite as much by considerations of convenience in teaching as by notions of logical relationships. In short, I have tried to give the student a better perspective of his chosen field; I have told a story as little complicated as possible, but I hope not so incomplete as to be misleading.

Sixth, there is need to impart a vast deal of plain information about our legal system and how it operates. For this reason I have cast the main part of this book in the form of an expository text. Much of what I say is so familiar to lawyers and teachers that it is quite taken for granted; as, for example, what a lawsuit is, how statutes are enacted, and what the judge's normal functions are. Just because the lawyer takes such matters for granted and because the layman does not know them, the lawyer has difficulty in explaining to the layman what a concrete legal situation really involves.

The law teacher, if he does not leave the student entirely to his own resources, throws in a bit of background here and there, in disconnected and unsystematic form, as the discussion of particular cases demands. The law student at the beginning of his course is in essentially the position of a layman. Much that the law-trained man takes for granted the student does not know. I believe that all this assumed background material should be brought together in a unified picture and explained in familiar terms, so that the beginner can see what he is doing and where he is going.

Finally, I have coupled with the textual material a variety of problems for discussion. This is in line with the problem method which we use consistently in legal instruction. The problems take the form of queries suggested for the student's consideration, of excerpts from various writers which are posed for critical discussion, and of briefly stated cases (though a few cases are stated in full). Problems are as necessary as the text. A bare text without problems does not take hold of one's mind. Problems are needed in order to develop an appreciation of the meaning of the text and to furnish exercise in its application. On the other hand, a casebook of the usual type seems to me impractical for the purpose of an introductory course. It does not furnish, or allow time to present, the much needed general picture of the legal system.[6]

The material here presented can be covered fully in about thirty classroom hours. It can be covered in as little as fifteen hours if the last chapter is omitted and if parts of the other chapters are pruned to a substantial degree. The material can be used independently as a separate course; or it can be used, as it is here at the University of Michigan Law School, in conjunction with other introductory work such as

---

[6] Some introductory materials recently published are open to objection on this account; they contain little, if any, descriptive material, restrict the range of discussion too narrowly, and force the instructor to stick too closely to the traditional method of case analysis.

instruction in legal bibliography and instruction in the history of the forms of action.

4. For Whom Intended

As already indicated, *Our Legal System and How It Operates* has been prepared primarily for the use of beginning law students. However I think it might also serve, in the hands of a properly trained instructor, as a textbook for juniors or seniors in college; I have never used it for this purpose, but I see no reason why it would be more difficult for the student to grasp than the standard treatise on economics.

The mature general reader, if he is curious about the legal system and desirous of obtaining general impressions of its nature and operation, may also find this book worthy of perusal.

The practicing lawyer or judge will find in this introductory book nothing of interest except the mode of analysis and the approach. If he has not been doing an extensive amount of "reading and using the newer jurisprudence," he may profit from a reinterpretation of familiar material in terms of this jurisprudence. Particularly he may find this a useful introduction to the items on legal theory which are suggested in the bibliography and which commonly assume that the reader is already familiar with the theoretical field.

The law teacher will see in this textbook chiefly an attack on a pedagogical problem.[7] He will be concerned to see whether I have developed, out of familiar stuff, a useful teaching tool. On this score I have nothing to add to what

---

[7] The teacher will note, for example, that I have put the discussion of Legal Policies and Policy Making at the conclusion rather than at the beginning of the course. Logically I might begin (and I do, with advanced students of legal method) with a discussion of legal policies, but pedagogically I am convinced—after trying both modes of arrangement—that the appreciation of the student develops more naturally if he is introduced first to the structure of the law and the acts and activities of the persons who make the legal wheels go around.

I have already said in this foreword and what will be obvious from a perusal of the text itself.

5. Debts

My general debts to Dewey, Pound, Holmes, Wigmore, Dickinson, Llewellyn, and others will be apparent to all who have read in the field of legal theory. However, I have not felt that it was necessary, as a rule, in a series of elementary lectures such as these, to acknowledge specific debts by citations. The lectures are intended for the information of persons unfamiliar with the field; citations would not be especially useful to them and would only clutter up the text. At various points in the book I have inserted bibliographies; these embrace the items to which I am chiefly indebted.

Table of Contents

PAGE

Chapter 1

Introduction: Scope of Lectures—Use of Language in Law

Subject Matter and Method [1]

Sec. 1–01. Purposes and program. The general purpose of these lectures is to furnish you, who are beginning the study of law, with an over-all view of the legal system and with certain general notions of the way it operates.* This purpose is not unlike that which is served in the field of economics by an introductory textbook on that subject. In

---

[1] Throughout this work two types of footnotes will be found: first, notes intended for the beginning student which will be numbered in the usual manner; second, special footnotes intended for the initiated reader (i.e., lawyer and legal scholar), which will be indicated by an asterisk and be introduced by the initials I.R.

* (I.R.) *General Bibliography.* The following items are suggested for further reading. It is not recommended that the beginner read anything beyond the text of these lectures until after he has completed the first year of legal study.

Arnold, Thurman W., The Symbols of Government, New Haven, Yale Univ. Press (1935).

Cairns, Huntington, Law and the Social Sciences, New York, Harcourt, Brace (1935).

Cardozo, Benjamin N., The Nature of the Judicial Process, New Haven, Yale Univ. Press (1921).

Cohen, Morris R., Law and the Social Order, New York, Harcourt, Brace (1933).

Columbia Associates, An Introduction to Reflective Thinking, Boston, Houghton Mifflin (1923).

Dewey, John, How We Think, Boston, D. C. Heath & Co. (1933).

Dickinson, John, "Legal Rules: Their Function in the Process of Decision," 79 U. of Pa. L. Rev. 833 (1931).

Dickinson, John, "Legal Rules: Their Application and Elaboration," 79 U. of Pa. L. Rev. 1052 (1931).

Frank, Jerome, Law and the Modern Mind, New York, Brentano's (1930).

Frank, Jerome, "Are Judges Human?", 80 U. of Pa. L. Rev. 17, 233 (1931).

Fuller, Lon L., "American Legal Realism," 82 U. of Pa. L. Rev. 429 (1934).

Fuller, Lon L., The Law in Quest of Itself, Chicago, Foundation Press, (1940).

this sense these lectures might properly have carried the title, *Introduction to the Study of Law.*

But different kinds of introduction are possible. In treating law or any other subject matter, different features may be studied, different aspects marked out for special consideration. I shall start with the legal system as a going concern, as an operating mechanism; and put about equal stress on its structure and its functioning.[2] My two main objectives will be to show you how the legal system is put together and what makes it tick; or, if I may borrow a comparison from medicine, to give you a combined anatomical and physiological treatment of the law. And I have sought to suggest

Holmes, Oliver W., Collected Legal Papers, New York, Harcourt, Brace (1920).

Lerner, Max, The Mind and Faith of Justice Holmes, Boston, Little, Brown & Co. (1943).

Llewellyn, Karl N., The Bramble Bush (1930); republished with an additional chapter, New York, Oceana Publications (1950).

Llewellyn, Karl N., "A Realistic Jurisprudence—The Next Step," 30 Col. L. Rev. 431 (1930).

Llewellyn, Karl N., "On Reading and Using the Newer Jurisprudence," 40 Col. L. Rev. 581 (1940).

Llewellyn, Karl N., "The Normative, the Legal, and the Law-Jobs: The Problem of Juristic Method," 49 Yale L. J. 1355 (1940).

Paton, George W., A Textbook of Jurisprudence, Oxford, Clarendon Press (1946).

Pound, Roscoe, Introduction to the Philosophy of Law, New Haven, Yale Univ. Press (1922).

Pound, Roscoe, "The Theory of Judicial Decision," 36 Harv. L. Rev. 641, 802, 940 (1923).

Pound, Roscoe, Law and Morals, Oxford Univ. Press (1926).

Pound, Roscoe, Social Control Through Law, New Haven, Yale Univ. Press (1942).

Radin, Max, The Law and Mr. Smith, Indianapolis, Bobbs-Merrill Co. (1938).

Radin, Max, Law as Logic and Experience, New Haven, Yale Univ. Press (1940).

Stone, Julius, The Province and Function of Law, Sydney, Associated General Publications Pty. (1946); reprinted, Boston, Harv. Univ. Press (1950).

In addition to the above general bibliography the reader's attention is directed to special lists of suggested reading appended to various sections below.

[2] The reasons for this choice of subject matter have been stated in the Preface; the justification for it will, I hope, be made out by what follows.

in the title, *Our Legal System and How It Operates,* something of this twofold emphasis.[3]

Our discussion will be confined to the typical American legal system—the system which one finds in any of the states in the United States.[4] We are not going to embark on a consideration of law in general or legal systems in general. This would take us too far afield and cover too much ground. Legal systems vary with differing forms of political organization. They vary with changing social conditions. Law has a different character in Russia from what it has in the United States; it is not quite the same in nature in France or in Italy or even in England as it is here. Sufficient unto the day are the difficulties and peculiarities of our own system. It is strongly colored by the American constitutional system and by American social conditions. Its study will require us to take account of American governmental organization and of characteristic American attitudes. We shall be especially interested in the ways in which our peculiar constitutional organization and our attitudes affect the making, the enforcement, the application, and the interpretation of law.

In courses such as Contracts, Property, Torts, Criminal Law, Procedure, Equity, Constitutional Law, and Business Associations, you will examine specific parts of our law; you will treat the detailed rules, methods, and problems of limited fields. By contrast, in the present course we shall examine together certain processes which characterize the

[3] Other adequate and accurate titles would have been *Introduction to Legal Method* and *Introduction to Legal Processes.* My objection to these titles, and reason for rejecting them, was that they are more abstract, and therefore less familiar and suggestive to the ordinary reader than the title which I have chosen.

[4] Hereafter I shall refer sometimes to the American legal system and sometimes to American legal systems in the plural. By *the* American legal system I shall mean the legal organization characteristic of all the states in this country. When I use the plural I mean to stress the peculiarities of each state's law and legal organization; there are differences as one passes from state to state, but in the main our interest centers on the features of likeness common to all.

American legal system and cut across lines between specific fields. These are the processes by which the behavior of persons are controlled, the processes by which law is made and formulated, the processes by which law is applied and interpreted, and the processes by which controversies among persons are adjudicated. The discussion of these various processes should give you a perspective of the legal system as an operating whole and an understanding of the functioning of its parts.

In order to lay before you our general program, I cannot do better than to give the titles of the chapters which will follow, and append a word of explanation as to each and a list of subtopics to be covered.

Chapter 1. *Introduction: Scope of Lectures—Use of Language in Law*—This chapter will be devoted, after a few more preliminary remarks about the subject matter and method of our course, to a discussion of the role of communication in the operation of the legal system.

    Subtopics: Subject Matter and Method
             Place of Language in Legal Work

Chapter 2. *Standards for the Individual's Acts*—The standards which are prescribed by the lawgiver, to guide the acts of the individual, are to be the chief subject of discussion in this chapter.

    Subtopics: Standards for Acts
             Significance of Standard Acts
             Effectuation of Standards
             Uses of Standards to Guide Action

Chapter 3. *Standards for Official Acts*—This chapter will deal with various official acts and the standards applicable to them, in particular with executive acts and with the processes of criminal prosecution and civil action.

Subtopics: Official Acts and Their Significance
Effectuation of Standards for Officials
Use of Standards for Officials

Chapter 4. *Legislation*—In this chapter the processes of creating explicit standards of all types will be dealt with, as well as the significance of these standards in various respects.

Subtopics: The Legislative Process
Standards for the Lawmaker
Subsidiary Lawmaking
Lawmaker's Statement of Standards
Significance of Legislation

Chapter 5. *Interpretation of Legislation*—In this chapter, the need for interpretation of standards and the resources and methods of the interpreter, will be treated under the following subheads:

Subtopics: Role of Interpreter
Sources and Standards of Interpretation
Typical Interpretive Problems

Chapter 6. *The Common Law*—This chapter will deal with the case law and the ways in which it is created and changed; it will cover among other items the doctrine of precedent.

Subtopics: The Creation of Law by Decisions
"Common-Law" Rules for Using, Finding, Interpreting, and Changing Standards

Chapter 7. *Legal Policies and Policy Making*—The subject matter of discussion here will be the policies of the state and law; the chapter will furnish an inventory of the major policies of government today.

Subtopics: Policies Regarding the Individual
Policies Regarding the Community
Policies Regarding Organized Groups
Determinants of Policies

Sec. 1–02. Is this course practical? No one of you needs to be "sold" on the importance of a course in Contracts or a course in Property. Some of you may also perceive right off the value of a course such as we are embarking on. But some of you, like many Americans and Englishmen, have a strongly developed feeling of suspicion, or at least of doubt, about matters theoretical; you may react uneasily to my suggestion of a program for this course. In fact, the list of chapter titles may sound somewhat abstract, and accentuate your feeling of doubt.[1] I hasten to say that I sympathize with your feeling up to a certain point, and that I wholly endorse the demand for the practical. I am just as much irked as any of you may be, by sterile academic discussions of theories that have no relation to the work of the lawyer, and I am just as determined as any of you might be to cut my cloth to the practical pattern.

But the practical-minded individual is sometimes prone to go even further than a doubt about theory; he may assume tacitly that the general or theoretical is necessarily opposed to the practical and is, therefore, to be rejected by the practical man. I remember hearing, when I was a student many years ago, some young fellows tell of an excursion through the "red-light district" in Detroit. According to their story, they entered a certain house of prostitution and created a "rough-house"; the "madam" in charge quelled the disturbance and said she would have them know she was running a "decent house." To one who starts with the assumption that theory and practice are opposed, the suggestion that a study of legal processes has practical value may sound like

[1] The list of chapter titles has been included because I felt that it would be helpful to give you a quick, though dim, glimpse of our course as a whole. I hesitated to do this for the very reason suggested in the text. The titles probably sound to you more abstract than the material which they represent will be found to be. Partly they sound abstract because they stand for unfamiliar material; on this basis the chapter titles in a casebook on Torts or Crimes also have an abstract ring.

a contradiction of similar character. But the assumption of an opposition is quite untenable, as I shall show in a moment. It is an assumption and never explicit opinion. It is an assumption only made by the unthinking. No one who stops to think things out ever expressly adopts this position.

Why, then, should theory and practice ever be assumed to be opposed? The blame for this perverse assumption has lain on both sides. Too much theorizing has been of a useless character, theorizing for its own sake, theorizing unchecked by practice. A good deal of legal theorizing has been of this character—"pretty poor stuff"—as Justice Holmes called it. And such theorizing has tended to give all theoretical activity a bad name and to make the practical-minded person look upon all of it as irrelevant and idle. On the other side, the assumed opposition between theory and practice has been fostered by a superficial view of men of action: they are in a hurry to get things done or at least to get to the task of doing. They want to learn how to do things and not spend time in discussing how they are done. What they fail to realize is that all important activities are reduced to standard methods and that the minimum "know-how" which they seek to obtain is nothing but theory under another name.

Actually, theory and practice are essential to one another and cannot be separated. On this, all thinkers and writers of today would agree. Practice is essential to prevent theory from becoming mere dreaming, essential to bring and hold it down to earth, so to speak. But theory represents the general ideas which organize experience. Theory is essential to good practice. Without general ideas to bring phenomena together, man would be forever floundering in a morass of particular experiences; he would not see the forest for the trees. To use another figure, general ideas are like the compass and the map which enable the traveler to traverse the forest without losing his way.

You will not penetrate far into the legal forest before you sense its endless variety and complexity. You will start grasping for means of putting things together. The multitude of rules is quite overwhelming, and the variety of fact situations which can arise is infinite. You will soon come to realize that you cannot memorize all of the rules, and you cannot possibly foresee all the bewildering array of fact situations to which your stock of rules may become applicable. You will learn that the most you can do is "to learn to think like a lawyer." You will find that the way to get about in the legal forest is not to memorize the characteristics of the particular trees but to develop methods of laying out and blazing paths. You will discover that the way to increase your grasp of the law is not to remember particular cases and how they were decided, but to develop an understanding of the methods of deciding them, of the broader principles on which they were determined. In the course on Contracts you will lay out paths through a part of the law; in the course on Property, paths through another part. In this course, I am trying to provide you with a larger legal map which will enable you to see the forest all together and to recognize the paths by which to pass from one part of it to another.

Justice Holmes has spoken regarding the importance of legal theory in the following terms: [2]

"We have too little theory in the law rather than too much. . . . Theory is the most important part of the dogma of the law, as the architect is the most important man who takes part in the building of a house. The most important improvements of the last twenty-five years are improvements in theory. It is not to be feared as unpractical, for, to the competent, it simply means going to the bottom of the subject. For the incompetent, it sometimes is true, as has been

[2] This and other quotations from Holmes found in this section are taken from his epoch-making essay, "The Path of the Law," 10 HARV. L. REV. 457 (1897).

said, that an interest in general ideas means an absence of particular knowledge. . . . The danger is that the able and practical minded should look with indifference or distrust upon ideas the connection of which with their business is remote."

It is important to notice, apropos of Justice Holmes' last remark about remoteness of theory, that this is not a course in Jurisprudence. Our chosen field of discussion is not remote from the work of the lawyer. The study of the structures and processes of the American legal system is as closely related to the practice of American law as are the study of anatomy and the study of physiology to the practice of medicine. Anatomy and physiology represent aggregates of theories regarding the structure and functioning of the human body. Without these general ideas the physician could not treat a disorder in a particular area, such as the stomach, intelligently. His thinking would not go beyond that of the layman who thinks of the stomach as a thing by itself and who can only deal with such a phenomenon as an acid stomach as an isolated affair to be relieved by some such immediate remedy as the administration of baking soda. The physician sees his problem in its wider relations. He asks what causes this acid condition: a temporary situation such as nervous overstrain or an eating spree? Or a more serious and continuing disturbance of gastro-intestinal functions? And what can be done about it, beyond providing a temporary palliative? Obviously, the doctor cannot analyze his case in this way without an ample fund of theories about bodily structures and functions. And the position of the lawyer is no different. He must understand the structure and functioning of the legal body if he wants to work effectively as a lawyer. He may learn how to draw a simple deed or contract—some stenographers and realtors can do this—but he will not be a successful draftsman and will not be able to take care of difficult problems of drafting without an adequate grasp of legal policies and legal ways and means. He may learn how to look up the law and write a brief on a legal point, but he will not be able to present hard and novel cases properly unless he has a real appreciation of the judicial process, of how judges work, of how they reach and how they justify their conclusions. He may learn to apply clear and unambiguous statutes to simple cases, but he is not prepared to deal with statutes which raise doubts and difficulties of application, without a comprehension of the processes by which statutes are made and the methods by which they are interpreted. In short, an understanding of the basic legal processes is essential, if one expects to be a legal architect rather than a legal mechanic, fit to do only routine jobs.

In conclusion, regarding the practical value of our course, I shall only add that I have tried to select material and problems which have importance to the lawyer. I accept the test of practical value, for theorizing as well as for other forms of activity. I can not demonstrate here and now that I have always made successful choices. To do this would require me to rehearse everything that is to be covered in the course. A large part of the proof of the pudding will be in the eating. But, as a token of my sincerity of purpose, I shall welcome at any time such questions from you as: "What relation does this topic in our course have to a lawyer's work?" "Why are we discussing this problem or that?" I not only regard such questions as proper; I feel that you should be propounding them constantly; and I shall do my best to give satisfactory answers if you cannot find answers for yourselves.[3]

Sec. 1–03. Material and method of study. A few words of explanation are in order, before we start on our main

---

[3] If some teacher finds it impossible to guess why I included this or that, he can either skip it with a profane reflection on the author, or write a letter to inquire.

undertaking, relative to the form of the material contained in these lectures, the organization of the material, and the use which you are expected to make of it.

The major part of the material here presented was originally delivered orally in traditional lecture style. I have retained the personal forms of address—"you," "we," and "I," which are common in lectures—because they make the text less formal and easier to read. However I have put the text itself in printed form, so that you can go over it before class and as often as you find necessary. This saves classroom time and allows you to prepare properly. When the class begins I shall assume that you are already familiar with the text, and shall conduct the discussion on the basis of this assumption.

After you have studied the text, devote an ample amount of time to the problems and queries stated for your consideration. These will be the principal subject matter for discussion in class and should be carefully weighed and answered beforehand. They are intended to give you an opportunity to apply the general statements made in the text. There is no way of developing appreciation of the meaning of general statements, comparable to actual exercise in their application.

What I aim to do in this course, as all the teachers in the law school aim to do, is to stimulate you to think in legal terms. I want you to develop an inquiring mind as regards all legal problems. Formulate your own opinions about what you read. Ask yourself, "Is that so, and Why?" Cultivate an "I'm from Missouri" attitude. Read critically, not passively. I do not want to give you exercise in memorizing a picture of the legal system. I do want you to understand the system, and understanding is an achievement. If you succeed in understanding, whatever needs to be remembered will stick without any special effort in that regard.

PLACE OF LANGUAGE IN LEGAL WORK

Sec. 1–04. Lawyer uses language. The man of the law works with language at every turn. Whether he be lawmaker, practitioner, judge, or scholar, his every move requires communication. Now he is using language in drafting a statute; [1] now in framing a deed, will, contract, or pleading; now in eliciting the testimony of witnesses or making an argument to the jury; now in instructing the jury or issuing an order; now in writing or reading an opinion; now in reporting a case or referring to a case already reported; now in interpreting a statute; now in preparing and writing a treatise or article on some special branch of the law. As one educator remarks, "The law appears—at least to a layman like myself—to be a highly verbal profession." [2] And another author writing recently observes half facetiously:

"When Hamlet was asked by Polonius what he read he made the oft-quoted response, 'Words, words, words.' The reply would have been equally apt if the old man had asked him for a definition of the law. The painter works with a great palette of colors, the etcher with lines and lights and

[1] I speak here of the legislator as a lawyer, for, while many members of our legislatures are not lawyers, almost all drafting is done by lawyers or passes their critical scrutiny. For our purpose this means that all the language used in statutes can be treated as language chosen or used by lawyers.

[2] The remark is made by Professor Crawford in discussing the kind of tests necessary for measuring legal aptitude. His statement continues:

"Ability on the part of the lawyer to express what his client intends to express in terms which are unequivocal and which, throughout as long as may be necessary, will be distinctly understood by others, necessitates a mastery of language on his part. This in turn demands a highly developed and precise use of words. Therefore, the test itself (legal aptitude test) is largely composed of verbal material and measures ability to use words in connection with such mental processes and problems as involve analysis, analogies, and the application of general principles to specific questions. By this means we attempt to measure not only the level of an individual's potential ability; but also whether he can use that ability *in the way* a law student is expected to do. We have found that mathematical and scientific thinking or the three-dimensional thinking required of the engineer is quite different from that which is related to this ability for legal studies." "Use of Legal Aptitude Test in Admitting Applicants to Law School," 1 BAR EXAMINER 151 at 154 (1932).

shadows, the musician with majestic chords or lilting melodies, but the lawgiver must confine himself to words, words, words.

"Words, words, words. The legislator puts his law into words. To know the law, the populace must know the meaning of those words. If words had an exact meaning legal troubles would end instead of beginning at this point. But since few if any words have exact meanings, being among the most slippery and evasive inventions of man, courts must be set up to interpret the words of the lawgiver and tell the puzzled populace—by means of more words—what the lawgivers mean by the words their laws make use of. And then, with many more words, the lawyers try to help the courts in their quest of truth by calling attention to previous words used by that and other courts in the interpretation of words of a like nature promulgated by lawgivers at some earlier time in even more words, words, words." [3]

In view of his almost continuous use of language, you will readily see how the man who labors in the vineyard of the law needs to give careful attention to the communicative process. As well might the medical student omit to consider the nature of available medicines and surgical instruments as for the prospective lawyer to fail to scrutinize his verbal tools and to learn about the uses to which they may be put.

Sec. 1-05. Communication analyzed in terms of verbal acts. The common man is accustomed to take the communicative process wholly for granted; he does not try to analyze it. It is like the air he breathes; he uses it constantly; yet never notices its character, its limitations, or its defects. When some important feature of the communicative process is called to his attention, he is in about the same condition as M. Jourdain in Molière's play, who was surprised to learn that all his life he had been speaking prose.[1] The result of

---

[3] PARTRIDGE, THE COUNTRY LAWYER 151 (1939).

[1] This reference to M. Jourdain has become a commonplace of late. So far as I can discover, Bentham was the first to refer to this example. See WORKS (Bowring's ed.) VIII, 122 (1843).

this lack of analysis is that the common man—and I might add, some of his more learned brethren, too—is forever dogged by a horde of verbal monsters, some prehistoric and many mythical. He is plagued by many needless verbal puzzles which vanish when the communicative process is broken down and its functions are understood. As Cardinal Newman has well said:

"Half the controversies in the world are verbal ones, and, could they be brought to a plain issue, they would be brought to a prompt termination. Parties engaged in them would perceive, either that in substance they agreed together, or that their difference was one of first principles. . . . When men understand what each other mean, they see, for the most part, that controversy is either superfluous or hopeless." [2]

Accordingly I shall begin with the assumption that communication is not the simple, single process that it is usually supposed to be; and our first job will be to subject it to further analysis.

Communication, like legal control, can be analyzed in terms of human acts; and this is the mode of analysis which I shall adopt in regard to both. This will bring out the functional aspect of communication as it will the operative side of the law. It will have the advantage, too, of reducing the process of communication and the process of legal control to common terms: acts. And since legal control is almost wholly exerted through words, this is an important point.

Each communicative act, each use of language, I shall call a *verbal act*. This expression is shorter than "use of language" and has the virtue of emphasizing the fact that each use is an act. "Verbal act" will be employed, accordingly, in a very general sense to include every distinct use of language, *spoken* or *written,* and to include every use of language whether small or comprehensive. The sudden cry of "Fire" is a verbal

2 OXFORD UNIVERSITY SERMONS 200.

act in this sense; as is the statement, "It's a fine day today," and the command of a father to his small son, "Willie, get my pipe." A letter is a verbal act and so is a speech. In the legal realm, the question put orally to a witness is a verbal act, and the response elicited from the witness is also such an act. In the same class fall written transactions such as contracts, deeds, and wills. Likewise, the passage of a statute is a verbal act, and the rendering of a judgment or an opinion in a lawsuit. And finally, the production of a large and important treatise such as a lawbook must also be regarded as a verbal act. Each of these acts represents, according to common understanding, a separate and distinct type of activity. Each of them bears a specific type name in ordinary speech and usage. Each of them represents a separate and distinguishable use of language. In these respects each of these acts meets the specifications of our definition of verbal act.

Sec. 1-06. Parties to communication. Communication may begin and end with a statement by a speaker, S.[1] He uses language in a verbal act; he addresses his act to a hearer, H. It is in this sense that we speak of S's act as communicative. But the verbal act of S may originate in a question by H which calls for an answer, or S's use of language may be sandwiched into an extended series of diverse statements such as a conversation. And the roles of speaker and hearer are constantly shifting. Everyone is now speaker, now hearer. The specific role of an individual in any protracted body of discourse changes from moment to moment.

Moreover, communication need not occur in a simple one-one exchange between a speaker and a hearer as it does in the ordinary face-to-face conversation. Quite often the par-

---

[1] Henceforth S will be used to indicate speaker; H to indicate hearer. These two parties will be taken to typify the parties in communication. Either may represent a plural meaning though the singular form be used. And speakers will be understood to include writers, and hearers to include readers.

ticipants in discourse are numerous. The speaker may share his role with several or many persons. Thus the members of the legislature speak as a group when they enact a statute. And S may address his message to large, indefinite and mixed groups of hearers. An orator may address a large audience; a writer may address his book to an indefinite audience; and a witness tells his story for the benefit of a mixed audience including judge, jury, parties, attorneys, miscellaneous on-lookers, and perhaps finally an appellate court. Nevertheless, effective analysis requires simplification of material, and except where some complex situation needs to be indicated, I shall treat communication as if it were merely a two-party affair in which S meets H face-to-face to transmit a message.

Sec. 1–07. Speaker's purposes. The speaker may act verbally for many reasons. His purposes for speaking or writing may be as varied as his purposes for any other kinds of activity. He may intend to influence the behavior of other persons whom he addresses; he may want to impart information; he may seek to obtain information; he may aim to make a prediction, and so on. In the following discussion, I shall divide the speaker's purposes into two main kinds and subdivide each kind into further types: [1]

1. The purpose to control others (sec. 1–08);
2. The purpose to give or obtain information (sec. 1–11).

---

[1] *Associative and expressive uses of language.* To make our discussion complete we ought to consider at least two more functions of language, but as these two functions have very little relation to legal work, I shall dispose of them with a brief reference.

Language may be used as Dewey says "to enter into more intimate sociable relations" with others. This kind of use is illustrated by the type of conversation which frequently goes on between persons who have nothing in particular to say. Thus, A says to B, "It is a fine day," and B answers, "Yes, very fine." For all practical purposes these remarks have no other meaning than "Let's talk." A great deal of our waking time and conversation consists of such interchanges of remarks, designed to keep up social contact, or to maintain "phatic communion," as Malinowski calls it.

Language may also be used to express one's feelings. Everyday expressive uses are found in exclamations of pain, joy, surprise, and so forth. The expres-

Sec. 1–08. Directive acts. Verbal acts are done by S to control others, to influence their activity, to give them directions as to what he wants them to do or not to do. S's act may vary in tenor from a blunt command to a mild request or even an expressed desire for action. When a father says to his son, "Willie, get my pipe," or "Willie, don't make so much noise," he is making a directive use of language. He undertakes to control Willie's behavior by an order. But control of behavior is no less attempted when Willie pleads with his father for a soda.

In law, frequent and important use of directive acts is made. Indeed verbal acts of this sort constitute the primary and basic legal uses of language, i. e., to control and influence people. These legal uses range all the way from the unqualified mandates of statute and judicial order to requests and petitions, as where a litigant requests relief from a judge and where a group of citizens petitions the legislature for the enactment of desired legislation.

Sometimes directive acts are very narrow and specific. A particular speaker may address a particular hearer and tell him just what to do. This kind of situation is exemplified by the case already mentioned where the father directs Willie to get his pipe. Similar specific orders also find a place in the operation of the legal system; specific directions are given by specific officials to specific individuals directing them to do or to refrain from doing specific acts. For example, the policeman may order the speeding motorist to "Pull over to the curb"; or a judge may issue an order to his bailiff to eject a particular person from the courtroom; or the judge may command the defendant in a case which he has heard, to do or to refrain from doing certain acts.

sive use of language is especially important in the field of art; it is represented by the employment of language in poetry, song, and drama, though in all these uses the expression of feeling is always coupled with the purpose to influence others or to convey information to some extent.

But some directives are *general* in character and scope, and these are the most important for our present purpose. They are the directives which fix general standards of behavior: laws, rules, regulations, principles and doctrines. Among them are general or natural principles such as principles of morality, which appear among us without the stamp of enactment by any particular authority. Others, such as the Ten Commandments, appear as the mandates of a Divine Legislator. Others are the declared rules or policies of such particular groups as labor unions, e. g., not to cross a picket line. And finally, there are the standards of behavior in which we are primarily interested, the general directives which we call in the aggregate, *law*. These are the rules, regulations, principles, and doctrines promulgated for the guidance of individuals and officials by various organs of the state.

Speakers who issue general directives and the hearers who receive them are often far removed from one another in time and place. An outstanding instance of this sort is the enactment of legislation. The speaker in this situation is an official agency endowed with authority to declare standards of behavior, a lawmaker.[1] He promulgates directions and addresses them to a distant and indefinite group of persons. He usually "speaks his piece" at a place far from most of the persons to be controlled; he acts at the state capitol, and his message is transmitted through various channels until it reaches the members of the group to which it is directed. And the members of this group are not only not named by individual or proper names, they are usually addressed as "anyone who" and constitute a fluctuating and changing group. Moreover, the legislative message is always put in permanent, i. e., written or printed, form. The lawmaker's verbal act is intended to exert a continuing influence. You and I receive

---

[1] The lawmaker may also issue specific orders such as the command of the father to Willie. He may, for example, order a particular official to make a certain payment. Compare sec. 1–10, problem 6.

today the legislative mandates of lawmakers who spoke a century or even several centuries ago.

Sec. 1–09. Distinguish control by force and by verbal acts. Lumley, a well-known sociologist, divides the methods employed in social control into two: 1. the physical force method, and 2. the symbol method.[1] Physical force has to be used in the control of inanimate objects. It may also be used in the control of human beings; in fact, there are some situations in which physical force is the only feasible means of controlling them. Thus, a mother has to employ physical force when she wishes her small child to have a bath. She has no choice but to pick up the child, carry it to the tub, and do the scrubbing. In like manner, legal control of behavior may sometimes have to be exerted through physical force; the policeman may have to restrain the violent acts of a wrongdoer by physical suppression.

The symbol method, on the other hand, involves the use of language or other symbols to induce or deter acts of the person controlled. When the child is old enough, it can be told to take a bath. When the individual can read he can be directed by published rules to do or not to do certain acts. The symbol method represents a great saving in the energy of persons who exercise control and causes much less social friction than the use of physical force. Legal control is almost wholly symbolic; it employs words, and words belong to that most important of all symbol systems, language. The standards of the law are stated exclusively, as I have already pointed out, in verbal form; and most official acts which are done in the effectuation of legal standards are verbal acts.

Sec. 1–10. Problems. 1. Suppose a city installs a traffic light on one of its streets for the purpose of regulating the movement of vehicles and pedestrians. Which of the two methods of control does this involve?

[1] MEANS OF SOCIAL CONTROL 14 *et seq.* (1925).

2. Suppose a policeman gives a driver a ticket for a traffic violation which directs him to appear in police court at a specific time to answer the violation charged. Which of the two methods is employed?

3. Suppose that a policeman arrests a man for an act of physical violence on the street and conducts him to the police station. Is this an instance of symbolic control or control by physical force?

4. A law provides that persons are obliged to appear and testify regarding matters pending in court whenever they are summoned for this purpose by a formal subpoena issued by the court. What type of directive verbal act is represented by this law?

5. A court issues a subpoena under the law aforesaid requiring W to appear and testify regarding matters involved in a lawsuit between P and D. What type of directive is involved here?

6. In 1531 there occurred in England a number of deaths by poisoning, afterwards known as the Lambeth Poisonings. These were traced to food served by the Bishop of Rochester. The English Parliament, having apparently satisfied itself that the Bishop's cook, Richard Roose, had wantonly put poison in a vessel of yeast, passed an act declaring that Roose and any other poisoner be adjudged a traitor and be executed by being boiled to death. Roose was accordingly boiled at Smithfield a few days after the act was passed.[1] What type or types of directive act were involved in this Act of Parliament?

Sec. 1-11. Informative acts. Man, like other animals, learns by direct experience. This is his original mode of obtaining information. Beginning as an infant each individual uses eyes, ears, and other sense organs to inform himself regarding his surroundings, animate and inanimate. And man

---

[1] FAY, HANGED BY A COMMA 77 (1937).

has the faculty of speech, a faculty which other animals do not have; this faculty opens up to him another mode of obtaining information. Without speech, organic life is individual and detached; experience remains the property of the organism which has it. Learning must be direct, and education is nonexistent. By the use of language the speaker can transmit reports of his experiences and, what is important for our immediate purpose, the hearer can share in the experiences of the speaker. Every human being, as speaker, transmits information of his experiences in this manner. Every human being, as hearer, receives an even larger amount of information regarding the experiences of others. The primary advantage is on the side of the hearer. The area of his contacts with the world is widened. He transcends the immediate limits of his senses. He has verbal experience of many things beyond the range of direct observation. Through S's verbal report, H can hear about the plan which S is now entertaining, and view the fight that S saw last year. He can learn of the opinion expressed by Lord Coke centuries ago regarding the natural rights of Englishmen. All these are matters which can be reported to H by speech, orally or in writing, but which could not be directly perceived by him.

Informative verbal acts may be divided into two main kinds: those by which information is imparted and those by which it is obtained. The first kind will need to be subdivided into several subtypes.

Three subtypes of verbal act impart information about specific situations. First may be mentioned the *statement of present fact*. S says to H, "It is raining outside." Similarly the bailiff tells the judge that a witness is waiting to be called; or the defendant's lawyer writes to the plaintiff's lawyer to say that the defendant is willing to make a settlement. Second, the informative act may concern a past occurrence and may properly be called a *narrative* use of language. S tells about a historical event or about a previous happening in his personal experience as where a witness relates what he saw at the scene of a crime. Third, S may make a prediction of a future occurrence. He may foretell a specific future event and in this sense make a *predictive* or prophetic use of language.[1] S says it is going to rain tomorrow, or he prophesies a bad end for X; the attorney tells his client that he expects the judge to decide their case in favor of the other side. These three subtypes of informative act are sufficiently familiar and call for no further comment.

A fourth, and very important, informative use of language is represented by the *general assertion*. This is a summation of experience, either of the speaker's personal experience or of experience which has been reported to him by others. The general assertion may be a simple summation in popular terms of the result of common experience, observations of natural phenomena, "Water runs down hill," or reports regarding typical human behavior, "Every man has his price." Or such assertion may be worked out and formulated on the basis of systematic and carefully controlled observation in the form of what we call scientific laws. Boyle's Law regarding the relation of pressure and volume of gases and Newton's Law of Gravitation are assertions of this scientific kind. These two laws relate to natural phenomena. But scientific assertions may also be made regarding human behavior; they express the observed constancies of habit and reaction among human beings. The construction of these generalizations constitutes the main objective of the modern sciences of psychology and sociology. In the legal field we encounter not a few generalizations regarding the behavior of individuals and officials and their reaction to the methods and processes of legal regulation. Whether these generalizations deserve the scientific

---

[1] This does not necessarily mean that the speaker uses the future tense. Predictions often take the form of a statement of present expectation or of present purpose to act. And, of course, predictions like assertions may be general as well as specific.

label or whether they are still on the level of common experience, we need not decide. In any case, we are constantly using and developing generalizations regarding the course of legal affairs.

The general assertion refers to common or scientific knowledge and not to a specific event. In this respect it differs from the specific informative acts first mentioned. But a general assertion like any other may be made by a particular speaker to a particular hearer on a particular occasion. Thus S may say to H on a particular occasion, "Every man has his price." The information transmitted is general and so is the assertion; but the communicative act is particular. Similarly, in a lawsuit in which a patient is suing a doctor for malpractice and is claiming that the fracture of his leg was not treated properly, another doctor may testify regarding approved medical procedures in treating fractures. He may say that good practice requires that the doctor take X-rays in case of known or suspected fracture. This statement about approved practice is a general assertion, and yet it is made on a particular occasion. It is to be used along with proof that the defendant doctor set the plaintiff's fracture without taking an X-ray (a specific occurrence) to establish the defendant's negligence and the plaintiff's right to recover.

However the general assertion does not have to be addressed to a particular hearer. Like the general directive referred to in section 1–08, the general assertion may be addressed to a more or less undefined audience. This is the case with many statements regarding common experience and popular usage. It is the case with most scientific work; indeed, with most serious writing.[2] Aristotle addressed his remarks to mankind in general, and the information which he gathered

---

[2] It is possible for a speaker to address a specific statement of fact on a particular occasion to an undefined audience but this is not too common. One thinks of such cases as statements made over the radio and statements and predictions made in historical writing.

and formulated is still being read and used by men of today. Lord Coke wrote about the English law as it stood more than three centuries ago, and his general assertions are still quoted and cited in judicial opinions of the present.

No less important than statements of present fact, narrative statements, predictions and general assertions, are interrogations, a fifth type of verbal act. Interrogations are the means through which a speaker seeks information. The first four types of informative act are used to give information to others; questions are used to obtain it for oneself. Questions are used when the speaker's information is doubtful, incomplete, or entirely lacking on some subject. It matters not whether the doubt or lack arises from the questioner's simple want of knowledge, as where he asks, "What time is it?" or whether the doubt or lack attaches to some prior statement which another party has made, where the father who tells Willie to get his pipe is met by the response, "Which pipe?" or "Where is it?" or "What did you say?" All these questions express the need for further information. A similar need may impel the lawyer to ask his client about the way in which the latter conducts his business or about the way in which business is usually conducted in the field where the client is engaged. This information may be obtained from the client, in other words, rather as a result of the lawyer's questions than as a consequence of voluntary informative statements by the client himself. In the trial of a case, the evidence which is presented to the jury is almost all obtained by means of interrogation of witnesses. Moreover, the judge may ask questions of lawyers and parties from the moment when he asks counsel whether they are ready to start the trial up to the very conclusion of the case. So that you must see that both in ordinary life and in legal work the use of interrogations to elicit information is hardly less common or important than the use of declarations to impart it. The two forms of use are complementary to one another. Strangely enough, however, students of logic and language have devoted almost all their attention to the role of declarations and have given very little notice to the role of questions.

Sec. 1–12. Problems. Consider the following items in relation to the foregoing discussion of directive and informative uses of language.*

1. *Cook:*

"The object of any science is to obtain general statements which will accurately describe those aspects of past events which have been noted and also serve as aids in forecasting future events. In the field of the so-called natural sciences, such general statements are called 'laws of nature' or 'natural laws'—the law of gravitation, the law of falling bodies, etc. . . .

"The phenomena which furnish the subject matter of legal science consist primarily of the conduct of certain societal agents—judges and similar officials. The records of the past conduct of these societal agents are found in the law reports. On the basis of these records and his knowledge of the behavior-patterns of the existing societal agents—members of the present Supreme Court of the United States, of the New York Court of Appeals, etc.—and using a logical technique fundamentally similar to that of other scientists, the student of law endeavors to formulate general statements which will summarize as accurately as possible these past phenomena and also serve as an aid in forecasting future phenomena—i. e., future decisions of whatever group of societal agents he is at the time interested in. . . ." [1]

What uses of language are made by the legal scientist, according to Cook?

* (I.R.) There has been much recent discussion of the general distinctions here suggested, notably in the writings of Holmes, Pound, Cook, Frank, Dickinson, Llewellyn, and Fuller. Obviously I cannot expect the beginner to go far into this subject; I only want him to make a start in noting differences between statements made in the operation of the legal system and statements made about the operation of the legal system.

[1] "The Present Status of the 'Lack of Mutuality' Rule," 36 YALE L. J. 897 (1927).

2. *Dickinson,* after referring to scientific laws, says:

"Human laws, on the other hand, are designed precisely for the purpose of producing relations in the real world which would not otherwise exist. Their object is not to describe the operation of forces, but to set them in motion. They are 'addressed to voluntary agents who may obey or disobey them.' In so far as human laws are applied and obeyed, they thus introduce, and are intended to introduce, a new factor, an active causative element, into an existing situation; for a different chain of physical consequences will follow on the judicial act applying them from that which would result if they were not applied or were altered.

"Thus jural laws are not, like scientific 'laws,' descriptive statements of verifiable relations between persons or things— relations which exist and will continue to exist irrespective of whether human choice and agency enter into the situation. Rather they are prescriptions of specific consequences to be attached by judicial—i. e., human—action to particular relations, which would not follow from those relations without the interposition of human volition; and more remotely, through the supposedly deterrent or persuasive effect of these consequences, they operate, and are intended to operate, to actively promote certain kinds of physical relations in which it is supposed that human beings *should* stand, as contrasted with others in which it is equally possible as a matter of physical fact for them to stand." [2]

How would you relate the distinction which he makes— between scientific and human laws—to our discussion of directive and informative verbal acts?

Can you reconcile what Dickinson says here with what Cook says about *legal science?* What use of language does legal science make?

3. Suppose that a person sticks his finger on a hot stove and observes the painful effect which follows. Can he derive a directive statement from this experience? An informative statement? What does this suggest?

[2] "The Law Behind Law," 29 COL. L. REV. 285 at 289 (1929).

4. In drafting a statute the lawmaker acts upon known principles of behavior. For instance, he may act upon the observations of economists regarding the buying behavior of persons who "play the stock markets." What does this suggest as regards the relation and the distinction between scientific laws and human laws?

5. Which use of language predominates in this book, judging by what you have seen of it so far? The informative or the directive?

6. "Judges follow precedent"—informative or directive?

7. "Judges ought to follow precedent"—informative or directive?

8. Suppose a lawyer advises his client of the danger of criminal liability in a particular line of conduct. Would you classify this advice as directive or informative?

9. How would you classify a client's request for advice? Does the answer to this question suggest any difficulty about our classification of interrogations?

Sec. 1–13. The mixed message. Unfortunately for simplicity's sake, the various types of verbal act which we have discussed are not always found in pure form. Indeed, it is probably safe to say that actual verbal acts are more often complex than simple. They are compounded from different directive and informative elements.

Both directive and informative elements may be combined in the same verbal act, even in the single sentence or smallest verbal act; and more often in larger complex acts such as a statute or legal treatise. For example, the father may say to Willie, "Fetch my pipe; it's in the library," or "Fetch my pipe from the library." Either way his statement is a compound of direction and information. Such compounds are very common in legislation. A typical statute begins with a recital of mischiefs, such as the prevalence of certain harmful activities (informative element), and concludes with the prohibition of them (directive element).

Also, different directives may be coupled together in one verbal act. These directives may be of different types. A specific and a general directive may be joined in one provision. This was done in the Parliamentary mandate to boil the Bishop of Rochester's cook (sec. 1–10); the penalty was prescribed for the cook specifically and for any other person who might subsequently commit the same offense as he had. And even more important, directives may be addressed to different persons in one statute, just as if a hunter were to try to bring down two ducks with one charge of shot. A typical instance of this sort is the statute which issues a command to A, B, and C and also gives directions to officials as to what they are to do if A, B or C fails to do what is commanded. In fact, this is probably the most common form which legislation takes.

In parallel fashion various informative elements are often linked with one another in verbal acts. A speaker gives one general assertion as the reason for another. The average man is hostile to railroads; therefore, the average jury finds for the plaintiff in suits against railroads for personal injuries. Or a speaker may make a compound declaration in which he includes a general assertion and a specific prediction based upon it; he may declare that juries usually find for the plaintiff in the manner just stated (general assertion), and that he expects the jury to do just this in a particular pending case.

Other combinations of elements are possible; these are enough to make the general point. Any verbal act must be analyzed. It cannot be safely assumed that it is wholly directive or informative. The mixed message is very common in actual practice.

Sec. 1–14. Verbal acts in discourse. The verbal act may not only be itself a complex affair as was pointed out in the last section, but any verbal act may form a part of a larger body of discourse. Usually, in fact, the statement of one speaker does not stand isolated and alone. It is coupled with the verbal acts of other persons in larger bodies of discourse and cannot be understood or interpreted apart from the discourse of which it is a part. The question by S is followed by an answer by H. The father's command to get his pipe is followed by Willie's question, "Where is it?"; this in turn by the father's reply that it is in the library. Verbal acts, as one might say, are woven together in a continuous process of communication. This process comprises a series of verbal acts all of which are connected together in execution. Consider, for instance, the following trivial conversation between students, a typical example of the connectedness in the process of communication:

S: "Where are you going?"
H: "I am going to class."
S: "What class?"
H: "Professor Jones' lecture in Zoology."
S: "What sort of fellow is he?"
H: "He is a funny old bird. His lecture is always pretty dull."

Here you can readily see how the separate statements which make up this conversation are woven together in one piece. Each new statement is tied into what had gone before. No statement stands alone. For instance, the meaning of the word lecturer in the last sentence of this series depends upon the verbal expressions which have gone before. The same observation applies to other elements in the series of statements, such as the word "he," "class," etc. Two parties participate alternately as speaker and hearer; the joint product of their verbal activity is regarded as a unity or whole. This composite whole also bears a type name—a conversation.

Substantially similar observations might be made regarding a lawsuit. This also is a continuous process of communication, a unified body of discourse. But, at the same time, it includes a number of subordinate steps or distinguishable verbal acts: the summons, the declaration, the answer, the demurrer and other pleadings, the testimony of witnesses, as well as written evidence, the instructions, the arguments of counsel, the verdict, the judgment and other orders, the various steps on appeal, the appellate court's opinion, etc. While each of these verbal acts may be regarded as separate for some purposes, we do also commonly regard them as parts of a whole. They have a coherence with one another, i.e., in relation to a single controversy between X and Y, which makes us treat them as a single entity, a complex legal conversation, which we know as a lawsuit.

We shall have frequent occasion to refer later to bodies of legal discourse. Most important legal processes can be regarded as extensive legal conversations. The process of law-making, the process of interpretation, the process of adjudication, and the process of expounding law in textbook form can be so regarded and will be treated and analyzed in these terms. But I have said enough for the present; I merely wanted to point out to you here how verbal acts are tied together in discourse and, correspondingly, how larger bodies of discourse are built up as aggregates of individual statements.

Sec. 1–15. The indirect message. Doubtless the original form of communication is the direct message delivered face-to-face. This form is still much used and very important but is seriously restricted in range. The range of communication is widened if messages can pass indirectly from speaker to hearer through intermediaries.[1] Mediation may be accomplished at the instance of the speaker when he delivers to

---

[1] The telephone, telegraph, and radio have widened the scope of person-to-person communication, though such communication is hardly face-to-face and usually involves the aid of intermediaries.

R a message which R in turn is to transmit to H; or where R on his own initiative reports to H the words said by S; or where H sends R to S for a message. These cases differ as regards the person who takes the initiative in transmitting the message; they are alike in that an intermediary figures in the process. The fact that R can mediate between S and H enhances the possibilities of communication both in space and time. Spatially, it enables S's message to reach H even when these parties are too far apart for direct communication to occur. Temporally, a similar widening of range is made possible. The learning and traditions of one age are passed on to succeeding ages, by word of mouth, through numberless intermediaries.

With the invention of writing, and later of printing, another form of indirect communication is established; and communicative range is further expanded both in space and time. Moreover, the durable quality of writing and printing makes possible a degree of certainty and definiteness which oral communication seldom has.[2] For example, Aristotle's words are still available to us, though more than two millennia have passed since he lived, and available just as he wrote them. In written and printed form human knowledge is accumulated and stored for the benefit of those who want to use it.[3] These means of indirect communication have played a tremendous role in building, transmitting, and storing our social heritage of knowledge. Legal traditions and ideas are a part of this heritage and have come down to us for the most part in written or printed form.[4]

[2] And very recently sound recording has been added to the means of perpetuating what is said.

[3] The writings themselves are ordinarily transmitted by third parties so that written communication also involves the intervention of intermediaries.

[4] For the present purpose it seemed necessary to distinguish printing and writing, as printing is a relatively modern invention. Writing and printing have also had quite different significance socially and historically. However for ordinary purposes writing is used to include printing and I shall follow this common usage from this point on.

However, this widening of communicative range is fraught with certain perils. The dangers of communicative failure, which are present even when S communicates with H face-to-face, are greatly multiplied. When a manuscript is handed down as Aristotle's work, there is always the chance that it is not what it purports to be. When a letter is sent by messenger or by mail, it may be lost in transit; a face-to-face message could not miscarry in this way. When S's message is reported by R to H, especially when the message and the report are both oral, the dangers that R will misunderstand the message and that he will misstate its true tenor are added to the normal dangers of misunderstanding in direct communication. And when statement is piled upon statement, as where A says that B says that C says such and such a thing; or direction is piled upon direction, as where father tells Willie to tell mother to tell Johnnie to mow the lawn, we can easily lose ourselves in the very maze of our own discourses, to paraphrase a remark by Hooker.[5] Legal transactions and legal discussion have not always escaped these pitfalls as we shall see in later chapters.

Sec. 1–16. Problems. Consider the following items in relation to the discussion of the five preceding sections.

1. Suppose A is called for jury service and says to the judge, "My wife is ill and I would like to be excused." Analyze the mixture of statements involved here.

2. A witness, on a trial of D for robbery of P, says, "Then I heard D say to P, 'Stick up your hands.'" Analyze.

3. "In general, the law admits the testimony of a witness only as to what he has himself observed; it does not permit him to testify in reference to what others have told him or to what he has heard them say. This is the so-called 'hearsay' rule. Behind this rule are two basic reasons: first is a sound distrust of rumor and second-hand report. Second is a specific purpose to subject all testimony to the check of cross-exam-

---

[5] HOOKER, ECCLESIASTICAL POLITY, V, chaps. 2, 4 (1662).

ination; the story of many a witness sounds different after it has been tried by this acid test. All students of methods of proof agree that there is a solid foundation for the hearsay rule, as a general proposition." [1]

What do you find in section 1–15 to justify this legal rule?

4. The paragraph above quoted continues, "Nevertheless the rule has had to give way in practice to a long list of exceptions." Of these I shall mention only two:

"*Pedigree exception:* No person knows of the time of his own birth or his parentage and relationships, except by second-hand report. Likewise of the birth, parentage, and relationships of others. Statements made to a witness by deceased members of the family are admissible to establish said facts.

"*Scientific matters:* Every physician or other learned person, obtains his knowledge largely from books; so far as he testifies on the basis of this learning he is giving a second-hand report of the experience of others, nevertheless he is permitted to testify on this basis."

How would you explain or excuse these exceptions?

5. Suppose S makes a New Year's resolution, e. g., "I'll never touch another drop." Can this be viewed as a directive use of language? If so, who issues the direction? To whom is it addressed? Whose behavior is to be controlled by it? Can the resolution be viewed as an informative use of language? If so, to whom is the informative verbal act addressed?

Sec. 1–17. Summary. Communication lies at the heart of the legal processes. Verbal acts are done to direct others and to convey or obtain information. The legislature communicates its directives to the populace in verbal form. Most of the acts which officials do are verbal acts. And the lawyer spends most of his time in doing or guiding or interpreting verbal acts. You must see therefore why I think it is important for the legal neophyte to become "language conscious."

[1] The passages quoted in this problem are taken from the syllabus of my lectures in MEDICAL JURISPRUDENCE 26–27.

You must understand also why I regard training in the use and analysis of language as most fundamental both in the preparation for legal study and in legal study itself. The lawyer must know his verbal tools: he must be a verbal artisan of no mean skill.

CHAPTER 2

Standards for the Individual's Acts[1]

Sec. 2–01. Lawmaker's messages—coverage and analysis.
The lawmaker, L, issues general directives to the community as the owner of a factory might issue instructions, blueprints, and models to guide the work of the men in his factory. These directives we call collectively "law" and severally "laws," so that law is a general term embracing a multitude of laws. Laws differ from one another in many respects, as we shall see later on.[2] They are alike in that all are formulated by some determinate law-making agency, a lawmaker; they are alike also in that all laws are intended to guide the behavior of all or part of the members of the community.*

The number of laws issued by L is very great, and the fields covered by them are many. From these facts it might easily be inferred that laws cover every kind of human activity. This is not the case, however; actually the coverage is far from complete. L provides guidance only in limited

[1] Throughout the remainder of this book I shall often designate important parties by capital letters as follows: the lawmaker by L, the individual actor by A, the individual's counselor by C, the official by O, and the law student and/or legal scholar by S.

Each one of these terms, and the corresponding letter, represents a class of persons and not a specific person. "The individual," "the individual actor," or "A" means a class of individuals, "the anyone who" is referred to in a general legal mandate.

[2] See especially chapter 4.

* (I.R.) In the early chapters I shall speak only of statutes. I shall take them as the prototype for all laws and avoid mentioning case law, as well as constitutional law, and administrative regulations. This restriction of material is made for the purpose of simplifying the teaching job. I believe that the nature of legal standards can be adequately developed with statutory material and have organized the matter in chapters 2, 3, and 4 on that assumption. While this method neglects differences in the ways in which standards are formulated and differences in the places where they are found, I do not believe that ignoring these differences at the start leaves any final misconception. All these differences are fully discussed later; and the simplification of treatment which results from disregarding them for the time being, is considerable.

areas of behavior. The greater part of what A does is left free from any legal constraint. Besides such activities as eating and greeting friends, the way A uses his land and what he does with his money, where he goes and what he says, fall almost wholly beyond the scope of legal provisions. For practical reasons or reasons of policy L does not attempt universal control of A's conduct; he leaves most of it unguided and untouched by his legal mandates.

Almost all laws promulgated by the lawmaker are complex; they are what we have called mixed messages; [3] they attempt to guide more than one type of act, and they may impart a great deal of collateral information besides. The usual statute, for example, contains not only instructions to A but also instructions to various officials, and it often contains a statement of the reasons why the statute was passed and of the general objectives which it is intended to promote.** In order to compare the important parts of different laws with one another and to discuss the relations of laws to various types of acts, it is necessary to break down these complex legal structures into smaller common units. The

---

[3] See sec. 1–13 above, regarding the nature of the mixed message. Note how many different acts are forbidden by the following statute:

"Any person who shall falsely make, alter, forge or counterfeit any public record, or any certificate, return or attestation of any clerk of a court, public register, notary public, justice of the peace, township clerk, or any other public officer, in relation to any matter wherein such certificate, return or attestation may be received as legal proof, or any charter, deed, will, testament, bond or writing obligatory, letter of attorney, policy of insurance, bill of lading, bill of exchange, promissory note, or any order, acquittance or discharge for money or other property, or any acceptance of a bill of exchange, or indorsement, or assignment of a bill of exchange or promissory note for the payment of money, or any accountable receipt for money, goods or other property, with intent to injure or defraud any person, shall be guilty of a felony, punishable by imprisonment in the state prison not more than fourteen (14) years." Mich. Stat. Ann. sec. 28.445.

What features do these acts have in common? In what respects are they different?

** (I.R.) And the matter which one finds in case law, constitutional provisions, and administrative regulations, is equally mixed and heterogeneous. Compare note * above.

basic unit which I shall adopt for this purpose is the legal standard.

The standard is a pattern for a particular type of action. It is a legally defined action picture, i. e., a standardized act. All legal directives, all laws, no matter how simple or how complicated, can be analyzed in terms of this legal unit. Their essential parts can be reduced to standards or combinations of standards. The advantage of treating the standard as the unit of law is that it corresponds with the unit of behavior which we have chosen, the act. Accordingly, we shall employ from this point on the *legal standard as the unit of law* and the *act as the unit of behavior controlled by law.*

Sec. 2–02. Scope of chapter. In the next preceding section I have defined the legal standard. The remainder of this chapter and the two chapters to follow, will treat the relations of standards to human acts. The standards of which we shall speak fall into two main types. Some standards are prescribed by the lawmaker primarily for the guidance of the individual's acts; other standards are designed for the guidance of official acts.[1] Standards of these two main types are, of course, very numerous; many types of human activity, individual and official, are standardized. Each of the main types will call for further subdivision into subtypes of standard acts.

The present chapter will be devoted to standards for the individual's acts. These will be taken up and discussed under the following headings:

Standards for Acts.

Significance of Standard Acts.

Effectuation of Standards.

Uses of Standards to Guide Action.

---

[1] In addition to standards for the individual and standards for officials, we shall also have occasion to mention standards regulating the activities of groups such as the church, the club, the labor union, the professional association, etc. See sec. 7–28 *et seq.*

STANDARDS FOR ACTS

Sec. 2–03. Kinds of standard acts. The traditional discussions of law are carried on in a manner to suggest that the lawmaker is concerned with just two kinds of standard acts: prohibited acts and obligatory acts. He tells persons what they must not do and what they must do; he undertakes to restrain them from doing certain acts and to compel them to do others. The impression which one gets is that law consists merely of prohibitions and commands. For instance, Blackstone's definition of law conveys this meaning; he says that a law is "a rule of civil conduct, prescribed by the supreme power in the state, commanding what is right, and prohibiting what is wrong." [1] And similar definitions of law and of the standards which it prescribes are common in legal texts and judicial statements even in our own time.

No doubt laws do prohibit some acts and make other acts obligatory, as I shall point out in the following sections; but it does not follow that legal prescriptions define only these two kinds of acts. On the contrary, I think we need to make room for at least four other kinds of legally defined acts: permitted acts, discretionary acts, effective acts, and ineffective acts. All these types of acts have always been important in fact. But it seems not to have been generally perceived by analysts and writers how important they are, nor how different essentially they are from acts which are prohibited or obligatory; nor to have been generally understood how much of our law actually formulates standards for effective and permitted acts. This traditional neglect makes it the more necessary to consider here all these types of acts and to compare and distinguish them. Accordingly, in the six sections to follow I shall treat six types of standards for acts, or, if you prefer, six types of standardized acts: (1) prohibited acts;

---

[1] BL. COMM. *28 (1765). [The * here represents star paging.]

(2) permitted acts; (3) obligatory acts; (4) discretionary acts; (5) effective acts; and (6) ineffective acts.

Sec. 2–04. Prohibited acts. First among legally standardized acts are those which the individual must not do, prohibited acts. Here falls most of that large class of acts, commonly called crimes: such acts as killing a person, stealing another's goods, disturbing the public peace. These acts are legally regarded as injurious to the public; the basic legal aim is to protect the community against them;* and accordingly the individual, A, is forbidden to do them. A is confronted with detailed pictures of these acts which he is prohibited from doing and usually threats of punishment are coupled with their prohibition.

Acts of A are also prohibited because they are harmful to some other person, B. A legal duty is imposed upon A to refrain from doing such acts. If A does a prohibited act of this sort, in violation of his duty, he is required to make compensation to B for the harm done. Action contrary to standard is regarded as a private wrong, or in the terminology of the law, a *tort.* Typical tortious acts are the intentional injury of another's property, the injury of another's person through the negligent driving of an automobile, and the injury of another's reputation by an unjustified defamatory statement.

Accordingly, legally prohibited acts may be divided into two grand types, crimes and torts. The standards for both

* (I.R.) Here I use the expressions "legally regarded" and "legal aim"; I shall also employ from time to time such expressions as the "law forbids" and the "legal system provides." All these expressions are metaphorical and elliptical; they suggest that the "law" and "the legal system" are persons who have wishes and do acts. This suggestion can lead to misunderstanding; personification of an abstraction is always dangerous. However these forms of expression are terse and convenient; they carry about the same meaning as the lawmaker regards or aims or forbids or provides, and thus offer serviceable alternatives for the constant reference to the lawmaker. And "the lawmaker" is a personified abstraction, too, as we shall see later, so that whatever objections apply to these other abstractions apply to "the lawmaker." The actual factors involved in action by the "legal system" or by "the law" or by "the lawmaker" will be elaborated in chapters 3, 4, 5, 6 and 7.

types of acts are alike in that they serve a negative function as regards the actor; they tell him what he must not do; they are patterns of action to be avoided. They differ from one another as regards the interests which are violated by A's act; the crime is a wrong to the public, the tort is a private wrong. They differ from each other in a parallel way as regards the actions which may be brought for violation of the prohibition; a crime is prosecuted by public authority; a tort is the basis for private action by the injured party. However, it is important to notice that one and the same act may constitute both a crime and a tort; it may be both a public and a private wrong. A's act of striking B may be a criminal battery and a tortious injury to B. A's act of carrying away B's goods may constitute theft and may also furnish ground for a private action by B against A.

Our interest centers primarily on acts prohibited by law. Crimes and torts are acts of this sort. But parties may also prohibit acts by agreement or voluntary undertaking. If a valid contract is made by which A promises not to do a certain act, this promise establishes a specific pattern of action which A must not pursue. The contract restricts A's freedom of action; a failure to obey the restrictive provision is a breach of contract, and breaches of contract constitute an important type of legally prohibited act. Thus, a doctor may sell his practice in a particular town, and agree not to treat patients there for a period of five years. The doctor, by his agreement, puts shackles upon himself. His agreement is obviously an agreement not to act—a self-imposed prohibition. Inasmuch as this prohibition is legally enforced, it becomes a legal prohibition.

Sec. 2–05. Permitted acts. Legal provisions may define acts which are permitted, as well as acts which are forbidden. For lack of a better name, the legal provision which thus expressly defines a permitted form of action may be called a legal permission. It constitutes, you will notice, a type of provision just the opposite in effect from a legal prohibition. It expresses a position of the law which is essentially neutral toward what A does. Such a provision declares, for example, that A may do what he pleases with his own property, that he may move about in regard to his own affairs, that he may speak his mind about matters which he chooses to discuss, that he may defend himself against attack, and so on. The most basic of these permitted activities are defined in our constitutions. They are the liberties for which our ancestors fought and died: freedom of religion, freedom of speech, freedom of the press, freedom to acquire and hold property, freedom to engage in an occupation of one's own choosing.

The legal provision which defines permitted action is sometimes couched in positive terms, sometimes in negative terms. When it takes the positive form, the provision may simply state that it is lawful for A to act thus or so; or the provision may employ the verb "may," as do the provisions which I have already cited, to indicate that A's activity is allowed; or if the provision declares the lawful character of A's activity in terms of nouns, it uses such permissive expressions as "freedom," "liberty," and "privilege." When the legal provision defining permitted action takes the negative form, it declares that certain activities are not unlawful, not contrary to law, not forbidden or not prohibited. In actual use the negative form is less common than the positive. The reason for this is fairly obvious. Why go to the trouble of using a double negative "not unlawful" when a simple affirmative, "lawful," will do as well?

Wide areas of A's activity are untouched by law as I have already pointed out.[1] In these areas freedom from legal restraint is existent simply because restraint is not mentioned; and most free areas are free in this sense. Everybody from

[1] See sec. 2–01.

the lawmaker (L) on down proceeds on the assumption that what is not forbidden is allowed; that what is not expressly prohibited is impliedly permitted. The absence of a legal provision is treated as tantamount to the definition of an area in which A may do what acts he pleases. Accordingly, one way in which L can establish areas of legal nonrestraint is to make no reference to them whatever and thus leave A's freedom to implication.

Why, then, does L define any areas of free action in express terms? Why does he set up explicit standards for permitted acts? Why not leave them all to implication? Is any function served by express definitions of lawful or nonprohibited acts? The answer to these queries is found in L's general purpose to provide guidance for A's behavior.[2] If A is in the middle of the wide ocean, he does not need to be told that navigation in any direction is possible and safe, but if A is in shallow waters or in the neighborhood of solid land he is well served by an instruction that navigation in a certain place or along a certain course is possible and safe. And guidance is furnished to A no less when he is told, "This is a safe channel to navigate," than when he is told, "Over there are certain rocks which you must stay away from." By the same token A is no less guided when L declares, "Here is a course of action which you may freely take" than when he declares, "There is a course of action which is prohibited." Both are useful as guides to A. In areas where prohibitions are close by, A needs to be told what he can safely and properly do. For example, it is useful to tell him that he is permitted to kill another in the necessary defense of his own life. Ordinarily A may not

---

[2] Contracts often provide that certain acts are permitted. Such contractual provisions are inserted by parties for essentially the same reasons that dictate the establishment of legally permitted acts. The parties agree that A is to be allowed to do certain acts so as to avoid doubt or controversy in regard to A's freedom of action. Compare what is said in the last paragraph of sec. 2–04 regarding prohibitions established by contract.

kill another, but in this situation he is allowed to do so.[3] Again, in areas where officials are tempted or inclined to interfere with A's action, as in regard to free speech, free press, and free exercise of religion, the express mention of these freedoms is useful for other reasons. The declaration that these acts are free, serves as a direct admonition against official interference with them, and as an encouragement to A to stand up for his rights when, as, and if such interference occurs.* Accordingly, the answer to the general queries, with which this paragraph began, is that express standards for permitted acts, like all other forms of standards for acts, are intended to furnish guidance to actors, individual and official; and their practical value in this regard is beyond question.**

[3] In fact, the prohibition of killing is usually stated in such broad and general form that it covers every killing, so that it needs to be supplemented by this exception in order to give an accurate picture of the law.

* (I.R.) The problem of *drawing lines* between the area of permitted action and the area of prohibited action is reserved for discussion in chapter 4. Problems connected with the *generality* of legal provisions—whether they define prohibited acts or define permitted acts—are reserved for discussion in chapters 4 and 5. To introduce these problems here would cloud unduly our examination of the permitted act as a type.

** (I.R.) Indeed it can be argued that the creation of permissive standards is more natural and logical than the establishment of prohibitive standards. The former are positive standards, the latter negative. Permitted acts are those which it is lawful for A to do; prohibited acts are those which it is unlawful for him to do; and it is simpler and more usual to issue mandates in positive than negative form.

Even if we accept this contention, it amounts to no more than the assertion of a rule of preferred usage. But negative terms and negative declarations are used and useful as well as positive terms and declarations. We do make informative statements in negative as well as positive form; and we do find in the law and elsewhere standardized acts which the actor is not to do as well as standardized acts which he is expected to do. Actually prohibited acts, i.e., acts which we are assuming for the moment are negative, are to be found in legal provisions with greater frequency and in greater number than permitted acts are. We cannot say that one type of legal standard or one form of legal declaration is necessary, or that one type or form is more fundamental than the other. Both positive and negative standards and positive and negative declarations are usual and useful. Usage and utility are the only criteria we have. If a type of standard or a form of statement is usual and useful, I see no alternative but to make a place for it in our classifications.

Another circumstance which militates against the argument which asserts a preference for positive standards, is the fact that the distinction between

Sec. 2–06. Obligatory acts. Third among the types of legally standardized acts—and somewhat less common than the prohibited and the permitted act—is the act which the individual must do, the obligatory act. The standard act is commanded or, what amounts to the same thing, a legal provision declares that it is the duty of the individual to act. For example, A is told that he must register for the draft; that he must serve in the armed forces; that he is required to file an income tax return. Such an act is required for the general public benefit. The failure to perform this type of act is usually declared to be a public offense, or crime, and penalized more or less seriously.[1]

In addition to the standard acts which A must do for the benefit of the public, he must perform certain acts for the benefit of other individuals. He must support his wife, B; he must care for and educate his child, C. In these particular cases, perhaps, we might properly say that A's acts are required both for the benefit of B and C and for the welfare

positive and negative is a relative one; it depends entirely upon the viewpoint. Who shall say whether a permitted act is a positive or negative category? Who shall say whether the prohibited act is to be viewed as positive or negative? That the two are opposites is clear; this fact inheres in the difference in L's positions toward them—one act he disapproves, the other he does not disapprove; one act he restrains, the other he does not. But which of these positions is positive and which negative? Is approval or is restraint positive? May one not regard prohibited acts as controlled acts and permitted acts as noncontrolled acts? The point is that there is no positive or negative category outside of the attitude of the classifier. The belief in an intrinsic distinction of this type is merely a hangover from outmoded beliefs in necessary ideas. Certainly the mere form of words, whether positive or negative, is not decisive. Words shift from negative to positive connotations as usage changes, and vice versa. The word "independent" will serve as an example. Originally this word was a negative term opposed to the term "dependent," but today there is no doubt that independence is thought of as a positive quality, like self-assurance, of which it is the substantial equivalent. Both our terms, permitted and prohibited, are in a somewhat ambiguous condition; both are used today with connotations which are sometimes positive and sometimes negative. Which is stressed depends on the interests and approach of the user. And whether either or both were originally positive or negative terms does not seem very important now.

[1] So that the category of crime includes both the doing of acts which are prohibited and the failure to do obligatory acts. Prohibited acts are much the more common among crime pictures.

of the public.* However, there are obligatory acts which are owed strictly to other individuals. The most important acts of this sort are those which A has taken upon himself to perform pursuant to *contract* or other voluntary engagement; for example, acts of service which he has agreed to perform, or payments of money which he has promised to make. Contractual undertakings are legally enforced at the instance of the parties benefited. In this sense, the acts that contracts call for, fall both in the class of obligatory acts and in the class of acts owed to other individuals.[2]

Sec. 2–07. Discretionary acts. Discretionary acts are those which A is not required by law to do, nonobligatory acts. They are opposed to obligatory acts as permitted acts are opposed to prohibited acts. When we say that an act is discretionary we mean that it is free from legal compulsion; when we say that it is permitted we mean that it is unrestrained by law. A discretionary act is one which A is free to do or not do. If done, the act is voluntary; A is free to act or to sit back and do nothing. For example, bringing a lawsuit is discretionary with the injured party; he may sue or, if he chooses, allow the injury to go uncompensated. Being a Good Samaritan is discretionary; the actor may help his fellow man in trouble or he may pass by on the other side. Supporting an indigent father or sister may be a moral duty, but in the eye of the law it is discretionary; the son or brother may furnish support or decline to do so.[1]

Just as most areas of human activity are free from legal prohibitions, so most acts of which A is capable are untouched

* (I.R.) I have not tried to make a neat distinction here between obligations implied by law and obligations arising from agreement. The aim is to do no more than make a beginning with problems of classification and division. Compare sec. 2–05, note *.

[2] Compare what is said in the last paragraph of sec. 2–04 regarding prohibitions arising from contract.

[1] Ordinarily the law makes a man responsible only for the support of wife and child; however, there is some modern legislation which makes him responsible for the care of other relatives.

by legal commands. These acts are discretionary because the law does not say anything about them. The absence of a legal command is treated as the recognition of an area in which A does not have to act unless he chooses to do so. Discretion is implied from the lack of command.

Discretion may also be conferred by express provision, and the act of A which is thus expressly declared to be free from legal obligation is the discretionary act with which we are now concerned.[2] In actual practice this kind of act is not as often mentioned as is the act which is expressly permitted; in fact it is not often mentioned at all. However, the discretionary act is not unimportant; and as we shall have to refer frequently to discretionary acts when we come to discuss the acts of officials, I introduce it here as one of our six kinds of acts.[3]

Sec. 2–08. Problems. In section 2–03, I have divided standardized acts into six general types. Of these we have now considered four: 1. prohibited acts, or those which A *must not* do; 2. permitted acts, or those which A *may* do; 3. obligatory acts, or those A *must* do; 4. discretionary acts, or those A is *not required* to do. I believe it will facilitate understanding to discuss a few problems involving the application of these four categories before we proceed with the remaining two types of standard acts.

1. A statute provides for the punishment of any act of cruelty to an animal. Which type of standard act is involved? For whose benefit is such act banned?

2. The law forbids the indecent exposure of one's person (nudism, exhibitionism, etc.). Where would you place this type of act?

---

[2] Discretion may also be expressly given by contract, as where X is given an option to buy a piece of real estate within a specified period of time. The consummation of the purchase rests in X's election; it is a discretionary act.

[3] See chapter 3 *passim.*

3. Suppose that the law provides that an individual or group of individuals of one sex may bathe in the nude in streams or lakes at places remote from dwellings or highways. How should such bathing be classified?

4. The law allows a husband to recover damages from a third party who alienates his wife's affections. How would you classify the third person's act?

5. The First Amendment to the Federal Constitution provides that "Congress shall make no law . . . abridging . . . the right of the people peaceably to assemble and to petition the government for a redress of grievances." What types of acts of individuals are defined by this constitutional clause?

6. Consider the following statements of law governing the doctor-patient relation. How would you classify each of the acts indicated by the italicized words in terms of standardized acts?

(a) The relation of doctor and patient commences when the patient *calls* the doctor and the latter undertakes the case.

(b) There is no obligation on the doctor to serve patients, i. e., *take* cases; and this means that the doctor can arbitrarily decline to accept patients.

(c) The general rule is well-established that before a doctor nay *treat* a patient or *operate* on him, the doctor must obtain the consent either of the patient, if competent to give it, or of someone authorized to give consent for him. If the doctor *acts without such consent*, he will be liable for the resulting damages.

(d) The doctor must *care for* his patient with reasonable skill and diligence while the doctor-patient relation continues.

(e) The doctor-patient relation may be terminated at any time by the patient's *dismissal* of the doctor.

(f) The doctor may not *abandon* the case at will; he can withdraw from the case by giving reasonable notice to the patient of such intention and allowing a reasonable time for the latter to obtain another doctor.

Sec. 2–09. Effective acts. The lawmaker also defines many acts which A can do with the purpose and intent of producing legal effects. These standardized acts are established for the use and benefit of A.* L tenders official aid to A if he calls for it in prescribed ways; he offers official services to A if A does certain acts.[1] He tells A what aid he can expect from the legal system and what acts he must do to obtain that aid.

Thus in the law of *property*, which you will pursue in your first year, you will find the definitions of various acts which are to be done in order to acquire property. The wild animal has to be killed or captured in order to obtain ownership of it. By doing either of these acts, the legal actor, A, pulls about himself the mantle of legal protection which we know as ownership; he becomes entitled to the services of the agents of the legal system in protecting his control. You will find also in your study of the law of property that there are standard acts, such as gift and sale, by which the chattel can be transferred; gift and sale are acts of donor and seller which invest the donee and buyer respectively with the perquisites of ownership. Interests in land can also be acquired and transferred by acts; the commonest of these we

---

* (I.R.) Some modern analysts speak of "juristic acts" or "legal transactions" at this point. However, the lawyer does not use such expressions frequently; their vogue is limited to the technical fraternity of jurisprudence. As I find no settled expression in general use, I feel free to create one which more definitely connotes what I have in mind, i.e., acts done with foresight of legal consequences. For this purpose I have chosen "effective acts." This term also includes (as I want to do) such an act as filing a pleading, which I doubt if either of the other expressions would embrace.

[1] This aid need not be demanded in so many words, though often it is so demanded; but in any case the individual must indicate a need for legal assistance by doing the acts prescribed by law. These acts are the effective acts in which we are presently interested.

know as "taking possession," "making a deed," and "making a will." The legal system in all these cases presents A with model acts which he can do in order to produce legal effects. One might liken these legal acts to the order blanks which a mail order house furnishes to its prospective patrons for use in obtaining desired goods. The legal patron is furnished with a variety of formalized acts which he can use in calling upon the legal system to carry out his desires.

Similar to the acts by which A can acquire or transfer property is a whole arsenal of useful acts which he may do in the transaction of business. Most of these can be lumped together under the caption of *contractual acts*. In the contract, two acts are usually involved; the offer by A and the acceptance by B. These two acts in combination constitute an agreement which gives rise to contemplated legal effects, i. e., contractual obligations. Contractual acts have in view the performance of services, the subsequent transfer of goods, and many other objectives. Contractual arrangements may be simple as where two parties, A and B, make an agreement directly with one another; they may be more complicated as where P by contract appoints an agent, A, who in turn makes a contract with C for and on behalf of P. They may be even more complex as where an individual draws a check or bill of exchange—an act which involves a whole series of possible consequences and arrangements between himself, a bank, a payee, indorsers, and other persons. An individual may participate in the formation and operation of a corporation, in which case his acts join with the acts of many others to produce legal consequences which he alone could not produce. As to each of these types of situation, simple or complex, the legal system provides beforehand both what it is necessary for A and others to do and what the legal effects of their acts will be. More than upon any other factor, transaction of business depends on the ability to act with foresight of results. This is where these standardized legal transactions fit into the business picture. Indeed, our commercial life could hardly go on if these standard legal transactions, coupled with standard and foreknown legal consequences, were not provided and available for use.

And so I might go on through almost every branch of our law. The law of court procedure, for example, provides A with a variety of standardized pictures of acts which he is to perform in the prosecution of his claims and the assertion of defenses; he is told what he must do and what kind of paper he must file at each step of a lawsuit. But it is unnecessary to pursue the subject further. The law is replete with these standard acts which A can do with a foresight of legal results; with acts which A can do for the purpose of calling upon the agents of the legal system for their services in one respect or another.

You will note how different is the position of the law toward these legally effective acts from its position toward an obligatory act or a prohibited act.[2] The law which authorizes A to dispose of his property by will, does not, for example, command him to make a will or forbid him to die without making a will. A is told, instead, that *if* he makes a will, certain legal effects will follow. A legal provision informs A that, by doing a specified act, he can invest his property at his death in persons of his choice. Every legal provision establishing a standard effective act and defining its consequences, follows essentially the same lines. The legal provision serves as a promise by the legal system that if the individual acts in the specified manner, certain legal consequences will ensue. The primary objective of the legal provision is to offer certain services to a prospective actor,

[2] Compare what is said in sec. 2–11 regarding the positions adopted by the law toward different types of acts.

to instruct him regarding ways and means of obtaining desired legal results.**

Sec. 2–10. Ineffective acts. This is a category opposed, as its name indicates, to the category of effective acts.* Ineffective acts are attempted effective acts; they are undertaken as effective acts but fail to take effect as intended.** The effective act must be undertaken for a lawful *purpose*, and the act must be done in the *manner* prescribed by law. Two reasons why an act may fail of effect correspond to these two major requirements.[1]

First, the legal actor may act for an unlawful purpose and his act may be denied legal effect for this reason. This type of act may be called an *illegal act*. A contract by A according

** (I.R.) Regarding the metaphorical and elliptical character of such expressions as the "position of the law" and "a promise by the legal system," see sec. 2–04, note *.

* (I.R.) Some readers may challenge the need, or desirability, of creating the category of ineffective acts. Such a challenge is always proper. Some may even assume that this category is on a par with Hohfeld's "no-right" and that we are talking of a "no-act" here. These assumptions are, however, not correct. We are definitely interested in a real act which A does with the intent to produce legal effects. In other words the negative quality here attaches to the effectiveness, and not to the occurrence, of the act. Everything else aside there is some convenience in pursuing the classification of acts in terms of three primary categories and their three opposites, even though some of the opposites are not quite as frequently used as the three primary categories. I could, of course, discuss ineffective acts at the point where I consider the significance of acts (sec. 2–15 *et seq.*). But I think it is quite as natural and convenient to consider them here along with other categories of acts. In other words, there are certain types of acts which are intended to have legal effects, and do have; there are other acts which are intended to have legal effects, but do not have such effects, i.e., the illegal acts and the defectively executed acts mentioned in the text.

** (I.R.) These statements are not accurate for all purposes; they do not take full account of cases where effectiveness and ineffectiveness depend on factors other than the actor's intent; cases of fraud and estoppel, for example. However, the statements are sufficient for the present purpose; they do cover the two types of ineffective acts which I want to discuss here, illegal acts and defective acts.

[1] Two other main types of ineffective acts are worth mention, though we have not the time to treat them here: 1. Acts by persons lacking in legal capacity; 2. Acts which are tainted in the doing by the actor's mistake or by fraud, duress, etc., practiced on him by another.

to which he is to pay B $1000 for services is valid and binding on A if executed in proper form. But if the service which B is to perform is unlawful, then A's promise is illegal and he is not bound. Thus if A promises to pay B $1000 if B will give C a thrashing, B cannot collect the $1000 after he has administered the thrashing because the promise of A was made to achieve an unlawful purpose, and the courts will not enforce a promise directed to such an end. Similarly, if A and B enter into an agreement to monopolize a market, the purposes of both men are unlawful, and their contractual acts (offer and acceptance) are ineffective. The agreement will be unenforcible by either A or B, and probably both parties will be exposed to tort liabilities in reference to specific parties injured by their contract, and to criminal prosecution for the violation of statutes which prohibit such a contract.

Second, A's act may fail of its intended effect because it is not done in the manner prescribed by law. This type of act may be called a *defective act*. If the law provides that certain contracts be written or that a will must be attested by two witnesses, A has no reason to be surprised or disappointed if his unwritten contract or his will attested by only one witness, is not given legal effect. The law has specified the terms and conditions on which his act will be effective; he must satisfy those terms and conditions; his act is ineffective by reason of defect in execution. Invalidity is inferred from failure to comply with explicit legal specifications. Ineffectiveness is implied from the fact that certain requirements are set up and are not met. However, the ineffectiveness of certain acts may also be expressly declared, not left to implication. Thus the Statute of Frauds provides that certain types of contracts are to be unenforcible unless they are in writing. Notice that it does not declare that contracts must be written, and leave to implication the conclusion that they will be unenforcible if they are not written; but rather it declares that unwritten contracts are to be ineffective. Either way the unwritten contract is a standardized ineffective act; in the one case by reason of an implication, in the other by virtue of an express provision.

Sec. 2–11. Distinction and interrelation of kinds of acts. In the foregoing sections we have talked of six kinds of acts; we ought not to conclude the discussion of them without a few words about how these kinds are distinguished and interrelated.

All these acts are alike in that they are the doings of our hypothetical individual, A. What is the basis on which we have *distinguished* one act of A from another and divided his acts into classes? The acts have been classified on the basis of differences in the lawmaker's attitudes toward them. These acts differ from one another only as respects the position which L (or if you prefer, the law or the legal system) adopts in regard to them. One kind of act L disapproves and forbids, the prohibited act; another type of act he approves very strongly and commands A to do, the obligatory act; another type he assures A will evoke certain services from the minions of the law, the effective act; another type he approves and tells A he may do, the permitted act; and another type L leaves to A's judgment, the discretionary act; and a last type he refuses to support by the aid of the legal system even though effectiveness be the desire and intent of A in doing the act, the ineffective act. In short, it is important to realize that we have been classifying A's acts but classifying them in terms of L's attitudes toward them.

Three of these classes are *opposed* respectively to three of the others: the prohibited act to the permitted act, the obligatory act to the discretionary act, and the effective act to the ineffective act. There is nothing inherent or necessary about the opposition of these categories; they merely represent opposing attitudes of the lawmaker, as for example in the case of prohibited and permitted acts, the one type he disapproves and the other type he does not disapprove. These categories are opposed simply because the lawmaker adopts contradictory attitudes toward them.

However some of our categories *overlap* one another in large degree. The same act may be classified under two or more categories. We find acts which are effective, permitted and also discretionary; as, for example, the act of getting married, the act of enlisting in the army, or the act of making a contract, a deed, or a will. We find acts that are obligatory and effective, too, such as the filing of an income tax return, or the act of registration for the draft. We find acts which are prohibited and ineffective, e. g., the agreement to commit a crime. And we even find acts which are prohibited but effective; as where A wrongfully takes B's goods, thereby becoming possessed thereof; A's act is effective to give him legal control as against third parties even if it is a wrong to B. The point I want to make is that you must not take these six categories as mutually exclusive of one another; some are and some are not.

Also important is the fact that the categories of acts are often *connected* together in series. A's acts are joined with B's as they are actually done so that the state cannot prescribe standards for A's acts without reference to B's. Standards have to be developed to cover and include the acts of both A and B. Standards have to be stated in chains or sequences in which A's act and B's act are combined.[1] For example, in the making of a contract, we find such a standardized combination of acts: an offer followed by an acceptance. Likewise, in the situation where B defends himself against attack by A; attack and self-defense represent a conjoint action picture in which the activities of two persons are

[1] On this matter of interconnected acts, see sec. 2–27.

legally essential. And legal standards in both these instances are set forth in terms of sequences or combinations of acts.

Finally, for fear that I have made these categories appear more formidable and solid than they really are, I want to add two admonitions: First, do not look upon the six categories as final or necessary. Another classifier might make up an entirely different set with as much justification as I have for these. The categories are modes of classification and nothing more; they are merely useful pigeonholes into which you can put various activities of A which are the concern of the law. Second, do not try to memorize this list of categories as such, or try to keep in mind the definition of any category, or try to recall specifically which category is the opposite of which. Such efforts are unnecessary here as well as elsewhere in our course. If you read the text with care and attention and work out the problems in terms of the text, you will retain all that needs to be remembered about these types of standard acts.[2]

Sec. 2–12. Problems. 1. Suppose A offers to work for B for ten days at ten dollars per day and B accepts this offer. This concludes a contract between the parties on the terms indicated. What kind of acts are involved in the making of the contract, i. e., the offer and the acceptance? What kind of acts are involved in the performance of the contract, i. e., the ten days' service by A and the payment of $100 by B?

2. L, a landlord, executes a lease of a house for five years to T, a tenant, at $1200 per annum. What kinds of standard acts are involved in the making of the lease? In the performance of its terms?

---

[2] This admonition about memorizing has already been given (sec. 1–03). If I did not know from long experience that students come to law school with a fixed notion that learning consists in memory work, and that this notion is very hard to eradicate, I would not regard it as necessary to repeat the admonition from time to time.

3. The law allows a husband to recover damages from a third party who alienates his wife's affections. How would you classify the third person's act? The husband's act of bringing suit?

4. What is the difference in the actor's attitude toward legal effects when he commits a legally forbidden act such as theft, and when he does a legally effective act such as the making of a will?

5. Under the rules of the common law the making of a bet is declared to be contrary to good morals, but is not punishable as a crime. The winner of a bet cannot be compelled to repay what the loser has paid. Under these rules, how would you classify the loser's promise to pay? Is it an effective act? A prohibited act? An illegal act?

Under the common law rules how would you classify the loser's act of payment? Is it illegal? Is it effective?

Sec. 2–13. Individual's acts are physical and verbal. Before we leave the problem of classifying A's acts, I ought to refer again to what was said earlier about two ways of controlling people—by physical force and by verbal acts (sec. 1–09). The individual's acts may be divided in parallel fashion into physical acts and verbal acts. Both may be the subject of legal control. What is meant by physical act is sufficiently obvious and familiar. Among physical acts which may be legally important are such acts as striking another person or carrying away his goods, moving about in one's business and the operation of a factory on one's land. Verbal acts I have already defined as all uses of language, in speech or writing. The expression covers any form of statement made, question asked, or command given, by the individual.[1]

---

[1] In secs. 1–08 and 1–10 we discussed the use of verbal acts (laws and orders) to control A. Here we are interested in verbal acts by A himself which may call for the establishment of legal standards of action.

The division of A's acts into physical and verbal cuts across the sixfold division of standard acts which we have just considered: [2]

There are physical acts which are *prohibited*, such as striking another person. And there are verbal acts which are likewise forbidden, such as the publication of a defamatory statement.

Both physical and verbal acts are to be found under the class of *permitted* acts. For example, freedom of locomotion involves freedom of physical activity, while freedom of speech involves permitted verbal acts.

There are physical acts which are *obligatory*, e. g., furnishing food for one's child. And there are verbal acts of like

[2] Physical and verbal acts are distinguishable as is indicated in the text, and it is often useful in legal discussion to distinguish them. But it is also important to remember that the two kinds of behavior, physical and verbal, are closely related to one another. First, behavior is often partly physical and partly verbal, and these parts are often *interconnected* and mutually qualifying. Thus physical acts may take a large part of their meaning from accompanying or preceding or succeeding verbal declarations. Suppose, for instance, S says to H, "Lend me a dollar." H forthwith hands S a dollar without remark. Here the physical act of H can only be understood in the light of S's request. And if S then says, "Thank you," his thanks too must be interpreted in reference to the verbal act and the physical act which have gone before. All these acts take color from one another. None of them can be interpreted apart from the others. *Second*, physical and verbal acts are largely *interchangeable*. They serve similar functions and can be substituted for one another to some extent. Consider again S's request for a loan. To this verbal act H may respond as aforesaid by the simple handing over of a dollar (physical act); or H may hand over a dollar with the statement, "Here is a nice new one" (physical plus verbal act); or H may reply, "I haven't a dollar with me; I'll give you one this afternoon" (verbal act promising a later physical act). Now all these combinations of physical acts and verbal declarations are substantially equivalent—provided, of course, that H hands over the dollar in the last case as promised. They all result in substantially the same legal obligation of S to repay the dollar at a later time.

In short, we must recognize that physical and verbal acts are conceptually distinguishable, just as we may distinguish a leg from the rest of the body; but in actual human activity the two forms of behavior are not ordinarily separated any more than legs are usually found separated from bodies. In actual life situations, physical behavior and verbal behavior are woven together like the warp and woof of one fabric; no part of the whole can be appreciated without taking account of the rest. (*Cf.* sec. 1-14.)

character, e. g., registration for the draft and filing an income tax return.

There are a few effective acts which are physical, though not many, e. g., the capture of a wild animal. The great bulk of effective acts is verbal. The making of a will is a verbal act; also, the making of a conveyance or a lease. The execution of a contract usually involves verbal declarations by two parties. And the steps which a party and his attorney must take in the course of a lawsuit are practically all verbal.

Similar observations might be made about discretionary and ineffective acts—but it is not worth the pains to pursue the subject or to produce further examples.

To the lawyer the verbal activity of A is far more important than the physical as has already been shown. Verbal acts engage most of the lawyer's attention in practice. And, I might add, these verbal acts are chiefly planned for legal effect; they are legally effective acts such as making wills, deeds, or contracts, or the incorporation of companies. The lawyer's main tasks are to guide the effective verbal acts of his clients and to perform such acts himself on their behalf.

Sec. 2–14. Problems. 1. There is an old saying, "With sticks and stones you break my bones but words will never hurt me." Consider in this connection the provisions of a Texas statute:

"Although it is necessary to constitute homicide that it shall result from some act of the party accused, yet, if words be used which are reasonably calculated to produce, and do produce an act which is the immediate cause of death, it is homicide; as, for example, if a blind man, a stranger, a child, or a person of unsound mind, be directed by words to a precipice or other dangerous place where he falls and is killed; or if one be directed to take any article of medicine, food or drink, known to be poisonous and which does produce a fatal effect; in these and like cases, the person so operating on the mind or conduct of the person injured shall be deemed guilty of homicide." [1]

Obviously the acts here referred to are verbal. Would you regard them as informative verbal acts (sec. 1–11)? As directive verbal acts (sec. 1–08)?

Where would they fall in our sixfold classification of acts?

2. *Commonwealth v. Randolph:* [2]

"It may be conceded that the mere intent to commit a crime, where such intent is undisclosed, and nothing done in pursuance of it, is not the subject of an indictment. But there was something more than an undisclosed intent in this case. There was the direct solicitation to commit a murder, and an offer of money as a reward for its commission. This was an act done, a step in the direction of crime; . . . It needs no argument to show that such an act affects the public policy and economy in a serious manner. . . .

"The authorities in England are very full upon this point. The leading case is Rex v. Higgins, 2 East 5. It is very similar to the case at bar, and it was squarely held that solicitation to commit a felony is a misdemeanor and indictable at common law. In that case it was said by Lord Kenyon, C. J.: 'But it is argued that a mere intent to commit evil is not indictable without an act done; but is there not an act done when it is charged that the defendant solicited another to commit a felony? The solicitation is an act; . . .'"

What act is made criminal here?

3. "No damages shall be awarded in any libel action brought against a reporter, editor, publisher or proprietor of a newspaper for the publication therein of a fair and true report of any public and official proceeding. . . ." [3]

What is the status of this type of defamatory statement, under the terms of this statute?

[1] Tex. Rev. Stat., Ch. 10, Art. 656 (1895).
[2] 146 Pa. 83 at 94, 95 (1892).
[3] Mich. Stat. Ann. sec. 27.369.

4. *Iddings v. Iddings.*[4]

A will was read over to the testator and duly signed by him. The scrivener who drew the will made a mistake as to the meaning of the word "cancel" so that the will directed that the accounts of his children (for advances) were not to be cancelled; the testator had intended just the opposite meaning. On appeal the court held that evidence of the scrivener to prove this error was inadmissible. The court said:

"But, if mistakes were to be corrected by the scrivener's recollection of his conversation with the testator, it would open such a door for perjury and confusion, as would render wills of very little use. The rule of law therefore, is that the writing is not to be *altered,* or *explained* by evidence *aliunde.* . . ."

What is the effective legal act here? Does the act operate as intended?

SIGNIFICANCE OF STANDARD ACTS

Sec. 2–15. Act and significance. Thus far I have focused attention on standard acts of the individual; these are acts which are legally significant. I have directed only incidental or passing notice to the significance of these acts. It is now time to turn attention to the matter of significance.[1] In what ways is the act of A important? What is the legal standing

---

[4] 7 Serg. & R. Pa. 111 (1891).

[1] From here on I shall often refer to the "legal significance" of A's acts. Significance seems to me the most appropriate word. However, there are other terms which are substantial equivalents and which are sometimes used herein as well as elsewhere—such as legal meaning, legal importance, legal operation, legal effects, legal consequences. Significance is preferred because it gives the idea that A's acts have meaning to other persons, including officials; they do not operate on others as a physical force does. A's act of striking B operates physically on B, of course; but the physical character of the act and its physical effect are something different from its legal significance. The latter consists of the meaning of A's act, and its physical consequences, within the legal system—viz., what rights, powers, and privileges arise from the striking and what officials are going to do about the striking.

or legal meaning of his act? These are the questions to which we shall now turn.

The legal system furnishes patterns for A's acts. Important acts which he may do are standardized. The significance of his acts is likewise standardized. The significance which is attached to what A does is patterned out and prescribed just as his acts are.* In fact, significant act and legal significance of the act, are but two sides of one coin. They are coupled together and imply one another.

$$\text{Standard} \quad \xleftrightarrow{\hspace{3cm}} \quad \text{Standard}$$
$$\text{Act} \qquad\qquad\qquad\qquad \text{Significance}$$

We cannot think and talk of the one without taking the other for granted. Nevertheless we can, at different times, stress one side or the other of this act-significance relationship; in the present and succeeding sections we shall keep our eye primarily on the significance side of this legal coin.

Sec. 2–16. Significance of acts—standard forms. The legal importance, or meaning, of A's acts is expressed in various standard forms, of which four are sufficiently common to call for specific mention:

1. Significance in terms of relations to the other person, B;
2. Significance in terms of effects on A himself;
3. Significance in relation to the state (or legal system);
4. Significance in terms of official (O's) acts.

* (I.R.) One reason why I have not used the terms *act* and *consequence* is that consequence is also used in a factual sense. If consequence is used, it becomes necessary to make and maintain a distinction between factual consequence and legal consequence. The failure to keep the two things apart results in great confusion in the consideration of causation problems. Factual causes and consequences (effects) are parts of standard action pictures. Legal consequences are the significance which we attach to these pictures. For example, the driving of a car may result in killing a pedestrian; in this sense it is the factual cause of his death and the death is a consequence of the driving. But the driving is not the legal cause and the death not the legal consequence of the driving, unless it appears that the driver was at fault in some way. If we use the term "significance" (instead of consequence) this kind of problem presents less difficulty of explanation and comprehension. Compare what is said in next preceding footnote.

Accordingly we can say that A's acts are significant in different respects or in different directions, and we can represent these different directions thus:

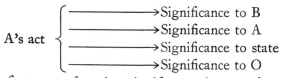

A's act
→ Significance to B
→ Significance to A
→ Significance to state
→ Significance to O

The first way of stating significance, in regard to B, will be discussed rather fully in the next several sections; the second, in regard to A himself, will be treated in section 2–24; the third and fourth ways of stating significance, in regard to the state and in terms of acts of officials, will be developed in section 3–02.

Sec. 2–17. Significance of act—in relation to others.* To meet the need to discuss the bearing of A's acts upon other persons, our law has standardized the ways in which A's acts

---

* (I.R.) On the subject matter of sec. 2–17 *et seq.*, see generally:

Corbin, Arthur L., "Jural Relations and Their Classification," 30 Yale L. J. 228 (1921).

Corbin, Arthur L., "Legal Analysis and Terminology," 29 Yale L. J. 163 (1919).

Corbin, Arthur L., "Rights and Duties," 33 Yale L. J. 501 (1924).

Goble, George, "A Redefinition of Basic Legal Terms," 35 Col. L. Rev. 535 (1935).

Goble, George, "Affirmative and Negative Legal Relations," 4 Ill. L. Q. 94 (1922).

Goble, George, "Negative Legal Relations Re-examined," 5 Ill. L. Q. 36 (1922).

Hohfeld, Wesley N., Fundamental Legal Conceptions 35 *et seq.* (1923).

Kocourek, Albert, "Basic Jural Relations," 17 Ill. L. Rev. 515 (1923).

Kocourek, Albert, Jural Relations (1927).

Kocourek, Albert, "Non-Legal-Content Relations Recombated," 5 Ill. L. Q. 150 (1923).

Kocourek, Albert, "Plurality of Advantage and Disadvantage in Jural Relations," 19 Mich. L. Rev. 47 (1920).

Kocourek, Albert, "Polarized and Unpolarized Legal Relations," 9 Ky. L. J. 131 (1921).

Kocourek, Albert, "*Tabulae Minores Jurisprudentiae*," 30 Yale L. J. 215 (1921).

Kocourek, Albert, "The Hohfeld System of Fundamental Legal Concepts," 15 Ill. L. Rev. 24 (1920).

Kocourek, Albert, "Various Definitions of Jural Relation," 20 Col. L. Rev. 394 (1920).

may have significance in relation to them. It has developed a standardized relational terminology. To connect A's doings with B, it employs such terms as duty, right, privilege, discretion, power, and liability. These are the common terms found in the legislative statement of the significance of standard acts; they are the common terms found in legal instruments, in orders, and in textbooks. Indeed, the greater part of all discussion of the legal significance of acts is carried on in these terms. For this reason, I shall devote the next several sections to the explication and illustration of the meanings of duty, right, privilege, discretion, power and liability.

You will find that this discussion is closely linked with our previous discussion of standard acts. Duty and right are connected with prohibited and obligatory acts; privilege with permitted acts; discretion with nonobligatory acts; power and liability primarily with effective acts. However, the treatment of these terms will carry us considerably beyond the subject of acts, and will tie up acts with other persons as well as the actor.

Sec. 2–18. Actor's duty to another. The legal importance of A's act may inhere in the fact that it is one which A must do for someone else's benefit, or an act which he must refrain from doing on someone else's account. The common terminology here is that of duty to act or duty not to act. In other words, the significance of an act is stated in terms of an actor's legal duty to act or his legal duty to refrain from action. Terry, a well-known writer, thus defines the meaning of duty: "A person who is commanded or for-

Page, William H., "Terminology and Classification in Fundamental Jural Relations," 4 Am. L. S. Rev. 616 (1921).
Pound, Roscoe, Introduction to Study of Law (1924).
Pound, Roscoe, Outline of Jurisprudence, 5th ed., 144 *et seq.* (1943).
Radin, Max, "A Restatement of Hohfeld," 51 Harv. L. Rev. 1141, 1153–1156 (1938).
Salmond, Sir John William, Jurisprudence, 6th ed. (1920).

bidden by law to do an act is under a legal duty to do or not to do it. A legal duty is a condition of one who is so commanded or forbidden." [1] Terry further says that a legal duty implies these elements: (1) a person on whom the duty rests; (2) a person to whom it is owed; (3) certain acts or omissions constituting the content of the duty. [2] This connects up the duty with someone, "a person to whom it is owed"; it emphasizes the relation of A's act to another person.

Accordingly, the legal meaning of obligatory and prohibited acts can be, and often is, stated in the terms of an actor's duty to someone else. Legislatures, courts, draftsmen, and writers in declaring the significance of acts, probably talk more often in terms of duty owed by A to B than in any other terms. In this sense, acts which are beneficial to B and which A is obliged to do (sec. 2–06), are acts which he is under a duty to do; and acts which are injurious to B and which A is prohibited from doing (sec. 2–04), are acts which A is under a duty not to do. The significance of A's acts in both these situations is commonly expressed in terms of duties owed by A to B.

Sec. 2–19. Right of another against actor. The importance of these same standard acts may also be expressed in another way. Their significance may be stated in terms of B's claim rather than A's duty. B has a claim that A perform an act or refrain from acting.* This mode of statement makes the

[1] PRINCIPLES OF ANGLO-AMERICAN LAW, sec. 1–08 (1884).
[2] *Ibid.* sec. 1–10.
* (I.R.) According to this definition, a right is always a right to an act or an omission by some other person. A great deal of confusion would be avoided in the discussion of rights if we were in the habit of stressing this aspect of them. I do not believe my definition of right is, in any essential, opposed to that of Hohfeld or his followers. However, they are accustomed to define rights in a way which leaves them practically without content. Hohfeld speaks of a right as correlative to a duty and says that right is synonymous with claim. (FUNDAMENTAL LEGAL CONCEPTIONS 35 *et seq.* (1923).) But he does not state what the nature of the claim is. This leaves

nonactor, B, the center of the picture. The claim, which we commonly call a right, belongs to him. For example, an act beneficial to B, and which A is under a duty to do (sec. 2–06), can equally well be characterized by saying that B, who would be benefited by the doing of the act, has a right that A shall do it. A similar mode of expression in terms of rights may be adopted in stating the legal significance of an act injurious to B, and which the actor is forbidden to do (sec. 2–04). Here it is usual to say that B has a right that A shall not do the act in question.

In fact, it is the common practice to state the significance of obligatory and prohibited acts in terms of both rights and duties at the same time. When B has a right, A has a duty. The significance of obligatory and prohibited acts is expressed in terms of a correlation between B's rights and A's duties. The imposition on A of a legal obligation to act for B's benefit is, at the same time, the creation of a claim on B's part to have the act done. The prohibition of A's action to B's injury is, at the same time, the creation of a claim or right on B's part to have the injurious act not done. The right or claim on B's part is, by definition, treated as the invariable correlative of a duty on A's part, to act or not to act.

completely unexpressed the very important and useful connections of rights with human acts. The effect is especially unfortunate in view of the tendency in all discussion of rights to treat them as independent things and to separate them from actual human activity. Even the reference, which is common in defining rights, to persons who have them and to persons who are subject to them, fails to counteract the devitalizing effect of the omission of all reference to action; and the same is true of the emphasis, in some discussions of rights, on their relation to things. All these modes of speaking of rights serve to hypostatize or reify them. What is needed is a form of expression which makes clear that the term "right" is merely a convenient mode of referring to human acts which ought, or ought not, to be done. These acts, of course, involve actors and persons affected by acts. They also involve things. But, starting with the general postulate that legal standards are norms for the guidance of human acts, it must be apparent that we are omitting something which is of the first importance when we state the significance of those standards in terms which entirely omit reference to human activity.

You will note from the above that we have tacitly defined right in two ways: (1) as a claim that A refrain from doing certain acts or that he perform certain acts; and (2) as the correlative of a duty.

We may also say, paralleling the analysis of a legal duty given in section 2–18, that a legal right implies these elements: (1) a person to whom the right belongs; (2) a person on whom the duty rests; (3) certain acts or omissions constituting the content of the right.**

Sec. 2–20. Actor's privilege to act. In section 2–05 we spoke of permitted acts and pointed out that permissive legal declarations are functionally justified by the need to tell the prospective actor how far he may go in his actions. But other persons are also concerned with A's liberties of action. Such a permissive declaration merely asserts that a particular type of action by A is permitted. We can, however, relate this liberty of action to other individuals who are affected by A's act. In this sense, we say that A has a privilege, or liberty, of acting in relation to B. Essentially, then, the privilege is merely a permissive declaration of law, stated in relation to other persons than the actor. Examples are the privilege of A to defend himself against attack by B; and the privilege of the doctor to operate on a patient who has consented to an operation.[1]

The privilege, you will notice, has quite a different connection with the actor than the right has, though the two notions are often confused in discourse. A privilege belongs

---

** (I.R.) At this point, it would be logical to insert a discussion of the distinction between *rights in personam* and *rights in rem* (and also of Hohfeld's paucital and multital rights). However, this topic seems to me far too complicated for inclusion in an introductory course, and I have, therefore, decided to omit it. On this topic, see SALMOND, JURISPRUDENCE, 6th ed., sec. 81 (1920), and HOHFELD, FUNDAMENTAL LEGAL CONCEPTIONS 67 *et seq.* (1923).

[1] Sec. 2–06, problem 6. See also sec. 2–14, problem 3, in which a privilege of defamation was involved.

to an actor, A; it is the freedom of A to act without treading on B's toes in the legal sense; it is an opportunity of A to act without justifiable objection by B.[2] The right, by contrast, always belongs to a nonactor, B, and this right represents a restraint on A's freedom of action; it means that A must refrain from acting in a manner to injure the right-holder, B. This is a distinction which we shall have to refer to repeatedly in discussing the problems in section 2–25.

Some writers have felt the necessity of conjuring up a correlative to match A's privilege to act.* They have said that A has a privilege to act and that B has a "no-right" that A shall not act. This kind of "no-right" seems to me both unnatural and unnecessary. There is no reason, of course, why we cannot say in an ordinary way that B has no right to object to certain lines of behavior on the part of A. But inasmuch as all we are trying to say is that an actor, A, is free to act without valid legal objection by B, I do not see any reason why we should not say just that, and dispense with this correlative cast in negative terms.

Sec. 2–21. Actor's discretion to act. The important legal aspect of an act may be that it is not obligatory on the actor. It may be necessary to express the fact that an act does not have to be done. It may be necessary to indicate the absence of obligation on A to do an act for B's benefit. In speaking of acts in these terms, and developing their significance in this way, we are simply looking at the other side of the coin described in terms of discretionary acts.[1] And the examples earlier mentioned also serve as illustrations of what is meant here. A owes no obligation to be a Good Samaritan, and a

---

[2] However, A may have a right against B and a privilege in regard to B at the same time. Thus A (as nonactor) has the right not to be struck by B (as wrongful actor), but A (as privileged actor) is allowed by law to defend himself against attack by B (a wrongful actor).

* (I.R.) This position is taken by Hohfeld and some of his disciples. See the items by Hohfeld, Corbin, and Goble cited in sec. 2–17, note *.

[1] Sec. 2–07.

doctor owes no obligation to accept a patient who calls for his services.[2] The reason it is worth mentioning these cases again is that there are times when it is useful to connect up A's discretion to act with other persons and point out the absence of obligation toward them.

Sec. 2–22. Actor's power over another. The primary meaning of "power" is the *ability to do an effective act* which affects another. In this sense, power expresses the possibility of A's doing an effective act, the possibility that A's act will be effective when, as, and if, done. On the other hand, it expresses the idea that A's act will affect B. Accordingly, power is defined as the ability, by an effective act, to change the legal position of another person. The potential actor, A, is the center of reference; the other person is passive and is simply affected by what A does. Examples are the power to adopt a child; the power to bring a civil action, e. g., a suit for damages; the power of the owner of land to make an effective conveyance to another; the power of a principal to invest an agent with authority to act on the principal's behalf; the power of a principal to terminate the authority of his agent; etc.

However, power is sometimes more broadly defined. It is used to include not only the ability to affect others by effective acts such as those mentioned, but also used to include the ability to affect others by wrongful acts, as by commission of a tort or a breach of contract.[1] In this sense, A is said to have power to commit a battery by striking B, and to have

---

[2] Mentioned in sec. 2–08, problem 6.

Suppose, however, that a doctor stops at the scene of a collision on the highway; that the principal person hurt is the wife of X; that the doctor declines to care for W because he has previously had a serious personal difference with X; that X draws a revolver and, standing over the doctor, compels him to give the needed medical service. The doctor not only has discretion about serving, but also has rights not to be coerced. *Cf.* sec. 2–20, note 2.

[1] Llewellyn: Power refers to what A ". . . *can* do, and so affect what the court will do." THE BRAMBLE BUSH 84 (1930).

power by refusal to perform, to breach his contract. The only point that needs to be noted about this broader use of the term power, is the necessity to make sure in any given case which usage is being adopted. Is the speaker employing the word power in the narrower sense of ability to do an effective act affecting another, or in the wider sense of the ability to do any legally significant act which affects B?

A power in either of the senses just defined is a notion radically different from a right as defined in section 2–19, though right and power are often confused. Power is defined in reference to an actor, A. To say that A has a power is to assert that A can, by an act, produce legal effects; that he can do a legally significant act. Right is defined in reference to a nonactor, B; it expresses B's claim that another, A, refrain from acting or that he act positively in favor of the right-holder, B. This is a distinction which we shall have occasion to develop in discussing the problems in section 2–25.

Sec. 2–23. Liability to effects of another's act. In discussing powers, I pointed out that B is often subject to the effects of acts which A does, and that we often want to speak of the fact that B's legal position will be affected when, as, and if A acts. The legal significance of A's act may be cast in terms of B's liabilities quite as well as in terms of A's powers. By a liability, I mean subjection to the effects of the act of another person; or, one might say, exposure to the effects of such an act. B's liability expresses the possibility of having his legal position altered by the effective act of another person. The liability of B is the correlative of the power of A, whose act can affect B. In other words, liability is the correlative of the power, by an effective act, to affect another's legal position. Examples are the liability of B, who has breached his contract with A, to suit by A; the liability of a tenant to the landlord's act of terminating the lease by re-entry for breach of condition; and the liability of the judgment debtor to a levy of execution on the judgment by the judgment creditor.

Liability, like power, may be given a broader definition. It may be defined, as I have defined it above, as the subjection to another's effective act, but it may also be defined more comprehensively to include also the subjection to wrongful acts of another, such as tortious acts and breaches of contract. In this sense, B is exposed to wrongful acts such as a battery by A, and B is also exposed to breaches of contract by the other party to a contract. However, though there is no reason why one cannot define liability in this wide sense to correspond with the wide use of power, I think it is rather unusual to use the word liability in this way.

Sec. 2–24. Significance of act to actor himself. In the foregoing sections, I have discussed and defined terms in which we are accustomed to express the legal importance of A's acts to B. Within a somewhat narrower range, it may be important to express the legal significance of A's act to A himself. The terminology of rights and duties is hardly appropriate for this purpose. That terminology is essentially relational. It presupposes at least two persons to be related to one another. While we do sometimes say that a person owes it to himself to do or not to do some act, this usage is rather a reference to moral considerations or is to be taken as a figurative use of terms. We do not seriously mean that A is at one and the same time the claimant of acts and the person bound to act. He does not have rights against himself, nor owe duties to himself.

Similar observations apply to the use of the terms "privilege" and "discretion." When these terms are used in a meaningful way, I believe a relationship to someone else is understood. A's privilege to act means his freedom from objection by others, not his freedom from complaint by himself. His discretion to act refers to the fact that others have no obligatory claim upon him, not to the fact that he can act in a manner to affect himself.

But when we speak of the significance of A's powers in regard to A himself, we introduce a new element. Power can be defined as A's ability by an act to affect the legal position of B—the definition given and used in section 2–22 above. But power may be defined as A's ability by an act to affect his own legal position. This latter is the sense in which the term power is used when we speak of A's power to make a will, or his power to abandon the chattel that he owns. These are both acts which immediately and primarily affect the legal status of A himself. This usage of power constitutes a third meaning to be added to the two already mentioned. And again, as I have said before, the chief point that needs to be noted about these three possible meanings of power is the necessity to make sure in any given case which usage is being followed.

Sec. 2–25. Problems. Unfortunately, the terms we have just defined are used in all sorts of confusing ways. This holds equally of use by legislatures, courts, lawyers, scholars, and students. Of these terms, the term "right" is probably the most loosely and multifariously employed. "Right" is used not only in the strict sense defined in section 2–19; it is also used in the sense of privilege (sec. 2–20) and of power (sec. 2–22). A similar confused use of "duty" is often found. The term is employed in the sense defined in section 2–18, but also in a sense which blends or confuses it with liability (sec. 2–23).

Ambiguity and carelessness in the use of language are facts with which we must reckon in law as elsewhere. No matter how careful we may be in our own use of terms, we always have to look out for careless and misleading use by others, just as we have to be on the lookout for others who drive carelessly on the highway. Both for the purpose of keeping your own use of terms clear and for the purpose of detecting loose use by others, it will be helpful for you to practice discriminating the six important conceptions which I have defined. Which of the six terms would you use in each of the following statements?

1. *Right* of a creditor of A to repayment of $100 which he has loaned to A.

2. The *claim* of X, the owner of land, that Y, a third party, stay off the land.

3. The *obligation* of Y to stay off X's land in the case last put.

4. The *right* of X to transfer his land to Y.

5. The *right* of L to lease his land to P.

6. The *right* of a landowner to use and enjoy his land, as by building a house on it, plowing it, and walking over it.

7. Every man's house is his "castle" as the law declares. In this connection, Gray says: ". . . a householder has the right to eject by force a trespasser from his 'castle.' " Would you say *right, power,* or *privilege* here?

8. Suppose that X, the owner of land, gives Y a *license* to come on his land to hunt. How shall we characterize Y's opportunity to hunt? How shall we characterize the giving of the license?

9. The ownership of land is a complex aggregate of rights, powers, privileges, duties, and liabilities. On the basis of the preceding examples and what you know generally, what rights, powers, and privileges of the landowner come to mind? Do you think of any duties which rest upon the landowner? Do you think of any liabilities which rest on the landowner as such?

---

[1] NATURE AND SOURCES OF THE LAW, sec. 53 (1909).

10. A does *not have any duty* to support his indigent brother. Which category?

11. The *right* of A to acquire ownership of wild animals by capture.

12. The *right* of a tenant from month to month to terminate his lease by one month's notice.

13. It is sometimes said that either party to a contract has a right to breach his contract inasmuch as either is able to break the contract and pay damages for the breach. In this case, should one say that either party has a *right* to breach the contract? A *privilege* to breach it? A *power* to do so?

14. The *right* of workmen to organize a union without interference by their employer. Should one speak of a *privilege* to organize? A *right* to organize? A *power* to organize?

15. My *right* to swear out a warrant for the arrest of a suspected thief. Suppose, first, that I act justifiably on the basis of reasonable cause to suspect that X has stolen my watch. Then suppose that I swear out such a warrant without justifiable cause. Would you use the term "right" in this case? Power? Privilege?

16. Sec. 4 of the *Restatement of Torts* (1934) declares:

"The word 'duty' is used throughout the Restatement of this Subject to denote the fact that the actor is required to conduct himself in a particular manner at the risk that if he does not do so he may become liable to another to whom the duty is owed for any injury sustained by such other of which that actor's conduct is a legal cause."

Is the word "duty" used here in a sense which agrees with our definitions? Is the word "liable" so used?

17. It is said that the owner of a house is "bound" to make repairs on floors and walls of his house if he wants them to be made. How do you interpret the word "bound" here? Does this statement refer to a duty or something else?

18. Compare the statutory language quoted in section 2–14, problem 3: "No damages shall be awarded in any libel action," with the language of the fourth section of the Statute of Frauds which declares that, "No action shall be brought . . . upon any contract or sale of lands . . . or any interest in or concerning them . . . unless the agreement upon which such action shall be brought, or some memorandum, or note thereof, shall be in writing, and signed by the party to be charged therewith. . . ."

The defamatory statement does not give rise to a cause of action, and the unwritten contract is not a basis for an action, either. Is this an adequate statement of the effects of these statutes? The effect of the one statute is to make the actor's act privileged. What is the effect of the other statute, i. e., the Statute of Frauds?

19. Suppose A sues B for damages for false imprisonment. The evidence on the trial of the action shows that B locked A in a cellar overnight as a practical joke. The court and jury award damages in the amount of $500 to A. How would you analyze this result in terms of rights, duties, powers, privileges, etc., as between A and B?

20. A undoubtedly has discretion (as well as power) to convey his home by deed to B. Now suppose that B by threats of bodily harm coerces A to make a deed to this effect; the deed to B would be ineffective and would be ordered cancelled in a proper suit by A. How would you express this result in terms of legal right, power, and discretion?

Sec. 2–26. Significance of circumstances—natural conditions. A's act is not an isolated phenomenon; it takes its place among the phenomena of nature. The law recognizes the importance of the natural and social conditions surrounding A's act. These conditions are considered both in fixing a standard for A's act and in fixing the significance of his act.

Standard and significance are part of the social machinery through which A's act is integrated and harmonized with B's needs and acts. The natural and social bearings of what A does, have to be reckoned with in deciding whether his act is to be socially approved, disapproved, or what not; they have to be reckoned with also in deciding what effects the act shall entail if it is done. Thus A, who drives an automobile on the highway, carries on an activity under given weather conditions and at a given place where others are driving. The legal provision, which declares that he must drive with reasonable care under the circumstances, takes account of both natural and social conditions. And the accompanying legal provision, which declares that A shall be liable for damages to B if he fails to exercise reasonable care, likewise involves a reference to both weather conditions and conditions of traffic. Both the standard for A's act and the significance of his act involve a consideration of factors outside the act itself.

Accordingly we see that the act alone does not determine legal significance. We cannot look alone to what A does. We have to look also to the circumstances in which he acted. Legal significance is determined both by what A does and by other factors which we have called circumstances or surrounding conditions:

Among the natural circumstances which help to determine the significance of A's act are many common facts. The circumstance may be a *previous* natural event. Thus, the significance of A's act in selling grape juice or cider may depend not only on the act of sale, but on the question whether the juice or cider has previously passed through the natural process of fermentation; if it has, A's act constitutes a sale of intoxicating liquor and the violation of a prohibition law.

The important natural circumstance may be a factual condition *accompanying* the act, such as the weather conditions previously mentioned; the liability of A to B for negligent driving may depend not only on the speed at which he was driving, but on the question whether it was raining at the time, so that the pavement was wet and slippery; or whether it was snowing, so that A's range of vision was reduced.

And finally, the important circumstance may be the *subsequent* occurrence of a natural event; this event may be essential to the operation of a previous act, as the testator's death is essential to the operation of the will he has executed. Or the event may change or vitiate the legal significance of an act which has already been done. If A is the owner of a music hall and enters into a contract to lease the hall to an artist for a particular concert, the contract gives rise to an obligation on A's part to do what he has agreed; but, if the hall be destroyed accidentally by fire before the date of the concert, the obligations of the parties under the contract are terminated. The significance of A's act in entering into the contract is affected (i. e., completely wiped out) by the subsequent fire. In these three examples we see that the significance of A's act in a given situation may depend on a previous natural event, or on accompanying natural conditions, or on a subsequent natural event, as well as on the nature of the act itself.

Sec. 2–27. Significance of another's acts. The significance of A's act may also depend on the acts of B, as I have already pointed out. Indeed B's acts raise legal problems more often than natural circumstances do, and in this sense his acts are more important to us from a practical viewpoint.

B's *previous* act may be important in determining the effects of A's act. Thus if A fatally stabs B with a knife,

A's act is murder. But if it appears that before A stabbed B, the latter struck A a blow in the face with his fist, then A's act of killing B would ordinarily be adjudged manslaughter, not murder. The prior blow by B mitigates A's crime; it changes and qualifies the significance of A's act. In a similar way B's *simultaneous* activity may be important in determining the significance of A's act. The case of A's driving on the highway may be used again to illustrate this point. The legal standard requires A to drive with reasonable care under the circumstances. What is reasonable will depend largely upon the amount of traffic. This means the number of other persons who are driving. As a driver, A is bound to act in a manner which takes account of the driving which others are doing. And the *subsequent* act of B may be important too. If A and B have made a contract and if B subsequently breaches the contract, this breach by B excuses performance by A. It excuses the obligation of A to perform. In short, the acts of B prior to, simultaneous with, and subsequent to, the act of A, have a part in determining its effects.

Another noteworthy angle of the relation of A's act to B's is this: legal significance often attaches to two or more acts only when they are coupled together in a certain way.

$$\begin{array}{ccc} \text{A's act} \\ \textit{then} & \longleftrightarrow & \begin{array}{l}\text{Legal} \\ \text{Significance}\end{array} \\ \text{B's act} \end{array}$$

Thus, in the case of the killing above mentioned, the *temporal sequence* of the acts is important. B strikes A first. If B had struck A after A gave the fatal stab, B's blow would not have mattered. Neither would the blow by B have had its mitigating effect if the sequence of events had been first a blow by A, then a blow by B, then the fatal blow by A. Here A would have been liable for murder because he struck the first blow as well as the one which was fatal. Another example of the same sort is the making of a contract. Normally a contract is made when two acts are coupled in this order: offer by A and acceptance by B. Legal significance attaches to the combination of the two acts.

Or sometimes the law requires that one or more acts *occur together*—simultaneously or essentially at the same time— alone neither act will produce legal effects:

As an illustration of this kind of legal provision, I refer you to the statute set out in the fourth problem of section 2–28 below, which requires that all the witnesses to the execution of a will be present at the same time and attest together. If all are not present at the same time and acting together, the will is not effective and the testator's act and the attestation of it are utterly without legal force.

Accordingly, we find that legal standards are often stated in regard to sequences, or combinations of acts: A's act, then B's act; or B's act, then A's act; or A's act and B's act together. And we find that, while legal significance may attach to A's act alone, often such significance only attaches to a sequence or combination of A's act with B's, or that the significance of A's act is different when it occurs in a sequence or combination with B's, from what it would be if it occurred alone. These points about the essential interrelations of acts and about their combined significance will be further developed by the problems which follow.

Sec. 2–28. Problems. 1. Suppose a statute provides that a person who makes a public offer to pay for a service to be rendered (e. g., to pay a reward to anyone who finds and returns a lost article) becomes bound to make compensation according to his offer, whenever another person meets the conditions of the offer and renders the service requested. If B loses his watch, and A finds it and returns it an hour later, would B be bound under the above statute to pay a reward? Why?

2. Suppose that A shot and killed B but it appears that B was attacking A with a pistol when A shot, so that A acted in the necessary defense of his own life. Here A would be exonerated completely.

Analyze this case in terms of interrelated acts and their significance.

Suppose B attacked A yesterday and A shot B today.

3. A and B enter into a contract under which A is to perform some service for B at $10 per day for 10 days. B later defaults and A sues for damages. Consider this situation as a sequence of interdependent acts which form the basis for A's suit (see sec. 2–27). In other words, what acts must A prove, or do, in order to recover damages?

4. A statute of the State of Michianna provides:

Execution of wills. Every will must be in writing and must be executed and attested as follows:

(1) *Subscription.* It must be subscribed at the end thereof by the testator himself, or some person in his presence and by his direction must subscribe his name thereto. A person who subscribes the testator's name, by his direction, should write his own name as a witness to the will, but a failure to do so will not affect the validity of the will.

(2) *Presence of witnesses.* The subscription must be made, or the testator must acknowledge it to have been made by him or by his authority, in the presence of both of the attesting witnesses, present at the same time.[1]

(3) *Testator's declaration.* The testator, at the time of subscribing or acknowledging the instrument, must declare to the attesting witnesses that it is his will.

---

[1] Most states do not specifically require that the testator have all the attesting witnesses present at the same time. ATKINSON, WILLS 295 (1937). But this is always the safe procedure to follow.

(4) *Number of witnesses, attestation.* There must be at least two attesting witnesses, each of whom must sign the instrument as a witness, at the end of the will, at the testator's request and in his presence. The witnesses should give their places of residence, but a failure to do so will not affect the validity of the will.

Suppose the testator asks the attesting witnesses to sign first, which they do; and that the testator signs immediately afterward. Would his will be validly executed under the statute quoted?

5. *Aikens v. Wisconsin.*[2]

"Malicious mischief is a familiar and proper subject for legislative repression as are also combinations for the purpose of inflicting it, and liberty to combine to inflict such mischief, even upon such intangibles as business or reputation, is not among the rights which the Fourteenth Amendment was intended to protect. . . .

"Section 4466*a*, Wisconsin Statutes of 1898, prohibiting combinations for the purpose of willfully or maliciously injuring another in his reputation, trade, business or profession, is not in conflict with the Fourteenth Amendment so far as the section applies to such a combination made from solely malevolent motives. . . ."

Mr. Justice Holmes:

"But if all these general considerations be admitted, it is urged nevertheless that the means intended to be used by this particular combination were simply the abstinence from making contracts, that a man's right so to abstain cannot be infringed on the ground of motives, and further, that it carries with it the right to communicate that intent to abstain to others and to abstain in common with them. It is said that if the statute extends to such a case it must be unconstitutional. The fallacy of this argument lies in the assumption that the statute stands no better than if directed against the pure nonfeasance of singly omitting to contract. The statute is directed against a series of acts, and acts of sev-

[2] 195 U. S. 194 (1904).

eral, the acts of combining, with intent to do other acts. . . . When the acts consist of making a combination calculated to cause temporal damage, the power to punish such acts, when done maliciously, cannot be denied because they are to be followed and worked out by conduct which might have been lawful if not preceded by the acts. No conduct has such an absolute privilege as to justify all possible schemes of which it may be a part. The most innocent and constitutionally protected of acts or omissions may be made a step in a criminal plot, and if it is a step in a plot neither its innocence nor the Constitution is sufficient to prevent the punishment of the plot by law. . . ."

Consider this decision in relation to our discussion in section 2–27.

EFFECTUATION OF STANDARDS [1]

Sec. 2–29. Standards do not per se control behavior. The legal standard is not self-effectuating. It is an expression of a pattern of action—it is a standard act which the lawmaker prohibits, commands, assures of effect, permits or leaves to the discretion of the actor. As such, the standard is a mere verbal formula, just words. It is not enough that the lawmaker formulate his standard, he must also think about how to make it effective in controlling the acts of A. The words of which the standard is composed have no effects on A per se. Words have no influence over things, and they do not control persons unless these persons understand them and are ready to be guided by them.

---

[1] By "effectuation of a standard" I mean the process of bringing about the kind of action which the standard is intended to secure. A command is intended to secure action of the type commanded so that the standard is effectuated when action of this type is done. A prohibition is intended to warn against action of the type forbidden, so that the standard is effectuated when action of this type is avoided. Another way of putting the same general idea is to say that effectuation is the process of making a standard operative in the actual activities of someone. These rough definitions will suffice for the time being; later we shall have to examine more closely the meanings of such expressions as "operative" and "effective."

Despite these obvious truths, men have always been prone to ascribe intrinsic or magical effect to words. They have been ready to suppose that words can exert direct effects on things, events, and human behavior. King Canute gave commands to the waves; spells and incantations have often been used to sway natural forces; and persons have been assumed to be pushed about by words as if words were physical instruments instead of mere conventional symbols through which ideas are conveyed.

While it is not common today to commit so gross an error as King Canute's, and most of us have passed beyond the belief in the efficacy of spells, it is not uncommon even now for the lawmaker, and other speakers as well, to forget that his message is intended to influence people, and that its effects in this regard will depend first and foremost on the attitudes and reactions of the people addressed. It is not unusual for those who propose or who enact laws to assume that all the lawmaker has to do is to declare, "Be it enacted that . . . ," and that in some indefinite way the standard becomes realized in fact. Nothing could be further from the truth.

The national prohibition law of recent unhappy memory illustrates the point I have in mind. This forbade the manufacture, possession, transportation, and sale of intoxicating liquor. It was hardly enacted before it was violated almost openly in many parts of the country. Why was this? Because the lawmaker had not given adequate consideration to the attitudes of the population and to means of enforcement. The law ran counter to the customs and desires of too many people. The legal machinery of enforcement which was available was not equal to the task of eradicating the drinking habits and suppressing the thirst of a large proportion—in some areas, the majority—of the population. In reality the lawmaker had done little more than declare a prohibitive standard; he had implicitly assumed that his declaration would somehow effectuate itself. He had not adequately considered the problem of enforcement.[2]

Sec. 2–30. "Law in the books" and "law in action." Not only is the legal standard not self-effectuating but it is also never 100 per cent effective. There is always some discrepancy between the "law in the books" and the "law in action." * Some murders are committed despite the threat of direst penalties. The law in the books expresses what the law-maker wishes to achieve or avoid; the law in action always falls short of this ideal. The difference between the prohibition law and other laws which we regard as satisfactorily enforced is merely one of degree. If the gap between the legal standard and its enforcement is too wide we speak of a "breakdown" of law; if it is not too marked we consider the situation more or less normal. The point can be illustrated by referring to the legal norms which regulate driving on the highway. Many drivers, as we all know, exceed the legal speed limit and pass other cars on hills. The regulations covering these acts fall far short of complete enforcement. To make such traffic regulations completely effective would require a vast police force. It would cost more than the public is willing to pay, to provide enough policemen on urban and rural roads to supervise driving and to prevent all infractions. With present machinery of enforcement, the public has to be satisfied with a reasonable degree of observance of these standards, or perhaps with something less than that.

[2] I use effectuation as the broad general term for all methods of bringing about approved types of action; enforcement, which is a term more often heard, is narrower. Enforcement refers only to coercion of the actor by threats or by physical force. Effectuation includes the use of threats and physical force but also includes the use of rewards, and the creation of favorable habits. See sec. 2–40, note *, for further explanation of the terminology here employed.

* (I.R.) The ideas here developed go back to Ehrlich and Holmes. They have been heavily stressed by Llewellyn and other so-called realists. The contrasting phrases, "law in the books" and "law in action," are Pound's.

And the discrepancy between standard and actuality is not limited to the commands and prohibitions of the criminal law; the standards relative to private injuries and benefits are likewise only imperfectly realized in practice. Personal injuries are suffered and not redressed. Contracts are broken and nothing is done. Property is damaged and compensation is never made. Perhaps the individual who causes the injury or commits the breach of contract can not be found or can not pay, or perhaps the amount involved is small and the injured party can not afford the trouble of a lawsuit. There is always a substantial discrepancy between the standard and its effectuation in real life.

The lawmaker, therefore, will not expect the impossible. He will realize that commands are not always obeyed; that forbidden acts are done; that boundaries of permitted action are sometimes overstepped; that prescribed formalities for effective action are not always complied with. He will realize that persons who are subject to regulation often defy, or attempt to evade, applicable standards of behavior, or they fail to act in prescribed ways through carelessness or ignorance. The realization of these facts is the beginning of legislative wisdom, but it is not the whole of it. While the lawmaker will not hope for perfection, he will try to hold to a minimum the discrepancy between his standard and its fulfillment.

Sec. 2–31. The actor's existing attitudes. The standard is a pattern of behavior addressed to A for his guidance. In preparing such a standard L must consider A's existing attitudes as the maker of a wooden object must consider the grain of the wood on which he is about to work. A's attitudes are the springs of his action; they are at the center of the problem of controlling what he does. What are these attitudes? How far can they be influenced or changed? What can A fairly be expected to know or do? How far is it necessary to stimulate action along approved lines or deter action along disapproved lines? What devices are available for these purposes, and how will they operate on A? All these questions must be carefully considered and answered by the lawmaker who establishes standards with an intelligent appreciation of what he is doing.

If the attitudes of persons to be controlled run counter to a proposed standard, as the attitudes of a large part of our population were set against the prohibition law, L must concern himself seriously with problems of changing them. He must consider whether he will be able to induce action along desired lines, whether he has the means available to arouse adequate law-abiding motives, and whether in regard to the particular standard the benefit attained will be worth the cost of attaining it.

On the other hand, if existing attitudes of persons to be controlled are in harmony with what L desires, the legal task of coercion or persuasion is reduced. If he can rely upon favorable habits or if such institutions as the church and the family inculcate and enforce essentially the same standard as his own, e.g., a prohibition of lying and stealing, L may have to concern himself only with the problem of creating motives for favorable action in a relatively small group. As regards most of the population, the standard will be realized in fact through existing habits. The problem of enforcement will be minimal.

Indeed the task of enforcing legal standards without the aid of law-abiding habits and extralegal sanctions would be quite impossible. On the asset side of the law enforcement ledger must always be reckoned the fact that not all actors need to be coerced or persuaded, or at least that most standards do not require enforcement against more than a small number of persons simultaneously. Just as the bank relies upon the fact that not all its depositors will want to withdraw their money at any one time, so the state counts on the fact that it will not need to enforce its standards of behavior against more than a small part of the community at any one time.

A reference once more to the fiasco of national prohibition will show what part established habits and extralegal factors play in the effectuation of legal standards. Even at the worst period of prohibition enforcement, most persons did not violate the law; they did not want to. They conformed because they were not accustomed to using, making, or selling intoxicants, so that the law did not run counter to their habits; or because they lived in dry communities and were restrained by the opinions of their neighbors; or because they belonged to church groups which regarded the use of intoxicants as immoral. Or they obeyed the prohibition law on principle, regarding obedience to law as a moral or social duty. Habitual attitudes or extralegal sanctions were sufficient, along with legal disapproval, to keep these persons out of the way of the law's ban. The breakdown of this law did not mean, therefore, that no one whatever observed its mandates; it meant only that the lawmaker 'had failed to reckon with the hostile attitudes of a large dissident group. This was the group which needed to be controlled if the law was to be effective, and this was the group which set the law at naught.

These observations sound obvious enough, and yet they have only too often been neglected or overlooked. As a result, the problem of effectuating standards has sometimes been conceived as a much larger problem than it is, i.e., as a problem of inducing all acts of all persons at all times. In this view, the job looks too big and L does not undertake all that he might. Or else L, if he is not critical, passes a law and overestimates his accomplishments; like the dog that chases the car down the street and comes back with his tail in the air, L cheerfully assumes that he made all people do what many were going to do anyhow. But the opposite mistake is the more common; the problem is not perceived to be as large as it is. L fails to realize that he is enacting a standard of behavior which is opposed to the habits of many persons, which therefore needs to be backed up by strong and effective sanctions, and which breaks down in practice when these sanctions are not provided.

Sec. 2–32. Problems. 1. In an earlier problem we spoke of a case where a city installs a traffic light on one of its streets for the purpose of regulating the movement of vehicles and pedestrians (sec. 1–10). This was treated as an example of control by the use of symbols. What control factors lie behind this symbolic device and its use?

2. What is the point of these bitter words of *Anatole France:* " 'The law in its majestic equality forbids the rich as well as the poor to sleep under bridges, to beg in the streets, and to steal bread' "? [1] What does this mean as regards legal prohibitions?

3. In an address delivered in 1897 Justice Holmes said that if you want to know how the law (in our terms, legal standards) is going to operate you must look at it as the bad man does.

"You can see very plainly that a bad man has as much reason as a good one for wishing to avoid an encounter with the public force, and therefore you can see the practical importance of the distinction between morality and law. A man who cares nothing for an ethical rule which is believed and practiced by his neighbors is likely, nevertheless, to care a good deal to avoid being made to pay money, and will want to keep out of jail if he can. . . . If you want to know the law and nothing else, you must look at it as a bad man, who cares only for the material consequences which such knowl-

[1] Cohen, Ethical Systems and Legal Ideas 79 (1933).

edge enables him to predict, not as a good one, who finds his reasons for conduct, whether inside the law or outside of it, in the vaguer sanctions of conscience." [2]

Do you agree? Why?

4. Consider in this connection the following passage from an article by *Llewellyn:*

". . . most pieces of law affect only a *relatively* small number of persons ever or at all, with any directness—or are intended to. Where that is the case, the *organization, attitude, present and probable behavior of the persons sought to be affected* is what needs major consideration, from the angle of getting results (or of understanding results). Indeed, the very *identification* of those persons may be a pre-condition calling for much study. Which is a somewhat absurdly roundabout way of saying that unless those matters are studied, the rules drawn, and the administrative behavior adapted to the persons in question, results will be an accident. *'To the persons in question,'* and, indeed, 'to those persons *under the conditions in question.'* It cannot be too strongly insisted that our attitude toward 'rules' of law, treating them as universal in *application,* involves a persistent twisting of observation. 'Rules' in the realm of action *mean* what rules *do;* 'rules' in the realm of action *are* what they do. The *possible* application and applicability are not without importance, but the *actual* application and applicability are of controlling importance. To think of rules as universals—especially to think of them as being applicable to 'all persons who bring themselves within their terms'—is to muffle one's eyes in a constitutional fiction before beginning a survey of the scene. To be sure, constitutions purport to require rules of law to be 'equal and general.' But most rules, however general as to the few they cover, are highly special, when viewed from the angle of how many citizens there are. And most rules 'applying to' all who come within their terms (all those who set up barber shops, or are tempted to commit murder, or to bribe officials, or to embezzle from banks or certify checks without the drawer having funds, or to adopt a child, or run

---

[2] "The Path of the Law," 10 HARV. L. REV. 457 at 459 (1897).

a manufacturing establishment employing five or more persons) do not and will not, realistically considered, ever be 'applicable' in any meaningful sense of the term, to *most* people in the community. Such rules are indeed open. Persons do move in and out of the sphere of their applicability. But that sphere is much more clearly seen, when viewed (as compared with the community) as narrow, as special, as peculiar." [8]

How are Llewellyn's observations related to our present topic?

5. In this country the established practice is to pass vehicles which one meets by driving to the right; this practice is sometimes called a "rule of the road." Suppose a general traffic statute were being prepared, would it not be important from the lawmaker's point of view to know this prevailing practice and to adopt it?

What would be the effect of adopting the English rule which requires drivers of vehicles to pass to the left?

Compare the situation dealt with by Mussolini when he came to power in Italy; right-hand driving was customary in some parts of Italy and left-hand driving in other parts. In deciding to establish a uniform rule what facts should have had weight with Mussolini?

Sec. 2–33. Enforcement by physical force. When the lawmaker has given due attention to the existing attitudes of persons whom he wants to control, he will pass on to the problem of methods of shaping their behavior to his desires; he will consider the devices and incentives through which he can deter or stimulate their action.

First, physical force may come in question. This includes physical restraint and physical compulsion. The application of force may be the only method available for controlling

[8] "A Realistic Jurisprudence—The Next Step," 30 COL. L. REV. 431 at 459–460 (1930).

certain insane actors; force may have to be applied as a last resort to other recalcitrant actors. Some persons, like the wild bull, can only be prevented from doing harm to others by physical constraint or by extermination. Certain persons can only be induced to do what is legally required, by the application of physical force.

But the physical force method of enforcing standards is costly and narrow in application. Our society could not possibly exist in its present form if only this method of control were available. As Lumley says, "But, with physical control as the *only* means for the management of human beings, the maintenance of a *social* order would be impossible. Let us follow the series through, for purposes of contrast—in a world with nothing but physical force to move men. If it is desired to take the culprit to jail, two or three policemen would have to be assembled at the spot, and be forced to pit their strength against that of the victim. But how would the two or three policemen be assembled? They would have to be forced there by others. They could not be *called* there. But who would the others be and who would push or drag them around to push or drag the several policemen to the required spot?" [1]

Sec. 2–34. Enforcement of prohibitions by penal threats. More serviceable and more widely used than actual physical force is the penal threat. Control by threat is symbolic control.[1] The penal threat is conveyed by words [2] and usually accompanies a legally stated standard such as a prohibition or command. Let us consider first its use in connection with the prohibition. A is forbidden to do such an act as murder, robbery or arson and the prohibition is coupled with the

---

[1] LUMLEY, MEANS OF SOCIAL CONTROL 14–15 (1925).

[1] The distinction between control by force and control by verbal acts is discussed in sec. 1–09 above.

[2] But compare the implied legal mandate and implied threat conveyed by a traffic light, sec. 1–10, problem 1.

threat of penal consequences such as imprisonment or hanging. It is not the mere prohibitory language that controls A's behavior; it is the penal threat that deters him from committing the prohibited act. The prohibitory standard tells him what he must not do and the threat of punishment supplies a motive for not doing it.

It is not to be inferred from the examples just given that only the prohibitions of criminal law are supported by penal threats. Penal threats are found in other parts of the law, in fact in every part. In the law of procedure, for instance, important prohibitions are coupled with penal consequences. I need only mention the fact that persons may be punished for disorderly conduct in court, and that a party may be committed for contempt in violating a prohibitory order of the judge, such as an injunction. Likewise in the field of tort, where A is prohibited from striking B or injuring B's goods, A is threatened with the exaction of compensation to B if he does either of these forbidden acts. From A's point of view, this exaction is a penalty with which he is threatened; it operates on A's motivation in a manner analogous to the threat of punishment for crime.[3]

Sec. 2–35. Deterrent effect of penal threat. What is the nature of the penalties threatened? Penalties may vary widely in character and in the way they affect A. The penalty may be imprisonment; it may be death by hanging or otherwise; it may be the exaction of a fine; it may be the payment for damage which A has done to someone else; it may be the

---

[3] This, however, is looking at the matter only from A's point of view. From B's point of view and from the social viewpoint, the protection of B against injury is the main thing. The threat of loss to A if he acts improperly, and the requirement of payment for B's loss, are both means directed to one end: the protection of B. The threat and the exaction of payment are simply two stages in this protection. One stage represents the effort to prevent improper action by A; the other stage represents an exaction of compensation if A does act improperly. Compare what is said in sec. 2–35 about the effect of penal threats and their execution.

performance of some disagreeable act such as repairing damage or making an apology; [1] it may consist in a loss of certain legal advantages such as civil rights; and so on.[2] But all penalties have one feature in common—a feature which accounts for their motivating force upon A's behavior. All are detrimental consequences to A or his pocketbook; all are consequences which A will presumably wish to avoid.

The purpose of the threat is to create motives in A which will make it unnecessary for the threat to be carried out. If the threat of penalty is effective, of course the penalty is not imposed. The thing threatened is a mere substitute for performance along desired lines. If the threat operates as intended, this substitute does not have to be exacted.

However, the threat does have to be executed sometimes, or at least the probability of its execution must be real; if not, the penal threat loses its motivating force on A's action. This force depends on three factors: First, it depends on what is threatened—the nature of the penalty. A threat of death obviously will have a stronger effect in deterring or coercing A's act than a threat of a short term of imprisonment or a small monetary fine.[3] Second, the remoteness of the penalty in time is important. If the penalty will be exacted immediately it will be more influential on A's behavior than if it is to be exacted a long time from now. It is common knowledge that some of us take plenty of chances on eternal damna-

---

[1] In certain European countries the unsuccessful defendant in an action for defamation is required to publish an apology.

[2] This list is not exhaustive. Many other penalties have been used at some time or some place in world history. Of these, loss of bodily members, killing in cruel fashion, selling into slavery, would no longer be tolerated; in fact, they would conflict with various provisions of our constitutions.

[3] The law proceeds on a quantitative calculus of penal consequences which is often of doubtful validity—at least of doubtful accuracy from the viewpoint of psychological science. I can put these questions to make the point. Does the threat of five years' imprisonment for theft deter the bum in the same degree that it deters a respectable citizen? How much more deterrent effect has a ten-year term in prison than a five-year term? Is its motivating force twice as great? What about the deterrent effect of a threatened $2000 fine as compared with a threat of a fine of half that amount?

tion because that seems a long way off. Third, the certainty of the exaction of the penalty is important in determining its force. Where there are enough policemen patrolling the streets and the speeder is very likely to get caught and punished, the deterrent effect on speeding is at a maximum.

Sec. 2–36. Deterrent effects of taxation and other governmental measures. The lawmaker is not confined to out-and-out prohibitions. He may endeavor to discourage rather than forbid certain acts by A. A common method of checking activity by A is to impose high or discriminatory taxes upon it. The power to tax, like the power to penalize, may be used to deter action. Taxes may be made so high as to be prohibitive; as the great Chief Justice Marshall once said, "The power to tax is the power to destroy." But more often disfavored acts are visited with discriminatory taxes.[1] Examples are the taxes with which the production and sale of oleomargarine until recently have been burdened both by our federal and state governments.

Restrictive regulations are often used as checks on disfavored activities. There can be no doubt, for example, that the liquor business has long been a problem child for the lawmaker. Even when he does not go so far as to prohibit the manufacture, sale or possession of intoxicating liquor, he closely regulates dealings in this commodity. The lawmaker

---

[1] If a real prohibition is intended, taxation usually seems too indirect a method of achieving the end desired, though this has not always proved true. The federal government has used special taxes in order to drive notes issued by state banks out of circulation. Veazie Bank v. Fenno, 8 Wall. 533 (1869). And the Congress of the United States once attempted to use its taxing power to prevent the products of child labor from using the channels of interstate commerce. The Supreme Court held this exercise of power invalid; its conclusion, however, was rested primarily on the ground that Congress could not bar such products from interstate shipment. Bailey v. Drexel Furniture Co., 259 U. S. 20 (1922). Today, as a result of the Court's broader conception of Congressional power, either the tax or the prohibition on the products of child labor would be sustained. There can be no question that generally our state and federal governments can employ taxes to restrict or prevent acts which they are empowered to prohibit.

permits sale only by licensed persons to particular persons and at particular times and places; he controls the manufacture with equal care. These limitations on sale and manufacture reflect a continuing frown of the lawmaker and achieve in large degree the same results as a complete prohibition.[2]

All of which leads to the conclusion that we greatly oversimplify when we treat prohibited acts as a neat clear category standing by itself. Prohibited acts shade over into disfavored acts. The lawmaker does not always speak with a full and certain voice; he does not always impress an unqualified "no" on behavior by A. Certain of A's acts may be not forbidden but handicapped by discrimination or discouraged by restriction.

Sec. 2–37. Problems. 1. A statute provides:

"If any person drawn or summoned as a juror, shall take anything to give his verdict, or shall receive any gift or gratuity whatever, from any party to a suit, for the trial of which such person shall be drawn or summoned, in addition to any criminal punishment to which he may be subject by law, he shall be liable to the party aggrieved thereby in ten times the amount or value of the thing which he has taken or received, in addition to the actual damages sustained thereby."

What prohibited act is involved here? What three methods (acts) of effectuation are mentioned?

2. It is often said that certainty of punishment for crime is more important than severity of punishment. Thus it might be argued that it is more important that most traffic offenders

---

[2] Of course these limitations themselves usually take the form of prohibitions, e.g., a prohibition of sale after certain hours or a prohibition of sale to minors. But my point is that the liquor business is permitted although it is not favored. These subordinate prohibitions are, as regards the liquor business, restrictions on the way it is carried on. At the same time they indicate an unfriendly legislative attitude toward this line of activity.

be caught and fined $5 than that an occasional offender be caught and fined $50. Do you agree? Explain in terms of motivation by threat of penalty.[1]

3. "In England the punishment for suicide was at one time forfeiture of goods and an ignominious burial, but both modes of punishment have been done away with. In the United States the person committing suicide is not punished, and it has been held that suicide is not a crime on that ground. This reasoning makes the existence of a crime depend on the punishment, whereas the punishment should depend upon the existence of the crime. Where suicide is a crime, the mere fact that the offender by this act places himself beyond the reach of punishment no more serves to make his act not a crime than would the fact that one after killing another person should commit suicide and thus make his punishment impossible. . . ."[2]

Was there any effective threat of penalty in the old English law? Is there any effective threat now, in the English law or in ours?

What do you think of this author's arguments pro and con on the question whether suicide is still a crime: suicide is no crime because it is not punished, and suicide is a crime though not punished? How would you restate these arguments in terms of standards and means of effectuation?

4. A generation ago the nature and purpose of tariffs on the importation of foreign-made goods was much debated. On the one hand it was contended that these tariffs should be used for purpose of revenue only. On the other hand it was argued that these tariffs should be made sufficiently high to protect American industry and labor against competition with the products of other countries where living and working standards were relatively low. How would you restate this problem in terms of methods of effectuating standards?

[1] See sec. 2–35, last paragraph.
[2] MILLER, CRIMINAL LAW 272 (1934).

Sec. 2–38. Enforcement of commands by penal threats.
We have already discussed the use of penal threats to deter
A from doing forbidden acts. Such threats are also used in
an opposite sense, to coerce A to do obligatory acts. A is
commanded to register for the draft or to file an income tax
return, and is threatened with fine or imprisonment if he fails
to do the act prescribed. Witnesses are required by law to
appear and testify when properly summoned by court order.
If the witness fails to appear or refuses to testify he may be
punished by fine or imprisonment. If A assumes certain obligations by contract he may likewise be penalized for failure
to perform them. For example, if A agrees by valid contract
to convey his farm Blackacre to B, his obligation to do so
may be enforced by threat of exaction of damages for breach
of contract or by threat of imprisonment for contempt if he
refuses to comply with the court's order to make the conveyance promised.[1]

*Sec. 2–39. Government spending and the effectuation of
standards.* You will not see the processes of effectuating
standards in proper perspective unless you see them in relation to the total functions of government. L has at his command the fiscal powers of the state, the power to tax and
the power to spend public money, as well as the powers of
creating standards of behavior and of providing machinery
to make them effective. The fiscal powers are just as important as regards the effectuation of standards as are the power
to define standards and the power to create enforcement machinery. Indeed all these powers are interlocking and interdependent in their operation.

Tax monies furnish the sinews of enforcement and the
means of effectuation in other ways. To make standards effec-

---

[1] The damage remedy is much the more common as you will find in your
courses in Contracts and Equity. Both remedies have a coercive tendency as
regards A. Compare what was said in sec. 2–34, note 3, regarding the deterrent effect of the threatened exaction of compensation for tort damages.

tive, officials must be provided and paid.[1] When a new standard of action, prohibitive or obligatory, is being considered, L must weigh its probable financial cost as well as its desirability as such. If he is about to create a liquor prohibition law or to establish an income tax law, L will probably have to provide for an increase in the number of police and other officials in order to insure the effectiveness of this new standard of behavior. He will have to lay additional taxes to meet new costs. At some point the financial burden will be regarded as too heavy, and the legislative proposal will be modified or abandoned. And the matter is not always thought out thus clearly beforehand. A law is sometimes passed with vicious looking teeth in it; but, when L considers the machinery of enforcement he is seized by a fit of economy. As a result the funds necessary to administer its provisions and police its operation are not forthcoming and the law falls flat. Which all goes to show the essential dependence of law enforcement on financial considerations and of lawmaking powers on fiscal powers.

In everyday life prizes and premiums play an important part in the motivation of behavior. Probably offers of reward, and other advantages to the actor, are as common devices for obtaining socially desirable conduct as threats of penalties. Willie is induced to act as often by promise of a soda as by fear of a spanking. To some extent L also offers rewards for legally approved behavior, and here again his fiscal powers become important because it is through them that he obtains the means of so doing. He offers a reward to persons who furnish information regarding the criminal conduct of others; he offers bonuses and subsidies to persons who produce certain kinds of goods, e.g., wheat, cotton, or potatoes; he offers special advantages to persons who enlist in

---

[1] We have already noted how taxation may be used to achieve the same objectives as prohibitions coupled with penalties (sec. 2–36). This fact also shows the close interconnection of fiscal and regulatory powers.

the armed services; and he offers tax exemptions to certain charitable enterprises such as hospitals and colleges. These are all ways of effectuating standards of approved behavior.

This type of "bought" behavior is closely related to behavior which is made legally obligatory. Both are socially needed types of action. The one type is induced by benefits offered, the other by penalties threatened. Obligatory acts are those that are deemed by L especially important and which are therefore commanded and coupled with strong sanctions. Where L does not feel that it is necessary or feasible to enforce unqualified commands, he leaves the act to A's discretion and offers a premium to A for doing the act. Which mode of inducement is used will depend on various circumstances. Thus, if service in the armed forces is deemed sufficiently pressing, men may be required to enter the forces by compulsory draft coupled with penalties for failure to register and serve. But, in times of less pressure, men may be induced to enlist by promise of high pay and other advantages. Again, though it may be important that the farmer raise certain crops it would hardly be practical for the government to command him to raise them and threaten him with penalties for failure to do so. Instead the government allows him to raise what crops he will but offers him a subsidy for raising the crops desired. Accordingly we must realize that obligatory acts do not stand as a class apart. They are one type of act which L views as socially desirable; they stand alongside other types of favored acts which L tries to induce A to do by assuring him of special benefits.

Sec. 2-40. Indirect methods of effectuation—education. The control of the purse also gives L many ways of controlling behavior indirectly. Social welfare measures may be undertaken. Slums may be cleared and housing provided at public expense; parks and playgrounds may be established for wholesome recreation; old age pensions and unemployment compensation may be set up to guarantee the individual against financial need; the public health may be protected in various ways; medical service may be provided for indigent individuals. All such measures tend to reduce the pressures toward illicit behavior, due to economic need or unhealthy living conditions.

But more important than other measures which L may adopt is a system of education at public expense. We have already spoken of the importance of law-abiding habits in the community. The state, through schools and other public agencies may take a hand in building such habits into the individual.[1] This at least is the theory of our prevailing system of popular education. It is intended to implant in the child both available knowledge and approved behavior patterns. Of chief interest to us are the latter; the child can be brought up with sound attitudes and ideals, with settled notions of sportsmanship, honesty, democracy, and consideration for his fellows. All these attitudes and ideals contribute directly or indirectly to law-abiding behavior. In this sense education is to be viewed as a long-range method of controlling behavior, as contrasted with penal threats and offers of reward which are used in the immediate inducement or deterrence of action.*

[1] To be sure, the state with all its devices plays only a secondary part in the training of the child. Parents play the leading roles; and are backed up by such social institutions as the church. And when we speak of good habits we must not forget that threats of penalty and offers of reward have a place in habit formation. When sound behavior has become habitual, penalties and rewards become virtually unnecessary. But the course of proper training like "the course of true love never did run smooth"; in the process of habit building, penalties and rewards and physical force have always had a part.

* (I.R.) *"Effectuation" and "enforcement"*—a note on terminology. Effectuation of standards is commonly treated in terms of enforcement, and enforcement is taken to mean deterrence or compulsion by force or by penal threats. This treatment of the subject requires a word of caution because it results in a wholly penal conception of the effectuation of standards. It gives an incomplete view of the motivation of A's acts and of the ways of making standards operative. It involves a tacit assumption that A's acts are controlled exclu-

Sec. 2–41. Maintaining standards for effective acts. By
and large, standards for effective acts are established by L
in order to serve the needs of A. These standards are methods
by which A can achieve desired results. L examines the usual
attitudes and objectives of A and tries to furnish convenient
methods of satisfying A's desires.* A wants to acquire chat-
tels and L provides standard acts through which A can
acquire them. A wants to transmit his property to relatives
and friends at death, and L establishes a testamentary act by
means of which this desire can be accomplished. A wants to
obtain advantages through the co-operative acts of other persons, and L makes this possible by providing standard forms

sively by force or threats and that legal standards are effectuated wholly by
these means. As a matter of fact, the lawmaker must rely largely on existing
law-abiding habits of A as well as legal threats, to motivate A's action (sec.
2–31). He may also rely on the offer of rewards or benefits to stimulate
the action of A in desired directions (sec. 2–39). And finally, throughout
a large and important area of human behavior, the lawmaker may rely on
long-range training to direct A's behavior into desirable channels (sec. 2–40).
All these devices must be added to penal threats and physical force when we
are listing the means and methods of controlling behavior, and all fall outside
of a penal theory of effectuating standards.

You will see, therefore, that a purely penal conception of the effectuation
of standards is open to objection; it gives an incomplete and even misleading
view of the motivation of behavior and of the methods which are used by the
legal system to effectuate standards. You will also see why I prefer to speak,
as a general matter, in terms of effectuation rather than of enforcement of
standards. Enforcement is an adequate and convenient term when we want
to refer to effectuation through force or threats; but it is not as broad a term
as effectuation; and enforcement can not be safely used where it might be
understood to include the whole ground covered by the broader term.

The penal theory of the operation of the legal system has been associated
with, if it is not an outgrowth of, the old notion that the exclusive functions
of the law are to command and to prohibit. This long-standing association
of penal theory and legal function was one reason why I went to so much
pains to point out earlier that law is concerned with effective and permitted
acts as well as prohibited and obligatory acts. When we see this, we are
also ready to appreciate the roles of existing habits and the creation of new
habits and the role of premiums and rewards, as well as threats of penalties,
in the effectuation of legal standards.

* (I.R.) To be sure, forms for effective acts are sometimes antiquated and
obstructive rather than helpful. They are not always framed or maintained
with the clearly conceived purpose of serving the needs, or following the
habitual practices, of the typical actor. However, the existence of nonfunctional
or obstructive forms represents mainly a blind retention of the traditional,
without critical consideration of its utility. The retention is not strictly inten-

of contracts and other legal transactions which A can use to obtain these desired advantages. Usually L does not undertake to induce A to do the effective act nor does he endeavor to discourage A from doing it. The act is ordinarily permitted and discretionary as well as effective. Whether the act is performed or not depends on the existing self-interest of A and not on any legally stimulated motivation. So far as the law prescribes the purpose for which an effective act may be done or the manner in which it may be done, the common sanction is failure of effect. If A attempts to accomplish an unlawful purpose through an effective act, as where he enters into a contract in unreasonable restraint of trade, his contract is illegal and unenforcible. Likewise, the sanction for failure to comply with legal provisions prescribing the way the act is to be executed, is ineffectiveness. For example, if the law requires that A sign his will and have his signature witnessed by two persons, his will is a nullity if it is witnessed by only one person. In both the case of the illegal contract and the case of the defective will, A fails to comply with the terms and conditions under which legal services are tendered and the result is that the services are withheld.

However, there is no reason in the nature of things, why the lawmaker must adopt an attitude of neutrality toward the act which is effective.[1] There is no reason why he cannot combine effectiveness with sanctions of various sorts. There is no reason why he cannot make an act effective and forbid

tional, but rather results from inattention or inertia. The statement of the text expresses what L should do in the establishment of patterns for effective action. Whether or not L's action or nonaction always produces this result is another question. If a discrepancy exists it is merely another instance of the discrepancy between the ideal and the actual in the legal processes.

[1] In general, the legal system also adopts a "hands-off" policy toward *permitted, discretionary,* and *ineffective* acts; it does not punish or reward them; it does not seek to deter A from doing them nor does it try to encourage him to act. The legal attitude is neutral or indifferent. For this reason it does not seem necessary to discuss further the relations of sanctions to these types of acts. Nothing essential would be added to what is said in this and the preceding sections about the operation of sanctions.

it too, or why he cannot make A's act effective and also command A to do the act. If the lawmaker sees fit he can declare an act effective and at the same time try to deter or encourage the actor who does it. This is all to say that effectiveness is but one of several types of consequences which L may attach to the doing of an act and that the several types of consequences are not mutually exclusive.[2] In fact, in earlier sections it was pointed out that effectiveness and other consequences are not infrequently combined. I refer again to the following:

(1) The wrongful seizure of another's goods which is effective for certain purposes even though it is prohibited;

(2) Filing an income tax return and registration for the draft, which are effective acts and at the same time obligatory;

(3) Enlistment in the army which is an effective act but which is favored by special inducements such as high pay, etc.;

(4) Engaging in the liquor business—a series of effective acts—which may be discouraged by various restrictions and tax burdens.

Sec. 2–42. Problems. 1. Consider the provisions of section 1092 of the Civil Code of California (enacted 1872): A grant of an estate in real property may be made in substance as follows:

"I, A B, grant to C D all that real property situated in (insert name of county) County, State of California, bounded (or described) as follows: (here insert description, or if the

---

[2] In a similar way the legal policy of indifference toward discretionary, permitted and ineffective acts is not invariable (see sec. 2–11 above). For instance, a discretionary act may be rewarded by a subsidy or benefit which encourages the doing of the act. And an act which is declared ineffective may also be punished, as where a contract in restraint of trade is unenforcible and visited with criminal penalties as well.

land sought to be conveyed has a descriptive name, it may be described by the name, as for instance, 'The Norris Ranch.')

"Witness my hand this (insert day) day of (insert month), 18—.

"A B."

How would you interpret these provisions in relation to the discussion in section 2–27 above?

2. The 4th section of the Statute of Frauds enacts that:

"No action shall be brought . . . upon any contract or sale of lands . . . or any interest in or concerning them . . . unless the agreement upon which such action shall be brought, or some memorandum, or note thereof, shall be in writing, and signed by the party to be charged therewith. . . ." [1]

This section obviously makes writing and signature by the party to be charged requisites of a binding contract for the sale of land.

What is the effect of the lack of these formalities?

Would you regard this effect as a penalty for not using writing?

3. P swept manure from the street into piles intending to haul it away on the following day. D, however, hauled it away before P returned to get it. In a suit to recover the value of the manure the court held that P had taken possession thereof in a sense sufficient to be entitled to recover the value of the manure from D.[2]

How would you characterize P's act of sweeping the manure into piles? How does the law figure in the problem?

Suppose P had only decided that he would sweep up and haul away the manure the next day; and that D had swept it up and taken it away as he did, knowing of P's decision. Would the result have been the same? Why?

[1] This is a celebrated statute first enacted in England in 1660 and adopted in substantially the same words by the various states of the United States.
[2] Haslem v. Lockwood, 37 Conn. 500 (1871).

4. Informers are frequently offered inducements by law to furnish information leading to the conviction of criminals or to the recovery of taxes and other money due to the government. For example, at the present time, the federal government offers to pay a certain percentage of the amount recovered from A who fails to make a correct income tax return, to B who gives information leading to such recovery. Note here that four important acts are involved:

(1) The legislative act of creating a standard applicable to A.

(2) The act of A (filing a return) required by the legal standard.

(3) The offer of a reward to B for giving information.

(4) The act of B in giving information.

What is the ultimate act which government is trying to induce? Would you regard the offer of a reward to B as a method of enforcement? How does this offer appear to B? How does this offer differ from a subsidy offered to the farmer for raising certain crops?

Why not simply command everyone (B) who has information regarding tax evasion, to furnish it to the proper authorities?

5. When A drives his car recklessly and collides with a car which is being driven properly and carefully by B, what standard is involved? Suppose that B's car is damaged to the extent of $25, but that it will cost him $50 for fees and costs to pursue a lawsuit to a conclusion? How would you criticize this situation in terms of motivation of acts? Of effectuation of standards?

6. Consider the following provisions of the Michigan statutes regarding *wagers:*

"All notes, bills, bonds, mortgages, or other securities or conveyances whatever, in which the whole or any part of the consideration shall be for any money or goods, won by playing at cards, dice, or any other game whatever, or by betting on the sides or hands of such as are gaming, or by any betting or gaming whatever, . . . shall be void and of no effect, as between the parties to the same. . . ." [3]

"Any person who by playing at cards, dice, or any other game, or by betting or putting up money on cards, or by any other means or device in the nature of betting on cards, or betting of any kind, shall win or obtain any sum of money or any goods, or any article of value whatever shall, if the money, goods, or articles so won or obtained be of the value of fifty dollars or less, be guilty of a misdemeanor. If the money, goods, or articles so won be of the value of more than fifty dollars such person shall be guilty of a misdemeanor, punishable by imprisonment in the county jail for not more than one year, or by a fine of not more than five hundred dollars." [4]

"Any person who shall lose any sum of money, or any goods, article, or thing of value, by playing or betting on cards, dice or by any other device in the nature of such playing or betting, and shall pay or deliver the same or any part thereof to the winner, and shall not, within three (3) months after such loss, . . . , prosecute with effect for such money or goods, the winner to whom such money or goods shall have been so paid or delivered, shall be guilty of a misdemeanor, punishable by a fine not exceeding three (3) times the value of such money or goods. Such loser may sue for and recover such money in an action for money had and received to the use of the plaintiff. . . ." [5]

What is the general standard sought to be effectuated here? Can each of these sections be regarded as making provision for a method of effectuation?

7. *Thompson v. Commonwealth.*[6] Opinion of the court by Judge Bennett:

"The appellant was convicted of the crime of robbing J. R. Barnes. The money that the appellant is accused of robbing

[3] Mich. Stat. Ann. sec. 18.933.
[4] Mich. Stat. Ann. sec. 28.546.
[5] Mich. Stat. Ann. sec. 28.547.
[6] 13 Ky. L. R. 916 (1892).

said Barnes of, was won by Barnes from the appellant that evening at an unlawful game; and the appellant, thereafter, presented his pistol on Barnes and compelled him to return him the money thus won.

"Under our statute the title to the money won by Barnes did not pass to him or from the appellant; nor did the right to its possession pass to Barnes as against the appellant.

"It is a uniform rule that a person is not guilty of stealing that that belongs to him and to which he has a right. Robbery is larceny, accompanied by violence, and putting the person from whom the property is taken in fear. Here the fact that the appellant was entitled to the money, and Barnes' possession of it was not rightful as against the appellant, stripped the appellant's act of feloniously taking the property of another with the fraudulent intention of permanently depriving the owner of it.

"The judgment is reversed, and the cause is remanded for further proceedings consistent with this opinion."

What method of effectuating an antiwagering standard does this decision allow?

8. Suppose the state adopts a policy of trying to reform the persons confined in its prisons. Where would its efforts along this line fit into our scheme of methods for effectuating standards?

Uses of Standards to Guide Action *

Sec. 2–43. Uses generally—use by lawmaker (L). We have now examined the standards applicable to A's acts and the ways in which these standards are effectuated. There remain for consideration the intentional uses of these standards to guide action. How are they used and by whom? How does the lawmaker use them? How does the actor, A, use them? What do officials do with the standards? And the legal

---

* (I.R.) The uses of standards to guide action will be discussed further in chapter 3, "Standards for Official Acts." The division of material between that chapter and this is largely dictated by considerations of convenience in teaching.

counselor? And the student of Law? The discussion of these questions will occupy us in the next several sections.

The discussion of the use of standards to guide action will follow closely what has already been said about the use of language for the purpose of guidance. This is not remarkable inasmuch as standards are patterns in verbal form and any use of a standard is a use of language. The creation of a standard is a directive use of language and the other uses to be considered are all responses or reactions to what the lawmaker has declared as a standard.[1] First, then, of the lawmaker's use of standards.

The lawmaker, L, is in the position of a speaker. He issues verbal directives for the guidance of others.[2] He uses standards instrumentally, to control the behavior of others. He creates them as one might devise tools for particular purposes. He sets them up in order to achieve results which he wishes to bring about.** These observations hold equally of all standards; whether for obligatory, prohibited, effective, permitted, discretionary, or ineffective acts. All standards alike are related to a maker as his handiwork; all are employed to guide the activity of others, by furnishing them with verbal patterns to follow.

Sec. 2–44. Use of standards by A and his counselor (C). The standards with which we are now concerned are addressed to the individual actor, A. He is in the position of hearer, and is intended to shape his acts by reference to the

---

[1] In addition to *standards*, which are directive uses of language (sec. 1–08), we shall also have occasion to speak of habit patterns, which are informative uses of language (sec. 1–11). These observed patterns of behavior are used primarily in predicting the acts of others. Their discussion does not fall strictly within our title, "Uses of Standards to Guide Action"; but an understanding of their role is essential to our present job. See sec. 2–46 below.

[2] This is not the place to go into the ways in which standards are created; the modes of their creation are reserved for detailed discussion in chapters 4 and 6. It is only essential for you to note at this point that a standard is produced by a lawmaker for the guidance of others.

** (I.R.) See sec. 2–01, note * above.

standards. In this sense they are standards for A's use; they cover, in more or less detail, important acts which he may do or think of doing. They are patterns which he can use in planning action of any kind. They tell him when and how he must act; they tell him what he must not do, what he must do, what he can do effectively, and so on.

When A is planning to act he will probably think first of safe lines of conduct; he will use standards for prohibited acts as criteria of what he must avoid, and use standards for permitted acts to determine how far his range of activity is free, and in that sense, safe. When he wants to know whether he must act or not, the standards for discretionary acts will be instructive. When he is undertaking obligatory action he will be anxious to fulfill legal requirements in all respects; he will use the standards as models with which to compare his own proposed act to make sure that it satisfies all requisites. And when he is aiming to do an effective act, he will treat the standards for effective acts, and their opposites, as check lists against which to measure the act he is doing so that he will omit nothing essential to its effectiveness.

But the legal system presents a vast arsenal of standards applicable to A's conduct, an arsenal so large that it is quite impossible for him to be familiar with them all. Many of these standards are set forth in technical legal terms which A cannot understand. Many of them are very complicated or indefinite in nature so that A does not know how to interpret or apply them. The result of all these factors together is that A frequently cannot apply the appropriate standards without assistance. He cannot act safely and effectively on his own and he cannot determine for himself the significance of acts that he has done. Whether he is trying to plan action or to determine the consequences of action already taken, he must be aided by an expert in the law, a legal counselor.

This legal counselor, whom I shall henceforth call C, is a man trained in the art of dealing with legal standards. He is familiar with many more of the established standards than the ordinary man is. Yet C does not know all the standards that are in the law books; not even learned judges do, nor professorial oracles of legal doctrine; there are far too many standards to be known and remembered by anyone. C's value to his client lies quite as much in his mastery of legal method as in his knowledge of the law. He knows how and where to find the relevant legal standards; he knows how to read a statute and how to analyze a case; he knows how to interpret and apply standards to cases; and he knows the standards and methods by which courts and other official agencies operate. In short, C is familiar with the legal processes; he can "reason like a lawyer" and find his way about in the legal labyrinth.

With his knowledge of legal standards and his experience in their use, C is prepared to aid A in planning action. He steers A's activities along safe and effective lines. He warns A away from the rocks and shoals of forbidden action; he advises A as to the best ways of bringing about desired results. For instance, such questions as these may have to be determined: Is it better to organize A's business in the form of a partnership or in the form of a corporation? What advantages and what dangers are involved in each form of organization? Or again, is it better for A to convey Blackacre to his son by deed in A's life, or by will to him at A's death? Is it better to convey to the son outright, or to set up a trust and allow the son to have only the income therefrom? The answers to such questions will depend largely on relevant legal standards and the way they are applied. The answers will involve the weighing of A's general objective successively with reference to possible standard acts and their consequences, and the making of a choice between acts on the basis of what will most nearly accomplish A's objective.

Frequently A requires more than the advice of a lawyer; he has to have the latter's help in the actual doing of acts which will conform to standard. He may require the lawyer to do acts on his behalf, and he may require the lawyer to draft papers for him. When A embarks upon a lawsuit, he needs the knowledge and skill of an advocate who will draw and file pleadings on his behalf and carry his case through the intricacies of legal procedure. When A wants to join with others in the organization of a corporation, he requires the services of a legally skilled draftsman to prepare the necessary papers for himself and his associates to execute. Even when A knows that he wants to dispose of his estate by will and knows whom he wants to make his beneficiaries, A needs for safety's sake to have a lawyer draw the instrument in assured legal terms and form.

But only too often A does not plan his action in reference to applicable standards; he fails to evaluate his act beforehand in terms of legal patterns of conduct. He drives at a reckless rate of speed and strikes and injures B, and then worries about consequences. He enters into a contract with X without proper advice or deliberation, and later comes to appreciate the improvidence of what he has done. In such cases, standards first enter A's calculations when he realizes that he has landed in trouble and tries to take stock of his situation. Is he liable to B for damages? Has he any defenses? Is the contract with X binding? Legal standards furnish A with answers. Moreover, standards furnish him with patterns for further possible acts by which he can extricate himself from his present difficulties, such as settling or litigating the respective claims of B and X.

And incidentally, it is of special interest to us as lawyers that it is just at this point—where A must have answers to questions like these—that he is apt to call on his legal counselor to help him, to decide on the significance of what he has done or to suggest ways of getting out of trouble with as little pain as possible. When he is threatened with prosecution or lawsuit or bankruptcy, A calls upon C. C gives his opinion on the facts as A states them, and decides whether A has failed to do what he should, has done a forbidden act, has exceeded the limits of permissible action, or has executed a legally effective contract.[1] If the answer to any of these queries is in the affirmative, C must decide what the effects of A's acts are and then advise him what to do. When this point is reached, C finds himself once more engaged in planning future acts. He is using his knowledge of legal standards and legal procedures as a basis for guiding A's acts. Usually such a situation presents to C and A a choice of courses of action. In the case of the collision, A may plead guilty to a criminal charge or may elect to go to trial. He may admit his liability for damages for reckless driving and pay the injured party; he may decide to fight the case, especially if there is doubt as to the facts; or he may deny liability but try to make a settlement of some kind. A may have to consider similar alternatives with reference to an improvident contract: performance, defending a lawsuit by the other party, or even bankruptcy. C advises A in his choice in the light of the consequences which are applicable to the various alternatives.

Sec. 2–45. Use of standards by O. The standards which we are considering are addressed immediately to A, the individual, and are intended to guide his behavior. But these standards are also of great interest to official agencies (which we shall designate generically by "O"): the policeman, the prosecutor, the court. Their official acts are largely concerned with steering or pushing A's activities along approved lines of behavior. By the same token their acts are tied to his acts and involve important uses of the standards applicable to his acts.

---

[1] In such a case, C must size up the situation in terms of existing standards in about the same way that the judge does. See the next following section.

First, the standards which are applicable to A's acts also define the *occasions* when O, the agent of the social giant, is to move. In this sense, the standards which are directed primarily to A carry secondary messages to O; the latter is to act *if* A acts in certain ways. When A commits a crime, O must see that he is punished; when A commits a tort, O must aid A's victim to obtain compensation; when A does an act which the legal system has undertaken to make effective at his behest, O must carry out A's verbally expressed desires according to the legal assurance which was given.

The use which the court makes of standards applicable to A's act may be taken as typical of the use of such standards by officials generally.[1] The court must decide whether A's act fits a particular standard and hence calls for action on its part. The court uses the standard as the doctor uses the standardized picture of disease in medical diagnosis.[2] The doctor checks off the features of his patient's condition against the list of symptoms which constitute a disease syndrome such as typhoid. He notices perhaps just one symptom, e. g., a fever, belonging to the typhoid picture; this suggests that the rest of the symptoms may also be present. He then examines the patient to determine whether the other symptoms can be found, and if they can be, he proceeds with treatment for typhoid. If he fails to find the other symptoms, he compares the case with another disease picture, and another, until he finds a standard picture which it fits. And the court proceeds in a similar way. It compares a presented case with a legally established behavior pattern to see if it fits.[3]

---

[1] As we have not yet discussed the separate functions of judge and jury, I speak here of the court as a unit embracing both. The functions of judge and jury will be treated in chapter 3.

[2] See COLUMBIA ASSOCIATES, AN INTRODUCTION TO REFLECTIVE THINKING 31–32 (1923).

[3] An appreciation of the judicial method of applying standards to cases, here analyzed and illustrated, should be helpful to you in understanding the cases which you read in your casebooks. Most of what appears in a judicial

Suppose, for example, that A is charged with larceny (theft) of an automobile. It is shown that he took an automobile which he saw standing on the street to use it for a "joy ride" of an hour or two. Can he be held for the crime charged? Larceny is defined as the act of taking and carrying away the goods of another with intent to deprive the owner permanently thereof; this definition fixes a standard criminal act for the court to apply. A, in our supposed case, would not be guilty of larceny, because one of the elements of the crime is lacking; he did not intend to deprive the owner permanently of his automobile. However, the prosecuting authorities might find another standard pattern of crime which A's act would fit, e. g., unlawfully driving away an automobile, and might then prosecute him for the latter offense. When and if the court finds that A's act fits a legally prescribed pattern, it acts: it metes out to him the legally specified consequences of what he has done, quite as the doctor applies the remedy which the patient's case demands.

So much for the first and most general use which O makes of a standard applicable to A's act: to decide whether an occasion is presented which calls for action by himself. But there is a second important use which O often makes of this kind of standard.[4] He uses it in planning what he shall do as well as in deciding whether he shall act. He treats the standard as the delineation of a goal for his own action. This is just another way of saying that O recognizes it as his task

decision is an exposition of the reasons for applying or not applying a particular standard to a presented case.

Thus far we have referred chiefly to the standards which are found in statutes; many of the standards which decisions involve are found in the case law rather than the statutes. We shall have a great deal to say about the case law later on. But for the moment we are interested only in the method of applying standards and this method is essentially the same whether the standards be found in the statutes or in the case law.

[4] Other incidental uses of standards applicable to A's act will be mentioned in chapter 3. These uses seem to be less closely associated with A's act than with O's, and are therefore reserved for discussion along with official acts.

to effectuate the standard. It means that the remedy that O gives follows the lines of the standard applicable to A's act. Consider again, for example, a case previously mentioned, where A agreed by a valid contract to convey his farm Blackacre to B.[5] If A refuses to convey, his obligation may be enforced by a court's order to make the conveyance agreed. In this case the court shapes its act, i. e., order to perform, so as to bring about the obligatory act which a legal standard imposes upon A. This standard marks out for the court what it shall put in its order; and the order is an act which makes the standard effective in this particular instance.* Suppose, for another example, that O, a policeman, arrives on the scene when A is robbing B. O stops the robbery and takes A into custody. O does not have to wait until a robbery is complete; he is entitled to act when a robbery is in process; he acts to prevent its consummation.[6] In this sense the standard fixes the objective of O's act (as well as the occasion for it) and this objective in turn defines the kinds of acts which O can appropriately do, such as arresting A, or frightening him away, or pursuing him, or killing him if necessary.

Not all remedial acts by O are so obviously tailored to a standard applicable to A's acts as are the two remedies just mentioned. Most remedies are mere substitutes for what a standard calls for, as where A is required to pay money damages for a barn of B which A has wrongfully destroyed. The property is gone and nothing can restore conditions

---

[5] See sec. 2–38.

* (I.R.) My purpose in citing remedial examples in this and the following paragraph, is very limited. For this reason I do not attempt to state all the "ifs" and "ands" of the law applicable to the remedies mentioned.

[6] This case is also interesting because the standard has to be applied to an act by A which is *underway* rather than complete. This change in the facts makes no real change in the use which O makes of a standard. The standard is used as a basis of comparison with A's activity whether that activity be complete or only begun. The difference in the time at which the standard is applied to A's act does not affect the method of applying it to measure the quality of A's conduct.

which should now exist.[7] However, so far as O acts to enforce or effectuate a standard, O is necessarily guided by what the standard provides. He must consider the standard in order to devise a suitable substitute. He must consider the nature and value of B's barn which would now be standing but for A's violation of a standard, in order to decide how much A must pay B by way of damages. To take another example, a legal standard requires A to support his child according to its need and his own financial ability. If A fails in his duty to provide shelter and necessaries for his child, a court will, in a proper suit by those who furnish these things, compel A to pay therefor. The court's judgment in this case is intended to achieve as nearly as may be the results which the legal standard requires. The amount of bills chargeable to A will be measured by reference to the child's needs and to A's ability to pay, just as the legal standard measures A's obligation to support. In other words, the remedy follows the lines of the standard of activity required of A.[8]

Sec. 2–46. Use by A of standards applicable to B—reliance on B's habits. Our ubiquitous individual, A, frequently has occasion to apply standards to the acts of another individual, B. This results from the fact that B's acts affect A in various ways and he must determine the significance of B's acts in

---

[7] Similar observations hold of criminal penalties (see sec. 2–35 above). The imposition of a penalty does not restore, in fact it does not even approximate, the *status quo ante*. The murderer's victim cannot be revived by anything that is done to the murderer. And yet the size and character of the penalty is always affected in some degree by the character of the standard which is violated. This is true whether we are concerned with the penalty imposed by law or the penalty imposed in the individual instance by the sentence of a court.

[8] Many of A's acts affect *other persons*. For this reason, the standards applicable to his acts are important to them as well as to officials and to A himself. These persons use the standards in essentially the same way that officials use them in deciding whether to act and what to do.

Compare sec. 2–46, where I mention the reverse situation, in which A applies standards applicable to B's acts.

relation to his own undertakings. When A applies standards to acts done by B, he uses the standards in essentially the same way as officials use them who are deciding whether to act and what to do. A, who is loaning money to B, asks and answers the question whether B has executed his promissory note in due and proper form; A, who has been injured in a collision with B, asks and answers the question whether B's conduct fits the standard for a negligent act in order to determine whether to sue B for damages; and so on.

But A's concern with acts of B is not confined to acts which B is doing or has already done; it is not confined to questions whether B's actual acts measure up to prescribed standards. A often wants to figure out what B is going to do at some future time. He needs to predict the future behavior of B. As a basis for prediction, A relies not so much on standards as on another kind of behavior pattern, the pattern which summarizes and describes B's habits of action.[1] A knows, as we all do, that human behavior manifests certain constancies which enable him to forecast the ways of future action. These constancies are the observed patterns of the past behavior of B. When A is in possession of such observed patterns of behavior, he is in a position to prophesy the lines which B's future action will take. He knows what to expect from B.*

Of course, A may, and sometimes does, use the prescribed standards of the community as a basis for predicting B's behavior. This A is able to do because he can assume that

[1] Notice that here we are returning to a distinction earlier made—the distinction between directive and informative uses of language. (secs. 1–07 to 1–12.) There we looked at this distinction primarily from the speaker's viewpoint. Here we are interested in A's utilization of directions and information as guides for his action.

* (I.R.) This section, regarding actual behavior of B and A's forecasts of B's behavior, parallels a later section (3–32) relative to O's behavior. The statements of the text are intended to express the views of a miscellaneous group of modern writers often lumped together under the name "realists." In sec. 3–32, note *, will be found a short bibliography of items representing and discussing the realist viewpoint.

B, l ke other members of the community, has habits which conform to these standards. Thus, A may take for granted that B will pay his debts, and drive with proper care. But what A must not forget in such a case is that he is resting his calculations on assumed law-abiding habits of the community, and that he is also assuming B's habits are like those of the rest of the community in this regard.[2]

If standards covered every act which B might do, and if standards were always effectuated to the letter, A might in all cases rely upon legal standards as bases of predicting B's conduct. A might simply look to the applicable legal standards and say, "This is what legal standards prescribe for B, and I expect him to behave accordingly." But most of B's conduct falls beyond the range of coercive legal standards. Most of the acts which he may do are neither prohibited nor obligatory; they are privileged, or discretionary, or both. When A wants to formulate a prediction of what B will do in this nonregulated area, A can only rely on B's habits and B's declarations. Thus, if A as host issues a dinner invitation to B, he relies upon the verbal acceptance of his invitation. B is not legally obliged to come, even if he has promised to.[3]

[2] Constancies of observed behavior may be: 1. patterns which describe behavior of persons generally (any B), or 2. patterns which describe the behavior of a particular person (specific B). Of the first type is the observation that businessmen usually pay their debts. Of the second type is the observation that a specific B is a conscientious person and always inclined to perform his duties. Both types of pattern put the observer in a position to predict future action by a specific B. Both are patterns based on past conduct. Both are general, the one a generalization of the conduct of the many, the other a generalization of B's modes of behavior.

Also included in the factors on which A relies are the habits of officials. Just as A assumes that B, like the rest of the community, habitually performs according to standard, so he makes this kind of assumption about O. He assumes that O's habits of action conform to prescribed standards. This factor will be considered later, in sec. 3–32.

[3] See secs. 2–05, 2–07 and 2–11, regarding the *unregulated* areas of individual action. We have already considered the importance of the actor's motives for action in these areas. At the moment we are interested in bases of prediction, and are therefore concerned with B's habits rather than his motives. Nevertheless, it is worth noting that motives other than those legally

However, A knows that guests usually make a practice of coming when they say they will. He knows that B is accustomed to keep his promises, and he has B's declaration of intention to come. And again, if A is a dealer in men's suits, and is about to lay in a stock for sale to the spring trade, he procures a stock based on his knowledge of the buying habits of his clientele. He makes his best guess as to what, and how much, that clientele will want. As none of his clientele is obliged to buy from him, A can only count on their habits of so doing.[4]

Furthermore, even where legal standards are applicable, B does not always conform to them. There is always some divergence between prescribed standards and the forms which B's behavior actually takes. Indeed, A, who is planning action and trying to forecast what B will do, may find observations of B's past behavior more useful in making these calculations than he does the prescribed patterns of the law. Thus, if A is a banker and about to loan money to B, he probably counts more on what he knows about the habits of businessmen like B in paying their debts, or on what he knows of B's character in particular, than he does on the abstract legal requirement that B must repay the loan.

What is said of the basis for A's predictions and calculations applies no less to those of his counselor. The counselor draws heavily on his fund of experience with the actual behavior of clients, witnesses and opponents. Trying cases, drawing papers, advising clients, are not just matters of knowing

induced may determine B's conduct. B may not want to accept, or may not want to go after he has accepted; but social pressures such as fear of group disapproval or of deprival of business may coerce performance. Whatever the reasons, A may count on his coming.

[4] Popular and business journals are replete with prognostications of future behavior of groups and individuals. Typical is the following calculation of future buying behavior which is taken from *Newsweek* for December 11, 1950: "A General Electric official said, 'The company expects a 25–30% drop in next year's demand for electrical appliances. Higher taxes and prices, credit restrictions, and less residential building would cause the decline.'"

legal standards, or knowing where to find them. The successful pursuit of his professional tasks involves knowledge of people; it involves experience in dealing with people. It involves the ability to predict what people will do. It is hardly less important that the counselor be acquainted with business practices and with the actual ways of life in his community, than that he have knowledge of the legal standards which are applicable to them.

Sec. 2–47. Use by student of law (S). We have now examined characteristic uses of standards by lawmaker, by actor, by officials, and by legal counselor. To these uses, which may be regarded as uses by actual participants in the legal drama, we must add the uses of another class of interested persons who view the operation of the legal system from the outside, somewhat as the theatergoer views the play. This class of observers of the legal scene includes many persons.[1] But I propose to notice only a limited group of them— students of law, whom I shall designate henceforth by the letter S. I have picked the student group for attention because it includes both you and the more experienced students who serve as your instructors. S's methods of using standards are those which you will employ as you work alone. S's methods are those which you will employ as you and your instructors

[1] Other serious and significant groups of observers of the legal scene are legal scientists, legal scholars, and legal historians. Their work is most important; but their uses of standards present no features not illustrated by the uses herein discussed. In fact, in most essentials, the uses which scholars and scientists make are like the uses of the student, and the uses of the historian are like applications to past acts which are made by A and O.

Observers include also the ordinary citizen when he is not immediately involved in a legal problem. They include writers and readers of detective fiction who see in legal standards and their applications merely dramatic opportunities, opportunities to portray distortions of law, technical hardships, and clever evasions. This attitude toward legal standards is well expressed in the following publisher's blurb attached to Arthur Train's *Tutt and Mr. Tutt:* "Come Right In! Here Is Your Ringside Seat! Any law case in the hands of Ephraim Tutt, America's best loved lawyer, is as much fun as a ringside circus."

analyze decisions together, and apply standards in your various law courses.

Standards are used by S in two distinctive ways; both underscore the fact that he is a nonparticipant in the operation of the legal system. First, S considers how others have applied standards to actual cases. He observes and talks about cases which others have already disposed of. However S is not a mere passive spectator. Though he is outside the legal drama, he is by no means indifferent to what transpires in it. He follows the applications of standards which judges and others make, and does this critically. S may be likened to the drama student who thinks about the action of a play and decides how he would have acted the various roles if he were playing them.[2] S reads the reported case, such as you have in your casebooks, and notes how the judge applied standards to the facts of the case. S then acts in the sense that he makes imaginative applications of standards to the case himself. This imaginative application of standards to cases gives S necessary exercise in the use of standards. He develops skill in the methods of using them and develops his critical faculties as regards their use. This reworking of the work of others prepares him for the day when he will be an actual participant in the operation of the legal machine as counselor, as advocate, as judge, or as lawmaker.

The second distinctive use which S makes of standards is the hypothetical use. He deals with hypothetical acts, hypothetical applications of standards, and even hypothetical standards. He propounds hypothetical cases and tries to find appropriate standards to apply; he makes up supposed case

---

[2] The lawmaker, the actor, the judge, and others can also put themselves in imagination into other roles than those which they are playing. As Hamlet could tell the players how they should speak their lines, any player can project himself into another role. But the fact remains that the legal players are primarily concerned with doing legally significant acts. They do not often find time to look at the operation of the legal system from the outside as S does.

after supposed case to see whether each case fits some existing standard; and he also engages in debate about what the standard ought to be rather than what it is. All this means that S is interested in possible applications of possible standards to possible acts, and not merely interested in actual applications which he sees others make to actual acts.[3] This kind of speculation is not mere idle play, however; it is not a pointless use of standard pictures and imaginary cases. Practice in applying standards to cases is the core of legal training; and a potent legal imagination is the most valuable instrument that a lawyer can have. Practice gives readiness to deal with the ordinary or easy case as it arises; and imagination represents the capacity to deal with the novel or difficult case. Working with hypothetical cases and hypothetical standards greatly expands S's range of practice; he handles hypothetically many times the number and variety of cases that he finds reported in decisions. And working in this speculative way develops his legal imagination. For these reasons the neophyte in law should give full rein to his curiosity as regards possible standards and their uses, and labor with all the manifold acts and standards and applications that his ingenuity can muster.

Beyond these abstract exercises in the use of legal standards, the lawyer's training must include practical experience in preparing pleadings, in trying cases, in advising clients, in

---

[3] The hypothetical use of standards is quite characteristic of S. For this reason I have treated this type of use in connection with S. However speculation is not limited to students of law; all persons who plan action make speculative applications of standards as they plan. The judge, for example, makes such applications as he ponders the decision to make in a particular case; he thinks out possible applications and their consequences; he weighs the arguments for applying this standard or that to the case. In his own planning the actor likewise considers the possible applications of standards to what he is about to do. And the counselor makes similar speculative applications. But the thinking of all these persons is normally limited by the needs of particular situations. They confine themselves to consideration of standards applicable to actually presented cases. S is not so restricted; he is not tied down, by time or purpose, to actual cases. He can and should venture as far as his imagination will carry him into the outer reaches of legal possibilities.

using the library, in drafting instruments. His training must include experience with business usages and with various kinds of people. The necessity for training in these respects has been suggested in the preceding sections where I have mentioned the work and the functions of the counselor.[4] However, I think it will be better to reserve the discussion of these practical phases of a lawyer's training for a later point; they raise questions which we are not yet ready to treat. Sufficient it is for the present to stress the law student's need to learn the traditional methods of using legal standards, of applying standards to cases and of fitting cases to standards. Whatever additional learning may be necessary, a familiarity with these methods is basic in the making of a lawyer.

Sec. 2–48. Problems. The last several sections have indicated the ways in which standards are used by lawmaker, actor, official, counselor, and law student. Consider the standards which are involved in the following problems, in relation to the materials of these sections.

1. A statute provides: "Whoever shall wilfully and maliciously wound or inflict bodily harm upon any person, either with or without any weapon or instrument, shall be guilty of a felony." D is charged thereunder with wilfully and maliciously wounding P. The undisputed evidence at the trial shows that D set fire to a haystack on the farm of X with the intent to injure X; that P was a tramp who was sleeping in said haystack; and that P received serious burns as a result of D's act.

Is D liable for the crime charged? How is the statutory standard used in answering this question? Whose use of the standard is the focus of our interest here?

Suppose another statute of the state provides: "Whoever shall wilfully and maliciously destroy or injure the personal

---

[4] See secs. 2–44 and 2–46.

property of another, shall be guilty of a felony." Would D be liable under this provision? Would he be liable for the wounding of P?

2. *State v. McGowan:* [1]

"The statute of this state prescribes the punishment of arson, but it does not define the crime. We look to the common law for its definition.

"Arson, by the common law, is the wilful and malicious burning of the house of another. The word *house*, as here understood, includes not merely the dwelling-house, but all outhouses which are parcel thereof. 1 Hale 570. 4 Bla. Com. 221. 2 Russ. on Crimes 551.

"This information charges the accused with burning a dwelling-house and the question in the case, is, whether the building, which was in fact burned by him, was a dwelling-house, within the meaning of the common law on this subject? That it was a dwelling-house, as distinguished from a building of any other kind, is certain.

"The building is described to be one built and designed for a dwelling-house constructed in the usual manner. It was designed to be painted, but was not yet finished, in that respect, and not quite all the glass were set in one of the outer doors. The building had never been occupied, and it was not parcel nor an appurtenant of any other.

"We think this was not a dwelling-house in such a sense, as that, to burn it, constituted the crime of arson. In shape and purpose, it was a dwelling-house, but not in fact, because it had never been dwelt in—it had never been used, and was not contemplated *as then ready* for the habitation of man.

"Arson, as understood at the common law, was a most aggravated felony, and of greater enormity than any other unlawful burning, because it manifested in the perpetrator, a greater recklessness and contempt of human life, than the burning of any other building, and in which no human being was presumed to be. Such seems to be the spirit of the English cases on this subject, and especially the late case of *Elsmore v. The Hundred of St. Briavells*, 8 B. & C. 461. In that case,

[1] 20 Conn. 244 (1850).

Bayley, J., in speaking of the building therein described, says, 'It appeared to have been built for the purpose of being used as a dwelling-house, but it was in an unfinished state, and never was inhabited. There can not be a doubt, that the building in this case, was not a house in respect of which burglary or arson could be committed. It was a house intended for residence, though it was not inhabited. It was not therefore a dwelling-house, though it was intended to be one.' "

Where did the court find the standard defined? Why was it not applicable to the case before the court?

Suppose a statute had penalized the act of setting fire to a building. Why would this have been important?

3. Suppose you are an attorney practicing in the state of Michianna. The statute quoted in section 2–28, problem 4, is in force there. You are asked by John Smith to draw a will for him leaving all his estate to his wife, Sarah. You take down from the shelf your book of legal forms and draw the following will according to a form therein contained. In what respect is this will insufficient to show execution according to the requirements of the statute?

I, John Smith, a resident of the city of Ypsi-Ann, county of Washtenaw, state of Michianna, and residing therein at 205 Green Street, being over the age of twenty-one years and of sound and disposing mind and memory, and not acting under duress, menace, fraud, or undue influence of any person whomsoever, do make, publish and declare this my last will and testament, in the manner following, to wit:

1. I direct that my executor hereinafter named pay and discharge all of my just debts and expenses.

2. I hereby give, devise and bequeath unto my beloved wife, Sarah, all my property and estate, both real and personal, of whatsoever nature or wheresoever situated, to have and to hold the same absolutely.

3. I hereby nominate and appoint Bank of Ypsi-Ann the executor of this, my last will and testament.

Lastly, I hereby revoke all former wills and codicils to wills heretofore by me made.

In witness whereof, I have hereunto set my hand and seal this 10th day of September, 1950.

John Smith

The foregoing instrument, consisting of one page, was at the date hereof signed, sealed and published by said John Smith, and declared by him to us to be his last will and testament who at his request have signed our names as witnesses hereto.

Richard Jones
Residing at 1010 Main Street, Ypsi-Ann, Michianna

Henry Brown
Residing at 915 First Street, Ypsi-Ann, Michianna

4. *Cochrane v. Moore:* [2]

Action to try the right to one-fourth of the proceeds of the sale of a horse called Kilworth. The plaintiff Cochrane claimed the entire proceeds under a bill of sale. The defendant Moore claimed a one-fourth interest in the horse by virtue of a prior transaction in which Benzon, the then owner of the horse, purported to give said interest to Moore.

The relevant facts, as they appear in the judgment of Lopes, L.J., and in that part of the evidence to which he attached credence, are shortly as follows:

"The horse was in June, 1888, the property of Benzon, and was kept at the stables of a trainer named Yates, in or near Paris, and on the 8th of that month was ridden in a steeplechase by Moore, a gentleman rider. In consequence, as it appears, of some accident, the horse was not declared the winner, and on the same day, according to the view of the evidence taken by the learned judge, Benzon by words of present gift gave to Moore, and Moore accepted from Benzon, one undivided fourth part of this horse.

"A few days subsequently Benzon wrote to Yates, in whose stables the horse was, and told him of the gift to Moore. But

[2] L. R. [1890] 25 Q. B. D. 57.

he did not inform Moore, nor did Moore know of any communication to Yates of the fact of the gift."

In the following month Cochrane made several large advances of money to Benzon by way of loans, and finally Benzon executed a bill of sale of Kilworth and other horses to Cochrane by way of security for repayment of the money which Cochrane had advanced.

"It is proved by the evidence of the witnesses, whom the learned judge believed, that, before the execution of the bill of sale, Benzon, with the assistance of a friend, Mr. Powell, was going through the list of horses to be included in the schedule, and that when Kilworth was mentioned Powell spoke of Moore's interest in the horse, and that thereupon a discussion arose as to what was to be done with it, and that Cochrane undertook that it should be 'all right.' After this the bill of sale was executed by Benzon.

"On these facts, it was argued that there was no delivery and receipt of the one-fourth of the horse, and, consequently, that no property in it passed by the gift. The learned judge, has, however, held that delivery is not indispensable to the validity of the gift."

In the Court of Appeal Lord Justices Fry and Bowen and Lord Esher, M.R., were unanimous in holding that the attempted gift from Benzon to Moore was ineffective for the lack of delivery. Fry, L.J., reviewed the authorities and concluded that according to the old law no transfer of a chattel whatever was effectual without delivery, and that on that doctrine of the old law two exceptions had been grafted: one, the case where the chattel is transferred by deed and the other, the case of a contract of sale, where the intention of the parties is that the property shall pass before delivery. He declared that in these two exceptional instances title may pass without delivery but in all other cases, including the case of the oral gift, delivery is essential to the transfer of title.

However, the Court of Appeal did support Moore's claim to a one-fourth interest in the horse and dismissed Cochrane's appeal from the judgment of Lopes, L.J., on the theory that "what took place between Benzon and Cochrane before Benzon executed the bill of sale to Cochrane, constituted the latter a trustee for Moore of one-fourth of the horse Kilworth."

Here the Court of Appeal mentioned four possible effective acts. What were they? The court considered two verbal acts done by Benzon. What were they?

The court chiefly discussed oral gift; it came to the conclusion that Benzon had not made a good gift of the one-fourth interest in the horse to Moore. Why not?

However the court held that Benzon had created a valid trust in Moore's favor. Do you think Benzon intended to create a trust? (Of course you have not yet learned what a trust is; but it is not necessary that you should know more than that a trust is an arrangement under which one person holds property for another's benefit.)*

Not all courts would conjure up a trust as this court did. If you were a legal counselor today for a party (like Benzon) who wanted to make a present of a one-fourth interest in a horse to another (like Moore), what would you advise your client to do?

Sec. 2–49. Summary. The foregoing chapter has been centered on the acts of the individual, A, and the standards which the lawgiver establishes to guide A's acts.

---

* (I.R.)
"In the early days, before the evolution of the informal contract, if any one of the formalities requisite for the consummation of a contract under seal was not observed, no contractual obligation whatsoever resulted, regardless of the intention of the parties. In the modern law this is not always so, since an undertaking which fails to become a contract under seal, or deed, for want of observance of some necessary formality, may nevertheless have the force of an informal contract, if the requisites for the formation of such a contract be present." GRISMORE, LAW OF CONTRACTS, sec. 79.

In the first subtopic we considered the various kinds of acts which are standardized by the lawgiver, and the significance of these acts. Six kinds of standard acts (or standards for acts) were described: prohibited, permitted, obligatory, discretionary, effective, and ineffective, acts. And two ways of stating the significance were discussed in some detail. In the first of these ways, the significance of A's acts was cast in terms of relations of A and B: duty, right, privilege, discretion, power, and liability. We spent a substantial amount of time in applying these various relational concepts as they are much used in all forms of legal discussion. In the second way, the meaning of A's acts was put in terms of their effects upon A's own legal status.

In the second subtopic we dealt with problems of effectuating standards established to control A's behavior. These were found to be chiefly problems of habituation and motivation. The lawgiver's aim must be either to play upon habits or motives which A is known to have, or to create habits or motives which will result in action along lines which the lawgiver approves.

In the third subtopic, we looked at standards from the point of view of application. We considered what the lawgiver uses standards for, how A and his counselor use them to guide A's actions, and what uses are made of standards by various officials and by the student of the law. The methods of using standards in the cases herein presented, are typical of methods of applying standards to acts and of fitting acts to standards. And finally, I have suggested to you that both A and his counselor must rely on established habit patterns of others in their calculations. Success in applying standards in real life depends on the ability to predict the behavior of people; it involves a wide acquaintance with people, their habits and modes of living, as well as familiarity with legal standards and their use.

This second chapter constitutes the first major division of our examination of the structure and operation of the legal system; it is intended to serve as the foundation for all of the rest of our study.

CHAPTER 3

Standards for Official Acts

Sec. 3–01. Regulative function of government—analysis.
To regulate the behavior of the individual, A, is the primary
function of government.[1] The regulative process involves on
the one hand activities of A whose conduct is controlled; and
on the other, activities of officials in a complex governmental
organization intended to control A's behavior. We began our
study of the regulative process by analyzing it first in terms
of A's acts and of the significance of his acts to B and to A
himself. These and other aspects of A's acts were covered in
the last chapter. But A's acts may be significant not only in
relation to B and to A himself; they may be significant also
to the state and to officials.[2] In other words, significance in
the latter respects represents two other ways in which A's
acts are meaningful. They call for attention before we move
on to the main topic for discussion in this chapter, "Standards
for Official Acts."

*Sec. 3–02. Significance of A's acts in relation to state and
to officials.* The significance of A's acts to the *state* can be
represented in relational terms similar to those which were
used when we were discussing the acts of A and their signifi-

---

[1] Hereafter, I shall speak of "the state" or use the term "government" when
I wish to refer to government in general; I shall speak of "the federal government," or "the states," or use the name of a particular state, e.g, state of
Michigan, when I want to make a distinction between the specific parts of our
federal system.

[2] In sec. 2–16, we noted in passing that the significance, or operation, of
A's act can be expressed in several ways:
  1. Significance in relation to the other person, B.
  2. Significance in regard to A himself.
  3. Significance to the state (or legal system).
  4. Significance to officials.
The first and second of these ways of stating significance were considered in
secs. 2–17 to 2–25. The third and fourth ways, significance to the state and
significance to officials, now call for discussion. See sec. 3–02.

cance to B. The state can be treated as another individual which is affected by A's acts, or by A's acts in combination with B's:

Standard Act	Standard Significance
─────────── ←──→	───────────
Of A (or of A and B)	Rights, powers, etc., of A and of the state

Thus A is said to owe to the state a duty not to be cruel to animals, and the state is regarded as holding a corresponding right that A refrain from this type of action.* And a man and woman, M and W, owe a like duty to the state not to cohabit without the sanction of marriage. Certain acts of A may be regarded as obligatory in relation to the state; for example, A is obliged to register for the draft and to file an income tax return. Indeed, similar rights of the state and duties of A can be taken to be the legal meaning of each and every criminal act defined by law.[1] A's freedom of religion and freedom of speech are outstanding instances of A's privileges in regard to the state. And all of A's powers, e. g., his power to make a will, or his power to maintain a lawsuit, involve acts by which A calls upon the state for its

---

* (I.R.) General usage decrees that we speak of a *duty* of A not to be cruel to animals, and of like duties not to commit other crimes. But there is no agreement as regards the corresponding rights and their allocation. Some writers ascribe the rights to the state; others ascribe the rights to the public; others refuse to speak of, or allocate, any rights whatever corresponding to these duties. Actually, the matter is merely a problem of definition. If one defines duty as the invariable correlative of a right, then if A owes a duty not to commit crimes, corresponding rights must be conjured up and allocated to someone, i.e., to the state or to the public. Some definers prefer one of these allocations, and some the other. On the other hand, if one does not define duty so narrowly, but recognizes duties which are owed to no one in particular (i.e., if one defines duty independent of any correlative right) then one has no real trouble with the placement of these cases; they are simply cases in which there is a duty without a correlative right. See on this point, SALMOND, JURIS-PRUDENCE sec. 72 (6th ed., 1920); POUND, INTRODUCTION TO STUDY OF LAW sec. 6 (1924); and PATON, JURISPRUDENCE 217 (1946).

[1] Usually, however, we speak in such a case of a crime against a particular state, such as the state of Michigan, or a crime against the federal government. The crime is created and defined by the law of a particular government, and is prosecuted in its name.

aid. The state makes A's act effective upon his demand. In the case of A's contract with B, the state attaches legal effect to their conjoint acts. Under its own promise and undertaking, the state makes itself liable or subject to A's and B's calls for assistance.

The significance of A's acts can also be expounded in the form of fixed relations between A and various *officials* (O). The operation of his act can be spelled out in terms of official duties, powers, liabilities, etc., which attach to it. The meaning or bearing of A's act is indicated in some such form as this: if such and such an act is done by A, then such and such an act must be done by O (duty), or can be done by O (power), with such and such effect. Indeed, this is a favorite mode of statement with lawmakers; most statutes take this form:

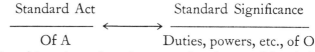

Standard Act	Standard Significance
⟶	
Of A	Duties, powers, etc., of O

But either the action picture or the picture of legal significance may be complex. As in other cases already mentioned, the essential action picture may consist of B's act as well as A's. A may make a defamatory statement about B, but this defamatory statement has no special meaning to courts and other officials unless and until B brings suit. Only when suit is brought does O have the various powers and duties involved in adjudicating B's claim for relief. And the standard significance of A's acts is, even more often, complex. It consists of duties and powers not of one official, but of many. For example, if A kills X, his act imposes duties on a number of officials, and invests them with powers to act. One official agency is bound to charge A with crime. Another is bound to arrest him. Another is bound to try him. And each of these agencies has powers in acting in regard to A, and A is subject to liabilities correlative to these official powers.

Finally, it ought always to be remembered that there is no reason why the significance of A's acts must be stated solely and exclusively in any one of the four ways that I have mentioned: in relation to B, in relation to A himself, in relation to the state, or in relation to officials. They can be combined; and we have a more complete view of the significance of A's acts if we do combine them. For instance, the significance of A's tortious act in striking B is better understood if we see not only what it means to B but what it means to officials who may be involved in a suit by B against A. Likewise, the legal operation of A's breach of contract involves both claims and powers of B and powers and duties of officials. Moreover, it is quite common to express the significance of A's acts in hybrid form. For example, A's criminal acts are usually spoken of in terms of duties to the state, but the processes of prosecution are more often analyzed and described, not in terms of powers of the state, but rather in terms of duties and powers of specific officials.

Sec. 3–03. Scope of chapter—official acts. But one can begin with an analysis of the regulative process at the other end. Instead of starting with the acts of A, one can take the acts of government as a starting point. In this sense, one can treat the state as an actor and expound the significance of the state's acts to A in terms of the conventional legal relationships: rights and duties, powers and liabilities, etc.[1]

Standard Acts	Standard Significance
Of State	Rights, duties, privileges, powers, liabilities of A and of the state

---

[1] As lawgiver, the state speaks as an entity. It speaks to A as one person addressing another. And in its declarations it relates itself to A and declares what it wants A to do, not to do, etc. See sec. 2–11. The state speaks in the same manner as an individual person who says to another, "I want you to remember that you owe me $10."

There are many clauses in the federal and state constitutions wherein acts of the federal government and acts of the states are referred to.[2] And there are likewise clauses in which their powers and duties are declared. For example, the Federal Constitution provides that "The United States shall guarantee to every State in this Union a Republican Form of Government, and shall protect each of them against Invasion; . . ."[3] and provides that "No Title of Nobility shall be granted by the United States";[4] and declares, "No

[2] In the United States, the function of regulating the behavior of A is divided between the *federal government* on the one hand, and the several *states* on the other. Accordingly, when relations between government and A are stressed, these are most often stated as relations of A to the federal government, or relations of A to a specific state, such as the state of Michigan.

Each state has its sphere of action, and corresponding powers, defined by its own constitution; its sphere and powers are also limited to an important extent by the Federal Constitution. The federal government has its sphere and powers fixed by the Federal Constitution.

The state's powers are general and varied. The state controls almost all matters which fall in the fields of contract, property, tort, crime, and personal and domestic relations. The state also possesses extensive powers of taxation; it lays taxes on property, on incomes, on transfers (sales), on inheritances and on licenses and franchises. In fact, the state issues the great bulk of the laws and fiscal regulations which the legal practitioner is called upon to use and apply in this practice.

Among the matters subject to state regulation is the practice of law. The state in which a lawyer practices establishes standards of education and conduct; it provides for the issuance of a license and for the forfeiture of the license for misbehavior. To be sure, a lawyer must also apply for admission to practice before the federal courts; but the admission to practice therein is usually a mere formality; if he is a state practitioner in good standing the federal courts admit him to practice as a matter of course.

By contrast with the state, the federal government is one of limited powers; it exercises only those powers which are specifically granted to it by the Federal Constitution or which are necessary and proper for the execution of the granted powers. The federal powers of greatest importance are the regulation of interstate and foreign commerce, the collection of taxes and expenditure of public funds to provide for the general welfare, the control of money and currency, the establishment and maintenance of armed forces, and the control over foreign affairs. But the limits on federal powers are rather than apparent than real. While it is true that federal powers are formally specific and limited, they are not so in practical operation. In actual fact the owners of the federal government are so far-reaching that they touch almost very aspect of the life of the country; especially its control over commerce and its vast fiscal powers give the federal government such dominance in the economic sphere as tends to throw the state's activities into the shade.

[3] Art. IV, Sec. 4.

[4] Art. I, Sec. 9, Cl. 8

state shall enter into any Treaty, Alliance or Confederation; grant Letters of Marque and Reprisal; coin money; . . ." [5] And the Fourteenth Amendment provides that, "No state shall deprive any person of life, liberty, or property without due process of law." This provision is at once an expression of a type of prohibited state action, a declaration of a duty of each state not to take this kind of action, and an implied assertion that this kind of action, if attempted, will be ineffective. The same can be said of the Fifteenth Amendment which provides that the right of citizens of the United States to vote shall not be denied or abridged by the United States, or by any state on account of race, color, or previous condition of servitude. These constitutional clauses are prohibitions of governmental action which can be regarded and interpreted in terms of governmental duty to refrain from action, and of corresponding claims or rights which can be asserted by A. But it is not necessary to list further examples. Much of the material in the remainder of this chapter can be regarded as illustrative of acts of government which are obligatory or effective in regard to A, or which are prohibited for his protection. [6]

However, when we talk of the state generally, or of the federal government, or of a state government, and say that any of these entities performs acts or owes duties, or has powers, or holds rights, we must realize that we are speaking in terms of rather "high order" abstractions. Government is an organization of people—a very important organization, to be sure—but still an organization of human beings. Government does not act in the ordinary sense; only individual human beings do acts. The acts of government are the acts

---

[5] Art. I, Sec. 10, Cl. 1.

[6] However, for the most part, the Federal Constitution refers not to acts and powers of the United States but to acts and powers of particular organs or officials of the United States, such as Congress (to regulate commerce), the Senate (to ratify treaties), the President, and the Supreme Court. Such acts and powers come properly within the scope of the following sections where we deal with acts and powers of officials.

of particular officials. These officials act on behalf of government or in its name. Governmental control is control of one man's activity by another's activity, control of some persons by others. A government acts through its lawmaking organs to establish standards of behavior for individuals and officials. It acts through other officials to effectuate these standards, and it acts through its courts to administer justice in controversial cases. Hence, it is clearer and more realistic, and is, in fact, more common, to analyze and represent regulative function of government in terms of acts and powers of officials rather than in terms of acts and powers of the state or of the federal government. And this is the method of exposition I shall adopt throughout the remainder of this chapter.

Accordingly, I shall now turn to an examination of the acts of officials and the standards which regulate them. The persons who perform public functions are as much in need of guidance as the ordinary man is. I shall deal with their acts and the standards which guide them in a manner parallel in all essentials to our treatment of standards for the individual's acts. This subject matter will be taken up under the following heads:

Official Acts and Their Significance
Effectuation of Standards for Officials
Use of Standards for Officials

Official Acts and Their Significance

Sec. 3–04. Official acts—standards—kinds of acts. Acts of officials are standardized. The standards are verbal patterns, and similar in most respects to standards applicable to the individual's acts. It will not be necessary, therefore, to repeat here, in full detail, what has already been said about the standardization of acts.[1]

---

[1] See secs. 2–03 to 2–14, inclusive.

We classified the acts of the individual, A, into six kinds: prohibited and permitted, obligatory and discretionary, effective and ineffective.[2] We can classify official acts on the same bases, and in the same manner. However, we find that the relative importance of these kinds and the relative frequency of acts of these respective kinds are not the same in regard to O's acts as in regard to A's.

Whereas the number of acts which A is prohibited from doing is very large, embracing most crimes, torts and breaches of contract, the number of acts which the official, O, is explicitly *forbidden* to do is relatively small. And whereas permitted acts of the individual loom large in any discussion of his significant acts, the *permitted* activities of O are, by contrast, not too frequently mentioned. Partly no doubt, this reduced attention to prohibited and permitted acts of officials is due to the fact that O is supposedly a properly bred animal and not expected to stray off the reservation as often as a member of the common herd might. But partly, the small number of expressly forbidden and permitted official acts is due to the fact that O, as an individual, is subject to the same general rules of law as A, so that the standards provided for A also cover the bulk of possible deeds and misdeeds by O.

---

[2] In speaking of the individual's acts, I distinguished between physical and verbal acts. Official acts may be divided and classified in the same terms. Most official acts are verbal. Now and then an official act may require the use of physical force; the policeman may suppress by physical force a person who is committing an assault on another. Much more often the policeman acts verbally, as when he arrests A by declaring to him: "You're under arrest; come with me." There is a threat of physical compulsion behind the invitation to the arrestee to come along to the police station; this does not alter the fact, however, that the normal activity of the officer is verbal. The prosecutor likewise carries out his functions almost wholly through verbal acts; he questions suspects; he interrogates possible witnesses; he frames a written charge and a sequence of other written papers; and he does all the oral acts which are involved in the trial. Similarly, the chief executive acts almost invariably in oral or written form. The jury's verdict is, of course, a verbal act. Practically all the acts of the judge are verbal; these include rulings on motions, orders to parties, orders to witnesses, orders to attorneys, and the final judgment or sentence. So that we can say that, all up and down the line, official activity is predominantly verbal activity.

The number of acts which are *obligatory* on O is relatively large. You will remember that we were able to mention only a few acts which A must perform, outside of those which he undertook by contract to perform. But officials perform many obligatory acts. The sheriff is bound to serve process upon the defendant when it is delivered for service by the plaintiff or his attorney; the policeman is required to arrest the speeder whom he catches in the act of reckless driving; and the judge is bound to instruct the jury at the proper time and pass sentence on a convicted defendant, and so on. And the *discretionary* or nonobligatory character of certain official acts is also not infrequently recognized in legal provisions. Discretion is very common where O is given authority to do an effective act. He is left free to exercise this authority when, as, and if he thinks proper.

Moreover, standards defining official acts which will be *effective* are, like the similar standards defining effective acts of the individual, numerous and very important. The constable can levy on the goods of a judgment debtor with certain effects; the policeman can arrest A with specified legal consequences; and the judge can render judgment in a civil case with predetermined legal results. And *ineffective* acts are also frequently defined in provisions relating to officials. This is due to the fact that O's acts are limited by a great number of constitutional and statutory provisions, so that it often becomes important both to O and to other persons to know whether a certain act of O transcends the limits of his powers. The instances in which his acts are ineffective as well as those in which his acts are effective tend to become crystallized in standard forms. An arrest in a certain manner is effective; an arrest in another way is ineffective. A levy in a certain way is legally approved and fully operative; a levy of another type is invalid and inoperative; an instruction in certain terms is proper; an instruction in other terms is a ground for reversal.

To sum up: whereas in regard to A, prohibited and effective acts are the types most commonly defined and most important in practice, in regard to O the most common and important standardized acts are the obligatory, the effective, and the ineffective.

According to our American tradition, official acts and powers are divided on another basis. They are separated into three kinds: *legislative, executive* and *judicial*. This division is made in regard to the acts and powers of federal officials. It is made in regard to the acts and powers, of all state officers. Certain persons constituting the legislature, make the laws; other persons who collectively compose the executive branch, enforce the laws; and other persons, the courts and their functionaries, adjudicate controversies regarding the laws.

Despite certain inadequacies of this traditional threefold division, which I shall point out later,[3] I shall use it in developing the ensuing analysis of official acts. I adhere to the traditional division of functions, first, because it is a classification which is adopted by our constitutions; second, because it is the classification which is ordinarily used in elementary and college courses in government so that you are already familiar with it; and third, because this classification works out conveniently for the purpose of dealing with the processes of regulation in which we are primarily interested.

However, I do not intend to follow the conventional order of treatment. This would require us to begin with the legislative process, then to discuss executive activities, and then to treat the activities and functions of the judicial branch.[4] Instead of following this order I shall deal first with the

---

[3] See especially secs. 3–20 and 3–21.
[4] The lawmaking process will be the subject of chapter 4.

activities of executive officials and then with the functions and activities of the courts. The activities of these two branches of government are closely interwoven with one another; I shall not try to keep them neatly apart. They constitute together the official acts with which we shall deal in this chapter.

Sec. 3–05. Significance of official acts. In the last chapter I spoke of the significance of individual acts in terms of fixed legal relations between the actor and other individuals. A similar analysis can be made of the significance of official acts in terms of standard relations between the official actor and the individual:

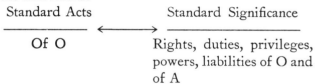

Standard Acts		Standard Significance
Of O	←——→	Rights, duties, privileges, powers, liabilities of O and of A

This mode of stating significance is especially appropriate in regard to executive and judicial acts. These acts are chiefly concerned with the effectuation and enforcement of the standard applicable to A. As such, the standard applicable to A's act is merely an empty pattern.[1] It is like the pattern for a dress or the architect's plan for a house. It is only the design for an act which may, or may never, be executed. Whether or not A does an act which fits the standard, depends upon A's motivation. The threat of penalty and other devices for controlling A's motivation are reducible in the last analysis to acts of officials, threatened or promised: the threats of penalties or threats of official activity, and the promises of benefit or assurances to A of beneficial acts by officials.

Some of O's acts are done or threatened for the purpose of *preventing* prohibited acts by A. By physical force O

---

[1] As I have already pointed out in sec. 2–29 *et seq.*

prevents A from doing a physical injury to B. By the threat of arrest, to be followed by prosecution and punishment, O preserves the public peace, and deters A from the commission of thefts. By patrolling the highway O forestalls such acts as driving at excessive speed; the speeder checks his propensity to hurry in a locality where he knows that police officers may be encountered. It is a distinct advantage from everybody's point of view if prohibited acts can be thus prevented, rather than punished as a deterrent to others.

Other official acts are done or threatened for the purpose of *inducing* performance of obligatory acts by A.[2] Thus, A is induced to perform his contract by fear of the consequences which will ensue if he fails to perform the acts which he has bound himself to do. Where a statute requires the factory owner to install certain safety devices to protect his workmen from injury, the threat of prosecution or suit for damages may operate as an adequate incentive for the performance of his obligation. But probably more effective will be the expectation of periodic visits from a safety inspector whose business it is to make sure that proper safety devices are installed and in operation. Even though failure to install such devices is threatened with heavy penalties, common experience shows that some employers will take a chance on such consequences unless they are continuously checked by official inspection. Lesser penalties are far more effective than heavy, if the lesser penalties are backed up by regular inspection and the certainty that the penalties will be exacted.[3]

---

[2] I shall not dwell again on the use of rewards or subsidies to induce acts by A; this matter has been adequately covered in sec. 2–39.

[3] Official action is no less essential to A's privileges and liberties. The founding fathers did not have a clear appreciation of the positive functions which government must serve. They were chiefly concerned to prevent abuses of powers such as had characterized the activities of the government of Great Britain. (See further discussion of this point in secs. 7–05, 7–12, and 7–17.) They did not realize how fully A's liberty, as well as his security, depends on governmental protection against aggressive acts by B. A's freedom of speech, for example, is not merely the privilege of speaking without inter-

Other official acts may be regarded as essentially *remedial* in character. The acts which O does where A has already committed an injury to B are of this type. O's acts are intended to force A to compensate B for the damage which he has done. Similar observations apply to O's acts intended to compel A to pay damages to B for a breach of his contract with B.

And many acts of O simply represent the performance of *services* which government has undertaken to render for A. Here, of course, fall all those official acts which are done by government agents when A calls upon them, by doing an effective act: the acts which O does by way of securing A's claims to property, the acts that O does by way of carrying out A's testamentary disposition, the acts which O does by way of recording and preserving deeds, mortgages, and so forth for the benefit of A.

But an act of O does not ordinarily stand by itself. Seldom, and perhaps I should say never, are the functions of government served by an isolated act of an official. An official act is normally a part of a complicated series of acts which are, in combination, significant. The series contributes to one common purpose or function. Thus, for example, as we shall see later, the enactment of a statute is not a simple single act. The process of putting a law on the books involves many distinguishable acts of different persons. A law is suggested, formulated, debated, adopted by each of the two houses of the legislative branch, and is then approved by the chief executive. All these acts enter into the legislative process; they culminate in the establishment of a statute. Then, after the statute is on the books, establishing, let us say, a speed regulation for those who drive on the public highways, this

ference by the federal government and without interference by state government, though both are important. To be fully secured, A's freedom to speak must also have governmental protection against interference by B, the other individual.

statute must be enforced; and here again we encounter a series of acts contributing to one general function, the function of enforcement. The policeman's act in arresting A for exceeding the speed limit is merely the initial step in a succession of acts which carry the process of enforcement through the courts. While we shall talk henceforth chiefly about separate acts of officials and about the standards applicable to these acts, we must not lose sight of the important fact that any one of these separate acts is really just an element in a complex series of acts, which have a combined significance.

Furthermore, the relations of O and A do not exhaust the legal significance of O's acts. An official act may be important to other officials as well as to A. One official act may be a condition precedent to another, as is suggested by the material in the last paragraph. The jury cannot try and convict a man until he has been charged by the proper authorities, and the judge cannot sentence him until he has been properly charged and properly convicted. So that we could, if we wished to pursue our methods of analysis further, state the effects of the acts of O on the powers and duties of other officials. And by the same token, we might point out that the acts of O are important to the state itself. And we might express this importance in terms of duties which O owes to the state, as well as powers and liabilities, operative between O and the state for which he acts. But I do not feel that it is necessary to pursue these lines of analysis further. My main point has been to show the various directions in which official action has legal import, and I believe that I have now sufficiently developed that point.

Sec. 3–06. Acts of executive officials. In the last two sections, I have classified official acts and suggested the ways in which these acts may be significant. In this and the following section, I propose to specify, more definitely, the officials who do acts on behalf of government, the acts which these officials do, and the ways in which their acts are significant. I begin with acts of executive officials.

Inferior executive officials do many acts in the processes of effectuating standards applicable to A. The acts of police, sheriffs, constables, and other peace officers come first to mind in this connection. Their acts are involved in the enforcement of both prohibitive and obligatory standards. Their acts are involved also in the execution of a court's order or sentence, as when they serve papers for the court, seize and sell property of a debtor, imprison or execute a convicted criminal.

To these acts of peace officers in enforcing standards must be added executive acts which impose special obligations on A, such as the tax assessor's act in levying assessments on A's property. Then there are the acts of such officials as the register of deeds who makes and preserves records of conveyances by and to A. Also to be counted among minor executive acts are those of various officials who issue licenses to A on his application, such as the building permit, the license to drive a car, and the license to engage in the liquor business. Their acts make effective A's demand for the privilege of engaging in certain activities, a privilege which he would not otherwise enjoy.

The acts of inferior executive officials are commonly governed by standards similar to the standards which are applicable to the acts of individuals. Their duties and powers are set forth specifically and in detail. Thus legal provisions specify the situations in which an officer can make an arrest and the manner in which he is to make it; they determine what the effects of an arrest are to be, as regards the arrestee, the arresting officer, and interested third parties. In a similar way legal provisions prescribe every step to be taken in the levy and collection of taxes. They prescribe the way in which a deed is to be filed for record and the way in which land records are to be kept, and they fix the consequences of recording as regards the grantor, the grantee and other parties.

Furthermore, the acts of inferior executive officials are largely controlled by general rules or specific orders of their superiors. In a police department, for example, many routine matters are regulated by general rules. The hours of duty may be fixed in this way as well as the occasions for making reports and the methods of making them. And the chief of the police department, or one of his lieutenants, may order an officer to investigate a particular case, send him out to stop a disturbance, or direct him to make a report on an investigation which he has already made.

Nevertheless the control of the minor official's acts is never complete. The legal system does not attempt to control all of the acts of A, as I have already pointed out.[1] Neither does it undertake to furnish the individual policeman with patterns for all the acts he must or may do. It would neither be practical nor desirable for the lawmaker or for his superiors to provide the policeman with complete standards to go by. It is not possible to foresee all the contingencies which the policeman will have to face. His acts have to be adapted to circumstances. Life is too complicated and variable to be foreseen and regulated to the last detail. Accordingly, the policeman is left with a substantial degree of discretion or freedom of action. He is left to decide, for example, whether the fair speeder shall receive a traffic ticket or be let off with a warning. And generally speaking, as we proceed upward in the executive hierarchy the extent of discretion increases.

The governor of a state is the chief executive of the state government; the President of the United States is the chief executive of the federal government. Each of these officials

[1] See secs. 2–01, 2–05, and 2–07 regarding the extent to which A's behavior is left free from legal control.

is the principal law-effectuating agent of the government which he represents. He directs the operation of his government from the top. However, we must not suppose that the executive branch in either of these governments is a well integrated hierarchy with complete and perfect control from the top. Rather the lines of control are loose and indefinite so that many parts of the executive branch have no effective superiors. Thus the mayor of a city or a local public prosecutor or the head of a government department may be subject to hardly any control from above, especially if he is an elective official and answerable only to local or state voters for his acts.

In the ordinary case the acts of the chief executive affect the individual only indirectly through the activities of subordinate officials to whom he issues general directions and specific orders. However, his effectuative acts are nonetheless important though their effects are indirect and though they are hardly noticed when affairs run along smoothly. The importance of his powers becomes apparent when it is necessary to exercise the whole power of government to enforce the order of a court in a time of public clamor, or when the governor finds it necessary to issue a declaration of martial law. Such a declaration is made when serious disorder occurs or impends in a community. The executive issues his declaration and sends a detachment of soldiers into the community to keep order. This declaration changes the whole status of law enforcement in the community affected. It confers enforcement authority upon the military commander and supersedes the authority of local officials to a very large degree; it works important changes likewise in the liberties and rights of individuals, to assemble together, to have access to the courts, and so on.[2]

[2] See 34 MICH. L. REV. 417 (1936) for a discussion of the effects of a declaration of martial law.

The acts of the chief executive are controlled by standards just as the acts of his inferiors are. These standards are found in the constitutions and the statutes, state and federal. He is charged in general terms with the duty of enforcing the law. Typical is the provision in the Federal Constitution which declares that the President "shall take Care that the Laws be faithfully executed." [3] Some duties of more specific character are imposed on chief executives by the constitutions; and somewhat more frequently specific duties are imposed by statutes; but duties of general character are more characteristic. In fact, as we proceed upward in the executive hierarchy from minor officials to the governor or the President, duties are more and more broadly and generally expressed.

Most of the standards which apply to the chief executive are cast in terms of power, rather than duty, to act. The executive is empowered to do this or that. Such powers, like executive duties, are commonly expressed in the most general terms. Typical are the two following sections of the Federal Constitution:

"The President shall be Commander-in-Chief of the Army and Navy of the United States, and of the Militia of the several States, when called into the actual Service of the United States; he may require the Opinion, in writing, of the principal Officer in each of the executive Departments, upon any Subject relating to the Duties of their respective Offices, and he shall have Power to grant Reprieves and Pardons for Offenses against the United States, except in Cases of Impeachment.

"He shall have Power, by and with the Advice and Consent of the Senate, to make Treaties, provided two thirds of the Senators present concur; and he shall nominate, and, by and with the Advice and Consent of the Senate, shall appoint Ambassadors, other public Ministers and Consuls, Judges of the supreme Court, and all other officers of the

[3] Art. II, Sec. 3.

United States, whose appointments are not herein otherwise provided for, and which shall be established by law; . . ."[4]

And as you will notice even the exercise of these very broad powers is left to the President's discretion. He has power to grant pardons, but is not required to do so in any case whatever. He "may require the opinion" of the head of a department, but again this is a matter lying wholly in the President's good judgment.

Sec. 3–07. Problems. 1. Suppose a policeman, O, commands a speeder, A, to pull over to the curb and stop. A stops as directed and O gives A a traffic ticket. How is O's act related to the standard applicable to A? Would you regard O's act as obligatory? As effective?

2. The Fourth Amendment to the Federal Constitution provides:

"The right of the people to be secure in their persons, houses, papers, and effects, against unreasonable searches and seizures, shall not be violated, and no Warrants shall issue but upon probable cause, supported by Oath or affirmation, and particularly describing the place to be searched, and the person or things to be seized."

Translate this passage into standards applicable to the acts of enforcement officials. How do A's acts enter the picture?

3. A statute provides: Sec. 1. Every register of deeds shall keep an entry book of deeds and an entry book of mortgages, each page of which shall be divided into six columns, with title or heads to the respective columns, in the following form, to wit:

(1)	(2)	(3)	(4)	(5)	(6)
Date of Reception	*Grantors*	*Grantees*	*Township* where the land lies	*To whom delivered* after being recorded *and date*	*Fee* Received

[4] Art. II, Sec. 2, Cls. 1, 2.

Sec. 2. In the entry books of deeds, the register shall enter all deeds of conveyance . . . , and in the entry book of mortgages he shall enter all mortgages . . . noting in such books, the day, hour and minute of the reception and other particulars, in the appropriate columns in the order in which such instruments are respectively received, and every such instrument shall be considered as recorded at the time so noted.

The statute then specifies the effects to be attached to the entry of deeds and mortgages in the entry books aforesaid; in particular, the statute provides that the entry of these instruments in the record books shall constitute notice of the instruments and their contents to all subsequent purchasers and mortgagees.

The register of deeds, R, is obviously an executive official. Where do R's acts, here defined, fall in our sixfold classification of standard acts? Are they prohibited? Obligatory? Effective?

How would you classify A's act of filing a deed for record? What is the relation of R's act of recording to A's act of filing for record?

4. *The American League of the Friends of the New Germany of Hudson County v. Eastmead et al.*[1]

Bigelow, V. C. (in part):

"Complainant proposed to hold a meeting in Union City in a hall hired by it for the purpose, but the police acting under order of the city commission forbade the meeting. Complainant applies for an injunction to restrain police interference.

. . . The defendants (i. e., the police) say, in effect, that if the meeting takes place speeches will be made extolling the present government of Germany and advocating measures to abridge the rights of Jews in the United States; that Jews will thereby be incited to riot, and that defendants forbade the meeting in order to avert disorder and possible bloodshed.

[1] 116 N. Y. Eq. 487 (1934).

The explanation does not, in a legal sense, excuse defendants. Our law does not prohibit the public expression of unpopular views. It is lawful to advocate, for instance, the establishment of a dictatorship in America, or a soviet form of government, or a hereditary monarchy, or the abolition of religious freedom, or other changes in our political, economic or social system, no matter how unwise or how shocking. If lawless elements in the community, instead of ignoring such propaganda, or meeting it by sound argument, resort to riot, it is the duty of police to protect the lawful assemblage and to repress those who unlawfully attack it." (Injunction denied on other grounds.)

What is the significance of the fact that complainant league is held entitled to hold a meeting and entitled to police protection in so doing?

Would you say that the league has a *right* to hold a meeting? A *privilege* to hold a meeting? If so, against whom is the right or privilege respectively available?

5. In section 2–25, problem 20, we discussed the case of a landowner, A, who made a deed of his home to B as a result of coercion exerted by B. The deed would be invalid; the court would order its cancellation in a proper action. How would you express this result in terms of A's relations to the court (O)?

Sec. 3–08. Courts—functions—questions of fact and law. Courts serve important functions in the processes of effectuating standards applicable to A. Primarily courts deal with and settle cases in which the actual application of a standard is controverted. This is what is meant when it is said that courts are established to decide controversies.

The questions which the court may have to determine are of two sorts: questions of fact and questions of law. When the court has to decide what A did on a particular occasion or whether he did a particular act or whether he had a specific intent when he acted, we say that the court has a question of *fact* to decide. Was A present when X was killed? Did A strike the fatal blow? Did A drive at sixty miles an hour on a particular occasion? Did A hand a deed to B merely to look over, or did he hand it to B with the intent to make an immediately operative conveyance? These are all questions of fact. They all take the form of a dispute about whether an act of A actually occurred or whether some essential feature of the act actually existed.

But the controversy may involve a question about the nature or scope of one or more standards, not about the facts of a particular case; it may involve a question of *law*. The controversy may turn on the question whether a particular standard is properly applicable to the act which has occurred or which is assumed to have occurred. Thus the question may be whether a particular act constitutes larceny, e.g., whether driving away an automobile to take a joy ride fits the standard for this prohibited act.[1] Or the controversy may involve the question which of several standards is properly applicable to the act which has occurred or which is assumed to have occurred. Does the act with which A is charged constitute murder or manslaughter, i. e., which of these two prohibitive standards does his act fit? Or the controversy may involve the question of law, just what elements go into the standard itself. What are the elements of arson or the elements of an oral gift? The questions here relate to the essentials of the standard itself. The constitution of the standard is doubtful or uncertain in some respect. We have already dealt with two cases which illustrate this type of controversial question of law. In *State v. McGowan* the court had to decide whether a house, which had been finished, but which had not yet been occupied as a habitation, was a dwelling house for the purpose of the law of arson.[2] The controversy turned on a doubt as to the meaning of one element in the definition of arson: what is a dwelling house. The court held that a dwelling house

[1] This case is discussed in sec. 2–45.
[2] See sec. 2–48, problem 2.

must be inhabited. In so deciding the court settled a question of law; it made clear an uncertain feature of the standard for a prohibited act. In the other case, *Cochrane v. Moore*, the court also settled a question of law.[3] It had to determine what are the essential elements of an oral gift. It held that this effective act requires something more than mere words of present gift; it requires also an actual handing over of the thing given, a delivery. In so deciding the court determined a controversy regarding the essential elements of a legal standard; it decided a question of law.

Most actual cases involve both questions of fact and questions of law; the court may have to determine both what A has done and what legal standard covers what he has done. And usually the two kinds of questions are so intertwined that they have to be considered and weighed in connection with one another; both kinds of questions ordinarily have to be settled together in the decision of one case.

Sec. 3–09. Trial courts—jurisdiction.* Courts can be divided into two general kinds: trial courts and appellate courts. Both kinds handle controversial cases and both kinds deal to some extent with disputed questions of fact and law.[1] The general distinction between the two kinds of courts is that the trial court gives the initial hearing and decision of a controversy; the appellate court reviews the job which the trial court has done. It will be convenient to examine the work of each of these courts separately.[2] I shall begin with the work of the trial court, and treat first its *field* of work.

[3] See sec. 2–48, problem 4.

* (I.R.) See generally regarding the organization of American courts, Pound, *Organization of Courts* (National Conference of Judicial Councils, 1940). Problems of the selection, tenure and supervision of judges will be discussed later in secs. 3–26 and 3–28.

[1] The distinction between trial jurisdiction and appellate will be further developed in sec. 3–18.

[2] The work of the trial court is covered in secs. 3–09 to 3–17; the work of the appellate court in sec. 3–18.

The trial court's field of work can be designated and described in various ways. It can be called the role of the trial court, or the scope of its functions, or the extent of its powers. The common legal designation for this field, which I shall use from now on just because it is the common expression among lawyers, is the *jurisdiction* of the trial court.

No court is ever invested with authority to try all cases whatsoever; its competence is always limited to the trial of certain cases; and this fact is what makes it necessary to talk about jurisdiction and its limitations. The limitations on trial jurisdiction are commonly defined in terms of territory (place), or subject matter (kinds of cases), or both.**

In the states, the jurisdiction of the trial court is almost invariably limited to a specified district or area such as a county, a group of counties, a city, or a township. For this reason the trial court often bears the name of the County Court of X County, or the Circuit (or District) Court of the Second Judicial Circuit, or the Municipal Court of the City of Y. The trial court's jurisdiction is also usually defined in terms of subject matter. It may be given authority to dispose of all types of cases within the area where it sits, or it may be authorized to deal only with specific kinds of cases. If the court is authorized to handle all kinds of cases, large or small, civil or criminal, legal or equitable, we call it a court of general jurisdiction; and most states establish one trial court of this type for every community so that the entire state is blanketed by a system of trial courts of general jurisdiction. Most states also establish some courts whose juris-

** (I.R.) Two other common jurisdictional distinctions are passed over without mention here: (1) the distinction between jurisdiction of the person and jurisdiction of subject matter; and (2) the distinction between acts and transactions within the court's jurisdiction, and acts and transactions which fall outside it. The first of these distinctions is covered in courses on procedure; the second is treated in courses on conflict of laws and constitutional law. Both distinctions seem to me too difficult and refined for discussion in an introductory course.

diction is limited to the handling of specific types of cases.[3] The court may, for example, be authorized to try only criminal cases; the Recorder's Court of Detroit is limited in this manner. Or the trial court's jurisdiction may be confined to the administration of decedents' estates and related matters. This is the limitation of jurisdiction characteristic of the county, probate, surrogate, or orphans' courts which one finds in most states. And almost everywhere one finds petty courts which have jurisdiction of small money claims (not over $100, or some other fixed amount), of petty criminal cases, and of the preliminary steps in major criminal cases; the latter are usually called by such names as justice of the peace courts, justice courts, or municipal courts. Almost always, as I have already suggested above, the court whose trial jurisdiction is limited in terms of the kinds of cases to be handled, is also limited in terms of place, so that a county court which is restricted to the handling of decedents' estates can only do so within the bounds of a particular county.

In the *federal* court system, trial jurisdiction of practically all matters is vested in the district courts of the United States.[4] There is at least one district court in every state. In

[3] The supreme court of a state and other appellate courts are sometimes given jurisdiction to try limited types of cases. The following provision from the Michigan Constitution is typical: "The supreme court . . . shall have power to issue writs of error, *habeas corpus, mandamus, quo warranto, procedendo* and other original and remedial writs, and to hear and determine the same. . . ." Art. VII, Sec. 4, Constitution of 1908. This jurisdiction is not very frequently exercised.

[4] The principal matters falling within the competence of the federal courts are:

(1) cases involving the application or interpretation of the Federal Constitution;

(2) cases involving the application or interpretation of federal statutes (including crimes against the United States);

(3) cases involving the application or interpretation of treaties of the United States;

(4) controversies between citizens of different states ("diversity of citizenship"). Such cases are disposed of in a federal court but the law which is applied is the law of a particular state.

However, trial jurisdiction in these four types of cases (with the exception of a trial of federal criminal charges) does not belong exclusively to the

the less populous states, such as Nevada, the federal district is coterminous with the state. The more populous states are divided territorially into two or more districts. Michigan, for example, is divided into two districts and New York into four.[5]

On the whole it is agreed by writers on court organization that both the common kinds of limitation on trial jurisdiction can be obstructive of efficiency in the administration of justice. Territorial limitations and limitations on subject matter both tend to clog the wheels of the judicial machine. In the first place, such limitations involve a great deal of litigation about the question of jurisdiction itself. Which court is the proper one to try this case? Has this court jurisdiction to try it? Such questions consume an extraordinary amount of the time of courts yet they do not seem to add much to the output of justice if we can assume that all our courts are able to dispense the same product. Second, as population shifts and as business needs change, the amount of judicial business to be handled in the various judicial districts and in the different types of courts also shifts and changes. The result is that frequently one trial court is overwhelmed by work and badly in arrears, while courts in neighboring areas and courts which handle

federal district courts. Many cases of these types arise and are tried in the state courts; if they reach the federal system at all, they do so only by way of appeal to the Supreme Court.

Certain minor matters are handled not by the district courts, but by United States commissioners. The latter issue warrants and take other steps involved in the preliminary stages of criminal cases. They occupy a position in the federal system roughly analogous to that of the justices of the peace in the states' systems. However, they are appointed by the district judge and are, therefore, quite directly answerable to him.

The Supreme Court of the United States also has a very limited trial jurisdiction. The Constitution, in Art. III, Sec. 2, Cl. 2, provides: "In all cases affecting Ambassadors, or other public Ministers and Consuls, and those in which a State shall be a Party, the supreme Court shall have original Jurisdiction." The occasions for the exercise for this jurisdiction are, needless to say, very rare.

[5] Where a federal district contains a large city, such as New York City, Chicago or Detroit, there are several district judges over whom the senior judge in point of service presides.

limited kinds of cases, do not have enough to do. And the ups and downs of judicial work are often merely temporary so that they do not call for permanent additions to court personnel. Accordingly, it may be regarded as preferable to create just one court with the widest possible jurisdiction as to place and subject matter, and to provide that judges can be assigned freely to try cases in any place and to handle any type of case as the burden of work requires.

However, there are real obstacles to the simplification of trial jurisdiction which has just been mentioned. The federal system of courts approaches the ideal inasmuch as all federal trial jurisdiction is vested in one district court which operates in a rather wide area. But the adoption of the same plan in the states is not so easy. The state constitutions often fix the jurisdiction of courts from the highest to the lowest. Where this is the case, the simplification of court organization and the reduction of the number of the different kinds of trial courts, can only be brought about by the cumbersome process of constitutional amendment.[6] Moreover, there is a serious practical objection to the complete simplification which I have suggested, even if it is constitutionally feasible. The state courts have to dispose of a vast number of petty cases, civil and criminal.[7] It is most important to bring the handling of such cases as close as possible to the persons affected and to make the handling of the cases simple, cheap and expeditious. The best way to meet these objectives apparently is to create an ample number of local courts to dispose of petty cases. If this is done the state will continue to have at least two

[6] Without constitutional amendment some degree of alleviation of congested dock s can be achieved by the statutory authorization of the assignment of judges for work in districts and courts where help is needed. Usually the power to assign is vested in the chief justice of the supreme court or in some other presiding judge.

[7] The problem of handling petty cases is not so serious in the federal system. Most of the cases which are handled therein are important. While there is a certain amount of petty and routine criminal business to handle, this business is for the most part disposed of by United States commissioners.

types of trial courts: petty trial courts and trial courts to handle more important matters. The correctness of this solution is confirmed by the fact that in England and on the continent of Europe, where thoroughgoing court reorganization has been undertaken in recent decades, this twofold scheme for handling trial work has been adopted.

Sec. 3–10. The public prosecutor—functions—criminal charges. In the last section I pointed out that each state is divided into judicial districts in each of which one finds a trial court of general jurisdiction and that the United States is similarly divided into judicial districts in each of which is a federal court of general jurisdiction. The next point to note is that in each of its judicial districts the state has an attorney who represents the public interests and that in each of its judicial districts the federal government has an attorney who acts as its representative. This legal representative is known variously as the state's attorney, the prosecuting attorney, the county attorney, the district attorney (the name used in the federal system), and known generically as the public prosecutor. I shall refer to all of them henceforth by the generic name. The public prosecutor's primary function, from which he derives his name, is to prepare and prosecute criminal cases.[1]

The criminal prosecution is brought in the name of the state or the federal government, as the case may be. It begins with the filing of a formal charge, although sometimes the formal charge is not filed until after the accused person is in custody.[2] In many of the states and in the federal system,

---

[1] The prosecuting witness, or other person with information about a criminal act, may be responsible for the filing of a charge in the sense that he makes a preliminary complaint, or that he tells what he knows to the prosecutor or the police.

[2] Actually several steps often precede the formal charge: (1) the making of a sworn complaint by a prosecuting witness who has knowledge of a crime; (2) the issuance of a warrant for the arrest of the accused; (3) the actual arrest of the accused; (4) the production of the accused before the magistrate

the formal charge for the more serious crimes is known as an *indictment*. The indictment is found by a *grand jury*. This jury is a group summoned by the court to investigate possible public offenses and public grievances; it consists of not less than twelve nor more than twenty-three persons. The grand jury calls witnesses and examines evidence; it carries on its investigations with such assistance from the public prosecutor and other officials as it requires. If it finds that there is probable cause to think that someone is guilty of crime, it draws up a formal charge and presents it to the court. As a practical matter the charge is usually drawn up for the grand jury, by the prosecutor, as the jury is composed of laymen. The grand jury serves two general functions. On the one side, the grand jury is intended to represent the government interests by initiating criminal charges on its behalf; on the other side, the grand jury stands as a safeguard, since it is composed of laymen, against the filing of unfounded or improper charges against the individual.

The Federal Constitution and the constitutions of many of our states require that serious criminal charges be initiated by indictment.[3] The constitutions of other states authorize the prosecutor alone to initiate criminal proceedings by filing a formal charge, called an *information*.[4] Sometimes this infor-

who issued the warrant for his arrest; (5) the commitment of the accused to jail until the grand jury meets and presents (or refuses to present) an indictment; (6) the fixing of bail so that the accused can be released pending indictment (and trial). These steps have to be taken before indictment simply because the grand jury is convened only a few times a year. For this reason criminal suspects have to be held in jail or on bail until the grand jury can act.

[3] The Fifth Amendment to the Federal Constitution provides: "No person shall be held to answer for a capital or otherwise infamous crime, unless on a presentment of indictment of a Grand Jury, except in cases arising in the land or naval forces, or in the Militia, when in actual service in time of war or public danger; . . ."

[4] However, the information cannot be filed until the accused has had a preliminary examination before a magistrate (justice of the peace or judge). In this examination the magistrate must satisfy himself that the prosecution has sufficient evidence on which to hold the accused for trial. The preliminary examination is intended to protect the accused person against the filing of unfounded or improper charges (compare the next preceding paragraph of the text).

mation practice is made exclusive; sometimes either information or indictment may be used. Even in the federal system and in states where indictment must be used for serious charges, the information can be used in the commencement of proceedings against minor offenders. The information practice is less cumbersome and less costly than indictment by grand jury; for these reasons the information is much more commonly employed wherever its use is permissible.

In both the indictment practice and the information practice the real burden of investigating cases, of drafting charges, and of preparing cases for trial, rests upon the public prosecutor. He furnishes the motive power for criminal law enforcement. Generally speaking, he decides what cases to push and what cases to drop; he decides what cases to call to the grand jury's attention, where the grand jury method is in vogue, and what cases to prosecute where he proceeds by information. He tries the cases; and, if persons are convicted, he has the primary responsibility of seeing that sentences are carried out. The prosecutor ordinarily cannot perform all these functions personally. He has to have assistance of various sorts. In larger communities the prosecutor's office includes several assistant attorneys, a number of investigators, and a large staff of clerks.

Another important function of the public prosecutor is to advise other officials in regard to legal problems which confront them. Frequently, doubts arise whether a particular official has power to do a certain act or whether one method of procedure is better or worse than another. These doubts usually hinge on matters of law, and officials are entitled to obtain the prosecutor's opinions for their guidance. In this way the prosecutor serves as counselor for officials, essentially as the ordinary attorney serves as counselor for the individual client.

The public prosecutor is also commonly expected and required to draft public documents and technical legal instruments for the local officials in his district. If a deed or lease of county property is to be executed, or if a purchase of a site for a county courthouse is to be made the prosecutor will serve as the legal draftsman for the local authorities.

Finally, the prosecutor brings lawsuits on behalf of various government units. In this capacity he may be called on to bring proceedings to collect property taxes or to condemn land for use as a highway. Similarly, he may bring action to enjoin or abate a public nuisance.[5] In short, in any case where the public has proprietary interests which need to be protected, the local prosecutor is ordinarily the functionary who is obliged to act. He serves in such cases as the representative of the public. He initiates action and carries the action through all its steps to a conclusion.

The prosecutor is an executive official. His acts are governed by legal standards as other executive acts are. Nothing need be added to what was said in section 3–06 on this general subject, except to observe that the prosecutor is not a minor executive, but one well up in the executive hierarchy and one invested with a considerable degree of discretion.[6]

Throughout this section I have treated the local public prosecutor as the prototype for all public attorneys. This emphasis on the local prosecutor is justified by the great practical importance of his functions. It is justified from your point of view by the fact that you will often be reading about what the public prosecutor does or can do. However, it would leave an incorrect impression if we passed over the functions of other public attorneys without any notice whatever. In the states, the local prosecutor is governed to some

[5] If a nuisance, e.g., smoke or noise, is injurious to an individual landowner he may bring a civil action to enjoin or abate. If the nuisance is injurious to the public, the action to enjoin or abate is brought by the prosecutor.

[6] To some extent, the prosecutor's discretion in the handling of cases, especially criminal cases, is controlled by the judge of the court in which a criminal proceeding is pending. However, this judicial control is rather remote; in actual fact the prosecutor has almost complete freedom to push or to drop the ordinary case.

extent by the orders of an attorney general.[7] The latter is the principal law officer of the state; as such he gives opinions, drafts papers, and brings important actions on behalf of the state. His functions in these respects are parallel on a higher level, to the various functions which the public prosecutor performs locally. In the federal system, the district attorney is subject to a very real control by the Attorney General of the United States.[8] The latter is the principal law officer of the federal government. He is a member of the President's cabinet. His office, called the Department of Justice, is charged with the care of most of the legal interests of the United States; it exercises a great variety of advisory, supervisory, investigative (e.g., F.B.I.), and administrative functions. I do not believe that it is necessary for our present purpose to deal specifically with all the functions of these central law offices of the state and federal governments.

Sec. 3–11. Criminal trial—jury and judge. You now have before you descriptions of the principal agencies involved in the enforcement of criminal law: executive officials, the courts, and the public prosecutor. It is time to give you a sketch of the criminal trial.

The criminal trial more than any other legal proceeding has the features of drama. Ordinarily the act charged against the defendant involves human interest, and the trial itself is a great contest in which the defendant battles for his life or liberty against the power of the state. In this contest, which is co-operative as well as dramatic, the prosecutor, the defendant, the defense attorney, the witnesses, the jury and the judge all participate and perform their appointed roles. The proceedings prior to trial and the trial, too, may be viewed as a series of acts or scenes. Filing the charge is an act; like-

[7] And less directly by the orders of the governor.
[8] Indirectly, the district attorney is subject also to the orders of the President who is the immediate superior of the Attorney General.

wise the arrest of the accused; and the entry of a plea. The impaneling of a jury is a scene. The presentation of the evidence is a series of scenes in which each question put to a witness and each separate answer made is a distinguishable act. And, the concluding arguments of counsel, the judge's instructions to the jury, and the jury's verdict are acts which bring the legal performance to a conclusion.

The jury and the judge play the dominant roles in the trial. The jury, properly called the *petit jury*, consists of twelve persons. Its function is to hear the evidence and decide whether or not the accused is guilty as charged. In other words, its function is to determine the facts. The jury is selected by various methods in different legal systems, but one essential feature is characteristic of the jury in all Anglo-American countries: it is a body of laymen drawn from the general population. The jury is intended to introduce the elements of common sense and common fairness into justice, thus preventing the operation of the legal system from becoming over-technical; and is intended to check arbitrary acts of officials who might otherwise detain individuals without sufficient cause or deny them their lawful rights.

The *judge* may be likened to a player-producer. He acts in the play and has the general management of it. All the acts which the prosecutor, the defendant, the defense attorney, and the witnesses do, are standardized and governed by legal regulations. The judge supervises their conduct to see that they follow the regulations. The judge decides whether each piece of evidential material is admissible, as it is offered by one side or the other. He rules on the propriety of questions asked by counsel on the two sides. And, after the evidence has all been presented and counsel have argued the case to the jury, the judge instructs the jury on the law applicable thereto.[1] He says to the jury in

---

[1] This is the order of procedure at common law. In some states, however, statutes have changed the order of procedure; the judge instructs the jury prior to the argument of counsel.

effect: If you find such and such facts to be true as contended by the prosecutor, then you will find the defendant guilty; on the other hand, if you find such and such other facts to be true as contended by the defendant, then you will find him not guilty. Of course, the actual instructions go into more detail, but their essential purport is sufficiently indicated by this skeleton form.

The trial judge not only supervises all steps in the trial and instructs the jury, but he issues all the specific orders which need to be given during the course of the trial. For example, if the trial needs to be postponed, the judge gives the order for a continuance (postponement); if a witness fails to appear or refuses to answer questions, the judge issues the necessary order imposing penalties; if the evidence of the prosecution is insufficient to support a conviction, the judge directs the jury to return a verdict for the defendant; if the jury returns a verdict of "not guilty," the judge orders the defendant discharged; and if the jury returns a verdict of "guilty," the judge sentences the defendant according to law.[2] In short, a criminal trial has some of the elements of a game in which two champions try to overcome one another. This is a feature which goes all the way back to the days of trial by battle. The judge controls the contest. He acts as a sort of referee as between the two primary contestants, the attorney for the prosecution on the one hand and the attorney for the defense on the other. His job is to see that the contest is carried on according to the rules.

Sec. 3–12. Problems. 1. In framing his instructions to the jury, how far is the judge concerned with questions of fact? How far with questions of law? Who decides the questions of fact? The questions of law? Consider here the matter in sections 3–08 and 3–11.

---

[2] According to the practice in some states, the jury fixes the penalty in regard to some or all types of crime.

2. A statute provides:

"Any person having knowledge of the commission of any offense punishable with death, or by imprisonment in the state prison, who shall take any money, or any gratuity or reward, or any engagement therefor, upon an agreement or understanding, expressed or implied, to compound or conceal such offense, or not to prosecute therefor, or not to give evidence thereof, shall be guilty of a misdemeanor."

Why should the agreements here specified be prohibited and punished?

Suppose A is clerk in a bank; he embezzles $1000. His defalcation is discovered and his father offers to repay the $1000. Can the bank properly accept this offer?

3. In the Sixth Amendment to the Federal Constitution is a provision that "In all criminal prosecutions, the accused shall enjoy the right . . . to have the Assistance of Counsel for his defense." [1]

What is the practical basis for such a guarantee? Viewed from the standpoint of enforcement of standards, how does this guarantee operate?

4. The 5th Canon of Professional Ethics adopted by the American Bar Association declares:

"It is the right of the lawyer to undertake the defense of a person accused of crime, regardless of his personal opinion as to the guilt of the accused; otherwise innocent persons, victims only of suspicious circumstances, might be denied proper defense. Having undertaken such defense, the lawyer is bound, by all fair and honorable means, to present every defense that the law of the land permits, to the end that no person may be deprived of life or liberty, but by due process of law."

[1] This provision applies only to criminal trials in the federal courts. However, there are similar provisions in the constitutions or statutes of most of our states; and the lack of counsel in a state prosecution may constitute a violation of the "due process" clause of the Federal Constitution. Powell v. Alabama, 287 U. S. 45 (1932); Betts v. Brady, Warden, 316 U. S. 455 (1942); Foster v. Illinois, 332 U. S. 134 (1947).

According to this canon how far can a lawyer go in defense of his client?

Statutes of limitation commonly bar the prosecution of crimes (except murder and a few others) after a certain period of time has elapsed (e.g., three years). Should a lawyer plead such a bar on behalf of a client whom he knows to be guilty?

5. In section 1–10, problem 6, we discussed the case of the Lambeth Poisonings, involving one Roose, the Bishop of Rochester's cook. The English Parliament passed an act declaring that Roose and any other poisoner be adjudged a traitor and be executed by being boiled to death. Roose was accordingly boiled at Smithfield a few days after the act was passed.

As applied to Roose such an act would be unconstitutional in the United States, both because it is an ex post facto law [2] and because the legislative branch cannot thus usurp judicial functions. What other constitutional guarantees would this enactment violate?

Sec. 3–13. Bringing civil action. The civil action occupies a prominent place among methods of law enforcement. A, who is harmed by the act of X, or threatened with harm, calls upon the courts for aid in maintaining his rights. The outstanding feature of this method of law enforcement is that it is initiated by an aggrieved party, A. One whose rights are violated or threatened with violation calls upon the state's tribunal for a remedy or protection. However, A is not obliged to maintain his rights; he is empowered to take action to protect himself. He can, if he chooses, allow the actual or threatened injury to go unredressed. The legal system relies upon A's self-interest as a motive for action.

---

[2] An ex post facto law is one which makes an act criminal after the act has been committed.

The legal system does not guarantee complete and perfect protection to him; it comes to A's assistance when he calls for help. From the point of view of A, the legal system performs a service function. From the point of view of the state, A, by setting the wheels of justice in motion, serves as an agent of enforcement.

On the principle of party presentation, stated in the preceding paragraph, the legal system leaves to the aggrieved A full responsibility for taking each step in the legal procedure for effectuating his claims. He must discover the witnesses and other evidence necessary to support his case and produce them in court. He must call upon the agents of the law to compel witnesses to appear, if they are unwilling; and he must require persons to produce papers which are needed. Only rarely does the judge or any other official do any act on his own motion, by way of enforcing A's claims. A must present his own claims and take each step in pursuing them to a conclusion. But, while we speak of party presentation as characteristic of our legal system, A, who is an ordinary layman, is not able to carry on his suit without assistance. Usually he must have the aid of an expert, a lawyer. The actual presentation of the case is made by the lawyer at the instance of A. The lawyer brings the action and leads his client through the procedural mazes which baffle the ordinary citizen and even bewilder the conscientious law student at the start.

Sec. 3–14. Trial of civil action. The private action at law is triable by jury. In fact the action cannot be tried without jury unless both parties waive jury trial, inasmuch as jury trial is guaranteed by the federal, as well as the state, constitutions. The role of the jury in a civil action is similar to its role in criminal cases. The jury hears the evidence and finds its verdict in a similar way. The jury's activities are subject to similar judicial control. The judge rules on the admissibility of evidence and makes all the necessary orders during the trial. He instructs the jury essentially as he does in a criminal case. The judge also gives the final judgment. And, if there is an appeal, he makes the requisite orders regarding the appeal and the preparation of the record for appeal.

All the acts of jury and judge are covered by legal standards. These fix the functions of the jury and the powers and functions of the judge. They determine what evidence may be used by the parties and how it is to be admitted. They control the manner in which the judge is to instruct the jury. They determine when and how a judge is to enter a judgment or decree; when he is to take a case from the jury, direct a verdict, or set aside a verdict for error or for other reasons. These standards you will become familiar with in your courses in procedure.

No one can truly assert that the jury is an efficient agency for the trial of civil cases. It is ordinarily composed of persons whose knowledge and experience are quite inadequate to the exigencies of cases involving complex business deals and difficult problems of scientific fact. Nevertheless jury trial in civil cases will probably be with us for a considerable while to come. The civil jury had a prominent place in the processes of establishing our civil liberties, especially freedom of speech; and for this reason is secured by our constitutions. It seems quite unlikely that sufficient political support can be mustered in the foreseeable future to bring about the constitutional amendments which would be required to abolish jury trial in civil actions.[1]

However, jury trial can be waived as I have indicated above. If this is done, the case is tried by the judge alone; he decides both matters of fact and matters of law. The

[1] Most of the legal systems of the world have either never employed the jury in civil cases or else they have abandoned its use long ago. Only in the Anglo-American systems of law has the civil jury retained its vogue.

practice of waiving jury trial is a relatively recent development in trial procedure. This practice has reached a point in many parts of the country where most civil cases are now tried without jury.

The American legal systems have evolved from the system which prevailed in England prior to the Revolution. In the English system of prerevolutionary days certain types of civil cases were not tried by jury but by the judge alone. The principal cases which I have in mind went by the name of "suits in equity." [2] This is not the place to develop the early history of equity in England or its later history in the United States. Suffice it to say that *equity cases* did not fall within the jurisdiction of the English law courts, where jury trial prevailed, but belonged in the jurisdiction of the Court of Chancery, where cases were tried without jury by a judge known as the Lord Chancellor. The distinction between cases for law courts and cases for equity courts, and the distinction between the modes of trial therein, have been maintained down to the present day both in England and the United States. So that even now equity cases are tried by the judge alone as they have always been tried in the English practice. Equity cases constitute an important section of civil cases. You will hear a great deal more about equity cases, equity actions, and equity procedure in your various courses, and I shall have a few more words to say about them in the next section.

Sec. 3–15. Redress in civil action. In our legal system *money damages* are the normal form of redress. The judgment of the court in a civil action condemns the defendant

---

[2] In the English ecclesiastical, admiralty and probate courts of pre-revolutionary days cases were also tried without jury. This method of trial still prevails in the admiralty courts on both sides of the Atlantic. In the United States we have no ecclesiastical courts. In the probate courts of the United States jury trial is often provided for by statute, but in some states probate cases are still tried without jury.

to pay a certain amount by way of compensation. If the defendant has done a personal injury to another, if he has trespassed upon another's land, if he has carried away or misappropriated another's goods, he must pay damages. In parallel fashion if he has failed or refused to perform his contract obligations, he must pay damages. The damages given are intended to make the injured party whole in an economic sense; they are intended to restore him to the same position, as regards total assets, as he would have occupied if the wrong had not occurred or if the contract had been performed.

But the private action is not ended with the final judgment. As any lawyer knows, there is a difference between getting a judgment and collecting it. So it is important to look beyond the judgment to the means of realizing on it. To collect the damages which have been adjudged to him the judgment creditor must have *execution* levied on the goods or other property of the judgment debtor. This means that the creditor, or an enforcement officer, must find property on which to levy execution. The execution involves the seizure and sale of the debtor's property to obtain money to satisfy the judgment. If no property is found the creditor realizes nothing. The seizure and sale are carried out by a constable or other official on the court's order at the behest of the judgment creditor. Accordingly the normal legal remedy in a civil action can be summed up in two phases: judgment for money damages and levy of execution on property of the judgment debtor.

In a few situations our legal system undertakes to give the complaining party *specific redress* rather than money damages. This means that it undertakes to give him what he actually wants, not merely money in place of it. Three instances of specific redress, frequently called specific relief, will suffice for illustration:

First is the redress obtained in the action of *ejectment*. The plaintiff who has been ousted from the possession of land asks to be restored to possession. If the court gives judgment for the plaintiff, it orders the sheriff to put the defendant out of possession and to put the plaintiff into possession. This is an obvious instance of giving the plaintiff what he asks for.

Second, a proceeding for an injunction may be brought in certain cases. *Injunctions* fall within the jurisdiction of an equity court. They constitute one of the classes of equitable actions which I mentioned in the next preceding section. Consider for instance a case where a man maintains a factory on his land which discommodes his neighbors by the production of smoke or excessive noise. On such facts a neighbor who is injured may apply to the equity judge for an injunction. After the judge hears the case and finds that the plaintiff is entitled to this remedy, the judge issues a restraining order to the defendant. The order prohibits him from continuing to produce smoke or noise to the discomfort of his neighbor. What is also important for our present purpose is that this order is enforced by threat of imprisonment for contempt if the defendant does not desist. Of course, it is only rarely that a defendant will persist in the face of such an order. The judge is authorized to proceed summarily in case of a violation of his order, as any defendant knows. He will therefore abate his own nuisance as the court commands him to do, and the complaining party obtains the relief that he wants.

Third, a court of equity may issue a positive order, not merely a restraining order, commanding a defendant to do a particular act. Typical situations in which positive orders, called *mandatory* injunctions, are issued are (1) the case in which a defendant is adjudged to be bound to convey land according to a land contract, and (2) the case where he is ordered to remove an offending structure which encroaches upon the land of another. In both these cases the court orders the defendant himself to do the act which should be done. In one case the order commands him to make the conveyance as per contract, and in the other it requires him to remove the structure in question. These mandatory orders, like the injunctions first spoken of, are enforced by threat of imprisonment for contempt; they secure to the plaintiff the relief to which he is entitled.

Sec. 3–16. Judicial control of persons, estates, etc. In addition to their jurisdiction over criminal prosecutions and civil actions, courts are commonly invested with extensive authority (1) to care for persons who need care, (2) to change and determine the status of persons, and (3) to manage and dispose of estates of various kinds. This authority, you will observe, does not ordinarily involve litigation of any kind; it does not necessarily involve the settlement of any controversy of law or of facts. It falls outside of what we normally consider the judicial role. It calls for the doing of supervisory and administrative acts.

As instances of jurisdiction to care for persons I might mention the general protection which courts extend to infants (minors) and to incompetent persons (the insane, etc.). This kind of jurisdiction is usually vested in, and exercised by, probate courts.[1] They appoint a personal guardian for the infant who is an orphan or whose parents are unfit or incompetent to care for him; and they exercise supervisory control over the acts of the guardian. They remove the child from the custody of unfit parents. They place the neglected child or juvenile delinquent in an institution or in the custodial care of a proper person. They supervise the care, training, and education of children who are under guardianship, in custodial care, or in institutions. Similarly these courts appoint personal guardians for incompetent persons and exercise

[1] See sec. 3–09 in regard to the character of probate courts.

supervision over the guardians and over the institutions and individuals who have such persons in custody.

Courts also exercise authority to change or determine the status of persons. For example, a judicial proceeding is requisite in order to declare a person to be incompetent or insane, and in order to commit him to custodial care. The adoption of a child has to be approved and accomplished through a judicial proceeding. Divorce and annulment are also judicial acts whose essential operation is to change personal status.[2]

Instances of judicial management and disposition of estates are very common. I shall refer to a few of the more important. *First,* I might mention the appointment by a probate court of a guardian to manage the estate of an infant or an incompetent person. Such a guardian has to be distinguished from the guardian of the person previously mentioned. This guardian has the control and management of property. However, one and the same individual may be appointed both guardian of the person and guardian of the estate of an infant or an incompetent. *Second,* the judicial administration of decedents' estates is worth noting. This is also an instance of the judicial management of property. Decedents' estates are actually managed and distributed by administrators or executors. But the latter have to be appointed by the probate court; they derive their legal authority from it; and they must get the court's approval for every important act which they do in the processes of collecting assets, converting them into money, paying debts, and distributing shares to the parties entitled. *Third,* courts of equity supervise the administration of trusts.[3] The trustees are the primary actors but

2 This jurisdiction is always invested in a court of general jurisdiction, not in a probate court. As regards this distinction, see sec. 3–09.

3 Except in one state, courts of equity are no longer separate courts. Equity powers are exercised by the trial courts of general jurisdiction. See sec. 3–09 above.

their acts are subject to judicial supervision. These courts also appoint receivers to take over the possession and management of the estates of insolvent individuals and corporations. And *finally*, the United States district courts handle the estates of bankrupts. The courts, through trustees who collect claims due the bankrupt, take possession of the bankrupt's assets, and distribute his estate ratably to his creditors. In all the instances here mentioned courts appoint agents to manage and administer estates. Usually the agents are also subject to removal for cause by the appointing court. These agents are required to make reports of their actions from time to time to the courts which appoint them; and their management is subject to judicial control and supervision at all times.

Sec. 3–17. Problems. 1. *Ricketts v. Dorrel.*[1] The defendant wrongfully took 738 rails and 164 stakes belonging to the plaintiff and built a rail fence dividing the lands of the plaintiff and the defendant. The plaintiff brought an action of replevin to recover the possession of the rails and stakes. The court held that the plaintiff had brought the wrong kind of action and dismissed his suit. The court said: "The law affords him ample remedy if he rightfully chooses it; but it is no part of the duty of this court to instruct him as to what that remedy is."

Consider the last statement made by the court. Where does it fit into our discussion of the civil action?

2. Under statutes of the United States aliens may become naturalized citizens of the United States through a proceeding in a state or federal court. The alien is eligible to apply for naturalization if he has filed a declaration of intention and lived in the United States continuously for five years. The admission to citizenship involves an application for

[1] 55 Ind. 470 at 474 (1876).

naturalization by the candidate, a hearing by the court on this application, and a decree admitting him to citizenship.

Where would you place this judicial jurisdiction to naturalize aliens, among the types of jurisdiction mentioned in the preceding sections?

3. Suppose H sues W for divorce and the court grants the divorce as prayed. How does the relief granted differ from the types of redress mentioned in section 3–15?

4. In the last thirty years, statutes have been passed by most of our states and by the federal government providing for what are called *"declaratory judgments."* * A declaratory judgment is a binding declaration of legal relations as between parties, made where such relations are in controversy; the declaration is made on the basis of contentions of adversary parties and counsel as the ordinary judgment is made. The declaratory judgment fixes the existence of relations arising out of a legal instrument or transaction, but does not embrace any relief beyond a binding determination of legal relations. The ordinary legal action springs from the fact that the party defendant has already committed a legal wrong for which the court is asked to provide a remedy, or that the defendant is threatening the immediate commission of a wrong which the court is asked to prevent. The declaratory judgment also falls in the field of preventive relief. However, it is intended to prevent damage by removing the uncertainty of parties regarding their rights, usually in cases where both parties are acting in good faith and without the purpose to commit wrong. There are many situations in which a legal declaration of rights can thus prevent damage —as where there is a bona fide dispute as to the existence of a marriage, as to the legitimacy or sanity of an individual, as to the title of property, or as to the construction of legal documents, such as contracts, deeds, leases or wills. In the

* (I.R.) See generally on this topic, BORCHARD, DECLARATORY JUDGMENTS (2d ed., 1941).

absence of provisions for declaratory relief, persons must act at their peril in such cases; persons must act upon their own interpretation of their supposed rights and take the consequences. It is to remove uncertainty in these respects that the declaratory judgment has been adopted as a device of preventive justice in the civil law countries of Europe, in England, and in the United States.

In arguing in favor of statutes to provide for declaratory judgments, Sunderland says:

"In early times the basis of jurisdiction is the existence and the constant assertion of physical power over the parties to the action, but as civilization advances the mere existence of such power tends to make its exercise less and less essential.

"If this is true, it must be because there is something in civilization itself which diminishes the necessity for a resort to actual force in sustaining the judgments of courts. And it is quite clear that civilization does supply an element which is theoretically capable of entirely supplanting the exercise of force in the assertion of jurisdiction. This is respect for law. If the parties to the action desire to obey the law, a mere determination by the court of their reciprocal rights and duties is enough. No sheriff with his writ of injunction or execution need shake the mailed fist of the State in the faces of the litigants. The judgment of the court merely directs the will of the parties, and the performance of duty becomes the automatic consequence of the declaration of right.

"It is not to be assumed that the peaceful acquiescence of the highly civilized man in the legal findings of the court implies any loss of power in the court itself. Quite the contrary. The greater the ease with which the court's findings impose themselves on litigants the more the real power of the court is demonstrated. But the force behind the finding of the court has become a latent instead of an active force. This transition is possible, however, only when the existence of the force is so well recognized and so clearly understood that no one would think it worth while to put it to the test. The entire cessation of actual coercive measures on the part of the court would therefore mark, not the disappearance, but the perfection of the rule of force.

"The modern observer, noting this correlation between social progress and the decline in the need for outward display of force in the administration of justice, may well ask himself why we have not done better than we appear to have done. If the existence of force is enough, without its exercise, to sustain the court in its findings, why do we not show a realization of that fact in our remedial machinery? If the power of the state stands irresistibly behind our judicial decisions, why take so much pains to clothe them with the outward show of authority? Why display the sheriff and his writ with so much ostentation? We do not arm our traffic policemen with guns and cutlasses. Why insist that the court must always rattle the sabre?

"To make a specific application of this general criticism, let it be asked why our judicial system does not provide a means for merely determining and declaring rights. If our civilization is not a sham, and the state is understood to be equal to the task of enforcing the decrees of its courts; a mere declaration may serve every purpose of an order, and the order will become unnecessary. A declaration by the court that A is entitled to the immediate possession of a chattel in B's possession, should be equally effective in A's behalf as a judgment that A do have and recover of B the possession of the chattel. A judicial declaration that a certain city ordinance is invalid ought to serve equally well as an injunction against its enforcement. Furthermore, the remedial possibilities in such declaratory judgments are much greater than in judgments for relief, and they open up an entirely new field for judicial usefulness as will hereinafter be pointed out." [2]

As regards the matter of redress or enforcement, how does an action for declaratory relief differ from the ordinary civil action? See sec. 3–15.

In what important respects is the declaratory judgment like the ordinary judgment in a civil action?

[2] Sunderland, "A Modern Evolution in Remedial Rights—The Declaratory Judgment," 16 MICH. L. REV. 69 at 70 (1920).

Sec. 3–18. Appellate courts—jurisdiction. In section 3–08 I referred to the controversies of fact and law which it is the primary function of courts to determine. In section 3–09 I divided the jurisdiction of courts into two kinds: trial and appellate. Trial jurisdiction has been considered in the preceding sections, as well as certain administrative functions which courts perform. In the present section I shall speak as briefly as I am able about appellate courts and their jurisdiction.*

The appellate court reviews the record of the work which the trial court has done. It does not hear the evidence in the case again.[1] It examines the lower court's proceedings to determine whether they have been conducted according to legal standards. If they have been so conducted, the appellate court affirms the trial court's findings, judgment, or decree. If material error has been committed, the appellate court reverses the trial court's determination. It sends the case back

---

* (I.R.) Manifestly I cannot deal with so large a subject in a brief space and make every statement complete and accurate to the last detail; I hope the informed reader will bear in mind that I am merely trying to give a general picture of our appellate courts—a picture which will aid the beginning law student in his study of reported cases.

For more detailed treatments of the organization and procedure of appellate courts, the reader is referred to POUND, ORGANIZATION OF COURTS (National Conference of Judicial Councils) (1940); POUND, APPELLATE PROCEDURE IN CIVIL CASES (also a National Conference publication) (1941); American Law Institute, CODE OF CRIMINAL PROCEDURE (1931)—the sections on appeal with full annotations; and also items cited in sec. 3–26, note *, and sec. 3–28, note *.

[1] Appeal, as we are using the term, always involves the review of the record of a trial. Appeal presupposes that the case reviewed has been fully heard, both as to the law and the facts, by a court below. And review, or appeal, accordingly means the judicial examination of the record of what a lower court has done.

However appeal is sometimes used in a different sense and one which can lead to confusion. For example, it is sometimes provided that an appeal can be taken from a petty court to a court of general jurisdiction where the case which was tried in the petty court is to be tried again. This provision for a trial *de novo* is called an appeal. As the case is heard fully, both on the law and the proof, on the second trial as well as on the first, the second trial is obviously not an appeal in the sense in which I have used that word; it is a second trial, just as I have called it, not a review.

for a new trial or directs the lower court to give judgment for one side or the other; or, in the practice of some jurisdictions, the appellate court itself enters judgment for one side or the other.

The common errors which occur in jury trials are errors in rulings on the pleadings, errors in admission and rejection of evidence, errors in instructing the jury on the law, and errors in rulings on motions of the parties, e. g., motions for new trial and motions for directed verdict. The common errors in trials by the judge are errors in excluding evidence and errors in the judge's findings of fact and conclusions of law.

However, not all errors in the proceedings are fatal. Some errors may be committed which the appellate court regards as harmless or at least as too trivial to require the radical remedy of reversal. Other errors are committed but corrected by the trial court before the trial is over. And it must always be remembered that a party cannot ordinarily take advantage in the appellate court of an error in the proceedings below, unless he has entered a proper objection when the error was committed. He cannot quietly sit by, see an error committed in the proceedings below, and raise an objection for the first time in the court above. If he does not make a timely objection he waives the error. Furthermore, the party must call the error to the appellate court's attention in a proper manner and rely upon it for reversal.** The principle of party presentation, i. e., the principle that parties must represent their own interests, applies in appellate proceedings as well as in trials. So that it is never safe to assume that the mere fact that error has occurred means that the proceedings of a trial court will be reversed.

In each of our states there is at least one appellate court whose function is to review the proceedings of trial courts;

** (I.R.) Ordinarily these propositions hold but there are some errors, as every lawyer knows, which can be raised for the first time on appeal.

sometimes there are several appellate courts, as I shall point out presently. The most important of such appellate courts is a supreme tribunal or court of last resort. This supreme tribunal is usually called the supreme court, but in some states it is known as the court of appeals or the court of errors and appeals. In the federal system the supreme tribunal is the Supreme Court of the United States.[2] Every supreme tribunal consists of several judges who sit together in the hearing and determination of appeals. The number of judges ranges in the different states from three to nine. In the Supreme Court of the United States there are nine justices.

Some of the state judicial systems have only one appellate court, e. g., Michigan. This arrangement is ideal if it can be made to work. Under this system every party litigant has the benefit of a trial and then of the scrutiny of the trial record by an appellate court. But a single appellate tribunal often has difficulty in keeping abreast of all the cases in which review is sought. The court may fall far in arrears with its business so that justice is seriously delayed. Or the court may have to resort to "one man" opinions; this means that each case is really considered carefully by only one appellate judge. He goes over the record; he decides whether the case has been properly tried; he writes the supreme court's opinion. The scrutiny of the case by the other judges becomes more or less perfunctory and formal. This, of course, defeats the very purpose of having appellate tribunals composed of several judges. Litigants do not get the benefit of the collective opinion of an appellate bench, to which they are entitled.

One way to meet the problem of handling the heavy load of appellate work has been to introduce intermediate appellate courts. This expedient has been adopted in the federal system and in New York, Illinois, and other states. It is

[2] While almost all of the business of the Supreme Court of the United States and of the supreme appellate tribunals in the states is appellate in nature, each of these courts handles a certain amount of business in the first instance. This kind of business is referred to as original jurisdiction. See notes to sec. 3–09.

intended to take some of the load of appellate work from the supreme tribunal by making the determination of the intermediate appellate court final in a large proportion of cases. In the federal system the intermediate appellate court, called the court of appeals, seems to serve this function rather well. The United States is divided into ten circuits in each of which there is a separate court of appeals. This court has jurisdiction of most appeals from the district courts within its circuit; [3] and in most matters which come before it the determination of the court of appeals is final. It would certainly not be convenient to have all appeals heard by a single court sitting in Washington.

However, there is serious doubt among procedural experts whether the intermediate appellate court is the best device for meeting the excessive load of appellate work in the state courts. The existence of an intermediate appellate court always raises a multitude of questions regarding jurisdiction. Which cases go to the supreme tribunal? Which cases are to be decided in the intermediate tribunal? In which cases is the determination of the intermediate court final? The determination of such questions is unnecessary if there is only one appellate court. And, in those cases which do go to the supreme tribunal via the intermediate court, the intermediate hearing simply presents an added appeal. It means that the case is heard twice by appellate courts. And this double hearing substantially increases the expense and delay of judicial business.

An alternative for the intermediate appellate court, strongly supported by experts on procedure, is to maintain a single appellate court, but to have it sit in several divisions, each division or branch to hear appeals. It is clear that, in a populous state like New York, one appellate court sitting as a unit, could not give due consideration to all the appellate

[3] A few cases are appealable directly from the district to the Supreme Court.

work of the state. Some division of the task seems to be necessary. If the appellate court is sufficiently large and is split up into divisions, it can handle as many cases as can be handled by one supreme appellate court and several intermediate appellate courts; but duplicative appeals can be avoided as well as unnecessary jurisdictional questions. The court can sit as a whole (in banc) in cases which it deems of sufficient public importance and in cases wherein the judges of a division find themselves divided in opinion. This divisional method is essentially that employed in England. The supreme courts of ten of our states are authorized to sit in divisions, but so far this authority has not been exercised to any great extent.

In most cases the party who seeks a review is entitled to the same as a matter of right; he can carry his case to the appellate court if he chooses. This fact vastly increases the load of appellate work; it means that many unnecessary and unimportant cases have to be considered along with those which are of real consequence. Congress has met this difficulty in regard to the Supreme Court of the United States by making the review of most cases discretionary with the Supreme Court. The party who asks for review must satisfy the court that his case presents points of sufficient merit or doubt to warrant review. If so, the court allows him to bring his case before it for full hearing; if not, it denies the opportunity for a review. The result is that only a relatively small proportion of cases which are tried in the federal courts ever reach the Supreme Court. The great bulk of them is finally disposed of in the courts of appeals.

Sec. 3–19. Advisory opinions. From very early times, the judges of the high courts in England gave extrajudicial advisory opinions on questions of law to other governmental agencies (the King, the Privy Council, the House of Lords, etc.). This practice was well established in England at the time of the American Revolution. But the framers of the Federal Constitution did not follow the English model; they expressly rejected a proposal to confer on Congress and the executive the authority to require advisory opinions of the Supreme Court. The powers of the judiciary were separated from legislative and executive powers. And the Supreme Court has consistently held that judicial power embraces only the adjudication of actual cases and controversies; it has held that the rendering of advisory opinions does not fall within the scope of judicial power.*

This view of the scope of judicial power has usually been adopted by the supreme courts in the various states. However, the constitutions of a few states (Massachusetts, Maine, New Hampshire, Rhode Island, Colorado, Florida and South Dakota) impose upon the highest court of the state the obligation to render advisory opinions upon the request of the legislature or either house thereof, or of the governor. And two states (Alabama and Delaware) have sanctioned the advisory opinion by statute. But most states definitely would not uphold legislation of this type without explicit constitutional authority.**

Where the advisory opinion is allowed, the procedure for obtaining it is as follows: the executive, by a written request, or either house of the legislature, by resolution, propounds to the supreme court a number of questions relating to a proposed measure or action. Answers are given by the judges

* (I.R.) Hayburn's Case, 2 Dall. 409 (1792); and Muskrat v. United States, 219 U. S. 346 (1911).

See generally regarding advisory opinions: Hudson, "Advisory Opinions of National and International Courts," 3 HARV. L. REV. 970 (1924), and Frankfurter, "A Note on Advisory Opinions," 37 HARV. L. REV. 1002 (1924).

** Matter of the Senate, 10 Minn. 78 (1865); Reply of the Judges, 33 Conn. 586 (1867); Opinions of the Justices, 64 N. C. 661 (1870); State v. Baughman, 38 Ohio St. 455 (1882); Re Board of Public Lands, 37 Neb. 425 (1893); Matter of State Industrial Commission, 224 N. Y. 13 (1918).

of the supreme court, collectively or individually. While it is usually provided that the supreme court may require the aid of the attorney general or other counsel in reaching its conclusions, no satisfactory way of securing this aid has been devised and actually the aid of counsel is rarely asked or obtained. Furthermore, the court has no actual litigants before it so that it is not deciding a controversy. For these reasons, the court which gives an advisory opinion does not regard itself, or any litigant in a later case, as bound by such opinion. On the other hand, it is not to be expected that any court will lightly depart in subsequent litigation from an opinion earlier expressed in an advisory capacity.

The principal argument opposed to advisory opinions is the impracticability of devising ways for presenting and submitting questions to the court for advisory opinion. As I have already indicated, courts have never succeeded in obtaining the assistance of adversary counsel for their guidance in deciding questions presented. Not only is the argument of counsel necessary in the sense that the court may overlook important considerations unless it has this aid, but also the court has to give its opinion in the abstract, without reference to any concrete facts. The validity of legislation is often conditioned by the factual situation to which it will apply. As Frankfurter says, "Constitutionality is not a fixed quantity. In crucial cases it resolves itself into a judgment upon facts. Every tendency to deal with constitutional questions abstractly, to formulate them in terms of barren legal questions, leads to dialectics, to sterile conclusions unrelated to actualities." [1] And this holds true of any abstract question, alike whether a constitutional question or a question of the meaning of a statutory enactment or executive action.

[1] See Frankfurter, "Advisory Opinions," in I ENCYCLOPAEDIA OF SOCIAL SCIENCES 475 at 478.

A strong argument in favor of advisory opinions is that they make possible the prompt resolution of doubts about the validity and meaning of legislative and executive acts. If an act is to be later declared invalid, it is much better that the act should not be passed or done at all. Even more important is the fact that a substantial period of time normally elapses between the date when a statute is enacted or executive action is taken and the date when the supreme court passes upon the validity or interpretation of the enactment or executive act. During this interval, costly and perilous uncertainty regarding legal rights and relations prevails. For example, the National Industrial Recovery Act was passed in the early stages of the New Deal. The validity of the Act was doubted from the beginning, and many of its provisions were very obscure. The Act affected most of the important business enterprises in the United States, and most of these enterprises attempted to comply with its provisions, deeming this the only safe course. Nevertheless, after almost two years, the whole Act was declared unconstitutional by the Supreme Court of the United States.[2] This kind of situation shows the practical need for having questions about the validity and interpretation of acts decided in advance of their operation and enforcement. The protagonists of the advisory opinion claim that it meets just this need, that it avoids waste in doing invalid acts and delay in passing upon acts of doubtful validity or doubtful meaning.

Queries: (1) There is a serious question whether the advisory opinion meets the need last suggested. On the basis of what is herein stated, what do you think about this point?

(2) In what respect is the general purpose of the advisory opinion like the purpose of the declaratory judgment?

(3) Why is it easier to bring the declaratory judgment within traditional notions of judicial power than to bring the advisory opinion within such notions?

[2] See note in 33 MICH. L. REV. 1254 (1935).

Sec. 3–20. Acts of administrative agencies. * The constitutional separation of powers among three branches of
government could have been taken to mean that governmental power was divided exhaustively among the three
branches, so that no governmental power could be exercised
and no governmental act done, except by the legislative,
executive and judicial agencies provided for by the Constitution. But this has not been the construction adopted by
those charged with the interpretation of the Constitution.
The practical exigencies of government have required the
creation of a fourth kind of agency, not strictly identifiable
with any of the three traditional branches. These agencies
are often called administrative. They are typified by the
Interstate Commerce Commission, the Federal Communications Commission, the Federal Trade Commission, and
various independent boards and offices, in the federal system;
and are exemplified by workmen's compensation commissions,
public utility commissions, and a great variety of boards and
supervisory agents, such as insurance commissioners, banking
commissioners, and others, in the state systems.

It cannot be said that these administrative agencies are all
of one type, or that the powers they exercise, or the acts
they do, are all alike. For this reason, I can give only a rough
picture of the administrative agencies which function in our
federal and state legal systems. These agencies are all created
by or pursuant to statutes; in this respect they are like the
subordinate executive agencies created by Congress and the
similar executive agencies created by state legislatures.[1] And
usually, they are invested with certain duties and powers
which might fairly be called executive in character, such as

*(I.R.) For bibliography on this subject, see STONE, PROVINCE AND FUNC-
TION OF LAW 593 notes (1946) and POUND, OUTLINES OF LECTURES ON
JURISPRUDENCE 92 (5th ed., 1943); and note also the lectures by Stason, cited
in this section, note 2.

[1] Regarding the rule-making, or legislative powers, which most of these
administrative agencies have, see secs. 4–15 to 4–17, inclusive.

are involved in the supervision and enforcement of the laws with reference to banking, or the laws with reference to railroads, or utilities, or the laws relating to employer-employee relations. As regards functions, powers and duties, they are to be differentiated from the executive merely by the fact that they enjoy a more or less complete autonomy; in particular they are independent of the supervisory authority of the chief executive. They are given a special field of operation, such as one of the fields just mentioned, and enforce and effectuate the laws in that field. If they did not enjoy this independence and control of a special field, they would remain mere arms of the general executive branch, and we would not need to distinguish them from executive agencies which definitely fall within the executive branch.

Many of these administrative agencies are empowered to handle certain types of controversies between parties, controversies which are, in essentials, like private lawsuits. In this respect, these agencies serve functions similar to courts. They are authorized to decide both questions of law and questions of fact. For this reason, they are sometimes referred to as quasi-judicial agencies, and their powers are called quasi-judicial powers. But inasmuch as these bodies are authorized to follow simpler procedures than courts use, and inasmuch as they determine fact questions without jury, they cannot be regarded as ordinary courts. For example, a workmen's compensation commission is given authority to pass on the claim of an employee against his employer for injuries arising in the course of employment. The employee must proceed before the workmen's compensation commission. The commission decides how and when he was injured; and decides, according to a fixed schedule, what his compensation shall be. Formerly, this type of case would have been handled in a court proceeding by the employee against the employer. It would have been a matter for a court and jury to determine. This modern proceeding before an administrative body has superseded the old legal action. This substitution of another trial agency in place of a court would not have been possible if grants of judicial power had been interpreted to mean that all controversies between parties must be heard and determined by the judicial agencies and methods provided for in the constitutions. On the contrary, administrative bodies are commonly allowed, in fields where public welfare so demands, to perform functions like those of courts, though these agencies are not regarded as judicial bodies in the full constitutional sense.

Not only could the constitutional separation of powers have been taken to mean that all the legislative, executive and judicial powers of government must always be invested in the three respective branches mentioned in the constitutions, but it might also have been held that the three kinds of power must always be kept separate from one another. It might have been held that the three kinds of power cannot be combined in a single hand. This view has often been urged; but again the interpreters of our constitutions have had to yield to the practical exigencies of government and to recognize the possibility of combining, in a single administrative agency, power to make regulations, power to enforce them, and power to adjudicate controversies regarding their meaning. In fact, this combination of powers is one of the outstanding features of the modern administrative agency.[2] Instead of separating the regulative powers of government into three hands, the tendency in recent decades has been to separate powers of control in regard to different fields and subjects of human action. Thus, in the federal system, control over railroads is assigned to the Interstate Commerce Commission, control over radio transmission to the Federal Communications Commission, and control of certain employer-employee relations to the National Labor Relations

---

[2] As well as one of the chief grounds of objection to the typical administrative agency. See items cited in next footnote.

Board; and in the state systems, control of the insurance business is invested in an insurance commissioner, control of public utilities in public service commissions, etc. Control of such a field is invested in a single body or official, and this body or official is given authority to legislate, enforce, and adjudicate within this field of special competence. In other words, within this field, the separation of powers as a scheme of checks and balances is not followed out; powers of control are not separated, but are combined in one hand. The administrative body or official is at once lawmaker, executive and judge. Its special field of operation is marked out and separated from others on a principle which is essentially the economic theory of specialization or division of labor. The idea is that a body which specializes in the control of railroads or public utilities, can do a better job of creating rules for their control, and a better job of supervising their activities and enforcing the applicable rules, and a better job of deciding controversies in regard to their activities and rules, than can an agency which has to make all kinds of rules, or to enforce all kinds of rules, or to settle all types of controversies. The job of control will be better done not only because of the knowledge and experience which comes with specialization, but also because the combination of powers of control avoids the delays and possible conflicts of views which may result where the job of control is divided three ways.

Our courts had no little difficulty about recognizing the constitutional validity of these hybrid agencies, exercising powers part legislative, part executive, and part judicial. They helped themselves over the difficulty at first by calling the powers of these agencies quasi-legislative, quasi-executive and quasi-judicial, as if the addition of the "quasi" conferred a different odor on the roses in question. As a matter of fact, the real basis for the creation and recognition of these agencies with mixed powers was the need for specialization in governmental functions. And nowadays this basis is frankly acknowledged. Congress and the legislatures still have to decide when the public welfare demands that a governmental function be invested in an administrative body rather than in an executive officer or court. Indeed, Congress and the state legislatures are showing a definite inclination to put specific checks on the administrative agencies which they create in order to prevent abuses that can result from the combination in one agency of the functions of rule maker, rule enforcer, and judge.[3] However, such checks are matters for legislative determination. There is no longer any doubt about the constitutional status of administrative agencies. Congress and the legislatures can invest their creatures, established to control special subjects, with almost any powers or combination of powers that they deem necessary in the public interest.

Sec. 3–21. Nonregulative acts of governmental agencies. It is sometimes tacitly assumed that government does just one thing: it performs a regulative function. In fact, this assumption is made in the conventional statement of the separation of powers doctrine. In classifying governmental powers into legislative, executive, and judicial, that doctrine subdivides only the regulative powers of government. Certainly the primary function of the state, as I have already pointed out,[1] is to regulate the behavior of individuals; and certainly this regulative function of the state is that in which we, as lawyers, are most interested. Even the regulation of the behavior of officials must be regarded as secondary to the primary function of regulating the behavior of the individual.

But state agencies perform many acts which are non-regulative in character, and which fall quite outside the

---

[3] See STASON, ADMINISTRATIVE DISCRETION AND ITS CONTROL (Cooley Lectures delivered in 1950); Federal Administrative Procedure Act of 1946, 5 U. S. C., secs. 1001–1011; and the Uniform Administrative Procedure Act (an equivalent state act), Wisconsin Laws, 1943, chapter 375.

[1] Sec. 3–01.

threefold classification of governmental powers into legislative, executive, and judicial. Besides its regulative function, the state performs fiscal functions; it raises and spends money. It performs many public services, such as the maintenance of schools and highways and the keeping of records of various sorts. And it administers its own affairs as any private business concern would do. One sees the operation of these nonregulative activities of government most plainly in connection with the legislative branch. While the legislature takes its name from the fact that it enacts laws, legislative bodies in our American legal systems are not confined to lawmaking. The Congress of the United States, for example, is vested with sweeping powers of taxation. It authorizes contracts on behalf of the government; it procures and controls government property; it expends funds for the general welfare; it controls and issues money; it supervises and investigates the conduct of officials; it declares war and peace.

Similar acts of nonlegislative character are done by the legislatures of the states. These acts, of course, are confined to the fiscal and business affairs of the respective states. The executive agencies of the federal and state governments are, in their turn, required to carry out the legislative mandates affecting these fiscal and administrative activities of government, so that their activities also fall beyond the field in which conduct of individuals is regulated. And the judicial agencies of these governments are, in an analogous way, often concerned with controversies between agencies of government and other disputes which do not immediately relate to individuals. In short, we need to remember that its regulative activity is not the only function government performs. The conventional classification of governmental powers in regulative terms is, therefore, one-sided and not exhaustive. It suits our present purpose well enough, but sometimes we find it necessary to look at all the functions of government in order to understand the operation of regulative and effectuative measures.[2]

EFFECTUATION OF STANDARDS FOR OFFICIALS [1]

Sec. 3–22. Need for effectuation—control devices. In the last subtopic, I have mentioned the kinds of acts which officials do—chiefly acts which they do by way of effectuating standards applicable to the individual—and have called attention to the standards which are applicable to these official acts. I shall now pass on to the ways in which these standards for official acts are in their turn effectuated. Officials themselves are human beings and, like those whom they control, need not only standards to guide their actions but proper motives and habits to make them perform according to standards.

The problem of making effective the standards applicable to official acts is essentially like the problem of effectuating standards for the individual's behavior; it is a problem of insuring proper motivation and habits. However, it is not quite as easy to devise methods to control officials, and especially top officials, as it is to devise methods to control the individual. This is the point of a celebrated question asked by Juvenal regarding Plato's proposal of a state in which the "guardians" would exercise all governmental authority: "*Quis custodiet ipsos custodes?*" (Who shall keep guard over the guardians themselves?) [2] In general terms, the answer to this question of control is easy. Officials will be controlled by the acts of their superiors, by their education

---

[2] After all, the activities of government of every kind and character are woven together in an inextricable manner so that no part can be properly evaluated apart from the whole. This is a point which has already been stressed. See secs. 2–36 and 2–39. It is a point which I shall have occasion to dwell on again later. See secs. 7–17 to 7–27, inclusive.

[1] The discussion in the present subtopic parallels the discussion of methods of effectuating standards for the individual, secs. 2–29 to 2–42, inclusive.

[2] SATIRES, VI, 347.

and training, by promise of reward for good behavior, by threat of penalty for bad, and so on, just as any actor is controlled. But when we undertake to work out specific programs for the control of particular types of officials, acting in the varied situations where they must act, the problems of devising sanctions to control officials become most difficult and complex.

The methods devised and used in the American legal system can be reduced to four:

1. The use of independent officials as checks upon one another.

2. The selection of officials on the basis of proper habits and training.

3. The assurance of sound conditions of tenure.

4. The supervision and disciplinary control of officials by superiors.

In the next section, the first of these methods will be considered; in the sections immediately following, the other methods will be treated as they apply specifically to control of inferior executives, the chief executive, the trial jury, the trial judge, and the appellate judge.

Sec. 3–23. Checks and balances—separation and integration of powers. As I have already mentioned, a prominent feature of all the American constitutions, beginning with the federal, is the separation of governmental powers and acts into three kinds: legislative, executive, and judicial.[1] This separation was not made by the framers of the Federal

---

[1] Although the doctrine of separation of powers is embodied in all the state constitutions, I shall speak here only of the Federal Constitution because it was the original instrument in which the separation was definitely adopted, and because it will serve as an adequate illustration of the nature and effects of the doctrine. It should be noted, however, that the Federal Constitution does not mention the separation doctrine explicitly, as some of the state constitutions do. It simply makes a separation of powers in distinct and express terms; in Article I it provides for legislative power; in Article II, it allocates executive power and defines its scope; and in Article III, it defines the scope of judicial power.

Constitution merely as a matter of convenient classification; it was made as a matter of policy. The founding fathers were deeply impressed by the argument of Montesquieu in his *Spirit of the Laws* that such a separation is essential to the security and protection of the individual.* Behind the separation of powers of government in this manner was a policy of checks and balances. The notion was that by creating three separate branches of government, each would serve as a check upon the acts and activities of the others. No one branch would be able to exceed or misuse its powers, inasmuch as it would be restrained by the powers and acts of the other two. In other words, the founders of our government expressed in the doctrine of separation of powers their intention to make the three branches of government independent for a special purpose—the purpose of using each branch as a means of insuring proper behavior, i. e., behavior according to standard, by the others.[2]

The function of Congress as a check on the executive is seen in the fact that the great bulk of legal standards which the President is to enforce and effectuate are created by Congress. Most of his powers depend upon statute.[3] Moreover, the President cannot act without the aid of subordinate officials, and these officials occupy offices created by Congress

* (I.R.) The theory of checks and balances did not originate with Montesquieu; Locke expressed the theory in somewhat different form. And the notion of using one organ of government as a check upon another was advanced by Polybius, a Greek writer, before the Christian era. Also, the colonial governments were already organized on lines which resembled the division of powers made by the Federal Constitution.

[2] It must also be remembered that the separation of powers among three branches of government is not the only instance in which the principle of checks and balances appears in the framework of American government. The division of legislative power between a House and a Senate is a separation derived from the British Parliament. The division of powers between the federal and the state governments makes the general government and the state governments checks upon one another. Similar observations apply to constitutional divisions between state and local government, such as the Home Rule Amendments, which have been adopted in many of our states.

[3] A few important powers are conferred on the President by the Constitution; but most of his powers depend on statutes.

and supported by Congressional appropriations. And, while the appointment of higher officials is normally made by the President, any such appointment must be approved by the Senate. In all these respects we see, then, that Congress has a very real restraining authority over what the executive branch does. On the judicial branch, similar legislative checks obtain. All the federal courts except the Supreme Court depend on acts of Congress for their existence. All the powers of the courts in the federal system, except a few constitutionally defined powers of the Supreme Court, are fixed and defined by the Congressional will.[4] Judicial appointments can be made only with the approval of the Senate, or in such manner as Congress shall determine. Finally, Congress checks both executive and judicial behavior through its power to remove federal officials from office by impeachment. The House of Representatives is empowered to start removal proceedings by filing charges of misbehavior, and the Senate is invested with power to hear and determine such charges and enter judgment of removal.

The President's power to veto legislation, his discretion in initiating action of various sorts, and his control over officials who enforce law, serve to make him a check on the behavior of the legislative branch, especially as he owes his election to the people and not to Congress. The President has some checking power as regards the judiciary in his power of appointing judges.[5] More important perhaps is the fact that the President is the ultimate agency to enforce decrees of the courts, and in this sense serves as a check on their action. For ordinary purposes, the court's own marshal can accomplish whatever is required, but if military assistance becomes

[4] See Lockerty v. Phillips, 319 U. S. 182 (1943); Yakus v. United States, 321 U. S. 414 (1944). Congress also appropriates money to pay federal judicial salaries, though it cannot reduce a judge's salary during his term in office. Const. Art. III, Sec. 1.

[5] Also his power to pardon serves as a check on judicial action in the criminal field.

necessary, the courts must call upon the Chief Executive who has control of the military forces.[6]

The judicial branch serves as a check on Congress chiefly through what has come to be known as the power of judicial review. This is the power to pass on the constitutionality of legislation. This power stands in the way of efforts by Congress to exceed its legislative powers.[7] And the judiciary exercises an analogous check on the executive branch. The courts pass on the question whether executive action exceeds constitutional authority; or, where executive action purports to be taken under authority of statute, they decide whether such action is in harmony with the statutory authority conferred by Congress.

There can be no doubt about the importance or soundness of this system of checks in the American governmental scheme. But there has been a tendency at times to exaggerate the extent of the cleavage between the branches of our government and to forget the reason for their separation. The branches of government were intended to co-operate with, as well as to check, one another. The three branches of government are partners in the processes of regulation. The one branch is to establish regulative provisions, the second branch to see that they are enforced, and the third branch to settle controversies regarding the meaning and application of regu-

---

[6] This is the point of the remark, attributed to President Jackson, "Well, John Marshall has made his decision, now let him enforce it." The decision referred to was that of Chief Justice Marshall in Worcester v. Georgia, 6 Pet. 515 (1832). The State of Georgia was ready to defy the authority of the Supreme Court in this case. It seems probable that President Jackson never made the remark quoted. WARREN, SUPREME COURT IN UNITED STATES HISTORY, II, 219 (1922). Nevertheless, the effectuation of the Supreme Court's decrees against states or large groups does depend on executive action.

Also, the judges of the federal courts may depend on the executive for protection against personal attack. See In re Neagle, 135 U. S. 1 (1890), a dramatic case in which a disgruntled litigant assaulted Justice Field of the Supreme Court while the latter was acting as circuit judge in California. The attacker was killed by Neagle, a United States marshal, who had been assigned by the Attorney General to protect Justice Field.

[7] As to judicial review of the validity of legislation and the effects of such review, see also secs. 4–08 to 4–13, inclusive, and 7–36 to 7–38.

lations. The three branches are partially separated, but also interdependent.[8] The separation has to be interpreted in the light of its purpose—to prevent the abuse of power by any of the three branches of government involved in the processes of regulation. Each is intended to check, but not paralyze the others' action. The activities of all are integrated by a common regulative purpose, and the division between them is not intended to destroy their unified operation. As Woodrow Wilson once said, "Government . . . is a body of men, with highly differentiated functions, no doubt, in our modern day of specialization, but with a common task and purpose. Their cooperation is indispensable, their warfare, fatal." [9]

Sec. 3–24. Control of inferior executives. We have now considered the checking influences which distinct and separate branches of government may exert upon one another's behavior. We move on to other processes of control, and con-

[8] The system of checks demands that two branches join in governmental acts. If the action of each were quite independent of the other, there would be no checking. Thus, two houses of Congress check one another and at the same time cooperate in legislation, taxation, impeachments, etc. The President and Senate participate in appointments and in treaty making. See LUCE, LEGISLATIVE PROBLEMS 104–139 (1935). The Congress is checked by the courts because legislative acts have to be applied by them in litigated cases. Indeed, all the instances of checking mentioned in the text are at the same time instances of co-operative action.

[9] CONSTITUTIONAL GOVERNMENT IN THE UNITED STATES 56 (1908). The most important instances of checks, extending to the point of paralyzing effective governmental action, have been the cases of judicial assertion of power of review of any and all kinds of executive and administrative action of the federal and state governments. This meant, for example, that every hearing on utility rates had to be retried in a federal court, and the processes of rate making were slowed to a point where they were almost completely stalled. This was the practical situation as regards many forms of governmental activity in the 1920's. Since that time the Congress has limited the powers of judicial review in various ways, and since about 1938 the federal courts have adopted a strong presumption in favor of the correctness of executive and administrative action. This combination of statutory limitations and a hands-off policy of the courts has completely altered the picture in this important area. See for example Railroad Commission v. Rowan and Nichols Oil Co., 310 U. S. 573 (1940); Federal Power Commission v. Hope Natural Gas Co., 320 U. S. 591 (1944); and Yakus v. United States, 321 U. S. 414 (1944).

sider the efficacy of methods of selection, of conditions of tenure, and of supervision and disciplinary measures as applied to various types of officials. I shall begin with inferior executive officials.

First, the behavior of inferior executive officials is determined by the way in which they are selected. Undoubtedly, the best way to insure proper official behavior is to pick persons with sound qualifications. Three methods of selection are commonly used. All are theoretically intended to secure men who by habit and training are most likely to perform the acts which their respective jobs call for. One method of selection is *appointment.* The power to appoint is usually vested in a single person, such as the President, or the governor of a state, or the head of a department or bureau. The appointing official, if competent and honest, can satisfy very well the need for a choice based on an estimation of qualifications and training. This method emphasizes the personal judgment of the appointing official regarding the personal qualities of candidates; it is especially suited for use in choosing higher officials who will be called upon to determine policy questions to some extent, and whose qualifications for this purpose can hardly be measured by any fixed standard.

Another method, and one which has quite wide vogue in this country, is *popular election.* This method of choosing fit candidates for such offices as sheriff, prosecutor, etc., goes back to the full flush of Jacksonian democracy. As a method of choosing officials to enforce the law, it has little to recommend it. Popular election has its place in government; we should by all means elect those who make our laws; we should all have a voice in shaping the policies of government. But, when it comes to the application and enforcement of those policies, when it comes to the administration of law, we need impartiality, not popular impulse; we need the man who knows his business and who applies the law as it is, honestly and fearlessly. Popular election does not get such men; in fact, it works the other way. The major fault of popular choice is that you and I and other citizens cannot obtain the information necessary to pass on a candidate's fitness for sheriff, register of deeds, or prosecutor. We have no way of getting the facts regarding his ability, his training, his habits, his disposition or his fairness. And probably one is too optimistic in supposing that the mass of voters attempt to choose the best man. Many voters forget the question of merit entirely. They vote for a candidate because of friendship, or they cast a straight party ballot, or they vote against an incumbent official because he has done an act adverse to them or their friends, regardless of whether the act was right and proper or not. In short, election of officials is an indiscriminate affair. It has little to do with fitness for office. It reflects chiefly the ability of the particular candidate to make a direct personal appeal to voters, or his readiness to make promises to particular persons, or to political or economic groups, in exchange for their support.[1]

A third method has come to be used more and more in recent decades. It gives promise of supplanting the other methods wherever this is constitutionally possible. This method we may call the *civil service* method. It relies primarily on the written examination to test the qualifications of candidates. The examination is generally open to all who fulfill certain formal conditions of training and experience. The examination is usually given by a board or by officials acting under the supervision of a board. In addition to the examination, there is usually a certain amount of weight attached to personal experience and to a face-to-face interview in which the personal qualities of each candidate are rated. Furthermore, the board does not actually choose a

[1] The faults of popular election, here mentioned, are most noticeable in choosing officials for large urban communities. In rural communities and small towns, where electors usually know the candidates and their backgrounds, popular election can work with a reasonable degree of satisfaction.

particular man for the job in question, but sends the names of the highest qualifiers, e. g., three persons, to the head of the agency for which a person is to be chosen. The head of the agency is left free to appoint from the candidates so suggested.

The conditions of official *tenure* are no less important than the methods of selection. In order to secure the most efficient and impartial service from officials, it is essential to guarantee to them indefinite tenure of office, or, as it is more commonly called, tenure during good behavior. At this point, government is confronted by an apparent dilemma: either to give all officials security and independence, which may involve a continuation of weak and incompetent persons in office for life; or to reserve a power to terminate official tenure at any time, which, of course, enables government to get rid of its unfit officials. If the first course is chosen, unfit men may be kept long in office. If the second course is chosen, all officials are deprived of that feeling of security and independence which is the very foundation of unselfish devotion to duty. On the whole, the balance of arguments is in favor of secure tenure, especially if this tenure is coupled with sound methods of selection and removal. If officials are chosen on the basis of merit, not too much unfit timber should find its way into the official structure. At least, the number of unfit persons should, on the average, be lower than the number who will fill offices when all candidates are chosen on a partisan and temporary basis; and even civil service need not stand in the way of removal from office for such causes as fraud, disobedience, or neglect of duty.

Compensation also needs to be reasonable in amount. Inadequate compensation has three harmful tendencies. It introduces a temptation to dishonesty and corruption; it results over the years in the resignation of the more energetic officials; and it diminishes the enthusiasm for service of those who remain in office. Compensation should also include a provision for that deferred type of payment which we commonly call a pension; such pension is essential to give security and thus independence to the officeholder. The combination of secure tenure, reasonable pay, and adequate pension, is calculated to secure for government services and abilities which would command substantially higher returns if devoted to private business.

Behavior according to approved standards can also be insured by supervision and threat of disciplinary measures by executive superiors. Most officials are subject to supervision by superiors who can issue direct orders for action, require reports on action taken, and scrutinize or criticize the work of their inferiors. Usually, this kind of supervision is coupled with authority to remove for misconduct or neglect of duty. Where civil service is in force, removal from office can be accomplished only after a hearing by an impartial agency and only for stated causes. These restraints on removal are essential to guarantee the secure tenure and independence at which the civil service system is aimed.

Besides the disciplinary measures just mentioned, the public prosecutor can, in many instances, proceed criminally against inferior executive officials for abuse or misuse of powers, or for neglect of duty. He can also employ "extraordinary legal remedies," such as *quo warranto* to question the exercise of official power, *prohibition* to prevent the exercise of power not possessed, and *mandamus* to compel the exercise of official power; and he can often use equitable remedies by way of injunction for purposes not unlike the functions of these extraordinary legal remedies.

The individual also enjoys adequate civil remedies against inferior executives whose misbehavior causes, or threatens, injury to him. From the public viewpoint, these remedies serve as sanctions to enforce behavior according to approved standards. For example, if a sheriff makes an unjustified arrest, he is liable for false imprisonment; if he makes an unauthorized seizure of an individual's property, he may be required to pay the full value of the property by way of compensation. If an official fails to do an act which he is commanded to do for the benefit of an individual, the latter may ordinarily hold him liable for damages, e. g., where an official negligently fails to serve process in an action by A against B and damage results to A. And official duties may also, in some instances, be enforced by equitable or extraordinary legal remedies at the individual's behest.

Examples need not be multiplied. You will realize by this time that the obligatory and prohibitive standards directed to minor executives, their duties to act or not to act, are backed up by formidable sanctions and control devices. Nevertheless, you will find only too often a considerable difference between the standard for official behavior as it appears in the books and the behavior of officials as it works out in actual practice.[2] Just as there are private persons who ignore applicable standards or consciously violate them, so there are public officials who fail to act in cases where they should act, or who do not carry out duties in the manner prescribed by standards. There is a great difference between an alert policeman and an indifferent one. This kind of difference counts heavily all the way up the scale to the chief executive.

Finally, there is a large and important part of official behavior which is not covered by obligatory or prohibitive standards. The official is given discretion or power to act or both. In these cases, action is left to the official actor's judgment. His acts are intended to be free and uncontrolled. Beyond furnishing him with patterns for effective action, to

[2] On this point, compare what is said in sec. 2–29 *et seq.*, regarding the discrepancy between standards for the individual's act and their effectuation.

use if he chooses to act, the lawmaker does not concern himself greatly about effectuation or enforcement. Even the traffic officer has some discretion in the performance of his duties. The element of discretion increases as one proceeds upward in the hierarchy, as I have already said.[3] Standards of behavior become more general; they do not prescribe behavior so definitely and so specifically. Sanctions for departure from standards are less immediate and direct. Thus, the public prosecutor as compared with the ordinary policeman has a very wide discretion. He has a great deal of leeway in deciding what cases to prosecute and what cases to disregard. He may take into consideration the strength of the evidence, the character of the person accused, and the hope for his reform if he be given another chance. This kind of discretion is a very good thing in the hands of a sound official, but it is hard to draw the line between proper use of discretion and the neglect of duty. An incompetent or dishonest prosecutor can go pretty far before the sanctions of the law will strike him.[4]

Sec. 3–25. Control of the chief executive. The chief executive is always chosen by popular election. While no one can deny that some very weak and some dishonest men have been elected to the highest executive offices in this country, I doubt if any serious student of our democratic

---

[3] Sec. 3–06.

[4] For example, in the days of prohibition the breakdown of enforcement was in large part due to the refusal of prosecutors to institute prosecutions for violations of the liquor laws. One could not blame the prosecutor in an urban community too severely for this neglect of duty. Quite apart from possible corrupt motives for his neglect, the prosecutor knew that it was most difficult to secure convictions by juries drawn from a population which was largely opposed to prohibition and that his ardor in favor of enforcement would not be appreciated by the wet voters whom he would have to face in a campaign for re-election. Hence, the prosecutor was naturally inclined to make a big show of prosecuting violators, but actually to do no more than was necessary to keep the drys from becoming aroused and organizing a campaign for his defeat.

institutions would substitute any other method of choosing
our chief executives for choice by popular election. Some
changes in the methods of nominating candidates and in the
machinery of election might be suggested, but on the whole
I believe that popular election of the President and governors
meets with approval.[1] Popular election works reasonably well
in regard to chief executives because of the prominence of
the officers involved. The successful candidate must almost
always be a man who is well known and who has maintained
himself in the public eye for a substantial period of time. He
usually runs on a more or less definite platform. The average
voter realizes that the chief executive has a hand in determining important public policies. For these reasons the voter
is apt to scrutinize the chief executive's qualifications more
carefully than he does the qualifications of candidates for
inferior offices, especially in states where the number of
elective offices is very large and the voter must indicate
choices for every office from lieutenant governor and secretary of state to dogcatcher.

The tenure of office of the chief executive is ordinarily
fixed at a relatively short period of years—four years in the
case of President of the United States and of most state
governors, though in a few states the governor holds office
for only two years. In a number of the states the governor
is explicitly made ineligible for re-election. Short terms and
denial of re-election were both dictated by the purpose to
prevent the perpetuation of men in office—a reaction against
the former British practice of hereditary succession to, and
life tenure of, many executive offices. It was intended to
make the control of policy by the electors direct and imme-

[1] I have not made mention here of any of the details of nomination or
election, such as party conventions, nominating primaries, or the federal elec-
toral college. These subjects are very important, to be sure, but I regard them
as more properly topics for courses in government, which I assume that most
of you have had, than as topics for discussion in the present course.

diate. However, the short tenure of governors has its draw-backs, too. In Michigan, for example, where the governor holds office for two years, the chief executive has an insufficient time in which to formulate and push through a program. He is hardly settled in office before he must again run the gauntlet of popular approval or disapproval.

The President of the United States needs and receives a substantial compensation, $100,000, plus large allowances for expenses. The pay of governors is also ample in some of our states. In other states, an unwise financial policy has been pursued by the legislature of keeping the governor's salary at an insufficient level, or else the salary is fixed by the constitution so that changes cannot be made to meet rising costs. The result of this kind of false economy is that the man who is elected governor must either be a rich man and spend freely of his own funds, or he must make political commitments to persons who furnish the funds to finance his election campaigns. Either result is contrary to the public interest.

However, the length and security of tenure and the adequacy of pay, count for less in relation to the office of chief executive than in relation to most other offices. The candidate for chief executive is largely actuated by the desire for honors and influence. And, in the case of the candidate for governor, the job is often looked upon as a stepping-stone to such offices as United States senator, ambassador, cabinet member, etc. So that in general, the quality of our chief executives has been relatively high, despite some of the disadvantageous tendencies mentioned in the foregoing paragraphs.

There are no very effective ways of enforcing the standards of behavior applicable to the official, who is himself the highest law-enforcer. To start with, his range of discretion is very wide, and the standards which apply to his activities are usually broad and ill-defined. Then there are no ways of compelling the chief executive to perform his positive duties, such as his duty to employ the military forces to suppress disorder, his duty to set in motion machinery to enforce laws, or his duty to appoint officials to fill vacancies. His prohibited acts, which violate the rights of others, may be challenged before the courts in litigated cases; improper acts may be held to be forbidden or ineffective. And the chief executive's underlings may be prevented from carrying out his orders by threat of suit on behalf of persons injured, e. g., if a sheriff undertakes to carry out an unlawful order of the governor. Yet there are no judicial remedies of any consequence which are operative against the chief executive directly. He may, of course, be impeached and removed from office if his conduct be flagrant enough. But impeachment is remote and cumbersome; it is rarely attempted and not often successful. Also, the chief executive may be defeated for re-election, if the voters disapprove of his behavior. But this, too, often fails as a method for visiting on an incumbent the proper consequences of misbehavior. It is only too easy for the demagogue to explain away the bad features of his deeds to an electorate which cannot be too well informed on the facts. In short, the obligations of the chief executive are without effective legal sanctions. The proper behavior of the chief executive is guaranteed principally by the quality of the man himself and by the impact upon him of the opinion of his leading associates and of the general public.

*Sec. 3–26. Control of the trial judge.** The chief actor in the adjudicative process is the trial judge. He controls the jury; he has wide discretion in many matters; he often

---

* (I.R.) In regard to the subject matter of this section, see generally HAYNES, SELECTION AND TENURE OF JUDGES (National Conference of Judicial Councils) (1944), and the following articles by the present author: "Pensions for Judges," 27 MICH. L. REV. 134 (1928); "Federal Judges—Appointment, Supervision and Removal—Some Possibilities Under the Constitution," 28 MICH. L. REV. 485, 723, 870 (1930); and "Retirement and Removal of Judges," 20 JOUR. AM. JUD. SOC. 133 (1936).

has to pass on matters of vital importance to individuals. For all these reasons we hope for, and expect from him, the utmost degree of fairness and objectivity in making his determinations. The control of his behavior, like the control of inferior executives, takes us back to fundamental questions of selection, tenure, compensation, supervision and discipline. In order to get and keep good judges, men who will perform their functions according to prescribed standards, important problems of training, habits and motivation need to be solved.

In the federal system, judges are appointed by the President with the approval of the Senate. On the face of it, this method of *selection* might seem to promise satisfaction. But, unfortunately, the appointment of inferior federal judges has come to be heavily involved in local partisan politics. The President has, to a large extent, abdicated his power of selection, and leaves the real choice to members of the Senate or to the politicians who stand behind them.[1]

In most of our states, trial judges are chosen by popular election.[2] This method of choosing judges is open to all the

[1] "This has come about because political interest in district and circuit judgships is local rather than national, because the President does not have time to investigate the reputation and standing of candidates and is forced to seek information and advice from local leaders, because senators and other influential persons of the state in which a vacancy occurs will naturally be consulted by the Senate when it passes upon an appointment, and finally because the President himself is in the midst of politics, and is forced to cede local patronage for political support. But whatever the causes, there is no doubt of the facts. Appointments of inferior judges and promotions to the circuit courts of appeal are dictated today by the senators from states where the vacancies exist, at least if they are influential and of the President's own party; if the senators are members of the opposition party, then naturally the President turns for 'suggestions' to the local chiefs of his own party. Every vacancy results in a wild scramble and pulling of political wires which is only less hurtful to judicial independence and disinterestedness than is a popular primary or election. I ask the reader candidly whether we dare view this situation with indifference, whether we dare look on without concern while this last citadel of justice according to law is engulfed by the rising tide of politics." Shartel, "Federal Judges—Appointment, Supervision and Removal—Some Possibilities Under the Constitution," 28 MICH. L. REV. 485 at 488 (1930).

[2] According to Haynes, judges are popularly elected in all but thirteen of the states. In Connecticut, "Most judges are appointed by the Governor with

objections that can be made to its use in the choice of inferior executives.[3] In addition to the fact that the average voter is quite unable to pass upon qualifications for judicial office, the popular election and the mudslinging which goes with it scare away many of our best potential judges. A campaign for popular favor disgusts men of fair and independent type, the very men who would make good judges. Such men do not need to curry favor with anyone in private law practice. They refuse to subject themselves to the political obligations which popular elections involve. The consequence is that the choice of judges is limited, generally speaking, to the lesser lights of the bar. In saying this I do not mean to say that we do not obtain some good judges by popular election. We all know elected judges who have served ably and well. But I do mean to say that the tendency of the system is wrong, and that we have probably obtained more good men than we were entitled to expect.

In recent decades there has been a strong and persistent movement among civic leaders and members of the bar in the several states to introduce methods of selecting judges on a merit basis.[4] There seems to be fairly complete agreement that judges should be appointed, and that their appoint-

---

the consent of the General Assembly, i.e., both houses of the legislature. In Delaware and New Jersey, nearly all are appointed by the Governor with the consent of the Senate. In Maine, Massachusetts and New Hampshire, most of them are appointed by the Governor with the consent of the Governor's Council. In four states (Rhode Island, South Carolina, Vermont and Virginia), virtually all are elected by the two houses of the legislature in a joint meeting." HAYNES, SELECTION AND TENURE OF JUDGES (National Conference of Judicial Councils) 9 (1944). Since this book was published, the State of New Jersey has adopted a constitutional amendment under which all judges are appointed by the governor with the approval of the state senate.

[3] Sec. 3–24.

[4] This movement is one phase of general efforts to promote improvements in our court organization. Various bar groups, national, state and local, are active in fostering such improvements. Especially active in this respect has been a voluntary association of lawyers known as the American Judicature Society, which was founded in 1913 "To promote the efficient administration of justice" and which publishes a useful journal dealing with problems of court and bar organization.

ment should be hedged about by safeguards against the making of political appointments.[5] The methods proposed usually combine appointment with checks to insure a scrutiny of qualifications and to eliminate political wirepulling. Most of the proposals have taken one of three forms. One proposal would vest the power of appointment in the chief justice of the particular judicial system, a proposal which has, so far, not been adopted anywhere in this country.[6] Another proposal would vest power to nominate in a nonpartisan commission, which is obliged to investigate the qualifications of candidates and suggest a list of names to the governor for appointment; the governor's choice would be limited to the persons whose names are thus submitted to him. This method of selection has been adopted in Missouri as a mode of choosing trial judges in the St. Louis and Kansas City areas, as well as all judges of the supreme and intermediate appellate courts.[7] A third proposal of this sort would provide for appointment by the governor with the approval of a nonpartisan commission; it would place the initial selection in the governor, and give a sort of veto to the nonpartisan body. This method has been adopted in California as a mode of choosing appellate, but not trial, judges.[8] Obviously, the make-up of the commission which proposes or approves judges under these various schemes is most important. It is

[5] In the states, gubernatorial appointment with the approval of the state senate (or equivalent body) seems not to have worked badly; and in the recent New Jersey constitution, this is the method of judicial selection which was adopted. Const. 1947 Art. VI, Sec. 6.

[6] Judicial selection of judges has been proposed by a number of writers. Appointment of inferior federal judges by the Chief Justice with the approval of the Supreme Court, is the method which I have urged in an article, "Federal Judges—Appointment, Supervision and Removal—Some Possibilities Under the Constitution." 28 MICH. L. REV. 485 (1930).

In England, judicial appointments are made by the Lord Chancellor, who is the highest judicial officer of the realm and who might, therefore, be compared to the Chief Justice of the Supreme Court of the United States. However, The Lord Chancellor does not hold his office as such permanently, but only so long as the ministry of which he is a member holds office.

[7] Const. Amend. 1940 Art. VI, Sec. 1.

[8] Const. Art. VI, Sec. 4a.

desirable to give various interests representation on the commission; it is desirable to have on the commission some men who have had judicial experience, some who are practicing lawyers, and some who are representative of the lay public.[9] If the members of the commission be chosen to represent various informed interests, and if they be given fairly long and staggered terms, I believe that politics in judicial appointments can be reduced to a minimum, and that the chances of getting a uniformly high-grade judiciary would be much improved.

Tenure during good behavior is guaranteed to judges of the federal courts by the Constitution; and judges of the superior courts of Massachusetts, New Hampshire and Rhode Island enjoy the like tenure.[10] Under the new constitution of New Jersey, the judge holds office on first appointment for a term of seven years, and on reappointment remains in office during good behavior. Trial judges in the other states hold office for limited terms of years. In most of these states, the term is relatively short—four to six years; but in a few of them, the trial judge's term of office is relatively long, e. g., in New York fourteen, and in Pennsylvania, ten years. Any limitation of tenure to a period of years, especially to a short period, is inimical to judicial independence. But actually, the harmful effects of repeated

[9] Such a nonpartisan commission was represented by a constitutional amendment proposed a few years ago by the State Bar of Michigan. It would have provided for appointment of supreme court judges by the governor on nomination of a judiciary commission of nine persons, to be chosen as follows:
"The judiciary commission shall consist of a justice of the supreme court elected by the justices of that court, a circuit judge elected by the judges of the circuit courts, a probate judge elected by the judges of the probate courts, three electors of this state not licensed to practice law therein appointed by the governor, and three members of the bar of this state appointed by the commissioners of the state bar of Michigan."

[10] See HAYNES, SELECTION AND TENURE OF JUDGES (National Conference of Judicial Councils) 10, 30–50 (1944). The superior quality of justice, which is usually dispensed in our federal courts, must be ascribed to the secure tenure and adequate pay of the judges and to the prestige which their office involves. Certainly one cannot attribute it to sound methods of selection (see above, this section) nor to effective methods of discipline (see below, this section).

exposure to popular caprice have been considerably reduced in many places by the activities of bar associations in supporting incumbents for re-election, and by the gradual development in many localities of a tradition of re-electing the sitting judge. If the end of each term always meant for the judicial incumbent a real battle for re-election, I believe that we would have a much less competent judiciary than we have in most of our state courts. Only by making popular elections more or less a form has this mode of choice been able to produce passable results.

The *pay* of trial judges varies greatly.[11] The United States district judge has a salary of $15,000. In 1948, the salaries of some trial judges of general jurisdiction in the states of Kansas, Oklahoma and Utah were as low as $4,000. In New York, judges in the more populous departments now receive $28,000; in the less populous, $18,000. In Pennsylvania, the judges of superior courts receive $21,000. In Michigan, the salaries vary between $7,000 and $16,500 in different counties. In the great majority of cases, trial judges are paid salaries of $6,000 to $7,000. In these days when the most ordinary labor is paid one dollar and fifty cents or more per hour and skilled workmen receive two to three dollars per hour, there can hardly be a doubt in anyone's mind that $6,000 is inadequate as pay for the kind of work which the judge does and the kind of responsibility which rests on his shoulders. When inadequacy of pay is added to the drawback of short terms and the possibility of defeat for re-election, it is hardly to be supposed that the best lawyer will choose to remain long in judicial office. If such a man does seek a judgeship, he does so for the sake of the experience and the profes-

---

[11] If the reader wishes to see complete and specific figures regarding the salaries of state judges, I refer him to 31 Jour. Am. Jud. Soc. 150 (1948).

Adequate *pensions* are hardly less important than adequate pay. See discussion of this point in sec. 3–24 above; and on the subject of judicial pensions, see generally my article "Pensions for Judges," 27 Mich. L. Rev. 134 (1928); for recent figures on pensions, see 31 Jour. Am. Jud. Soc. 147 (1948).

sional prestige which he will enjoy after he has held such an office.

So far, I have spoken of problems of selection, tenure and compensation of trial judges. I cannot say that we have been quite successful, on the whole, in dealing with these problems. Nor can I give a more favorable report about our handling of problems of discipline and supervision.

The first and most important of existing checks on the behavior of the trial judge is threat of *reversal* for error. The Supreme Court will upset his judgment in a civil case, or his sentence in a criminal case, if the trial judge commits a substantial error of law or fails to comply with the standards which control him in any essential respect. The threat of reversal is effective as far as it goes; no judge wants to have his acts publicly exposed as erroneous.[12] The difficulty is that this remedy does not cover enough. It does not cover personal misconduct, unless it is obvious enough to get into the record and unless it is clearly prejudicial to a complaining party. Misconduct, such as drunkenness in or out of court, inattention on the bench or arbitrary refusal to listen to argument, manifestation of bias in front of the jury, and abuse of lawyers, cannot ordinarily be reached through threat of reversal.

A second possible check on the trial judge is threat of criminal liability for his acts. This threat applies to judges as well as to other persons; but it is not practically very important, since judicial misconduct, if it occurs, is not likely to be criminal in character. And civil liability of the judge as such, to individual parties is not recognized at all.

"Judges have always been accorded complete immunity for their judicial acts, even when their conduct is dictated by 'malicious' or improper motives. The reason is not a desire

---

[12] Furthermore, orders of the Supreme Court are enforcible against the trial judge by threat of personal punishment for contempt; so that we can say that they are backed by effective sanctions.

to protect the misbehaving official, but rather the necessity of preserving an independent judiciary, free from the undue influence of the threat, or even the possibility, of subsequent damage suits." [13]

The third check on the trial judge, operative where judges are elective, is the threat of *defeat* for re-election. The fear of such defeat may indeed check some kinds of misbehavior. The judge who has to be elected from time to time is inclined to be more polite than he might otherwise be to influential parties and attorneys. Only, defeat for re-election is indiscriminate; it cuts down the courageous and honest judge who has to make an unpopular decision as often as the judge who misbehaves in a way to displease the public. It is like a drastic medicine which kills disease but kills the patient, too. Its net effect is to destroy independent judicial behavior of all sorts.

Finally, there is the threat of removal from office by impeachment.[14] While the judge is legally subject to removal for personal misbehavior, this remedy is hardly ever used. The houses of the legislature are too busy with other things to deal with impeachments. Especially in states where judges are popularly elected, the disposition of the legislature is always to "pass the buck" to the electors. Impeachment proceedings are not even attempted, as a rule, except in the most flagrant cases of misconduct. Fortunately, judicial misbehavior is relatively rare, but I feel that it is nonetheless essential to have effective methods of removing judges when cases calling for removal do occur. In recent years in Detroit, for example, two judges have been repeatedly charged in the newspapers with drunkenness and other scandalous mis-

[13] PROSSER, TORTS 1075 (1941).
[14] In many states, judges are also removable by joint resolution of the houses of the legislature, called "address." If the reader is interested in a detailed discussion of methods of removal, I refer him to my article, "Removal and Retirement of Judges," 20 JOUR. AM. JUD. SOC. 133 (1936). This method is patterned after the British practice. It is applicable, either expressly or according to general understanding, to such cases as disability and incompetence, and not to cases of misconduct. It is even less frequently used than impeachment.

behavior. If these men are innocent it is not fair that such accusations go unheard; if they are guilty, it is not right that they remain in office. Yet nothing has been done about the charges against them; and there is no way now existing to eliminate an offending judge other than impeachment.

What is needed is a judicial method of removing judges for misconduct. The supreme court, or an administrative council composed of judges, should be vested with power to remove any misbehaving trial judge or judge of an inferior appellate court, after notice and hearing. This method of removal is used in other countries, and is provided for in a few states in this country.[15] Jurisdiction to remove judges for cause is not unlike jurisdiction to disbar attorneys. It should be exercised in a manner similar to disbarment proceedings.

Just as much needed as effective methods of removal is provision for *judicial supervision* of the personal conduct of the trial judge. One of the most common objections to judicial tenure during good behavior is that the judge who enjoys this tenure tends to become arbitrary and high-handed. Certain federal judges are pointed to as examples. As I have said in another place:

"Perhaps this objection is sometimes made by attorneys who are only aggrieved by the fact that they are not allowed to run wild in the federal courts as they are too often allowed to do in state courts where judges are afraid of political consequences. But one would not be warranted in assuming that this particular criticism is quite without basis in fact. The trial judge acts alone. He has a very wide discretion in many matters. He sits in hotly contested cases where essen-

[15] Alabama, Louisiana, Nebraska, New Jersey, New York, Oregon and Texas, provide for judicial removal of some or all judges for misbehavior. Provisions for such removal were introduced in New Jersey by the Constitution of 1947; they apply to judges of superior and county courts. Const. Art. VI, Sec. 6 (4). In 1947, New York, which had long provided for removal of justices of the peace and other petty judges, after trial by an appellate division of the supreme court (Const. Art. VI, Sec. 17), also made provision for removing judges of superior courts by judicial proceedings. Art. VI, Sec. 9–A.

tial facts are disputed and feeling runs high. He is on the firing line, so to speak, and subject to the greatest stress and strain. And in this connection it is worthy of note that the trial judge is the one most often charged with arbitrariness, high-handed conduct, and abuse of discretion. An occasional reversal of a case does not have that immediate and essential effect to restrain him in his everyday conduct. Even though his lapses may not be frequent, they should not go unchecked. The high-handed conduct of a single judge not only works serious injustice to individuals but through his conduct the entire bench suffers a serious impairment of its reputation and of public trust. It seems, therefore, desirable that there should be devised some supervision over the daily conduct and discretionary acts of the trial judge." [16]

In an earlier article, proposing a method of supervision for the federal bench, I discussed the form which such supervision should take:

"The officials best suited to exercise this supervision are the Chief Justice and the presiding circuit judges. The Chief Justice should give attention to the conduct of all federal judges; the presiding circuit judges should oversee the conduct of district judges. These supervisory authorities should undertake to restrain arbitrary and high-handed demeanor, abuses of discretion, and other minor judicial improprieties. They should suggest, criticize and admonish. Most of the common causes of complaint against federal judges should soon vanish if the Chief Justice and the presiding circuit judges were to act in the manner suggested, and especially if the power to supervise were reinforced by effective methods of removal in case of persistent misconduct. Each judge would have the feeling on all occasions that his conduct might come under the eye of the Chief Justice or the presiding circuit judge. He would constantly feel the need, as we ordinarily express it, 'to watch his step.'" [17]

[16] "Retirement and Removal of Judges," 20 Jour. Am. Jud. Soc. 133 at 134 (1936).
[17] "Federal Judges—Appointment, Supervision and Removal—Some Possibilities Under the Constitution," 28 Mich. L. Rev. 485, 723, 870, at 727 (1930). For an elaboration of this plan for supervision, see continuation of passage quoted.

If, as is certainly true, most of our trial judges do behave themselves as they should, this is because they have sound personal habits and the training of lawyers, and are controlled by social and extralegal sanctions, such as the opinion of fellow members of the bar and of other persons with whom they come in contact. It is not because of well-worked-out methods of disciplinary control. In fact, existing disciplinary methods of checking what I have called personal misconduct, are almost completely lacking or ineffective.

Sec. 3–27. Control of trial jury.* The jury is part and parcel of our adjudicative machinery.[1] Although its members are laymen and private citizens, the jury constitutes collectively an official agency. The function of the jury, as it is ordinarily stated, is to find the facts. There are various standards which govern the jury's activities and procedures, such as the rule which forbids the jury to talk about the case to outside persons during the course of the trial, rules regarding burden of proof, etc. In the aggregate, the rules are all intended to insure a fair consideration and determination of the facts by the jury on the basis of the proofs which are presented to it. The effectuation of these standards for jury behavior presents many distinctive problems, which I believe it is desirable to discuss separately from problems regarding control of other official agencies involved in the adjudicative processes.

---

* (I.R.) See generally regarding the trial jury, WILLOUGHBY, PRINCIPLES OF JUDICIAL ADMINISTRATION 482–512 (1929).

On the subject of jury selection, see Blume, "Jury Selection Analyzed; Proposed Revision of Federal System," 42 MICH. L. REV. 831 (1944), and Knox, "Jury Selection," 22 NEW YORK UNIV. L. Q. R. 433 (1947). See also the new federal statute relating to jury selection, 28 U. S. C. A., Sec. 1861 *et seq.*; Report to the Judicial Conference of Senior Circuit Judges of the United States of the Committee on Selection of Jurors (1942); Thiel v. Southern Pacific Company, 328 U. S. 217 (1946); and Fay v. New York, 332 U. S. 261 (1947).

[1] See sec. 3–11 above regarding the constitutional requirement of jury trial in criminal cases; and sec. 3–14 regarding the requirement of juries in civil cases.

Methods of selection are basic in the control of the jury as in the control of other official actors. Many methods have been employed since the early days of the English common law jury. Today, jury selection is governed by statutes in all jurisdictions, and these statutes vary greatly in substance and detail. It would only be confusing to try to describe all the methods of selection which have been, or which are now, in use. I shall give you only a description of common methods used, and of the usual agencies involved in the processes of jury selection.

In the older practice, a jury was often drawn by the sheriff pursuant to a specific order of the judge, to serve in the trial of a specific case. Today it is still possible in some instances to draw juries for the trial of specific cases; but usually the statutes provide for the preparation of a *comprehensive list* of eligible jurors in advance of need, and require that juries for most cases be drawn from this list. In our larger cities, this eligible list may embrace several thousand names, and in smaller localities, the number of names usually runs into the hundreds. The list is prepared in some jurisdictions by the sheriff, in some by a jury commissioner, and in many places today by a jury commission, consisting of two or more persons. From this eligible list, the clerk of the court, or some other specified official, draws by lot a smaller list, or *panel,* to serve on juries during a particular term of court. The reason for the large list, as well as the choice by lot, is to avoid the possibility of packing juries with persons of known views. The list and the juries to be drawn from it are supposed to represent a "cross section" of the community.

Persons drawn for jury service must meet certain statutory *qualifications.* They are usually required to possess: 1. physical capacity (e.g., be able to hear); 2. mental capacity (e.g., be of "sound mind and discretion"); 3. of good moral character; 4. a definite political status (e.g., citizenship or right to vote); 5. residence in the district of jury service; 6. a definite economic status (e.g., be a property owner or tax-payer), though this qualification is by no means universal. Persons who do not have these qualifications are normally to be excluded from the jury list by the sheriff or other official agency which makes up the list of persons eligible for jury service; though, of course, the judge will eliminate disqualified persons himself if any such get by the initial sifting procedures.

The make-up of jury lists and panels is further reduced by various statutory *exemptions*. For example, public officers and employees and persons engaged in certain professions, such as doctors, lawyers and teachers, are commonly exempt from jury service. An exempt person may serve or not at his election; the exemption belongs to him personally, and must be claimed by him; in this respect it differs from a disqualification.

Persons may also be *excused* from jury service if they satisfy the court in which they are called to serve that they have a valid reason for not serving at the particular time, such as an illness in the family which requires their presence at home.

Finally, constitutional provisions and statutes uniformly contain provisions intended to insure that the jury which is to try the particular case will be made up of persons who are able to hear and determine that case without *bias*. The application of these provisions involves selective activities of the judge and the parties concerned in the case to be tried. Accordingly, when a group of veniremen (persons called for jury service) is drawn for the trial of a case, the judge and counsel for the parties examine the proposed jurors to determine whether each one is impartial and able to perform his duties as juror properly. Each is asked whether he is opposed to the law applicable to the particular case, e.g., in a case in which the capital penalty may be involved, whether he is opposed to capital punishment. He is asked whether he has already formed and expressed an opinion concerning the facts of the case. He is asked whether he is biased for or against any of the parties in the case. He is asked whether he is interested (financially) in the outcome of the case. If it appears from the examination that the prospective juror is not impartial, he is challenged by interested counsel "for cause," or may be excused by the court on its own motion. In addition to the dismissal of persons for cause, statutes very commonly provide that parties are entitled to a certain number of peremptory challenges. Such challenges are to be used to get rid of persons whom the party in question (or his counsel) regards as likely to be hostile or unfavorable to his side. The general aim is the same as the aim of challenges for "cause." The difference is that no actual showing of bias must be made to appear; the peremptory challenge can be exercised without any explanation or statement of a reason for challenging the juror.

Theoretically, this combination of selective devices, starting with the preparation of a comprehensive jury list by an official agency, and followed by the drawing of a panel by lot, by exempting and excusing persons, and by striking off other persons for reasons of bias in the particular case, and finally by peremptory challenges, is supposed to result in a jury which is at one and the same time a cross section of the community, unbiased in its views, and satisfactory to all persons who are involved in the case to be tried. Actually, however, the average jury can hardly be said to represent a fair cross section of the community. Most of the ablest and busiest persons are able to avoid jury service by claiming exemptions or making excuses, and usually it is definitely to the interest of one party or the other to challenge the more intelligent jurors. The consequence is that only too often juries, especially in cities, are constituted of persons whose experience and capacity are below the average of the community. But I doubt if the remedy for this situation is to be found in the abandonment of jury trial—though as I have already pointed out, trial without jury is growing in popularity in some fields [2]—rather the practical remedy for inferior juries is to be sought in better and more discriminating methods of selection, in reducing the number of exemptions and excuses, and in improving the pay and other conditions of jury service.[3]

Inasmuch as the jury is made up of laymen, it cannot be expected to know the rules which are applicable to its official activities, the rules which apply to its weighing of evidence and its determination of facts. The judge always instructs the jury on request and, in fact, is required to instruct the jury as to its duties and procedures in determining the facts. But there are two kinds of verdicts which the jury may be required to give: a special verdict and a general verdict. A *special* verdict is a simple determination of facts which are disputed between the parties. Usually it takes the form of specific answers to specific questions of fact, e.g., "Did the defendant make such and such a promise?" and "Did the defendant perform this promise?" Such a verdict decides

[2] At its best, jury trial is not a very satisfactory device for settling civil litigation; it is cumbersome, costly in time and money, and unpredictable as regards results (see sec. 3–14). Waiver of jury trial, with consequent trial by the judge, is occurring with ever-growing frequency. In criminal cases I doubt if anyone, familiar with the jury's historic role in the development and protection of our liberties, would want to do away with the jury. Anyhow, abolition of jury trial would require constitutional amendment, and this could not be easily accomplished (see section 3–11).

[3] It is a common opinion today that the service of women as jurors has raised the quality of juries, since many well-qualified women have the time to serve. If this opinion be accepted as correct, it is unfortunate that the statutes in some states allow women to claim, as such, an exemption from jury service.

Regarding possibilities of improving methods of selecting juries, see the items cited in note * above.

only fact questions and leaves to the judge the task of applying the law to the facts found. The functions of finding facts and of applying law are, in effect, completely separated. The *general* verdict is of quite a different sort; it represents the more common practice in this country. It is applicable to all criminal cases and is employed in most civil cases. In rendering a general verdict, the jury performs two functions; it determines the disputed facts and applies the law to them. For instance, in a case where D is charged with the theft of X's goods, and defends on the grounds that he took the goods believing they were his own, and that he was insane at the time of the act, the jury does not specifically report in its verdict whether D took the goods of X, and if so, whether he thought they were his own, or if he was insane at the time he took them; instead the jury declares simply that D was guilty or not guilty of the crime charged. Such a verdict obviously requires that the jury not only decide what happened, i. e., the facts, but also that it employ the rules of law applicable to what happened. This in turn makes it necessary that the jury be instructed about the rules of law applicable to the facts in issue. The court must tell the jury what the law requires it to do in connection with all the possible fact conclusions which it may justifiably reach on the evidence presented to it. This often calls for very elaborate instructions; and the jury is left with the task of applying them to the actual facts.

From what has already been said you will realize that the judge exercises a substantial control over the jury. Indeed, he controls the jury's performance of its functions in several important ways. First, he determines *what evidence* is to be admitted for the jury's consideration. He passes on the admissibility of this evidence, bit by bit, as it is presented. Second, he *instructs* the jury regarding its own functions and procedures, and regarding the law of the case where a general verdict is to be found. Third, the trial judge in the common law practice was accustomed to *comment* on the weight of the evidence; he gave the jury the benefit of his opinion and advice in relation to the facts of the case. This practice is still followed in the federal courts, and in a substantial number of state courts.[4] However, in the majority of states this practice is no longer permitted; the judge is prohibited from indicating his opinion on the evidence in any way. Fourth, he is empowered to scrutinize the evidence which has been presented, and if he finds that the evidence on one side is altogether insufficient to support a verdict, he must *direct* the jury to find a *verdict* for the other side. As a recent writer says:

"In present-day practice a directed verdict is a device for taking a case from the jury when there is no issue of fact for the jury to decide. The jury brings in a verdict, but it is clearly recognized that the act of the jury is merely a matter of form. This practice must be carefully distinguished from (1) instruction on the law and (2) advice on the facts."[5]

Fifth, the judge may *set aside* the jury's *verdict* if he concludes that it is contrary to the great weight of evidence, or is supported by insufficient evidence. Thus, if a jury has found D guilty of a crime, the judge may set this verdict aside if he finds that the verdict is based on insufficient evidence to justify a finding of guilt beyond a reasonable doubt.[6]

---

[4] See Capital Traction Co. v. Hof, 174 U. S. 1 (1899) in regard to the judicial role in jury trial in the federal courts.

[5] Blume, "Origin and Development of the Directed Verdict," 48 MICH. L. REV. 555 (1950). It is almost impossible to give an accurate characterization of the directed verdict in a sentence or two. And this observation holds in somewhat less degree of the other devices herein mentioned. My purpose here is to point out methods of controlling jury action, not to furnish complete summations of the law. If the reader wishes further information regarding the directed verdict, he can profitably consult the article above cited.

[6] The double jeopardy clauses of our constitutions (which forbid an accused to be twice put in jeopardy for the same offense) are ordinarily construed to

In short, the judge supervises and checks the jury's fact-finding process in various ways just mentioned. The standards which require the jury to perform its functions in a certain manner are effectuated in a very real sense by this judicial control. However, it must not be supposed that the control of the judge over the jury's verdict is complete. The jury can ignore the judge's instructions with impunity. There was a time when juries in criminal cases were punishable for contempt in ignoring the court's instructions, and when juries in civil cases were liable to injured parties for returning improper verdicts.[7] But for almost three centuries now it has been established in all Anglo-American jurisdictions that a jury cannot be penalized, criminally or civilly, for rendering a wrong or perverse verdict. And inasmuch as the jury has a wide range of discretion anyway, in drawing its conclusions of fact from the evidence, it must be apparent that the jury has considerable freedom of action. The standards which control the jury, like all other standards which we have discussed, are only partial in their coverage and are by no means completely enforcible. The judge's control merely represents elements of guidance and enforcement of standards within the limited range where enforcement is feasible.

Sec. 3–28. Control of appellate judge.* The appellate judge, like all other persons involved in the adjudicative

---

forbid all attacks on a jury's verdict of acquittal. Such a verdict cannot be overturned by appeal or otherwise; it matters not if the most obvious errors have been committed, or if conclusive proof of guilt be later found; the jury's verdict of acquittal is final as to the prosecution of the defendant on the particular charge. However, a state can construe its double jeopardy clause differently and can accordingly provide for appeal by the prosecution without violating the due process clause of the Fourteenth Amendment; and two states have so provided. Palko v. Connecticut, 302 U. S. 319 (1937); and see AMERICAN LAW INSTITUTE CODE OF CRIMINAL PROCEDURE, sec. 428 and annotations at 1203 *et seq.*

[7] I HOLDSWORTH, HISTORY OF ENGLISH LAW 337–347 (1924).

* (I.R.) On the subject matter of this section, see generally the items cited in sec. 3–26, note *. In addition the reader should consult a study which has

process, is governed by standards. And the effectuation of standards in his case raises many of the same problems as the effectuation of the standards applicable to the trial judge; methods of selection are usually the same and methods of removal are also the same.[1]

But there are two important differences between the work of the appellate, and the work of the trial, judge. The trial judge normally sits alone. Every appellate court is made up of several men; often as many as nine sit and work together. The conduct and determinations of each appellate judge are, to a considerable extent, restrained and supervised by his fellow members on the court. Furthermore, the appellate judge works in a more quiet atmosphere than the trial judge; he works chiefly on legal problems far removed from the emotional strains of battle over facts. Both these differences mean that there is less need for checks on personal misbehavior of the appellate judge, such as outbursts of temper, etc.

And the control of the supreme court judge differs from the control of the trial judge and the intermediate appellate judge in another way. As in the case of the chief executive, the supreme court is not controlled or affected by any very direct or immediate legal sanctions.[2] The court has no superior. The proper behavior of supreme court justices is guaranteed chiefly by the quality of the persons who man the court. These men are almost invariably lawyers of long

been prepared for the Council of State Governments by Spector and which has just appeared in preliminary draft. The study is entitled *The Courts of Last Resort of the Forty-Eight States* (1950). It covers selection, compensation, removal and retirement of state supreme court justices as well as other important features of supreme court organization.

[1] See sec. 3–26.

[2] Only the threat of impeachment and defeat for re-election are worth mentioning. Both are remote, and the latter is indiscriminate. Nevertheless there does not appear to exist any pressing need for additional ways of checking or removing supreme court judges. Thoroughly bad individuals are not apt to reach the supreme court; and, if a judge in that high office misbehaves, his conduct is likely to evoke action where the misdeeds of an inferior judge might not.

training and experience; their ideals and purposes are derived from this legal background. If such men are swayed at all by outside influences, they are moved chiefly by a regard for public opinion and especially for the opinion of their brethren at the bar. As a matter of fact, both appointment and popular election work better in relation to supreme court judges than they do in relation to judges of inferior courts. Thus, I think it is clear throughout the years that most appointees to the Supreme Court of the United States have been outstanding men; [3] and even the elective process which is employed in most of our states has worked reasonably well in the selection of supreme court judges. The prestige of such judgeships means that many good lawyers are ready to accept appointment or election; political bosses who use their power over the choice of other officials almost openly to serve their own ends, do hesitate to install venal men or men of questionable reputation on the supreme bench. Furthermore, judges of our supreme courts are chosen, if they are elected, for terms which are usually longer than the terms of trial justices; [4] their pay is also better, and the tradition of re-electing them is more common; so that these judges enjoy a greater degree of independence than trial judges do. I do not think that our methods of choosing and controlling the judges of our supreme courts are by any means ideal; and yet it is only fair to say that the average of men

[3] Some persons may be inclined to challenge this statement. They will point to the appointment of many New Dealers to the Supreme Court by President Roosevelt. I shall have to answer that whether one likes the social philosophy of these appointees or not, practically all of them were men of outstanding ability. So long as the President has the power to appoint, and so long as the Supreme Court makes the important policy determinations that it does, we shall have to expect that the President will choose appointees whose social views are in general accord with his own.

[4] For example, in Pennsylvania, justices of the supreme court are chosen for twenty-one years: judges of the principal trial courts, for ten years; and in Michigan, supreme court justices are chosen for eight years, judges of the circuit courts for six.

on our supreme courts is far above the average of government personnel, in regard to both ability and integrity.

Sec. 3–29. Problems. 1. *Tumey v. Ohio.*[1] Chief Justice Taft delivered the opinion of the court:

"The question in this case is whether certain statutes of Ohio, in providing for the trial by the mayor of a village of one accused of violating the Prohibition Act of the State, deprive the accused of due process of law and violate the Fourteenth Amendment to the Federal Constitution, because of the pecuniary and other interest which those statutes give a mayor in the result of the trial. . . .

"All questions of judicial qualification may not involve constitutional validity. Thus matters of kinship, personal bias, state policy, remoteness of interest, would seem generally to be matters merely of legislative discretion. *Wheeling v. Black,* 25 W. Va. 266, 270. But it certainly violates the Fourteenth Amendment, and deprives a defendant in a criminal case of due process of law, to subject his liberty or property to the judgment of a court the judge of which has a direct personal, substantial, pecuniary interest in reaching a conclusion against him in his case.

"The Mayor of the Village of North College Hill, Ohio, had a direct, personal, pecuniary interest in convicting the defendant who came before him for trial, in the twelve dollars of costs imposed in his behalf, which he would not have received if the defendant had been acquitted. . . . But the pecuniary interest of the Mayor in the result of his judgment is not the only reason for holding that due process of law is denied to the defendant here. The statutes were drawn to stimulate small municipalities in the country part of counties in which there are large cities, to organize and maintain courts to try persons accused of violations of the Prohibition Act everywhere in the county. The inducement is offered by dividing between the State and the village the large fines provided by the law for its violations. The trial is to be had before a mayor without a jury, without oppor-

[1] 273 U. S. 510 at 514–15, 523, 532, 533 (1927).

tunity for retrial and with a review confined to questions of law presented by a bill of exceptions, with no opportunity by the reviewing court to set aside the judgment on the weighing of evidence, unless it should appear to be so manifestly against the evidence as to indicate mistake, bias or willful disregard of duty by the trial court. The statute specifically authorizes the village to employ detectives, deputy marshals and other assistants to detect crime of this kind all over the county, and to bring offenders before the Mayor's court, and it offers to the village council and its officers a means of substantially adding to the income of the village to relieve it from further taxation. The Mayor is the chief executive of the village. . . . He is charged with the business of looking after the finances of the village. It appears from the evidence in this case, and would be plain if the evidence did not show it, that the law is calculated to awaken the interest of all those in the village charged with the responsibility of raising the public money and expending it, in the pecuniarily successful conduct of such a court."

Accordingly, the Court held that the defendant, tried for offenses against the Ohio prohibition law in the circumstances above indicated, had been denied due process of law; and the judgment of the Supreme Court of Ohio, upholding his conviction, was reversed.

The decision of this case is expressed in terms of the lack of due process. How would you restate the court's conclusions in terms of motivation of judicial behavior and of the effectuation of standards applicable to such behavior?

2. Consider the following discussion of methods of retiring disabled and superannuated judges: [2]

"Another device for eliminating disabled or superannuated judges is compulsory retirement at a fixed age. This particular device is chosen in order to escape the difficulty of passing on individual cases and of making invidious distinctions between individuals affected. Often the individual who ought

[2] Shartel, "Retirement and Removal of Judges," 20 JOUR. AM. JUD. SOC. 133 at 137, 138 (1936).

to be retired does not realize that he has ceased to be able to perform his functions. It is not easy for others to tell him that he has lost his fitness for his job. A compulsory retirement makes the process of elimination easy and quite impersonal. But while the administrative difficulty is thus avoided, the legislative problem is not. Is it feasible to fix a uniform age for compulsory retirement? If so, what shall be the age thus fixed by constitution or statute? The fact is that not all men become incapacitated at the same age. Some men are old at 50, while occasionally a man retains his faculties and full vigor until 90 or over. Whatever age of retirement is set, some waste of competent man power will result; the judicial system will lose the experience and ability of some men who still have all their faculties though they have passed the fixed age. Against this waste must be balanced the advantage of eliminating dead timber. That it is not easy to fix a uniform age for retirement is attested by the not uncommon opinion of competent persons that such an age is not possible to fix and by the marked diversity of opinion among other persons as to what the proper age should be. But admitting the difficulties it does not seem to the writer that fixing an age for judicial retirement is different in kind from fixing an age for any other significant act or event. The age for majority is typical; not all persons arrive at the age of discretion at the same time. Nevertheless we must and do fix such an age on the basis of a general estimate. And no one has ever felt that the fact that some good professors or army officers or business executives will be put on the shelf by an automatic superannuation provision constituted a conclusive reason against such a requirement. If provision is made for part-time service by retired judges, the waste of man power need not be great; almost all states have overcrowded dockets. The retired judge can always sit if he is willing, and be assigned to the types of matters for which he is best fitted."

Can one regard methods of retirement as devices for controlling judicial behavior? Compare methods of retirement with methods of selection, in this respect.

3. *Hancock v. Elam.*[3] Nicholson, C. J., delivered the opinion of the Court:

"This suit was brought by Hancock to recover of Mary L. Elam $228 for work and labor, in repairing a mill. The jury found a verdict for defendant, and plaintiff has appealed. . . .

"In this case, after the jury had been out from eleven o'clock until dinner time, which we suppose was about one o'clock, upon returning into Court and announcing that they could not agree, and that they did not disagree as to the evidence, or the charge of the Court, the Sheriff was peremptorily ordered 'to lock them up until they should agree,' and that, without allowing them to have their dinners before being locked up. The jurors might very well understand from this order, that they were required either to agree or to submit to indefinite confinement and starvation. They were ordered to be locked up until they should agree. They did agree in the course of several hours, but whether their disagreement was harmonized, under free, patient investigation and deliberation, or under the apprehension of prolonged confinement and starvation, we have no means of determining. We can see, however, that under the influence of such an arbitrary order, jurors may have yielded their convictions, in order to avoid the threatened consequence of continued disagreement. . . .

"The verdict is, therefore, set aside, and the judgment reversed."

How would you state the prohibitive standard applicable to the judge's act in this case? How is this standard enforced?

4. *Thiel v. Southern Pacific Co.*[4]

Plaintiff brought action in a California court against the defendant railroad for injuries caused by the latter's negligence. The case was removed to a federal court on the ground of diversity of citizenship. At the start of the trial, plaintiff moved to strike the jury panel because the jury

[3] 62 Tenn. 33 (1874).
[4] 328 U. S. 217 (1946).

commissioner and clerk of the court had excluded all daily wage earners from the jury. These officials testified that the exclusion of wage earners was motivated by knowledge that the federal district judges had consistently excused such persons from jury service because of pecuniary hardship (i. e., the pay for jury service was only $4.00 per day). The district court denied plaintiff's motion. The jury found a verdict for defendant, and on appeal the circuit court of appeals affirmed a judgment for defendant. The Supreme Court granted certiorari. Held—the exclusion of daily wage earners in drawing the jury panel was improper, and the judgment was reversed.

Murphy, J., speaking for the Supreme Court said in part:

"The American tradition of trial by jury, considered in connection with either criminal or civil proceedings, necessarily contemplates an impartial jury drawn from a cross section of the community. *Smith v. Texas*, 311 U. S. 128, 130; *Glasser v. United States*, 315 U. S. 60, 85. This does not mean, of course, that every jury must contain representatives of all the economic, social, religious, racial, political and geographical groups of the community; frequently such complete representation would be impossible. But it does mean that prospective jurors shall be selected by court officials without systematic and intentional exclusion of these groups. Recognition must be given to the fact that those eligible for jury service are to be found in every stratum of society. Jury competence is an individual rather than a group or class matter. That fact lies at the very heart of the jury system. To disregard it is to open the door to class distinctions and discriminations which are abhorrent to the democratic ideals of trial by jury. . . .

"The undisputed evidence in this case demonstrates a failure to abide by the proper rules and principles of jury selection. Both the clerk of the court and the jury commissioner testified that they deliberately and intentionally excluded from the jury lists all persons who work for a daily wage. They generally used the city directory as the source of names of prospective jurors. In the words of the clerk, 'If I see in the directory the name of John Jones and it says he is a longshoreman, I do not put his name in, because I have found by experience that that man will not serve as a juror, and I will not get people who will qualify. The minute that a juror is called into court on a venire and says he is working for $10 a day and cannot afford to work for $4, the Judge has never made one of those men serve, and so in order to avoid putting names of people in who I know won't become jurors in the court, won't qualify as jurors in this court, I do leave them out. . . . Where I thought the designation indicated that they were day laborers, I mean they were people who were compensated solely when they were working by the day, I leave them out.' The jury commissioner corroborated this testimony, adding that he purposely excluded 'all the iron craft, bricklayers, carpenters and machinists' because in the past 'those men came into court and offered that (financial hardship) as an excuse, and the judge usually let them go.' The evidence indicated, however, that laborers who were paid weekly or monthly wages were placed on the jury lists, as well as the wives of daily wage earners.

"It was further admitted that business men and their wives constituted at least 50% of the jury lists, although both the clerk and the commissioner denied that they consciously chose according to wealth or occupation. Thus the admitted discrimination was limited to those who worked for a daily wage, many of whom might suffer financial loss by serving on juries at the rate of $4 a day and would be excused for that reason.

"This exclusion of all those who earn a daily wage cannot be justified by federal or state law. Certainly nothing in the federal statutes warrants such an exclusion. And the California statutes are equally devoid of justification for the practice. . . .

"It is clear that a federal judge would be justified in excusing a daily wage earner for whom jury service would entail an undue financial hardship. But that fact cannot support the complete exclusion of all daily wage earners regardless of whether there is actual hardship involved. Here there was no effort, no intention, to determine in advance which individual members of the daily wage-earning class would suffer an undue hardship by serving on a jury at the rate of $4 a day.[5] All were systematically and automatically excluded."

Frankfurter, J., and Reed, J., dissented. Jackson, J., took no part in the decision of the case.

How is this decision related to the methods of controlling a trial jury above discussed? Does the decision really meet the problem presented by the $4.00 per diem allowance for jury service? [6]

USE OF STANDARDS FOR OFFICIALS

Sec. 3–30. Use by executive officials. We have now mentioned the standards applicable to various official acts, and have examined the ways in which these standards are effectuated. It is necessary to consider also the intentional uses of these standards, the ways in which they are used to guide action. How are these official standards used, and by whom? How does O, the official actor, use them? What use do courts make of them? How are they used by the individual and his legal counselor? And in what ways are they used by the student of the law? [1]

The standards with which we are now concerned are addressed primarily to the official actor, O. He is in the position

[5] The compensation of jurors is now fixed at $7.00 per day in the federal courts, "except that any juror required to attend more than thirty days in hearing one case may be paid in the discretion and upon the certification of the trial judge a per diem fee not exceeding $10 for each day in excess of thirty days he is required to hear such case." U. S. C. A. tit. 28, § 1871.

[6] Regarding the decision in this case, see note in 59 HARV. L. REV. 1167 (1946), and article by Fraenkel, "The Supreme Court and Civil Rights: 1946 Term," 47 COL. L. REV. 953 at 959 (1947).

It is interesting to compare the effects of systematic racial discrimination in the drawing of juries. Smith v. Texas, 311 U. S. 128 (1940) and Akins v. Texas, 325 U. S. 398 (1945); and the effects of the selection of so-called special or "blue ribbon" juries for criminal trials in state courts. Fay v. New York, 332 U. S. 261 (1947), noted in 46 MICH. L. REV. 262 (1947) and discussed in the article by Fraenkel above cited.

[1] The discussion in the present subtopic parallels the discussion of ways of using standards for the individual, secs. 2–43 to 2–48, inclusive.

of hearer, and is intended to shape his acts by reference to the standards. In this sense they are standards for O's use; they cover, in more or less detail, important acts which he may do or think of doing. But these standards are not quite independent; in very large part they connect O's act with A's. Very frequently, the official begins by using a standard applicable to the individual's act in the manner described in the last chapter.[2] Thus O, a policeman who is patrolling the street, applies such a standard for individual action when he notes that A, the driver of a car, is speeding. On the basis of this observation regarding A's conduct, O will employ a standard applicable to his own official act, a standard which tells him what to do on such an occasion.[3] As you see, O is called upon to apply two sets of standards, those applicable to A and those applicable to himself; he considers whether A is subject to arrest, and, if so, how he shall make the arrest. In both respects O makes use of legally prescribed standards; he checks the elements of an act (A's or his own) against the specifications of a standard. O's method of applying standards is not essentially different from the method employed by A when A uses standards in planning his acts or in sizing up their effects.[4]

The chief executive or any superior official may make similar uses of standards applicable to individual and official acts. A police chief, for example, may have to test a series of acts, including his own, by the applicable standards. Thus, he may first have to decide whether there is sufficient evidence to indicate that A was speeding or that he was driving while drunk; then, whether O who arrested A behaved according to the standards applicable to an arrest; and finally the chief may have to decide what the presented facts require him to

---

[2] Sec. 2-45.
[3] Here, O's use of a standard to guide his own action parallels the individual's use of a standard to guide his acts. Sec. 2-44.
[4] Sec. 2-44.

do and the manner in which he is to do it. If he believes that A cannot be shown to have violated any standard or that O acted improperly in arresting A, the chief may be bound to order A's discharge. If he thinks that A is probably guilty and that his subordinate has acted properly, the standard applicable to his own act requires that he have A detained and produced before a magistrate on the morrow. The performance of his proper functions may require such a superior executive to use not only the standards applicable to A's acts, but also the standards governing the acts of his inferiors and those which govern his own.

Sec. 3–31. Use by the courts. The trial judge is often called upon to apply the proper standards to the acts of individuals. The method which he uses in applying such standards has already been described.[1] He applies standards to the acts of officials and official agencies in essentially the same manner. And his own acts are also governed by standards. These he must look to and use in laying out his own courses of action.[2] They determine his powers and functions; they define the acts which he must do in supervising and conducting a trial. They specify methods he must use in bringing the case to issue, and in admitting evidence to the jury; they determine the manner in which he is to instruct the jury, and enter judgment or sentence; they determine when he is to direct a verdict, set a verdict aside, and so on.

The supreme court, in its turn, may be called upon to use standards applicable to the acts of A, to the acts of O, to the acts of the jury, and to the acts of the trial judge; the court may have to decide whether any or all these acts have been performed according to applicable standards. In examining these prior acts of individuals and official agencies, and in taking action based thereon, the supreme court is also

---

[1] See sec. 2–45.

[2] Here the judge's use of a standard, i.e., to guide his own action, parallels the individual's use of a standard to guide his acts (sec. 2–44).

guided by standards; it applies them in its own acts. So that the supreme court's use of standards may represent a sequence of applications comparable to the series of acts described in "The House That Jack Built."

Sec. 3–32. Use by A and his counselor—reliance on O's habits. All standards are addressed primarily to a limited group of persons, but all standards are important also, in a secondary sense, to other persons than the addressees, because these others are affected one way or another by what the addressees do. In this sense, A may be concerned with the standards applicable to acts which O has done.[1] His rights may depend on O's acts, and he may have to know whether O has acted effectively. He may be injured by an act that O has done, and need to decide whether O has behaved in a manner which will warrant his recourse to the courts for an injunction, or other remedy. These secondary uses of standards addressed to O hardly require further elaboration, in view of what has already been said about multiple uses of standards, and inasmuch as the methods of applying such standards to O's acts are essentially the same as various other applications of standards already discussed.

But A's concern with acts of O, like his concern with acts of B, is not limited to past acts of O, to acts that O has already done. On the contrary, A often needs to predict the future behavior of O.[2] He has to rely on what O is going to do. For the purpose of prediction, A rests his calculations on observations of the past behavior of O. Sometimes A may use the prescribed standards for official behavior as a basis for predicting what O will do; A expects O to perform his duties and exercise his powers as prescribed by legal stand-

[1] Compare the discussion of A's application of standards to acts which B has done (sec. 2–46).

[2] The discussion in this section of the bases for predicting O's behavior parallels the discussion in sec. 2–46 of the bases for predicting B's behavior.

ards; A predicates this expectation on the general law-abiding habits of officials. But the standard itself merely tells A *what* O is supposed to do; it does not form a basis for predicting *whether* he will act according to its terms. O's known habits are the basis for that kind of calculation.

If legal standards covered every act which O might do, and if these standards were completely effectuated, A might in all cases rely on legal standards as a basis for prediction. But much of official conduct falls beyond coercive legal standards. A large part of O's conduct is privileged, or discretionary.[3] What will O do in areas where he is free to act or not to act? So far as A's planning depends on what he can expect O to do, A has just two things to rely on—O's habits and his declared intentions. For example, if A is a busy doctor and is called as a witness in a suit between X and Y, he hopes to be put on the stand at once and without delay. Can he count on this courtesy? Or must he expect to cool his heels for a half day while he waits for his turn to be called to the stand? The answer lies in the discretion of Judge Jones, presiding at the trial. A may rely on the known practice of Judge Jones to interrupt the course of a trial and put the busy witness on the stand out of turn. Or he may rely on the personal assurance of Judge Jones that this will be done. Moreover, officials do not always act according to standards. And what is just as important, their activities do not always eventuate as they are supposed to do. On the one side, there is the discrepancy between prescribed standards and the forms which behavior actually takes. On the other, there are various practical factors which may defeat the operation of legal remedies.* Thus, in the case of a

[3] See sec. 3–04 regarding the unregulated areas of official action; and compare secs. 2–05, 2–07, 2–11 and 2–46 regarding the unregulated areas of individual action.

* (I.R.) These two propositions constitute for me the gist of the "realist" position. The relevant items regarding the realist point of view are very numerous; I shall suggest only a few, in order of date of publication. These

banker who is about to loan money to B, the capacity of B to repay it may loom larger than B's legal obligation. The banker may be more interested in the fact that the legal means of collection may fail for various reasons, that official aid may be very costly, or may be futile in the sense that a judgment may be uncollectible. Or again, A, whose car has been damaged in a collision through the fault of B, must consider not only whether a jury ought to give him a full recovery for his loss, but also the question whether there is some chance that the legal processes through which he will obtain compensation may go awry at some point. B may have ways to evade or defeat A's claim. B's witnesses may contradict A's, and the jury may believe B's witnesses. Or the jury may be prejudiced against A, and may reject his claim in spite of all the evidence in his favor. And finally, if A is one of the "bad men" about whom Holmes speaks,[4] he counts upon the discrepancies between legal standards and official acts for his own advantage. Let us say he contemplates opening a gambling establishment. He knows well enough that he will be acting contrary to legal standards. He bases his calculations of profit on his ability to evade official sanctions and to corrupt certain officials and to make gains large enough to offset the costs of fines and losses. In all the cases I have mentioned, A has to look first of all to actual patterns of official behavior. He uses them as bases for calcu-

represent different attitudes toward the realist viewpoint. A full citation of articles maintaining the realist point of view is appended to Llewellyn's second article cited below (at pages 1257–1259).

Ehrlich, Fundamental Principles of the Sociology of Law (1912), a translation from the German in Harvard Studies in Jurisprudence, 1936.

Frank, Law and Modern Mind (1930), reprinted in 1950.

Fuller, "American Legal Realism," 82 U. of Pa. L. Rev. 429 (1934).

Holmes, "The Path of the Law," 10 Harv. L. Rev. 457 (1897).

Llewellyn, "A Realistic Jurisprudence–The Next Step," 30 Col. L. Rev. 431 (1930).

Llewellyn, "Some Realism about Realism," 44 HARV. L. REV. 1222 (1931).

Pound, "The Call for a Realistic Jurisprudence," 44 Harv. L. Rev. 697 (1931).

[4] See sec. 2–32, problem 3.

lating possible acts of O. He is justified in resting his calculations on legal standards only so far as these can be identified with the lines that official behavior will probably take.

A's legal counselor has a large part in A's forecasts of official action, and in planning the practical results of A's own action. Both the counselor's knowledge of law and his experience with legal affairs are brought to bear in these respects. The successful counselor learns early in his practice to weigh his chances of achieving actual results. He learns how important it is to think out and provide for the various contingencies which may arise under a contract, deed, mortgage or will that he is drafting. He learns that promises are not always kept; that doubtful promises are usually construed by each party according to his self-interest; that vague or inadequately drafted instruments may entail the necessity for court action to determine meaning. He learns to appreciate the difference between the standards in the books and the results which can be achieved through official aid.[5] He learns—and advises A accordingly—that there is a vast difference between having a lawsuit and having the means of proving it; that even when evidence is available, the processes of proof are uncertain and fraught with hazards, such as the disappearance or impeachment of a key witness; that it is usually better to settle a lawsuit at a substantial discount than to incur the cost, suffer the delays, and run the risks of litigation; that there is no point in pursuing an expensive lawsuit to a conclusion against a defendant who is uncollectible; that the bias of juries counts heavily in certain cases. In short, he has to learn how to plan his client's lawsuit

[5] The importance of this aspect of the lawyer's role was first clearly stated by Justice Holmes. He said that the real meaning of legal rules inheres in their probable application by judges and other agents of the state, that the lawyer must be able to foretell what these officials are going to do, that the lawyer's primary function is that of prophecy. See "The Path of the Law," 10 HARV. L. REV. 457 (1897).

and draft his client's documents, and guide his client's acts in the light not only of knowledge of legal standards but also of experience with human contact, especially official conduct.

Sec. 3–33. Use by student of official standards and habit patterns—academic and practical training. In the foregoing section and others,[1] I have tried to give you a picture of various kinds of work which the legal counselor is called upon to do. These materials suggest at the same time important lines of preparation and training which the legal counselor needs to have. They suggest uses of official standards which the student of the law must learn to make, and uses of official habit patterns which he must become familiar with. In the present section, I want to deal with these necessary skills and the times and methods of acquiring them, in other words with the what, when, and how of these parts of S's legal education.

S, the student of the law, must first of all learn to use legal standards, to analyze fact situations, and to fit them to legal standards. The importance of this side of his training has been stressed in our discussion of uses which he makes of standards applicable to the individual.[2] We saw how S follows and criticizes the applications of standards which others have made in actual cases, and how he makes manifold hypothetical applications of standards, and thus acquires experience in their use. Standards applicable to officials are used by S in the same ways. He can make similar examinations of others' applications of standards to official acts, and make similar hypothetical applications of official standards.[3] In

---

[1] See secs. 2–44, 2–46, 2–47.

[2] See sec. 2–47.

[3] And if we are thinking of S's experience in applying standards to official acts we must also count here the numerous standards and methods to be mentioned in subsequent chapters: in Chapter 4, standards and methods which govern the legislator's act; in Chapter 5, those which control the inter-

fact, there are no marked differences between the uses he makes of the two kinds of standards. Everything I have said about uses of standards for the individual is relevant here; and everything I shall say here about uses of official standards applies equally to the use of both kinds of standards. I aim chiefly to expand and drive home some of the points already suggested regarding the place in legal education of exercise in the use of standards.

As our law schools are set up and operate, the law student's work is preponderantly theoretical. This is another way of saying that he is a nonparticipant in the legal scene. He studies the operation of the legal system from the outside. His detachment from the legal scene carries certain advantages and also involves certain limitations. Both advantages and limitations are reflected in the uses which he makes of legal standards.

One advantage of S's detached position is that it allows him to wrestle with a very wide variety of problems of applying standards. The variety far exceeds the bounds of the direct experiences which S might have with actual cases. The law reports make available a large supply of materials for re-examination. And these materials are found in a form to show how a court has worked out a problem of application. They are well adapted for study and the development of the capacity to think in legal terms. In these respects, the reported cases constitute a fund for instruction hardly equalled in any other art or science. When we add to S's opportunity to work with reported cases, his chance for discussing, analyzing, and dealing with hypothetical situations,

preter's act of construing legislation; in Chapter 6, those which guide the judicial lawmaker's acts of finding, making, and unmaking law; and finally in Chapter 7, those which determine or shape the acts of various policymakers. All these important official acts and the standards applicable to them can be, in fact must be, studied by S in the same manner as the official standards mentioned in the present chapter.

we find that S has an almost unlimited scope for exercise in the use of standards.

Another advantage of S's detached treatment of cases is the fact that it makes possible an objective attitude towards the standards themselves and their applications. S can view a legal problem impartially from every side. He does not have to apply standards in cases which affect his interests or sympathies in any way. For this reason, he can be free of the natural bias of those who are touched by the actual operation of the legal system. A, who drives a car and collides with another car, cannot be expected to view the event with the same detachment as S; A is naturally swayed by the impulse to justify what he has done or failed to do. Even his counselor's thinking tends to take on the color of A's interest. Nor is S required to apply individual or official standards to a concrete occurrence, which may affect the lives of real human beings—as judge and jury must do. To be sure, judge and jury are normally more objective than the parties themselves, or their witnesses, because judge and jury have no personal stake in the decision of the controversy before them, and because they are chosen by methods which are designed to eliminate the element of bias as far as possible. Nevertheless, judge and jury see the parties and hear their "real life" stories; judge and jury cannot be entirely unaffected by factors of human sympathy or prejudice. S is one step further removed from the actual facts. He does not have to make a decision which will have practical effects. He can, if he will, view each case from all angles. He can, if he tries, acquire habits of objective judgment. Such habits will serve him well even when, later on, he assumes the position of counselor and representative of a particular point of view. He will need to anticipate the points which his opponents can make as well as those which he ought to make himself.

But the law student is getting ready for the time when he will make actual uses of legal standards in the practice of the law. His exercise in analyzing cases and applying standards is only preparatory for his functions as counselor and advocate; it has to be supplemented by exercise in doing the practical work of a lawyer. Ultimately he has to acquire experience as adviser, as draftsman of instruments, as pleader, and perhaps as judge and as draftsman of legislation. The student needs to learn how to use the law library, i. e., how to find the standards which he is to apply. He needs to learn how to prepare briefs, i. e., how to use previous applications of standards in decided cases in order to support his own lines of argument. He needs to learn to draft important instruments, and to try cases.

The whole approach to these practical jobs is different from the approach which one takes to the study of decided or hypothetical cases. In the study of cases, one tries to multiply all the legal possibilities and to resolve them as far as one can. One tries to develop a grasp of legal standards by making all possible applications of them, normal and abnormal. One tries to develop a sense for distinctions by working them out into the greatest refinements. By contrast, in doing a practical job the actor aims primarily to insure desired results. He wants to accomplish something constructive, not merely analyze situations in legal terms. Above all he is minded to do a safe job. He does not see how close he can come to legal shoals, but adopts a safe course. He draws a pleading, so far as he can, which does not raise legal questions. He draws an instrument, such as a long-term lease or a contract, in which all probable points of dispute between his client and the other party are covered and provided for. He is not interested in peculiar situations and difficulties as such. Rather, he aims to avoid difficult legal problems if he can. He uses his experience with legal standards and legal methods as means of avoiding legal problems.

There is no question in anyone's mind about S's need for practical training for law practice. The only questions are when and how this kind of training is to be given. Some older practitioners think extensive practical training should be given in the law schools; and are inclined to criticize the schools for sending their graduates out incompletely prepared for practice. On the other hand the law schools acknowledge only a minimum obligation to give the student practical training. They recognize an obligation to give him some experience in the use of the law library, some experience in the drawing of pleadings and argument of disputed points of law, and some experience in the drafting of important instruments. But almost all law teachers are convinced—and their views determine the policies of the schools—that the place to learn to practice law is in actual law practice, that the law school cannot go far in training the student to practice law, that the law school has neither the time nor the facilities for giving such training efficiently. Three years is felt to be little enough time in which to introduce the law student to the various fields in which he has to make use of legal standards and legal methods. If there were any slack time, over and above what is needed for a sound academic training (plus a minimum initiation in practical methods), I believe, and I think most experienced law teachers believe, that the law student should be detached from the law school by just that much sooner, and sent out into practice where he can learn most speedily and efficiently how to write briefs, to advise clients, to draft instruments, and to try cases.

Legal education is sometimes compared unfavorably with medical, in regard to this matter of practical training. It is pointed out that the medical student is given not only academic training in medical science but a substantial amount of practical training in medical work—contact with patients and experience in use of medical and surgical procedures. Even the general practitioner of medicine has to have at least one year of interneship beyond the normal period of four years in medical school, in which he learns to use the medical science with which he has become familiar. And the specialist has to put in several additional years beyond that. The suggestion is then made or implied that the processes of legal education have nothing to correspond to the practical training of the physician. But the difference in this regard between legal and medical education is merely apparent. Probably the actual academic part of the training for the two professions does not differ greatly in quantity. Most of law school training is of the academic type for a period of three years, and I think it is safe to estimate that no less than three years of the five or more which the young physician must spend in school and in the hospital are really academic in character. Probably the young lawyer needs as long a subsequent period of practical work as the young physician in order to get a grasp of his professional tasks. This is recognized in a few jurisdictions by specific provision for an apprenticeship in law practice before the young lawyer is admitted to the bar.[4] Likewise, in most European countries service of an extended apprenticeship is a prerequisite to admission to the profession. This kind of service corresponds in all essentials to a medical interneship. But in most states in this country no such requirement of practical preparation exists; this does not signify any essential difference, however, between the two professions in regard to academic and practical training. It only means that the young lawyer gets his license to practice before he is fully prepared; he has to obtain the bulk of his practical training after he is admitted to the bar.

[4] Until almost the end of the 19th century the predominant form of legal training in the U. S. was of the apprentice type. Relatively few of the men who went to the bar were trained in school. The law student prepared himself in a law office under the supervision of a practitioner. This form of training resulted in an undue emphasis of the practical, and a serious neglect of theoretical and systematic preparation. Blackstone and a few other texts were read by the student, but the bulk of the training of the young lawyer was derived from observing and aiding the work of his practitioner-teacher.

In recent years the law student's preoccupation with legal standards and their application has been vigorously criticized from another angle, by a group of so-called "realists." * These writers say that legal standards are abstract and give S a totally misleading impression of the activities, and the relations, of individuals and officials. They say the traditional approach involves a neglect of realities, that descriptions of behavior are more significant than standards of behavior, that what is needed by S is an appreciation of the way individuals and officials behave in actual life.[5] They stress the habit factors which were mentioned in the last and other sections. As regards the law student, they declare that he needs to be taught to perform the prophetic functions which Holmes ascribes to the lawyer. He needs to be made to realize that legal standards are not descriptions of reality, but merely ideal pictures. Lawyers and judges come to the realization of this fact through their experience with the actual operation of the law. And the law student should have the difference between the ideal and the actual hammered into him so that later on he will properly evaluate his own observations along this line, and so that he will be spared the disillusionment entailed by having impossible ideals destroyed by his future experiences in practice.

* (I.R.) See bibliography on the realists in sec. 3–32, note *.
[5] Toward the end of the last, and the beginning of the present, century our American legal scholarship and teaching were justifiably criticized, too, for dealing with their subject matter in a social vacuum. Writers and teachers took law as it was and hardly asked about its social functions. Lawyers, writers, and students (and I was a student myself when this was the case) concentrated on the technical niceties of existing law. That was the day of what Pound has called "mechanical jurisprudence." Lawyers lived in a "heaven of juristic conceptions." The social background of the law and its relations to real people were hardly mentioned in those days. Holmes, Pound, and Wigmore were the spearheads of a general attack on this traditional approach which neglected social functions and the ends of law. Most of what these pioneers stood for and taught, has now become well accepted; it constitutes the most important part of our present-day notions regarding legal policies. I mention this change in approach in passing only because it also affected the direction of legal education. I shall leave consideration of policies to our last chapter: Legal Policies and Policy Making.

No doubt these writers have helped to correct a one-sided stress on legal standards and their manipulation. No doubt the lawyer does need to know business practices, the ways of life, and the habits of all kinds of people. When I was a law student this sort of thing was hardly mentioned. The modern law teacher tries to complete his classroom presentation with all the material he can muster, regarding the actual operation of the legal system and regarding the habits of individuals and officials so far as they are relevant to the operation of the legal system. He points out the discrepancies which do often exist between legal standards and their effectuation. He tries to fill out his classroom discussion with necessary references to the practices of business and actual modes of living. You will note, indeed, that I have given you a great deal of material of this realistic type in this and the next preceding chapter; and you will find that the same approach and presentation of material is adopted in most of your regular law courses.

However, I have two reservations to offer regarding the theme of the "realists." Without these reservations, I think some of their expressions of opinion might leave you with misleading impressions. In the first place, I think some of the more ardent "realists" are guilty of overstressing the need to study actual behavior of officials and individuals. Their emphasis on the prophetic function of the lawyer is just as one-sided as the abstract viewpoint which it was aimed to correct. There is no call here to fly from one extreme to the other; no call to exchange one one-sided viewpoint for another. There is no occasion to conclude that legal standards are of secondary importance, as some of the extreme "realists" seem to do, simply because the operation of standards is not one hundred per cent perfect.** Certainly, we as

** (I.R.) Among items in which such a one-sided emphasis is laid on habit patterns and attitudes and on the lawyer's function of prediction, see items

lawyers need to understand the role of standards. We need to know how they are made, how they are applied, how they are interpreted, how far they are realized in practice. Even when we describe human behavior or prophesy what the behavior of individuals or officials is going to be, we cannot afford to ignore the patterns set up to guide behavior. The primary purpose of our legal system is to furnish guidance for behavior. And guidance for behavior involves the use of standards, models of action established beforehand, or, if you will, prescribed plans of action. We see their character most plainly in connection with effective acts. It is absurd to suppose that plans or patterns are unimportant because they are not always perfectly carried out. Important as it is to call attention to deficiencies in execution and effectuation, the core of legal training will always be the legal standards and their application.

In the second place, I have some question about the extent to which a knowledge of people and their ways can be taught in law school. In prelegal courses, such as psychology, social psychology, sociology, economics, and political science, and in law courses, such as jurisprudence and sociology of law, most of what is scientific in the field of human behavior can be given to the student. These sciences represent the sum total of what our thinkers and writers have been able to achieve by way of systematic descriptions and observations of human attitudes, habits, and practices. But these sciences

from Frank, Arnold, and Radin, cited in sec. 1-01 note *, and Rodell's *Woe Unto You, Lawyers!* (1940).

Among items in which a balanced stress on standards and habit factors is adopted, see items by Holmes, Pound, Dickinson, and Fuller, cited in sec. 3-32, note * and Llewellyn, "The Normative, the Legal and the Law-Jobs: The Problem of Juristic Method," 49 YALE L. J. 1355 (1940). Ten years earlier I think Llewellyn would have had to be counted among the writers who overstressed the realist viewpoint; at that time he referred to legal rules as mere "paper rules"; the "real rules" were for him the official patterns of behavior, "A Realistic Jurisprudence—The Next Step," 30 COL. L. REV. 431 (1930).

of behavior hardly touch the practical bases for predicting official and individual behavior. That is a type of knowledge which is not easily described, set down in books, or taught. It is the kind of knowledge which comes through personal experience, experience which each lawyer must have for himself. How can a school, for example, develop in its students a sense for detecting a lying witness, or a capacity for negotiating the settlement of a damage case, or an ability to figure out when the court will put a defendant on probation? There is no reason why the teacher should not contribute anything he can along these lines, but I do not think it can be very much. Most of the kind of information, which the practitioner needs and gets, regarding individuals, witnesses, and judges, is not generally available; it can only be acquired by S after he is a practitioner, not while he is in law school. The most that the law teacher can do about such information is to call S's attention to the importance of it, when, as, and if he can come by it. Accordingly, I have a feeling that most of the talk about the deficiencies of law schools in failing to teach practical material of this kind is far removed from pedagogical realities, quite as far removed from realities as was the old-fashioned doctrine which some extreme protagonists of realism so vociferously talk about and criticize.

Sec. 3–34. Problems. 1. *Ex parte Hardcastle.*[1] Morrow, J., delivered the opinion of the court:

"This is a habeas corpus proceeding in which the relator is held under an order of the city health officer of San Antonio, by virtue of quarantine regulations established in accord with chapter 85 of the Acts of the Fourth Called Session of the Thirty-fifth Legislature, under a statement of the order of arrest that, according to the information of the health officer, relator is affected with gonorrhea. . . .

[1] 84 Tex. App. 463, 208 S. W. 531 (1919).

"The Legislature, under the police power, has authority to authorize the establishment of quarantine regulations for the protection of the public against contagion from those persons whose condition is such as to spread disease, and, incident thereto, to authorize the arrest and detention of such persons: and such, we understand, is the purpose of the statute in question. Under its terms, the proper health officer may issue a warrant by virtue of which a lawful arrest may be made without preliminary thereto affording the person affected a hearing; but if, after arrest, such person challenges the right of the authorities to continue the detention, the fundamental law accords him the right to have the legality of his detention inquired into by a proper court in a habeas corpus proceeding. . . . The health authorities causing the arrest of relator derive their power to do so from the alleged existence of the fact that the relator is affected with the disease mentioned, and that her detention is required in the public interest to prevent contagion. If those facts do not exist, the officer has no jurisdiction to continue the restraint and the court in the habeas corpus proceeding has authority to inquire whether the facts essential to jurisdiction exist. Ex parte Degener, 30 Tex. App. 566, 17 S. W. 1111. . . .

"We conclude that, under the act of the Legislature in question, the relator had the right to a hearing on writ of habeas corpus, and therein to prove the nonexistence of the facts necessary to authorize her continued detention and thereby obtain release. Facts essential to determine whether she should or should not be held not being available in this court, it is ordered that the writ of habeas corpus prayed for be granted, and that it be referred for hearing to Hon. R. B. Minor, Judge of the Fifty-Seventh Judicial District of Texas."

What important standards for official acts are here involved? Who is called on to apply them?

2. Judge Jerome Frank says in a recent article:

"Litigation is the ultimate reference for the lawyer. By and large, in the last analysis, legal rights and duties, so-called, are nothing more or less than actual or potential successes or failures in lawsuits. A lawyer who has inadequate acquaintance with litigious processes is, relatively, an impotent lawyer. Indeed, the lawyer is differentiated from other men by the sole fact that he, more expertly than others, is supposed to know the way of courts. (When I speak of courts, I include administrative agencies, which constitute a special sort of court.)

"When you come to practice and, acting for your client, Mr. Shadrach, draw his will, or pass on a bond issue, or organize a corporation, or negotiate the settlement of a controversy, or draft a legislative bill, you will—or you should be—concerned with how the courts will act. If you are competent, you will, as best you can, try to answer this question: 'What will happen if those specific documents or transactions hereafter become a part of the drama of a trial?' For the legal rights and duties of your client, Mr. Shadrach, under any given document, or in connection with any given transaction, may mean simply what some court, somewhere, some day in the future, will decide at the end of a trial in a future concrete lawsuit relating to Shadrach's specific rights under that specific document or in connection with that specific transaction. In the last push, when your client gets into litigation, he has a legal right if he wins the lawsuit, a legal duty if he loses it.

"You will note that I have emphasized trials and trial courts. In that respect, I differ from most law teachers. With a very few notable exceptions, the kind of so-called 'law' taught by most professors in schools consists of deductions from upper-court opinions. The schools, generally speaking, are upper-court law schools. But upper courts, courts of the sort in which I sit, are relatively unimportant for most clients. Why? Because the overwhelming majority of lawsuits are never appealed, and, in most of the small minority which are appealed, the appellate courts accept the facts as 'found' by the trial court.

"This brings me to the transcendent importance of the facts of cases. A legal rule, principle or standard, says merely this: 'If the facts are thus and so, these are the legal consequences.' In a lawsuit, any particular rule, then, should be applied only if the facts invoking that rule's application are found to exist. If you, as a lawyer, assert that a given rule should govern your client's case, you will therefore fail, you will lose your suit, unless either the opposing lawyer concedes that those are the facts (which he seldom does), or you persuade the trial court (a jury or a trial judge sitting without a jury) that those are the facts.

"Now the actual facts in a suit do not walk into the courtroom. For they are past events, events which occurred before the suit began. The trial judge or jury, in most cases (i.e., those in which the facts are disputed) can usually learn about those past facts in but one way—through the courtroom narratives of witnesses. The witnesses, being human, may make mistakes in their original observation of the facts, in their memories of what they thus observed, or at the trial in their reports of their memories. Some witnesses deliberately lie. Many others are biased, and, because of bias, unconsciously distort their stories. The trial judge or juries, who are themselves merely fallible human witnesses of the witnesses, must guess which, if any, of the witnesses accurately testify about the actual past facts.

"A guess it must be, since there exist no mechanical instruments for weighing evidence or for determining the honesty and accuracy of the respective witnesses. We have not yet perfected a foolproof lie detector; we certainly now have no detector of the unconscious distortions of prejudiced but honest witnesses; and almost surely, we will never have a contrivance for correcting a witness' original mistaken observation of the facts.

"The facts, then, for decisional purposes are no more than what trial judges or juries guess—what they think the facts are (or, more accurately, what they publicly say or imply they think the facts are). The 'facts' consist, therefore, of the fallible subjective reactions of the trial judge or jury to the fallible reactions of the witness. Consequently, subjectivity, in two ways, inheres in trial-court fact finding—in the subjective reactions of the witnesses, and in the subjective reactions to the witnesses of the jury or trial judge. Specific decisions frequently turn on such subjective reactions, culminating in such fallible findings of the facts. In court-houses, the legal rules are never self-operative, are always at the mercy of those findings and often of that subjectivity. I can perhaps most easily indicate the practical significance of that subjectivity by quoting what I have said elsewhere with respect to the trial judge: 'What we call the "facts" of a case constitute, often, the most important ingredient of the trial judge's decision. But when the testimony is in conflict,—as it is in thousands of cases—the "facts" of a lawsuit consist of the judge's belief as to what those facts are. That belief results from the impact on the judge of the words, gestures, postures and grimaces of the witnesses. His reaction—inherently and inescapably subjective—is a composite of the way in which his personal predilections and prejudices are stimulated by the sights and sounds emanating from the witnesses. Now these personal attitudes of the judge reflect the subtlest influences of his experience and of the manner in which he has moulded them into what we describe, loosely, as his "personality." Where he was born and educated, his parents, the persons he has met, his teachers and companions, the woman he married, the books and articles he has read—these and multitudinous other factors, undiscoverable for the most part by any outsider, affect his notion of the "facts." All kinds of obscure, unarticulated community moral attitudes thus play their part in his fact determination.' As I recently said, on behalf of our court: 'Democracy must, indeed, fail unless our courts try cases fairly, and there can be no fair trial before a judge lacking in impartiality and disinterestedness. If, however, "bias" and "partiality" be defined to mean the total absence of preconceptions in the mind of the judge, then no one has ever had a fair trial and no one ever will. The human mind, even at infancy, is no blank piece of paper. We are born with predispositions; and the process of education, formal and informal, creates attitudes in all men which affect them in judging situations, attitudes which precede reasoning in particular instances and which, therefore, by definition, are prejudices. Without acquired "slants," preconceptions, life could not go on. Every habit constitutes a pre-judgment; were those pre-judgments which we call habits absent in any person, were he obliged to treat every event as an unprecedented crisis presenting a wholly new problem, he would go mad. Interests, points of view, preferences, are the essence of living. Only death yields dispassionateness, for such dispassionateness signifies utter indifference. "To live . . . is to have an ethics or scheme of values, and to have a scheme of values is to have a point of view, and to have a point of view is to have a prejudice or bias . . ." An "open mind," in the sense of a mind containing no preconceptions whatever, would be a mind incapable of learning anything, would be that of an utterly emotionless human being, corresponding roughly to the psychiatrist's descriptions of the feeble-minded. More directly to the point, every human society has a multitude of established attitudes, unquestioned postulates. . . . Much harm is done by the myth that, merely by putting on a black robe and taking the oath of office as a judge, a man ceases to be human and strips himself of all predilections, becomes a passionless thinking machine.' For obvious reasons, the point becomes markedly sharper when cases are tried by juries.

"Never forget that courts do business at retail, not wholesale. All decisions are specific decisions in specific suits. In advising a client of his rights and duties, a lawyer is attempting to predict, to guess, what decision will be rendered in a specific bit of litigation. Often that requires him, before any suit is begun or even threatened, to guess whether, should litigation arise, there will be a dispute about the facts, and, if so, whether conflicting testimony will be introduced at the trial, and what trial judge or jury will try the case, and what will be the reaction of that as yet unknown trial judge or jury to that as yet unknown testimony.

"Prediction of specific decisions is hazardous, then, not primarily because of uncertainty about the legal rules but usually because of the obstacles to guessing what the trial courts will guess to be the facts. Due presumably to the difficulty of such guessing, Learned Hand, our greatest American judge, declared, after a long period on the trial bench, 'I must say that as a litigant I should dread a lawsuit beyond almost anything else short of sickness and death.' Sir William Eggleston, the present Australian Ambassador, an experienced trial lawyer, wrote this year, 'With regard to the trial of pure questions of fact, I am of opinion that the results are . . . much a matter of chance.'

"Because, fixing their attention on upper courts, they neglect that crucial aspect of court-house government, many leading law teachers do their maximum worst in gravely miseducating their students. Repeatedly they assert that clear and precise legal rules usually prevent litigation, and imply that the difficulty of predicting decisions stems largely from uncertainty in or about the rules. That amounts to saying that if all the legal rules were settled and precise, or if parties to controversies always could agree on the pertinent rules, there would be little or no litigation. That is pure, unadulterated tosh. In most suits, no disagreement arises about the rules, and the disputes relate solely to the facts. Decisions in such suits, says many a professor, quoting Cardozo, leave 'jurisprudence . . . untouched.' That is true, provided you so conceive of 'jurisprudence' that it stays aloof from the affairs of ordinary men. But such a decision often means death or imprisonment or poverty or a ruined life to some mere mortal who, in his benighted ignorance, has more regard for his own welfare than for the aesthetic delights of pure 'jurisprudence.'

"Uncertainty about some of the legal rules exists; one comes upon it in the 'marginal' (or 'unprovided' or 'new' cases). Cardozo correctly said that such uncertainty ought not to be exaggerated. However, the point he missed, because he was an upper-court lawyer or an upper-court judge during most of his career, is this: The major cause of legal uncertainty, which is vast in extent, inheres in the unknowability of the 'facts' of cases. For I repeat that few cases are appealed and that, even when a case is appealed, the upper court usually accepts the facts as found by the trial court. Appellate courts deal principally with the legal rules. For that reason, upper courts are relatively unimportant. Trial courts—trial judges and juries—are the pivotal factor in the judicial process. . . ." [2]

What difficulty about the application of standards does Judge Frank stress? Is this point brought out in your law studies?

[2] "A Plea for Lawyer-Schools," 56 YALE L. J. 1303 at 1305–1311 (1947).

What proportion of contracts made between citizens A and B give rise to litigation, i.e., disputes in court regarding law or facts? What does this suggest?

Sec. 3–35. Summary and concluding observations. The main theme of this chapter has been the control of official acts by legal standards. We have been concerned with methods of controlling official acts which are, in turn, mainly significant as means or methods of controlling individuals.

First, we dealt with the standards which are established to control officials, and the ways in which official acts are significant. The discussion here included an analysis of executive acts, a discussion of the functions of courts and court procedures, and a brief description of the activities of administrative agencies and certain nonregulative acts of governmental agencies.

Second, we discussed the ways of effectuating standards for officials. Here, methods of motivating official behavior along desirable lines, methods of selecting officials, and methods of checking official acts were treated.

Finally, we considered the important uses which are made by various persons of the standards prescribed for official acts: how these standards are used by executive officials, by the courts, by the individual and his counselor, and by the student of law.

The stress throughout both this chapter and the preceding, has been on legal methods—methods of controlling people and methods of using and applying standards. This stress is justified by the fact that the principal thing which one gets in law school is a knowledge of legal methods—methods of analyzing fact situations and methods of applying legal standards to a case. No one can acquire a knowledge of all the law; no one can remember for long even a major part of the law which one covers in law school. Every practitioner and every teacher has learned, analyzed and digested—and then forgotten—a great quantity of law. One often hears the practitioner say that he could not take a bar examination, or that he never knew so much law as when he graduated from law school. What he has carried away and kept are methods of analyzing fact situations, methods of applying legal standards to a case, and a feeling for the ways in which legal principles can be and will be developed and applied. Just as one who has learned to swim never loses his sense for the way to keep himself afloat and propel himself through the water, a legal trainee never loses his sense for, and ability to use, the legal methods into which he has been initiated.

CHAPTER 4

Legislation *

Sec. 4-01. Lawmakers and legislation. Several kinds of governmental agencies create standards for the guidance of individuals and officials. These agencies include the convention or assembly, which establishes the basic instrument of government called the constitution; the legislature (or in the case of the federal government, the Congress) whose function is to enact statutes, sometimes called acts, public acts, or laws; cities, towns and villages, which enact ordinances; various executive and administrative officers and boards which exercise rule-making authority; and the courts, which lay down rules, principles and doctrines in the decision of cases.

To the extent that these various agencies produce standards of behavior, I shall speak of them henceforth as lawmakers, speak of their grist as law, and call their activity lawmaking. The word legislation, however, I shall reserve for enacted law and distinguish between legislation on the one hand and judicial lawmaking on the other. Accordingly, legislation will

* (I.R.) Suggestions for further reading:
Field, David Dudley, Centenary Essays (New York University, 1949), a group of papers dealing with codification and law reform.
Pound, Outlines of Lectures on Jurisprudence (5th ed., 1943) 124–139, furnishes a comprehensive bibliography on legislation and codification.
Pound, "Sources and Forms of Law," 21 Notre Dame Lawyer 246–314 and 22 *ibid.* 1–80 (1946), discusses sources of law, the traditional elements in law, and the imperative element; the last title covering legislation and codification.
Read and MacDonald, Cases and Materials on Legislation (1948), a very useful collection of material.
Sutherland, Statutes and Statutory Construction (3rd ed. by Horack, 1943), a large treatise recently revised; contains material on the legislative process as well as the interpretive process.

include three types of law: (1) constitutional provisions (2) statutes (3) executive or administrative rules.[1]

Sec. 4–02. Scope of chapter—statutes as chief subject. The present chapter will be devoted to legislation as above defined. The process of judicial lawmaking will be considered fully in a later chapter. However, it does not seem to me necessary to consider all three types of legislation in equal detail. Statutes constitute the most prominent type of enacted law. The legislature is a body established for the very purpose of enacting statutes; it acts frequently and prolifically; it creates the lion's share of standards applicable to individuals and to officials. I believe therefore that the character and significance of legislative activity will be amply developed by a discussion of the making and the effects of statutes. And, apart from occasional remarks about the effects of constitutional provisions and three sections in which subsidiary lawmaking is briefly considered, all the following discussion of legislation will center on the acts of the legislature.[1]

The material of this chapter will be taken up under the following heads:

The legislative process.

Standards for the lawmaker.

Subsidiary lawmaking.

Lawmaker's statement of standards.

Significance of legislation.

---

[1] Patterson uses "legislation" in essentially this manner. He includes in the term all forms of law which are characterized by "textual rigidity." He mentions as specific examples the Constitution of the United States, treaties, federal statutes, federal executive orders and administrative regulations, state constitutions, state statutes, administrative regulations, municipal ordinances, and rules of court. DOWLING, PATTERSON, AND POWELL, MATERIALS FOR LEGAL METHOD 21–29 (1946).

[1] Except where I specifically refer to the Congress or to a state legislature, I shall use the word *legislature* henceforth in the generic sense to refer to the Congress, to a state legislature or to either without distinction. This usage will avoid a cumbersome reference to the Congress each time I wish to refer to the act of statute making.

THE LEGISLATIVE PROCESS

Sec. 4–03. Enactment of statute—a series of steps.
A statute does not spring full-blown from the legislative
brow as Minerva did from the brow of Jove. The process
of getting a law on the books usually extends over a considerable period of time. It involves many distinguishable
acts of different persons.[1] A law is suggested, formulated,
debated, revised, amended, and adopted. Its completion
involves such separate steps or acts as the preparation of
a bill, the introduction of the bill in one house of the
legislature,[2] the reference of the bill to a committee, the
consideration, revision, and redrafting of the bill by this committee, the return to the house of the bill with the committee's report, the debate on the bill in the house, its adoption
by the house, the signature and certification of adoption by
the presiding officer and clerk, the repetition of all these steps
in the second house of the legislature, the signature or veto
by the chief executive of the state, the repassage of the bill
by the necessary majorities in case of veto, and finally the
publication of the enacted law in some official form. In other
words the legislative process is not a solid indivisible unit but
a series of interconnected steps; it is not a simple instan-
taneous occurrence but a sequence of acts.

Sec. 4–04. Occasion and purpose of legislation. The legislative act, like all forms of human action, originates in a felt
need to change the environment.[1] In the legislative situation

---

[1] The adoption of a constitution or a specific constitutional provision is
also a series of acts in which various agencies participate. There are not only
distinguishable acts in the constitutional convention itself, but the work of the
convention is ordinarily submitted to the voters to be accepted or rejected.

[2] Before the process of enactment is complete the proposed law is commonly
called a bill or draft. When the process of enactment is complete the bill
or draft becomes an act, statute or law.

[1] By "change the environment" we can mean either an alteration of the
environment itself, or a change of the environment in the sense that the actor

the actor recognizes a need to change the patterns of action which govern the behavior of his fellows. He becomes aware of the fact that these patterns of action, or standards, are not the best available or that they are not as effective as they should be under prevailing conditions. He recognizes the need to change standards or to set up new ones. Often the perception of the need for change originates outside the legislature; the legislature's attention is directed to the need by some individual or group of persons. But in any event the legislature itself must recognize this need. The need is the occasion for legislation; it is, to paraphrase a statement of Lord Coke, the mischief and defect for which the existing law does not provide.[2]

Closely related to the occasion for legislation is the purpose of legislation. In fact this purpose is nothing more than what the legislature aims to do about the need which it recognizes. The purpose of action and the occasion for action cannot really be severed from one another; the purpose of action springs from an existing occasion. The lawmaker acts to meet a need, as I have just said. His action is remedial; his purpose is to change existing standards. First of all he has to decide upon a general purpose—what he wants to accomplish by amending or creating standards. What behavior of A or O does he wish to foster or bring about? What ends or objectives does he wish to achieve by amending or creating legal standards? It is not too important how we characterize such questions: whether we call them questions of objectives or ends, or whether we call them questions of purpose or of policy. All of these characterizations—and they are all used—come to about the same thing. All mean that the

moves from one environment to another. The legislative change in the environment is, needless to say, of the former type. It involves a change of surrounding social conditions by altering prevailing legal standards.

[2] Heydon's Case, 3 Co. 7a (1584). Coke is speaking of the factors which have to be considered in interpreting a statute. Among them he counts "what was the mischief and defect for which the common law did not provide."

lawmaker has to face the problem of deciding what is socially desirable; he has to decide what results he wants to bring about by amending or creating legal standards. This is the basic legislative problem.

Suppose, for example, it is suggested to the lawmaker that there is a liquor problem, a need to eliminate the use of intoxicants by establishing and enforcing prohibitory standards. He must decide whether it is a real need and, if so, what to do about it. He has to make a choice among such alternatives as these: (1) to undertake to prevent the harm, individual and social, that flows from overindulgence in intoxicants, perhaps by outright prohibition of the traffic in intoxicants; (2) to check the misuse of intoxicants, by forbidding their sale at certain times, e.g., after midnight, or by preventing their use by certain persons, e.g., minors; (3) to induce the individual to be temperate in the use of intoxicants, by employing the educational machinery of the state; (4) to adopt a hands-off policy and so allow each individual to decide for himself how far he will indulge in the use of intoxicants, or at least allow him to decide for himself except as he is checked by the standards of other social institutions, such as the family or the church; (5) to pursue a policy quite the opposite of that which is suggested and encourage each individual, by education or otherwise, to make the most of his opportunities for alcoholic indulgence, on the theory of the saying "eat, drink, and be merry for tomorrow you may die." All these are possible alternatives for the lawmaker. Which of these alternatives is to be chosen? Which is to be the objective of the state as expressed in its legal standards?

Ordinarily, the occasion for enactment is not mentioned in the legislation itself, nor is the purpose for which it is intended announced. The lawmaker takes need and purpose for granted and simply issues directives for the guidance of individuals and officials. This, I mean to say, is the common type of legislative act; it sets forth standards of behavior without indicating the reasons of need and purpose which lie behind them. But only recently the Congress and the legislatures of some of our states have revived the practice, not unusual several centuries ago,[3] of declaring in their important legislative acts the needs on which they are based and the purposes to be promoted by their enactment. The following section from the federal Fair Labor Standards Act is typical of this modern practice:

"*Congressional finding and declaration of policy.* (a) The Congress finds that the existence, in industries engaged in commerce or in the production of goods for commerce, of labor conditions detrimental to the maintenance of the minimum standard of living necessary for health, efficiency, and general well-being of workers (1) causes commerce and the channels and instrumentalities of commerce to be used to spread and perpetuate such labor conditions among the workers of the several States; (2) burdens commerce and the free flow of goods in commerce; (3) constitutes an unfair method of competition in commerce; (4) leads to labor disputes burdening and obstructing commerce and the free flow of goods in commerce; and (5) interferes with the orderly and fair marketing of goods in commerce.

"(b) It is declared to be the policy of sections 201–219 of this title, through the exercise by Congress of its power to regulate commerce among the several States, to correct and as rapidly as practicable to eliminate the conditions above referred to in such industries without substantially curtailing employment or earning power."[4]

The importance and helpfulness to the interpreter of a declaration like this, can hardly be overestimated. The point

---

[3] Good examples of the former practice are two famous statutes which you will encounter in your first-year property course: the Statute De Donis Conditionalibus, 13 Edw. I, Westm. II, c. 1 (1285) and the Statute of Uses, 27 Hen. VIII, c. 10 (1536). Both statutes contain elaborate statements about the need for legislation and the purposes intended.

[4] 52 Stat. 1060, sec. 2, 29 U. S. C., sec. 202 (b), June 25, 1938.

is one which you will see better when we consider, in the next chapter, the roles played by legislative need and legislative purpose in the processes of interpretation.*

Sec. 4–05. Legislative provisions as means. The first major problem of the lawmaker, as I have just said, is to determine what he wants to accomplish. His next problem is to decide *how* he will accomplish the purpose or purposes which he has set for himself. This is the problem of choosing means. What are the appropriate standards to establish for individuals and officials in order to accomplish his general objective? What are the best devices to use to effectuate the standards he sets up, and thus carry out his general plan? [1]

Various phases of the problem of means have already been discussed. In section 2–01 it was pointed out that the lawmaker uses legislation as a means to ends; it was said "The lawmaker, L, issues general directives to the community as the owner of a factory might issue instructions, blueprints and models to guide the work of the men in his factory." In section 2–43 it was said that the lawmaker "uses standards instrumentally, to control the behavior of others. He creates them as one might devise tools for particular purposes. He sets them up in order to achieve results which he wishes to bring about. These observations hold equally of all standards; whether for obligatory, prohibited, effective, permitted,

*(I.R.) Discussion of the occasion for legislation and of legislative purpose, arises most often in connection with interpretation. Until a doubt about the meaning of legislation arises these factors are taken for granted; and, as I have said in the text, they are not usually mentioned in the legislative enactment. However, the importance of these factors in interpretation derives from the fact that need and purpose represent important aspects of the legislative act. And I believe that the student obtains a better conception of the legislative act and of the relation of legislation to interpretation, if he is introduced to legislative need and legislative purpose as factors in the legislative process.

[1] From this viewpoint, both the standards which his statute establishes and the effectuative devices which he provides for (e.g., penalties, etc.) are means used by L to accomplish his legislative purpose.

discretionary or ineffective acts. All standards alike are related to a maker as his handiwork; all are employed to guide the activity of others, by furnishing them with verbal patterns to follow." And in sections 2–29 to 2–42 we dealt in some detail with problems of effectuating standards. Here the problems were all essentially problems of choosing appropriate means; in particular the need to consider the attitudes of persons to be controlled by standards was emphasized, and available methods and devices for motivating their behavior were discussed. In chapter 3 similar problems relating to methods of controlling officials were analyzed. All these materials have illustrated the approach to legislative provisions which we are talking about. The materials do not need to be discussed again. I have only referred to them here because they represent an important approach to the legislative process and one that is essential to a well-rounded view of the lawmaker's job.

However, legislative ends and means cannot be weighed quite independently of one another. Means signify nothing apart from an end or purpose which they serve, and an end is only realized through the use of appropriate means. Like legislative occasion and legislative purpose, legislative purpose and the means of execution are inseparable in practice. Try, for example, to distinguish between purpose and means in the legislative problem mentioned in the following news item in the *Detroit Free Press,* April 23, 1949:

"SENATE DELAYS LIQUOR BILL. The [Michigan] Senate almost stopped grocery clerks under 21 years from carrying a customer's case of beer.

"In a drive to prevent all persons under 21 years of age from handling liquor, the Senate passed the bill.

"Then Senator Henry R. Kozak, Detroit Democrat, induced the Senate to reconsider the bill so he could offer an amendment.

"But the amendment was so broad it was considered as bad one way as the bill was the other way and the whole question was put over till Monday."

Obviously, the Michigan Senate could not completely divorce the purpose to keep intoxicants out of the reach of minors from the problem of devising ways to carry out this purpose. The distinction between the lawmaker's purpose and the means of accomplishing it is not a final physical division of matter, like sawing an object in two; it is just a useful differentiation of two approaches to the legislative problem. Both approaches are possible and both are fruitful, but often the two approaches show us pretty much the same matters.

Sec. 4–06. Sources of legislative provisions—social context. What are the sources of statutory enactments? Where does the lawmaker find the standards and legal ideas which he declares in statutory form? He must find them somewhere in his own social heritage. His ideas do not spring from nowhere; he is limited by the knowledge of his time; he acts within a social context or background.* Genuine legislative inventions are rare; ordinarily the legislator does not show marked originality. Types of legislative provisions grow and change with the centuries, but they change very slowly. The great mass of legislation repeats, imitates, and adapts oft-used models.

* (I.R.) The social background of the lawmaker's act—what we here call the social context—serves four important functions: (1) It furnishes materials on which the lawmaker may draw in composing an enactment; it is a source of legislation in this sense. (2) The social context provides standards for the lawmaker's own act; thus provisions of the constitution govern L's act and the standards of moral, natural or divine law may set limits to L's activity; all these are background of L's act and in this sense are part of its social context. (3) The social context provides material for the process of interpretation; the interpreter performs a supplementary legislative function and draws on source materials just as the lawmaker himself does. (4) The context also provides standards to guide the interpreter. The first of these functions is developed in section 4–06 of the text; the second in secs. 4–08 to 4–11 and 4–31; the third and fourth functions of social context, in chapter 5.

Sometimes the lawmaker borrows statutory provisions verbatim from the statutes of another state, as where he copies the Workmen's Compensation Law already in force in the other state. Often he finds the essential pattern for a statutory provision in the decisions of his own or another state. Or he finds the suggestion of the need for legislation in the decisions of his own state and works out the details of an enactment by following the lines of analogous legislation of his own or another state. Or he derives the suggestion for an enactment from the standards of Holy Writ, or the moral ideas of the community,[1] or the writings of some author who discourses on legal or social subjects. Or he finds and adopts a standard already formulated, more or less definitely as the norm of some social institution, such as a church, a professional association, or a labor union. Or he finds a standard already implicit in the habits and practices of the majority of the community, as where he finds that most persons are accustomed to drive in a certain manner and, framing a traffic code, adopts the common practice as the legal rule for driving.

Sec. 4–07. Problems. Analyze the two following items in terms of *occasion, purpose, means,* and *sources* of legislation:

1. *Enactment of the Mann Act* (White Slave Act).[1] Before considering specifically the enactment of the Mann Act in 1904, it will be worthwhile to set forth some of the legislative and social background within which the enactment falls. As early as 1875, Congress had taken steps to prohibit "the importation into the United States of women for the

---

[1] In sec. 7–45 we shall discuss the "higher law" theory according to which human law is ultimately derived from natural law or Divine Law.

[1] 36 Stat. 825, sec. 2, 18 U. S. C., sec. 398, May 18, 1904. Both this statement regarding the enactment of the White Slave Act and the statement about the enactment of the Wisconsin Workmen's Compensation Law were prepared for me by Mr. Charles Hanson of the law class of 1950.

purposes of prostitution." [2] That this prohibition apparently proceeded through both houses of Congress without the slightest degree of opposition is evidence of the fact that in so acting, the Congress was merely giving voice to a community standard of conduct definitely opposed to such practices.[3] This and succeeding acts, however, left much to be desired with respect to the solution of the problem of the white slave traffic, a trade which by the early part of the 20th Century had reached considerable proportions.[4]

The reasons for the inadequacy of the then existent legislation were several. First, although in 1904 the United States had entered into a multi-nation treaty for the purpose of stamping out the traffic, this agreement proved to be of little practical worth.[5] Without considerable aid at foreign points of debarkation, enforcement of the immigration laws as a sole means for eliminating the trade were almost bound to prove insufficient. In addition, even completely effective operation of such laws could not strike strongly at the large number of persons already engaged in the traffic within the borders of this country.[6] Further, the participants were not easily amenable to state regulation since it was discovered that they moved frequently from place to place.[7] In addition, because of the absence of federal legislation, the interstate

[2] Act of March 3, 1875, 18 Stat. 477, sec. 5.

[3] Further confirmation of this view may be had by examining statements made in the course of Congressional debates and others appearing in Congressional reports with respect to later, but closely allied measures. See 45 CONG. REC. 1037, 1039, 61st Cong., 2d Sess., "Importing Women for Immoral Purposes"; SENATE DOCUMENT, No. 196 (Jan. 26, 1910) 32, 61st Cong., 2d Sess. (Dec. 10, 1909).

[4] SENATE DOCUMENT, No. 214, Report of the Commissioner General of Immigration, part 2, 5, 61st Cong., 2d Sess. (Dec. 7, 1909); 45 CONG. REC. 821, 61st Cong., 2d Sess. (Jan. 19, 1910).

[5] SENATE DOCUMENT, No. 196, "Importing Women for Immoral Purposes," 33 (Dec. 10, 1909).

[6] SENATE DOCUMENT, No. 214, Report of the Commissioner General of Immigration, part 2, 14, 61st Cong., 2d Sess. (Dec. 7, 1909).

[7] SENATE DOCUMENT, No. 196, "Importing Women for Immoral Purposes," 28 (Dec. 10, 1909).

traffic was looked upon as being safer than that carried on intrastate.[8] This was the situation facing the draftsmen of the Mann Act, section 2 of which will be considered here.

The objects of this legislation, although not fully spelled out in the enactment itself, are indicated to some degree in the title: "An Act to Further Regulate Interstate and Foreign Commerce by Prohibiting the Transportation Therein for Immoral Purposes of Women and Girls, and for Other Purposes." Further elucidation of the societal changes sought to be accomplished, can be gotten from an examination of several previously noted references. First, the measure apparently was designed to supplement the immigration laws in solving the problem of excluding new additions to the trade by providing for further penalties as to interstate activity. These additional sanctions were perhaps considered valuable as providing a degree of deterrence which would serve to limit the number of persons who might attempt to run the immigration gauntlet where the penalties imposed by the immigration laws taken alone would not so operate.[9] Secondly, because of the prevalence of interstate activity in the trade, it was felt that a step toward preventing its existence could be taken by preventing such movement.[10]

To achieve these objects, penalties were imposed upon those who violated the provisions of section 2 of the Act through use of the instrumentalities of interstate or foreign commerce for the transportation of females for immoral ends. These penalties consisted of a fine of not more than $5000 and of imprisonment of not more than five years. It should be mentioned in passing that since, as previously noted, the white slave traffic existed in opposition to the established

[8] HOUSE REPORT, No. 47, 61st Cong., 2d Sess. (Dec. 21, 1909).

[9] SENATE DOCUMENT, No. 124, Report of the Commissioner General of Immigration, 14, 61st Cong., 2d Sess. (Dec. 7, 1909).

[10] HOUSE REPORT, No. 47, 61st Cong., 2d Sess. (Dec. 21, 1909), submitted by Rep. Mann from the Interstate and Foreign Commerce Committee.

social standards of the country, no broad problem of effecting social change was involved, and utilization of federal officers to apprehend the relatively few engaged in the trade would seem to have been appropriate.[11]

2. *Enactment of the Wisconsin Workmen's Compensation Law.*[12] "It is a matter of common knowledge that this law forms the legislative response to an emphatic if not a peremptory, public demand. It was admitted by lawyers as well as laymen that the personal injury action brought by the employee against his employer to recover damages for injuries sustained by reason of the negligence of the employer had wholly failed to meet or remedy a great economic and social problem which modern industrialism has forced upon us, namely, the problem of who shall make pecuniary recompense for the toll of suffering and death which that industrialism levies and must continue to levy upon the civilized world. This problem is distinctly a modern problem. In the days of manual labor, the small shop with few employees, and the stagecoach, there was no such problem, or if there was, it was almost negligible. Accidents there were in those days and distressing ones, but they were relatively few, and the employee who exercised any reasonable degree of care was comparatively secure from injury. There was no army of injured and dying with constantly swelling ranks marching with halting step and dimming eyes to the great hereafter. This is what we have with us now thanks to the wonderful material progress of our age, and this is what we shall have with us for many a day to come. Legislate as we may in the

---

[11] At the time immediately preceding the passage of the act there was considerable doubt as to whether Congress had the means at its disposal under the commerce power for preventing the use of interstate and foreign commerce for the transportation of women for immoral purposes (45 CONG. REC. 809, 61st CONG., 2d Sess., Jan. 19, 1910). However, fortified by the "Lottery Cases," 188 U. S. 321 (1902), the sponsors of the bill succeeded in meeting this objection.

[12] Ch. 50, Laws of 1911, Stats., Secs. 102.01 to 102.65.

line of stringent requirements for safety devices or the abolition of the employer's common-law defenses, the army of the injured will still increase, the price of our manufacturing greatness will still have to be paid in human blood and tears. To speak of the common-law personal injury action as a remedy for this problem is to jest with serious subjects, to give a stone to those who ask for bread. The terrible economic waste, the overwhelming temptation to the commission of perjury, and the relatively small proportion of the sums recovered which comes to the injured parties in such actions, condemn them as wholly inadequate to meet the difficulty.[13]

To remedy this situation it was recognized at the outset that the legal relationship between the employer and the employee would require a basic reconsideration. As one writer stated the matter, "Many suggestions have been made as to a remedy, but commissions on Employer's Liability are strongly of the opinion that the industry itself should bear the burden and not the employee. The industry now bears the burden of the wearing out and destruction of machinery necessarily resulting from its use, and civilization now demands that the industry bear also the burden of the wearing out and destruction of the efficiency of the human machines without which the industry could not survive. . . . When a man's life is lost, or his efficiency decreased through injury in his employment, humanity demands that his dependents in case of his death, and he himself in case of injury, shall be cared for." [14]

[13] Borgnis v. Falk, 147 Wis. 327 at 347, 133 N. W. 221 (1911). For a summary of a consideration of the problem by a New York commission, see BULLETIN OF THE UNITED STATES BUREAU OF LABOR STATISTICS, WORKMEN'S INSURANCE AND COMPENSATION SERIES: No. 5, Whole Number 126, p. 19 (1913).

[14] 1 BOYD, WORKMEN'S COMPENSATION AND INDUSTRIAL INSURANCE 10 (1913). This view was concurred in by the Wisconsin Special Committee on Industrial Insurance. BULLETIN OF THE UNITED STATES BUREAU OF LABOR STATISTICS, WORKMEN'S INSURANCE AND COMPENSATION SERIES: No. 5, Whole Number 126, p. 26 (1913).

To achieve this end, the Wisconsin legislature drafted a law making several changes in the employer-employee relationship. First, the defenses of negligence of a coworker and of assumption of risk were eliminated; and secondly, a comprehensive scheme was provided whereby any substantial injury received by the employee, in the course of or incidental to his employment would be compensated for according to certain definite rules laid down by a simultaneously created administrative agency.[15] A further avenue for effectuating the desired social change lay in making application of the law compulsory.[16] However, because there was considerable authoritative opinion to the effect that such a law would be later declared unconstitutional,[17] the bill as passed required an affirmative election on the part of both employer and employee before the provisions of the act were applicable.

Thus, on September 1, 1911 when the Act became effective, Wisconsin was added to the growing list of jurisdictions which, led by Germany in 1883,[18] had recognized the impact of the Industrial Revolution on the employer-employee relationship, and had softened that impact by bringing about conformation of this relation to the altered social need.

STANDARDS FOR THE LAWMAKER

Sec. 4–08. Standards—where found. The acts of all our lawmakers are themselves guided and controlled by standards. To be sure, the framers of the original constitution begin with a slate which is clean and perform their funda-

---

[15] Borgnis v. Falk, 147 Wis. 327 at 346, 133 N. W. 221 (1911).

[16] It should be noted that some legislative bodies felt that this was the only practical way of enforcing such a law. BULLETIN OF THE UNITED STATES BUREAU OF LABOR STATISTICS, WORKMEN'S INSURANCE AND COMPENSATION SERIES: No. 5, Whole Number 126, p. 27 (1913).

[17] BULLETIN OF THE UNITED STATES BUREAU OF LABOR STATISTICS, WORKMEN'S COMPENSATION AND INSURANCE SERIES: No. 5, Whole Number 126, p. 26 (1913); Borgnis v. Falk, 147 Wis. 327 at 350, 133 N. W. 221 (1911).

[18] For a historical review and analysis of the German scheme, see I BOYD, WORKMEN'S COMPENSATION AND INDUSTRIAL INSURANCE 25–52 (1913).

mental legislative acts with no other guidance than the traditional legal ideas of the community.[1] After a constitution is once established, however, the amendment of it (and even the adoption of a new constitution) usually has to be carried out according to the tenor of an amendment clause of the existing instrument.[2] The acts of the legislature in enacting statutes are covered by a variety of constitutional provisions. The legislature itself also establishes statutory standards to govern the processes of lawmaking; and each house of the legislature creates rules of procedure for the governance of its legislative and other business. The legislative acts of subordinate lawmaking bodies, such as cities and administrative agencies, are governed by constitutional provisions to some extent, but in the main by statutes. And finally, in the course of the centuries, the courts have developed many common-law standards which regulate their own lawmaking activities as well as the lawmaking activities of other organs of government, insofar as the latter are not controlled either by provisions of the constitution or by statutory enactments.

The standards controlling the *enactment of statutes* will be considered in the following sections; they fall into three types:

1. Constitutional provisions which confer general and specific power to legislate

---

[1] This of course was true only of the original thirteen colonies, which adopted their own constitutions, and also of the Republic of Texas. Other states which have been formed were controlled by the provisions of the Federal Constitution and to some extent by acts of Congress.

[2] Certainly this is the normal conception of the manner in which change is to be effected; but change can be brought about by revolution, and in our own constitutional history there are a few instances in which changes have been wrought without obeying the mandates of the earlier instrument. The adoption of the Federal Constitution itself is an outstanding example. The Articles of Confederation of 1777 required that amendments be adopted by unanimous consent of the states. These Articles were superseded by our Federal Constitution by a method which did not conform to the Articles, i.e., when nine of the thirteen states approved. As we all know, all of the states did ultimately approve but ratification did not depend on unanimous consent.

2. Provisions of constitution, statute, or rules of order, which prescribe the form and manner in which legislative power is to be exercised

3. Constitutional provisions which prohibit certain kinds of legislation.

Sec. 4–09. Grants of power to legislate. The first type of standard applicable to statute making, and obviously the most basic and important type, is the constitutional grant of power to legislate.[1] Such a grant confers authority on the legislature to do effective acts. The constitution maker announces to the world that L can establish standards for the guidance of others; he determines the purpose for which, and the field in which, L's acts shall be effective. For example when the Federal Constitution provides that the Congress shall have "power to regulate commerce . . . among the several States," it authorizes Congress to create effective standards for the regulation of conduct in a particular area. The analogy is close between such a grant of legislative power and the grant to A of power to do an effective act such as the making of a will; both grants provide for acts which will have effects within the legal system and both provide for acts which are to be done with foresight of these effects. The analogy is even closer between the grant of power to legislate and the statutory grant of authority to executive officials; the lawmaker and the policeman alike are authorized to do effective acts, the one to create legal standards, the other to enforce them.[2] So that I think I am warranted in

[1] The reader must not forget that I am speaking here of the typical American legal system, in which statute making always stands on a constitutional foundation.

[2] There are differences in the bases of different effective acts. The effects of L's acts are determined primarily by constitutional clauses; usually the effects of O's acts depend on either constitution or statute or both. But these differences of foundation are not important in the present connections; the acts of L, A, and O alike produce intended legal effects, i.e., they have purposive significance within our legal system.

saying one prime characteristic of the statute maker's act is that it is an effective act, an act depending for its operation on a constitutional grant of power.

The constitutional grant of legislative power may be general or specific. The general grant of legislative power is characteristic of our state constitutions. These instruments ordinarily confer legislative power in broad terms which authorize the legislature to enact standards of behavior in any field whatever. But there are also constitutional clauses which make specific grants of power—power to legislate in specific fields or in regard to specific subjects. This type of provision, while not uncommon in the state constitutions, is predominant in the Federal Constitution. In terms of traditional doctrine, the Federal Constitution establishes a government of limited powers; this means simply that the legislative branch of the federal government (and other branches too) can do effective acts only in specified areas. Thus Congress is not given a general power to enact standards on any subject; instead, the Federal Constitution contains provisions that Congress shall have power "to regulate commerce with foreign nations and among the several States, and with the Indian tribes"; "to define and punish piracies and felonies committed on the high seas, and offenses against the law of nations"; and power "to promote the progress of science and useful arts by securing for limited times to authors and inventors the exclusive right to their respective writings and discoveries." [3] Of course the distinction between general and specific grants of power is one of degree; even the specific grants of power to the Congress are very wide and comprehensive in practical application as I have previously pointed out.[4]

[3] All of the grants herein quoted are found in Art. I, Sec. 8.

[4] See sec. 3–03, note 2. And the grant of power to lay and collect taxes to provide for the common defense and general welfare of the United States, would have to be regarded as a general grant of power, by any criterion of generality. See Art. I, Sec. 8, Cl. 1.

One might even maintain that provisions granting legislative power are not only enabling but obligatory in effect. They can be said to be obligatory in the sense that they implicitly impose a duty to exercise the power granted. They tell the legislature what it is expected to do, i.e., make standards for the community to live by. However, while such an implication of duty can perhaps properly be spelled out of any investiture with power, the fact remains that the constitutional provisions in question are actually expressed as grants of power, not as impositions of duty. Furthermore, a duty to legislate for the welfare of the community has little meaning except so far as the legislature itself recognizes an obligation. The exercise of its lawmaking power lies almost wholly within the legislature's discretion. If it fails or refuses to act when it should, there is no real remedy except to choose a new legislative body that will act, or, more specifically, to replace its inactive or obstructive members by others who will do what needs to be done. The duty, if any, of the legislature to act for the general good is vague and tenuous; the dominant element in these constitutional clauses is power, not obligation.*

Sec. 4–10. Formal requirements. The second type of standard applicable to L's act is that which prescribes the form and manner in which his authority to legislate is to be exer-

* (I.R.) As regards legislative acts lawyers and judges are almost exclusively preoccupied with the questions whether the act is effective and if so, what its effects are. This fact will explain why I find it desirable to look at the legislative act chiefly as an effective act and why I do not try to work out a sixfold classification of legislative acts such as I used in discussing acts of individuals. Most of the categories of acts in our sixfold classification would be empty, or almost empty, if we were applying them to acts of the legislature. The legislature is not expected to commit crimes or torts in the performance of its lawmaking functions. The standards which one finds in constitutions or elsewhere do not mention any such injurious acts. Nor does one find among these standards any reference to the legislature's privilege of enacting law. The great bulk of standards applicable to acts of the legislature are cast in terms of what the legislature can do, and cannot do, effectively. This means, to refer again to the sixfold classification, that almost everything falls under the head of standards for effective acts.

cised. Some standards of this type—the most fundamental —are found in constitutional provisions. Thus, common constitutional provisions require that statutes be entitled in specified ways; that they be enacted a certain period of time before they take effect; that they be published in a certain manner; [1] that they be adopted by both legislative houses; that adoption by the respective houses be certified by the signatures of the presiding officer and clerk thereof; that statutes be signed by the governor, except when they are passed over his veto; and that the houses of the legislature keep certain records or journals of their proceedings. Other standards to control the legislature's act are found in statutes or resolutions adopted by the two houses and in the rules of order of the separate houses of the legislature. Ordinarily these statutes, resolutions, and rules deal with less important matters than the constitutional provisions and go into more detail; they are analogous to the rules of form and procedure which one finds in the bylaws of a society or corporation.

Sec. 4–11. Prohibitions. The third type of standard applicable to L's acts is that which expressly or impliedly prohibits lawmaking of certain types or on certain subjects. Examples of *express specific* prohibition are the Contracts Clause of the Federal Constitution which declares that "No State shall . . . pass any . . . Law impairing the Obligation of Contracts . . ."; and the clauses of most, if not all, of the constitutions which forbid enactment of ex post facto laws: i.e., legislation which would operate to make an act criminal which was not so when done. Wider and more general prohibitions are represented by the Due Process clauses of the Fifth and Fourteenth Amendments to the Federal Constitution, which forbid the federal and state governments respectively to deprive persons of "life, liberty or property,

---

[1] As regards the requirement of publication, see also what is said in sec. 4–18 below.

without due process of law." These clauses do not, in terms, apply to legislative acts, but their terms are general and embrace any and all acts of government, including legislative acts; and, according to the settled interpretation, this is their effect.

Implied prohibitions are exemplified by the negative side of the "separation of powers" doctrine. According to this doctrine, prohibitory implications are to be drawn from the fact that the constitutions invest the legislature with the power of making laws, the executive branch with the power of administering the business of government and enforcing laws, and the judiciary branch with the power of adjudicating controversies. The fact that the constitutions invest the legislature with the lawmaking power is treated as an implied prohibition against its exercising other kinds of power, i.e., executive or judicial. Parallel results can be implied from the fact that executive and judicial powers are invested explicitly in those respective branches.

These prohibitory provisions and implications applicable to L's acts bear an obvious resemblance to the prohibitory standards applicable to A's acts; in this respect they appear to impose negative duties upon L. However, L cannot be sued or punished if he violates a prohibition, as A might be. The only important effect of a prohibition, such as that barring ex post facto legislation, is that it renders L's countervailing act ineffective. The courts do not approach the consideration of the question whether an act of the legislature is violative of a constitutional provision as if they were concerned with a duty problem. They talk and think in terms of legislative power or the lack of it; and so do all the rest of us.*

---

* (I.R.) The situation is similar to that in which we consider whether a particular contract is violative of law. It is true that one can commit crimes and other wrongs by making contracts, e.g., by contracts in restraint of trade. Yet contracts are acts which raise chiefly questions of legal effects; they are

Sec. 4–12. Problems. Consider the following items in relation to the matters presented in sections 4–08 to 4–11 above:

1. The Michigan Constitution, like many other state constitutions, provides that "No law shall embrace more than one object which shall be expressed in its title." [1]

Which of the three types of standards applicable to legislative acts is represented by this clause?

Suppose you were called upon by an interested group to draft a bill to be submitted to the legislature. You were expected to prepare provisions to achieve the following objectives: (1) to provide for the sterilization of mental defectives, (2) to authorize sterilization of such defectives on court order and also to authorize voluntary sterilization of such persons, (3) to prohibit the advertisement and sale of contraceptive devices, (4) to make punishable the acts of any doctor who performs a sterilization operation on a patient for purely contraceptive purposes. What would you do in view of the provisions in the foregoing constitutional clause?

2. "No law shall be revised, altered or amended by reference to its title only; but the act revised and the section or sections of the act altered or amended shall be reenacted and published at length." [2]

To which of the three types of standards does this clause belong? Just what does this clause require be done?

3. "Congress shall make no law . . . abridging the freedom of speech, or of the press. . . ." [3]

Which type of standard is here employed?

4. "The Congress shall have Power . . . To regulate Commerce with foreign Nations and among the several

acts done with the purpose of producing legal effects. And so of statute-making. The power to legislate can be misused but this does not alter the fact that legislation is essentially an effective act.

[1] Mich. Const. 1908 Art. V, Sec. 21.
[2] *Ibid.*
[3] U. S. Const., 1st Amendment.

States, and with the Indian tribes. . . ." [4] This is a specific grant, as is stated in section 4–09. This clause allocates control of interstate commerce to Congress. Other clauses of the Constitution recognize that the power to regulate intrastate commerce is preserved to the states. What prohibitive standards might be implied from these allocations of power?

Sec. 4–13. Effectuation of standards—discretion. As stated above, the positive obligation of the legislature to create enactments for the general welfare, has little meaning beyond the needs which the legislature itself recognizes. There are practically no sanctions within the legal system to induce the legislature to exercise its functions. The exercise of law-making power lies almost wholly within the legislature's discretion.

But the standards which limit legislative powers to certain fields or subjects are capable of effective enforcement under our American constitutional system. The courts can, and do, refuse to give effect to laws which transcend constitutional grants of power, or which offend against prohibitions in the constitutions. This method of refusing judicial recognition to a legislative act, i.e., holding it ineffective, would for example strike down a statute which violated the prohibition of ex post facto legislation. The method is equally efficacious in regard to constitutional standards which prescribe formalities or methods for the enactment of laws; the courts consistently refuse to give effect to laws which do not comply with these requirements.[1]

---

[4] U. S. Const., Art. I, Sec. 8, Cl. 3.

[1] However, according to the usual view, the deficiency must be evident on the face of the statute; e.g., the defects involved in problems 1 and 2, sec. 4–12. The court does not go behind the certificate of proper officials that standards governing methods of enactment have been complied with: e.g., it will not permit a showing that a quorum was not present when an act was passed, or that an act was passed by less than a majority of votes. See generally **Field v. Clark,** 143 U. S. 649 (1892).

Sec. 4–14. Legislative inertia—law revision commissions.
The lawmaking process, especially as carried on by the legislature, is strongly affected by inertia. Laws are not made and
changes are not brought about when they should be. Laws
often remain on the books long after they have ceased to
serve any useful end. Sometimes they remain after they
become positive detriments to the community. More often
they simply lose their practical importance by reason of
change of circumstances. They are in a class with a regulation,
which I understand still stands among the house rules of
one of the Harvard dormitories, penalizing any resident
student the sum of one dollar for rolling a cannonball down
the hall. This may have been an appropriate prohibition right
after the Civil War, when men were returning to school
with souvenirs of this type in their possession, but the rule
has ceased to serve any real function. And so of some of our
laws; regulations of hitching posts, of fords over streams and
of other subjects once important have become practically
inoperative.

The reason for legislative inertia in the matter of revision
and change is not hard to discover. The legislative process,
like other legal processes, is motivated chiefly by immediate
interests of individuals. The members of the legislature are
busy. They have many pressing matters to attend to, matters
in which their constituents are vitally interested, especially
matters of taxation and of local expenditure. The legislator
who has a pet project for the expenditure of money in his
own district will be very active in promoting it, and he will
also press for a particular measure which many of his constituents want. But he has little incentive to push through
a measure which neither he nor a substantial body of his
constituents finds immediately urgent. When, for example,
a revision of some detail in the law of property is needed,

the necessary pressure for change is apt to be lacking; probably only a limited group of persons is aware of the need for change, and this group is too little interested, or too small in number to set the legislative mill grinding. The consequence is that legislative needs of real, but less immediate, interest are often crowded out and are completely neglected for years.

The need for methods of activating the processes of legislative revision is recognized by all persons familiar with the subject. A meritorious experiment to this end has recently been tried in a few of our states, notably in New York. The method is to create a permanent agency responsible for suggesting revisions to the legislature. In New York two bodies are established by law and charged with the functions of examining the existing law of the state, searching out needed changes in it, and drafting and proposing to the legislature, bills through which the changes can be made. One of these bodies is the Law Revision Commission, which studies and proposes changes in the body of the substantive law, i.e., the ordinary rules of law governing the rights and relations of individual to individual, and of individuals to the public. The other body is the Judicial Council, which performs similar functions as regards the law of procedure and the law governing the administration of justice. The work of such agencies results in calling the legislature's attention to needed changes and saves the effort and delay which is involved in preparing legislation for passage. Several other states have developed similar devices, and I believe that other states will eventually follow suit. While too much must not be expected from any single improvement in legislative procedures, devices are badly needed to keep the law up to date and eliminate outmoded legal standards from the statutes and the common law of the state.

SUBSIDIARY LAWMAKING

Sec. 4–15. Subsidiary agencies—delegation of legislative authority. The constitution and statutes of all our states contain provisions investing local agencies such as cities, villages, townships, and counties with legislative authority in reference to matters of local concern. The subjects of legislation include local highways and traffic, the use of land and methods of building thereon, and similar subjects. Furthermore, legislatures invest a great deal of rule-making authority in boards and administrative agencies. Thus the state bank examiner is authorized to make regulations for the business of banking, the state insurance commissioner for insurance companies and agencies, the public service commission for public utilities and transportation companies. In the federal field, rule-making authority of the Interstate Commerce Commission, the Bureau of Internal Revenue, and the Federal Trade Commission, exemplifies a similar delegation by Congress of regulatory power to subsidiary lawmaking agencies. In short, we must count legislation by local and administrative agencies, agencies with limited and specialized functions, as an important type of legislation to be put alongside statutory enactments.

You will encounter in your reading of cases the frequent assertion that legislative power cannot be delegated, or the somewhat broader statement that delegated authority cannot be delegated *(delegata potestas non potest delegari)*. Such statements cannot be accepted without substantial qualification. Of course, the legislature cannot turn over the whole of its legislative authority to some other agency to exercise. But the legislature can, and does, empower various subsidiary agencies to make standards. Until relatively recent times courts were reluctant to admit the existence of this type of delegation of authority; instead of doing so, they often made a distinction between delegation of legislative authority, which was said not to be possible, and delegation of quasi-legislative authority, which was said to be permissible. The resort to such a distinction was, of course, simply a method of saving the face of the nondelegation doctrine which was cast in absolute and unqualified terms, at the same time allowing actual delegations by calling them by another name. Today courts no longer resort to this device. They acknowledge that legislative authority can be delegated as such.

Sec. 4–16. Problems: reasons and conditions of delegation. The only serious questions which remain are questions regarding the extent of authority which can be delegated and the conditions which must be attached.

Consider these two excerpts in the light of the foregoing observations:

1. Taft, C. J.:

"The Interstate Commerce Commission was authorized to exercise powers the conferring of which by Congress would have been, perhaps, thought in the earlier years of the Republic to violate the rule that no legislative power can be delegated. But the inevitable progress and exigencies of government and the utter inability of Congress to give the time and attention indispensable to the exercise of these powers in detail, forced the modification of the rule." [1]

According to this statement by Chief Justice Taft, what is the reason or basis for the delegation of rule-making authority?

2. Lamar, J.:

"It must be admitted that it is difficult to define the line which separates legislative power to make laws, from administrative authority to make regulations. This difficulty has often been recognized, and was referred to by Chief Justice Marshall in *Wayman* v. *Southard*, 10 Wheat. 1, 42, where

---

[1] 257 U. S. xxv–xxvi (1921).

he was considering the authority of courts to make rules. He there said: 'It will not be contended that Congress can delegate to the courts, or to any other tribunals, powers which are strictly and exclusively legislative. But Congress may certainly delegate to others, powers which the legislature may rightfully exercise itself.' What were these non-legislative powers which Congress *could* exercise but which might also be delegated to others was not determined, for he said: 'The line has not been exactly drawn which separates those important subjects, which *must* be entirely regulated by the legislature itself, from those of less interest, in which a general provision may be made, and power given to those who are to act under such provisions to fill up the details.'

"From the beginning of the Government various acts have been passed conferring upon executive officers power to make rules and regulations—not for the government of their departments, but for administering the laws which did govern. None of these statutes could confer legislative power. But when Congress had legislated and indicated its will, it could give to those who were to act under such general provisions 'power to fill up the details' by the establishment of administrative rules and regulations, the violation of which could be punished by fine or imprisonment fixed by Congress, or by penalties fixed by Congress or measured by the injury done." [2]

What are the limitations suggested by Justice Lamar as regards the delegation of rule-making authority? Note that this Justice, speaking in 1911, was not quite willing to recognize that the authority which was delegated by Congress is "legislative."

Congress has delegated a large degree of power to the Supreme Court to make rules of procedure for actions at law, suits in equity, criminal prosecutions, etc. Similar delegations of rule-making authority have also been made in many of the states. What is the advantage of this type of delegation of power?

[2] United States v. Grimaud, 220 U. S. 506, at 517 (1911).

Sec. 4–17. Standards for the subsidiary lawmaker. The rule-making activities of subsidiary legislative agencies are controlled by a variety of constitutional and statutory standards. To start with, all the constitutional limitations which apply generally to the exercise of legislative power apply to them, such as the prohibition of ex post facto legislation and legislation which deprives persons of life, liberty, or property without due process of law. But there are also particular limitations which define the legislative competence of these subsidiary agencies and regulate the manner in which their rule-making authority is to be exercised. The authority of the city council to enact ordinances is restricted to certain subjects of local concern and the manner of enactment is definitely prescribed. The administrative body can establish rules and regulations only in a certain narrow field and only in the manner authorized by law.

It is interesting to note how some of these legislative acts depend upon others and how some furnish standards for others. Take for example the enactment of a city ordinance such as we have been discussing. This enactment really involves a series of three legislative acts: (1) the act of the constitution maker, (2) the statute establishing a city government and conferring the power to make ordinances, and (3) the ordinance in question.[1] The ordinance is dependent upon the other two acts. It presupposes them, so that when one speaks of a city ordinance regulating parking of automobiles, one is merely giving attention to the last of a series of law-making acts which establish standards of behavior for the public, and is taking for granted two more fundamental acts on which the ordinance is predicated and which furnish standards for the ordinance-maker.[2] A like analysis may be

---

[1] This series of three acts represents the typical situation; but in some states the constitution confers power directly on cities. In such cases only two acts are involved; the constitution and the ordinance.

[2] The same analysis can be applied to the enactment of a statute, except that only two distinct and interrelated acts are involved. The first is the basic

made of the rules and regulations of an administrative body. These likewise constitute the third in a series of three legislative acts: a constitutional provision, a statute which confers and governs rule-making authority, and the exercise of that authority by the adoption of rules. To be sure, it is not necessary to mention on every occasion the basic and presupposed elements in such a series. One need not speak of the constitutional and statutory basis of a city ordinance or administrative rule every time one mentions the ordinance or rule. But for some purposes it is important to make explicit the precedent elements which are presupposed, notably when there is reason to doubt whether the dependent act stands on a solid foundation of authority, or whether it conforms to all the standards which pertain to its enactment.

Lawmaker's Statement of Standards

Sec. 4–18. Communication of legislative message. In preparing and issuing his message, the lawmaker has three major problems to consider: (1) the problem of fixing a purpose or policy, i.e., what general results he wishes to bring about through his legislative act (section 4–04 above); (2) the problem of means and methods, i.e., what standards and what effectuative devices are appropriate to bring about the purpose he aims to achieve (section 4–05 above); and (3) the problem of communicating his message to those to be affected by it. The first two of these problems have already been stressed. The third is no less important; the communication of his message ought to be planned no less carefully by the lawmaker than its content. The problem of communication really falls into two—the problem of *stating* his message so that it will be understood and the problem of

act by which the constitution is adopted, establishing the framework of government and authorizing the legislature to enact statutes. The second is the act of the legislature in enacting the statute in question. The constitutional act confers legislative power and governs the form and manner in which statutes are to be enacted.

transmitting it so as to make sure that the message reaches the ears of the persons to be guided or controlled.

The problem of *stating* the message, which will engage our chief attention throughout the rest of this subtopic, is one of the most difficult that I know of. A poorly drawn statute can cause more confusion and upset more applecarts than almost any act under heaven. The slightest looseness or slip in phrasing can result in serious problems of interpretation; it can cause uncertainty, delay and costly litigation, to individuals and officials who have to act or refrain from acting and who must carry cases to the Supreme Court for the clarification of points which affect their actions. Realizing the momentous consequences of what he says and does not say, the conscientious lawmaker will do all he can to state his meaning so clearly and certainly that it will be understood, and understood in the same sense, by everybody. Yet the lawmaker can never be quite successful in this aim. His messages are addressed to a great variety of persons, persons of every degree of intelligence, education, and language background, from the most intelligent and highly educated, to the very dull and illiterate. Drafting a statute which will be read in the same way by persons of all kinds and degrees is out of the question; the lawmaker simply does the best that he can.

The problem of *transmitting* the legislative message is intensified by two facts earlier mentioned: that the lawmaker sends his message over wide reaches of space, and that he hands it down through indefinite stretches of time.[1] These facts require that the lawmaker, above all speakers, transmit his message in a form which cannot miscarry or be lost to view. Moreover, the problem of transmitting the legislative message, like that of stating the message, is enhanced by the

[1] See sec. 1–08.

variety of persons addressed. In regard to transmission the
lawmaker needs to consider not only levels of intelligence
and education but also the alertness of the persons addressed.
Are they ready to seek out what he enacts? Or are they
inclined to wait for casual information about what he has
declared? If his message is intended primarily for lawyers,
he can probably depend upon real effort to discover what
he has laid down. If the message is directed to the common
man, he will probably have to expect that knowledge of enactments will reach its intended hearers chiefly through the
newspapers and through neighborhood gossip.

Under the circumstances mentioned in the last two paragraphs you will understand why the statement and the transmission of his message are not minor problems for the lawmaker. But our constitutions do not provide much guidance
to the lawmaker in regard to the way he states his mandate
or the way in which he transmits it to persons affected. These
problems are left by the constitutions almost wholly to the
lawmaker's discretion and ingenuity for solution. He can
state his legal mandate in any manner he chooses, so long
as he does not violate the requirements of form previously
mentioned,[2] and does not state it so indefinitely that the
courts will declare it void. Also the constitutions do require,
expressly or by implication, that laws be put in printed form
as they are enacted. The Michigan Constitution, for example,
requires that "All laws enacted in any session of the legislature shall be published in book form within sixty days after
final adjournment of the session. . . ."[3] But, in almost all
states, statutes become operative when they are passed by
both houses of the legislature and signed by the chief executive. The process of enactment is then complete. Even under
a provision like that just quoted from the Michigan Consti-

[2] See sec. 4–10.
[3] Const. 1908 Art. V, Sec. 39.

tution, the operation of a statute does not depend upon publication. Publication is not a part of the process of enactment in the Anglo-American systems as it is in the systems of the states of continental Europe.[4] Whatever is done by way of advertising the fact that a law has been passed, is done by the legislature in its discretion, or is undertaken unofficially by newspapers or other news disseminating agencies, or by interested groups such as trade and bar associations.

Sec. 4–19. Parts of statute. Statutes, for the most part, follow traditional lines of form and structure. (1) There is usually a *title clause* describing more or less accurately the content of the enactment; this clause is made mandatory by constitutional provisions of many of the states. (2) Following the title clause is often found a *preamble* in which the occasion of the legislation, its purpose, or both, are explained. Sometimes these explanations are found not in a preamble but in the first sections of the body of the act. (3) After these preliminaries comes the *main body* of the act. This is usually introduced by some such clause as "Be it enacted that." The body of the act is divided up into sections, if the statute is one of any size and complexity. The sections set forth standard acts of individuals and officials, which are to be done, not done, etc., together with their consequences and legal significance. All the sections are interconnected so as to constitute a unified legislative plan. (4) Following the main body of the act, one often finds a section which contains *definitions* of important terms used in the act; sometimes, however, the section containing definitions is placed ahead of the main body of the act. (5) Another section commonly found in statutes is one which deals with the possible contingency that part of the act be held *unconstitutional.*

[4] In a few states publication is made a prerequisite to the effectiveness of a statute. For example, the Kansas Constitution provides: "No law of a general nature shall be in force until the same be published," Art. II, Sec. 19. See also Wisconsin Constitution, Art. VII, Sec. 21.

(6) Most statutes contain a concluding section *repealing or amending* other acts which are inconsistent in whole or in part with the statute in question. Such a provision is not absolutely necessary (see section 4–32 below) though it is desirable and is almost always included.

You will appreciate the parts and structure of a statute more readily if you see an example. I have chosen for the purpose a federal statute, enacted in 1932, to control the *issuance of injunctions in labor disputes.* I quote the first three sections in full and also the last two sections of the Act; the others I state in summary form:

"AN ACT [1]

"To amend the Judicial Code and to define and limit the jurisdiction of courts sitting in equity, and for other purposes.

"*Be it enacted by the Senate and House of Representatives of the United States of America in Congress assembled,* That no court of the United States, as herein defined, shall have jurisdiction to issue any restraining order or temporary or permanent injunction in a case involving or growing out of a labor dispute, except in a strict conformity with the provisions of this Act; nor shall any such restraining order or temporary or permanent injunction be issued contrary to the public policy declared in this Act.

"Sec. 2. In the interpretation of this Act and in determining the jurisdiction and authority of the courts of the United States, as such jurisdiction and authority are herein defined and limited, the public policy of the United States is hereby declared as follows:

"Whereas under prevailing economic conditions, developed with the aid of governmental authority for owners of property to organize in the corporate and other forms of ownership association, the individual unorganized worker is commonly helpless to exercise actual liberty of contract and to protect his freedom of labor, and thereby to obtain acceptable terms and conditions of employment, wherefore, though he should be free to decline to associate with his

[1] 47 Stat. 70.

fellows, it is necessary that he have full freedom of association, self-organization, and designation of representatives of his own choosing, to negotiate the terms and conditions of his employment, and that he shall be free from the interference, restraint, or coercion of employers of labor, or their agents, in the designation of such representatives or in self-organization or in other concerted activities for the purpose of collective bargaining or other mutual aid or protection; therefore, the following definitions of, and limitations upon, the jurisdiction and authority of the courts of the United States are hereby enacted.

"Sec. 3. Any undertaking or promise, such as is described in this section, or any other undertaking or promise in conflict with the public policy declared in section 2 of this Act, is hereby declared to be contrary to the public policy of the United States, shall not be enforceable in any court of the United States and shall not afford any basis for the granting of legal or equitable relief by any such court, including specifically the following:

"Every undertaking or promise hereafter made, whether written or oral, express or implied, constituting or contained in any contract or agreement of hiring or employment between any individual, firm, company, association, or corporation, and any employee or prospective employee of the same, whereby

"(a) Either party to such contract or agreement undertakes or promises not to join, become, or remain a member of any labor organization or of any employer organization; or

"(b) Either party to such contract or agreement undertakes or promises that he will withdraw from an employment relation in the event that he joins, becomes, or remains a member of any labor organization or of any employer organization."

Sec. 4. Expressly enumerates various acts of participants in labor disputes which do not constitute grounds for the issuance of an injunction, such as refusal to continue employment relations, retention of organization affiliations, giving publicity to disputed facts, peaceably assembling, etc.

Sec. 5. Declares that concerted acts of disputants do not constitute unlawful combinations.

Sec. 6. Declares that organizational officers are not liable for acts of individual members unless they participate in those acts or ratify the same.

Sec. 7. Regulates the issuance of injunctions and the procedure in connection with the hearing thereof.

Sec. 8. Provides that the complainant shall not be allowed an injunction unless he has fully complied with his own legal obligations.

Sec. 9. Defines the findings which must be made by the court in order to justify injunctive relief.

Sec. 10. Deals with procedure for review.

Secs. 11 and 12. Deal with proceedings for contempt in violating injunctions issued.

Sec. 13. Contains definitions of important terms used in this Act, such as labor dispute, association, etc.

"Sec. 14. If any provision of this Act or the application thereof to any person or circumstance is held unconstitutional or otherwise invalid, the remaining provisions of the Act and the application of such provisions to other persons or circumstances shall not be affected thereby.

"Sec. 15. All Acts and parts of Acts in conflict with the provisions of this Act are hereby repealed.

"Approved, March 23, 1932."

Sec. 4–20. Statement in popular and in technical language. The lawmaker may state his directive message in popular or in technical language. By popular language I mean that which is in common use in the community. By technical language I mean the special terminology used by men belonging to a particular craft or profession. The peculiar terms of almost any profession may be used in statutes, e.g., a building code may use terms ordinarily used only by contractors, plumbers, and carpenters, and a statute regulating the sale of drugs may use names known only to pharmacists and physicians. But the technical terms in which we are primarily interested and which are most commonly found in legislation are the peculiar terms of the legal craft. Statutes are usually drafted by lawyers. They are chiefly read and used by lawyers. They are applied by judges who are legally trained. It is not surprising, therefore, that statutes do contain a great deal of lawyers' language.

The facts just stated may explain the use of legal terms in statutes; do they justify this use? Is the introduction of these technical terms into legislation desirable? Why should not all legislation be cast in popular terms? Popular terms have the advantage of being understood by everybody or at least by everyone who has had a moderate amount of education. Technical terms are understood only by the few who have undergone technical training.

Before we address ourselves to these questions it must be noted that the vast majority of the words which even the technical man employs are of the popular sort. Legal terms do not constitute a complete language. The lawyer cannot express himself exclusively in legal terms. Like everyone else the lawyer uses such common terms as "and," "the," "house," "street," "go," and "kill." He inserts legal terms only when he is discussing subject matter and activities which are of peculiar interest to lawyers. Accordingly our question about the desirability of using technical terms is considerably narrower than it might appear to be at first glance. The question is why it is desirable or necessary to use *some* legal terms in legislation, since legislation is never cast wholly in such terms.

One reason for using a technical term may be the fact that there is no popular term for the subject matter involved. "Carburetor" and "penicillin" are examples; such terms are unique; there are no equivalents for them in the common language. However, if their subject matter is important and becomes generally known, these technical terms become popular by a gradual process of adoption. In this sense one finds many legal words for which there can hardly be said to be any popular equivalent. And, on the other hand, there are not a few legal words which have in the course of time become popular words by adoption, such words as "possession," "contract," "corporation," "crime," and others. There can be no valid basis for objecting to the use either of unique legal terms or of legal terms which have become popular, in the enactment of statutes; although, if a unique term is to be used, it should probably be specifically defined in the statute itself.

Another reason for the use of technical terms is that they can be and usually are carefully chosen and defined. This means that technical terms can be used more specifically and accurately than popular terms. The latter are almost always indefinite in meaning and loosely used. The use of technical terms is, therefore, justified by the needs for accuracy and certainty. These needs are especially felt in relation to the execution of effective acts. Where individuals and officials act with foresight of results and where specific guidance of acts is aimed to be furnished by legal standards, the actor must be told specifically and accurately what he is to do and what the consequences of his act will be. The needed degree of definiteness and certainty can usually be attained only by employing technical legal words whose meaning has been brought out and fixed by long experience and use. Moreover, in regard to effective acts which are normally done or engineered by lawyers, such as the drafting of pleadings, deeds, and wills, the organization of corporations and the preparation of contracts, statutes usually employ many technical terms. The ordinary lay client need not understand the statute applicable in such situations; he hires a lawyer to do a legal job for him and whether the lawyer is guided by a statute couched in popular or in technical terms is of no consequence to him. It is no more necessary for the client himself to understand the technical jargon which the lawmaker introduces into such statutes than it is for the patient to understand the medical jargon in which a medical textbook instructs the doctor in the diagnosis and treatment of ailments.

Sec. 4–21. Problems. 1. Is the last argument to justify the use of technical terms in statutes entirely convincing? Here I make the fact that a transaction is one which is usually engineered by lawyers, the criterion for the use of technical terms in the relevant statute. Is there a possible fallacy in making this fact the basis for the use of technical terms in legislation? Does one who uses such an argument lift himself by his own bootstraps?

2. Bentham, writing in the early 19th century, compared the use of technical terms in jurisprudence and other sciences as follows:

"The case is, that in the language of every branch of art and science that can be named, a more or less extensive stock of words of a peculiar nature, in addition to all the words in familiar use, is an indispensable appendage: applied to these, what the appellation technical imports is nothing more than peculiar, as above, to some branch of art and science: to wit, in contradistinction to those which, being likewise employed in discourse relative to that same branch of art and science, have nothing to distinguish them from the words in universal use belonging to the common stock of the language;—or the import of them, from the import attributed to those same ordinary words. But the difference between these jurisprudential peculiar words, and the other peculiar words, is this: in the case of the other peculiar words, the deviation from ordinary words is matter of absolute necessity, and on the occasion of framing them the whole attention and skill possessed by the framers was commonly employed in the rendering them as expressive as possible; whereas in the other case, the deviation from ordinary language being as wide commonly as can be imagined,—no attention has been paid to render it expressive, by rendering it as near akin as possible to the words appertaining to that same common stock;—to that end no attention whatsoever was employed, the attention, if any, applied to the subject, having the direct opposite end, viz., that of rendering them as inexpressive as possible, as unlikely as possible to convey correct conception;—the only purposes to which they are applicable or designed to be applied, are either conveying to the persons in question no conception at all, or if any, such as shall have the effect of leading them into error, either productive of burden to the persons thus deceived, or benefit to the deceivers.

"Terms of art, jurisprudence must have as well as every other branch of art and science. But in English practice, the terms of art are to what they ought to be, what the terms of astrology are to the terms of astronomy. . . .

"In medical art and science, improvement is rapid and extensive at all times and in all places; in legislation and jurisprudence, everything is either retrograde, or at best stationary.

"The cause is no secret. In medicine it is the interest of every practitioner to promote improvement, and to promote it to the utmost, to make whatsoever addition to the stock his faculties admit of his making:—of no judicial practitioner is this the interest—his interest is directly opposite."[1]

Bentham recognizes the need for technical legal terms. What is he complaining of? Is he correct in contrasting medicine with law? Do you agree that the legal profession attempts to render its language "as inexpressive as possible, as unlikely as possible to convey correct conceptions"?

Sec. 4–22. Incomplete statement of legislative message. The lawmaker's handiwork is always incomplete. His message is never set forth in a manner to fully define a standard act or to declare all of its significance. Only a relatively small portion of any legal action picture and its meaning are expressly set out in the enacted provision. However, this is not a peculiarity of constitutional or statutory enactments; all verbal acts are incomplete in this sense. Since this incomplete-

[1] III WORKS OF JEREMY BENTHAM 270–271.

ness is characteristic of verbal acts generally, a few observations regarding the expression of meaning seem appropriate and even necessary at this point.

Incomplete statement is to a considerable extent unavoidable. No matter how careful the speaker, his statement will always be unfinished, due to the inadequacy of his knowledge of existing conditions and his inability to foresee future events. The speaker can never make a complete and all-embracing statement for the simple reason that he cannot think out a complete and final plan on which to base prescriptions of this kind. In addition, there is always the necessity of cutting his expression short at some point. No statement can be complete in an absolute sense. To express any meaning in complete detail would carry the speaker to the end of time, since each statement would have to be explained and each explanatory proposition further explained and elaborated, ad infinitum.

But in both planning and expression the speaker always stops far short of practicable limits. He does not even try to figure out and state a full meaning. He leaves gaps as a matter of economy of effort. He does not state any more than he feels is necessary for the purpose in hand. Speakers may vary in their feeling of obligation to develop and express meaning. One speaker may act with meticulous care to avoid misunderstanding and oversight. Another may mention only immediately important points, and for the rest, like the bridegroom as he says "I do," he may trust in a benevolent Providence to shape the consequences of his verbal act in a proper way. Every speaker, careful or careless, takes many things for granted. He treats many facts as understood and known to the hearer, as well as to himself, and therefore as unnecessary to be expressed in verbal form. He leaves much unsaid which might be said, expecting the hearer to supply it. In short, any verbal act embodies only a part of the meaning which the speaker might express. The hearer is relied on to fill up the gaps in what is said, from what he knows or what he can find out, if and when supplementation of meaning becomes relevant or necessary.

Economy of expression on the speaker's part does not imply neglect or fault. Reliance on the activity of the hearer to supply implicit elements from context, makes possible an enormous saving of time and effort. Only the bore or pedant explains the obvious. The ingenious speaker expresses just what he needs to express, neither more nor less. And, since the hearer and the speaker act in the light of the same context, no additional burden is cast upon the hearer in the normal case. In fact, the hearer is hardly aware that he derives the meaning of the speaker's verbal act quite as much from context and circumstances as from the words he hears. But, if the speaker misjudges the elements which need to be stated, if he takes too much for granted, if he leaves too much to Providence, the hearer will have to supply the lack by efforts of his own. The speaker's saving of effort is bought at the cost of even greater effort on the part of the hearer, who has to fill up the blanks in an inadequate declaration.

The lawmaker's declarations are incomplete as other verbal acts are and for the same reasons. There are unavoidable gaps due to the fact that the lawmaker cannot know everything about the situation he tries to control and cannot foresee future developments, and due to the fact that he cannot express his plan and desire in complete detail. There are also careless gaps and plain oversights in legislation.

But of greatest practical significance is the fact that the lawmaker, like other speakers, takes many things for granted. He economizes his own effort in expressing his legislative plan and thus leaves blanks which may, as conditions later develop, need to be filled by explicit judicial rulings. Suppose for example that the lawmaker passes a statute creating a new crime. The statute uses common and legal terms without defining them; it refers to ordinary life situations without describing them; it implies a knowledge of many facts which it does not refer to even indirectly. The lawmaker assumes that the interpreter and other persons affected by the statute, will know, or can find out, the meanings of terms and other matters of common knowledge. The statute provides for a specified punishment, but it says nothing about the details of procedure in prosecution, nor about the functions of public officials in relation thereto. The lawmaker takes for granted that prosecution will follow the forms of existing criminal procedure except as the statute makes specific provision for a different form. He assumes that existing officials will perform their typical functions in reference to this crime as in reference to others. All these are matters which the lawmaker could have put into the statute but did not deem it necessary to mention. His expression of meaning is left in truncated form which will require supplementation by individuals and officials affected by its provisions.

Sec. 4–23. Statement of message in general terms. The lawmaker uses many general or class terms in framing his message. He employs such terms as "person," "contract," "injury," "prosecute," and the like. In fact the use of general terms is unavoidable. But a general term is to some extent, indefinite and in this sense incomplete, so that generality of expression involves incompleteness of statement. And generality varies in degree. Some terms and statements are more general and therefore less definite than others. Most legislative enactments are couched in terms which fall between the extremes of broad generality and minute specification.

From the lawmaker's viewpoint general terms have the advantages of flexibility in application and of applicability to unforeseen cases. If his statute specifies details of appli-

cation with undue particularity, there is always the danger
that important situations will be omitted, and that the language will fail to cover cases which the lawmaker would have
wanted to cover if he had had sufficient foresight and could
have stated his meaning perfectly. General provisions are
adaptable to whatever conditions may arise.

"Statutes framed in general terms apply to new cases that
arise, and to new subjects that are created from time to time,
and which come within their general scope and policy. It is
a rule of statutory construction that legislative enactments
in general and comprehensive terms, prospective in operation,
apply alike to all persons, subjects, and business within their
general purview and scope coming into existence subsequent
to their passage." [1]

However, the flexibility and adaptability of general terms
are bought at the price of indefiniteness and incompleteness
as I have already pointed out. A general provision is very
like one in which the lawmaker has failed to set forth his
meaning fully. There is a formal difference between them;
incomplete legislative statement leaves a subject quite untouched though it be taken for granted (see next preceding
section); while the general statement covers the subject
formally but in an undefined way. The coverage of detailed
situations by general terms is rather apparent than real. As
Holmes has said, general propositions do not decide cases.
A general provision is one which is unfinished; the applier
has the burden of supplying details of meaning which are
only implied or suggested by the general terms.

The lawmaker may also use general language in order
to conserve his own efforts in thinking out more detailed
provisions; or he may recognize that he cannot give the close
attention to rule-making for specific cases which is needed,
or that he has not the facilities for investigation and for the

[1] 25 R. C. L. 778.

framing of detailed rules. He therefore delegates the job of detailed legislation to others. These are the cases of subsidiary lawmaking we have heretofore discussed. The lawmaker intentionally leaves to an administrative agency the task of filling in details of a broad legislative plan which he lays out. Theoretically, the lawmaker might make all the rules which the administrative agency is to apply, but for reasons of convenience, in order to provide rules which are flexible and well adapted to specific types of situations, the legislature is content to lay out a general design, and to authorize another agency to write in specific elements of the regulative scheme. Insofar as an administrative agency has to fill in these elements, it is clearly functioning as a supplementary lawmaker. The same is true of the processes by which ordinances are made by a city council. And one can fairly ask (and we shall do so in the next chapter) whether the activity of the judicial applier in filling in details of general legislation is not essentially the same. To be sure, the judge's activity is not usually called legislation; it goes by the name of interpretation. Yet it is nonetheless apparent that the judge is writing something into a general regulative scheme in the same manner as an administrative or other subsidiary lawmaker does.

So far as a standard is general, it fails to furnish assured guidance. To the applier it represents the necessity of exercising unguided judgment in the act of filling in details. To the person intended to be guided, generality represents uncertainty; it means reduced guidance value; a general standard fails to present a fully developed pattern of action. The person is told broadly what he is expected to do or not do, and that the rest of the pattern will be filled in by a subsidiary lawmaker as occasion requires. This spells for him the possibility of arbitrariness in application by officials who have to fill in detailed rules before they can apply them.

Sec. 4–24. Problems. 1. Consider again the case of *State v. McGowan,* set out in section 2–48, problem 2, where a statute penalized the act of arson.

Spell out: (1) Some of the details of the general terms of the statute which the court had to supply; (2) some of the principal elements which were taken for granted by the lawmaker and not mentioned at all.

2. Consider in a similar way the Commerce Clause of the Federal Constitution, which reads as follows: "The Congress shall have power . . . to regulate commerce with foreign Nations and among the several States. . . ." [1]

Note the principal general terms used. Would you know from reading this clause whether Congress can control interstate transportation of passengers as distinct from commodities of trade? What about transmission of radio messages?

Again, what are some of the important elements of the control over commerce which are taken for granted and not even referred to?

3. Dickinson:

"It is therefore clear why the broader and more fundamental principles of the law are themselves almost never capable of being applied directly as rules of decision for the settlement of controversies. On the one hand the principle may be so broad—as e.g., that property rights should be protected—that it will embrace within its scope both the opposing interests in a particular controversy, and therefore give no clue as to which should prevail over the other. Thus in a nuisance case both parties can appeal to their right to have their property protected. On the other hand, if the principle is less broad in its scope, it is likely to express the interest of only one of the parties to the controversy, and so come into square collision with another equally valid principle expressing the interest of the opposing party. Take the case of a nuisance again. On one side stands the principle that

[1] Art. I, Sec. 8.

a man may lawfully do as he wills with his own. On the other stands the principle, *Sic utere tuo ut alienum non laedas.*" [2]

How are these statements related to our discussion in section 4–23? What does Dickinson add to the statement of Holmes that general propositions do not decide cases?

4. "The Legislature shall pass no local or special act in any case where a general act can be made applicable, and whether a general act can be made applicable shall be a judicial question." [3] Similar prohibitions of local and special legislation are to be found in many state constitutions.

When is legislation general by contrast with special in the sense of this prohibition? Suppose a statute enacts a health code for all cities of ten thousand. Is this code general legislation? Suppose another health code applies to cities of one million, and there is only one such city in the state.

Does the constitutional clause prescribe the form of statutory statement? Suppose, for example, the legislature passed a health code applicable to "the City of Detroit." Can you state the purport of the constitutional clause in terms of a distinction between general and specific directives, i.e., standards and orders (see section 1–08)?

Does the constitutional clause fix the number of items to which a statute must apply? Is it satisfied if the legislature makes a bona fide effort to classify cities, etc. according to their needs?

*Sec. 4–25. Codification.** Now and again a legislature undertakes to adopt a comprehensive and systematic statute, called a code, to embrace all the legal provisions applicable

---

[2] Meaning: so use your own as not to injure another. "The Law Behind Law," 29 Col. L. Rev. 285 at 298 (1929).

[3] Mich. Const. 1908 Art. V, Sec. 30.

* (I.R.) See bibliography on this subject in sec. 4–01 * note.

to a general field. The general purposes of codification are to render the law clear, certain, systematic, and complete.[1]

On the continent of Europe almost all states, building on the foundation of the Roman *corpus juris*, have codified their laws quite completely. The same is true of the South American countries.[2] In England the process of codification has not gone far. In this country the development of codes has been rather irregular; most states have only codified part of their law but New York, California and a few other states have codified the law of most important fields.

Common types of codes adopted in the last century and a half have been a *civil code*, dealing with matters of property, contract, tort, family relationships, etc.; a *code of civil procedure* or a general practice act, dealing with practice and procedure in the courts; a *commercial code*, covering matters such as sales, negotiable paper, etc.; a *code of criminal law*, commonly called a penal code; and a *code of criminal procedure*. Narrower fields of law may also be covered in a systematic form, by what may be called minor codes. Of this character are general acts dealing with the subject of corporations, traffic on the highways, or probate matters, as well as the various uniform acts which have been developed by the Commissioners on Uniform Laws and adopted in most of our states (e.g., the Uniform Negotiable Instruments law, the Uniform Sales law, etc.).

The process of codification does not begin with a blank legal sheet. It is always a reworking of existing legislation and of law as laid down in judicial decisions. It not only revises and amends pre-existing law but builds upon it and

---

[1] An additional purpose has often been to unify the law of the country in which several competing systems exist in different states or provinces. Unification was one of the main reasons for codification in both France and Germany.

[2] The original modern codes were drafted in France at the time of Napoleon. All subsequent codifications in Europe and South America have built on the Napoleonic codes.

out of its materials. The task of reworking and reforming these legal materials to constitute a clear, simple and unified code, is no mean undertaking. It is an undertaking which requires a considerable period of time. The difficulty of the job and the time which it requires, exclude the possibility of preparing and enacting a code in any single legislative session. Either the legislature borrows a code already enacted elsewhere, or it authorizes the preparation of a code which its successors will have to accept or reject. Moreover, the preparation of a code requires a degree of expertness which the ordinary legislature does not find within its own ranks. Consequently codes have usually been framed at the instance of a legislative body by a group of experts and submitted in the form of drafts for adoption by the legislature itself. The German Civil Code, for example, was framed by a select group of lawyers, judges, and professors of law. It went through several drafts and was twenty years in preparation. While the Field Codes, which have been the foundation of the principal codes in this country, were not drafted with quite the meticulous care of the German, Swiss and recent Italian codes, their preparation did extend over a considerable period of time and involved great effort by David Dudley Field and his collaborators.[3]

In the early part of the 19th century it was supposed that codification could be carried to the point where every case or situation would be provided for in advance. Bentham, the great English law reformer of that period, entertained this view; he stressed the idea that the law should be made "cognoscible," by which he meant that the law should be put in such form that everyone could know his legal rights without the least uncertainty. Accordingly the aspiration of codifiers of that day was to codify law completely and finally.

---

[3] You would find interesting H. M. FIELD's LIFE OF DAVID DUDLEY FIELD (1898). Chapters 7 and 8 give a brief account of the battle for codification in New York in the 1850's and 1860's, and of the adoption of codes in the western and midwestern states.

But time has proved that the hope of making complete and final codes is a vain one. We fall far short of this ideal, as we do of all other legal objectives. The possibilities of human behavior are too varied to be specifically provided for in advance. Life conditions change too rapidly to be anticipated in a roster of patterns of prescribed behavior. The lawmaker has to be satisfied, in the main, with general statements which can be adapted to innumerable and changing situations. The ideal of a complete and final codification, good for all cases and all times, has had to be abandoned; it has been replaced by a practical working notion of a codification which is good for a particular place and time, but which will require periodic revision to meet changing needs.

Sec. 4–26. Compilation, consolidation, annotation and indexing of statutes. Even where the statutes of a state are not integrated in codes, they are usually grouped and organized according to topics. This work of compilation is sometimes done at the instance of the legislature and at public expense. Sometimes it is done unofficially by a publisher as a commercial venture. The objective in either case is to make the separate enactments of the state more readily available for use and reference by lawyers and individuals. This is a desirable objective since the person who wishes to find the statutes on a particular topic is thus spared most of the effort of seeking for them throughout the miscellaneous assortment of laws which are passed from year to year in the sessions of the legislature.

Sometimes the process of integration is pushed one step further. All the statutes dealing with a particular subject matter are consolidated. Such a consolidation does not ordinarily attempt to unify the case law with the statute law, nor does it aim primarily to improve existing statute law. It merely brings together in a unifying statute all existing legislation on a particular topic (e.g., a British consolidation of 132 statutes dealing with perjury). The process of consolidation necessarily requires the ironing out of inconsistencies and the systematization of the existing statutes to some degree, but it is not intended to produce a complete statement or a systematic expression of the law.[1]

The statutes of the United States and of the states have also been annotated with reference to decisions construing their various paragraphs and provisions. These annotations are very useful to the lawyer as they bring together statute law and case law.

Indexing is another method employed to make statutory material readily available. A great deal of attention has been given to this type of work in recent years. Most if not all of the statutes, federal and state, have now been completely and minutely indexed.

Two general criticisms apply to the compilation, consolidation and indexing that has been done. First is the lack of uniform plans according to which material is arranged and catalogued. The plans vary greatly from state to state so that the lawyer has to familiarize himself with new schemes of arranging and cataloguing each time he examines the laws of a different jurisdiction. The second criticism results from the nature of all these devices. None of them integrates the statutory provisions with which it deals. All of them represent an organization which is extrinsic to the statutes. They constitute an organization of material which is imposed from the outside, a mere arrangement of existing material and not a reworking of the material handled. In this respect consolidation and indexing are different from the type of organization which is injected by the lawmaker when he creates a code

---

[1] Names are not always safe guides in this respect. For example, the so-called United States Code is really a consolidation rather than a codification of the federal statutes. "No new law is enacted and no law repealed." The code is "the official restatement in convenient form of the general and permanent laws of the United States" in force on the date when the code is issued.

and fits each of its provisions into a pattern with the rest so as to establish a unified, complete, and systematic whole.

Sec. 4–27. Problems. In an article in the AMERICAN LAW REVIEW,[1] DAVID DUDLEY FIELD said:

"I will mention here four *reasons* for codification, and four *sophisms* against it:

"*First.* There are certain propositions which have become maxims of government, one of which is that the legislative and judicial departments should be kept distinct, or in other words, that the same person should not be both law-giver and judge. There is no need of arguing about it. The maxim is founded on philosophy and experience. It has taken ages of struggle to establish it. And here it is. We profess to take it for absolute truth; we talk of it as one of the fundamental doctrines of modern government; we write it at the head of our constitutions; but we violate it every hour that we allow the judges to participate in the making of the laws.

"*Second.* Another of these maxims is, that they who are required to obey the laws should all have the opportunity of knowing what they are. These laws are now in sealed books and the lawyers object to the opening of these books. They can be opened by codification and only by codification. Do not say that this is a figurative expression which proves nothing. It proves everything. The law with us is a sealed book to the masses; it is a sealed book to all but the lawyers; and it is but partly opened even as to them. It is an insult to our understanding to say that the knowledge of the law is open to everybody.

"It should be open. That none can deny who has common understanding and a decent regard for truth. How can it be opened? In one way, and one only; writing it in a book of such dimensions and in such language that all can read and comprehend it. What if lawyers should say unwritten law is good enough for them? They are used to delving in it; they like it; they live by it. What then? Supposing it to be so does not mend the matter, unless it be assumed that the law is made for the lawyers and not for the people.

[1] Field, "Codification," 20 AM. L. REV. 1 at 2 (1886).

"These two reasons for codification should of themselves be decisive.

"*Third.* Another and a third reason is the lawyer's own experience; the experience, I might say, of every lawyer. What does he do when a case is brought to him, for the courts or for his private opinion? The first question he asks himself is, has the point been decided? He looks for a decision. Where does he look? First in the volumes of his own State reports. It may be that he finds a case just decided in the highest court on all fours with his own, and he fancies that he may rely on that. Can he? We lawyers know that there is still a chance of mistake. Look at the list of 'cases cited, criticised, distinguished, or overruled.' This is the very best aspect of the lawyer's position in the case supposed. But what if there be no such decision? Then he looks into the decisions of inferior courts in his own State. If he finds one that he thinks is applicable, he ventures to take it, though with less confidence, because he knows that he is to go through the ordeal of the higher court, and his chances there are uncertain. Should he happen to find no decision at home applicable to his purpose, he goes abroad into other States or across the sea. Now he has got beyond the hundreds of volumes of his own State he resorts to the thousands of volumes of other States and countries. What 'a codeless myriad of precedents' to look through! What 'a wilderness of single instances' to explore! Consider the nature of the search and what is found, after all? He peers into volumes upon volumes, with no other guide than an index at the end of each volume, or a compilation or collection of indexes called digests, of many volumes. These are made sometimes by men of sense, and sometimes by men of no sense, without any agreement upon a plan or classification of subjects. The result is, as might have been expected, that the lawyer, with an earnest desire to get the 'best opinion' or the 'weight of opinion' has, after all, to make a guess. Now, if he had been asked at the outset whether he would not prefer to look for an authoritative statement of the rule for his case in a statute-book, IF HE COULD FIND IT THERE, he would have answered yes.

"*Fourth.* The fourth reason that I will mention is that no people, which has once exchanged an unwritten for a written law, has ever turned back. One might as well expect the sun to return upon the dial. Even where the written law has been imposed upon a conquered people, to whom it must have been at first distasteful for that reason, it has held its place after the foreign domination has departed. The eagles of Napoleon were driven back across the Rhine, but the code which went forward with the eagles did not return with them. These facts are arguments worth all the theories in the world. Scholars may write as many treatises as they will; the experience of mankind is worth all the books that were ever written. You cannot explain away this experience; you cannot reason it down; it proves the superiority, beyond dispute or cavil, of written to unwritten law, of statute law to case law, or, as it might be better called, to guess-law.

"Now for the sophisms against codification:

"*First.* It is said that the law will be 'cabined, cribbed, confined,' if it be written. . . .

"*Second.* A second sophism is that a perfect code can not be made, and therefore, inasmuch as none but an imperfect one is possible, there had better be none at all.

"*Third.* A third sophism is this one: we have grown strong and prosperous without a code, why get one now? What need is there of a change? . . .

"*Fourth.* A fourth sophism is, that legislatures are always at work changing the laws, and therefore if a code is made it will be subject to continual change and so it is better to have none of it. . . ."

Do you agree with FIELD's four reasons for codification? How would you answer each of the four sophisms?

SIGNIFICANCE OF LEGISLATION

Sec. 4–28. Significance in various aspects. In preceding chapters we have analyzed the operation of laws in terms of effects on persons. We have considered the ways in which standards for the individual affect the individual himself and the significance which they have for officials and other individuals. We have discussed standards for officials in similar manner.

It is also possible and quite common, to relate the operation of legislation to place, time, and other legislation. Where does the legislation operate? How long does it operate? And how does it affect prior existing, or subsequently created, laws? The answers to these questions are found in the same places as the laws themselves: in constitutional provisions, statutes, and decisions. They are to be the subject matter of the following sections.

Sec. 4–29. Territorial operation. Generally speaking, the Anglo-American legal systems adhere to a theory of "territorial jurisdiction." [1] Applied to the operation of legislation, this theory means that standards which are found in the constitution, statutes, and decisions of a state or country, operate only within the territorial limits of that state or country. An act of the legislature of Michigan regulates only things, persons, and acts within the State of Michigan; a federal statute only matters which fall within the domain of the United States. This theory is implicit in many provisions of the constitutions, especially in those which distinguish between state and state, county and county, etc. It is a fundamental postulate of common-law thinking. There are some exceptions to this general theory, some instances in which Michigan legislation will affect persons and transactions beyond the borders of the state, or in which federal legislation affects persons and transactions beyond the territorial boundaries of the United States. But the theory of territorial jurisdiction to legislate, holds good on the whole; it states a common limit on the operation of legislation in the Anglo-American legal systems.

Sec. 4–30. Time of operation. Acts of Congress take effect from the date of passage if no other date is specified therein.

---

[1] Among jurisdictions where this theory prevails are Great Britain and its dominions, and the United States and its states and territories.

The same principles apply to the enactments of the various states, apart from controlling constitutional clauses. However, many states do have constitutional provisions which fix the ordinary date at which statutes are to become effective at sixty or ninety days after enactment or at some specified date such as July first following enactment. Even in these states, the legislature always has authority to give immediate effect to emergency legislation.

Ordinarily the operation of a statute is of indeterminate duration. Once established by the lawmaker, a legal provision continues in effect indefinitely in time. Or as we would more often say, a statute remains in force until changed. Of course the legislature can, and not infrequently does, include in a statute a specific provision limiting its operation to a definite period.

There are nevertheless important limits on the temporal operation of legislation. Most significant is the principle that legislation is to have only future operation.[1] The federal and state constitutions contain a number of provisions which bar retroactive changes in existing law. These aim to protect vested rights and established expectations. It is not worth our while to specify all these provisions in the present place. They are exemplified by the Due Process clauses which bar changes in the law that destroy the owner's existing property rights. They are also illustrated by the prohibitions against ex post facto legislation and against laws impairing the obligation of contracts. Our points of interest here are that, so far as clauses of this type furnish standards for the legislative act, they put existing laws beyond the reach of legislative change; and that so far as they declare limits on the operation of legislative acts, they mean that the lawmaker can change

---

[1] Also important is the type of constitutional provision which permits a legislative act to operate only after a certain period of time has elapsed following the date of its enactment.

existing legislation, but only for the future; that new laws can be established, but only with a prospective operation.

Sec. 4–31. Constitutional provisions and other legislation. Since we have more than one lawmaking agency within the state—the framers of the constitution, the legislature, various subsidiary agencies, and the courts—we need criteria (standards) by which to decide whose lawmaking act prevails in case of conflict or overlapping. The most basic of these criteria, that which governs the case of conflict between a statute and a constitutional provision, has already been frequently referred to. Needless to say, a constitutional provision prevails over legislation of any other kind; statute, decision, or subsidiary rule. The distinction between fundamental legislation represented by our constitutions, and ordinary but subordinate legislation, represented by statutes, common law, etc., is fundamental in the American legal system. It marks the most important departure from English models made by the founding fathers.

Sec. 4–32. Repeal and amendment of statutes. The operation of a statute may be terminated by repeal or changed by amendment. In the most general sense this involves the principle that where two statutes of the same state are in conflict with each other, the statute which is later in time prevails. The repeal or amendment of a statute is tantamount to making a new statute. The legislature's power to repeal or change law is as complete as its power to enact law originally,[1] and the standards which govern the processes of lawmaking are applicable to the legislative repeal or change of existing laws.[2]

[1] But see final paragraph of sec. 4–30 above.
[2] The relations of statutes and common law will be discussed in chapters 5 and 6.

But the legislature does not always explicitly repeal or change an existing statute. Often it merely enacts another statute which is inconsistent, wholly or partially, with existing legislation.[3] Here the later statute also prevails, on the principle already mentioned; but we speak of implied, not express, repeal or amendment. The principle of implied repeal, like that of the prevailing force of the later statute, is one common to all the Anglo-American legal systems.

Sec. 4–33. Federal versus state legislation. In our federal system there are not a few possibilities of conflict between federal and state action. There are areas in which the Congress and the state legislature exercise concurrent legislative power. For example, Congress is authorized to regulate interstate commerce, yet the state legislatures have always adopted certain types of local regulations which affect interstate commerce. Which of these regulations is to prevail in case of conflict or inconsistency, the federal or the state? A similar question can arise out of a conflict between a treaty with a foreign nation, and the statute of a single state. Suppose for instance that a statute of the state of Washington forbids aliens to engage in certain occupations, but a treaty between the United States and a foreign state permits citizens of the latter to engage in those occupations anywhere in the United States. Which is to control, the United States treaty or the state statute? The answer to both these questions is furnished by a section of the Federal Constitution which provides:

"This Constitution, and the Laws of the United States which shall be made in Pursuance thereof, and all treaties made, or which shall be made, under the Authority of the

---

[3] It is obviously preferable to repeal explicitly all prior statutes, or parts of statutes, which are in conflict with the new enactment; this avoids difficult questions whether such prior enactments do conflict and whether they are repealed—questions that may only be settled by litigation.

United States, shall be the supreme Law of the Land; and the Judges in every State shall be bound thereby, anything in the Constitution or laws of any State to the Contrary notwithstanding." [1]

The purport of this section is that where there is any conflict between federal and state legislative acts the federal act prevails. It not only supersedes any pre-existing state legislation of contrary tenor, but stands as an insurmountable obstacle to any subsequent state statute which runs counter to it. [2]

Sec. 4–34. Problems. 1. It is often said that the legislature cannot pass an irrepealable law. Which of the foregoing general propositions regarding the operation of legislation (sections 4–28 to 4–33) declares substantially the same idea?

2. It is a generally accepted view that a statute cannot be repealed by desuetude, i.e., abrogated by disuse.[1] Which of the above propositions regarding the operation of legislation is, in effect, another way of stating this view? Is there a difference?

3. Suppose a city council enacts an ordinance forbidding driving within the city limits at any speed exceeding 15 miles per hour; a later general statute of the state is passed prohibiting driving in residential districts of cities and towns, at any speed in excess of 25 miles per hour. Would the state law repeal the ordinance? Would it matter if the statute were prior in time?

What would be the proper conclusion if the ordinance provided for a maximum of 25, and the statute for one of 15, miles per hour?

---

[1] Art. VI, Sec. 2.
[2] It need hardly be said that these statements assume that the federal act is a valid one.
[1] See generally GRAY, THE NATURE AND SOURCES OF THE LAW (1916), secs. 4–01 to 4–19, 7–06 to 7–19.

Sec. 4–35. Summary. In the above chapter I have tried to give you a general view of the legislative process. (You will get a much more complete view later if you elect the course called Legislation.) I have laid emphasis on the human factors involved in the making and operation of legislation. More specifically, I have indicated when, how and why statutes are made; how far their enactment is controlled by standards; and the extent to which legislative power may be delegated. I have called your attention to certain important problems of stating the legislative message so that it will be clear and available to the persons who will be affected by it. And finally I have tried to furnish you with basic notions of the manner in which any piece of legislation operates as regards time, place, and other legislation.

CHAPTER 5

Interpretation of Legislation *

Sec. 5–01. When interpretation is needed—scope of chapter. In the preceding chapter we viewed the processes of legal control primarily from the side of the agency which formulates a legislative message; we stressed the problems of the lawmaker. At this place we shift our point of view and look at the processes of legal control from the side of persons to whom the legislative message is addressed; we look at the message as it appears to persons who must use or apply its directives. However, we shall not undertake to discuss all aspects of the application of legislation. We have already covered a large part of this ground; [1] we have already discussed cases where the legislative message is clear and understandable and where its provisions are applied without effort. The only cases that need to be discussed further are those where the application of legislation raises doubts or difficulties in the mind of the person who must apply it.

If language were a perfect vehicle of communication, and if human beings thought out their intentions with complete foresight, and if they expressed their aims and desires fully and perfectly, one might expect to find legislation which

---

* (I.R.) Suggestions for further reading:
"Symposium on Statutory Construction," 3 VANDERBILT L. REV. 365–596 (1950), an excellent series of papers, including a full bibliography on this subject, "Legal Writings on Statutory Construction," 569–584.
SUTHERLAND, STATUTORY CONSTRUCTION (3rd ed. by Horack, 1943).
READ AND MACDONALD, CASES AND MATERIALS ON LEGISLATION (1948).
See also items cited herein in sec. 5–14, note *, and sec. 5–17, note *. The voluminous material on this topic is found for the most part in the Law Reviews. It is not necessary to cite it all here as it is referred to or quoted in the works above cited.

[1] Notably those parts of chapters 2 and 3 where we discussed the *use* of standards for the individual (secs. 2–43 to 2–48) and the *use* of standards for officials (secs. 3–30 to 3–34).

needed no interpretation. However, there are deficiencies in language itself, in human foresight, and in the ability to express ideas; all these contribute to the general result that verbal acts of all kinds require interpretation. The use of language in legislation, like any other use of language, may be insufficient or obscure; it may be ambiguous, self-contradictory, vague or incomplete. If legislation is defective in any of these respects there is work for the interpreter to do.

This chapter will be devoted to the work of the interpreter, to cases where the meaning of legislation is problematic and has to be settled before it can be applied. This subject matter will be taken up under the following heads:

Role of interpreter.

Sources and standards of interpretation.

Typical interpretive problems.

ROLE OF INTERPRETER

Sec. 5–02. Who interprets—dominance of judiciary. On occasion, almost anyone may be confronted by the necessity of interpreting a legislative provision, just as he may have to apply one. An important new labor law, such as the Fair Labor Standards Act, raises at once questions of interpretation for every employer of labor: whether this statute applies to his contracts with his employees, and if it does, what are the effects of its provisions regarding wages and hours in his case. Only after a considerable length of time do such questions receive authoritative answers, and until and unless they do, the individual affected must make his own guesses as to how the act will be applied and enforced.[1] In like manner,

[1] In a speech last year Justice Jackson said:

"I read from time to time of laws enacted by Congress of which it is said it will require several years to learn how the Courts will apply them and what meaning Courts will give to them. . . . This seems to be accepted as necessary and usual, but it really indicates that there is something wrong in the process by which law is communicated to this country." "The Meaning of Statutes," 34 A. B. A. J. 535, 537 (1948).

an official who is under obligation to enforce a legislative provision may have to figure out the meaning of its terms before he embarks on the performance of his duties. Also the trial judge frequently must construe a legislative provision of doubtful meaning before he takes action or decides the case before him. And finally, the Supreme Court counts among its chief functions the settlement of questions of constitutional and statutory interpretation, that is to say questions which come up on appeal from the courts below. So that we can truly say that the interpretation of legislation is a function which may have to be performed on occasion by everyone.

But judicial interpretations of constitutional and statutory clauses have a peculiar significance which does not attach to the interpretations of other officials or of individuals. And from this peculiar significance has developed the common notion that the power of interpretation belongs exclusively to the judiciary, or more specifically, to the supreme court of each jurisdiction. There is no real contradiction here. The one proposition is to the effect that anyone may have to interpret legislation before he acts; the other to the effect that the supreme court gives the final and conclusive interpretation when it does speak. The latter proposition emphasizes the predominant role of the supreme court in settling the meaning of legislative provisions.

The predominance of judicial interpretations is best appreciated if we note the status in our American legal systems of judicial decisions construing constitutions and statutes. Such decisions are recorded and followed. A judicial interpretation of a legislative provision virtually becomes part of that provision's meaning; what the court says adheres to the legislative text. The interpretation is a judicial precedent; it is treated by all concerned as part and parcel of the provision's effective meaning, quite as if written into the provision itself.

The supreme court which rendered the decision so regards its prior interpretation. Courts of other jurisdictions and text writers do likewise. And lawyers always deal with a construed provision of a constitution or statute as if the construction were embodied in the provision; they do not simply cite the text of the provision, they also quote what the supreme court has said that the text means.

In view, then, of the dominance of judicial interpretations of legislation and of the fact that the judicial process typifies the interpretive process generally, I shall from this point on discuss judicial acts of interpretation (except where some other interpretive act is indicated) and shall use "interpretation" to mean judicial interpretation.

Sec. 5–03. Three theories of interpreter's role—"legislative intent" theory. What is the interpreter's role or function? Three theories have been propounded in answer to this question. I believe it will help us to understand the processes of interpretation if we examine each of these theories rather closely. These theories, and the conceptions of the interpreter's role which they express, are:

1. "Legislative intent" theory, to discover L's intent.
2. "Verbal meaning" theory, to arrive at the settled meaning of the words L used.
3. "Free interpretation" theory, to interpret as the interpreter chooses.

First, then, of the "legislative intent" theory. This is the conventional theory of interpretation. It declares that the judicial interpreter is expected to discover the legislator's intent. Statements to this effect appear over and over in the cases. Sometimes this theory purports to be a description of what the interpreter does; sometimes it is essentially a rule of method for the interpreter, telling him that the discovery of the legislator's intent is controlling or that his proper goal is to find out what the legislator meant. Offhand, these statements sound plausible; and probably in cases where the meaning of legislation is fairly clear under all the circumstances, such modes of stating objectives do no particular harm. But in cases where the legislator's meaning is not clear, in cases where real problems of interpretation confront the person who must apply legislation, these ways of stating the interpreter's objective serve to obscure the real nature of the interpretive process and the factors which are involved in it; they misdescribe the process which occurs and misdirect the attention of the interpreter in a manner which may be positively harmful.

Sec. 5–04. Problems. 1. Gray says of this theory:

"A fundamental misconception prevails, and pervades all the books as to the dealing of the courts with statutes. Interpretation is generally spoken of as if its chief function was to discover what the meaning of the Legislature really was. But when a Legislature has had a real intention, one way or another, on a point, it is not once in a hundred times that any doubt arises as to what its intention was. If that were all that a judge had to do with a statute, interpretation of statutes, instead of being one of the most difficult of a judge's duties, would be extremely easy. The fact is that the difficulties of so-called interpretation arise when the Legislature has had no meaning at all; when the question which is raised on the statute never occurred to it; when what the judges have to do is, not to determine what the Legislature did mean on a point which was present in its mind, but to guess what it would have intended on a point not present to its mind, if the point had been present. If there are any lawyers among those who honor me with their attendance, let them consider any dozen cases of the interpretation of statutes, as they have occurred consecutively in their reading or practice, and they will, I venture to say, find that in almost all of them it is probable, and that in most of them it is perfectly evident, that the makers of the statutes had no real intention, one way or another, on the point in question; that if they had, they would have made their meaning clear; and that when the judges are professing to declare what the Legislature meant, they are, in truth, themselves legislating to fill up *casus omissi.*" [1]

How would you state Gray's objection to this theory? Why does his view, if correct, make it difficult to accept the "legislative intent" theory?

2. Why does the following case make difficulty for the "legislative intent" theory?

State v. Partlow. [2] "The defendant is indicted for selling one quart of spiritous liquor to one Rutherford within three miles of Mount Zion church, in the county of Gaston, in violation of the Act of 1881, ch. 234.

"It was in evidence that the liquor was sold as alleged; and that there were two churches (about fifteen miles apart) each called "Mount Zion church," in said county—one for the white people and the other for the colored people. And there was nothing in the statute indicating to which of these two churches the name applied or had reference.

"With a view to apply the statute, the state introduced a witness who was a senator in the general assembly at the time the Act in question was passed, and the court allowed him to testify, after objection, that it was intended to apply to the church mentioned by himself and the other witnesses, and this he knew, because the provision of the Act in respect to Mount Zion church was inserted upon his motion, made in response to petitions praying for the prohibition of the sale of spiritous liquor within three miles of Mount Zion colored church, signed by colored people whom he knew. The defendant excepted, and further insisted that the statute was ambiguous and therefore void.

"Verdict of guilty; judgment; appeal by the defendant. . . ."

Merrimon, J.: "The Act of 1881, ch. 234, prohibits the sale of spiritous liquors within designated distances from

[1] THE NATURE AND SOURCES OF THE LAW, sec. 370 (1916).
[2] 91 N. C. 497 (1884).

many churches and other places named therein. So much of it as is material to this case provides, 'that the sale of spiritous liquors shall be prohibited within three miles of . . . Mount Zion church in Gaston county.'

"It appeared on the trial that there were two churches bearing the name 'Mt. Zion' in Gaston county, and there is nothing in the statute indicating to which of them it applies.

"It is plainly the duty of the court to so construe a statute, ambiguous in its meaning, as to give effect to the legislative intent, if this be practicable. . . . But the meaning must be ascertained from the statute itself, and the means and signs to which, as appears upon its face, it has reference. It cannot be proved by a member of the legislature or other person, whether interested in its enactment or not. A statute is an act of the legislature as an organized body. It expresses the collective will of that body, and no single member of it, or all the members as individuals, can be heard to say what the meaning of the statute is. It must speak for and be construed by itself, by the means and signs indicated above. Otherwise, each individual might attribute to it a different meaning, and thus the legislative will and meaning be lost sight of. Whatever may be the views and purposes of those who procure the enactment of a statute, the legislature contemplates that its intention shall be ascertained from its words as embodied in it. And the courts are not at liberty to accept the understanding of any individual as to the legislative intent. . . .

"Now, the clause of the statute before us simply refers to 'Mount Zion church in Gaston county,' and there are two churches of that name in that county. There is nothing in the statute that in the remotest degree indicates to which of the two it refers. There are no means or signs of any kind appearing in it, in terms, by implication, by reference, or by any possible construction, that go to point to one of the two churches any more than to the other. It must, therefore, be as inoperative as if there was no church, or fifty churches of the same name in that county.

"The testimony of the witness, who was a senator at the time the statute was enacted, was wholly incompetent for the reasons already stated.

"We are constrained to declare that the clause of the statute under consideration is, because of its ambiguity, inoperative and void.

"Error. Reversed."

Sec. 5–05. The "verbal meaning" theory. On the basis of reasoning like that of the *Partlow Case* just quoted, a second theory of the interpreter's role has been evolved. This theory I call the "verbal meaning" theory. It declares that the interpreter is concerned strictly with the established meaning of the language which the lawmaker has used. In the words of another court, "Whether we are considering an agreement between parties, a statute or a constitution, . . . the thing we are to seek is *the thought which it expresses.* . . . That which the words declare, is the meaning of the instrument; and neither court nor legislatures have a right to add to or take away from that meaning." [1]

As a description of the interpretive process this theory has the advantage of frankly converting the process of interpretation into an inquiry based on objective materials. The job of the interpreter becomes an investigation of the established meaning of what the legislator has said. This conception of the interpreter's task represents an advance in realism insofar as it discards any fictitious and irrelevant subjective element suggested by the "legislative intent" theory; it represents a sound policy inasmuch as it refers the interpreter to objective material, the legislative text, which is also available to persons affected by the legislation.

Those who announce this "verbal meaning" theory have usually assumed that the proper meaning of a legislative text is simple and single; they have usually assumed, if not stated, that the proper meaning inheres in the words used and can be directly read off. Thus Justice Story, who emphatically announces the view that the correct meaning of

[1] Johnson, J., in Newell v. The People, 7 N. Y. 9 at 97 (1852).

the clauses of the Federal Constitution is to be derived from the words used, also takes for granted that there can be only one proper meaning of those words. As he says:

"Nothing but the text itself was adopted by the people. And it would certainly be a most extravagant doctrine to give to any commentary then made, and a fortiori to any commentary since made, under a very difficult posture of feeling and opinion, an authority which would operate as an absolute limit upon the text, or should supersede its natural and just interpretation." [2]

Here Story takes for granted that the text has one natural and just interpretation. In another part of the same section, he says, "The Constitution was adopted by the people of the United States, and it was submitted to the whole upon a just survey of its provisions as they stood in the text itself." This learned author takes great pains at the same time to point out that the parties who adopted the language of the Constitution may have had different views as to what its language meant.

Sec. 5–06. Problems. 1. If the proper interpretation of language, or as Story calls it "the natural and just interpretation," is as obvious and uniform as his theory assumes it to be, how is it possible for courts to differ as widely as they often do, regarding the correct interpretation of a statutory or constitutional clause? Story himself was a member of the United States Supreme Court when it thus differed in opinion with the supreme appellate tribunal of New York in the celebrated case of *Gibbons v. Ogden*.[1] The difference concerned the proper interpretation of the simple language of the Commerce Clause of the Federal Constitution. The United States Supreme Court gave the clause a wide and comprehensive interpretation, to bring all kinds of intercourse

---

[2] THE CONSTITUTION (5th ed.), sec. 406 (1905).
[1] 9 Wheat. 1 (1824). See full discussion of this case in WARREN, THE SUPREME COURT IN UNITED STATES HISTORY, I, 797 *et seq.* (1937).

between states within the legislative power of Congress; the New York Court would have restricted Congressional control to commerce in the sense of traffic in goods. Both interpretations were possible, both were reasonable from any ordinary point of view, and each was adopted by a bench of judges whom we number among the leading lights of our legal history.

Why does such a difference of opinion, as was found in the *Gibbons Case* in regard to the meaning of the Commerce Clause, make difficulty for the "verbal meaning" theory as Story and others have declared it?

2. Jethro Brown: "As a matter of fact, however, the statute does not mean—cannot mean—to one generation just what it meant to a preceding generation." [2] Brown here speaks of a statute. His remarks would apply with great force to such ancient legislation as the Statute de Donis and the Statute of Uses. What he says would apply equally to legislation such as our Federal Constitution and to important constitutional documents, such as Magna Charta. If what he says is true, how does it bear on the "verbal meaning" theory?

Sec. 5–07. The "free interpretation" theory. This brings us to the third theory of interpretation: that the interpreter can and does make the statute mean whatever he wants it to mean. The theory, which has had considerable vogue recently, I have called the "free interpretation" theory; it stresses the creative role of the interpreter; in fact, it converts this role into a complete theory of interpretation. On this point Gray quotes a venerable writer as follows: "Nay, whoever hath an absolute authority to *interpret* any written or spoken laws, it is *he* who is truly the Law Giver to all intents and purposes, and not the Person who first wrote and spoke them." [1] In similar vein, Chief Justice Hughes, when he

---

[2] "Law and Evolution," 29 YALE L. J. 394 at 396 (1920).
[1] THE NATURE AND SOURCES OF THE LAW, sec. 276 (1916).

was Governor of New York, said of the power of the United States Supreme Court to interpret the Constitution: "We are under a Constitution, but the Constitution is what the judges say it is." [2]

Sec. 5–08. Problems. 1. Why would you not be ready to accept the "free interpretation" theory? What would be its necessary effect?

2. How would you state a theory to combine the virtues of all three theories? In other words what do you think ought to be the interpreter's role and method of interpreting a statute?

SOURCES AND STANDARDS OF INTERPRETATION

Sec. 5–09. The interpreter's act and his sources. The interpreter's act starts with the legislative text. This is the primary subject matter of interpretation.[1] However, interpretation always occurs in a problematic situation. If the application of the legislative text raised no doubts, there would be nothing for the interpreter to do as such; if the text were not unclear or incomplete there would be no call for interpretation. In other words, the interpreter's act is partially creative, it adds elements not expressed in the legislative text itself. At the very least the interpreter is called upon to restate or explain what the legislator has said; and he may have to go so far as to correct the legislative statement or to supply gaps in it.

While the creative side of the interpreter's act is indisputable, the nature and amount of his contribution will vary

[2] Unlike some who have since quoted his words, the learned Chief Justice probably did not intend his statement as a complete characterization of the process of interpretation.

[1] Unless one accepts the theory of "free interpretation" in an absolute and unlimited form (of course, we do not, and I doubt if anyone does), one always begins with the legislative text.

from case to case. For this reason there does not seem to be much point in trying to separate and distinguish neatly between elements contributed to the final meaning by legislator and by interpreter respectively. It can never be quite clear, either in reference to a specific interpretive act or in reference to the process of interpretation generally, how much the interpreter derives from what the legislator has said or suggested and how much he adds to the legislative text which he is interpreting. What the legislator says passes by imperceptible degrees into what he implies or takes for granted. What the legislator implies or takes for granted, is not clearly distinguishable from what he would have said, if he had thought of the problem which is now presented to the interpreter. And what the legislator would have wanted and would have said, shades into what the interpreter thinks ought to be the meaning of the legislative provision, purely as a matter of policy.

A more promising undertaking than to try to measure the specific contributions of legislator and interpreter to the final product, is to analyze the interpretative process itself in order to see what materials the interpreter works with and what he does with these materials. These at least are the tasks which we shall set ourselves in the remainder of this chapter. In the present subtopic we shall examine primarily the materials out of which the interpreter develops his interpretation. In the subtopic to follow we shall see how he goes about solving typical interpretive problems.

Turning now to the materials which the interpreter uses in his act of interpretation we find that he has two important sets of materials to work with: (1) the language which the legislator has used; and (2) the context in which the language is used. The interpreter deduces his interpretation from the text of the legislation and the context of its use. Both these factors are objective, and open to investigation and determination by the interpreter; both contribute to the final interpretation which he adopts.

The necessity of considering the *text* of the legislative provision is obvious enough. That is what the interpreter is construing. But the nature and role of context is not so obvious. What is the *context* which is important? What do we mean by the term and what does it include? In a general sense context means setting. It embraces all the conditions and circumstances which attend the use of language. In the case of the interpreter we can regard context as just another name for the sources on which he draws in developing his interpretation. In context he finds the materials and ideas on the basis of which he reworks the legislator's text. So that context is to the interpreter what sources are to the legislator; and ideally we hope that both legislator and interpreter act in the light of the same context or, otherwise stated, draw on the same sources for their verbal acts. If not, we shall find that when the interpreter says what the legislator meant, the meaning as declared will not correspond with the real meaning of the legislator.

For the purpose of further analysis and discussion, I shall differentiate three kinds of context:

1. The general context, i. e., the general knowledge of the time.

2. The legal context, i. e., other law existing at the time of enactment.

3. The history and circumstances of enactment of the particular legislative provision.

Sec. 5–10. The general context. Any verbal declaration, oral or written, must be interpreted against the cultural background in which it is made. The culture consists of the entire fund of knowledge which belongs to the community. This background is implied in all uses of language, and in every application thereof. In this sense any legislative declaration must be read and interpreted in relation to the general context in which it is enacted and applicable. Exactly the same statutory provision would, and should, have a different meaning and application in India from what it would have in England; in England, from what it would have in the United States. Where habits, knowledge, and modes of living are different, the interpretations of one and the same legal provision are bound to be different.

Prominent in the general context are the facts of *common experience* in the community. Matters of common knowledge, such as the facts that cattle eat grass and that milk requires special care to prevent contamination and spoiling, are presupposed and taken for granted in the enactment and the interpretation of legislative provisions regarding cattle raising and milk marketing. The legislator has to assume that he is addressing an interpreter, as well as ordinary individuals, who know the common patterns according to which people in the community live and move about, e.g., what they use an automobile for. Of course, a man from Mars would not know these facts and could not interpret what the legislator has enacted; and even the mundane interpreter may have to make facts of common knowledge explicit, whenever they become relevant to a problem of interpretation.

Another important part of the general context consists of the various branches of tested knowledge which we know by the collective name of *science*. Here belong the pure sciences, e.g., biology, physics, chemistry, and astronomy, as well as medicine, engineering and other fields of applied science; and we use science in a broad enough sense to include all branches of special knowledge such as agriculture, lumbering, plumbing, carpentry, etc. We shall see presently that one of the recognized rules of interpretation requires the interpreter to give technical words their technical signification. "Technical" is used here as substantially equivalent to "scientific" in the broad sense just suggested. If a scientific word or a word peculiar to a special profession or trade is employed in a legislative enactment, the interpreter must draw upon the proper field of knowledge for its definition.[1]

The *general history* of the community constitutes another part of the context which may have to be used or examined by the judicial interpreter. Historical conditions of the past are often important in determining the meaning of legislation. Even today the Supreme Court of the United States frequently refers to general conditions in America at the time when the Revolution occurred and when the Constitution was framed.

And finally, though our enumeration is not intended to be exhaustive, the general background includes all the established *usages of language*. It includes the standard meanings of words, the usages of grammar, rules of punctuation, and other related matters. Language symbols by themselves are abstract and meaningless.[2] Meaning attaches to them through repeated and continuous use. The interpreter, like the legislator, must be able to use and apply standard language devices; he must know, for example, what the words "automobile" and "driving" mean. Language devices and all they imply are taken for granted in the processes of enacting, applying, and interpreting legal provisions. Familiarity with language is something distinct from the common knowledge and the scientific knowledge mentioned, although both kinds

[1] Compare sec. 4–20 above, where the use of popular and technical terms in statutes is discussed.

[2] Accordingly, a particular group of language symbols—a legislative or other text—means absolutely nothing except in terms of a particular cultural background. And this dependence of the significance of symbols upon established cultural background holds true of all symbols whatever. For example, the word "gift" in an English setting, means a donation; in a German setting, means poison. What this all signifies philosophically is that the distinction between text and cultural context is really a distinction between one part of the cultural heritage and another part; it is a distinction between the prevailing symbol system and the rest of the culture. Nevertheless, the distinction is a practical one which is commonly made; and I have not hesitated to use it for the present purpose.

of knowledge are definitely hooked up with language devices. However, it is quite possible that a Frenchman may be conversant with the knowledge of today but unable to interpret a statute written in English. The interpreter must not only be possessed of knowledge; he must also be familiar with the particular language devices which refer to it.

Sec. 5–11. Problems. 1. A Michigan statute provides:

"Words imputing to any female a want of chastity shall be deemed to be actionable in themselves. . . ." Mich. Stats. Ann. § 27.1370. Plaintiff, a married woman, brought action for slander based on this statute. The defendant admitted that, in an argument over some horses, he had called the plaintiff "you damned old bitch." The trial court instructed the jury that these words "did impute the want of chastity to Mrs. Warren" and that she was entitled to recover. The Supreme Court reversed the case on account of this instruction. It declared "We are of the opinion that the court erred in instructing the jury that the language admitted to have been used by defendant, under the circumstances alleged by him, was slanderous per se."

This was all that was said on the subject by the court.[1]

On what basis would you say that the court reached its decision?

2. *McBoyle v. United States.*[2] Mr. Justice Holmes delivered the opinion of the Court.

"The petitioner was convicted of transporting from Ottawa, Illinois, to Guymon, Oklahoma, an airplane that he knew to have been stolen, and was sentenced to serve three years' imprisonment and to pay a fine of $2,000. The judgment was affirmed by the Circuit Court of Appeals for the Tenth Circuit, 43 F. (2d) 273. A writ of certiorari was granted by this Court on the question whether the National Motor Vehicle Theft Act applies to aircraft. Act of October 29,

[1] Warren v. Ray, 155 Mich. 91 at 93 (1908).
[2] 283 U. S. 25 (1931).

1919, c. 89, 41 Stat. 324; U. S. Code, Title 18, § 408. That Act provides: 'Sec. 2. That when used in this Act: (a) The term "motor vehicle" shall include an automobile, automobile truck, automobile wagon, motor cycle, or any other self-propelled vehicle not designed for running on rails; . . . Sec. 3. That whoever shall transport or cause to be transported in interstate or foreign commerce a motor vehicle, knowing the same to have been stolen, shall be punished by a fine of not more than $5,000, or by imprisonment of not more than five years, or both.'

"Section 2 defines the motor vehicles of which the transportation in interstate commerce is punished in § 3. The question is the meaning of the word 'vehicle' in the phrase 'any other self-propelled vehicle not designed for running on rails.' No doubt etymologically it is possible to use the word to signify a conveyance working on land, water or air, and sometimes legislation extends the use in that direction, e.g., land and air, water being separately provided for, in the Tariff Act, September 22, 1922, c. 356, § 401 (b), 42 Stat. 858, 948. But in everyday speech 'vehicle' calls up the picture of the thing moving on land. Thus in Rev. Stats. § 4, intended, the Government suggests, rather to enlarge than to restrict the definition, vehicle includes every contrivance capable of being used 'as a means of transportation on land.' And this is repeated, expressly excluding aircraft, in the Tariff Act, June 17, 1930, c. 997, § 401 (b); 46 Stat. 590, 708. So here, the phrase under discussion calls up the popular picture. For after including automobile truck, automobile wagon and motor cycle, the words 'any other self-propelled vehicle not designed for running on rails' still indicate that a vehicle in the popular sense, that is a vehicle running on land, is the theme. It is a vehicle that runs, not something, not commonly called a vehicle, that flies. Airplanes were well known in 1919, when this statute was passed; but it is admitted that they were not mentioned in the reports or in the debates in Congress. It is impossible to read words that so carefully enumerate the different forms of motor vehicles and have no reference of any kind to aircraft, as including airplanes under a term that usage more and more precisely confines to a different class. The counsel for the petitioner have shown that the phraseology of the statute as to motor vehicles follows that of earlier statutes of Connecticut, Delaware, Ohio, Michigan and Missouri, not to mention the late Regulations of Traffic for the District of Columbia, Title 6, c. 9, § 242, none of which can be supposed to leave the earth.

"Although it is not likely that a criminal will carefully consider the text of the law before he murders or steals, it is reasonable that a fair warning should be given to the world in language that the common world will understand, of what the law intends to do if a certain line is passed. To make the warning fair, so far as possible the line should be clear. When a rule of conduct is laid down in words that evoke in the common mind only the picture of vehicles moving on land, the statute should not be extended to aircraft simply because it may seem to us that a similar policy applies, or upon the speculation that, if the legislature had thought of it, very likely broader words would have been used. *United States v. Thind,* 261 U. S. 204, 209.

"Judgment reversed."

Where does Holmes get his information about the meaning of "vehicle"? How does he happen to know the manner in which planes move? How far are these points dealt with in the text of the statute?

Ordinarily the court goes to the dictionary and other standard books of reference, if it is in doubt about the meaning of an expression which it is interpreting. Does this seem proper?

Suppose the expression is defined in the statute itself, e.g., "motor vehicle" in the statute involved in the *McBoyle Case.* What difference does this make?

Sec. 5–12. The legal context.[1] Maitland once declared, in words often quoted, "The law is a seamless web." His words express neatly the idea that the mass of legal rules, principles,

[1] The sociologist regards the law as part of the culture of a community. In this sense he would treat the legal background as a mere part of the general

and doctrines, constitutes an integrated whole of which any particular law is only a part, and at the same time suggest the idea that the entire body of law is a general background for any individual legal provision. In this latter sense the law-maker who frames a law really weaves a small strand into an already existing legal web; he takes an established legal fabric for granted and attaches his legislation to it. And, by the same token, the interpreter assumes and relies on the existing legal context; he can understand a particular legis-lative provision only in relation to it. In working out the meaning of any provision, he must trace out connections between its terms and the existing legal setting.

The legal context is traditionally divided into common law and legislation, and in line with this division we find several recognized rules of interpretation which are intended to guide the interpreter in developing the relationships of new pieces of legislation to established law. One declares that every statute is to be interpreted in the light of the *common law;* or, to use a quaint metaphor of Coke, "To know what the common law was before the making of the statute is the very lock and key to set open the windows of the statute." Another rule declares that statutes in derogation of the common law are to be strictly construed—a rule of somewhat doubtful virtue since its general tendency is to perpetuate antiquated common law at the expense of modern legislation.

The integration of new legislation with existing legislation is equally important; and there are helpful rules to guide the interpreter in this part of his job. One part of the estab-lished legal background consists of the *constitutions.* The interpreter must, if he can, harmonize a new statute with

---

cultural background. But the legal background is so important for our purpose that I feel justified in treating it as something separate and distinct. See the remarks made in sec. 5–10, note 2, regarding a similar distinction between language and culture.

these. If a statute conflicts with a constitutional provision, of course it is void; but this is not the only significance of constitutions. The interpreter presumes that the legislator did not intend his act to run afoul of constitutional provisions; the interpreter is required to adopt a construction which will avoid these consequences. Furthermore, the constitutions commonly state important policies regarding the public welfare, the liberties of the individual, and other matters. These statements of policy have substantial weight in the interpretation of statutes. Where the judicial interpreter has a choice between two interpretations he is always ready to choose that one which tends to effectuate, or which is in harmony with, such a constitutionally declared policy.

Another part of the established legal background is made up of existing *statutes*. The interpreter draws on this existing material for aid in construing a new statutory provision and also tries to harmonize the latter with the existing law. Such efforts are in line with well-recognized rules of interpretation. For example, one such rule declares that any piece of legislation is to be interpreted in relation to existing legislation on the same subject. This rule is commonly called the *in pari materia* doctrine. According to this doctrine, if a new statute be passed dealing with some special feature of the law of corporations, this statute is to be interpreted in the light of existing legislation governing corporations; a new larceny statute is to be fitted into the existing law of larceny; a new tax regulation into the body of law and regulations on this subject; in short any legislative act is to be read in the light of other legislation on the same subject.

And we cannot say that the legal background is limited merely to existing enactments and existing common law. Existing law has behind it a long history. The interpreter may consider this history to discover instructive trends. Such trends may be useful to him in guiding his choice between different possible interpretations. Furthermore, he may travel outside the body of existing law to consider doctrines which have been developed by writers on legal subjects. Textbooks, encyclopedias, and other works on law, may furnish the interpreter with instruction or inspiration for his creative role, just as they serve the legislator as sources for ideas and materials which he embodies in enactments. So that we have to recognize that the sources on which the interpreter draws and the materials which he considers, include not only common law and legislation but also these extralegal writings about law.

In connection with what has just been said about the use of legal background as a source of ideas, it is worth pausing to note more specifically how the interpreter may use legal background as a source of materials and what important materials he derives from it. In the legal background he may find four important kinds of material: (1) general notions of the ends of law; (2) definitions of legal ideas and existing classifications of legal material; (3) existing provisions which define the functions of officials and control their modes of action; (4) existing law dealing with the acts of individuals. Each of these four elements requires a word of comment as regards its status as part of the legal background.

1. Prevailing notions of legal policy (ends of law) are part of the wider background of the legislator's act: preservation of the general peace, protection of property, freedom of contract and trade, safeguarding family relations, and so on. The lawmaker may or may not refer to these policies explicitly. But even if he says nothing about them, the interpreter assumes that the lawmaker had them in view. Recognized legal policies are frequently cited by the interpreter as reasons for choosing one interpretation rather than another, for cor-

recting or limiting the operation of the text, or for filling a gap in the text.

2. Definitions of legal ideas and existing classifications of legal material constitute an important part of the legal background. These definitions and classifications are found in various parts of the existing common and statutory law and in writings about law. The legislator usually expects the interpreter to find them for himself; the legislator does not feel obliged to state them out every time he enacts a new legislative provision, though occasionally a provision will contain definitions of important terms which it employs, as well as specifications of the way in which they are to be construed in relation to existing law.

3. Existing rules and principles which define the functions of officials and govern their acts also constitute a major element of the background of any new legislation. They are taken for granted by lawmaker and by interpreter; they are assumed to be part of the legislation just as if they were explicitly stated in it. The legislator who creates a new action for damages does not ordinarily say anything about the rules of pleading or procedure which are to govern the action. Nor does he undertake to tell the court how to interpret the legislation in question. He expects all these effects of the legislation to be handled according to existing principles and techniques of the legal system. Only if the lawmaker wants to make some special provision relative to the way in which the new legislation is to be applied, enforced, or interpreted, does he take the trouble to refer explicitly to general functions and techniques of officials. Nevertheless, those general functions and techniques constitute part of the significance of new legislation in the sense that they must be drawn upon as occasion requires and read into its terms by the interpreter.

4. New legislation affecting the individual is also incomplete and takes much for granted. Existing rules and principles of law, which relate to acts and activities of the individual, supply the material which is to be read into the gaps and blanks of this new legislation. They furnish the materials for supplementing the express provisions of the new law so far as supplementation is later needed. In this respect the function of existing materials is analogous to the materials mentioned in the last preceding paragraph.

Sec. 5–13. Problems. 1. In *State v. McGowan* (sec. 2–48, problem 2) a state statute provided simply that "arson" should be punished in a certain manner. The court had to decide whether setting fire to a new house, not yet occupied as a dwelling, constituted the crime of arson. More specifically the question was whether such a house was a dwelling for the purpose of this crime. Where did the court find the definition of arson, and the answer to the more specific question?

2. It should be noted that the parts of a statute are to be construed in relation to one another. Any part finds an immediate verbal setting in the other parts. Each section is to be construed in the light of others, any clause in relation to other clauses and to the whole. Indeed, any word has to be construed in connection with the words which surround it. There are many established norms which recognize this method of construing parts with reference to one another. I shall mention only one, the maxim of *ejusdem generis*. This maxim is to the effect that general words, following an enumeration of specific things, are to be interpreted as limited to things of the same kind *(ejusdem generis)* as those specifically enumerated. (*Cf.* remarks of Holmes, J., about the enumerated forms of motor vehicles in sec. 5–11 above.) This maxim and its application illustrate very well the

dependence of the meaning of one phrase or clause upon the phrases or clauses with which it is associated.

3. *Hoff v. State of New York.*[1] Appeal from a judgment, entered November 26, 1937, upon an order of the Appellate Division of the Supreme Court in the fourth judicial department which affirmed a judgment in favor of defendant entered upon a decision of the Court of Claims dismissing on the merits a claim of the appellant.

Lehman, J.:

[1] "The claimant on March 6, 1936, while confined to Tonawanda State Hospital under an order of the court, signed and verified a petition for a writ of habeas corpus and placed it in a stamped envelope addressed to his attorney, A. Stanley Copeland. The claimant had been adjudged insane. It is the duty of an employee of the hospital, acting under the direction of the superintendent, to examine all the mail of patients confined in the hospital before the mail is sent out. The claimant, believing that he was sane, had written to many men in public life asking their assistance. The claimant's wife had been annoyed by inquiries from persons who have received such letters. She requested that all letters written by the claimant should be sent to her. The superintendent of the hospital acceded to her request and, by his directions, all mail, including the letter addressed to the claimant's attorney and containing the petition for the writ of habeas corpus, was forwarded to claimant's wife who suppressed the letter. On March 25th, Copeland presented a new petition verified by himself to the County Judge of Erie county.

[2] "The writ was made returnable on March 30th before a jury. On April 2, 1936, the claimant was discharged from custody after the jury had determined that he was sane. Our constitutional guarantees of liberty are merely empty words unless a person imprisoned or detained against his will may challenge the legality of his imprisonment and detention. The writ of habeas corpus is the process devised centuries

[1] 279 N. Y. 490 (1939).

ago for the protection of free men. It has been cherished by generations of free men who had learned by experience that it furnished the only reliable protection of their freedom. The right of persons, deprived of liberty, to challenge in the courts the legality of their detention is safeguarded by the Constitution of the United States and by the Constitution of the State. The Legislature could not deprive any person within the State of the privilege of a writ of habeas corpus. (N. Y. Const. art. 1, Sec. 4.) The superintendent of the hospital by diverting to claimant's wife the letter and petition for a writ of habeas corpus obstructed the claimant's right to test the legality of his imprisonment. Doubtless the superintendent acted in the honest belief that the claimant was insane. Nevertheless, his act delayed for a time a test of the claimant's sanity which, when made, resulted in his discharge. . . .

[3] "The right of the superintendent in the exercise of a reasonable discretion to censor the ordinary mail written by a patient who has been adjudged insane is not challenged. The question is whether the superintendent of a State hospital for the insane may in the exercise of his discretion obstruct or delay a challenge of the legality of detention by a patient held under a court order. To that question one answer is clearly dictated. The State cannot under the Constitution withhold the privilege of the writ of habeas corpus. It has not attempted to do so. On the contrary, the Legislature has provided that 'any one in custody as an insane person, . . . is entitled to a writ of habeas corpus, upon a proper application made by him or some relative or friend in his behalf.' (Mental Hygiene Law (Cons. Laws, ch. 27), § 204.) An officer of the State . . . may not by indirection accomplish what the Constitution forbids to the State. He may not lawfully withhold from a person so detained the opportunity to apply for a writ of habeas corpus. .' . .

[4] "The Legislature in the Civil Practice Act has made clear that under no circumstances may the grant of the writ of habeas corpus, or a hearing upon the writ when granted, be refused or delayed. A judge authorized to grant the writ 'must grant it *without delay*' whenever a petition therefor is presented and for violation of that command a judge

forfeits to the prisoner $1,000. (§ 1235.) It may not be disobeyed for any defect of form. It may be served even on a Sunday (§ 1242) and 'the court or judge before which or whom the prisoner is brought by virtue of a writ of habeas corpus . . . must *examine, immediately after the return of the writ*, into the facts alleged in the return and into the cause of the imprisonment or restraint of the prisoner.' (§ 1251.)

[5] "The act of the superintendent was an act of misfeasance, and the State may be held liable for any damages caused by that act. (*Martindale v. State*, 269 N. Y. 554.) In this case the damages were probably very small but there can be no doubt that the claimant's challenge, ultimately successful, was delayed for approximately two weeks.

"The judgments of the Appellate Division and of the Court of Claims should be reversed and a new trial granted, with costs to abide the event."

(This decision by one of our leading courts is interesting to us because of the manner in which the court reaches its conclusion; it is also interesting because, as a note writer in the Michigan Law Review says, "No case has been found to parallel this decision.") [2]

In arriving at his decision is Judge Lehman warranted in considering the provisions of the Mental Hygiene Law (referred to in paragraph [3]) and the provisions of the Civil Practice Act (referred to in paragraph [4] of this opinion)? In what way are these materials relevant to his conclusion?

What is the relevance of the judge's view that "The writ of habeas corpus is the process devised centuries ago for the protection of free men. It has been cherished by generations of free men who had learned by experience that it furnished the only reliable protection of their freedom."?

We have been talking of interpretation here. Have you paused to think just what it is we are interpreting? Is it the

[2] 38 MICH. L. REV. 103 (1939).

clause of the New York Constitution mentioned in paragraph [2]? Is it the Mental Hygiene Law mentioned in paragraph [3]? Is the court merely elaborating the scope of the common law action for false imprisonment? Or do you have some other suggestion regarding the subject matter (text) of interpretation?

Sec. 5–14. History and circumstances of enactment: extrinsic aids. We have now discussed the general context of enactment and the legal context. It remains to consider a third contextual factor, the history and circumstances of the specific provision's enactment. This context is often characterized by the plural title "extrinsic aids." It includes the occasion for enactment, e.g., the existence of a depression or a crime wave; the legislative history of the passage of the provision, embracing all changes in its wording from introduction to final approval; the report of the legislative committee or official agency or outside group, which prepared the draft of the provision for submission to the legislative body; the report of a committee to which the draft was referred for examination and recommendation; and statements of persons charged with steering the provision in question through the legislative processes, made during its consideration and enactment.

There is no sharp line to divide the specific history from the general background. The latter may be regarded as the more remote circumstances of enactment; the "history and circumstances," in which we are now interested, as the immediate circumstances. And there is no clear-cut distinction between the specific legal conditions (occasion) out of which the enactment in question evolved, and the wider legal background. But distinctions are not useless because they are not clearly or sharply marked. There are practical differences between the significance of general context and legal context on the one hand, and specific conditions and origins on the other. Courts have recognized and acted on these differences in the processes of interpreting statutes; the courts have appreciated that general conditions, cultural or legal, can be taken to be commonly known, while specific historical materials cannot be supposed to be open to everyone who must act on the basis of the legislation.[1]

For the reason just stated, not all courts have been ready to resort to these "extrinsic aids" to interpretation. The English courts have, generally speaking, refused to consider them at all.[2] The federal courts in this country make full use of these extrinsic aids. The state courts do not reject them outright, but have made much less use of them than the federal courts have done. It is not worth our while to go into detail here regarding the actual holdings of the cases.* Such a discussion would require more complete information than you possess, regarding technical rules of evidence and other matters. It will suffice, for our present purpose, to state for your consideration (in the next section) a relatively recent case in the United States Supreme Court, which

[1] See Justice Jackson, "The Meaning of Statutes: What Congress Says or What the Court Says," 34 A. B. A. J. 535, 537–8 (1948).

[2] See Davies, "The Interpretation of Statutes in the Light of Their Policy by the English Courts," 35 COL. L. REV. 519 (1935).

* (I.R.) The initiated reader may be interested in a reference to a few instructive articles on this difficult subject. See Chamberlain, "The Courts and Committee Reports," 1 U. OF CHI. L. REV. 81 (1933); Davies, "The Interpretation of Statutes in the Light of Their Policy by the English Courts," 35 COL. L. REV. 519 (1935); tenBroek, "Admissibility and Use by the United States Supreme Court of Extrinsic Aids in Constitutional Construction," 26 CALIF. L. REV. 287, 437, and 664 (1938); tenBroek, "Use by the United States Supreme Court of Extrinsic Aids in Constitutional Construction," 27 CALIF. L. REV. 157 (1939); Powell, "Construction of Written Instruments," 14 IND. L. J. 199, 309, 397 (1939), same article in abbreviated form in 25 A. B. A. J. 185 (1939); Jones, "The Plain Meaning Rule and Extrinsic Aids in the Interpretation of Federal Statutes," 25 WASH. UNIV. L. Q. 2 (1939); Jones, "Extrinsic Aids in the Federal Courts," 25 IOWA L. REV. 737 (1940); Nutting, "The Relevance of Legislative Intention Established by Extrinsic Evidence," 20 BOSTON UNIV. L. REV. 601 (1940); De Sloovere, "Extrinsic Aids in the Interpretation of Statutes," 88 U. OF PA. L. REV. 527 (1940).

will show the variety of extrinsic aids which can be resorted to for the purpose of interpreting a federal statute.

Sec. 5–15. Problems. 1. *Nye v. United States.*[1] E, as administrator of his son's estate, had entered suit against B and C for the wrongful death of his son. One hundred miles from the courthouse, M and N, by plying E with liquor, induced him to terminate the action. E was illiterate and "feeble in mind and body." N, through his lawyer, prepared and mailed letters to the trial judge asking that the case be dismissed, and filed a final administration account, for which he paid the fee. E was promised, and received, nothing for the dismissal. Upon the motion of E's attorney, an order to show cause why M and N should not be attached and held for contempt of court was issued. The district judge found that the intent and effect of the actions of M and N were to prevent a trial on the merits and adjudged them guilty of contempt. The judgment was affirmed by the circuit court of appeals. On certiorari the Supreme Court reversed the judgments below.

Douglas, J., speaking for the Court, said in part:

[1] "The question is whether the conduct of petitioners constituted 'misbehavior . . . so near' the presence of the court 'as to obstruct the administration of justice' within the meaning of § 268 of the Judicial Code. That section derives from the Act of March 2, 1831 (4 Stat. 487). The Act of 1789 (1 Stat. 73, 83) provided that courts of the United States 'shall have power . . . to punish by fine or imprisonment, at the discretion of said courts, all contempts of authority in any cause or hearing before the same.' Abuses arose, culminating in impeachment proceedings against James H. Peck, a federal district judge, who had imprisoned and disbarred one Lawless for publishing a criticism of one of his opinions in a case which was on appeal. Judge Peck was ac-

[1] 313 U. S. 33 (1914).

quitted. But the history of that episode makes abundantly clear that it served as the occasion for a drastic delimitation by Congress of the broad undefined power of the inferior federal courts under the Act of 1789.

[2] "The day after Judge Peck's acquittal Congress took steps to change the Act of 1789. The House directed its Committee on the Judiciary 'to inquire into the expediency of defining by statute all offences which may be punished as contempts of the courts of the United States, and also to limit the punishment for the same.' Nine days later James Buchanan brought in a bill which became the Act of March 2, 1831. He had charge of the prosecution of Judge Peck and during the trial had told the Senate: 'I will venture to predict, that whatever may be the decision of the Senate upon this impeachment, Judge Peck has been the last man in the United States to exercise this power, and Mr. Lawless has been its last victim.' The Act of March 2, 1831, 'declaratory of the law concerning contempts of court,' contained two sections, the first of which provided: 'That the power of the several courts of the United States to issue attachments and inflict summary punishments for contempts of court, shall not be construed to extend to any cases except the misbehaviour of any person or persons in the presence of the said courts, or so near thereto as to obstruct the administration of justice, the misbehaviour of any of the officers of the said courts in their official transactions, and the disobedience or resistance by an officer of the said courts, party, juror, witness, or any other person or persons, to any lawful writ, process, order, rule, decree, or command of the said courts.'

[3] "Sec. 2 of that Act, from which § 135 of the Criminal Code (35 Stat. 1113, 18 U. S. C. § 241) derives, provided: 'That if any person or persons shall, corruptly, or by threats or force, endeavour to influence, intimidate, or impede any juror, witness, or officer, in any court of the United States, in the discharge of his duty, or shall, corruptly, or by threats or force, obstruct, or impede, or endeavour to obstruct or impede, the due administration of justice therein, every person or persons, so offending, shall be liable to prosecution therefor, by indictment, and shall on conviction thereof, be

punished, by fine not exceeding five hundred dollars, or by imprisonment, not exceeding three months, or both, according to the nature and aggravation of the offence.' . . .

[4] "Congress was responding to grievances arising out of the exercise of judicial power as dramatized by the Peck impeachment proceedings. Congress was intent on curtailing that power. The two sections of the Act of March 2, 1831 when read together, as they must be, clearly indicate that the category of criminal cases which could be tried without a jury was narrowly confined. . . .

[5] "Mindful of that history, we come to the construction of § 268 of the Judicial Code in light of the specific facts of this case. The question is whether the words 'so near thereto' have a geographical or a causal connotation. Read in their context and in the light of their ordinary meaning, we conclude that they are to be construed as geographical terms. . . .

[6] "We are dealing here only with a problem of statutory construction, not with a question as to the constitutionally permissible scope of the contempt power.* . . .

[7] "We may concede that there was an obstruction in the administration of justice, as evidenced by the long delay and large expense which the reprehensible conduct of petitioners entailed. . . .

"The fact that in purpose and effect there was an obstruction in the administration of justice did not bring the condemned conduct within the vicinity of the court in any normal meaning of the term. It was not misbehavior in the vicinity of the court disrupting to quiet and order or actually interrupting the court in the conduct of its business. *Cf. Savin, Petitioner, supra,* at p. 278. Hence, it was not embraced within § 268 of the Judicial Code. If petitioners can be punished for their misconduct, it must be under the Criminal Code where they will be afforded the normal safeguards surrounding criminal prosecutions. Accordingly, the judgment below is *Reversed.*" [2]

---

* (I.R.) The constitutional question here mentioned was considered and decided in Bridges v. California, 314 U. S. 252 (1941).

[2] A large part of the majority opinion, in which the Court considered and overruled Toledo Newspaper v. United States, 247 U. S. 402 (1918), has been omitted.

Stone, J., wrote a dissenting opinion in which the Chief Justice and Roberts, J., concurred.

Note the first four paragraphs of Justice Douglas' opinion. What are the principal factors which he invoked as aids in construing this act of Congress? How would you distinguish the directions of the House to its Committee on the Judiciary and the remarks of James Buchanan (in paragraph [2]), from the statement of the sponsor which was denied consideration in the *Partlow Case* in section 5–04 above?

2. In the *McBoyle Case*, section 5–11, problem 2, Holmes, J., said:

"Although it is not likely that a criminal will carefully consider the text of a law before he murders or steals, it is reasonable that a fair warning should be given to the world in language that the common world will understand, of what the law intends to do if a certain line is passed. To make the warning fair, so far as possible the line should be clear. When a rule of conduct is laid down in words that evoke in the common mind only the picture of vehicles moving on land, the statute should not be extended to aircraft simply because it may seem to us that a similar policy applies, or upon the speculation that if the legislature had thought of it, very likely broader words would have been used."

At another point in his opinion he said "Airplanes were well known in 1919 when this statute was passed, but it is admitted that they were not mentioned in the reports or the debates in Congress." Suppose airplanes had been mentioned and suppose it had been clear from the reports and debates that airplanes were intended to be included in the term "vehicle," should the statute have been construed to apply to McBoyle's act?

3. Suppose the occasion and purpose for a statute are set forth in a preamble or in a preliminary section (see for example the federal statute regarding issuance of injunctions in labor disputes, which is quoted in sec. 4–19). What difference should this explicit statement make?

Sec. 5–16. Nature of rules of interpretation. The acts of the interpreter are guided by rules just as the acts of the legislator are. In fact, the rules which prescribe standards for the interpreter are part and parcel of the rules applicable to officials. They are rules which apply to a judge when he does a particular kind of act, i. e., interprets legislation. The existence and operation of these rules furnish added reasons for not accepting the "free interpretation" theory without reservations. The interpreter's act is not unrestrained; it is not freely creative as is the act of the legislator who enacts the text to be interpreted. The interpreter's act is not only tied to the legislative text, but is controlled also by established rules of interpretation.[1]

Some of the rules which guide the interpreter have already been noted incidentally in the preceding sections; this notice could hardly have been avoided in view of the important functions of these rules in the interpretive process. But I saved the discussion of their nature and operation until this point; I felt that it was necessary to dispose first of the interpreter's role and of the material with which he works. The rules of interpretation are primarily concerned with the ways in which the interpreter handles the legislative text and its context. Having finished the consideration of the text and context as such, we are now ready to examine the rules which guide the interpreter in the performance of his functions.

The rules with which we are concerned are rules of method; they are techniques. They tell the interpreter how he is to handle text, when and how he should refer to context, how to resolve ambiguities, how to eliminate inconsistencies, and how to restrict, expand, or supplement the language of legislation. On the whole, these rules have been judicially

---

[1] In fact, the obligation of the interpreter to begin with the text, i.e., with the language used, can be regarded as itself a rule of interpretation, the most fundamental of all such rules.

developed, that is to say they are part of the common law. They are rules which the courts have worked out over the centuries for their own guidance in elaborating, correcting and supplementing the legislative product. But some of these common law rules have been deemed so important that they have been embodied in constitutional provisions. And in recent decades some of the states have, by so-called "statutory construction acts," wholly or partially codified the judicially developed rules and in some particulars modified them.[2]

In their character of rules of method, the rules of interpretation have to be differentiated from ordinary rules of law. They are *rules for interpreting rules*. They do not serve the same function as rules which govern the activity of Tom, Dick and Harry, and fix their relations to one another. They do not have the same role in the legal system as the common rules which govern the activities of officials. The rules which govern individuals and officials constitute the subject matter with which the interpreter works, whereas the rules of interpretation tell him how to do his work. Only the greatest confusion of thought can result from the failure to keep the interpretive rules clearly in view, from the failure to distinguish them from the rules being interpreted. If we were concerned with the repair of a house, we would not need to be warned against confusing the house with the methods used in repairing it; nor would there be danger of confusing methods of repair with the physical materials which go into the repair of the house. But when we leave the physical realm and deal with processes of correcting and supplementing legal rules we find ourselves in serious danger of blending the rules we are interpreting, with rules of interpretation, and with other existing legal rules which constitute a major part of the background for the interpreter's work. To specify further there are three kinds of rules to distinguish and to

[2] Typical is the Pennsylvania Statutory Construction Act, PURDON'S PA. STAT. ANN. tit. 46, § 501 *et seq.*

keep clearly in view: First, there are the legal rules which are the subject matter of interpretation; these are analogous to the house which is to be repaired. Second, there are the rules of method which govern the interpreter as he corrects and supplements the legislation which he is interpreting; these are parallel to the methods of repairing the house and are the rules of interpretation in which we are presently interested. Third, there are the rules, principles, and objectives of the law, already established and existing, which form a background for our interpretive problems; these are comparable to the material which is used in the repairing of the house and like that material they may be built into and added to the rule which is being interpreted. Confusion is easy here because subject matter, methods, and material are all rules or guides for conduct. To overlook the rules of interpretation is likewise easy because rules of interpretation are more or less taken for granted and do not have the prominent place in attention which is occupied by the subject matter of interpretation or the existing law to which it is being related. The interpretive rules need to be clearly seen as rules of a distinct and special kind which tell the interpreter how to clarify, correct and supplement the rules set forth in legislative texts.

Sec. 5–17. Problems—types of rules. 1. The expression "rules of interpretation" is commonly applied to a wide variety of guiding standards for the interpreter. These standards have only the one feature in common, their guidance function; all tell the interpreter how he shall carry on some phase of the interpretive process. They range all the way from specific rules—rules in a strict and accurate sense—through principles and presumptions, to the most general doctrines and prescribed attitudes. For example the term may include such varied elements as the following: (1) a specific rule that when a period of time is referred to in any law, such period shall be so computed in all cases as to exclude the first and include the last day; (2) a principle that associated words explain and limit each other, or a principle that ordinary words are to be taken in their plain and ordinary sense; (3) a presumption, that the legislature does not intend a result which is absurd; and (4) a prescribed attitude, such as that which is expressed in the doctrine that penal statutes are to be strictly construed.

It would serve no good purpose to attempt to furnish an exhaustive list of rules of interpretation. The rules are listed in standard works on interpretation and are the chief subject matter of discussion in courses on legislation. It will be enough if I introduce you to a few of the common rules and give you an opportunity of "spotting" a few of them in a decided case. Accordingly, I suggest that you see how many such rules you can point out in the opinion of the court and in the opinion of the dissenting judges in the following case:

Caminetti v. United States.[1] Mr. Justice Day delivered the opinion of the court:

". . . The petitioner was indicted in the United States District Court for the Northern District of California, upon the sixth day of May 1913, for alleged violations of the act. The indictment was in four counts, the first of which charged him with transporting and causing to be transported and aiding and assisting in obtaining transportation for a certain woman from Sacramento, California to Reno, Nevada, in interstate commerce for the purpose of debauchery, and for an immoral purpose, to wit, that the aforesaid woman should be and become his mistress and concubine. A verdict of not guilty was returned as to the other three counts of this indictment. As to the first count defendant was found guilty and sentenced to imprisonment for eighteen months and to pay a fine of $1,500.00. Upon writ of error to the United States

[1] 242 U. S. 470 (1916).

Circuit Court of Appeals for the Ninth Circuit, that judgment was affirmed. 220 Fed. Rep. 545. . . .

"It is contended that the act of Congress is intended to reach only 'commercialized vice,' or the traffic in women for gain, and that the conduct for which the several petitioners were indicted and convicted, however reprehensible in morals, is not within the purview of the statute when properly construed in the light of its history and the purposes intended to be accomplished by its enactment. In none of the cases [2] was it charged or proved that the transportation was for gain or for the purpose of furnishing women for prostitution for hire, and it is insisted that, such being the case, the acts charged and proved, upon which conviction was had, do not come within the statute.

"It is elementary that the meaning of a statute must, in the first instance, be sought in the language in which the act is framed, and if that is plain, and if the law is within the constitutional authority of the law-making body which passed it, the sole function of the courts is to enforce it according to its terms. *Lake County* v. *Rollins*, 130 U. S. 662, 670, 671. . . .

"Where the language is plain and admits of no more than one meaning the duty of interpretation does not arise and the rules which are to aid doubtful meanings need no discussion. *Hamilton* v. *Rathbone*, 175 U. S. 414, 421. There is no ambiguity in the terms of this act. It is specifically made an offense to knowingly transport or cause to be transported, etc., in interstate commerce, any woman or girl for the purpose of prostitution or debauchery, or for 'any other immoral purpose,' or with the intent and purpose to induce any such woman or girl to become a prostitute or to give herself up to debauchery, or to engage in any other immoral practice.

"Statutory words are uniformly presumed, unless the contrary appears, to be used in their ordinary and usual sense, and with the meaning commonly attributed to them . . . while the title of an act cannot overcome the meaning of plain and unambiguous words used in its body . . . , the title of this act embraces the regulation of interstate commerce

[2] Three cases were heard and decided together by the Supreme Court: Caminetti v. United States, Diggs v. United States and Hays v. United States.

'by prohibiting the transportation therein for immoral purposes of women and girls and for other purposes.' It is true that § 8 of the act provides that it shall be known and referred to as the 'White-slave traffic Act,' and the report accompanying the introduction of the same into the House of Representatives set forth the fact that a material portion of the legislation suggested was to meet conditions which had arisen in the past few years, and that the legislation was needed to put a stop to a villainous interstate and international traffic in women and girls. Still, the name given to an act by way of designation or description, or the report which accompanies it, cannot change the plain import of its words. If the words are plain, they give meaning to the act, and it is neither the duty nor the privilege of the courts to enter speculative fields in search of a different meaning.

"Reports to Congress accompanying the introduction of proposed laws may aid the courts in reaching the true meaning of the legislature in cases of doubtful interpretation. . . . But, as we have already said, and it has been so often affirmed as to become a recognized rule, when words are free from doubt they must be taken as the final expression of the legislative intent, and are not to be added to or subtracted from by considerations drawn from titles or designating names or reports accompanying their introduction, or from any extraneous source. In other words, the language being plain, and not leading to absurd or wholly impracticable consequences, it is the sole evidence of the ultimate legislative intent. See *Mackenzie* v. *Hare*, 239 U. S. 299, 308. . . .

"The judgment . . . is *Affirmed*. . . .

"Mr. Justice McKenna, with whom concurred the Chief Justice and Mr. Justice Clarke, dissenting.

"Undoubtedly in the investigation of the meaning of a statute we resort first to its words, and when clear they are decisive. The principle has attractive and seemingly disposing simplicity, but that it is not easy of application or, at least, encounters other principles, many cases demonstrate. The words of a statute may be uncertain in their signification or in their application. If the words be ambiguous, the problem they present is to be resolved by their definition; the subject-matter and the lexicons become our guides. But here, even, we are not exempt from putting ourselves in the place of the legislators. If the words be clear in meaning but the objects to which they are addressed be uncertain, the problem then is to determine the uncertainty. And for this a realization of conditions that provoked the statute must inform our judgment. Let us apply these observations to the present case.

"The transportation which is made unlawful is of a woman or girl 'to become a prostitute or to give herself up to debauchery, or to engage in any other immoral practice.' Our present concern is with the words 'any other immoral practice,' which, it is asserted, have a special office. The words are clear enough as general descriptions; they fail in particular designation; they are class words, not specifications. Are they controlled by those which precede them? If not, they are broader in generalization and include those that precede them, making them unnecessary and confusing. To what conclusion would this lead us? 'Immoral' is a very comprehensive word. It means a dereliction of morals. In such sense it covers every form of vice, every form of conduct that is contrary to good order. It will hardly be contended that in this sweeping sense it is used in the statute. But if not used in such sense, to what is it limited and by what limited? If it be admitted that it is limited at all, that ends the imperative effect assigned to it in the opinion of the court. But not insisting quite on that, we ask again, By what is it limited? By its context, necessarily, and the purpose of the statute.

"For the context I must refer to the statute; of the purpose of the statute Congress itself has given us illumination. It devotes a section to the declaration that the 'Act shall be known and referred to as the "White-slave traffic Act." ' And its prominence gives it prevalence in the construction of the statute. It cannot be pushed aside or subordinated by indefinite words in other sentences, limited even there by the context. It is a peremptory rule of construction that all parts of a statute must be taken into account in ascertaining its meaning, and it cannot be said that § 8 has no object. Even if it gives only a title to the act it has especial weight. *United States* v. *Union Pacific R. R. Co.*, 91 U. S. 72, 82. But it gives more than a title; it makes distinctive the purpose of the statute. The designation 'White-slave traffic' has the sufficiency of an axiom. If apprehended, there is no uncertainty as to the conduct it describes. It is commercialized vice, immoralities having a mercenary purpose, and this is confirmed by other circumstances.

". . . Any measure that protects the purity of women from assault or enticement to degradation finds an instant advocate in our best emotions; but the judicial function cannot yield to emotion—it must, with poise of mind, consider and decide. It should not shut its eyes to the facts of the world and assume not to know what everybody else knows. And everybody knows that there is a difference between the occasional immoralities of men and women and that systematized and mercenary immorality epitomized in the statute's graphic phrase, 'White-slave traffic.' And it was such immorality that was in the legislative mind and not the other. The other is occasional, not habitual—inconspicuous—does not offensively obtrude upon public notice. Interstate commerce is not its instrument as it is of the other, nor is prostitution its object or its end. It may, indeed, in instances, find a convenience in crossing state lines, but this is its accident, not its aid.

"There is danger in extending a statute beyond its purpose, even if justified by a strict adherence to its words. The purpose is studied, all effects measured, not left at random— one evil practice presented, opportunity given to another. The present case warns against ascribing such improvidence to the statute under review. Blackmailers of both sexes have arisen, using the terrors of the construction now sanctioned by this court as a help—indeed, the means—for their brigandage. The result is grave and should give us pause. It certainly will not be denied that legal authority justifies the rejection of a construction which leads to mischievous consequences, if the statute be susceptible of another construction. . . . the Chief Justice and Mr. Justice Clarke concur in this dissent."

The rules of interpretation which are applied in this case, relate chiefly to the use of contextual factors: when is context to be referred to and when not. Why did the majority of the court feel bound to reject references to the history of this act?

2. In reading and interpreting the language of past works, historical, scientific, and literary, the reader is usually desirous of putting himself in the writer's position; he wants to know what the writer meant when he wrote, not what he would mean if he were writing today. And traditionally the judicial interpreter adopts the same approach to the legal mandates which have come down from the past; he assumes that he is expected to find out what the legislative mandate meant when it was issued. Indeed, the judicial interpreter regards himself as bound by a principle which requires him to read the legislator's declaration in the context in which it was enacted.

What would you think of a proposal to have the courts continuously reinterpret constitutional provisions in the light of present times and needs, i.e., present context?*

Suppose courts always interpreted statutes as if they were written today. Would this be the same method of interpretation as that represented by the "free interpretation" theory?

Typical Interpretive Problems

Sec. 5–18. Types of problems. So much for the role of the interpreter, the sources on which he draws, and the rules which control his operations. Now let us turn to some applications and illustrations of the principles that have been developed, to some typical interpretive problems. Suppose

---

* (I.R.) On the proposal here made, see the observations of Kohler in "Judicial Interpretation of Enacted Law," translated and quoted in *Science of Legal Method* (American Legal Philosophy Series) 187–200 (1917). Compare the following decisions of the Supreme Court which indicate a readiness to consider present context (needs) as well as context of enactment, in construing the Federal Constitution: McCulloch v. Maryland, 4 Wheat. 316, 407, 415 (1819); Hurtado v. California, 110 U. S. 516 (1884); Weems v. United States, 217 U. S. 349, 373 (1910); Missouri v. Holland, 252 U. S. 416, 433–434 (1920); Home Bldg. and Loan Assn. v. Blaisdell, 290 U. S. 398, 442–443 (1934); United States v. Classic, 313 U. S. 299 (1941); and United States v. South-Eastern Underwriters' Ass'n, 322 U. S. 533 (1944).

the language of legislation is ambiguous, how is the ambiguity to be resolved? Or suppose the language is general, how far is the interpreter free to fill in details or to extend the language or restrict its meaning? Or suppose the indications of the words and the indications of context point in different directions, is the meaning suggested by the words or the meaning suggested by extrinsic aids to be preferred? Or finally, suppose the language of legislation is incomplete, how far are the various elements of setting to be drawn upon to supply what the words do not declare? Such are the basic problems which confront the interpreter.

For the purpose of convenient treatment I shall divide the interpreter's problems into five main types:

Resolving ambiguity.

Reconciling inconsistency.

Reading details into general provision.

Restrictive interpretation of general provision.

Extensive interpretation of general provision.

Sec. 5–19. Resolving ambiguity. Here we start with a situation where the text itself points to two or more possible meanings. A rather trivial example will show what I mean. A business man receives a scribbled note reading, "Your suit is ready to try tomorrow. Smith." He hands the note to his secretary and says, "Look at that. I cannot tell whether it comes from my lawyer or my tailor. Both are named Smith." In this case, the word "suit" has two distinct meanings; likewise the word "try"; and the name Smith may refer to either of two persons. The note is ambiguous in the sense that I have in mind. Earlier in this chapter I mentioned the case of the statute which was similarly ambiguous; the statute which forbade the sale of liquor within three miles of Mount Zion Church, in Gaston County.[1] On its face, such a statute would appear to be clear and sufficiently definite, yet in actual

[1] Sec. 5–04.

application it turned out to be ambiguous, as there were two Mount Zion Churches in said county, one for white persons, the other for colored persons. Not a few such ambiguities develop even in the most carefully drafted statutes.

How do these ambiguities happen? Basically, the cause of ambiguity is to be found in the nature of language itself. It would be utterly impossible to have a specific symbol for each and every idea which anyone wants to express. The burden of creating, learning and retaining so many words would be overwhelming. Instead, we make every one of our verbal symbols serve in a number of different type situations; practically every important word in the dictionary has not one but many meanings. On the one side, this multiple use of symbols represents an economy of human effort. On the other side it entails danger of confusion; it is the basic cause of ambiguity. Yet multiple usage is not the only cause of ambiguity in actual life situations. The danger of ambiguity is a danger which varies with the way in which persons use language. A careful and explicit use of terms will eliminate much of the danger; carelessness, ignorance, or lack of foresight on the part of the one who uses language, increases the danger. For example, in the case of the note from the tailor or the lawyer, the ambiguity would not have existed if the writer had used his business stationery and perhaps not if he had signed his full name. The ambiguity would not have existed in case of the churches, if the framer of the statute had expressed a little more fully what he had in mind and had declared that the statute was applicable to Mount Zion Church for colored people. In short, while ambiguity is a danger which can never be completely avoided, it is a danger which can be greatly reduced by a careful and explicit use of language.

Whatever the cause, ambiguity means a problem for the interpreter, a problem of *choosing between competing mean-*

ings. Of course, the choice is not absolutely compulsory. The court which is called upon to apply a statute which is ambiguous in its application may treat the ambiguity as fatal; it may refuse to apply the statute at all.[2] But as regards most ambiguities, this is not the course taken by the interpreter. He feels obliged to choose if he can, and to give effect to one of the two or more meanings of which the statutory language is capable. This method of dealing with problems of ambiguity is the method in which we are interested. What does the interpreter do when he undertakes to resolve an ambiguity? On what basis does he decide in favor of one meaning or another?

In part the interpreter is guided by rules which aid in making a choice between possible meanings of language. One such rule requires that he adopt the popular meaning of words; it declares that the language of a legislative text is to be taken in its ordinary or popular sense. You will remember that Justice Holmes recognized and followed this rule in his opinion in *McBoyle v. United States*.[3] He had to decide whether an airplane was a vehicle within the meaning of a federal statute which penalized the transportation of a stolen motor vehicle from one state to another. He said, "No doubt etymologically it is possible to use the word to signify a conveyance working on land, water or air. . . . But in everyday speech 'vehicle' calls up the picture of a thing moving on land." He concluded, therefore, that, as an airplane did not fall within the meaning of "vehicle" in the popular sense, its transportation from one state to another was not punishable under this statute. The rule is one of preference, however; it establishes a mere presumption in

[2] In the Partlow (Mount Zion Church) Case, the court's language suggests that ambiguity is generally fatal; however, it is not quite clear that the court would have refused to choose between the two Mount Zion churches if there had been competent evidence (such as a record of debates) on which to predicate a choice.

[3] Sec. 5–11.

favor of the popular meaning, not an absolute prescription. The context or counter-presumptions may nullify its effect so that the interpreter derives only a tentative guidance from this rule.

As a general canon of interpretation, this rule appears founded on good reasons. In the first place, the legislative provision which is being construed is framed by a legislative body presumably drawn from all walks of life and composed of persons with different verbal backgrounds and different kinds of experience. These men have agreed upon a verbal text. It is natural to assume that the standard of usage, which this heterogeneous group has followed in adopting its text, is the common or popular standard. In the second place, legislative provisions are normally framed so as to be applicable to persons generally. So far as they do apply to the general population, the popular sense of terms offers the appropriate and expectable standard of interpretation.

Another general rule, which serves as a companion to the rule just discussed, and which may aid the interpreter in making a choice between possible meanings, is the rule that technical terms are to be interpreted in a technical sense. Different professions and occupations have their peculiar terms and these are sometimes used in legislation; where this is the case, the interpreter is directed to adopt the technical meaning in his interpretation.[4]

But it is sometimes hard to decide whether language is used in a popular or a technical sense; usages change; they are not clearly divided. As I have said earlier, technical terms often become popular, by a slow process of adoption. Thus the word "legacy" would usually be regarded as a technical legal term, a word used by lawyers to refer to a testamentary

[4] In regard to technical legal terms, the rule which requires that technical terms be interpreted in a technical sense is identical with the rule that requires the interpreter to find his definitions of legal (i.e., technical) terms in the common law and other repositories of legal learning.

gift of personal property. In popular usage, however, the word "legacy" is often employed in a more comprehensive sense to include testamentary gifts of personal property, or real property, or both. If the legislature uses the term "legacy" in a statute, the interpreter may well decide, as the Colorado Supreme Court did in a case of this sort, that the term bears a popular meaning.[5] In so doing the interpreter is aided by a rule of preference favoring the popular meaning and based on reasons set forth in an earlier paragraph.

Of material assistance in resolving ambiguities are also a variety of rules which instruct the interpreter in the use of the verbal context of the ambiguous word or phrase.[6] Typical are the rule of *ejusdem generis* and the rule that words are to be construed in relation to their associates. The former declares that general words (the ambiguous element) following an enumeration of specific things are to be interpreted as limited to things of the same kind (*ejusdem generis*) as those specifically enumerated. The other rule, which is more general and which may indeed be said to include the former, stresses the dependence of the meaning of one word or phrase upon the words or phrases with which it is associated in use. For instance the word "home" in one connection might refer to a man's dwelling house; in another connection it might refer to place of his origin or birth; in another connection it might refer to his legal domicile, as where I say, "The State of Michigan is my home." So that in one statute the word might receive one construction, in another a different construction, depending on the text of

[5] Logan v. Logan, 11 Colo. 44 (1888). In reaching its conclusion in favor of the popular and comprehensive meaning, the court relied chiefly on two points: the fact that the legislature had used this term in a popular sense in other statutes, and the fact that the broad popular meaning of legacy would give a result more nearly in accord with the aim of the particular statute and with established policies (equality of shares), than the technical meaning would have produced.

[6] Other typical rules govern the force and effect to be given to preambles, provisos, etc.

the statute as a whole or the text of the section in which the word is used, or even upon the associated words of the phrase or clause in which the word is used.[7]

Many other rules serve as guides in resolving an ambiguity. Some of them have already been mentioned in discussing the various kinds of context: the rules which require the interpreter to look to the general and historical background for information; the rule which requires him to find his definitions of legal terms in the common law; the rule that statutes in derogation of the common law are to be strictly construed; the rule that statutes are to be interpreted in relation to other legislation dealing with the same subject matter; the rule that penal legislation is to be strictly construed, etc. These and almost all the other rules of interpretation hereintofore or hereinafter discussed, can be invoked in the solution of ambiguity problems. But it would be tedious and superfluous to try to illustrate the application of all these rules to problems of ambiguity or to each and every other kind of interpretive problem. I shall refer, in the next section, only to two more types of ambiguity problems and the methods of dealing with them.

Sec. 5–20. Problems. 1. Abrams et al. v. United States.[1] This case involved a choice between different meanings of the word *intent.* The defendants had been indicted and convicted of conspiring to violate the Espionage Act of 1917. On appeal the Supreme Court held the evidence sufficient to sustain their conviction of violating said act by publishing certain circulars *intended* to provoke and encourage resistance

[7] An important type of situation where this rule applies—though it is not commonly so labeled—is the case of the statute which carries its own definitions of questionable terms. These definitions are part of the verbal context of the terms as used; they fix the meaning thereof, even though each term standing alone might have had other meanings.

[1] 250 U. S. 616 (1919).

to the United States in the war with Germany and by inciting and advocating, through such circulars, resort to a general strike of workers in ammunition factories for the purpose of curtailing production of ordnance and munitions essential to the prosecution of the war. The members of the Court differed in opinion as to the sense in which the word "intent" was used in the Espionage Act. Three different senses of this term are common in legal parlance—as Mr. Justice Holmes points out: according to one usage, a person intends what he *desires* and aims to bring about; according to a second, he intends what he *foresees* as a consequence of his action, even though he does not desire to bring the consequence about; and according to a third usage, he intends the *foreseeable* consequences of his act, even though he does not actually foresee, nor actually desire, those consequences.

Mr. Justice Clarke, speaking for the majority of the Court, adopted the second usage as the proper one; he stressed the highly inflammatory and dangerous character of the circulars which defendants had published. In part, he said:

"It will not do to say, as is now argued, that the only intent of these defendants was to prevent injury to the Russian cause. Men must be held to have intended, and to be accountable for, the effects which their acts were likely to produce. Even if their primary purpose and intent was to aid the cause of the Russian Revolution, the plan of action which they adopted necessarily involved, before it could be realized, defeat of the war program of the United States. . . .

"These excerpts sufficiently show, that while the immediate occasion for this particular outbreak of lawlessness, on the part of the defendant alien anarchists, may have been resentment caused by our Government sending troops into Russia as a strategic operation against the Germans on the eastern battle front, yet the plain purpose of their propaganda was to excite, at the supreme crisis of the war, disaffection, sedition, riots, and, as they hoped, revolution, in this country for the purpose of embarrassing and if possible defeating the military plans of the Government in Europe. . . ."

Mr. Justice Holmes (supported by Mr. Justice Brandeis) dissenting, thought "intent" in this statute should be understood in the first sense; he minimized the danger of evil which might result from the circulars published by defendants and emphasized the need for safeguarding freedom of speech. As regards the meaning of intent, he said in part:

"I am aware of course that the word intent as vaguely used in ordinary legal discussion means no more than knowledge at the time of the act that the consequences said to be intended will ensue. Even less than that will satisfy the general principle of civil and criminal liability. A man may have to pay damages, may be sent to prison, at common law might be hanged, if at the time of his act he knew facts from which common experience showed that the consequences would follow, whether he individually could foresee them or not. But, when words are used exactly, a deed is not done with intent to produce a consequence unless that consequence is the aim of the deed. It may be obvious, and obvious to the actor, that the consequence will follow, and he may be liable for it even if he regrets it, but he does not do the act with intent to produce it unless the aim to produce it is the proximate motive of the specific act, although there may be some deeper motive behind.

"It seems to me that this statute must be taken to use its words in a strict and accurate sense. They would be absurd in any other. A patriot might think that we were wasting money on aeroplanes, or making more cannon of a certain kind than we needed, and might advocate curtailment with success, yet even if it turned out that the curtailment hindered and was thought by other minds to have been obviously likely to hinder the United States in the prosecution of the war, no one would hold such conduct a crime. . . ."

On the basis of this condensed statement of the Abrams case, what would you infer was the basis of choice between meanings of the word intent? Was it a mere matter of following the commoner usage?

2. Suppose a statute is adopted in California which might have either of two possible meanings, meaning X and meaning Y; and suppose this statute is later interpreted by the Supreme Court of California in an opinion which adopts meaning X. Now suppose this same statute is later borrowed and adopted by the State of South Dakota. The Supreme Court of South Dakota will treat the California decision as controlling. In so doing, how does the South Dakota court resolve the ambiguity? How would you formulate the rule followed?

Sec. 5–21. Reconciling inconsistency. Ambiguity and inconsistency are quite similar in nature and in the problems which they pose for the interpreter. Ambiguity characterizes a text which points in two directions, which may have either of two meanings. Inconsistency involves separate texts or different parts of one text, which point in two directions. Ambiguity and inconsistency are alike in that the language which the legislator has used points in two ways, and in that the interpreter must make a choice between them.

The chief kind of inconsistency which I have in mind is conflict between different parts of a single legislative enactment. The possibility of inconsistency inheres in the fact that any extended enactment consists of a series of more or less independent and more or less overlapping statements; the lawmaker may not sufficiently consider each of his statements in relation to the others. He states a purpose in the preamble of his legislative act and states a specific mandate in the body thereof, which suggest conflicting meanings or which coincide with one another only in part. Or he states a standard of behavior for individuals in one section, and another standard in another section which is not quite consistent with the first. Or he states overlapping but different standards of behavior for officials in different sections of his act. In all such cases the interpreter has the task of reconciling the applications of the various parts of the text with one another.

How does the interpreter deal with these problems? He finds a few guides which are peculiarly applicable to inconsistency problems. These rules give preference to one part of the legislative act over another part, or to one kind of statement therein over another kind of statement. Of such rules the two following provisions of the Pennsylvania Statutory Construction Act,[1] are typical; the provisions are merely declaratory of common-law rules of interpretation:

Sec. 563. *Particular Controls General.* "Whenever a general provision in a law shall be in conflict with a special provision in the same or another law, the two shall be construed if possible, so that effect may be given to both. If the conflict between the two provisions be irreconcilable, the special provision shall prevail and shall be construed as an exception to the general provision, unless the general provision shall be enacted later and it shall be the manifest intention of the Legislature that such general provision shall prevail."

Sec. 564. *Irreconcilable Clauses in the Same Law.* "Except as provided in section (five) sixty-three, whenever, in the same law, several clauses are irreconcilable, the clause last in order or date or position shall prevail."

However, most of the rules and methods which the interpreter uses in reconciling inconsistencies are not peculiar to the inconsistency problem. For the most part, he proceeds in about the same way and uses the same methods and materials as he does in resolving an ambiguity. The same guiding principles apply, so that it is not worth our while to list again all those rules which aid in choosing between conflicting

[1] Purdon's Pa. Stat. Ann. tit. 46.

meanings or which guide the interpreter's reference to the general, legal, and the historical context, of the legal provisions which he is attempting to reconcile. Nor is it surprising that the interpreter sometimes finds, as he does in resolving ambiguities, that all other prescriptions fail, and that he has to choose between inconsistent textual provisions simply on the basis of what is desirable policy.

In the wide sense one may find inconsistency between a statute and the common law, or between a statute and an earlier statute, or between a statute and a constitutional provision. For such cases our legal system is prepared with general solutions of conflict which are relatively easy. The statute displaces the common law, the later statute repeals the earlier, and the constitution overrides the conflicting statute. Established rules regarding the operation of legal provisions leave the interpreter without any real problems of reconciling conflicts to struggle with. Only if the inconsistency in any of these cases be partial, does the interpreter have something to do. He must then decide how much of the common law, of the earlier statute, or of the conflicting statute, is inoperative and how much of it remains in force. Typical of this kind of problem and of the way our legal system deals with it, is the following provision of the Pennsylvania Statutory Construction Act, dictating the proper solution where a statute conflicts in part with a constitutional provision:

Sec. 555. *Constitutional Construction of Laws.* "The provisions of every law shall be severable. If any provision of a law is found by a court of record to be unconstitutional and void, the remaining provisions of the law shall, nevertheless, remain valid, unless the court finds the valid provisions of the law are so essentially and inseparably connected with, and so dependent upon, the void provision, that it cannot be presumed the Legislature would have enacted the remaining valid provisions without the void one; or unless the court finds the remaining valid provisions, standing alone, are incomplete, and are incapable of being executed in accordance with the legislative intent."

This statute is simply declaratory of principles which the courts had worked out for themselves independently of legislation.

Sec. 5–22. Reading details into general provision. In the last chapter I pointed out that the legislator always uses language which is more or less general; that he uses general language in order to conserve his own effort in thinking out more detailed provisions and in order to cover unforeseen cases which future conditions may present. If his legislation specifies details of application with undue particularity, there is always the danger that important situations will be omitted and that the language of his text will fail to embrace cases which he would have wanted to cover if he had had sufficient foresight and could have stated his meaning perfectly.

On the other side of the ledger is the fact that a general text is indefinite; that general language fails to furnish assured guidance to individuals and officials who need it. An extreme example will make my point. Suppose that a criminal statute were to provide simply that "any act prejudicial to the general welfare is punishable as a misdemeanor." Such a statute leaves everything undefined.[1] It fails in the prime function of a legal provision. It leaves the individual who may be punished, without guidance; and it leaves the judge who may have to apply the provision, likewise without proper direction.

[1] In fact a court would probably hold the very statute which we have supposed, invalid by reason of its indefiniteness. (See United States v. Cohen Grocery Co., 257 U. S. 81 (1921).) But this does not destroy its value as an example. Indefiniteness is a matter of degree. A somewhat slighter degree of generality and indefiniteness would escape the ban of invalidity. And constitutional provisions themselves escape this reason for judicial disapproval. The problem of dealing with indefinite provisions is one which the courts must face and which they do dispose of in the ways indicated in the text.

What is the judicial interpreter to do, when he is called upon to apply such an indefinite provision? Shall he declare the provision void for indefiniteness, and therefore refuse to apply it? Or shall he apply it in cases as they arise, according to his best judgment on the facts of each case, but leave the provision in its undefined state and let every individual continue to act at his peril?* Or shall he undertake to complete the meaning of the indefinite provision as he applies it from case to case, by establishing subsidiary rules to define what is, and what is not, prejudicial to the general welfare? All three of these solutions are possible and are at times adopted; we are interested now only in the last solution because it alone can be called interpretation, and because it is the common solution adopted by American judges.

This solution requires the interpreter to define or redefine the general terms of the provision to make them definite. In the words of Chief Justice Hughes in *Home Building and Loan Association v. Blaisdell,* the famous mortgage moratorium case: ". . . where Constitutional grants and limitations of power are set forth in general clauses, which afford a broad outline, the process of construction is essential to fill in details." [2] The Chief Justice means, though he does not say just this, that the interpreter must supply details which are not found in the constitutional provision he construes. When we connect this method of supplying needed details with the general doctrine that judicial decisions are con-

* (I.R.) Occasionally courts realize the danger of making their own, or the legislative, product too specific in operation (see first paragraph of this section) and warn that instances are not to be understood as definitive; they try to keep the operation of the provision which they are construing, general and undefined; consider, for example, the way equity courts have refused to tie themselves by definite notions of fraud and the way our Supreme Court has refused to formulate standards of due process more definite than the standard of reasonableness. Nevertheless specific cases are decided and cited as precedents even though the courts profess to keep their own hands free; so that the whole tendency is to convert general legislative standards into more specific, as is pointed out in the ensuing paragraphs of the text.

[2] 290 U. S. 398 at 426 (1934).

trolling precedents for future applications of the provision, we see that the details become essentially judicial additions to the original text. The court's decisions in one case after another furnish more specific rules in the general area covered by the original indefinite provision. A vague general provision is converted by interpretation into an aggregate of specific rules, all of which together constitute the effective meaning of the general provision.

Original indefiniteness is especially characteristic of constitutional provisions; in fact Chief Justice Hughes used the language above quoted in regard to the Contracts Clause of the Federal Constitution. The extent to which such a clause is rendered more definite by judicial interpretation can be illustrated by the development of the meaning of that clause. It reads: "No state shall . . . pass any Law . . . impairing the Obligation of Contracts. . . ." [3] The major terms here are all vague and general. What is a "law"? The Supreme Court has said that the term "law" includes state statutes, city ordinances, and state constitutional provisions, but does not include decisions by state courts. What is a "contract" which is protected against impairment? The term "contract" is held to embrace private and public contracts, executed and executory contracts, express and implied contracts; it includes franchises, corporate charters and public grants of land. Like questions have arisen and have had to be answered regarding the application of "obligation" and "impairing." The result is that in the century and a half since the clause was adopted a great mass of specific judicial propositions have been developed which are the real, practical meaning of the Contracts Clause. The exact wording of the clause itself has ceased to be of primary consequence. It is these details of meaning, supplied by adjudication, on which the lawyer's chief interest centers.

[3] Art. I, Sec. 10.

Moreover, this process of filling in details is not limited to obviously indefinite statutory provisions and sweeping clauses of a constitution. The process of filling in needed details occurs regularly in the application of any general term which may be found in legislation. As regards all enactments, there is a continuing process of reducing general terms to more specific. Thus, the judicial interpretations which have supplemented the general terms of the Statute of Frauds fill many volumes. One obtains no adequate conception of what that statute means by a mere scrutiny of its language. It was once said about Coke's elaborate commentary on Littleton's *Tenures,* that the book represented a little rivulet of Littleton running through a great meadow of Coke. No less can it be said that the text of the Statute of Frauds is almost lost to sight in the enormous judicial gloss erected about the legislative original. And while the accumulated volume of judicially supplied details is never quite so large in the case of modern statutes, it is nevertheless apparent enough. Phrase after phrase of the Uniform Negotiable Instruments Act has had to be construed, and these constructions constitute, in the main, detailed applications and refinements of the general terms of this legislation. Every term of a simple statute, such as a criminal statute prohibiting the carrying of concealed weapons, calls for the same kind of judicial exposition. What is a "weapon"? When is a weapon "concealed"? And what is "carrying" a weapon? Details have to be filled in, specific answers have to be furnished. And, in effect, these specific answers develop into a cluster of specific rules.

The process of filling in details is analogous to the process of resolving an ambiguity. Both processes are concerned with a legislative text not fully expressed. Both processes involve for the interpreter a choice between possible meanings. The means of solving an ambiguity and the sources of details are alike to be found in the context, general, legal, and historical;

and the rules of interpretation applicable to both problems are essentially the same. The difference between resolving an ambiguity and choosing between the various meanings which may be read into a general term, lies in the fact that the general term ordinarily allows the interpreter a wider choice of possibilities. He is not limited to a choice between two but may choose among several detailed meanings. In furnishing the details for the Contract Clause, for example, the Supreme Court was free to choose from a variety of senses of the words *contract, obligation, impair,* etc. It found the material of its choices in popular and legal usages of terms.[4]

Sec. 5–23. Restrictive interpretation of general provision. Sometimes a statute or a constitutional provision is couched in terms which literally include more ground or more items than the interpreter believes the framer would ever have wanted to include; and the question confronts the interpreter whether he ought to trim down the operation of the statute or constitutional provision by interpretation.*

The overinclusive provision may be due to any of the reasons already mentioned, which explain such defects as ambiguity, inconsistency and indefiniteness. But the prime reason for overinclusiveness is the legislator's effort to offset

[4] The choice was based on considerations of history and policy, considerations derived from context. See for example such cases as Fletcher v. Peck, 6 Cranch 87 (1810); Trustees of Dartmouth College v. Woodward, 4 Wheat. 518 (1819); Home Building and Loan Association v. Blaisdell, 290 U. S. 398 (1934); Gelfert v. National City Bank of New York, 313 U. S. 221 (1941).

* (I.R.) In strict logic restrictive interpretation might be regarded as a special instance of the process of filling in details (sec. 5–22); or, perhaps, the latter process as an instance of restrictive interpretation. Both processes involve the qualification or limitation of general language by reading limitative particulars into it. However, we are accustomed to think and speak of the two processes as different. Filling in details is regarded as a form of limitation which supplements or completes what is said; restrictive interpretation (including the introduction of exceptions) is regarded as a form of limitation which cuts across or contradicts what is said. This difference in traditional view and mode of speech is practical warrant for treating restrictive interpretation under a separate head.

his inability to foresee and specify all the situations to which he wants his provision to apply. The legislator wishes his provision to be inclusive enough, and therefore uses comprehensive terms. He wishes the provision to cover not only types of cases of which he has had experience, but also analogous types and new types which come into existence in the future. To this end he uses catchall phrases. Thus a statute may be enacted which prohibits individuals to carry dangerous weapons. This blanket provision would doubtless apply to a new form of atomic weapon even though such a weapon had never been dreamed of at the time when the statute was passed. By using comprehensive terms the legislator is able to cope with the problems of an expanding and indefinite future. However, in his effort to catch all the fish he wants to catch by casting a wide net of broad general character, the legislator runs the risk of sweeping up some fish in his net which he would not have desired to catch if he had had the vision of the "compleat angler."

How does the interpreter arrive at the conclusion that the legislator has overreached himself in this way? Actually the interpreter does this on the basis of the fact that important contextual factors suggest a narrower inclusion than the language suggests. Conventionally he talks in terms of a distinction between the purpose (or spirit) of the statute on the one hand, and its literal terms on the other. But the important point is not the matter of names; it is the fact that the interpreter recognizes a divergence between language and something else. It is not hard to see that the purpose (or spirit), which is not consistent with the language, is nothing but the purport of known contextual factors; indeed, that it is a mere deduction from them.**

** (I.R.) Sometimes a partial divergence between different parts of the language of a statute (inconsistency) is combined with divergence between the language and the spirit. In this case solution of an inconsistency is blended with restrictive interpretation.

What does the interpreter do when he uncovers such a conflict between the text and the purpose of legislation? Of course he might refuse to amend the legislator's work, apply the statute as it stands, and "pass the buck" back to the legislature to make any needed changes. But on the whole, courts are inclined to make free use of their corrective power; they are prepared to do a job of restrictive interpretation whenever they feel that contextual factors point with sufficient clearness to this result. The limits and details of this method of pruning down, or engrafting exceptions on, the language of a statute will be developed in the following cases.

Sec. 5–24. Problems. 1. State v. Gorham.[1]

Fullerton, J. "The appellant was convicted of a violation of the speed ordinances of the city of Hilliard. The facts are stipulated, and are in substance these:

"The city named lies within, and forms a part of, the county of Spokane. The appellant is a duly appointed, qualified and acting deputy sheriff of such county. On June 3, 1919, a charge of grand larceny was preferred against one William Agnew, and a warrant issued for his arrest. This warrant was given to the appellant for execution. The specific charge was the larceny of an automobile, and on inquiry the appellant was informed by a police officer of the city of Spokane that the accused had been seen on that day on the down town streets of the city driving an automobile bearing the license number of the stolen automobile. Upon further inquiry, the officer found a young man who knew the accused, and who stated to the officer that he had seen the accused only a few moments before that time driving an automobile 'at a good rate of speed' toward the city of Hilliard, on the main highway leading from the city of Spokane to that city. The officer immediately took up the pursuit of the accused on a motorcycle, and in passing through the city of Hilliard,

---

[1] 110 Wash. 330 (1920); WAITE, CASES ON CRIMINAL LAW (2d ed.) 62 (1937).

rode the motorcycle at a greater rate of speed than its ordinances permitted.

"In this court, the appellant . . . (contends) . . . that a sheriff is exempt from the operation of city ordinances regulating the speed at which a motor vehicle may be driven when he is in pursuit of a person accused of felony for whose arrest he has a warrant.

"The sheriff is made, by statute, the chief executive officer and conservator of the peace of the county. By statute, also, it is made his duty to keep the public peace, and to arrest and confine all persons who commit violations of the law, and especially is it made his duty to execute all process issued to him by a court of justice. His duties in these respects are public duties necessary to the safety of the state and its people, and necessary for the preservation of public and private property. In the performance of these duties, the sheriff has many privileges not accorded to a private individual, and statutes and ordinances directed against the individual do not generally apply to him when so performing them, especially where their enforcement would hamper and hinder performance.[2]

"That the enforcement against a peace officer of statutory or ordinance provisions limiting the speed at which a motor propelled vehicle shall be driven over a public highway would have a tendency to hamper him in the performance of his official duties, can hardly be doubted. The case in hand affords an illustration. Here the felon was fleeing with a stolen automobile. Naturally he would pay but little regard to the minor offense of exceeding the speed limit. And if the sheriff must confine himself to that limit, pursuit in the manner adopted would have been useless, since the felon could not have been overtaken. The rule contended for would

[2] Where a court is considering a choice between two interpretations of a legislative provision, it is very common practice to develop the consequences which will follow from the one interpretation and the other, and to allow the choice to be determined by the consequences which the court regards as preferable or as more nearly in accord with a general legislative purpose. See for example Hoff v. State of New York quoted in sec. 5–13, problem 3. The consequences of alternative interpretations are especially stressed by the court when it says, "Our constitutional guarantees of liberty are merely empty words unless a person imprisoned or detained against his will may challenge the legality of his imprisonment and detention."

also hinder the public peace officers in enforcing the statutes regulating traffic upon the state highways. These statutes contain somewhat stringent regulations as to the speed a motor propelled vehicle may be driven over them, and contain no exception in favor of the peace officers whose duty it is made to enforce them. If these officers may not pursue and overtake one violating the regulations without themselves becoming amenable to the penalties imposed by them, the old remedy of hue and cry is not available in such instances, and many offenders who are now brought to answer will escape.

"It is not meant to be asserted, of course, that there are no restrictions upon the speed a sheriff or a peace officer may travel in the pursuit of a fleeing criminal. Such officers may abuse their privileges in this respect as well as in others and must answer for such abuse. What is meant to be said is that the statutory regulations as to speed do not apply to them, and that for an abuse of their privileges in this respect they must answer in the manner they are required to answer for other abuses of privilege. . . .

"Our conclusion is that the trial court erred in adjudging the officer guilty of the offense charged. Its judgment will therefore be reversed, and the cause remanded with instruction to discharge the appellant."

On what contextual factors, does the court predicate an exception to the speed regulations here involved?

2. *Queen v. Tolson.*[3] Indictment and conviction for bigamy. An Act of Parliament provided that "whoever being married, shall marry any other person during the life of the former husband or wife . . . shall be guilty of felony"; the Act also contained a proviso that "nothing in this act shall extend to any person marrying a second time whose husband or wife shall have been continually absent from such person for the space of seven years last past, and shall not have been known by such person to be living within that time." D married her husband on September 11, 1880; he

3 (1889) 23 Q. B. D. 168.

deserted her on December 13, 1881. D, believing in good faith and on reasonable grounds that her husband was dead, married another on January 10, 1887. In December 1887 her husband, who had not died, reappeared.

On the question whether D was guilty of bigamy nine judges of the Court for the Crown Cases Reserved, held that she was not and that her conviction must be quashed. Several opinions were filed; the major arguments for the court's conclusion were that while the words of the Act literally applied to a case such as the one presented, the Act must be construed in the light of its purpose, of the harsh consequences of applying it here, and of the undoubted "principle of English criminal law that, ordinarily speaking, a crime is not committed if the mind of the person doing the act is innocent." On these grounds the court decided in effect that the Act did not apply to a person "who married believing in good faith and on reasonable grounds that the former husband or wife is dead."

A minority of five judges dissented; they thought D was guilty of bigamy on the ground that the language of the Act was plain and clear. One judge declared, "It is the imperative duty of the Court to give effect to it, and leave it to the legislature to alter the law if it thinks it ought to be altered."

What factors of context does the majority invoke as a basis for restricting the language of this Act?

What might be said to be the force and effect of the proviso?

A contemporary commentator said of the decision:

"The judgment of the majority of the Court will no doubt commend itself to popular opinion, and we do not assert that the judgment is wrong. It suggests however observations of some importance.

"If the judges are to qualify the plain language of a statute by the introduction of limitations and provisos as to which not a hint is to be found in the Act, statutory legislation must necessarily become hopelessly confused. If the Courts hold that Parliament cannot mean what Parliament says, then how is anyone to make sure as to what an Act really means? If Parliament had meant to make bigamy in all cases a crime, Parliament could not have used language more clear than the terms of 24 & 25 Vict. chap. 100, sec. 57.

"The popular idea that a code would remove all possibility as to uncertainty about the meaning of a law is shown by the *Queen v. Tolson,* if proof were needed, to be a delusion. Ambiguity arises in the main from the difficulty of framing rules accurate enough to meet the subtlety of nature. Human nature and the facts of life create cases which human sagacity fails to anticipate." [4]

Is there force in this commentator's general criticism of the decision?

3. *People v. Hatinger.*[5]

"Bird, J. Under an agreed statement of facts in the trial court, the respondent was convicted by a jury of a violation of the local-option law. He now seeks to have the conviction set aside by this court, on the ground that it is at variance with the law.

"It appears from the stipulation of facts that respondent, in the months of August and September, 1912, was operating a lunch and soft drink counter in the village of Edmore; that he had on sale what was known as 'Old Fort Cider,' which he purchased under a positive guaranty that it contained no alcohol; that the same was analyzed and found to contain 5.6 per cent alcohol; that as soon as the respondent learned that it contained alcohol he discontinued the sale. It is conceded by the people that respondent bought and sold the cider in good faith and with no intent to violate the law.

"It was the claim of respondent that under the case made by the stipulation he was entitled to a directed verdict of not guilty. This claim is based upon the concession of the people

[4] (1889) 5 L. Q. R. 449–450.
[5] 174 Mich. 333 (1913); WAITE, CASES ON CRIMINAL LAW (2d ed.) 57 (1937).

that respondent had no intent to violate the law. The contention of the prosecuting attorney was that the question of intent was immaterial, and was not a prerequisite to a conviction. The trial court agreed with the contention of the prosecuting attorney, and instructed the jury that it was their duty to return a verdict of guilty.

"The question raised is one of construction of the statute which is charged to have been violated. While most of the offenses defined by the criminal laws involve guilty knowledge or intent, it is admittedly competent for the legislature to forbid the doing of an act and make its commission criminal without regard to the intent of the doer. . . . If the legislature may create offenses with or without the element of intent, it becomes important to inquire what its intention was with respect to the passage of Act No. 183 of the Public Acts of 1899.

"Section 1 of the act prohibits in positive terms the sale of intoxicating liquors, and no language is used which indicates that the element of intent is to be read into it. Had the legislature intended to make the intent to violate the law an essential element, it would have doubtless used some appropriate language indicating its purpose. If it were necessary to prove intent to violate the law before a conviction could be had, the act would fall far short of doing what the legislature obviously intended it should do; and presumably in this can be found the chief reason why it did not incorporate into the act the element of intent. Laws forbidding the sale of intoxicating liquor and impure foods would be of little use if convictions for their violations were to depend on showing guilty knowledge. The fact, then, that respondent had no knowledge that the cider contained alcohol and that he purchased it and sold it in good faith, with no intent to violate the law, will not avail him in the face of his admission that he sold it and that it contained alcohol. . . ."

Here the court allowed the language to have its full effect and refused to exempt the respondent from liability. Why? What is the difference between this case and the *Tolson Case?* Is it a difference of the statutory language?

Sec. 5–25. Extensive interpretation of general provision.
The interpreter sometimes concludes that a provision is too
narrowly stated. It fails to cover certain cases which are
within its purpose (or spirit). The deficiency, you will notice,
is just the opposite of the defect last considered. Here, as
we assume, the provision is too narrow in terms; there the
provision was too inclusive. The questions here are whether
the interpreter shall stretch the provision to include cases
not normally within their meaning, or whether he shall go
even further and expand the scope of the provision by
analogy, to include cases not within its terms in any sense.*

The reasons for this defect, like other defects of statement,
may be lack of care in drafting and failure to foresee the
situations to which the enactment should apply. Particularly
the sponsor of legislation may have a special case in mind
and frame a specific rule to cover it, and his legislative
brethren may be indifferent or inattentive to the wording of
the act as they go through the steps of enacting it. Thus the
initiating legislator may think simply of the necessity for
regulating the catching of trout and may introduce a bill
fixing a limited trout season. He may not realize (or if he
does, not care) that catching of other fish needs to be likewise
regulated, or that a limited season should be similarly fixed
for each kind of fish. Shall the interpreter extend the application of an act so framed to cover all the kinds of fish within
the need for regulation?

As regards statutes, our judges are not inclined to indulge
in extensive interpretation of either sort. They are not usually
ready to stretch the statutory terms; and they refuse to
extend them to analogous cases. The courts ordinarily declare
that it is their function to apply a statutory provision as it
stands, not to amend it; and they argue that legislation will,
on the whole, be more carefully drafted if courts refuse to

---

* (I.R.) Extensive interpretation may also be combined with solution of
an inconsistency or resolution of an ambiguity. (*Cf.* sec. 5–23, note ** (I.R.).)

correct legislative errors by interpretation, and leave to the legislature the responsibility for avoiding or rectifying them.

Queries: Have these lines of argument any more relevance to extensive interpretation than to restrictive interpretation? Is there any logical or practical basis for making a distinction between the two types of correction? [1]

However, our courts often interpret constitutional clauses extensively, by stretching their terms to the farthest limits. On this point the great Chief Justice Marshall declared, in words which are frequently quoted: "We must never forget, that it is a Constitution we are expounding . . . a Constitution intended to endure for ages to come, and consequently, to be adapted to the various crises of human affairs." [2] Accordingly, the Supreme Court of the United States, in particular, has construed important clauses of the Federal Constitution in the most comprehensive sense. The Commerce Clause, for example, has been construed to include many things which are not "commerce" in the ordinary sense; the Due Process Clause has been given the widest possible meaning so as to cover many things which were certainly not originally included in the concept of "due process of law" in a historical sense; and the Contracts Clause has been interpreted to

---

[1] In this connection it is relevant to note that the courts in civil law countries (France, Germany, Italy, Spain and the Latin American countries) do interpret a *code provision* extensively; they apply a code provision to cases which are literally not included but which fall within the principle of the provision. See Pound, "Theory of Judicial Decision," 36 HARV. L. REV. 641 at 647 (1923); and compare the following:

"With the general assumption of complete codification goes a liberal attitude toward legislation. German legislation is readily construed to cover cases beyond its letter. Emphasis is put on the spirit or principle embodied in code provisions, rather than on the literal meanings of words. The general reliance of the German lawyer on legislation and his readiness to construe legislation as complete, i.e., liberally, stand in contrast to our own reliance on the common law to furnish the solution of doubtful cases and to our narrow construction of statutes, which are expressed in the propositions that the common law fills all gaps in the law and that statutes in derogation of the common law are to be strictly construed." Shartel and Wolff, "German Civil Justice," 42 MICH. L. REV. 863 at 866 (1944).

[2] McCulloch v. Maryland, 4 Wheat. 316, 407, 415 (1819).

embrace many types of transaction which have not been called "contracts" in any ordinary usages of that term.

Sec. 5–26. Problems. 1. Why should the Supreme Court indulge more readily in extensive interpretation of constitutional, than of statutory, provisions?

2. *International Stevedoring Co. v. Haverty,* 272 U. S. 50 (1926). The plaintiff was a stevedore employed by the defendant company. While he was engaged in storing freight in the hold of a vessel lying at the dock in Seattle, he was injured through the negligence of a fellow employee of the defendant company. He brought action in a Washington court to recover damages for the injury sustained. The defendant company contended that it was not responsible for the injury to the plaintiff on the ground that the fellow-servant rule was applicable. Under this rule, an employer is not liable for an injury to one servant caused by the negligence of a fellow servant. The plaintiff contended that his action was governed by a federal statute which abrogated the fellow-servant rule in actions by "seamen" against the vessel on which they are working, and made the vessel liable for all injuries occurring in the course of their employment. The trial court held the statute to be applicable, and gave judgment on a verdict in plaintiff's favor; the Supreme Court of Washington affirmed the judgment. A writ of error was granted by the United States Supreme Court. The question presented to the Supreme Court was whether or not the defendant company was liable to the plaintiff stevedore under the terms of this federal statute.

The court, speaking through Mr. Justice Holmes, affirmed the judgment of the Washington Supreme Court and held that the defendant company was liable to the plaintiff. In his opinion, the justice referred to the fact that before Congress enacted the statute in question, it had enacted a similar statute abolishing the fellow-servant rule in regard to suits against railroads by their employees. Among other things he said:

"It is true that for most purposes, as the word is commonly used, stevedores are not 'seamen.' But words are flexible. The work upon which the plaintiff was engaged was a maritime service formerly rendered by the ship's crew. *Atlantic Transport Co. v. Imbrovek*, 234 U. S. 52, 62. We cannot believe that Congress willingly would have allowed the protection to men engaged upon the same maritime duties to vary with the accident of their being employed by a stevedore rather than by the ship. The policy of the statute is directed to the safety of the men and to treating compensation for injuries to them as properly part of the cost of the business. If they should be protected in the one case they should be in the other. In view of the broad field in which Congress has disapproved and changed the rule introduced into the common law within less than a century,[1] we are of opinion that a wider scope should be given to the words of the act, and that in this statute 'seamen' is to be taken to include stevedores employed in maritime work on navigable waters as the plaintiff was, whatever it might mean in laws of a different kind."

This was a case in which the Supreme Court gave an extensive interpretation to a *statute*. What was the special factor which induced the court to do this? [2]

Would the Supreme Court have held either the statute regarding railroad employees or the statute regarding seamen to be applicable to employees of an airline or a motor carrier?

---

[1] "The rule that the employer was not liable for injuries caused by the negligence of a fellow servant first appeared in England in 1837, and almost immediately in the United States, where it was stated elaborately in a well-known opinion of Chief Justice Shaw of Massachusetts in Farwell v. Boston and Worcester Railway." PROSSER, TORTS 514 (1941).

[2] Another instance of extensive interpretation (or perhaps I should say interpretation by analogy) is the common extension of statutes of limitation, applicable literally only to suits for possession to cases involving prescriptive claims to easements. See, for example, Klin v. New York Rapid Transit Corp., 271 N. Y. 376 (1936).

Can you say that Holmes' opinion in the above case is consistent with his opinion in the *McBoyle Case* (sec. 5–11)? If "seamen" can include stevedores, why cannot "vehicles" include airplanes? In the *McBoyle Case* Holmes said: ". . . the statute should not be extended to aircraft simply because it may seem to us that a similar policy applies, or upon the speculation that if the legislature had thought of it, very likely broader words would have been used."

Sec. 5–27. Summary. Interpretation is necessary because legislative provisions are obscurely or inadequately expressed. As a matter of terminology we do not speak of interpretation except in instances where the meaning of legislation is problematic and has to be settled before it can be applied. The principal instances of this sort arise from the legislator's use of ambiguous or inconsistent terms, from his use of indefinite language, from the fact that he leaves gaps in his legislative plan, and from his employment of overcomprehensive or unduly narrow expressions. In the face of a deficient legislative provision the person who is called upon to apply it, may take one of three courses. Sometimes he may refuse to apply the provision at all; at other times he may attempt to apply the provision just as it stands even though the results be harsh or even absurd; and finally, he may undertake to correct the deficiencies in the legislative provision before he applies it. Ordinarily, and certainly within very wide limits, the last course is that which is chosen by our American courts. It is the course which has been discussed in the present chapter.

All the processes of interpretation are creative to a certain degree; they involve a limited amount of judicial lawmaking. The interpreter's act is aimed to restate and explain the legislator's verbal act. The interpreter's act revises or completes a job of legislation which is deficient or incomplete.[1]

[1] And the interpreter's own act, like any other verbal act, may be deficient or incomplete and call for subsequent interpretation.

The interpreter starts work with the language which the legislator has used. He draws material for correcting deficiencies from the context of the legislator's act. This context embraces matters of general knowledge, the existing legal background, and the specific history of the enactment to be construed. The interpreter derives his information about these extrinsic factors partly from his own previous experiences, partly from deliberate inquiry on the particular occasion, and partly from evidence offered by other persons.

The whole of the interpreter's procedure is controlled by rules of method. These purport to tie the interpreter to what the legislator has said; they instruct the interpreter's choice as between various linguistic meanings; they specify the extrinsic sources on which he may draw for aid in carrying out the process of interpretation; they establish a variety of presumptions in favor of this meaning or that; they define the ends and policies of the legal system. To be sure, these various rules do not bind the interpreter absolutely; they leave a great deal of play for his discretion and judgment. But in practical operation the established procedures and rules of interpretation do offer real guidance for the interpreter's activities; they do guarantee that he will not depart too far from the expectable applications of the text of the legislation he is interpreting. While we can say that the interpreter acts as a supplementary lawmaker, his action is markedly different from the original lawmaker's in that he is merely completing or amending a structure already built, and he is working according to instructions which specify in some detail the way in which he is to carry out even this limited task.

CHAPTER 6

The Common Law *

Sec. 6–01. Scope of chapter. A large part of what we ordinarily call law is found not in the statutes, but in the reports of cases decided by our courts. This case law consists of rules, principles, ideas and methods which are used in the decision of cases. The body of decisions runs backward continuously from today through our colonial period and into the earliest history of England. Our colonists began as subjects of the English King and derived their legal notions from English sources. After the Revolution, the American courts simply carried on in their decisions, the notions which had been worked out by the English courts. From the English cases they derived general ideas and legal methods as well as rules and principles to apply. The development of case law, based on this foundation, has gone on without interruption to the present day.

The continuous but rather loosely interrelated mass of case law in England, in this country, and in the British Dominions,

---

* (I.R.) Suggestions for further reading:
1. Regarding the common law
Future of the Common Law—Harvard Law School Conference (Harvard Tercentenary Publications, 1937). Two of the more important items in this collection of papers were published separately as articles: Stone, "The Common Law in the United States," 50 Harv. L. Rev. 4 (1936), and Pound, "What is the Common Law?," 4 U. Chi. L. Rev. 176 (1937).
2. Regarding the judicial process
Cardozo, The Nature of the Judicial Process (Yale Univ. Press, 1921).
Dickinson, "The Law Behind Law," 29 Col. L. Rev. 113, 285 (1929).
Frank, "Are Judges Human?," 80 U. of Pa. L. Rev. 17, 223 (1931).
Frank, Law and the Modern Mind (Brentano's 1930) (reprinted 1948).
Fuller, "American Legal Realism," 82 U. of Pa. L. Rev. 429 (1934).
Pound, "Theory of Judicial Decision," 36 Harv. L. Rev. 641, 812, 940 (1923).
3. Regarding sources of case law, see sec. 6–04, note *.
4. Regarding the doctrine of precedent, see sec. 6–12, note *.
5. Regarding the overruling of precedent, see sec. 6–18, note *.

is sometimes called "the common law" or "the Anglo-American common law." Though more often the mass of case law as a whole is not mentioned, but only certain methods, principles and doctrines common to the systems of law in England, the United States, and the Dominions, these common elements are called the methods, principles and doctrines of "the common law." From these usages of the phrase "common law" must be distinguished two others: First, the case law of England down to about the time of our Revolution, essentially as summarized in Blackstone's *Commentaries* (1765); this is sometimes referred to as the "English" common law or the "old" common law. Second, it is not unusual to speak of the case law of a particular state, e.g., New York, as the common law of that state. But usages are indefinite and not consistent; often a writer slips from one use of the phrase, the common law, into another within the confines of a single paragraph. Whatever use you may choose to make of this phrase, it is most important that you keep these various kinds of decision-law distinct from one another. The need for clarity of thought and usage in this respect will become sufficiently obvious as we proceed with our discussion of the problems to follow.

A century or more ago, most of the standards provided by our American legal systems were to be found in case reports. The man who wanted to know what the law was went to the reports; he had no other place to go. In the ensuing years the proportions of case law and statute law have changed. Legislation has intruded into more and more fields; the legislatures, federal and state, have added enormously to the bulk of the statutes, so that the predominant part of legal standards is now cast in statutory form. In a few states, such as New York and California, the process of codification has been pushed about as far as it can go. In most states, however, the statutory coverage is far from complete; statutes cover only certain fields and parts of fields; the intervening spaces are covered by case law. For example, the "law" regarding contracts, torts, property, trusts, etc., remains uncodified in most states. Where codification is relatively complete, the courts still look to "the common law" for definitions, methods and general principles. Indeed, in your work as law students you will find that your time and attention are taken up more with a discussion of case law than statute law. In any event, we would be leaving our picture of the American legal system and its operation quite unfinished if we were to stop without considering the important body of legal standards, principles and methods expounded in the case law.

The present chapter will be devoted to the common or case law. The discussion will fall under two subtopics:

Creation of law by decisions.

"Common law" rules for using, finding, interpreting and changing standards.

CREATION OF LAW BY DECISIONS

Sec. 6–02. Occasions for creation of law. When a case or controversy is properly presented to an Anglo-American court, the court recognizes an obligation to decide it. What does the court do if it finds no appropriate rule of law to apply to the case or controversy? Conceivably the court might, in such a situation, refuse to proceed to a decision. But this has never been the practice of courts anywhere, so far as I know, and certainly not the practice of any English or American court. It does not refuse to decide a case simply because it cannot find a ready-made rule to apply. It weighs the case, works out the rule that ought to apply, and then applies it. Nor is the Anglo-American court ever content to dispose of a new and precedented case with the simple declaration that the court holds for the plaintiff or for the defendant, without giving reasons. The court always feels obliged to decide the case that is brought before it, and equally obliged to give reasons for its decisions.[1] These reasons are the rules and principles of law which the court fashions for the occasion; they are the rules or principles according to which the court decides. They are rules or principles which apply to the case in essentially the same sense that statutory provisions, if there were any, would be held to apply to it.

Sec. 6–03. Rules and methods of judicial lawmaking. The lawmaking activity of a court is markedly different from the lawmaking activity of the legislature. Whenever the legislature recognizes the need to regulate the behavior of individuals or officials, it creates new standards for the purpose. Whenever it recognizes that standards need to be changed, it repeals or amends them, or substitutes new standards in their place. The court does not make case law in this broad and unrestricted fashion.[1] Judicial lawmaking is controlled by several restrictive rules of method: First of all, the court must not lay down a new legal rule except in relation to a case which it has to decide. Second, the court must not lay down a rule broader than is necessary to settle the case. In short, the court legislates only incidentally in the decision of a case. As Mr. Justice Holmes said, "I recognize without hesitation that judges do and must legislate, but they can do so only interstitially; they are confined from molar to molecular motions." [2] Third, the judicial lawmaker must stick to hallowed principles in choosing a new rule; he must

---

[1] In some states they are required by constitution or statute to declare their reasons fully and in writing.

[1] Judicial lawmaking is also narrow in another respect; it is limited to gap filling and does not generally extend to the making of changes in existing law. Certainly statutes cannot be amended by judicial decision nor do courts assert a general authority to change the case law as you will see in later sections.

[2] Southern Pacific Co. v. Jensen, 244 U. S. 205 at 221 (1917) (dissenting in regard to other matters). One can say that the reception of the Law Merchant in England and the reception of the English Common Law in this country are two instances in which judicial lawmaking occurred on a wholesale scale. But such instances are not typical of the processes of judicial lawmaking today.

reason by reference to the closest analogies and derive his results as far as possible from doctrines or policies which have been settled by the cases or declared by statute. The judicial lawmaker is not expected to be a daring innovator. He is to look first for a specific rule to apply. If he cannot find one, and if he is forced to declare a new rule for the occasion, he is to set forth a wider principle from which he deduces the rule laid down. He is to bring his decision of a case under a specific rule which can, in its turn, be regarded as a natural deduction from a general principle which is well recognized.

*Sec. 6–04. Sources of case law.** The sources of case law are in general the same as the sources of statute law.[1] The judicial lawmaker like the legislature, derives standards from the available knowledge of his time. He discovers standards to adopt primarily in the legal background. If he finds none there, he looks to the general social background.

Ordinarily he starts his quest with the scrutiny of the law of his own state. Even though there is no case law directly covering the case before him, he may be able to make an analogical extension of principles previously accepted by the decisions of his own state. If such extensions are not possible he looks to the case law of other jurisdictions. In fact the

---

* (I.R.) Throughout the rest of this chapter, I ask the student repeatedly to distinguish between sources of law and law. I also ask him to differentiate the various meanings of the term "common law." Of course, none of these distinctions is necessary. They are controlled by usage and are fluctuating in character. But I find that the effort to make and maintain such distinctions is a useful pedagogical device. The student has a clearer notion of our case law and its character after he has wrestled with these distinctions.

On the general subject of sources of law, see Pound, "Sources and Forms of Law," 21 NOTRE DAME LAWYER 247 (1946), and 22 *ibid.* 1 (1946). A full bibliography on this subject is contained in POUND, OUTLINE OF LECTURES ON JURISPRUDENCE (5th ed.) 115 *et seq.* (1943).

[1] As to the sources of statute law see sec. 4–06 and note*. The sources of case law are also essentially the same as the sources of interpretation which we discussed in the last chapter, especially the general and legal contexts of interpretation; see secs. 5–09 to 5–13.

judge who is preparing to lay down a new rule often proceeds in both of the ways mentioned. If he finds nothing suitable in either of these sources he may borrow a standard from the legislation of some other state or from a textbook on legal subjects.

Not infrequently the judicial lawmaker has to look beyond the legal background for a standard to adopt. He gives legal sanction to an existing folkway or custom, or to the standard of an extralegal institution, such as a church or trade association. By judicial recognition, the way, custom, or standard becomes a legal standard. However, it is worth noticing that these prior existing usages are sometimes spoken of by writers on law in a manner which is very misleading. They sometimes speak of these usages as if they were already existing law, not dependent upon judicial adoption for their legal character. By a logical sleight-of-hand, social usages are converted by these writers into law, without adoption by any agency of the state. Their method of statement has caused an enormous amount of confusion regarding the way law arises, by blurring or obliterating the distinction between law and its sources.

Sec. 6–05. Statement of law in cases. In an earlier chapter we dealt with the form in which the legislator's message is stated.[1] We discussed the terms in which it is stated, its completeness, its generality, its organization, and other matters. I believe that a similar examination of the form of the case law will be worth making.

The common law was often called "the unwritten law" by writers of a generation or more ago. It was given this name because it was identified with the customs of the community and these customs were not written down as statutes are. But "unwritten law" is a misnomer. Case law cannot

---

[1] Secs. 4–17 to 4–27.

properly be identified with customs. And while case law is not declared in the same clear-cut form that enactments of the legislature are, the case law is written. The decisions of cases, at least the decisions of appellate courts, are recorded in printed form no less solemn and permanent than enactments of the legislature. As regards written character, case law stands on essentially the same footing as legislation. And, what is most important for our purpose, the application of case law may involve all the problems that the application of any verbal statement does. Propositions of case law, like propositions of statute law, may have to be interpreted. When one applies a proposition of case law, one may have to determine first of all what that proposition means. In fact, I am sure that you will find, after perusing the material which follows, that these interpretive problems are more critical and more difficult to handle in regard to case law than in regard to legislation.

In the first place, such interpretive problems grow out of the fact that case law is not fully stated out. Case law, like legislation, takes much for granted. It deals with individual cases and does not profess to cover fields. An opinion may refer to many decisions in prior cases, but these references extend only to those rules and principles which are relevant to the points to be decided. The result is that anyone who reads case law with understanding, has to fill in a great deal from his knowledge of the legal background.

Most reported decisions employ a great deal of technical legal terminology. Even more than statutes, case reports are intended for the eyes of courts and lawyers. Only exceptionally can a case be read with full understanding by a layman. Usually the report states rules and principles in technical terms; it describes the procedural steps in technical terms; and it even sets forth facts and conclusions of fact in legal jargon which is quite incomprehensible to the person without legal training. So that it is almost invariably true that "it takes a lawyer" to extract the law from cases. As David Dudley Field remarks about case law in a passage already quoted:

"The law with us is a sealed book to the masses; it is a sealed book to all but the lawyers; and it is but partly open even to them. It is an insult to our understanding to say that the knowledge of the law is open to everybody." [2]

But the factor which makes case law most difficult of application, even for the lawyer, is the form in which case law is stated. It is not declared in a clear-cut legal text, as statutes and constitutional provisions are.[3] Case law is found in judicial opinions on particular cases. These opinions take the form of a discussion of a legal problem. The discussion may include a great variety of materials. Normally, it includes a statement of the facts in the case before the court; a formulation of the legal problem or issue, which the court has to decide; an exposition of various rules of law which may be relevant to the decision; an analysis of the facts of the particular case in relation to these various rules; the citation of the holdings in other cases and an analysis of their facts (some of which are analogous and some of which are different and distinguishable); and finally, a discussion of general principles on the basis of which the court chooses to adopt one rule rather than another. In other words, the proposition of law for which such a case stands seldom comes ready-made; it is interlarded with a discussion of the facts of the particular case; it is mixed up with a discussion of many other cases; it is put first in one shape and then another, here as a principle, there a rule. The person who approaches such a decision may sometimes find a clearly formulated proposition of law for which the decision stands. More often,

[2] See the excerpt from his article, quoted at some length in sec. 4–27 above.
[3] Statutes are characterized, as Patterson says, by "textual rigidity."

he has to formulate his own proposition. The legal element is "interstitial"; and it is not always easy to dig out of the interstices, as you have doubtless found in the reading of cases that you have done so far.

The mass of case law from which rules and principles have to be extracted would be quite overwhelming for the individual lawyer if he had to do all the extracting himself. He simply could not handle the job alone. The job of integrating and organizing the case law is done for the lawyer in partial fashion.

1. In digests of the cases, of which the most notable is the *American Digest,* which is part of the National Reporter System and covers all American decided cases.
2. In encyclopaedias, e.g., *Corpus Juris Secundum.*
3. In textbooks, e.g., Williston on *Contracts,* Prosser on *Torts,* Tiffany on *Real Property,* and Wigmore on *Evidence.*
4. In case annotations, e.g., *American Law Reports Annotated* (A.L.R.), which are selections of important cases with collections of other decisions relating to the same topics.

The persons who prepare these works attempt to select and extract the significant legal material from the cases, and to sort and arrange it by reference to subject, principle and rule. Their work is most helpful for practitioner, student and scholar. But it is unofficial and unauthoritative; selection, statement and arrangement are extrinsic to the material organized, in the sense that they are imposed from the outside by a person or persons who have no authority to make or formulate the law.

In the last two decades an important enterprise, similar to the preparation of textbooks on law, has been carried out by the American Law Institute. This is an organization of judges, practitioners and law teachers, formed "to promote the clarification and simplification of the law and its better adaptation to social needs, to secure the better administration of justice, and to encourage and carry on scholarly and scientific legal work." It has restated the law in the following fields: Agency, Conflict of Laws, Contracts, Judgments, Property, Restitution, Security, Torts, and Trusts. The Restatement in each of these fields was undertaken by a reporter, who was a specialist in that field and who had working with him a number of advisers, chiefly law teachers, also interested in the field. Frequent conferences were held, and the drafts as they progressed were submitted for discussion and criticism by the council and the annual meetings of the Institute.* Mr. William Draper Lewis, first director, thus describes the work which the Institute undertook to do and what it has accomplished:

"We started with the belief that out of the mass of case authority and legal literature could be made clear statements of the rules of the common law today operative in the great majority of our states, expressed as simply as the character of our complex civilization admits. The result shows that this belief was justified. The Restatement of each subject expresses as nearly as may be the rules which our courts will today apply. These rules cover not merely situations which

* (I.R.) For recent statements regarding the work of the American Law Institute, and the character and value of its work, see Lewis, "The First Restatement of the Law, and How We Did It," 25 NEB. L. REV. 206 (1946); and Goodrich, "Report to the American Law Institute," (1948). Both these items are set forth in FRYER AND BENSON, CASES AND MATERIALS ON LEGAL SYSTEMS 1067 *et seq.* In his article, Lewis cites the following earlier critical reviews of the work of the American Law Institute, which should also be of interest to the initiated reader: Clark, "The Restatement of the Law of Contracts," 42 YALE L. J. 643 (1933); Pollock, "Book Review," 47 HARV. L. REV. 363 (1933); Patterson, "The Restatement of the Law of Contracts," 33 COL. L. REV. 397 (1933); Goodrich, "Institute Bards and Yale Reviewers," 84 U. OF PA. L. REV. 449 (1936); Arnold, "Institute Priests and Yale Observers" *id.* at 811; Leach, "The Restatements as They Were In the Beginning, Are Now, and Perhaps Henceforth Shall Be," 23 A. B. A. J. 517 (1937); McDougal, "Restatement of the Law of Property," 32 ILL. L. REV. 509 (1937); Vance, "The Restatement of the Law of Property," 86 U. OF PA. L. REV. 173 (1937); McDougal, "Future Interests Restated; Tradition v. Clarification and Reform," 55 HARV. L. REV. 1077 (1942).

have already arisen in our courts, but by analogy rules applicable to situations likely to arise. The Restatement of a subject is thus more than a picture of what has been decided; it is a picture of present law expressed by foremost members of the profession. As a result of the way in which the work has been done and the persons who have labored on it, the Restatement has acquired an authority far greater than those of us who organized the Institute to do the work anticipated. Though the rules are expressed in the form of a code, except in sporadic instances, there never has been any desire to give them statutory authority. The Restatement is an agency tending to promote the clarification and the unification of the law in a form similar to a code. But it is not a code or statute.[4] It is designed to help preserve, not to change, the common system of expressing law and adapting it to changing conditions in a changing world."[5]

Sec. 6–06. Problems. Consider the following items in terms of judicial lawmaking and the sources therefor:

1. *Judge von Moschzisker:*

"The judge may discover the solution of the point for decision in the constitution or statutes of the jurisdiction involved, and when either of these sources supplies the guide, he is bound to stop there; if they both fail he must turn to the body of the law as previously laid down by his own court, and be guided by such relevant authorities as he may find there. Should his researches in that field prove fruitless, it is usual for him to look for decisions in other jurisdictions, and if none appears which appeals to him as furnishing the proper rule, then he who is fixed with the responsibility of deciding the case has 'to draw his inspiration from consecrated

---

[4] However, the American Law Institute did prepare three model codes for submission to the state legislatures: 1. a Model Code of Criminal Procedure, which has been adopted, in whole or in part, in about one-half the states; 2. a Model Code of Evidence, which has not so far been adopted anywhere; and 3. a Code of Commercial Law, which has only progressed to the stage of a tentative draft. This last-named code is a joint undertaking of the Law Institute and the National Conference of Commissioners on Uniform State Laws.

[5] "The First Restatement of the Law and How We Did It," 25 NEB. L. REV. 206 at 215–216 (1946). See also Goodrich, "Restatement and Codification" in DAVID DUDLEY FIELD CENTENARY ESSAYS 241 (1949).

principles,—he is not to yield to spasmodic sentiment, to vague and unregulated benevolence (but must) exercise a discretion informed by tradition, methodized by analogy, disciplined by system, and subordinated to "the primordial necessity of order in the social life." ' " [1]

Von Moschzisker gives a hierarchy of sources from which the judge derives the rule which he applies. How far are the various items which he mentions to be regarded as law and how far as sources of law? Suppose for example a judge in Michigan decides to follow a New York decision, there being no Michigan decision on the point. Is he treating the New York decision as law or as a source of law? What do you think von Moschzisker means by the suggestion that the judge must, if no other resources are available, "draw his inspiration from consecrated principles"?

Where would von Moschzisker place a textbook or a Restatement of the law? Is such a work to be regarded as law or a source of law? In what essential respect does a Restatement differ from a code?

2. *Petit v. Liston.*[2]

"Plaintiff, a minor, brings this action by his guardian to recover $125, paid by him upon the purchase of a certain motorcycle purchased from the defendants.

"The case involves the question of whether or not a minor, who has purchased an article of this kind, and taken and used the same, after paying part or all of the purchase price, can return the article and recover the money paid without making good to the vendors the wear and tear and depreciation of the same while in his hands. . . .

"Bennett, J. The amount involved in this proceeding is not large, but the question of law presented is a very important one, and one which has been much disputed in the courts, and about which there is a great and irreconcilable conflict

[1] "Stare Decisis in Courts of Last Resort," 37 HARV. L. REV. 409 at 411 (1923), quoting CARDOZO, THE NATURE OF THE JUDICIAL PROCESS 141 (1921).
[2] 97 Ore. 464 (1920).

in the authorities, and we have therefore given the matter careful attention.

"The courts, in an attempt to protect the minor upon the one hand, and to prevent wrong or injustice to persons who have dealt fairly and reasonably with such minor upon the other, have indulged in many fine distinctions and recognized various slight shades of difference.

"In dealing with the right of the minor to rescind his contract and the conditions under which he may do so, the decisions of the courts in the different states have not only conflicted upon the main questions involved, but many of the decisions of the same court, in the same state, seem to be inconsistent with each other; and oftentimes one court has made its decision turn upon a distinction or difference not recognized by the courts of other states as a distinguishing feature.

"The result has been that there are not only two general lines of decisions directly upon the question involved, but there are many others, which diverge more or less from the main line, and make particular cases turn upon real or fancied differences and distinctions, depending upon whether the contract was executory or partly or wholly executed, whether it was for necessaries, whether it was beneficial to the minor, whether it was fair and reasonable, whether the minor still had the property purchased in his possession, whether he had received any beneficial use of the same, etc.

"Many courts have held broadly that a minor may so purchase property and keep it for an indefinite time, if he chooses, until it is worn out and destroyed, and then recover the payments made on the purchase price, without allowing the seller anything whatever for the use and depreciation of the property.

"Many other authorities hold that where the transaction is fair and reasonable, and the minor was not overcharged or taken advantage of in any way, and he takes and keeps the property and uses or destroys it, he cannot recover the payments made on the purchase price, without allowing the seller for the wear and tear and depreciation of the article while in his hands.

"The plaintiff contends for the former rule, and supports his contention with citations from the courts of last resort of Maine, Connecticut, Indiana, Massachusetts, Vermont, Nebraska, Virginia, Iowa, Mississippi, and West Virginia, most of which (although not all) support his contention. On the contrary, the courts of New York, Maryland, Montana, Illinois, Kentucky, New Hampshire, and Minnesota, with some others, support the latter rule, which seems to be also the English rule.

"Some of the cyclopedias and some of the different series of selected cases state the rule contended for by plaintiff, as supported by the strong weight of authority; but we find the decisions rather equally balanced, both in number and respectability. . . .

"Our attention has not been called to any Oregon case bearing upon the question, and as far as our investigation has disclosed, there is none.

"In this condition of the authorities, we feel that we are in a position to pass upon the question as one of first impression, and announce the rule which seems to us to be the better one, upon considerations of principle and public policy.

"We think, where the minor has not been overreached in any way, and there has been no undue influence, and the contract is a fair and reasonable one, and the minor has actually paid money on the purchase price, and taken and used the article, that he ought not to be permitted to recover the amount actually paid, without allowing the vendor of the goods the reasonable compensation for the use and depreciation of the article, while in his hands. . . .

"We think this rule will fully and fairly protect the minor against injustice or imposition, and at the same time it will be fair to the business man who has dealt with such minor in good faith. This rule is best adapted to modern conditions, and especially to the conditions in our far western states.

"Here, minors are permitted to and do in fact transact a great deal of business for themselves, long before they have reached the age of legal majority. Most young men have their own time long before reaching that age. They work and earn money and collect it and spend it oftentimes without any oversight or restriction.

"No business man questions their right to buy, if they have the money to pay for their purchases. They not only buy for themselves, but they often are intrusted with the making of purchases for their parents and guardians. It would be intolerably burdensome for everyone concerned if merchants and other business men could not deal with them safely, in a fair and reasonable way, in cash transactions of this kind.

"Again, it will not exert any good moral influence upon boys and young men, and will not tend to encourage honesty and integrity, or lead them to a good and useful business future, if they are taught that they can make purchases with their own money, for their own benefit, and after paying for them in this way, and using them until they are worn out and destroyed, go back and compel the business man to return to them what they have paid upon the purchase price. Such a doctrine as it seems to us, can only lead to the corruption of young men's principles and encouraging them in habits of trickery and dishonesty.

"In view of all these considerations, we think that the rule we have indicated, and which is substantially the rule adopted in New York, is the better rule, and we adopt the same in this state."

How far do you regard this decision as creative of law for Oregon? Where did the court find the rules which it adopted?

3. *Daily v. Parker.*[3] Evans, Circuit Judge:

"The instant appeal raises this question: Have children living in Pennsylvania, a cause of action for damages against a woman living in Illinois who caused their father to leave them, their mother, and their home and go to Chicago and live with her and to refuse to further contribute to their maintenance and support? The District Court answered the question in the negative and dismissed the complaint. . . .

"Is the family relationship and the rights of the different members therein, arising therefrom, sufficient to support a cause of action in each, the father, mother, or children, against one who breaks it up and destroys rights of the said individual members?

[3] 152 F.2d 174 (1945).

"Appellee concedes that such a cause of action exists in favor of the father and within certain limits and certain jurisdictions, also in favor of the wife. She denies that such a cause of action, however, exists in favor of the children.

"The history of the development of the family and the family relations and the duties and obligations of the members of the family is a long one, covering centuries. Its development was slow, due to society's acceptance of the relative positions of the parties in the family and its reluctance to change such status. The husband was lord and master, and the rights of all of the members of the family were merged in him. He ruled. He spoke in the first person singular in all matters. He spoke authoritatively for all. Through the centuries, however, there came slowly a change. The father is still the master, it may be said, but the duties of the master have changed. Where it was said to be his duty to rule, he now serves. He recognizes rights of the others and his obligation to meet them.

"Perhaps he is still the titular head of the family. If so, his position merely carries with it greater duties and obligations. The duties of each member of the family are measured (at least in theory and in legal conception) by the position, the role, each takes in the family. Thus we see the wife, the breadwinner, and speaking for the family when the husband becomes incapacitated through sickness or invalidism. And children of tender years take on the family financial burdens when father is incapacitated and mother must attend him or for other reasons is unable to contribute to the financial support of the family. Relativity of rights and duties marks the rights and the obligations of the group and relativity is determined in each case by the situation of the family. But relativity does not eliminate or destroy the rights of any member.

"It is this conception of the family which must constitute our approach to the question at hand. . . .

"Defendant argues that such rights as here asserted have never been, and should not now be, recognized by any court until and unless legislation has been enacted creating such right. She argues that in the past, children's rights have not been judicially recognized, save after legislative enactment and she points to various specific acts which the Illinois Legislature enacted to give rights which were not previously recognized. . . .

"Plaintiffs, on the other hand, rely upon the maxim, Ubi Jus Ibi Remedium. Also they refer to the bill of rights of the Illinois Constitution (Sec. 19, Art. 2, Smith-Hurd Stats.) where it is provided 'Every person ought to find a certain remedy in the laws for all injuries and wrongs which he may receive in his person, property or reputation.' They contend that the absence of precedent affords no justification for denial of a common-law remedy where the right of an individual has been invaded by the wrongful act of another. . . .

"Instead of holding that there is no remedy, because there is no precedent, they argue for what they assert to be the better rule, and what Dean Pound calls judicial empiricism. In other words, the common law has been and is sufficiently elastic to meet changing conditions. We quote from Dean Pound's book, 'The Spirit of the Common Law,' page 183:

'Anglo-American law is fortunate indeed in entering upon a new period of growth with a well-established doctrine of lawmaking by judicial decision. . . . Undoubtedly. . .judicial empiricism was proceeding over-cautiously at the end of the last century. . . . If the last century insisted overmuch upon predetermined premises, and a fixed technique, it did not lose to our law the method of applying the judicial experience of the past to the judicial questions of the present.' . . .

"Our conclusion, without going further into the matter, is that a child today has a right enforceable in a court of law, against one who has invaded and taken from said child the support and maintenance of its father, as well as damages for the destruction of other rights which arise out of the family relationship and which have been destroyed or defeated by a wrongdoing third party. Likewise, we are persuaded that because such rights have not heretofore been recognized, is not a conclusive reason for denying them. . . .

"The judgment is reversed with directions to proceed in accordance with the views expressed in this opinion."

What sources are used by Judge Evans in his decision? Does he rely on constitutional sources? On common law sources? On general background?

Does he go beyond the consecrated principles to which Judge von Moschzisker refers? [4]

Sec. 6–07. The "discovered law" doctrine. Down until about two generations ago legal writers in this country were quite unwilling to admit that the judge actually creates law by his decisions. This reluctance was due chiefly to the prevailing "separation of powers" doctrine, according to which the legislature is to make laws, the executive to carry them out, and the judge to apply them to controversies. To admit that the judge makes law was to concede that he disregards this fundamental dogma. Adhering to a literal interpretation of the separation doctrine, these writers denied that the judge legislates, and in order to avoid ascribing a legislative role to him, they developed the so-called "discovered law" doctrine. Its purport was that the rules and principles that the judge announces in his opinions are merely discovered by him. They are supposed to have existed since the beginning of time, even though neither the judge himself nor anyone else was aware of their existence before they were judicially announced.

This "discovered law" doctrine involved an automatic or "slot machine" conception of the application of standards to cases. It denied entirely the judge's role in creating new law. It ignored entirely the judge's function of settling doubts and uncertainties regarding the law. By cloaking all these matters in a mystery, it prevented a rational explanation of the creative side of the judge's role.

Today practically all theoretical writers and most judges are ready to recognize the limited creative role of the judge.

[4] Compare Russell v. Men of Devon, 2 Term R. 667 (1788) quoted in sec. 6–17, problem 3.

They are ready to admit that the judge does of necessity make law. That he has many legal problems to solve, and in solving them contributes new law for the guidance of future judges. They regard the so-called discovery of pre-existent law as merely a pious fiction, invented to save the face of a doctrine of "separation of powers" stated in absolute form. They realize that interstitial legislation is a necessary consequence of the decision of doubtful cases. The recognition that lawmaking of this character attends the decision of cases, has meant a real advance in realism and in clarity of thinking about law and the judicial process.

One factor which probably contributed to the success and former acceptance of the "discovered law" doctrine, was the fact that the judge's creative work occurs only in small bits, as is pointed out above. His lawmaking is not on a large scale. No doubt his prime function in the mine-run of cases, is to apply standards to acts of individuals and officials, standards which can fairly be said to be already existing; judicial legislation is secondary and incidental. It is easy to overlook the element of judicial lawmaking as it occurs from case to case. This oversight is a good deal like the failure to see that a glacier moves because it moves so slowly. It is only when we look at the imposing structure of the common law as it has grown up and developed through the centuries that we get a real appreciation of the creative work that judges have done and are doing.

Sec. 6–08. Problems. 1. At one place in his *Nature and Sources of Law*, Gray asks the question regarding a group of common law rules, "What was the law in the time of Richard Coeur de Lion on the liability of a telegraph company to persons to whom a message was sent?" (Sec. 222.) What is Gray's point?

2. Suppose states X, Y, and Z have respectively three different common law rules regarding the same subject

matter: e.g., different rules regarding "attractive nuisances," or regarding the effects of a mistake in telegraphic transmission of a contractual offer, or regarding the test for insanity as a defense to criminal liability. Why does the existence of such differences create logical difficulties for the "discovered law" doctrine?

Suppose the differing rules are found not in judicial decisions but in statutes. Does this alter the logical difficulty? Why?

3. Does the fact that the legislature of state X passes different statutes at different times make logical difficulties for the "discovered law" doctrine? *

Suppose the Supreme Court of state ·X changes its view of the law in the course of time; first it adopts rule 1, later it adopts rule 2 on the same subject, still later rule 3, and finally it reverts to rule 1 again. What does this suggest?

"COMMON-LAW" RULES FOR USING, FINDING, INTERPRETING AND CHANGING STANDARDS

Sec. 6–09. Legal standards and rules for their use. The acts of the judge like the acts of any other official are controlled by standards. Some of these standards—the rules of pleading and procedure—have already been considered in the third chapter of these lectures. To be contrasted with these are the rules of method which govern his handling of

---

* (I.R.) Those who adhere to a "higher law" theory, are prone to accept the "discovered law" doctrine. There is, however, no necessary connection here. The "discovered law" doctrine is concerned only with judicial lawmaking and purports to describe (and prescribe) a relationship between judicial decisions and an existing body of law. There is no mention of a parallel relationship between legislation and an existing body of law; it is not denied that the legislature can and does lay down law which never existed before. But the "higher law," according to its protagonists, is a body of pre-existing principles which stand apart from human law; these principles serve as sources for legislative lawmaking and limitations on such lawmaking. Of course, this "higher law" can serve likewise as source and limit of judicial lawmaking. My quarrel with the "discovered law" doctrine is that it gives a special, different and unrealistic explanation of judicial lawmaking. See section 7–45 for further discussion of the "higher law" theory.

legal materials. Some of these latter rules have also been given sufficient consideration, such rules as those which tell the judge how to deal with conflicts between constitution and statute, and between statute and statute; and also the rules which govern the processes of interpretation. Besides these many rules of method, we have also referred to the rules which govern the judge's function as lawmaker. All these rules control the judge in handling legal materials. Some of them regulate his handling of statutory material, others his acts of creating case law. There remain a number of other important rules of method which control the judge's choice of legal rules, his use of legal rules, and his interpretation of the materials which he finds in the case law. These are to be the subject of discussion in the remainder of this chapter.

Sec. 6–10. Primary rules of use: follow statutes and follow decisions. First among the rules of judicial method is one which directs the court to apply the mandate of statutes in cases which come before it. This rule is taken for granted by the legislature whenever it enacts a statute. The legislature assumes that the standards which it declares will be used by the courts in the decision of cases. The courts themselves consistently recognize their obligation to follow statutes; no court would ever question that it is bound to carry out the mandates of a statute, provided of course, that the courts regard the statute as constitutional.

Occasionally this rule is explicitly stated; [1] more often the rule is taken for granted. The fact that the rule is not men-

---

[1] The rule appears explicitly in the clause of the Federal Constitution which declares that "the laws of the United States . . . shall be the supreme Law of the Land; and the Judges in every State shall be bound thereby, any thing in the Constitution or Laws of any State to the Contrary notwithstanding." (Art. VI, Cl. 2.) But this clause is apparently intended for the immediate purpose of declaring the obligatory force of federal statutes, etc., on state judges; their obligatory force on federal judges is taken for granted. Again, that clause of the Federal Constitution which provides that "judicial Power shall extend to all Cases in law and equity, arising under this Constitution, the Laws of the United States . . ." rather implies than states the binding

tioned frequently does not mean that it is any the less important. It does mean that its role in the operation of the legal system can be overlooked. The fact that the binding force of statutes is assumed and not mentioned, has resulted in a failure to analyze the controlling force of statutes on the court, and this in turn has resulted in some very obscure thinking about the binding force of standards. What needs to be noted is that a simple statute is a mandate to an individual or an official, and that this statute is supplemented by a very general superstandard which requires the judiciary to effectuate statutory provisions. This superstandard is analogous to the explicit provision of the Federal Constitution that the President "shall take care that the laws be faithfully executed." For example, a statute which penalizes reckless driving raises questions of the binding force of two standards. It is needful to inquire whether the statute furnishes a standard for individual action and also whether the court is bound to apply this standard by virtue of a standard applicable to it. The statutory provision does not per se bind the court; the court is rather bound by a general standard which directs it to use statutes in cases which come before it; in so doing it acts pursuant to a standard for applying standards, an established rule of judicial method.[2]

A second general rule of judicial method, parallel to the rule which requires courts to follow statutes, is embodied in the *doctrine of precedent,* or as it is sometimes called, the doctrine of *stare decisis.* This doctrine requires the courts to follow previous decisions. It was received by our colonial

force of federal statutes. Quite apart from provisions of this sort, the binding force of statutes upon courts is so ingrained in the thinking of judges and lawyers that it can fairly be called a part of their habitual attitudes. (Art. III, Sec. 2.)

[2] Even if the statute expressly provides that the court shall take certain action, a very common type of statutory provision as applied to trial courts, the situation is not changed. There are still two standards—the standard applicable to the individual and a second standard requiring the court to apply the first.

ancestors as part of their English common law heritage. As Salmond has said, "The importance of judicial precedents has always been a distinguishing characteristic of English law. . . . A judicial precedent speaks in England with authority . . . the courts are bound to follow the law that is so established."[3] What Salmond says of the English system holds equally of the American legal systems today.

Sec. 6–11. Problems. 1. Von Moschzisker says, in a passage quoted above:[1]

"The judge may discover the solution of the point for decision in the constitution or statutes of the jurisdiction involved, and when either of these sources supplies the guide, he is bound to stop there; if they both fail he must turn to the body of the law as previously laid down by his own court and be guided by such relevant authorities as he may find there. Should his researches in that field prove fruitless, it is usual for him to look for decisions in other jurisdictions, . . ."

How are this author's remarks related to the points about rules of method which are made in the last preceding section?

2. Consider the "choice of law" problems which the court had to deal with in the following case:

E. A. Stephens & Co. v. Albers.[2] The plaintiff, who operated a silver fox farm, paid $750 for a fox named, "McKenzie Duncan." Soon afterward this fox slipped through an inner gate inadvertently left unfastened at feeding time, and escaped. Next evening, the fox was shot by a ranchman who lived six miles distant, and who discovered the animal prowling near his chicken house. The ranchman did not know of the nature, value, or ownership of the animal, but removed his pelt and gave it to a trapper to sell

---

[3] JURISPRUDENCE (6th ed.) sec. 61 (1920).
[1] "Stare Decisis in Courts of Last Resort," 37 HARV. L. REV. 409 at 411 (1923).
[2] 81 Colo. 488 (1927).

on commission. The latter sold the pelt to the defendant for $75. The plaintiff later found out what had happened to the fox and located its pelt in the defendant's possession. Plaintiff brought suit for the value of the pelt, and recovered $75. Defendant appealed.

Burke, J.:

". . . Defendant says McKenzie Duncan was a wild animal whose possession was essential to ownership, and that when he escaped and pursuit was abandoned plaintiff lost title which the ranchman obtained by slaughter and passed to defendant by sale. Plaintiff says the fox was domesticated; that his disposition to return to his pen (*animum* (sic) *revertendi*) must be presumed; that irrespective of such facts foxes are taxable in this state, hence the common law rule as to domesticated animals applies; and that the common law rule as to wild animals is not applicable here. . . .

"For the common law we go to Blackstone who says: A qualified property may subsist in wild animals 'by a man's reclaiming and making them tame by art, industry and education; or by so confining them within his own immediate power, that they cannot escape and use their natural liberty. . . . These are no longer the property of a man, than while they continue in his keeping or actual possession; but if at any time they regain their natural liberty, his property instantly ceases; unless they have *animum revertendi* (the intention of returning) which is only to be known by their usual custom of returning. . . . The deer that is chased out of my park or forest, and is instantly pursued by the keeper or forester: remains still in my possession, and I still preserve my qualified property in them. But if they stray without my knowledge, and do not return in the usual manner, it is then lawful for any stranger to take them.'[3] . . .

"It should be borne in mind that when this common law rule was formulated the great wild animal menageries of the present day, with their enormous collections and vast investment, were in embryo, and the business of raising fur bearing animals in captivity was practically unknown in England. . . .

[3] 2 Bl. Comm. *391 *et seq.* (1765).

"Counsel for defendant further says this common law rule is in force in this jurisdiction by virtue of an act passed by our territorial legislature in 1861. 'The common law of England, so far as the same is applicable and of a general nature, . . . shall be the rule of decision, and shall be considered as of full force until repealed by legislative authority.' Sec. 6516, p. 1698, C. L. 1921.

"Applicability as to past or to future conditions would often be difficult, if not impossible, of ascertainment. That it is to be determined when claimed is clearly indicated by the language of Mr. Justice Beck, who, speaking for the court nineteen years after the passage of the statute, in a case where the common law rule as to damage done by trespassing cattle was involved, said, 'such a rule of law is wholly unsuited and inapplicable to the present condition of the state and its citizens.' *Morris v. Fraker,* 5 Colo. 425, 428.

"For the reason hereinbefore pointed out we think it equally clear that the common law rule now invoked 'is wholly unsuited and inapplicable to the present condition of the state,' the transaction in question, and the industry out of which it grew.

"Having then neither statute nor applicable common law rule governing the case we must so apply general principles in the light of custom, existing facts, and common knowledge, that justice will be done. So the courts of England and the United States have acted from time immemorial and so the common law itself came into existence.

"Counsel for defendant concedes he would have no title had the fox been released by a stranger or killed by one informed of its ownership. The thread is too frail to support its burden. McKenzie Duncan was held in captivity, semi-domesticated, escaped by accident, fled against the will of his owner, and pursuit was abandoned by compulsion. This defendant in fact had, or is charged with, knowledge that the pelt purchased was the product of a vast, legitimate, and generally known industry; that it had a considerable and easily ascertainable value; that it bore the indicia of ownership; that it has been taken in an unusual way; that the seller was not the owner; that no right of innocent purchasers had intervened; and that it was from an animal taken in a locality where its kind ferae naturae was unknown and in a state where large numbers were kept in captivity.

"We are loath to believe that a man may capture a grizzly bear in the environs of New York or Chicago, or a seal in a mill pond in Massachusetts, or an elephant in a corn field in Iowa, or a silver fox on a ranch in Morgan County, Colorado, and snap his fingers in the face of its former owner whose title had been acquired by a considerable expenditure of time, labor, and money; or that the rule which requires that where one or two persons must suffer the loss falls upon him whose carelessness caused it, has any application here. If the owner was negligent in permitting the escape the dealer was even more reckless in making the purchase.

"Under all the circumstances of this case we feel obliged to hold that the defendant obtained no title which it can maintain against the plaintiff.

"The judgment is accordingly affirmed."

What rule did the defendant contend was applicable here? Why did the court reject it?

How did the court dispose of the statute which adopted the English common law as "the rule of decision" in Colorado? Did this statute make the English law a *source* of law, or make it *law* for Colorado?

How do you interpret the paragraph beginning, "Having then neither statute nor applicable common law . . ."?

3. An important field of the law bears the name "conflict of laws." The bulk of the problems which are considered in this field are problems of the "choice of law." Suppose as an example that O, who lives in Michigan, is the owner of land in Ohio which he wishes to convey. What law controls such a transfer, the law of Michigan or the law of Ohio? Story states the answer thus: "All the authorities in England and America . . . recognize the principle in its fullest import, that real estate, or immovable property, is exclusively subject to the laws of the government within

whose territory it is situate." [4] Accordingly, the formal sufficiency of a conveyance is governed by the law of the place where the land lies; that law also determines what constitutes the delivery of a deed, who is a competent grantor, etc. However, statutes in some states have modified the requirement regarding formalities by providing that the conveyance of local land is valid, as regards form, if it complies with the law of the place where the conveyance is executed.

What rules regarding "choice of law" appear in the foregoing statement?

4. In 1789 the first Congress of the United States enacted the Federal Judiciary Act. Section 34 of this act provided:

"The laws of the several States, except where the Constitution, treaties, or statutes of the United States otherwise require or provide, shall be regarded as rules of decision in trials at common law, in the courts of the United States, in cases where they apply."

This section was intended primarily to specify the law which was to be applied in the federal courts in lawsuits between citizens of different states ("diversity of citizenship" cases). Justice Story, speaking for the Supreme Court in the famous case of *Swift v. Tyson* [5] held that "laws of the several states" referred only to statute law and that on matters of common law the federal courts were at liberty to follow their own ideas of the general common law. This interpretation was repeatedly criticized, but was adhered to by the Supreme Court until 1937. Thus *Black and White Taxicab, etc., Co. v. Brown and Yellow Taxicab, etc., Co.* [6] involved a contract between A, a citizen of Tennessee, and B, a citizen of Kentucky, made in Kentucky and to be performed there. There was no question but that the operation of the contract was to be governed by Kentucky law, nor that the contract was

[4] CONFLICT OF LAWS (8th ed.) sec. 428 (1883).
[5] 16 Pet. (U. S.) 1 (1842).
[6] 276 U. S. 518 (1928).

of a type which was *invalid* under the Kentucky decisions. However, in a suit to enforce this contract the Supreme Court held the contract *valid* and binding between the parties. The majority opinion declared:

"The cases cited show that the decisions of the Kentucky Court of Appeals, holding such arrangements invalid, are contrary to the common law as generally understood and applied. And we are of opinion that petitioner here has failed to show any valid ground for disregarding this contract, . . ." [7]

According to this decision of the Supreme Court, what is the common law of Kentucky applicable to this contract? What determines the content of the common law of Kentucky?

In this last case Holmes, J. (with Brandeis and Stone, JJ.) dissented. He said in part:

"Books written about any branch of the common law treat it as a unit, cite cases from this Court, from the Circuit Courts of Appeals, from the State Courts, from England and the Colonies of England indiscriminately, and criticise them as right or wrong according to the writer's notions of a single theory. It is very hard to resist the impression that there is one august corpus, to understand which clearly is the only task of any Court concerned. If there were such a transcendental body of law outside of any particular State but obligatory within it unless and until changed by statute, the Courts of the United States might be right in using their independent judgment as to what it was. But there is no such body of law. The fallacy and illusion that I think exist consist in supposing that there is this outside thing to be found. Law is a word used with different meanings, but law in the sense in which courts speak of it today does not exist without some definite authority behind it. The common law so far as it is enforced in a State, whether called common law or not, is not the common law generally but the law of that State existing by the authority of that State without regard to what it may

[7] *Ibid.* 528.

have been in England or anywhere else. . . . Whether and how far and in what sense a rule shall be adopted whether called common law or Kentucky law is for the State alone to decide. . . . The Supreme Court of a State does something more than make a scientific inquiry into a fact outside of and independent of it. It says, with an authority that no one denies, . . . that thus the law is and shall be. Whether it be said to make or to declare the law, it deals with the law of the State with equal authority however its function may be described." [8]

Under Holmes' view, how is the common law of Kentucky determined? What rule for choosing applicable law is to be recognized by the federal courts?

In *Erie Railroad Co. v. Tompkins*,[9] the Supreme Court speaking through Mr. Justice Brandeis overruled *Swift v. Tyson* and the whole series of cases following it. I need not go into the reasons for the conclusion in the *Erie Railroad Case*, as we are interested only in the views above expressed regarding the determination of common law. It is only important for our purpose that the *Erie Railroad Case* in effect adopted the views propounded by Justice Holmes above.*

Sec. 6–12. Judicial lawmaking and the following of precedent. Judicial lawmaking and the following of precedent are correlative acts. They are like proposal and acceptance of marriage. The judges who lay down a precedent offer it as a guide for subsequent decision; the judges who

[8] *Ibid.* 532–536.
[9] 304 U. S. 64 (1937).
* (I.R.) The distinction is now definitely made between state created rights and federally created rights, or, as I would prefer to say, between state created law (statute or common law) and federally created law. Regarding developments since Erie Railroad v. Tompkins was decided, see Guaranty Trust Co. v. York, 326 U. S. 99 (1945); and Clark, "State Law in the Federal Courts: The Brooding Omnipresence of Erie v. Tompkins," 55 YALE L. J. 267 (1946); Gavit, "State Rights and Federal Procedure," 25 IND. L. J. 1 (1949); Keeffe et al., "Weary Erie," 34 CORN. L. Q. 494 (1949); and Blume and George, "Limitations and the Federal Courts," an article to appear in the MICHIGAN LAW REVIEW in 1951.

follow the precedent accept it as a guide. The aims and intentions of these groups of judges are parallel respectively to the intentions of the legislature which enacts a statute and the court which applies it. Just as the legislature passes a statute with implicit confidence that its provisions will be applied by the courts in future cases, the supreme court as it lays down an original decision expects its opinion to serve as a guide for future decisions, and tries to make it a satisfactory and safe guide. On the other hand, judges in subsequent cases uniformly recognize the obligation to follow the precedent already established. This is one of the basic tenets of Anglo-American judicial method, as I have already pointed out. And the following of precedents is reinforced by the conscious judicial recognition that precedents ought to be followed as a matter of policy, and by judicial habits of mind which have become established through long training in our common law modes of thinking.

Acts of legislation and the following of precedents affect others than the judicial participants. Individuals, officials, and judges of lower courts rely upon the decision which has been made and upon its obligatory force on judges in subsequent cases. They rely upon the habits and practices of judges of following cases. They rely upon the authority of precedent. And further than this, they regard the judicial decision which establishes a precedent as an implied promise, and a solemn one, to adhere to the rules laid down therein. From the court's point of view the promise can be likened to a promise made to oneself—a resolution; but from the point of view of the outsider, the supreme court's declaration stands as a public confession of faith. The court says in effect: "This is what we hold now; it is what we are going to hold in like cases in the future." The court does sometimes go back on its resolution; it overrules a precedent. But no one likes to go back on a pious resolution openly announced, least of all judges who are trained to announce their intentions and to stick to them. The supreme court's assurance of continuity of decision is therefore a considerable bond on which to rely.*

Sec. 6–13. Varying force of precedents. Precedents are not self-effectuating. They do not control later decisions automatically. Precedents only control to the extent that they are accepted as binding by judges in later cases. Varying force is attached by judges to different kinds of prior decisions. The variation in weight or operation of precedents is apparent in several respects:

1. As regards the *place* and *court* in which the precedent is cited. A decision of the supreme court of state X has a different weight when cited in an inferior court than when it is cited in the supreme court itself. It also has another weight when it is cited in state Y; in the latter state it is usually regarded merely as persuasive authority, and courts there will follow it only to the extent that its reason commends itself to their judgment.

2. As regards the *character* of the judicial statement which is relied on. If the opinion is unanimous, it will have one force; if the court is divided in opinion, the weight of its decision is somewhat weakened.

3. As regards *the scope of acceptance* of the view expressed by the precedent. If, for example, a precedent is supported by an overwhelming weight of general authority, it is entitled to more weight than if it diverges from general views.

4. As regards *age* and *confirmation* in later cases. A new precedent, it is often suggested, may be overruled more readily than one which has been long and continuously followed.

* (I.R.) Status of the Rule of Judicial Precedent—Conference at Cincinnati Law School, 14 U. CINN. L. REV. 203–323 (1940); (Justice) Jackson, "Decisional Law and Stare Decisis," 30 A. B. A. JOUR. 334 (1944); (Justice) Douglas, "Stare Decisis," 49 COL. L. REV. 735 (1949). See also sec. 6–18, note *.

5. As regards the *subject matter* involved in the previous decision. Courts have less hesitation about overruling cases in some fields than in others, e.g., decisions on points of evidence and procedure than decisions on points of property law. Compare von Moschzisker, "Stare Decisis in Courts of Last Resort," 37 HARV. LAW REV., 409 (1924).

Sec. 6–14. Problem.

Salmond:

"Decisions are further divisible into two classes, which may be distinguished as authoritative and persuasive. These two differ in respect of the kind of influence which they exercise upon the future course of the administration of justice. An authoritative precedent is one which judges must follow whether they approve of it or not. It is binding upon them and excludes their judicial discretion for the future. A persuasive precedent is one which the judges are under no obligation to follow, but which they will take into consideration, and to which they will attach such weight as it seems to them to deserve. It depends for its influence upon its own merits, not upon any legal claim which it has to recognition. . . .

"The authoritative precedents recognized by English law are the decisions of the superior courts of justice in England. The chief classes of persuasive precedents are the following:

"(1) Foreign judgments, and more especially those of American courts.

"(2) The decisions of superior courts in other portions of the British Empire, for example, Irish courts.

"(3) The judgments of the Privy Council when sitting as the final court of appeal from the Colonies.

"(4) Judicial *dicta,* that is to say, statements of law which go beyond the occasion, and lay down a rule that is irrelevant or unnecessary for the purpose in hand. We shall see later that the authoritative influence of precedents does not extend to such *obiter dicta,* but they are not equally destitute of persuasive efficacy." [1]

---

[1] JURISPRUDENCE (6th ed.) sec. 63 (1920).

Does Salmond make a valid distinction here? In what way shall we describe the difference in the binding force of authoritative and persuasive precedents? Do courts ever overrule the former?

Do you accept his distinction between the force of a decision and a dictum? Would it be correct to say that a dictum of a court in state X is persuasive there, in the same way as a decision made in state Y?

Sec. 6–15. Dictum and decision.* Not all statements which one finds in a judicial opinion are regarded as having binding authority. Only those declarations of law which are made by the court upon questions which are necessary to the decision of the case before it, are binding in later cases. An opinion expressed by the court upon some question of law which is *not necessary* to the decision of the case before it, is dictum and not binding. Dictum may be persuasive, but it has not the force of *decision*. This all means that one must make the distinction between decision and dictum—a distinction which is not easy to make and which will cause you plenty of trouble as you proceed with your study of cases.

Under the caption, "What Does a Case Decide?" Oliphant points out three types of dictum and suggests the difficulty of distinguishing dictum from decision. He says in part:

"In the first place, a court, in deciding a case, may throw out a statement as to how it would decide some other case. Now if that statement is a statement of another case which is as narrow and specific as the actual case before the court, it is easily recognized as dictum and given its proper weight as such. In the second place, the court may throw out a broader statement, covering a whole group of cases. But, so long as that statement does not cover the case before the

---

* (I.R.) In addition to the item by Oliphant, cited in the next footnote, see Goodhart, "Determining the Ratio Decidendi of a Case," 40 YALE L. J. 161 (1930).

court, it is readily recognized as being not a decision, much less the decision of the case. It is dictum, so labeled and appraised. But, in the third place, a court may make a statement broad enough to dispose of the case in hand as well as to cover also a few or many other states of fact. Statements of this third sort may cover a number of fact situations ranging from one other to legion." [1]

Simply put, dictum is any statement of law by the court which is not necessary to the decision of the case before it. The third of the types of dictum mentioned by Oliphant is the one which makes most difficulty. It is the type in which the court has laid down a proposition in its decision which is more general than it needs to be in order to decide the case. It raises the question, when is a proposition broader than it needs to be? When is it too general? Oliphant supposes a case in which A's father induces her not to marry B as she has promised to do. If the court holds that A's father is not liable to B for inducing A to break her contract, what proposition should it base its conclusion on? Oliphant suggests the following possibilities among others:

"1. Fathers are privileged to induce daughters to break promises to marry.
"2. Parents are so privileged.
"3. Parents are so privileged as to both daughters and sons.
"4. All persons are so privileged as to promises to marry.
"5. Parents are so privileged as to all promises made by their children.
"6. All persons are so privileged as to all promises made by anyone."

And this author then asks:

"Where, on that graduation of propositions, are we to take our stand and say, 'This proposition is the decision of this case . . .'? Can a proposition of law of this third type ever

[1] "A Return to Stare Decisis," 6 AM. L. S. REV. 215 at 217 et seq. (1928).

become so broad that, as to any of the cases it would cover, it is mere dictum?'"

Sec. 6–16. Problems regarding dictum. 1. Now to pursue to the end the line of suppositions which Oliphant makes let us assume that the court which decides the case rested its decision on the sixth of the above possibilities: All persons are so privileged as to all promises made by anyone. Might not the court in a later case, involving a breach of promise of marriage induced by a neighborhood busybody, quite properly say that the previous decision only supported the second possibility, i.e., that parents are privileged to induce the breach of such promises? If the court in this later case determined to hold the busybody liable, it would call the proposition of law laid down in the first case dictum insofar as it went beyond what was necessary to decide the first case.

2. Suppose another later case arises in which Z has induced X to breach his contract to sell and deliver *lumber* to Y; on what basis might the court distinguish the original case involving A's father, and justify a conclusion that Z is liable for damages to Y?

3. The process by which the judge limits the application of a prior judicial declaration, which he calls dictum, closely resembles the process by which the judge restrictively interprets a legislative declaration in statutory form (secs. 5–23 and 5–24). Elaborate and explain the analogy.

4. What is the relation of dictum to the rules of method which limit judicial lawmaking (see sec. 6–03 above)?

Sec. 6–17. Analogical and extensive interpretation of precedents. Problems. When a novel case arises, one which is not clearly covered by a statute or by a prior decision, the court to which it is presented will develop a principle from its former holdings, and decide the case according to this principle. This method of decision obviously extends the holdings of the previous cases, although the court usually talks as if it were applying law which it found in them.

1. Let us return for a moment to the breach of promise cases discussed above. Suppose D, a father, induces his daughter to breach her promise to marry P, and P sues D for damages. Suppose, further, that the court which decides the action in D's favor, rests its conclusion on the proposition that a father is justified in inducing his daughter to breach a promise of this kind. Now, if a later case comes before this court in which a son has been induced by his mother to breach a promise of marriage, what would this court probably hold? How would it state the proposition of law of the second case? How would it state what was decided in the first case?

Can the method of extending the principle of a decision to a new case be reconciled with the traditional doctrine which limits the controlling force of a decision to what is actually decided?

2. *Commonwealth v. Hoxey.*[1] The indictment set forth that the inhabitants of Williamstown, on the 15th of March, 1819, were duly assembled in town meeting, for the choice of town officers for the political year then next ensuing; that a moderator was duly chosen, who called on the electors present to give in their votes for a selectman for the year ensuing; that the defendant, while the moderator was presiding in the meeting, and was receiving the votes for a selectman, with force and arms, intending as much as in him lay to prevent the choice of said selectman according to the will of the electors, and to interrupt the freedom of election, unlawfully and disorderly did openly declare that the old selectmen should not be chosen, and attempted repeatedly to take from the box, which contained the ballots of the electors, the votes of the electors; and so the jurors say, " 'that the said T. F. Hoxey, on &c., at &c., in the public

[1] 16 Mass. 385 (1820).

town meeting aforesaid, in manner and form aforesaid, did behave himself disorderly and indecently, to the disturbance of the peaceable and quiet citizens then and there assembled for the purpose aforesaid, in violation of the rights of private suffrage, against the peace of the commonwealth aforesaid, and *contrary to the form of* the statute in such case made and provided.'

"The defendant pleaded guilty to the indictment, and moved in arrest of judgment, 'because the said indictment purports to be founded upon a statute of law of the commonwealth; whereas there is no such statute in the state, making the facts set forth in the indictment an offence against the commonwealth; and because the facts set forth in the indictment do not amount to an offence at common law.' . . .

"*By the Court.* The indictment charges the offence to have been committed *contra formam statuti;* but no statute is found to describe the offence as alleged. The statute of 1785, c. 75, § 6, imposes a penalty of twenty shillings for disorderly conduct in town meetings, if the offender shall, after notice from the moderator, persist in his disorderly behavior, and shall refuse or neglect to withdraw from the meeting, after being directed to do so by the moderator. The offence laid in the indictment is not within this provision. . . .

"The remaining question is, Do the facts charged amount to an offence at the common law? On this question we entertain no doubts. Here was a violent and rude disturbance of the citizens, lawfully assembled in town meeting, and in the actual exercise of their municipal rights and duties. The tendency of the defendant's conduct was to a breach of the peace, and to the prevention of elections, necessary to the orderly government of the town, and due management of its concerns for the year. It is true that the common law knows nothing perfectly agreeing with our municipal assemblies. But other meetings are well known and often held in *England,* the disturbance of which is punishable at common law, as a misdemeanor. In this commonwealth, town meetings are recognized in our constitution and laws; and the elections made and the business transacted by the citizens, at those meetings, lie at the foundation of our whole civil polity. If then there were no statute, prohibiting disorderly conduct at such meetings, an indictment for such conduct might be supported.

"Motion overruled."

Would you regard such a decision as a creative decision? Why?

Is the court ready to extend the existing statutes to cover this new case? Do not the same objections apply to the extension of the principle of prior decisions to cover the new case?[2]

3. *Russell v. Men of Devon.*[3]

"This was an action upon the case against the *men dwelling in the county of Devon*, to recover satisfaction for an injury done to the waggon of the plaintiff's in consequence of a bridge being out of repair, which ought to have been repaired by the county; to which two of the inhabitants, for themselves and the rest of the men dwelling in that county, appeared, and demurred generally. . . .

"LORD KENYON, Ch. J. If this experiment had succeeded, it would have been productive of an infinity of actions. And though the fear of introducing so much litigation ought not to prevent the plaintiff's recovering, if by law he is entitled, yet it ought to have considerable weight in a case where it is admitted that there is no precedent of such an action having been before attempted. Many of the principles laid down by the plaintiff's counsel cannot be controverted; as that an action would lie by an individual for an injury which he has sustained against any other individual who is bound to repair. But the question here is, Whether this body of men, who are sued in the present action, are a corporation, or *qua* a corporation, against whom such an action can be maintained. If it be reasonable that they should be by law liable to such an action, recourse must be had to the Legislature for that purpose. But it has been said that this action ought to be

---

[2] See Hall, "Nulla Poena Sine Lege," 47 YALE L. J. 165, 172–180 (1937) and compare sec. 5–25 above.

[3] (1788) 2 Term R. 667.

maintained by borrowing the rules of analogy from the statutes of hue and cry: but I think that those statutes prove the very reverse. The reason of the statute of *Winton* was this; as the hundred were bound to keep watch and ward, it was supposed that those irregularities which led to robbery must have happened by their neglect. But it was never imagined that the hundred could have been compelled to make satisfaction, till the statute gave that remedy; and most undoubtedly no such action could have been maintained against them before that time. Therefore, when the case called for a remedy, the Legislature interposed; but they only gave the remedy in that particular case, and did not give it in any other case in which the neglect of the hundred had produced any injury to individuals. And when they gave the action, they virtually gave the means of maintaining that action; they converted the hundred into a corporation for that purpose: but it does not follow that, in this case where the Legislature has not given the remedy, this action can be maintained. . . .

"ASHHURST, J. It is a strong presumption that that which never has been done cannot by law be done at all. And it is admitted that no such action as the present has ever been brought, though the occasion must have frequently happened. But it has been said that there is a principle of law on which this action may be maintained, namely, that where an individual sustains an injury by the neglect or default of another, the law gives him a remedy. But there is another general principle of law which is more applicable to this case, that it is better that an individual should sustain an injury than that the public should suffer an inconvenience. Now if this action could be sustained, the public would suffer a great inconvenience; for if damages are recoverable against the county, at all events they must be levied on one or two individuals, who have no means whatever of reimbursing themselves; . . . .

"BULLER, J. and GROSE, J. assented.

"Judgment for the defendants."

Here the court refused to make an analogical extension of prior decisions and established principles. Why?

What do you think of the "strong presumption" which Justice Ashhurst mentions? If applied, what is its effect? [4]

Sec. 6–18. Overruling precedents. Problems. Courts do overrule their prior decisions. Even the clearest precedents are not absolutely binding. *Three theories* are expressed in the following excerpts as to whether courts should overrule previous decisions and if they are to overrule them, when they should do so.

1. In *People v. Tompkins* [1] the court said in part:

"The learned district attorney is clearly right in his assertion that the law of this state, as enunciated in the cases of Clough, Stetson and McCord, is at variance with the rule adopted by many other states in the Union. We are also impressed with the weight of the argument that in view of the constantly expanding ingenuity of intelligent criminals, which serves to render the administration of criminal justice more and more difficult, the law must be progressively practical in order to keep pace with the development of new forms of crime. But these arguments, impressive as they are, simply serve to suggest that it is the province of courts to give effect to existing rules of law and not to legislate. The law of this state, as set forth in the *McCord Case*, has been in existence since 1837. It has become a rule of personal liberty quite as firmly established in this state as the rule of property recently re-affirmed in the case of *Peck v. Schenectady Ry. Co.*, 170 N. Y. 298, 63 N. E. 357. Although it may be admitted that this rule, which exists only in New York and Wisconsin, is at variance with what now appears to be the more reasonable view adopted in at least twelve of our sister states, and although it may be conceded to be too narrow for the practical administration of criminal justice as applied to modern conditions, we are admonished that the remedy is not with the courts, but in the legislature. We

---

[4] Compare Daily v. Parker, quoted in section 6–06, problem 3; Pyle v. Waechter, 202 Iowa 695 (1926); and dissenting opinion of Grose, J., in Pasley v. Freeman, (1789) 3 Term R. 51.

[1] 186 N. Y. 413 (1906).

cannot change the existing rule without enacting, in effect, an *ex post facto* law. This cannot be done without ignoring the constitutional rights of many who may legally claim the protection of the rule. Neither can it be done without judicial usurpation of legislative power."

How would you state the theory here announced? Is there a real point in the statement that the court "cannot change the existing rule without enacting, in effect, an ex post facto law"?

2. In *Bricker v. Green,*[2] Bushnell, J., speaking for the court, said in part:

"We come, then, to the question of imputed negligence. In this case, a wife who, while riding with her husband as a passenger, was killed by a combination of his negligence with that of a third party. Under the authorities as they now stand in this State, she could not have recovered had she survived nor can her administrator now recover. This rule, which exists only in Michigan, has been consistently applied in this State since the decision in *Lake Shore & Michigan Southern R. Co. v. Miller,* 25 Mich. 274, 277, decided in 1872, and it has been just as consistently criticized both within and without this jurisdiction. . . .

"The *amicus curiae* brief of the State Bar of Michigan closes with this statement:

" 'In the typical case, there is presented, on the one hand, the plaintiff-passenger, wholly free of any negligence or wrongdoing. On the other hand, there is the tortfeasor whose negligence has brought harm to such passenger or contributed to such harm. The injured party brings suit. The court must choose between them, the one innocent, the other guilty. Which is to be preferred? Must we continue for all time to drag in this exploded and obsolete legal monstrosity with the sole result of throwing the loss on the innocent party? The "imputed negligence" doctrine prefers the wrongdoer. He is the favored one and he is allowed to go free of responsibility for his wrongdoing. The loss is thrown upon the innocent passenger. As has been pointed out, abolition of the pernicious

[2] 313 Mich. 218 (1946).

doctrine would affect only the wrongdoer and that only to the extent of preventing his escape from liability for his own negligence to one free from fault. At rock-bottom, the imputed-negligence doctrine is a denial of justice as between parties litigant. Hence, the rule of *stare decisis* should not be invoked in its behalf to perpetuate it through the many years to come. . . .'

"Ever since 1872 we have adhered to the imputed-negligence rule. We have recognized from time to time the changes brought about by the innovations of science and engineering, and we have carefully considered at much length the implications of the rule, its application, and the effect of its abandonment. As a result of our study and observation we are convinced that in the long run the application of the rule is more harmful than helpful and results in more injustice than it prevents; and that we should not continue the invariable application of the so-called imputed-negligence rule merely and solely on the ground that the injured person was a voluntary, gratuitous passenger in an automobile, the driver of which was guilty of negligence which was a contributing proximate cause of an accident and injury to such passenger. . . .

"The rule of imputed negligence as announced and applied in *Lake Shore & Michigan Southern Railroad Co. v. Miller*, 25 Mich. 274, and in subsequent cases of like character, is overruled, so far as pending and future cases are concerned. Notwithstanding the fact that the trial judge applied the law as laid down in our opinions, we must, in view of our present holding, set aside the judgment of no cause of action and order a new trial. . . ."

How would you formulate the theory here announced? What are its effects as regards the instant case? As regards the decision of future cases?

3. *Payne v. City of Covington.*[3] Opinion of the court by Creal, Commissioner:

"The framers of our Constitution who gave multiplied months to preparation of the instrument which was later

3 276 Ky. 380 (1938).

ratified and adopted by the people, knowing the general tendency of governments and especially subordinate taxing divisions thereof and their officials to run into debt and incur liabilities that would affect their faith and credit and impose onerous burdens upon the tax paying public placed these positive and wise limitations upon the powers of the counties, towns, etc., to incur debts or impose liabilities upon themselves beyond the limitations prescribed in the quoted provisions without referring the proposition to the voters for approval (section 157). Knowing also that the electorate through zeal or improvidence is often inclined to assume excessive and burdensome indebtedness, they inserted section 158 of the Constitution as a further safeguard limiting the total amount of indebtedness that might be incurred by a political subdivision in any manner whatsoever, even by a vote of the people. . . ."

The opinion then reviewed several of the court's prior decisions construing the provisions in question, and the decisions of other courts construing similar provisions; and the opinion continued:

"The rule announced in the domestic cases referred to lets down the barriers to the mischief obviously intended by the framers of the Constitution to be prohibited, and invited an orgy of maladministration waste of public funds and accumulation of indebtedness in counties and municipalities of alarming and in many instances ruinous proportions, which inevitably follow in the wake of judicial pronouncement removing restraint and limitations upon public expenditures and the creation of public indebtedness. The court can only view with regret the mischief already wrought under sanction of its decisions in giving a clearly strained and erroneous interpretation to the involved sections of the Constitution, however, and as will later be pointed out, the court is not by any rule of stare decisis or long continued erroneous construction rendered powerless to remedy the ills arising from its erroneous prior interpretations but may with propriety and so far as is consistent with vested rights acquired or acts done on faith of its decisions subordinate that rule when justice and public welfare make such a course preferable to perpetuation of error. . . .

"But it is said that the doctrine of stare decisis prevents us from overruling our former opinions and compels us to continue to follow them, howsoever erroneous they may be. . . .

"Of course, all of the authorities say that more hesitation will be indulged against overruling prior opinions establishing property rights than in cases where such rights are not established. But no case that we have been able to find attributes such binding force to the rule as compels courts to continue to follow prior erroneous opinions to the detriment of the public interest, and when prior erroneous opinions are not only without reason to support them, but are in direct conflict with what was intended by a statute, a Constitution, or by the parties to a contract. . . . We, therefore, conclude that if there ever was a case where the doctrine of stare decisis should not prevent us at this time from correcting the glaringly erroneous opinions heretofore prevailing on the question in hand, it is this one, and we unhesitatingly disallow its urged effect in this case.

"But it might be said that property rights have been created in following our prior interpretations of the sections of the Constitution referred to, and which is true. We conceive, however, it to be competent for a court, in overruling a prior adopted principle, to preserve in the overruling opinion all rights accrued under the prior declaration, the same as if they had been created or arose out of a former existing statute which was later repealed by the Legislature. . . .

"Therefore, in overruling our prior opinions and in declaring our disapproval of such erroneous interpretations herein dealt with, we do so with the express reservation that all rights heretofore created and accrued in favor of all persons interested, in any manner whatsoever, shall be preserved and the principles of this opinion will not apply to any transaction begun or in the course of completion, or finished before this opinion becomes final. But the various taxing units of the commonwealth embraced by the two sections of the Constitution, supra (157 and 158) shall, after this opinion becomes final, observe and be governed by the interpretation herein made, and shall contract no debts beyond the amount of revenue which they themselves provide under authority given to them by the Constitution or Statutes legally enacted thereunder. Therefore, if they wish to incur debts in any fiscal year they must not exceed in the aggregate what they themselves produce under the authority so given to them, and that any indebtedness in excess of what they do so produce, shall be void. As a consequence of the conclusions we have reached the opinions in the cases of *City of Providence v. Providence Electric Light Co., supra; Overall v. City of Madisonville*, 125 Ky. 684, 102 S. W. 278, 31 Ky. Law Rep. 278, 12 L. R. A., N. S., 433; *Carter v. Krueger & Son*, 175 Ky. 399, 194 S. W. 553, and all others following the interpretations therein made, are hereby expressly overruled; but with the reservation, supra, whereby the rights of all parties are preserved, and this opinion shall have a prospective effect only.

"However, the withholding of any retroactive effect of this opinion requires an affirmance of the judgment, since compliance is shown with the erroneous interpretations heretofore made. Wherefore, the judgment of the lower court is affirmed.

"The whole court sitting."

How would you formulate the theory here announced? What are its effects as regards the instant case? As regards the decision of future cases?*

Sec. 6–19. Summary. In this chapter the chief topics for consideration have been the ways in which case law is made,

---

* (I.R.) "But an overruling decision may be limited to prospective effect only, and thereby have the same general, future operation as a legislative enactment. In the overruling case, the court may apply the overruled decision to the case before it and announce a new rule which it will apply to jural relations that arise thereafter." Kocourek and Koven, "Renovation of the Common Law Through Stare Decisis," 29 ILL. LAW REV. 971 at 972 (1935). Two jurisdictions, Montana and Kentucky, have adopted this theory and method of overruling precedents. See editorial "Sensible View of Stare Decisis Gains Ground," 23 AM. JUD. SOC. JOUR. 32 (1939); Kocourek, "Retrospective Decisions and Stare Decisis and a Proposal," 17 A. B. A. J. 180 (1931); and Green, "Freedom of Litigation," 38 ILL. L. REV. 117, 248, 355 (1943–1944).

followed, and changed by our judges. We have analyzed the massive body of precedents, built up bit by bit by judicial decisions and known collectively as "the common law"; and have noted the ambiguity of the latter term. We have examined the more important rules that our judges have worked out to guide each judge in the handling of legal materials. These rules are superstandards of judicial method. They tell the judge where to find rules of law to apply, how to choose among possible rules, how and when to lay down a new rule or precedent, how far to follow precedents already established, and when to depart from or overrule such precedents. And the lawyer needs to understand the role of these rules of method no less than the judge. Without this understanding a lawyer cannot read a case intelligently, or write a law brief, or present a legal argument in court.

CHAPTER 7

Legal Policies and Policy Making *

Sec. 7–01. Scope of chapter: policies and how made. In the foregoing discussion, standards have been viewed primarily as means of achieving ends, as instruments through which the lawgiver tries to effectuate policies which he envisages.[1] We have not yet come to grips with the question of what the ends of law are. We have assumed in our discussion that legal standards are created to serve human ends. But what are those ends? What are the purposes which find expression in legal standards? Why does the legal system furnish guidance of various sorts? Why prohibit behavior of some kinds? Why command other kinds of behavior? Why permit certain activities? And, why does the law undertake to make many predefined acts effective? Until now, we have given only passing notice to such questions.[2] Thus far, we

---

* (I.R.) *Suggestions for further reading:* Pound, "A Survey of Social Interests," 57 HARV. L. REV. 1 (1943) (a rewriting of a paper originally published in 1921); POUND, AN INTRODUCTION TO THE PHILOSOPHY OF LAW (1913), chapter on Ends; POUND, SOCIAL CONTROL THROUGH LAW 63 *et seq.* (1942); STONE, THE PROVINCE AND FUNCTION OF LAW (1946), Chapters XV, XX, XXI, XXII; M. Cohen, "On Absolutisms in Legal Thought," 84 U. of PA. L. REV. 681 (1936); F. COHEN, ETHICAL SYSTEMS AND LEGAL IDEALS (1933); Dickinson, "The Law Behind Law," 29 COL. L. REV. 113, 285, especially at 296–307 (1929); Pekelis, "The Case for a Jurisprudence of Welfare," 11 SOCIAL RESEARCH 312 (1944); MacIVER, THE MODERN STATE, chapter 5 (1926).

[1] In thus treating law and its standards as instrumentalities devised to serve human ends, I have merely followed the modern trend of thinking here and elsewhere. Ever since the epoch-making work of Von Ihering, *Law As a Means to an End*, legal writers have been stressing the instrumental character of law. In this country, the great protagonist and popularizer of this viewpoint has been Roscoe Pound. As he says, "Making or finding law, call it what you will, presupposes a mental picture of what one is doing and why he is doing it." AN INTRODUCTION TO THE PHILOSOPHY OF LAW 59 (1913).

In the present work, the instrumental approach to law is represented especially by the discussion in secs. 1–07 *et seq.*, 2–01, 2–11, 2–15, 2–29, 4–04, 4–05, 6–02 and 6–17.

[2] More or less definite references to legal policies will be found in the following places: secs. 2–11, 2–29, 4–04, 4–05, 4–07, 5–12, 5–13 (problem 3), 5–20 (problem 1), 5–23, 5–27, 6–06, 6–11 (problem 2), 6–18 and 6–19.

have only carried the discussion of legal problems up to the point where we have found that questions involving legal policies were involved, and have stopped there. In the present chapter, I propose to take up these questions as such; I want to consider what our principal legal policies are, and show how these policies are fixed and formulated.

Sec. 7–02. Legal policies and policy makers. The creation of a legal standard is an intentional, a planned, act. The lawmaker who does his job properly works out a full plan; he works out the provisions of his standard with a clear appreciation of the ends he wants to accomplish by it. His planning encompasses both the provisions of the standard itself and the ends for which the standard is framed.[1] These ends serve as self-imposed guides for the framing of the standard.*

By a legal policy, I mean an end or objective of such a legislative plan. In framing a constitutional provision, the draftsman has certain ends in view; these are legal policies. In enacting a statute, the legislature likewise entertains purposes which are to be attained through the creation of a standard or standards; these are also legal policies. And the judicial lawmaker who establishes a standard by his decision visualizes certain objectives behind it; these objectives are legal policies, too. A legal policy, then, as I am using the term, is essentially a legislative policy; it is the objective

[1] For examples of statutes in which the legislative ends are definitely stressed, see secs. 4–07 and 4–19; and compare the general discussion in sec. 4–04 of the point here made.

*(I.R.) It is worth noting that the means-ends analysis can be developed in more detail; it can be applied in the following series: Legal remedy as means of securing legal right (end); legal right as means of recognizing legal interest (end); and remedy, right, and interest as means through which a legal policy is recognized. In the present chapter, I have chosen to use the means-ends analysis in the last sense. This is the sense which is useful in the present chapter. The choice of a terminology or a mode of analysis is largely dictated by the purpose in hand, though convenience dictates that one not depart too far from common usage.

of a lawmaker. So that when I speak of legal policies in the rest of this chapter, I shall be taking the legislative point of view and focusing attention on the purposes for which the lawmakers of our American legal system create standards.

The creation of a policy is a verbal act. It is a declaration of intention. Often it is a part of the same verbal act as the standard to which it relates. The framer of a legislative provision establishes standards and tells what he wants to accomplish by them, all in one breath. And the judicial lawmaker lays down a rule of law and in the same opinion declares what the purpose of the rule is. This method of coupling standards and policies has become the common practice with Congress, as I have already pointed out; it enacts various provisions regulating individual and official conduct, and joins with them an expressed declaration of policy.[2] Only too often, however, the policy maker's purpose is stated on a separate occasion, or is perhaps not thought out at all, or is merely assumed and taken for granted.[3] In all these cases, the interpreter of law has to discover the lawmaker's policy. In some cases, this means that he must conjure up something which, like the "little man," was "not there." The interpreter becomes, in effect, the policy maker of the legislation he is interpreting.

So policies and their declarations are always connected with human actors. Individual human beings may act on behalf of organized groups, as the lawmaker and other officials do when they entertain and express policies on behalf of the state.[4] But only individuals do acts and lay out plans. I stress

[2] See examples in secs. 4–04 and 4–19.

[3] See further regarding the incompleteness of legislative declarations, sec. 4–22.

[4] It is common usage to speak of the ends of law, the policies of government, and the interests of society as if law, government and society were persons who entertained ends, pursued policies, and asserted interests. This mode of speaking does no harm if one appreciates that it is metaphorical and elliptical. In fact, I shall not hesitate to follow this common usage myself throughout the rest of this chapter. But it must always be remembered that these modes of speech refer in the last analysis to ends, policies and interests recognized and adopted by officials. Cf. sec. 3–03.

this personal role of policy makers and other officials in order to forestall the type of thinking which loses sight of human acts in the midst of dry abstractions. Of course, I do not mean to limit our discussion to particular policies of particular lawmakers on particular occasions.** I do not mean that you and I can get along without generalized types of policies, or general ends of law as expressed in official actions on many occasions. We must make use of these general ideas; in fact, most of the policies with which we shall have to deal in the remainder of this chapter are general in the sense just mentioned. But the fact that they are general and commonly accepted, does not deprive them of their character as ends recognized by actual officials.

Sec. 7–03. Policies as guides for other officials. One of the lawmaker's primary aims is to give guidance to other officials. Correlatively, these officials look to him for guidance. The lawmaker ordinarily makes his instructions as detailed as possible. He tells other officials, in the form of specific stand-

** (I.R.) More specifically, my reason for recognizing the role of the policy maker in formulating and recognizing legal policies lies in the fact that it is so common to speak of legal policies, ends of law, legal interests, social interests, etc., in the elliptical manner mentioned in the preceding footnote. This usage neglects the personal side of legal policies and policy making. It leaves policies hanging in the air, and can, on this account, be seriously misleading. To speak of the ends of law is quite as if one spoke of the aims of poetry, or the purposes of philosophy. Poetry and philosophy do not, as such, recognize ends. In this connection, ends must mean, respectively, the general aims which are cherished by poets and the general purposes which are professed by philosophers. By the same token, what we mean when we speak of the ends of law are the purposes which are entertained by persons who create law, or who interpret and apply it. If this is not clearly realized, it is easy to fall into the fallacy of personifying the law itself. Much of the difficulty which I have found over the years in trying to explain the ends of law to law students seems to me to stem from the fact that law is regarded as if it were somehow endowed with a phantom personality which can pursue objectives of its own, and as if it had an independent existence apart from the acts of lawmakers, judges, and other officials. But if we look upon law merely as a set of standards established by human acts, and if we see the ends of law as objectives entertained by human lawmakers and intended to guide the acts of human officials, we shall not have too much difficulty in grasping the meaning of the ends of law or the policies of the legal system.

ards, what they must do and not do, what they may do, and what they can do effectively. But he may employ very broad and indefinite standards, including the type of broad statement in which we are at present interested, to wit, the declaration of policy. In other words, the lawmaker's explanation of his aims has guidance value, too, though this guidance may be rather remote and vague. If the lawmaker's plan of guidance by specific directions is adequate, and normally it is, then his vague and general declarations of policy play very little part. But sometimes specific directions turn out to be ambiguous or conflicting, or are found to be altogether lacking. In that case, the official who is looking for guidance must seek for directions outside the specific standards provided; he may find it in an explicit declaration of legislative policy, or a general policy of the common law, such as the policy of preserving the public peace, or a general policy of our constitutions, such as the policy of allowing the individual the maximum of freedom in deciding what contracts he will make. When other guides fail, legally recognized policies serve as secondary standards and furnish at least a minimum of guidance for official action.

Similar resort to general policies for guidance may be had by officials when the lawmaker intentionally fails to provide specific standards to go by. Of this type, as you will recall, are the instances where the legislature delegates subsidiary lawmaking authority to administrative agencies.[1] This kind of delegation does not leave the agency with an unlimited lawmaking discretion. Usually the agency is tied down by an explicit declaration of policy in the act which invests it with governmental authority; and besides this, the agency is to be guided by policies such as public convenience, the protection of life, protection of property, etc., which find general recognition in constitutional clauses, statutory provi-

---

[1] See secs. 4–15 to 4–17; and compare sec. 4–23.

sions, and judicial decisions. Of this same general type and purport are the cases of acts which are left to the free discretion of judges. For example, if a judge must pass on the question whether a particular type of contract operates as an unreasonable restraint of trade—a vague enough standard—he looks for and obtains some guidance in common declarations of policy, legislative and judicial. He finds some support in policies regarding free contract, freedom of business, protection of the public against monopoly, etc. Such policies serve as a secondary, but nonetheless helpful, guidepost to direct his conclusions. Again, if a judge has to decide whether a particular offender is to be put on probation or sent to prison, he does not find himself entirely without leads as to the proper choice to make. He is aided by declared policies of statute and decision, regarding reformation of offenders, the protection of the public against injury, etc. Alike in all these cases where specific standards are intentionally not provided, policy declarations of various sorts serve the official actor as general guides.

Sec. 7–04. Legal policies—classification—subtopics. Policies, like the private objectives of the individual, might be listed almost without number. They vary widely from one legal system to another. For classification and further discussion, I have selected the principal policies recognized by the American legal systems.*

* (I.R.) Also like motives (e.g., hunger and sex, self-regarding and other-regarding motives, self-preservation and socially directed motives), policies can be classified in a variety of ways. For example, policies can be related to the persons who announce them (officials and theorists); they may be policies which are adopted in fact and those which ought to be adopted; they may be related to things, tangible and intangible, to physical environment and to culture; they may be related to various kinds of personal subject matter, as individuals, groups and communities.

It is obviously not feasible to consider and mention all the policies that have ever been adopted. A selection must be made. It is also not feasible to analyze and classify the selected material except in limited ways. In fact, the selection of items for analysis and the classification of material selected,

All these policies have an *actual* and an *ideal* side. They are actual in the sense that they are, in fact, adopted by some or all the American legal systems. They are ideal in the sense that they are goals which may or may not be achieved; and ideal in the further sense that they are viewed as desirable or proper goals by those who adopt them.

Along with each policy presented, I shall refer to standards in which it is recognized, and to various governmental measures through which it is effectuated.[1]

The policies will be subdivided and described under three heads, to each of which a subtopic will be devoted:

Policies regarding the individual.
Policies regarding the community.
Policies regarding organized groups.

These three subtopics will be followed by a fourth and concluding head, entitled Determinants of Policies, in which you will see how policies are formulated and what shapes their development.

Policies Regarding the Individual

Sec. 7–05. Stress on the individual claim. The United States was born in the heyday of individualist thinking. The emphasis of political and economic writers of the time was on the claim of the individual, on his demand for liberty, equality and security. These writers were much impressed by the drawbacks of governmental interference with individual initiative, and by the dangers of governmental abuses of power. They regarded the individual as the best judge of his own interests, and felt that governmental restraints

always go back to what the classifier thinks is important. In this regard, the following treatment expresses my personal views of what is significant in this field.

[1] Consult section 3–01, note 1, regarding the senses in which the terms "government" and "state" are used in these lectures.

on his acts and choices should be held to a minimum. It is not surprising, therefore, that the practical policy makers of that day embodied these general views in the federal and state constitutions which they framed. It is not surprising that they gave emphatic recognition to the individual will, and adopted a hands-off policy for government which would allow the individual to work out his own salvation.

But this original concern with the individual's claims is more than a matter of historical interest; it continued without break or challenge almost until the end of the nineteenth century. It found expression in innumerable subsequent declarations of constitutions, statutes, and decisions. Even today the vast bulk of our private law is focused on the claims of the individual; we talk of his acts, his rights, his powers, his privileges, and his remedies, almost without end. So that the legal policies in which individual claims are recognized are still matters of prime, practical import to us as law students. They constitute a natural and convenient starting point for our discussion of legal policies.

The claims made by individuals and recognized by law I shall call "individual interests," following the terminology which is now commonly accepted. These are claims asserted by individual men, and also recognized as the subject matter of protection by the policy makers of our legal system. They may be said to have two aspects: an individual aspect and an official aspect. The individual aspect is found in the making of a claim for protection on the individual's part. The official aspect is found in the grant of that protection by policy makers. These two aspects of the policy of protecting an individual claim are linked together when we speak of the legal recognition of an individual interest or the legal protection of the individual.*

* (I.R.) The treatments of this subject by Pound and Stone seem to me to suffer from the fact that they do not develop this official aspect clearly. They do indicate that legal interests are claims asserted by people; they fail to

A convenient inventory of these recognized interests of the individual has been prepared by Pound. He lists three major groups of individual interests: 1. interests of personality; 2. interests in domestic relations; 3. interests of substance. I adopt the essential features of Pound's inventory in the three sections which follow.[1]

Sec. 7–06. Interests of personality. This group of recognized interests underlies a major segment of the law of torts as well as important parts of the criminal law. The group embraces such interests as the claims of the individual to live without molestation by others, to move about without restraint, to act freely, to believe and say what he chooses, and so on. These interests find recognition in constitutional provisions, which guarantee the protection of the life, the liberty, and the equality of the individual. They also find recognition in statutes and decisions, defining standards for individual action, and fixing the rights, powers, privileges and immunities of individuals in regard to other individuals and to officials.

The policy of protecting the individual's personality is subdivided by Pound further into:

a. *Protection of the integrity of his physical person—* against aggression or injury by others, such as assaults, batteries, and negligent harms.

b. *Protection of the freedom of his will*—against restraints on his freedom of movement and freedom of action; and against compulsion and fraud in the like respects.

---

indicate with equal clarity that legal interests, legal ends and legal policies are interests, ends and policies recognized and adopted by people, i.e., by officials. See POUND, OUTLINE OF JURISPRUDENCE (5th ed.) 96–97 (1943); POUND, SOCIAL CONTROL THROUGH LAW 68–69 (1942); STONE, THE PROVINCE AND FUNCTION OF LAW 487 *et seq.* (1946).

[1] OUTLINE OF JURISPRUDENCE, (5th ed.) 97–102 (1943). However, I have modified some items and have omitted others in order to simplify the presentation. See also STONE, THE PROVINCE AND FUNCTION OF LAW, chapter 21 (1946).

c. *Protection of his personal reputation*—against defamatory acts, i.e., libel and slander.*

d. *Protection of his freedom of belief and opinion*—against governmental interference and interference by others; the protection in this regard extends to religious tenets, political beliefs, and economic views; it covers freedom of speech and of the press and of assembly, as well as freedom of belief. All these freedoms are clearly recognized by provisions of the constitutions, by statutes, and especially by the decisions of the Supreme Court.

Sec. 7–07. Interests in domestic relations. The individual's interests in domestic relations cover his family relationships. They are, in a very real sense, an extension of his personality to include claims regarding his relations to others. Many of these claims are recognized in legal policies. For example, the claims of husband and wife to one another's society; the claims of husband and wife that third parties shall not interfere in their relations to one another; the claims of the parent to the control of the child, and to its society and services; [1] the claims of the child to the society and support of the parent.[2] It is not necessary to elaborate these claims or the policies behind their recognition; they are well known and find expression and recognition in a variety of familiar rights, powers, privileges, and remedies.

Sec. 7–08. Interests of substance. The individual's interests in the economic sphere are recognized in many important

---

* (I.R.) Pound also lists at this point, as a further head, the protection of the individual's privacy and sensibilities. No doubt this head represents a proper inclusion for a complete discussion such as Pound's, but as our purpose is merely to give a brief account of the recognition of individual interests, and as the inclusion of this item would require more explanation and discussion than our space allows, I have decided to omit it.

[1] See Pierce v. Society of Sisters, 268 U. S. 510 (1925), discussed in sec. 7–33, problem 4.

[2] See Daily v. Parker, 152 F. 2d 174 (1945), quoted in sec. 6–06, problem 3.

legal policies. These interests cover all of the individual's claims regarding property, contracts, and related matters. They constitute the subject matter of the law of property and the law of contracts. These interests are recognized and the policies behind them are announced in the provisions of the constitutions which guarantee the property and the liberty of individuals, as well as in numberless enactments and decisions, which expound the rights, powers, and privileges of the individual.

The recognized interests of the individual in this sphere can be subdivided into:

a. The individual's claim of the *opportunity to acquire* tangible things. This claim is commonly given recognition in the form of powers and privileges of acquiring tangible things in standard ways, as by occupation, by purchase, by gift, by exchange, by will, and by inheritance.

b. The individual's claim to *use and control tangible things* acquired. This claim finds recognition in various rights, powers, privileges, and immunities of ownership and possession. The policy behind the recognition of this claim to use and control tangibles is typical of the policies which lie behind the legal recognition of all the claims of the individual. The individual must be allowed to control his own destiny.[1] The individual who has property need not worry about the morrow. Hence, the legal policy of protecting his use and control of tangibles is a policy of encouraging him to make his own future secure.

c. The individual's claim of the *opportunity to choose a vocation*. Of this claim to free choice of vocation, a recent writer says:

"It is this aspect which a famous judge much later symbolized in 'the natural right to be an iceman.' The Jeffersonian

---

[1] This aspect of property is sometimes characterized by the phrase, "property for security." It includes not only the property-holder's security as regards his own future, but also his ability to assure the future living of other persons dependent upon him for support.

democratic spirit drew from the principle of equality of citizens the corollary that all men should have equal access to all offices, pursuits and professions. Though carried at times to remarkable lengths, it did draw attention to the important fact that the claim to free choice of vocation is not merely a claim of substance, to earn a salary. It is also an intimate claim of personality affecting the activities and environment of each man's life. . . ." [2]

The individual was guaranteed by our constitutions against certain governmental interferences with his choice of a vocation. But the policy of the law was far from any guarantee of a job to the individual. It was essentially a guarantee against discrimination. Equality of opportunity to engage in any ordinary line of work was guaranteed; in particular, limitations and inequalities of opportunity based on race and color were outlawed by the Federal Constitution.

d. The individual's claim of *freedom of contract*—his opportunity to make such contracts as he pleases. This claim has been recognized very fully by our law from the foundation of our country down to the present time. In the language of Jessel, M. R., a famous English judge, in a decision rendered in 1875, ". . . if there is one thing which more than another public policy requires it is that men of full age and competent understanding shall have the utmost liberty of contracting. . . ." [3] As we shall see presently, the modern social trend in legal policies is resulting more and more in limits on this freedom. Yet it is still substantially accurate to say with Sutherland, J., of our Supreme Court, that "freedom of contract is, nevertheless, the general rule and restraint the exception." [4]

e. The individual's claim to *enforce contracts* and other beneficial arrangements with others. Until A and B, the

---

[2] STONE, THE PROVINCE AND FUNCTION OF LAW 534 (1946).

[3] Printing and Numerical Registering Company v. Sampson (1875) L. R. 19 Eq. 462 at 465.

[4] Adkins v. Children's Hospital, 261 U. S. 525 at 546 (1923). However, see the further discussion of this statement in sec. 7–36.

parties to a contract, have concluded their arrangement, both enjoy freedom of contract. This is the individual interest last ·above discussed. But when their agreement has been completed, each enjoys a new and different interest, the interest in having the contract enforced. This interest also has been strongly stressed by our American legal systems, and still retains most of its pristine vigor.[5]

Often the original policy of our government in the economic sphere has been characterized as a policy of free enterprise, or as an adoption of the economic doctrine of *laissez faire*. These characterizations are good enough if one understands what the doctrines of our government have really been; if not, they can lead to misunderstanding. The danger lies in the fact that both these characterizations give expression to the individual's claims to liberty and omit to express his claims to security. "Free enterprise" has always involved the individual's economic claims in both respects. First, it has involved recognition of the individual's freedom of action, and second, it has involved the assurance to him of the fruits of his acts. These can be regarded as two distinct policies, or lines of policy, regarding his claims. Both are represented in the analysis above developed; both are fully recognized in our legal systems. The policy of allowing free scope for individual action in the economic sphere is clearly adopted by the Federal Constitution in clause after clause; freedom to create property is recognized; also freedom to acquire property and freedom of contract. But no less clearly are adopted the policies of protecting established property rights and established contract obligations. The liberties and expectations of individuals in both these respects have been ·announced with equal force by state constitutions down to the present day; likewise in judicial opinions interpreting the

---

[5] I shall have more to say about the claim to the enforcement of contracts when I come to discuss the social interest in the security of transactions; see sec. 7–15.

constitutional clauses or laying down general principles of law. And not infrequently both policies are stated in statutory form. Free enterprise meant originally, and still means, both freedom of the individual to establish claims and security for them when established.

Sec. 7–09. Alternative classifications and names of policies regarding the individual. The individual interests which have found recognition in government policies have been given a variety of names, such as individual wants, needs, claims, and "rights." [1] Each of these names has had in the past, and still has, some vogue. Each name has a connotation of its own, but all express an approach to legal problems which puts the emphasis on the individual's claim. For our present purpose, there is no great issue involved in choosing one name rather than another, but their substantial identity is worth noting so that we shall not become confused when a change of terms is encountered.

It may also have struck you that the individual's welfare can be broken down and analyzed in different ways. The classifications of individual interests adopted in sections 7–05 to 7–08 is by no means the only one available or in use. In fact, the traditional classification of individual interests is cast in terms of the liberty, the equality, and the security of the individual, rather than in terms of personality, domestic relations, and substance. However, liberty, equality and security, like the other three terms, are very broad and inclusive. They require further subdivision and specification. Liberty in what respects? In regard to the movement of one's person, the acquisition of property, the use of one's property, or in what other regard? And similarly of equality and security. When we work out answers to these questions we arrive at

---

[1] The word "right" is here used in a broad sense, which includes rights, powers, and privileges (e.g., A's "right" of ownership); and not in the sense of right as we define the term in section 2–19 (i.e., as the correlative of a duty).

about the same place and achieve a list substantially the same as our inventory of individual interests. Nevertheless, as the analysis of individual welfare is often made in terms of liberty, equality, and security, and is very common in judicial opinions, I have included below several problems which are cast in these terms or in some combination of them.

Any selection of material for discussion as well as any classification of it, has its virtues and its shortcomings. These inhere in the emphasis which the selection or classification gives. The analysis of individual welfare in terms of liberty has the advantage of stressing the privileges of the individual; the analysis in terms of security has the advantage of stressing his rights as against others; and the analysis in terms of equality has the virtue of stressing comparisons between one individual and another, so that unperceived discrimination does not enter into the legal treatment of A and of B. The analysis in terms of individual interests, that which we have presented, has the merit of stressing the general importance in legal affairs of the individual's claim; it serves to give weight to the point that a prime policy in wide areas of our law is to give effect and protection to the individual's will.

But you should note that the stress on the individual's claim, as well as the stress on his liberty, equality, and security, means a stress on his advantages. Individuals do not lay claim to burdens. Burdens do not appear in any of the classifications mentioned, except incidentally and as the obverse side of the individual claimant's interests. Of course, a good deal of the time, one man's advantage is another man's burden, and vice versa, so that indirectly the duties of the individual to other individuals are taken account of. But this cannot be said of social duties. The exclusive attention to the individual's claims led to a neglect of claims which were to be made on behalf of society generally. It tended to make lawyers and judges overlook the obligations of the individual in society, unless these obligations were very striking and clear. The result was that social considerations had a hard time achieving recognition with legal, and especially with judicial, policy makers; a slow and painful process which is to be the main theme of sections 7–12 and following.

Sec. 7–10. Conflicting interests—necessity of choice. Every individual interest mentioned in the foregoing sections is limited in scope. No interest is guaranteed without qualification. Even the most extreme individualist thinkers of the last century saw that individual interests overlap and cut across one another at some point. A's freedom to act becomes at some point a violation of B's personal integrity. A's freedom of speech is limited by a duty not to defame B. A's freedom to acquire property does not include the liberty to take property which belongs to another. The simple fact is that A and B alike want the whole world to hold and to move about in, and both cannot have this unrestricted scope for action. The scarcity of space and things imposes necessary problems of division which the policy maker must face in recognizing individual interests.

To furnish a method or general standard for resolving these conflicts of interest, various criteria have been suggested by those thinkers who cast their formulas in terms of individual welfare. For Bentham, the criterion is to be the solution which will procure the greatest happiness for the greatest number; for Spencer, the liberty of each individual is to be limited only by the like liberty for all; for Felix Cohen, a modern writer, the promotion of the good life for all is the criterion to adopt. Obviously such criteria of choice do not furnish ready or easy methods of resolving conflicts. The policy maker is left with a wide range of discretion, both in deciding what interests to recognize and in deciding how far to recognize and secure each interest. Such general standards do define a general approach to legal problems, a general line of attack on them; and the policy maker's approach or line of attack is not without importance, as I shall show later. In any event this kind of general standard is all that the policy maker has to guide his determinations.

But conflicts of interests do not stop with the conflict of A's interest with B's interest. A's interest frequently conflicts directly with a general interest of the community, such as the interest in the public peace or the interest in the public morals. A's freedom of action does not extend so far as to permit him to run naked through the public streets. His freedom of speech does not include the liberty to advocate the overthrow of the existing government by force and violence. At some point the line of demarcation must be drawn between conduct which is, and conduct which is not, permitted. This line is drawn by the policy makers of the community, in the light of the various individual and public interests which they recognize. Such conflicts and the methods of resolving them I shall refer to more in detail presently. For the moment it suffices to say that conflicts of this type are no easier to deal with than the conflicts already discussed, and the methods suggested for resolving them are equally indefinite and difficult to apply.

And finally, even at an early day, practical policy makers of the Anglo-American law realized that there were cases in which the individual, A, was to be protected against his own acts. A's will was not to control, even as to himself. A could not agree to the maiming of his person. The King, it was said, had an interest in maintaining his fitness as a soldier. Also, A could not agree to be killed so as to confer a good defense on his killer. And infants were protected against the effects of their own acts; they could not contract freely. Today we would say that these cases involve countervailing social interests, which the policy maker weighs and finds controlling. But formerly these countervailing interests were not too clearly perceived or named. Such cases were merely treated as exceptional and not allowed to overturn the general principle which made the individual the master of his own destiny.

Sec. 7–11. Problems. 1. Suppose that D states to X that P is a thief. In fact, D speaks on the basis of misinformation; P has not committed any theft, and his innocence becomes obvious upon investigation. D has violated a prohibitive standard, and P is entitled to recover damages for defamation. On what policy is this prohibitive standard based? If D acted in perfect good faith, can he not assert a countervailing interest? At first blush, it might seem that D has a meritorious defense; but we all know that our legal system has not recognized any such privilege on D's part. What does this mean in terms of conflicting interests, i.e., policies?

In the foregoing case, the interest of D is sacrificed to that of P. However, if P had formerly been a servant of D, and if D had, in good faith, answered an inquiry as to P's character, made by Y, another prospective employer, there would again be presented a conflict of interests. But the result would be different; D's act would be privileged (i.e., permitted). Why?

2. In *Ross v. State,* a Texas case decided in 1881,[1] the defendants were convicted of the murder of one Hall, a town marshal who had attempted to arrest them. The appellate court decided, in view of the testimony, that Hall had no legal right to make the arrest. The court stated its conclusion as follows:

"Hall, the deceased, having no right to arrest the defendants or either of them, what were the legal rights of the defendants, if, in preventing this illegal arrest, they or either of them slew him? . . .

"As the law, divine and human, gives the citizen the right to stand upon his individual rights, and to use force against

[1] 10 Tex. App. 455 at 463.

force to successfully prevent the attempted wrong, the citizen whose liberty is thus unlawfully assailed can not only use force, but can increase that force and continue to increase it even to the death if necessary to prevent the attempted wrong, and if he slay his adversary he will be held excused. Otherwise the lawless aggressor, the vindictive oppressor will be permitted to triumph over the rights and liberties of the citizen. Right will be made to do homage to wrong, and look to future redress in the courts of the country. This is not American law. The citizen has the right to maintain his liberty at all hazards, against any and all persons who attempt to invade it unlawfully, taking care not rashly to use or resort to greater violence than is necessary to its protection."

Do you think the court reached a proper solution of the conflicting individual interests here? In holding the defendant's act privileged, the court laid stress on the policy of freedom of movement for the individual. What important community interests (policies) does this court overlook? Compare the following statement in *Smith v. Commonwealth:* [2]

"While personal liberty is a very highly esteemed right, it is better to undergo the ill convenience of an unlawful arrest, from which the law will deliver, than that human life should be sacrificed, and a dispute as to whether an arrest is unlawful should not be decided with pistols, when it is a matter that the magistrate can speedily determine. . . ."

3. How can you justify a compulsory education law, i.e., a law which requires all children to attend school until they reach the age of sixteen? Suppose "little Willie" prefers to spend his time fishing rather than in school attendance?

4. Stephen:

"The result is that discussions about liberty are either misleading or idle, unless we know who wants to do what, by what restraint he is prevented from doing it, and for what reasons it is proposed to remove that restraint.

[2] Smith v. Commonwealth, 196 Ky. 479 (1922).

"Bearing these explanations in mind, I may now observe that the democratic motto involves a contradiction. If human experience proves anything at all, it proves that, if restraints are minimized, if the largest possible measure of liberty is accorded to all human beings, the result will not be equality, but inequality reproducing itself in a geometrical ratio." [3]

To illustrate the force of what Stephen says, let us suppose a case where twenty persons, including A and B, B, are competitors in a particular line of business operating on a national scale. A buys out two competitors; he is then able to obtain supplies at lower prices than B because he buys in larger quantities; he is also able to obtain more favorable treatment in regard to freight rates (rebates); and he can establish advantageous retail outlets for his product. A makes large profits and continues to buy out competitors until only B is left. A then lowers prices so that B is squeezed out of business. What does this story suggest in relation to the point last made by Stephen?

As a matter of fact, some or all of the acts of A above mentioned would be forbidden by federal statutes (Sherman Act, Interstate Commerce Act, Clayton Act, Robinson-Patman Act, etc.). I need not go into details regarding these cross-cutting prohibitions and restraints on A's liberty of contract. What is the general policy behind them?

Policies Regarding the Community

Sec. 7–12. Present-day stress on general welfare. Since the end of the nineteenth century, greater stress has been put on the general good as the objective of legal and governmental policies. Where formerly legal and political problems were discussed almost exclusively in terms of individual claims, discussion today is carried on more and more in terms of the general welfare. By the prevailing doctrine, the indi-

---

[3] Liberty, Equality, Fraternity 182 (1874).

vidual is no longer assumed to have an intrinsic value or to enjoy necessary rights.[1] He is no longer assumed to have essential claims to freedom, equality or security. Instead, there has developed a strong tendency to put the securing of interests on a social basis; a strong tendency to emphasize the good of the community or over-all group.

However, even the switch of attention to community welfare has not represented a complete change of legal policies. It has been, rather, a change of point of view. The policy maker pursues largely the same objectives; but he has a different slant which introduces the social or community welfare factor into his calculations. He recognizes the same policies and objectives under different names. The policy maker of today recognizes the individual's claims, not as such, but for the social good.[2] Thus the policy of recognizing individual interests of personality is justified by the community's interests in the individual's life. Sound and capable individuals may be regarded as necessary to a soundly functioning community. Hence, individual welfare readily be-

---

[1] No doubt the founders of our republic thought of certain individual rights as fundamental and beyond the reach of the policy maker. And in the philosophy of Kant, the individual is assumed to have an intrinsic value. His practical imperative reads: "*Act so as to use humanity, whether in your own person or in the person of another, always as an end, never as merely a means.*" Watson, *Selections from Kant* (Ed., 1927) 246. Probably it is correct to say that the modern exponents of the "higher law" in this country all maintain similar views. Compare discussion of "higher law" views in section 7–45. These writers hold that there are certain parts of human life which are sacred and not to be controlled for the public good.

[2] Individual welfare and social welfare do not, accordingly, represent completely divergent objectives. In a certain area the two kinds of welfare may coincide; the individual may be accorded what he wants because it is good social policy to do so; this is the area of legal recognition of his claims in the form of rights and legal interests. Beyond this area of positive recognition lies another where it may be a matter of indifference, socially speaking, whether the individual's wants are satisfied or not, and where the legal system adopts a policy of neutrality; this is the area of liberties. And beyond this area of indifference and neutrality is one where the individual's claims run counter to the general good, or the good of other individuals; this is the area of legal prohibition. Compare what is said in sections 2–03 to 2–11, inclusive. See also the remarks of Stone regarding the interchangeability of interests seen from different viewpoints. THE PROVINCE AND FUNCTION OF LAW 490–491 (1946).

comes a community objective. In this sense, the state, through its legal system, not only undertakes to secure benefits for its membership as a whole, it also treats the welfare of each individual member as a state objective.

To some extent, the social viewpoint of policy matters is a natural consequence of the fact that policy makers who formulate, and other officials who execute, policies, are social agents. They act for the community, and in its interests. In other words, the machinery of the state is social machinery. This fact tends to give all official thinking a social coloring.[3] It tends to make officials look at all objectives of their activity in terms of the community's welfare. But, in the American legal systems, this tendency to the social or official viewpoint will always be kept within bounds, so long as the present constitutions stand. These instruments prohibit many possible official inroads on the individual's claims. These instruments, together with our individualist tradition, make the individual and his claims the starting point for official action. These instruments take the individual's claims for granted, and have the effect of requiring that social interests be newly established and positively recognized. Our officials cannot forget the individual while they continue to operate under our existing frame of government.[4]

[3] In some parts of the world, this stress on the community interests has been almost as one-sided and exaggerated as the stress on individual welfare was here in the last century. Thus some governments, notably the recent Fascist and Communist regimes, have fallen into ways which sacrifice individual life and personality for some mystical racial goal or party advantage. As is indicated in the text, this extreme of emphasis on group interests would hardly be possible under our American legal systems without a complete change of our constitutions.

Of course, officials may also be controlled by selfish interests or the interests of smaller groups. See next general subtopic, POLICIES REGARDING OTHER GROUPS AND COMMUNITIES.

[4] In fact, our strong recognition of individual claims was achieved as a part of a revolution in which the existing government and its officials were displaced by the efforts of nonofficial individuals. These individuals were able to secure the protection of individual claims in setting up a new government. If English and American history prove anything, they show that an established officialdom does not on its own motion recognize individual interests and confer its blessing on individual claims.

In the following sections, I shall try to present an inventory of legal policies regarding the community. The objectives of these policies I shall call "social interests," following a terminology which has become current through the writings of Pound and others. I shall begin the inventory of social interests with those which are the most ancient and generally recognized:

> Social interests in internal peace and order (sec. 7–13)
> Social interests in security of acquisitions (sec. 7–14)
> Social interests in security of transactions (sec. 7–15)

and then move on to other social interests (secs. 7–18 to 7–24), which have been more recently recognized and adopted.

Sec. 7–13. Social interests in peace and order. Historically, the preservation of peace and order in the community appears to be the earliest objective explicitly recognized and avowedly pursued by politically organized society. It is also probably the most fundamental of all governmental policies, inasmuch as the achievement of most, if not all, other social interests depend upon order. And it is a most comprehensive social policy; it covers a large share of the protection given by government to individual claims against criminal and tortious aggressions by others; and it embraces several social interests to be presently discussed, if the phrase, "peace and order," be used in a broad sense.

Under the existing American legal systems, the chief responsibility for maintenance of peace and order rests with the states, though the federal government may have to act to preserve order in connection with its ordinary operations, e.g., the work of its courts, or may have to deal with an extraordinary situation, e.g., a general rebellion. The principal means employed by the states to preserve peace and order are state and local police forces, consisting of sheriffs, constables and other officers, and state military forces, commonly called militia.[1] The federal government maintains a system of United States marshals, a Federal Bureau of Investigation, and various inspectors and executive officers, as well as its military forces.

On the legal side, the policy of preserving peace and order is expressed or implicit in many prohibitive standards applicable to individuals, especially in the standards of the criminal law. This policy is the basis for punishing murder, rape, robbery, and other acts of violence. This general objective is also evident in many legal limitations on the individual's privilege of self-help. Keeping the peace is involved, too, in numerous correlative standards, applicable to officials. Legal provisions commonly require officials to arrest, suppress, and prosecute individuals who disturb the public order; and the governors and the President are authorized and required by constitutional and statutory provisions to declare martial law in case of serious public disorder.

Sec. 7–14. Social interests in security of acquisitions. You will see in the policy of protecting acquisitions an old familiar face. This policy cannot be regarded as a quite new item in our policy inventories. First, the social interests in the security of acquisitions are already familiar in the sense that they are roughly identical with the individual's interests in holding things.[1] Recognition of these social interests does not constitute any wide departure from the individualist point of view. The social interests merely represent the social bearing of the individual interests. Recognition of the social interests consists essentially in finding a social justification for the protection of individual claims to control things.

---

[1] The militia is a body of citizens of a state, enrolled in its military force on a part-time basis. The militia is not usually called together for actual service except in emergencies. In both respects, the militia is to be distinguished from a regular army, such as that maintained by the federal government.

[1] Sec. 7–08, subdivision b.

Second, the policy of protecting acquisitions may be said to be only a part, or at most, an offshoot, of the policy of preserving peace and order, and in either case, not a new policy. Obviously, the public peace and the security of acquisitions are closely connected. Many disturbances of the peace do relate to the acquisition or control of things; the robber disturbs the public peace at the same time that he violates the security of acquisitions. But the security of acquisitions is such an important phase of public order, and looms so large in legal discussions that it well deserves, and is usually given, a separate place among social interests.[2]

The social interests in protecting individual acquisitions lie behind all the various legal forms in which private property is recognized. As a recent writer says, ". . . substantially the whole law of real and personal property, as well as great parts of the law of torts and crimes, are directed to the security of acquisitions."[3] And these social interests find recognition (along with the individual) in the American constitutions, notably in the provisions forbidding government to deprive persons of property without due process of law, and in various provisions prohibiting retroactive legislation.

"Acquisitions" in this connection refers to acquisitions of land and tangible goods. "Security" refers to the protection given to the individual's claims to such land and goods. So that the social interests in security of acquisitions mean the legal objective of making secure the claims of those who establish control of land or goods in prescribed ways, such as by occupation, by transfer or exchange, by inheritance, etc. The individual claims thus recognized are commonly designated "property rights."[4] They are secured, so far as they

---

[2] After all, the number of policies which we distinguish and the distinctions between them that we make, are to be determined mainly by considerations of convenience and common usage.

[3] STONE, THE PROVINCE AND FUNCTION OF LAW 561 (1946).

[4] "Rights" is here used in a broad sense which includes rights, powers, and privileges.

are secured, by legal remedies, by private actions of different kinds, by limited self-help, and by public prosecution.

Sec. 7–15. Social interests in security of transactions.[1] The policy of recognizing the individual's claims to enforce contracts and other beneficial arrangements with his fellowmen has already been counted among policies regarding the individual. Now, I want to refer to the social reason given for recognizing this claim. All of modern economic life rests upon the sanctity of contractual undertakings. Goods are produced and distributed on the faith of promises by others. Services are performed on a like basis. Security in these respects is the foundation on which all forms of economic activity rest. This security is what Cardozo means when he speaks of the ". . . overmastering need of certainty in the transactions of commercial life."[2]

It is a basic policy of all modern governments to furnish the needed security of transactions. In some measure, this is done by providing preordained patterns for contractual transactions and obligations (forms for effective acts) so that all parties who enter into contractual undertakings can know beforehand what the effects of their acts will be, and thus avoid controversy and misunderstandings. But, of course, the ultimate basis for security of transactions is found in the availability of legal remedies to back up promises made. And, so that the assurance of governmental backing for contractual obligations will be doubly sure, the states are expressly forbidden by the Federal Constitution "to pass any . . . Law impairing the Obligation of Contracts. . . ."[3] This means

---

[1] Transfers of tangible things are also transactions in one sense. However, I have included these under the preceding head. I have followed the usual practice of distinguishing between contracts and other executory transactions on the one hand, and conveyances, sales, and other executed transactions on the other.

[2] THE GROWTH OF THE LAW 111 (1924).

[3] Art. I, Sec. 10.

that no state can legislate in a manner to change the obligatory force of an existing contract.[4]

Sec. 7–16. Problems. 1. The Constitution of the United States gives Congress power "to provide for the Punishment of counterfeiting the Securities and current Coin of the United States."[1] Acting under this authority, Congress has provided for the punishment of persons who counterfeit the money of the United States or attempt or conspire to do so, or who possess tools, plates, or instruments intended to be used for such purpose. Which of the policies (social interests) above mentioned is primarily involved in this constitutional provision and these statutory enactments?

2. Assume that larceny (theft) is defined by the common law as the act of taking and carrying away the goods of another with the intent to deprive the owner permanently thereof. What policy (social interest) lies behind the judicial recognition of this common law offense?

3. It is a settled doctrine of common law that the possessor of a chattel is entitled to legal protection of his control against all the world except a prior possessor or a person who has the immediate right to possession. Stated the other way around, a defendant in a suit for possession of a chattel cannot rely upon the title of a third person *(jus tertii)*; he cannot assert that someone else has a better claim to the chattel than the plaintiff has. These doctrines can result in sustaining against aggression even the control of a plaintiff who has come into possession of a chattel by wrong, e.g., a thief. Obviously, it is not the policy of our legal system to give

---

[4] Literally, the contracts clause seems to preclude any impairment whatever, but the Supreme Court has interpreted it in effect to mean that no state can *unreasonably* impair the obligation of a contract. See further, regarding the interpretation of the contracts clause, the discussion in sec. 5–22 above.

In some respects the due process clauses of the Federal Constitution also give some protection to the obligation of contracts; and the various clauses which preclude retroactive legislation have some protective effect in this regard.

[1] Art. I, Sec. 8.

protection to the wrongdoer as such. What is the policy behind this broad protection of the possessor's control?

4. Consider the following rules regarding the legal capture of a whale:

"In the Greenland whale-fishery, by the English custom, if the first striker lost his hold on the fish, and it was then killed by another, the first had no claim; but he had the whole if he kept fast to the whale until it was struck by the other, although it then broke from the first harpoon. By the custom in the Gallipagos, on the other hand, the first striker had half the whale, although control of the line was lost. Each of these customs has been sustained and acted on by the English courts, and Judge Lowell has decided in accordance with still a third, which gives the whale to the vessel whose iron first remains in it, provided claim be made before cutting in. The ground as put by Lord Mansfield is simply that, were it not for such customs, there must be a sort of warfare perpetually subsisting between the adventurers." [2]

Why is it necessary to have a standard effective act for such cases? What is the prime policy for the court to consider in dealing with such competing possessory claims?

Why do you assume that the English courts adopted a different standard for one place from the standard adopted for another?

5. In a case involving the contention that a foreign corporation, by seeking and obtaining consent to do business in a state, had impliedly agreed to be sued in any county of the consenting state, Holmes, J., dissenting, said:

"In order to enter into most of the relations of life people have to give up some of their Constitutional rights. If a man makes a contract he gives up the Constitutional right that previously he had to be free from the hamper that he puts on himself." *Power Company v. Saunders*, 274 U. S. 490 at 497 (1927).

[2] HOLMES, COMMON LAW 212 (1881).

How would you characterize the "constitutional right" which a man gives up when he makes a contract? What does Holmes mean by "the hamper that he puts upon himself"?

Sec. 7–17. Human control of environment—increased role of government—law and other means of control. Man is affected by his physical environment in many ways. His activities are shaped by the nature of the place and conditions in which he lives. But the effects of environment on him are not the whole story. The rest of the story has to be told in terms of his control over the environment, his use of the means which it provides, and his production of goods and services to meet his own needs. The environment acts upon man, but he reacts upon it. He remakes his surroundings. He prepares himself against the natural forces which he finds about him. He puts cushions between himself and "nature in the raw." He makes clothes, builds shelters, and lights fires to warm himself, and thus is able to live in climatic conditions for which his natural bare body is not adapted. And he makes use of Nature's resources and produces goods and services for his own ends. He cultivates the soil to produce food. He tames and breeds animals to furnish food and power. He takes minerals, coal and petroleum from the earth in order to create tools and produce energy. He builds roads and instruments of transportation. In short, the world in which man lives is largely a world of his own creation; the natural world puts limits on his activities, but man revamps natural conditions, uses natural resources, and creates goods and services to satisfy his wants.

Natural conditions surrounding the community have always been, and still are, reshaped mainly by individuals acting on their own initiative. For example, A ordinarily decides whether to build a house for himself and what kind to build, and he may build it with his own hands if he chooses.

Another individual, B, may specialize in building for others, as the carpenter or mason does. Both A and B are individual enterprisers, and typical of many individuals in the community. Collectively such individuals contribute heavily to the nature of the surroundings in which they and other members of the community live. Similar observations apply to the utilization of natural resources and to the creation of goods and services for the community. Individual enterprisers are the principal users of natural resources, and the principal producers of goods and services for the community. In fact, as I have already pointed out, our American economic system stands on a solid foundation of individual free enterprise.

But individual enterprise is not adequate to meet many of the needs of the community, and, as I have already pointed out, ours is a day of increasing stress on community interests. With this increased stress on community interests has come an increased demand for community services, and this demand it has fallen largely to the lot of government agencies to satisfy.[1] This has meant that government and law have assumed an ever-increasing role in modern society. This development is well illustrated in the history of our American legal systems.[2] Beginning at a period when governmental

[1] Here I have spoken of only two possibilities, individual action and governmental action. There are obviously other possibilities than these two. A man may provide shelter for his family as well as himself; an individual may furnish facilities for others for hire, and a group may provide for the welfare of its own members. But governmental activity is the subject of our story. For our purpose it is not essential to consider all the possible alternatives. It suffices to treat the individual's provision for himself as the only alternative for governmental provision, as this is the simplest and most fundamental alternative, and corresponds with our traditional emphasis on individual free enterprise.

[2] These systems began in a revolution against established authority. The result was an overstress on individual liberty and a belittling of the role of government. Liberty meant, to the men of that day, freedom from governmental restraint. What our Revolutionary forefathers saw in the large was that the liberties of the individual need to be protected and secured against official misdeeds. Governmental control of the individual was, in their eyes, an evil;

functions were held to a minimum, and legal ends were defined in terms of satisfying individual claims, keeping the peace, and securing acquisitions and transactions, government has gradually developed into an institution to perform a wide variety of community services.

" 'Under the compulsion of the changed conditions brought about largely by mechanical and technological development, the modern state has rapidly ceased to resemble the old political organization, whose chief functions were defense, the administration of justice, and the exercise of a rather narrow police power.'[3] 'Today, the state acts also as a doctor, nurse, teacher, insurance organizer, housebuilder, sanitary engineer, chemist, railway controller, supplier of gas, water and electricity, town planner, pensions distributor, provider of transport, hospital organizer, roadmaker, and in a large number of other capacities.' . . .[4]

" 'The supplying of money and credit has become an important government enterprise. In addition to acting as the authority to control the currency, the government has been forced to act as a great credit agency, lending money, either directly or through subsidies, to banks, railroads, insurance companies, private business undertakings, and owners of homes and farms. . . .' " [5]

We are, of course, interested primarily in the effects of this expansion of government functions upon the policies of the legal system. But law is merely one of the means employed by government to effectuate its ends. When we were examining the effectuation of legal standards, we found it necessary to look beyond the strictly legal machinery of

governmental control can always be abused, and is not to be extended beyond what is really necessary; the less government the better, one might say. Compare secs. 7–05, 7–08 and 7–11, problem 2.

[3] BLACHLY and OATMAN, ADMINISTRATIVE LEGISLATION AND ADJUDICATION 1–5 (Brookings Institution, 1934), quoted by FRYER AND BENSON, LEGAL SYSTEM 1089 (1948).

[4] Committee on Ministers' Powers, Vol. II, 1932, Minutes of Evidence, p. 52 (memorandum of W. A. Robson) *ibid*.

[5] BLACHLY AND OATMAN, *loc. cit*.

enforcement and to observe the effects of such governmental activities as taxation, spending, and education. So here, I think it is essential to see legal policies in relation to the policies of government as a whole. A legal policy is always a policy of government. Both law and legal machinery are instruments of government; they are created and maintained by government. The policies of government which are expressed in law are often intertwined with and dependant upon other purposes of government. Thus, for example, a statute which requires an income tax return from each potential taxpayer expresses a legal policy which is merely an adjunct or incident of a fiscal policy of the state. The legal requirement of a return is only intelligible in the light of the income tax setup. Likewise, a statute which limits the loads which may be carried by trucks on public highways is almost meaningless unless one sees that this limit is incident to a governmental undertaking to provide and maintain highways. In other words, the regulation of behavior by prescribed standards is only a part, and often only an incidental part, of government functions. The purposes behind regulations—especially regulations applicable to official acts—cannot be understood apart from the policies behind other functions of government.

Hence, instead of continuing in the following sections with a list of the social interests served by legal regulations, I shall try to provide you with a list of the social interests served by governmental measures of all kinds. The list will include the social interests which are recognized by law, and special emphasis will be put on strictly legal policies and measures. But, for the reasons just indicated, all the major policies and measures of our state and federal governments will be included.

Sec. 7–18. Social interests in natural resources. Man depends upon his natural environment for the basic means of livelihood.[1] The land, the air, the rain, the streams, the lakes, the sea, the forests, the minerals, the fish and other wildlife, are gifts of Nature. So far as these are limited in amount, or irreplaceable, the policy maker has to decide how such natural assets are to be controlled and utilized. He recognizes social interests in their exploitation; or as we commonly say today, he adopts a policy of conservation. He may assign some of these assets to private or individual control; others he may reserve for more or less complete public control. Varying dispositions have been made of different natural resources in different times and circumstances.

Without being too specific as to what we include under the term, we can readily agree that *land* is the most basic of natural resources. Land has been quite consistently assigned by our American legal systems to individual control and ownership. This was the conception of the proper disposal to make of land which prevailed at the time our federal government was founded.[2] The private ownership of land was accordingly recognized from the start, and it remains an established tenet of our governmental policy. However, the general recognition of private ownership has not stood in the way of important legal checks on the owner's control over this natural resource. First, there were checks on the owner's powers of disposition, intended to keep land free from fetters on use and to insure the free alienation of land. It was recognized by our courts and legislators, as it had been

[1] Man also prepares himself against the natural forces that he finds about him. Partly this preparation is the work of individuals, but to a not inconsiderable extent, preparatory and preventive measures of this type are undertaken by government, e.g., flood and fire control; and steps to prevent the spread of disease, e.g., quarantine, premarital examination, vaccination.

[2] Though the ownership of land had not been too general or widespread in England, from which our ancestors came, private ownership of land was the general rule there, and the English settlers all had the ambition, which most had not been able to gratify in England, to own land. Here, land was relatively plentiful; it could only be effectively utilized by individual farmers and settlers. It was natural that private ownership was accepted without question.

by English courts and lawmakers, that the owner of land ought not to be allowed to tie it up perpetually so that it could not be freely used and alienated. The social interests in the full use and free transfer of land were appreciated, and, as a result, the owner's individual interest was limited to a complete *usufruct* for life, coupled with powers to name his successors (by deed, will, etc.) and powers to control their use and disposition of the land for a moderate additional period. Furthermore, the general recognition of private ownership did not in the beginning, and does not now, exclude a considerable degree of governmental control aimed to prevent injury to others by the landowners' activities, e.g., the common-law prohibition of the maintenance of nuisances and statutory prohibitions of the maintenance of dangerous instrumentalities and statutory regulations intended to insure the construction and maintenance of safe and sanitary structures on the land. Nor has the principle of private ownership stood in the way of zoning legislation aimed to insure segregation of uses, and comfortable and, to some extent, aesthetic, conditions of living.[3] And finally, it must be realized that the principle of private ownership was not initially extended to all land. The federal government assumed control of the territories of the West and acted as a governmental proprietor thereof. In fact, the federal government still exercises a not inconsiderable control over the utilization of land through its ownership of vast areas in our western states and in our territorial possessions.[4] As owner, the federal government has

---

[3] Zoning legislation divides up areas, urban or rural, into zones, and permits only particular uses of land in particular zones, such as residential uses, business uses, uses for apartment houses, and factory uses. Usually the statutes which establish zoning confer a considerable degree of discretion on administrative agencies, to fix and change zones and to determine their application in particular cases.

[4] "In the western states the Federal Government owns vast tracts of land. The extent of this public domain may be realized from the following figures: in Arizona, 92 per cent of the lands within that state are owned by the United States Government; in California, 52.58 per cent; in Colorado, 56.67 per cent; in Idaho, 83.80 per cent; in Montana, 65.80 per cent; in Nevada, 87.82 per

been in a position to conserve the resources of this land, e.g., minerals and timber, and to insure its economical exploitation.[5]

Forests and solid minerals, such as coal, have generally been treated as part of the land, and subject to the same principles and policies as the land itself.[6] Oil and gas and subsurface water have usually been regarded as unowned until they are reduced to possession. The owner of the land on which they occur merely has a preferential right to reduce them to control. Nevertheless, the landowner's individual interest in these resources has been subjected to a great deal of legislation of the common regulatory type, intended to control the acts of the individual landowner and the acts of other individuals so as to prevent waste of these important natural resources. Statutes regulating methods of production, use, and marketing of oil and gas are of this type, as well as statutes regulating the utilization of natural water for sale, for power, and for irrigation.[7]

Wild animals, i.e., fish and game, have usually been treated as vacant property. If on private lands, the landowner has an exclusive right to appropriate them to his own use. If on public lands, our legal systems originally adopted the policy of allowing these resources to be freely appropriated by individuals. But in recent years our governments

cent; in New Mexico, 62.83 per cent; in Oregon, 51 per cent; in Utah, 80.18 per cent; in Washington, 40 per cent; in Wyoming, 68 per cent." KERWIN, FEDERAL WATER-POWER LEGISLATION 65 (1926).

[5] Whether the government has actually used its control to the best advantage is another question.

[6] You will be interested to know that in many countries of the world, notably those which belong to the civil law group, all or some of the minerals under land belong to the government and not to the owner of the surface. In those countries, such resources are exploited normally by persons or companies to whom the government grants concessions to search for and extract them from the land.

[7] See, for example, as regards legislation relating to oil and gas: Ford, "Controlling the Production of Oil," 30 MICH. L. REV. 1170 (1932); and as regards the use of water, Hathorn v. Natural Carbonic Gas Co., 194 N. Y. 326 (1909).

have asserted more and more control over wildlife, no matter where it may be, in order to prevent its depletion or complete extinction. This control has been exerted by the states and the federal government, either on the basis of a general social interest in conservation or in the name of public ownership of wildlife.[8]

Other natural assets, such as streams and lakes, are, to a limited extent, recognized as subjects of private ownership. But there is a distinct tendency in the law today to treat streams and lakes, along with the air [9] and the sea, as common property, strictly owned by no one, yet subject to public control of the most sweeping character. Public control is predicated on the policy of making these assets as fully and generally available for the use and enjoyment of all the population as is practicable.[10]

In addition to the above cases, in which the social interest in natural resources is recognized or asserted, we find numerous other instances within the last generation where our governments, especially the federal government, have taken extraordinary pains to safeguard these resources against destruction or injury by natural causes. Public funds have been freely spent to protect forests against destruction by fire, to secure property along rivers against erosion, to drain swamp lands, to reclaim desert lands, and to encourage farmers to use approved methods of land cultivation.

Sec. 7–19. Social interests in production of goods and services. Man creates goods and services to satisfy his own wants. He does not, like wild animals, depend wholly upon the table Nature has set. The individual man may provide

---

[8] See generally BROWN, PERSONAL PROPERTY, sec. 6 (1936).

[9] See Hinman v. Pacific Air Transport quoted in sec. 7–21, problem 1.

[10] See, for example, Collins v. Gerhardt, 237 Mich. 38 (1926), and a comment entitled "Federal Power Act—Jurisdiction and Functions of the Federal Power Commission—Constitutional Limitations," 39 MICH. L. REV. 976 (1941).

for his own needs, or he may, as a business enterprise, undertake to supply the needs of others. Or, in our politically organized society, government may recognize the community's needs for goods and services, and undertake to insure their production for the benefit of the community as a whole.[1] It is this general interest and the measures taken by government to stimulate and control productive processes that are to be the subjects of the present section.

At the end of the eighteenth century when our government was founded, free enterprise was an outstanding fact in this part of the world. Life was primarily agricultural, and each home produced most of its own goods and services. It was not unnatural to develop economic theories and policies based on this condition of affairs. The policy of free enterprise was explicitly formulated and remained the traditional and generally accepted policy into the nineteenth century. This policy recognized individual initiative as the principal means, if not the only means, of inducing the production of goods and services for self and for others. It saw production as a process depending on self-interest to create for oneself, and as a process relying on profits to motivate creation for others. While these theories of production prevailed, there was not too much scope for the recognition of social interests in the productive process, or for governmental interposition in the production of goods and services.[2]

Nevertheless, the policy of free enterprise was not absolute even in the beginning. It has long been recognized that some restraints might be placed on freedom of enterprise, and that some economic enterprises might be sponsored or undertaken

---

[1] Again, as in the last two sections, I limit myself to two alternatives: individual action and governmental action. It seems quite unnecessary for my present purpose to discuss other possibilities. See sec. 7–17, note 1.

[2] "The unfettered right to contract was pressed, as we have seen, during these phases as the indispensable means whereby individuals seize such opportunities, whether of work or profit, as the social and economic environment offers." STONE, THE PROVINCE AND FUNCTION OF LAW 533, 534 (1946).

by government itself. And the policy of free enterprise has suffered further serious inroads as a result of the practical needs of our times and their impact on the thinking of legislatures and courts. Even the individualist cast of our constitutions has not been able to stop these social trends. The scope of individual freedom of enterprise is being perceptibly reduced by the two expedients of increasing the number of governmental regulations on the one hand, and of increasing the number of governmental enterprises on the other. Both these expedients involve the recognition of new social interests, or the expansion of social interests already recognized. The shape which these developments have taken is illustrated in the following materials.

First, free enterprise may be directed to the production of the wrong kinds of goods. The profit motive is not always directed to the creation of useful goods, or the rendition of meritorious services. For example, the producer may be tempted to prepare unwholesome food or drugs for the market. Penalties and inspections may be employed by government in order to insure that his products are of proper quality. Or the producer may choose to prepare marijuana cigarettes, or quack remedies for the market; or he may elect to operate a gambling den, or house of prostitution. The community may decide through its policy makers that such goods and services are always coupled with injurious consequences; the community interest in preventing their production may be recognized and appropriate measures to this end adopted.

Second, the productive processes themselves may be carried out in a way, or with means, which are harmful to the community. Thus, coal needs to be mined, and clothing manufactured, but these industries should not be allowed to operate in ways which endanger the lives, limbs and health of persons who are employed in them. The community is interested in the working conditions in various productive enterprises. It requires the installation of safety devices. It enacts regulative provisions regarding hours and conditions of labor. It prohibits child labor. It charges the persons engaged in producing goods and services with the burden of compensating their workmen for personal injuries suffered in the course of their employment. And, as regards services, such as professional or technical services, government adopts standards to insure the competence and honesty of the persons who render them, e.g., requirements of training for medicine, law, and other professions.

Third, free enterprise may result in monopoly. One large fish may swallow all the rest, or one enterpriser may buy out all his competitors, or join them in restricting the quantity or quality of goods or services rendered to the public. Acts of entrepreneurs, e.g., contracts, conspiracies and consolidations, which result in a monopoly, or which tend to have this effect, may be forbidden outright by law, and administrative agencies may be created to supervise business in order to see that monopolistic trends are controlled. But some kinds of monopoly seem to be inevitable. Such monopolies call for regulation, instead of prohibition, in order to insure the production of the proper amount or kind of goods or services. Thus, the entrepreneur who establishes a local water works usually enjoys a monopoly in fact, as it is not feasible to have several concerns competing in furnishing water to one community. He is not to be left to decide at his discretion on the quantity and quality of service he will give. His monopoly gives him an undue power over others. Such power calls for public control; it has entailed the enactment of many legal regulations, and the creation of a variety of administrative officials to enforce them.

Fourth, the needed but unprofitable enterprise must be reckoned with by government. Since the turn of the century, it has been appreciated ever more clearly that not all the goods and services which the public requires will be produced through individual undertakings inspired by the profit motive. As these goods and services are definitely needed, there is a social interest in their production, and, as individuals do not have sufficient incentives to act, government has no choice but to take a hand in the productive processes. Some products and services can be made available if government becomes the purchaser thereof at an agreed price, e.g., guaranteed prices to farmers. The production of other goods and services can be induced by the offer of a subsidy of some kind, in order to reduce the producer's costs, e.g., subsidies by the federal government to the airlines and the merchant marine. Other goods are produced when government affords protection to the producer as against threatened competition, as in the case of the protective tariff to foster home industry. Other products and services will be forthcoming only if governmental agencies furnish them. Of this last type are public highways and the prosecution of atomic research.

Governmental productive enterprises have become a type so important and so common that they deserve special notice. Such governmental enterprises enter fields which cannot be developed profitably by the individual, fields which involve risks too great for the individual entrepreneur to run, fields which demand an amount of capital which the individual cannot obtain, and fields where the public is dissatisfied (justly or unjustly) with the kind of services rendered by private concerns, such as water works or other utilities. For any or all of these reasons, we find governmental agencies projected into the problems of financing and administering enterprises for the public benefit. Among the earliest ventures of this sort, embarked upon by American governments at public expense, were provisions for streets, highways, and bridges. These could hardly be called business enterprises as they were commonly maintained without cost to the user. More recent governmental undertakings have included water works, sewage disposal facilities, parking lots, transportation facilities and hospitals of various kinds.[3] In the same class fall the provision of parks and playgrounds, the clearance of slums, and the public financing of low-cost housing. And finally, under this head we can place the pending health insurance program of the federal government, which would provide medical and hospital insurance for everybody.[4] All these measures involve chiefly the use of fiscal and administrative powers; government undertakes to create and manage these enterprises to serve the needs of the community.

Sec. 7–20. Social interests in distribution of goods and services. The distribution of goods produced in a community also presents problems of planning for the policy maker.[1] His general end, we shall assume, is to achieve a fair distribution; but great differences of opinion prevail, both as to what constitutes a fair distribution and what are the best methods of bringing such a distribution about. For some collectivists, a fair distribution is an equal distribution of all the goods produced in the community; for others, a fair distribution is one which is relative to the need of the distributee, or to the productive effort which he has put forth. For individualists, the question of the fairness of the ultimate

---

[3] Thus, different branches of government establish hospitals and provide medical care for the indigent, the insane, the feeble-minded, the crippled, the blind and the tuberculous.

[4] Such a program was again urged upon Congress by President Truman recently, having been under discussion for several previous years. Whether this program in its pending form is desirable or feasible, or whether it is likely to be adopted in the near future, need not be debated here. The fact that it is seriously proposed, and the further fact that similar health programs have already been adopted in England, Sweden, and other countries of Europe, do point to a growing sense of responsibility of the modern community for the health of all its members, and to the possible assumption by government of a policy of health protection of a very broad scope.

[1] I use "distribution" to include both the process of distribution (exchange, sale, gift, etc.) and the end result of the process.

distribution is little stressed; it is simply assumed that freedom to produce and to exchange goods and services will result in a satisfactory distribution thereof.[2]

Then there are differences of opinion as regards methods of insuring a fair distribution. According to the theories of various collectivists, the state must intervene to insure a division of the product on whatever basis it determines to be fair. This intervention may involve the use of its regulatory or its fiscal or its administrative powers. The intervention may extend as far as the out-and-out appropriation by government of both production facilities and products, and the assignment of definite shares of the product to individuals by, and in the name of, the state. However, according to our traditional theory of free enterprise, the best method of dividing the product is to allow each producer to obtain whatever share he can by his own productive efforts and the processes of exchange.[3] Under this view, government adopts a hands-off policy as regards the distribution of goods within the community, and permits the economic processes of production and exchange to work themselves out in their own way; government only enters the picture to protect distributees in their holdings and to secure the processes of production and exchange against extreme forms of aggression by outsiders.

---

[2] This is true of the simon-pure advocates of free enterprise; they are not much concerned with the problem of fair distribution; they regard the economic processes of production and distribution as self-sufficient; they are inclined to assume that these processes will work out for the best, if only government does not interfere or tinker with them.

So far as the writers who maintain this view felt that it was necessary to justify the appropriation of a share by A, they found the justification in A's labor as a producer, or in a social compact of some sort. See LOCKE, TWO TREATISES ON GOVERNMENT (London, 6th Imp.) 215 *et seq.* (1764). The justification on the basis of A's labor as producer, is commonly called the "labor theory" of property.

[3] The first part of this statement is an expression of the "labor theory" of property, referred to in the next preceding note. As regards the functions of property, this statement suggests two: "property for use" and "property for exchange." Compare what is said regarding "property for security" in sec. 7–08, b, and "property for power," referred to later in this section (in the discussion of monopoly).

The tendency in the United States has been to make a compromise between extreme individualist and collectivist policies regarding a fair distribution of the community's product (goods and services). In making this compromise, government starts with a policy of distribution along traditional lines of free enterprise, but recognizes a variety of limited countervailing policies which cut down its scope. These countervailing policies are expressed in various regulative, fiscal and administrative measures intended to temper the rigors of free enterprise and protect the community against obvious defects of its operation. These countervailing policies, and the social interests which they recognize, and the governmental measures which they involve, will be the subject of discussion in the following paragraphs.

First, there are regulations intended to make sure that goods and services reach the right persons. For example, certain drugs and poisons and firearms are intended to reach only certain persons in the community. Their general and free distribution is found to be harmful. Opiates and barbiturates are needed by certain persons and may be obtained by them under proper safeguards; but their free use in the community is injurious since it leads to an increase in drug addiction. Pistols may be properly distributed to reliable persons for the purpose of self-defense and the defense of property; they should not be allowed to come into the hands of unreliable persons. Accordingly, these needs for restraints on free distribution are expressed in various restrictive and prohibitive legal provisions which are intended to prevent these products from reaching the hands of the wrong persons.

Second, going far back in Anglo-American law, there have always been some restraints on the opportunities of the "haves" to exact a price from the "have-nots." Some of the oldest examples are our usury legislation and analogous rules of common law and equity.[4] Bentham and other ardent individualists fought hard against usury legislation as a contradiction of the principle that each individual should be allowed to look after his own interests. But restraints on usury, and certain other forms of unfair exaction, persisted in spite of individualist attack; they represented an initial recognition of inequality of bargaining power among individuals, a realization of the truth of the New Testament statement: "Unto everyone that hath shall be given, and he shall have abundance; but from him that hath not shall be taken away even that which he hath." [5] These restraints express a social interest in protecting the weak and needy against the abuse of power by those who already possess a large distributive share of the world's goods. And legal prohibitions or regulations of monopoly are variations played on the same theme. The individual who gets a monopoly in the production of goods and services can exact an unreasonable price for them. This means an undue advantage in the distribution of goods. It means that he obtains an excessive distributive share in the total product of the community in return for what he delivers to others. This kind of monopoly power is either prohibited or is closely regulated. Usually some type of administrative agency is created to fix the price which the monopolist can exact for his product or service. Moreover, the monopoly category with its corresponding social interests and restrictive governmental measures, is assuming an ever-greater place in our legal thinking today. Monopoly is largely a function of time and circumstances. The very fact that a producer can demand a price of some kind for his product or service represents some degree of power over buyers. Temporary conditions may result in a shortage of almost any commodity or service, so as to give

---

[4] E.g., legal restrictions on (or invalidity of) transfers of expectancies by presumptive heirs, and the equitable doctrine that the mortgage debtor cannot waive his equity of redemption.

[5] Matthew XXV: 29.

an unfair advantage to the producer. During the recent war this happened in regard to a variety of commodities, and particularly in regard to rental properties. The situation was made the basis for emergency price regulations. Indeed, notions of monopolistic enterprises, of "business affected with a public interest," and of inequality of bargaining power, have now been so broadly defined by our Supreme Court that Congress and our legislatures are enabled to classify almost any enterprise under these heads, and authorized to regulate its charges and activities accordingly, provided the enterprise seems to these legal policy makers in their wisdom to be making unfair exactions from the public.

Third, government has sometimes used its various powers to guarantee to each individual the enjoyment of a minimum distributive share; not the absolutely equal share which is the professed aim of communism, but a fixed minimum below which the individual's "take" from the community income is not to be allowed to fall. Such a guarantee is seen in legislation which assures to A a minimum wage, an old age pension, employment insurance, workmen's compensation insurance, and health insurance. It is seen in the legislation which exempts his homestead and the tools of his trade from seizure or execution for debt. But on the whole, our legal systems have remained committed to the free enterprise system. Above a minimum they have not tried to guarantee to A an actual distributive share of any kind. Instead, they have guaranteed to A an equal opportunity to acquire a share by his acts. This opportunity is not a distributive share, because when B has acquired something it is no longer open to acquisition by A. And this opportunity is not a guarantee of a job, because when B takes a job, there may be none left for A; B's opportunity to work may exclude A's chance for a job. However, today the job holder is asserting, and to some extent, successfully, preferential and seniority rights with regard to employment. So far as this is true, the job holder has something more than an equal, but empty, opportunity to seek a job; he has a guaranteed opportunity to work, superior to that of others. It is only a few steps further, along this route of a legally secure opportunity to work, to the recognition of a workman's "right to his job"—a right which the protagonists of labor have been vigorously pressing for legal recognition ever since the day of the "sit-down" strike.[6] Whether such recognition will come, and whether it is desirable that it should, is not for us to decide; we are only interested in noting the trend of the times.

Fourth, government has used its tax powers to cut down the distributive share of A, who has acquired a substantial portion of the community's goods or income. If, then, government pays over the proceeds of the levies, directly or indirectly, to B, who has a small share or none at all, this obviously operates to reduce the difference between A's and B's financial positions. For example, our governments in this country have imposed income taxes, graduated to rest more heavily on large incomes; they have exacted estate and inheritance taxes, similarly graduated, from decedent's estates; and they have collected special dues from presumably opulent employers of labor. When government later pays out old age pensions from the proceeds of these impositions, taxes and dues, or when it compensates a workman for losses due to unemployment or injury, government is, in effect, cutting down one set of incomes and enhancing another set. Government is, in effect, charging the free enterprise system with the burden of collecting and paying a minimum share of the community's product to persons who would otherwise receive small, or negligible, distributive shares.

Finally, there are the enterprises undertaken by government which were discussed in the next preceding section

[6] See "Legal Status of the Sit-Down Strike—Legal and Equitable Remedies," 35 MICH. L. REV. 1330 (1937).

(sec. 7–19). I refer to roads, highways, parks, playgrounds, parking lots, water works, sewer systems, housing, hospitals, etc. These enterprises produce services at public expense. Sometimes, such enterprises furnish goods or services, i.e., distribute them, to all equally, gratis or at a nominal charge. Sometimes they furnish goods and services gratis to those who cannot pay, e.g., medicines and medical and hospital services for the indigent; and furnish the same goods and services at a substantial charge to those who can pay. And sometimes they furnish their products to the members of the public at a charge sufficient to sustain the whole burden of financing, as in the case of many modern building projects, parking lot projects, etc., commonly referred to as "self-liquidating."

Sec. 7–21. Problems. 1. Hinman v. Pacific Air Transport.[1]

Haney, Circuit Judge.

"From decrees sustaining motions to dismiss filed by defendants in two suits, appellants appeal and bring for review by this court the rights of a landowner in connection with the flight of aircraft above his land. . . .

"Appellants allege, in the bills under consideration, facts showing diversity of citizenship and that the amount in controversy exceeds $3,000 exclusive of interest and costs; that they are the owners and in possession of 72½ acres of real property in the city of Burbank, Los Angeles county, Cal., 'together with a stratum of airspace superjacent to and overlying said tract . . . and extending upwards . . . to such an altitude as plaintiffs . . . may reasonably expect now or hereafter to utilize, use or occupy said airspace. Without limiting said altitude or defining the upward extent of said stratum of airspace or of plaintiff's ownership, utilization and possession thereof, plaintiffs allege that they . . . may reasonably expect now and hereafter to utilize, use and occupy said airspace and each and every portion thereof to an altitude

---

[1] (U. S., 9th Cir., 1936) 84 F.2d 755 at 756 *et seq.*

of not less than 150 feet above the surface of the land. . . .'
The reasonable value of the property is alleged to be in
excess of $300,000.

"It is then alleged that defendants are engaged in the
business of operating a commercial air line, and that at all
times 'after the month of May, 1929, defendants daily,
repeatedly and upon numerous occasions have disturbed,
invaded and trespassed upon the ownership and possession
of plaintiffs' tract'; that at said times defendants have
operated aircraft in, across, and through said airspace at alti-
tudes less than 100 feet above the surface; that plaintiffs
notified defendants to desist from trespassing on said airspace; and that defendants have disregarded said notice,
unlawfully and against the will of plaintiffs, and continue
and threaten to continue such trespasses. . . .

"The prayer asks an injunction restraining the operation
of the aircraft through the airspace over plaintiff's property
and for $90,000 damages in each of the cases.

"Appellees contend that it is settled law in California that
the owner of land has no property rights in superjacent
airspace, either by code enactments or by judicial decrees and
that the ad coelum doctrine does not apply in California.[2]
We have examined the statutes of California, particularly
California Civil Code, § 659 and § 829, as well as *Grandona
v. Lovdal*, 78 Cal. 611, 21 P. 366, 12 Am. St. Rep. 121;
Wood v. Moulton, 146 Cal. 317, 80 P. 92; and *Kafka v.
Bozio*, 191 Cal. 746, 218 P. 753, 29 A. L. R. 833, but we
find nothing therein to negative the ad coelum formula.
Furthermore, if we should adopt this formula as being the
law, there might be serious doubt as to whether a state statute
could change it without running counter to the Fourteenth
Amendment to the Constitution of the United States. If we
could accept and literally construe the ad coelum doctrine, it
would simplify the solution of this case; however, we reject
that doctrine. We think it is not the law, and that it never
was the law.

"This formula 'from the center of the earth to the sky'
was invented at some remote time in the past when the use

---

[2] *Editor's note:* The court here refers to the old maxim, *"Cujus est solum
ejus est usque ad coelum,"* which meant literally that the owner of land owned
the airspace above it to an indefinite height (to the heavens).

of space above land actual or conceivable was confined to narrow limits, and simply meant that the owner of the land could use the overlying space to such an extent as he was able, and that no one could ever interfere with that use.

"This formula was never taken literally, but was a figurative phrase to express the full and complete ownership of land and the right to whatever superjacent airspace was necessary or convenient to the enjoyment of the land.

"In applying a rule of law, or construing a statute or constitutional provision, we cannot shut our eyes to common knowledge, the progress of civilization, or the experience of mankind. A literal construction of this formula will bring about an absurdity. The sky has no definite location. It is that which presents itself to the eye when looking upward; as we approach it, it recedes. There can be no ownership of infinity, nor can equity prevent a supposed violation of an abstract conception.

"The appellants' case, then, rests upon the assumption that as owners of the soil they have an absolute and present title to all the airspace above the earth's surface, owned by them, to such a height as is, or may become, useful to the enjoyment of their land. This height, the appellants assert in the bill, is of indefinite distance, but not less than 150 feet. . . .

"We believe, and hold, that appellants' premise is unsound. The question presented is applied to a new status and little aid can be found in actual precedent. The solution is found in the application of elementary legal principles. The first and foremost of these principles is that the very essence and origin of the legal right of property is dominion over it. Property must have been reclaimed from the general mass of the earth, and it must be capable by its nature of exclusive possession. Without possession, no right in it can be maintained.

"The air, like the sea, is by its nature incapable of private ownership, except in so far as one may actually use it. This principle was announced long ago by Justinian. It is in fact the basis upon which practically all of our so-called water codes are based.

"We own so much of the space above the ground as we can occupy or make use of, in connection with the enjoyment of our land. This right is not fixed. It varies with our varying needs and is coextensive with them. The owner of land owns as much of the space above him as he uses, but only so long as he uses it. All that lies beyond belongs to the world. "When it is said that man owns, or may own, to the heavens, that merely means that no one can acquire a right to the space above him that will limit him in whatever use he can make of it as part of his enjoyment of the land. To this extent his title to the air is paramount. No other person can acquire any title or exclusive right to any space above him.

"Any use of such air or space by others which is injurious to his land, or which constitutes an actual interference with his possession or his beneficial use thereof, would be a trespass for which he would have remedy. But any claim of the land-owner beyond this cannot find a precedent in law, nor support in reason."

How far does the court recognize the claims of Hinman, and another, to the airspace over their land? What social interest in this space does the court recognize? [3]

How does the court dispose of the old maxim according to which the possessor of land has "possession of the column of air situated above the surface to an indefinite height"?

2. *Crane v. Campbell, Sheriff.*[4]

Mr. Justice McReynolds delivered the opinion of the Court.

"The question presented for our determination is whether the Idaho statute, in so far as it undertakes to render criminal the mere possession of whiskey for personal use, conflicts with that portion of the Fourteenth Amendment which declares

---

[3] The scope of the social interest in the airspace over privately owned land has been variously conceived and defined in the case law and statutes. See Ball, "The Vertical Extent of Ownership in Land," 6 UNIV. OF PA. L. REV. 631 (1928); and RESTATEMENT OF TORTS, Explanatory Notes, Tentative Draft No. 7, 1931, p. 51. This matter is a subject for your further consideration in your courses in Torts and Rights in Land. For our present purpose, the only important points are (1) that a social interest is recognized where none would have even been suggested before 1900, and (2) that the individual land-owner's interest is correspondingly limited.

[4] 245 U. S. 304 at 305 *et seq.* (1917).

'No State shall make or enforce any law which shall abridge the privileges or immunities of citizens of the United States; nor shall any State deprive any person of life, liberty, or property without due process of law. . . .'

"It must now be regarded as settled that, on account of their well-known noxious qualities and the extraordinary evils shown by experience commonly to be consequent to their use, a State has power absolutely to prohibit manufacture, gift, purchase, sale, or transportation of intoxicating liquors within its borders without violating the guarantees of the Fourteenth Amendment. . . .

"As the State has the power above indicated to prohibit, it may adopt such measures as are reasonably appropriate or needful to render exercise of that power effective. . . . And, considering the notorious difficulties always attendant upon efforts to suppress traffic in liquors, we are unable to say that the challenged inhibition of their possession was arbitrary and unreasonable or without proper relation to the legitimate legislative purpose.

"We further think it clearly follows from our numerous decisions upholding prohibition legislation that the right to hold intoxicating liquors for personal use is not one of those fundamental privileges of a citizen of the United States which no State may abridge. A contrary view would be incompatible with the undoubted power to prevent manufacture, gift, sale, purchase or transportation of such articles—the only feasible ways of getting them. An assured right of possession would necessarily imply some adequate method to obtain not subject to destruction at the will of the State.

"The judgment of the court below must be

"Affirmed."

What individual interest did Crane assert here?

What social interests lay behind this Idaho statute, according to the Supreme Court?

How did the Court square the recognition of these statutory aims with the policies of the Fourteenth Amendment?

How did the Court connect the mere possession of liquor (like Crane's) with the production and distribution of this prohibited article?

3. *Adkins v. Children's Hospital.*[5]

Mr. Justice Sutherland delivered the opinion of the Court.

"The question presented for determination by these appeals is the constitutionality of the Act of September 19, 1918, providing for the fixing of minimum wages for women and children in the District of Columbia, 40 Stat. 960, c. 174. . . .

"The statute now under consideration is attacked upon the ground that it authorizes an unconstitutional interference with the freedom of contract included within the guaranties of the due process clause of the Fifth Amendment. That the right to contract about one's affairs is a part of the liberty of the individual protected by this clause, is settled by the decisions of this Court and is no longer open to question. . . . (Citations including *Adair v. United States,* 208 U. S. 161). . . . Within this liberty are contracts of employment of labor. In making such contracts, generally speaking, the parties have an equal right to obtain from each other the best terms they can as the result of private bargaining.

"In *Adair v. United States, supra,* Mr. Justice Harlan (pp. 174, 175), speaking for the Court, said:

" 'The right of a person to sell his labor upon such terms as he deems proper is, in its essence, the same as the right of the purchaser of labor to prescribe the conditions upon which he will accept such labor from the person offering to sell. . . . In all such particulars, the employer and employed have equality of right, and any legislation that disturbs that equality is an arbitrary interference with the liberty of contract which no government can legally justify in a free land. . . .'

"There is, of course, no such thing as absolute freedom of contract. It is subject to a great variety of restraints. But freedom of contract is, nevertheless, the general rule and restraint the exception; and the exercise of legislative author-

[5] 261 U. S. 525 at 539 *et seq.* (1923).

ity to abridge it can be justified only by the existence of exceptional circumstances. Whether these circumstances exist in the present case constitutes the question to be answered. . . ."

The Court (three justices dissenting and one justice not sitting) decided this question in the negative and held the statute unconstitutional.

What is the policy ascribed by the Court to the framers of the Fifth Amendment? What becomes of the social interest which the Congress of the United States recognized and attempted to protect?

However, in *West Coast Hotel Co. v. Parrish*,[6] the *Adkins Case* was overruled and minimum wage legislation was held to be valid (four justices dissenting).

"Mr. Chief Justice Hughes delivered the opinion of the Court.

"This case presents the question of the constitutional validity of the minimum wage law of the State of Washington. . . .

"The appellant conducts a hotel. The appellee Elsie Parrish was employed as a chambermaid and (with her husband) brought this suit to recover the difference between the wages paid her and the minimum wage fixed pursuant to the state law. The minimum wage was $14.50 per week of 48 hours. The appellant challenged the act as repugnant to the due process clause of the Fourteenth Amendment of the Constitution of the United States. The Supreme Court of the State, reversing the trial court, sustained the statute and directed judgment for the plaintiffs. *Parrish v. West Coast Hotel Co.*, 185 Wash. 581; 55 P. (2d) 1083. The case is here on appeal.

"The appellant relies upon the decision of this Court in *Adkins v. Children's Hospital*, 261 U. S. 525, which held invalid the District of Columbia Minimum Wage Act, which was attacked under the due process clause of the Fifth Amendment. . . .

"The point that has been strongly stressed that adult employees should be deemed competent to make their own

[6] 300 U. S. 379 (1937).

contracts was decisively met nearly forty years ago in *Holden v. Hardy*, supra,[7] where we pointed out the inequality in the footing of the parties. We said (*Id.*, 397):

" 'The legislature has also recognized the fact, which the experience of legislators in many States has corroborated, that the proprietors of these establishments and their operatives do not stand upon an equality, and that their interests are, to a certain extent, conflicting. The former naturally desire to obtain as much labor as possible from their employees, while the latter are often induced by the fear of discharge to conform to regulations which their judgment, fairly exercised, would pronounce to be detrimental to their health or strength. In other words, the proprietors lay down the rules and the laborers are practically constrained to obey them. In such cases, self interest is often an unsafe guide, and the legislature may properly interpose its authority.'

"And we added that the fact 'that both parties are of full age and competent to contract does not necessarily deprive the State of the power to interfere where the parties do not stand upon an equality, or where the public health demands that one party to the contract shall be protected against himself.' 'The State still retains an interest in his welfare, however reckless he may be. The whole is no greater than the sum of all the parts, and when the individual health, safety and welfare are sacrificed or neglected, the State must suffer.' . . .

"We think that the views thus expressed are sound and that the decision in the *Adkins Case* was a departure from the true application of the principles governing the regulation by the State of the relation of employer and employed. . . .

"There is an additional and compelling consideration which recent economic experience has brought into a strong light. The exploitation of a class of workers who are in an unequal position with respect to bargaining power and are thus relatively defenseless against the denial of a living wage is not only detrimental to their health and well being but casts a direct burden for their support upon the community. What these workers lose in wages the taxpayers are called upon to pay. The bare cost of living must be met. We may

---

[7] *Editor's note:* 169 U. S. 366 (1898).

take judicial notice of the unparalleled demands for relief which arose during the recent period of depression and still continue to an alarming extent despite the degree of economic recovery which has been achieved. It is unnecessary to cite official statistics to establish what is of common knowledge through the length and breadth of the land. While in the instant case no factual brief has been presented, there is no reason to doubt that the State of Washington has encountered the same social problem that is present elsewhere. The community is not bound to provide what is in effect a subsidy for unconscionable employers. The community may direct its lawmaking power to correct the abuse which springs from their selfish disregard of the public interest. . . .

"Our conclusion is that the case of *Adkins v. Children's Hospital, supra,* should be, and it is, overruled. The judgment of the Supreme Court of the State of Washington is

"*Affirmed.*"

This decision gave judicial sanction to the legislative recognition of a social interest in minimum wages. How would you characterize this interest? How is it to be reconciled with the policy of free contract expressed in the Fourteenth Amendment?

Sec. 7–22. Social interests in human stock. With Alexander Pope, the policy maker can say that the proper study of mankind is man. Almost everything that has been said from the beginning of our story has told how the policy maker concerns himself with ways of controlling and protecting an existing generation of men. But the policy maker may also be confronted by basic population problems. He may consider the future of the human stock. He may face problems which relate to the quantity and quality of tomorrow's population; he may take measures to control the number and kind of individuals who will make up the community.

As regards quantity, the dangers of overpopulation have been most often suggested by theoretical writers. For example, Malthus and others have stressed the tendency of population to outgrow the available food supply. Practical policy makers have occasionally made overpopulation an excuse for an aggressive foreign policy in which additional *Lebensraum* was sought. For the most part, however, practical policy makers have worried rather about the possibility that the human stock, or the particular branch of it to which they happened to belong, would die out. Occasionally in world history, some policy maker, like Hitler or Mussolini, has sung both songs at the same time, without any real regard for consistency. He has demanded more room and encouraged the production of more cannon fodder at the same time. In this country, government has, on the whole, pursued a policy of *laissez faire* in this area as in many others. While this policy can hardly be identified with a definite purpose to foster an increase in population, the net effect of *laissez faire* has been just that. The population of our country has increased, through births and immigration, many fold in the one hundred and seventy years of its independent existence. Most of us take pride in our rising population figures, national and local. Certainly, there is no indication yet of a serious legislative purpose to check or limit the number of persons who are to inhabit our country; and so far, there has not been any occasion for legislators to consider offering positive incentives for a population increase.

As regards the quality of our population, more concern has been manifested in recent decades and has found expression in governmental measures. Eugenists have been telling us for several decades that the human stock is rapidly degenerating in quality. They ascribe the degenerative trend to reverse selection in the processes of human reproduction. They declare that this reverse selection is due to wars which kill off the better, stronger men and thereby leave the next generation to be fathered by the less fit members who are not taken for military service; that it is due to reckless procreation by unfit persons, such as the feeble-minded, as compared with restraint and birth control exercised by the better stock, thereby increasing the proportion of the unfit in each succeeding generation; and that it is due to our general humanitarian measures, such as hospital and maternity care, sanitation, etc., which keep the unfit and weak alive so they can reproduce their kind, instead of allowing them to be eliminated by the operation of disease, starvation, and other natural causes. Not all scientists agree that this picture of degeneration is an established fact,[1] but many of our legislatures have accepted the statements of eugenists as correct and have made them the basis for laws to provide for the sterilization of unfit persons. The immediate purpose of this legislation is to check the downward trend of the human stock by preventing the further procreation of its inferior members. A secondary purpose is to reduce the burden of weak and unfit persons which future generations will have to care for and support.[2]

Query: The same persons who support the sterilization program also aid in the establishment of birth control clinics in many of our cities, to furnish contraceptive information and devices to the poor. Why? These same persons are also opposed to legislation prohibiting the dissemination of contraceptive information and devices; they claim that such legis-

---

[1] And some religious groups are strongly opposed to the eugenic program of sterilization as well as birth control clinics to aid in cutting down the birth rate among the poorer classes. Such measures are held to be contrary to divine law. See ENCYCLICAL OF POPE PIUS XI, "On Christian Marriage," Dec., 1930 (Paulist Press).

[2] Of late years also, more and more concern has been expressed about the increasing proportion of the aged in our population. This increase is ascribable chiefly to improvement in living conditions and to advances in medicine. The net effect of the increase in the percentage of elderly people will obviously be felt in the pension burden of the future, and probably in other ways which affect the taxpayers. However, thus far no policy makers have shown any indication of a desire to cut down the length of life, though perhaps some policy makers, in granting old age pensions, have been troubled by the prospect of an ever-growing burden.

lation operates as an adverse qualitative measure. Why do they say that this is its effect? In form, such legislation is merely a prohibition of individual checks on the quantity of population.

Sec. 7–23. Social interests in transmitting knowledge. Man's creative efforts as regards his environment do not stop with his immediate physical surroundings. Man develops a social environment as well.

"On top of the natural physical environment such as the ape-man and his kind had to deal with, our bigger brains have built an *artificial environment* made up of ideas, tools, customs, institutions, skills, techniques of all kinds, man-made and absolutely essential to our well-being. This is the social heritage, or *culture*." [1]

This artificial or man-made environment is transmitted from one generation to another. Each new generation is indoctrinated with the learning of the past. Thus, each new generation of men is enabled to begin with the fruits of the experience of its predecessors and not start with a clean sheet.

It is possible to leave the transmission of the cultural heritage wholly to the efforts of individuals. Much of the work of transmitting does occur in this way; parents instruct children, age instructs youth, and friend instructs friend. But this method can be modified and formalized by the organization of schools. The earliest schools in Anglo-American history were church schools or private schools. However, the fathers of our country cherished, and undertook to realize, an ideal of public education.[2] The states early as-

[1] COOLEY, ANGELL and CARR, INTRODUCTORY SOCIOLOGY 6 (1933).

[2] Interestingly enough, the fathers of our country adopted an exactly opposite policy as regards religion, and embodied that policy in our constitutions. They explicitly forbade the establishment of a state religion by the First Amendment to the Federal Constitution and by many of the state constitutions. This prohibition was the outcome of unfortunate experiences with established religions, both in Europe and in the American colonies. Religion was to be left to the free choice of the individual, or to groups voluntarily formed. Government was not to exercise any preference among religions, or to con-

sumed the task of bringing the knowledge which had been accumulated in past ages to our entire population. We who are committed to the tenets of democracy can hardly doubt the soundness of what Lowell once said: "But it was in making education not only common to all, but in some sense compulsory on all, that the destiny of the free republics of America was practically settled." [3]

The educational function is, of course, primarily concerned with the maintenance of schools for children. However, today we also find public agencies furnishing education to adults, sponsoring musical and artistic programs, furnishing instruction in farming methods, and providing informational radio broadcasts of many types. In some parts of the country, public or semi-public agencies also provide artistic and physical training, and furnish information regarding health and care of children. Indeed, I believe we can see in present trends a greater public interest in positive moral training. For example, a systematic sex education is now being given in some of our public schools, and ideas of fairness, sportsmanship, and proper social behavior are being stressed there in more definite form than they have ever been before.

Query: Why does the state undertake the task of education? Why not leave education of each individual to his own initiative or to that of his family? Why not leave education to the initiative of persons who start private schools? Why not leave education to such agencies as the church?

Sec. 7–24. Social interests in growth of knowledge—freedom of opinion and expression. The state may take account of the need to develop new ideas as well as the need to

tribute to their support. Jefferson and Madison were among the early protagonists of these views, and were largely responsible for their general adoption. For an interesting discussion of this whole problem as it stands today, see Everson v. Board of Education, 330 U. S. 1 (1947).

[3] AMONG MY BOOKS, "New England Two Centuries Ago" 237 (1877).

disseminate the knowledge which has been handed down from the past. Our American governments have always put great stress on the need for progress in knowledge.[1] They have adopted progress as a major objective to be pursued, and have recognized freedom of thought and expression as the primary means of achieving it.

New ideas originate with individuals, hence opportunity must be allowed to individuals to invent them. As Mill says, the function of liberty is to encourage "different experiments of living," which is another way of saying that individual liberty is the means of developing new ideas. As a state policy we find this objective of developing further knowledge expressed in constitutional provisions which guarantee freedom of the mind in the form of free thought and free opinion.[2] We find it expressed in the clause of the Federal Constitution which empowers Congress "to promote the Progress of Science and useful Arts by securing for limited Times to Authors and Inventors the exclusive Right to their respective Writings and Discoveries." [3] The one type of clause shows government guaranteeing freedom to think out new ideas; the other shows it offering positive encouragement for the use of this freedom along socially useful lines.

But new ideas have to be tested. Free discussion is recognized by our governments as the principal method of testing. It is recognized as the sieve through which new ideas must pass in order to become accepted. Accordingly, freedom of discussion is to be encouraged. As a state policy we find this

[1] Among social interests may be counted progress in various other respects, especially progress in regard to the material conditions of life. Several such social interests have already been mentioned, though the name "progress" has not heretofore been used. Thus, better peace and order in the community, greater security for acquisitions, enhanced security of transactions, better utilization of natural resources, more adequate production of needed goods, are all forms of progressive development.

[2] The First and Fourteenth Amendments to the Federal Constitution and similar provisions of state constitutions.

[3] Art. I, Sec. 8, Cl. 8.

objective expressed in constitutional clauses which guarantee freedom of speech, freedom of the press, and freedom of assembly. Our governments pursue a definite policy of *laissez faire* in this regard. Justice Holmes has expressed this policy in a passage which is one of the finest in our legal literature:

"Persecution for the expression of opinions seems to me perfectly logical. If you have no doubt of your premises or your power and want a certain result with all your heart you naturally express your wishes in law and sweep away all opposition. . . . But when men have realized that time has upset many fighting faiths, they may come to believe even more than they believe the very foundations of their own conduct that the ultimate good desired is better reached by free trade in ideas—that the best test of truth is the power of the thought to get itself accepted in the competition of the market, and that truth is the only ground upon which their wishes safely can be carried out. That at any rate is the theory of our Constitution. It is an experiment, as all life is an experiment. Every year if not every day we have to wage our salvation upon some prophecy based upon imperfect knowledge. While that experiment is part of our system, I think that we should be eternally vigilant against attempts to check the expression of opinions that we loathe and believe to be fraught with death, unless they so imminently threaten immediate interference with the lawful and pressing purposes of the law that an immediate check is required to save the country. . . ." [4]

This policy of free trade in ideas is still maintained by our governments, especially by the federal government. Although the policy of *laissez faire* has suffered serious inroads in the sphere of economic activity (business, property and contracts), the collectivist trend has not been effective to cut markedly into the sphere of freedom of opinion and freedom of expression. One finds these freedoms as rigorously upheld

[4] Dissenting opinion in Abrams v. United States, 250 U. S. 616 at 630 (1919).

in the recent decisions of the Supreme Court as they ever were in the early days of our history.

Sec. 7–25. Inventory as check list. The items mentioned in the last section complete our inventory of social interests. Before I leave the subject of social interests, however, I want to say a few words about the utility of such an inventory. The inventory is primarily useful to the policy maker. It consists of actual objectives pursued, adopted, or professed by policy makers of the past. It serves the policy maker of today as a list of possible objectives to consider. Like the list of purchases that I intend to make on a trip to town, an inventory of social interests serves the policy maker as a check list. With such a list in hand, the policy maker is insured against the possibility of overlooking or forgetting any item.

Two special dangers of overlooking social interests accentuate the need for a check list such as this inventory. The first danger inheres in the one-sided emphasis on the claims of the individual which has characterized our legal tradition from the beginning down to the present time. This emphasis invites a neglect of social interests which can result in some rather radical miscarriages of justice. You will remember, for example, the *Ross* case, where individuals were allowed to defend their liberty, even to the point of killing a peace officer who was attempting to arrest them without proper authority.[1] It is possible that not even a check list of social interests would have changed the results in that case, decided under the influence of frontier conditions. Nevertheless, an explicit notice of countervailing social interests would at least have prevented an inadvertent conclusion like that of this case.[2]

[1] See sec. 7–11, problem 2.

[2] This is the purport of a frequently quoted critical comment by Holmes, relative to the individualist slant of our judges at the end of the last century:

"I think that the judges themselves have failed adequately to recognize their duty of weighing considerations of social advantage. The duty is inevitable, and the result of the often proclaimed judicial aversion to deal with such

The second danger inheres in the fact that social interests have to be asserted by officials acting as the representatives of the general good. Individual interests are asserted ordinarily by persons motivated by their own selfish wants; [3] officials only enter the picture in the sense that they grant or withhold recognition to what the individual claims. But as regards social interests, officials not only grant recognition, but executive officials, e.g., prosecutors, are charged with the burden of asserting these interests as well. Their motives for asserting them are not so strong on the whole as the motives of individuals for asserting their own interests. If these social interests are not clearly stated or announced, it is easier for the public official to neglect or lose sight of them.

The inventory also provides a check list for the scholar and the student who try to understand, to predict, or to criticise the operation of the legal system. The social interests enumerated are basic objectives for all the legal processes; for the process of creating law, the process of applying or interpreting it, the process of repealing or changing it. If you, as students, attempt to explain or predict a particular statutory enactment, a particular judicial decision, or a particular type of official action, you will do so predominantly in terms of social welfare. If you approve a particular provision of statute, a particular judicial decision, or a particular type of individual or official action, your basic reason for approval will be that the provision, decision, or action harmonizes with one or more of the listed social interests or conduces to the achievement of one or more of such interests. If you disapprove a particular provision of statute, a particular decision, or a particular type of individual or official action, your basic reason for disapproval will be that the provision, deci-

considerations is simply to leave the very ground and foundation of judgments inarticulate, and often unconscious, as I have said." Holmes, "The Path of the Law," 10 HARV. L. REV. 457 at 467 (1897).

[3] Trustees, guardians, executors and administrators, however, assert claims on behalf of others.

sion, or action runs counter to one or more of the listed interests, or that it fails to take account of all the legal ends that ought to be considered in the situation where the provision, decision, or action operates. In other words, this inventory gives you a set of basic factors to use in explaining and predicting all types of activities which fall within the framework of the legal system, and a set of recognized criteria for judging the soundness of these activities.[4]

Sec. 7–26. Conflicting policies—necessity of choice. But policies conflict with one another; they overlap and cut across one another. The policy maker must choose between them. He cannot give effect to any of them without limit. The pursuit of each and every one of the policy objectives in our inventory has to be qualified by the pursuit of other crosscutting objectives. Even a man's right to life, or the community's interest in having his life continue, cannot be treated as absolute; the policy maker ordinarily calls upon the individual to risk his life in defense of the state, and often provides for the forfeiture of the individual's life as a punishment for crime. Similarly, the objective of maintaining the security of acquisitions may have to be qualified by the fiscal needs of the state. The owner of property will not be allowed to hold it without obligations. The man who has a large income may have the lion's share of it taken away under

[4] It is well to remember that different authors make different inventories of state policies and social interests. They classify objectives in various ways, and emphasize different aspects of the general welfare. I mention this point because I do not want to suggest that my inventory is anything more than a convenient one, one of many possibilities. I certainly do not regard this inventory as necessary, final, or complete. Compare, for example, Pound's inventory to be found in his *Outline of Jurisprudence* (5th ed.) 96 *et seq.* (1943).

Furthermore, variant names are used by different writers for what I have called "policies" and "interests." Judges often refer to them as "rights" and "public policies." Pound sometimes calls them "legal ends." More often, he refers to them as "social interests." The name which is chosen is not too important. It is important, however, to realize that substantially the same thing may be meant by different names. If this fact is not appreciated one may fail to recognize the rose when someone chances to call it by another name.

present legislation in the form of income taxation. The confirmed bachelor may be charged a heavy school tax to educate the children of others. The security of acquisitions is qualified by other public needs such as the need to support the state itself and all its varied undertakings.

So a mere inventory of policies is not enough. It will not resolve these conflicts. Even when he has an inventory before him, the policy maker must choose between conflicting and cross cutting interests. He still has the problem of weighing one interest against another, and deciding which is to be preferred where both cannot receive recognition. Can we offer the policy maker any guidance in making his choice? Do we give him any landmarks to go by in steering between conflicting social interests?

We can offer the policy maker a general picture of what he is trying to do. We can remind him that his over-all objective is to serve the welfare of the community; or, in line with the old tradition, to secure the claims of the individual. Or, we can give him a general picture in somewhat more detail, such as the following by Pound:

"For the purpose of understanding the law of today I am content with a picture of satisfying as much of the whole body of human wants as we may with the least sacrifice. I am content to think of law as a social institution to satisfy social wants—the claims and demands involved in the existence of civilized society—by giving effect to as much as we may with the least sacrifice, so far as such wants may be satisfied or such claims given effect by an ordering of human conduct through politically organized society. For present purposes, I am content to see in legal history the record of a continually wider recognizing and satisfying of human wants or claims or desires through social control; a more embracing and more effective securing of social interests; a continually more complete and effective elimination of waste and precluding of friction in human enjoyment of the goods of existence—in short, a continually more efficacious social engineering." [1]

Here, Pound views the law "as a social institution to satisfy social wants." This is its grand objective. It is intended to further the general welfare by recognizing and satisfying as far as possible "the whole body of human wants." The task of legal regulation is one of "a continually more efficacious social engineering." While these ways of defining the policy maker's problem are as good as any I have seen, they are chiefly valuable for the purpose of perspective. They define a point of view for the policy maker. They do not furnish him any easy criterion for resolving conflicts between social interests. He is merely admonished to bear in mind social wants and to try to satisfy as many of them as he can. Such suggestions to the policy maker are about on a par with the common admonition to an individual, "Be good." Nevertheless, they do define a social approach for the policy maker. In this sense they have significance in guiding his determinations.

Beyond such general pictures, one is not able to offer the policy maker much guidance in making his choice. Particular policy makers may be helped and controlled by rules and presumptions of various sorts, as we shall find in the next subtopic. But on the whole, the guidance which previous policy makers and theoretical writers can offer is not great. The reason is not far to seek. Social interests and individual interests are not quantitative ideas which can be measured in terms of size or heaviness. They cannot be reduced to units, laid on two sides of a scale, and weighed. The weighing of interests is rather a metaphor than a description of an actual process. Competing interests are incommensurable, and yet the policy maker must choose which interest to secure

[1] INTRODUCTION TO THE PHILOSOPHY OF LAW 98 (1922).

and how far to secure it. The weighing of interests reminds of Bentham's hedonistic calculus of happiness factors. In fact, Bentham's formula of justice, the greatest happiness of the greatest number, is not very different from Pound's general picture "of satisfying as much of the whole body of human wants as we may with the least sacrifice." Both schemes involve essentially the same problems of trying to measure the immeasurable. In the last analysis, much is left to the policy makers' unguided judgment and his unconscious reactions; the policy makers' choice is affected more by personal and social factors than by instructions regarding the method of choice.

Sec. 7–27. Problems. 1. Consider the relation to the growth of knowledge of such governmental projects as the recently developed research in atomic physics, the government supported program of research in medicine and general science, and the long-established research of the Department of Agriculture. Are these governmental measures consistent with the policy described in section 7–24? On what basis can such measures be justified?

2. What is the significance of the extensive research programs carried on by large industrial enterprises, such as General Motors, General Electric, and United States Rubber, which engage large numbers of experts as employees to work out problems of improving their respective products? How is this method of producing new ideas related to the policies described in section 7–24?

3. *Brown:*

"As the student has doubtless long since discovered it is frequently impossible for the law to mete out exact justice. Often contending parties each present claims which in themselves are worthy of recognition and protection, but which unfortunately so conflict that both cannot be satisfied. In such a situation the law has no other alternative than to make a choice, recognizing that in so doing one of the parties must be made to suffer in spite of his freedom from any fault. Such an occasion is presented when one who has no title to a specific chattel, and no right to sell it, nevertheless does so sell it to another who in good faith pays full value therefor to the wrongful vendor. Either the rightful owner must lose the goods, which are retained by the *bona fide* purchaser, or the *bona fide* purchaser must surrender the goods to the rightful owner and lose the price which he has paid to the wrongful seller. The recognition of the original owner's claim as against that of the innocent purchaser is moreover injurious to the interests which society has in fostering trade and commerce. Business will suffer if purchasers cannot be assured of the title to the goods which they buy. In this dilemma the common law, as well as the civil law, has chosen to prefer the claims of the rightful owner, though as will be seen considerable of a compromise has been made. . . .[1]

"The most notable exception to the rule that no title to property can be passed by one who is himself without title, is in the case of money and of negotiable commercial paper such as promissory notes, bills of exchange and bank checks. It is obvious that this exception is due to the exigencies of trade and commerce which demand that the media in which payment is made shall circulate freely from hand to hand without placing upon the recipient the burden of determining the state of the title of him who offers the money or commercial paper in payment, usually an impossible task. . . .

"This principle fully established in the common law is now codified in the Uniform Negotiable Instruments Act in force in every state of the United States." [2]

How far does Brown work out the solution here in terms of individual interests? How far in terms of social interests?

Specifically, what are the conflicting social interests here? Which interest is preferred and why?

---

[1] As a matter of fact, Brown is in error in his statement of the civil law. French law, as well as the law of Germany and other continental countries, has adopted the proposition that possession is the equivalent of title (*possession vaut titre*), and accordingly any possessor can confer legal title on a *bona fide* purchaser for value; only the thief and the finder are unable to give the purchaser a good title.

[2] BROWN, PERSONAL PROPERTY, secs. 67, 69 (1936).

4. Suppose the legislature of state X is considering the enactment of a compulsory vaccination law, and realizes that a large group of persons in the community adheres to the Christian Science faith and is opposed to vaccination. Which of the governmental policies mentioned in our inventory are involved? Which would probably be preferred in this situation? Why?

5. In *Gitlow v. New York*,[3] the Supreme Court of the United States upheld a New York statute punishing those who advocate, advise, or teach the duty, necessity or propriety of overthrowing or overturning organized government by force, violence or any unlawful means, or who print, publish, or knowingly circulate any book, paper, etc., advocating, advising or teaching the doctrine that organized government should be so overthrown. The majority opinion declared that this statute did not penalize the utterance or publication of abstract doctrine or academic discussion having no quality of incitement to any concrete act, but denounced the advocacy of action for accomplishing the overthrow of organized government by unlawful means. And the majority opinion held the statute to be constitutionally applied in prosecuting defendants for printing and publishing a "MANIFESTO" advocating and urging mass action which should progressively foment industrial disturbances and, through political mass strikes and revolutionary mass action, overthrow and destroy organized parliamentary government; even though the advocacy was in general terms and not addressed to particular immediate acts or to particular persons.

Mr. Justice Holmes dissented; he said:

"Mr. Justice Brandeis and I are of opinion that this judgment should be reversed. . . . I think that the criterion sanctioned by the full Court in *Schenck v. United States*,

---

[3] 268 U. S. 625 (1925). See accord, Dennis v. United States, 71 S. Ct. 857 (1951).

249 U. S. 47, 52, applies. 'The question in every case is whether the words are used in such circumstances and are of such a nature as to create a clear and present danger that they will bring about the substantive evils that [the State] has a right to prevent.' . . . If what I think the correct test is applied, it is manifest that there was no present danger of an attempt to overthrow the government by force on the part of the admittedly small minority who shared the defendant's views. It is said that this manifesto was more than a theory, that it was an incitement. Every idea is an incitement. It offers itself for belief and if believed it is acted on unless some other belief outweighs it or some failure of energy stifles the movement at its birth. The only difference between the expression of an opinion and an incitement in the narrower sense is the speaker's enthusiasm for the result. Eloquence may set fire to reason. But whatever may be thought of the redundant discourse before us it had no chance of starting a present conflagration. If in the long run the beliefs expressed in proletarian dictatorship are destined to be accepted by the dominant forces of the community, the only meaning of free speech is that they should be given their chance and have their way." [4]

What are the conflicting objectives here? Where does the majority opinion draw the line between them?

Where would Holmes and Brandeis draw the line between these conflicting policies? What do you think of Holmes' suggestion about allowing a proletarian dictatorship to have its way? What has been the policy as regards change and progress of the dictatorships which we have known in recent years? Should their known policy on this point have any bearing on the question whether a dictatorship should be allowed to have its way? [5]

[4] *Ibid.* 672–673.
[5] "Democracy ought to instruct its citizens in its own values instead of feebly waiting until its system is wrecked by private armies from within. Tolerance does not mean tolerating the intolerant." MANNHEIM, MAN AND SOCIETY IN AN AGE OF RECONSTRUCTION 353 (1940).

POLICIES REGARDING ORGANIZED GROUPS

Sec. 7–28. The state and other social institutions. One finds in human society a multitude of organizations which formulate standards of behavior and exercise control over behavior. The state, the school, the church, the club, the labor union, the professional association, the stock exchange, and organized baseball, are examples. These agencies are called social institutions.

Of the role and nature of social institutions *Park* and *Burgess* say:

"Every society and every social group, *capable of consistent action,* may be regarded as an organization of the wishes of its members. This means that society rests on, and embodies, the appetites and natural desires of the individual man; but it implies also, that wishes, in becoming *organized,* are necessarily disciplined and controlled in the interest of the group as a whole.

"Every such society or social group, even the most ephemeral, will ordinarily have (a) some relatively formal method of defining its aim and formulating its policies, making them explicit, and (b) some machinery, functionary, or other arrangement for realizing its aim and carrying its policies into effect. Even in the family there is government, and this involves something that corresponds to legislation, adjudication, and administration." [1]

Each of these institutions exists in a world of men where other institutions exist. All are organizations, more or less complete, of one subject matter, to wit, the members of the human race. The state is more prominent and fully developed than any of the other organizations. It embraces an entire community. Most of the other groups are merely partial organizations of a community of which the state is the all-inclusive organization. It is inevitable that the state and these other control institutions should interact and com-

[1] INTRODUCTION TO THE SCIENCE OF SOCIOLOGY 45–56 (1930).

pete with one another in various ways. The coexistence and activities of other control institutions within the community pose policy problems for the state. The state and its officials orient themselves in defined ways toward the activities of other groups organized within the community. Moreover, the state itself is an organization of men. The maintenance of this organization and the definition of its functions present policy problems for the state and its officials; the latter adopt definite policies regarding the continued existence and the functions of the state. And finally, the state and its officials must face policy problems regarding its relations to other states, i. e., politically organized communities. These policies regarding organized groups, within and without the community, are to be the matter for our attention in the present subtopic. They will be taken up in three subsequent sections, entitled as follows:

Policies regarding subordinate groups (sec. 7–30).

Policies regarding the state's own organization and functions (sec. 7–31).

Policies regarding other states (sec. 7–32).

Sec. 7–29. (Optional.) Features and functions of social institutions. You will appreciate better these problems of the orientation of the state toward organized group activities if we pause to compare the state and its functions with other social institutions and their functions. The state and other developed institutions involve these common features:

1. *Group of members.* A group such as the labor union or the American Medical Association has a definite but limited membership. The membership of the state embraces the entire population of a community.

2. *Division of members into two functional parts: Controllers and controlled.* In some of the simpler institutions such as the family, control may be exercised by a small

number of controllers or even by a single person. In the state, control is always exercised by many persons. We can for the present purpose refer to these controllers in the state as officials. There is a higher degree of specialization and subdivision of function among state controllers than among the controllers of any other institutions. State officials may be subdivided on a functional basis into legislative, executive, judicial, etc. They may be subdivided on a hierarchal basis into superior and inferior officials. They may be subdivided on a territorial basis between counties and other geographical units.

3. *Standards of behavior for members (the controlled).* The institution through its controllers establishes standards of behavior for its members. For example, the American Medical Association maintains its standards of right behavior commonly known as medical ethics. The labor union prohibits its members from working in a nonunion establishment, or from crossing a picket line. The state has special agencies, i.e., the legislature, the courts, etc., which formulate standards, and it has a more complete and detailed array of standards prescribed for the control of the behavior of its membership than any other institution.

4. *Machinery and methods for effectuating its standards.* Each institution develops its own machinery and methods for making its standards effective. A medical society, for example, can expel or suspend a member who is guilty of an infraction of its rules, or can deprive him of access to hospital facilities which are controlled by the association or its members. Similarly, a labor union can expel members or mete out lesser forms of disciplinary penalties to them. The church in a similar way can exclude from membership and can discipline members in various ways. It can threaten persons with what Ross calls "other-world sanctions," i.e., penalties in afterlife. But such sanctions are, I fear, less

effective today with the general population than they used to be. The state, in comparison with these other institutions, has a more complete arsenal of sanctions and control devices. It uses criminal prosecution, official supervision, the private lawsuit, the reward for individual action, and other methods which have been more fully considered at an earlier point.[1] In addition, it employs education through its public school system to mold the young and develop habits and attitudes which will insure the effectiveness of its standards.

5. *Standards of behavior for the controllers (officials).* The institution maintains standards for the behavior of its controllers. The controllers are the persons through whose acts standards of the institution are made effective; and the controllers, like those whom they control, need standards to guide their actions. Such standards define the times when control is to be exercised and the manner of its exercise. Collectively, they may be said to make up an institutional constitution. Every well-developed institution has a set of standards which define official operations in this sense. In the state, such standards apply to all persons who exercise its authority.

6. *Devices and methods of controlling the controllers.* In most social institutions machinery and methods of effectuating the obligations of controllers are rather indefinite and undeveloped. In the main, the pressure of group opinion upon those who are in charge of group affairs is relied upon to hold the controllers in check. In many institutions it is hardly worth while to establish more potent sanctions. How much difference does it make whether the president of the ladies' literary club misuses her power? But in other institutions, such as the labor union or the professional association, the consequences of abuse of power may be serious, and the need for restraints on controllers may be very real, since they

---

[1] See secs. 2–15 to 2–28.

exercise on behalf of the association power over the bread and butter of members, and since they affect the welfare of many persons outside the group as well. In the state, first reliance is put upon schemes of organization which establish one official agency in a position of supervisory authority over another. The weakness of such schemes is that there is no agency to check the top agency. To meet this difficulty, the modern democratic state relies upon the creation of co-ordinate official agencies which check one another, a scheme of checks and balances which sets off one group of controllers against another.[2]

7. *Institutional policies or objectives.* The institutional group pursues certain objectives as such. Medical practitioners are organized to promote the welfare of their profession. The labor union aims to improve the economic and social conditions of its membership. The objectives of the state are broader and more varied. The state is expected to secure the general welfare—the welfare of all the people within its sway, not a particular kind of good for a limited group; at least, that is the professed aim of American government in all its forms and parts. To analyze the state and its functions thus, in institutional terms, reduces to a common denominator the state and other social control agencies. I think you will find this helpful in understanding the interactions of the state with other institutions, and the policies of the state toward other institutions—about which I now want to speak.

Sec. 7-30. Policies regarding subordinate groups. Within wide limits, the state does not concern itself with the forma-tion or activities of other organized groups, e.g., a ladies' literary club or a neighborhood ball team. It neither favors nor opposes them; its policy is, on the whole, one of indiffer-ence toward them. Its policy-making agencies discover no

[2] See secs. 3-22 *et seq.*

special benefit and no special harm in the existence or behavior of these groups, and accordingly, they adopt a neutral position in regard to them. This area of indifference or neutrality parallels the area of liberty for the individual. There also government adopts a neutral or hands-off attitude. Here, government allows individuals to form groups and allows groups to act without interposing any restraints and without affording any support for their aims and activities.

But some organized groups serve highly useful functions in the community. The state, acting through its policy makers, recognizes in their existence and operations definite social interests. Such groups the state tries to foster in various ways and in varying degrees. For example, the state traditionally extends its protection to the family; it encourages the formation of families and safeguards family relationships against outside interference.[1] It establishes forms and requirements for entering into the marriage relation, and methods for terminating that relation by divorce or annulment; it penalizes adultery and fornication; it creates legal liability for the support of wife and child. And economic groups receive the state's blessing, too. The state encourages the formation of groups to carry on trade and business. It provides for the creation of business corporations and other business associations; it provides for the establishment of banks, insurance companies, transportation companies, etc. The state protects the operations of these groups and gives effect to their acts. To certain business groups, the state may give subsidies; to some groups, it may extend protection by enacting tariff laws to safeguard against foreign competition. In recent years, labor organizations have been strongly supported by our federal government and by many of the states. These governments have sought to guarantee to labor groups

[1] See the earlier discussion of individual interests of family members in sec. 7–07. Here we are concerned with the family group as a recognized social entity.

the opportunity to form and maintain unions without interference by persons on the outside. The formation of these
unions has been encouraged in order to equalize the bargaining power of workmen in dealing with the large employer
on whom they depend for a livelihood. Finally, the state
encourages the organization of groups for charitable, social,
and other nonprofit purposes. These, like business corporations, are invested with powers of acting as a legal unit,
powers of owning property, powers of making contracts, etc.
Charitable and religious and educational institutions fall under this head; they are often given exemptions from taxation
and other fiscal advantages. All these different group organizations are alike in that they perform needed community
services. They are encouraged and protected by regulative,
fiscal, or administrative measures of the state because they
serve the interests of the community.

Besides the specific functions which organized groups are
intended to serve, they also serve the community in a regulative capacity. They set up standards of behavior for their
members and enforce them through their own institutional
machinery. This regulative function of other social institutions is especially important in relation to the regulative
function of the law. So far as these institutional standards
coincide with legal standards, and so far as they are institu-
tionally effectuated, a part of the load of enforcement is taken
off the legal machinery. Thus, for example, organized medicine is not only important to the community because it aids
in the provision of medical services, it is also significant
because it maintains canons of ethics for its practitioners to
control their dealings with one another and with the public.
If these canons are in accord with the general welfare, the
state can well afford to back them up, wholly or in part, and
give aid to the organized medical profession in enforcing
them. Similarly, the state may find definite social interests

in protecting such institutions as the family and the church, not only because of the primary functions that they perform, but also because these institutions create and enforce standards which regulate the behavior of members of the community.[2] I have in mind such standards as those regarding truth telling. The church by its standards enjoins truthfulness and forbids lying. Similar standards are inculcated by training in most families. Such standards coincide generally with standards and objectives, recognized as desirable by the state. Our organized educational institutions, the public schools, normally support the same standards. And the legal machinery of the state is directed to the enforcement of the same standards. As regards testimony in court, the state enjoins truth telling and punishes perjury. As regards business transactions, the state requires correct statements of fact and backs up this requirement by threats of actions or penalties for fraud. As regards the dealings of officials with officials, involved in the operation of the legal system, the reliance of each official on the correctness of statements of others is taken for granted. Indeed, it is hard to imagine what the practices regarding truth telling would be in our community, and how legal machinery would be created adequate to carry the burden if these other social institutions were not in the picture, and were not enforcing standards substantially coincident with the standards of the law.[3]

On the other hand, groups may be organized whose activities run counter to state policies. The general ends of certain groups are so far opposed to state policies that the state attempts to prohibit their formation entirely. In this sense,

[2] We can, to use Pound's terminology, refer to the state's interest in maintaining these extralegal standards as the social interest in the *general morals*.

[3] In an analogous way, one might point to the regulative utility of family and church in many other respects. The standards of these institutions normally coincide with the standards of the law in regard to acts of theft and acts of sex intercourse outside the marriage relation. To the extent that these institutions work effectively in the processes of training and enforcement, the task of the law in these respects is reduced.

the state may try to prevent the organization of a gambling syndicate, or of a society whose purpose is to overthrow the government by force. Or the conflict with governmental policies may arise rather out of the methods commonly used by an organized group such as the Ku Klux Klan. The Klan may profess to work for good ends, but it operates secretly and employs violent means, both of which are ordinarily disapproved by organized government. The result may be an outright prohibition of this organization, intended to strike at the unlawful methods usually employed by it.

As regards other subordinate groups, the hostility of the state may be not complete, but partial. The state may only undertake to prevent certain acts of these groups which are injurious to persons who are inside or outside the group. Suppose, for example, that an association of merchants attempts to fix prices. From the point of view of the merchants, this may be regarded as a justifiable and desirable act; it may be intended by them to insure reasonable profits. But the fixing of prices in this manner is a practice which is or may be harmful to others; it leads to injury to the buying public, and is definitely prohibited by law. Similarly, labor organizations may resort to violence in labor disputes, or, in regard to persons outside their membership, may attempt to enforce demands by boycotts. These acts may be quite justifiable from the point of view of labor organizations, and may accord fully with the standards which the organization itself recognizes. But both acts may affect injuriously persons outside as well as inside their membership, and the state may adopt a policy of prohibition or restriction. The theory behind governmental interference in such cases is that the state as the representative of the whole community must move to suppress the activity of any group which seeks to promote its own interests at the expense of injury to an individual, injury to another group, or injury to the public as a whole.

Sec. 7–31. Policies regarding the state's own organization and functions. No less important than the policies which the state adopts regarding subordinate groups in the community are the policies which the state maintains regarding its own organization and functions. One can speak of them as policies of the state regarding itself.[1] In one aspect, all the policies which we have heretofore considered relate to the state; they are policies of the state in the sense that they are pursued by the state or in its name. But thus far we have considered only policies which were directed to an objective external to the state itself. The policies with which we are here concerned are those whose objectives are the state's own organization and some of the state's functions.

One basic policy question for the state relates to the change of its organization. Is this organization to be subject to change? The American governments are established under constitutions, and these constitutions provide definite machinery for the change and amendment of governmental organization. What about change by revolution? What about efforts of individuals or groups to overthrow the government by force? So far as I know, no government here or elsewhere has ever recognized this as a permissible form of change. Where such an overthrow has occurred, it has been accomplished despite the state. In countries where dictatorships are in power, usually revolution represents the only possibility for change. The policy of the established dictatorship is opposed to change of any kind. Democratic and liberal groups

[1] Also, we must not forget that policies of the state regarding its own organization and functions are really the policies or attitudes of its officials regarding the state's operations. This is one of the places where it is especially important for clarity of thinking, to realize the connection of policies with actual policy makers. See sec. 7–02, and note ** thereto.

are necessarily revolutionary groups, and the full power of the state is exerted to suppress them. They have no opportunity under such a state policy to bring about change in a lawful manner.

Other basic policy questions for the state relate to the use of the state's powers for its own support. I think it is proper to say that the state itself is a state-supported institution. By supporting itself and its own functions, the state serves indirectly to secure the various interests which it protects and fosters. Subordinate policy questions concern the means which the state will use in supporting itself: What tax sources will it draw upon? How far will it make exactions from the rich? How far from the poor? How will it distribute its available funds between one undertaking and another?

Government in the United States can deal appropriately with acts of individuals or groups which threaten its destruction. It can penalize the acts of those who advocate its overthrow by force. The federal government punishes treason, espionage, trading with the enemy, and acts of sabotage. All our governments restrain and punish acts of individuals and groups which interfere with the performance of governmental functions. They protect public property against theft or injury, and they accord special protection to government officials while they are acting in the performance of their duties.

Another important type of policy question concerns the functions which the state itself is to assume. The state may assume only a few and narrow functions. This was the traditional policy of our governments until relatively recently. Instead of assuming functions itself, the state may adopt a policy of encouraging individuals or organized groups to perform needed social services. In the last section I showed how the state may stop short of assuming functions itself and aid subordinate group organizations which perform social functions. Thus, the state has encouraged universities and colleges, privately endowed, to perform educational functions, and helped them in various ways, as by subventions and tax exemptions.

Or the state may assume many and wide functions. It may create organs of its own, designed to take over functions previously performed by private agencies, or create government agencies to render services not theretofore performed. I have already referred to the tendency of the modern state to take on more and more functions, exemplified by what has been done by governments in Europe as well as by our own governments, state and federal. These have created a multitude of agencies to perform social services. I do not refer here merely to government corporations, such as the Home Owners' Loan Corporation, though these are to be included, too. I have in mind organizations such as our system of public education, extending from elementary schools to universities. These represent the governmental assumption of the chief role in education. Public education is hardly a century and a half old. At an earlier time, education was the function of the family or the church, or was given in private schools. These schools are still, to a large degree, encouraged by our government. Nevertheless, the public schools and universities have now taken over the greater share of the burden of education in this country. And the public educational institutions of the American state are now as completely incorporated into its structure as are the courts and the organs of taxation.[2]

---

[2] The established church is historically important and still exists in many parts of the world, though it is no longer possible in this country to create such an establishment because of constitutional prohibitions. Usually the state furnishes the established church with most of its funds, and combines with it in a close union of members and enforcement machinery. Yet the established church is not merely an organ of the state. Accordingly, the established church falls between the complete assumption of government control and the independent group organization which is merely subsidized.

Under the recent fascist regimes of Italy and Germany, major business organizations and labor unions were, as I understand the matter, converted into semipublic agencies along lines similar to that of an established church.

Sec. 7–32. Policies regarding other states.[1] If we had in the world a superstate, it might be endowed with authority to control the relations of one state to another, and to fix the policies which each state should pursue in relation to other states. But no such central international power exists.[2] Each state asserts practically unlimited authority over its external affairs. One of the normal functions of every state is to deal with foreign states and their subjects. Through some agents or agencies each state determines what is commonly called its "foreign policy." In the United States, this role is assigned by the Constitution to the federal government,[3] and more specifically, to the President and Senate.[4]

The most aggressive policies regarding other states are represented by war, offensive and defensive. War is the crudest and most radical method of dealing with other nations. For the purpose of prosecuting war, armed forces are prepared and kept ready. Many of the acts and measures of our federal government are actuated by this war policy. The government creates and maintains an army, navy, and air force; it regulates by law the internal activities of the military forces as well as the relations of the individual citizen to them.[5]

[1] I have not overlooked the fact that some supernational institutions, such as the Catholic Church, bear both internal and external relations to the state. Such an institution organizes persons within the community, but its sway also extends beyond the community. Such organizations pose no new type of policy problems for the state. From the state's point of view, these problems are of two types; internal relations, like the relations to subordinate groups in the community, and external relations, like the state's relations to other states. I have not felt that an additional heading was needed in order to cover the policies involved in such double relationships.

[2] The League of Nations was a beginning. And the United Nations is another start; but so far its authority has not attained very considerable significance.

[3] The individual states are explicitly excluded from action in this area by several provisions of the Federal Constitution. See Art. I, Sec. 9.

[4] However, the House of Representatives also has a hand in shaping foreign policy. The influence of the House is exerted chiefly through its control over taxing and spending. But the House also makes its views felt by its participation in the lawmaking processes.

[5] You can see in the organization and maintenance of the military establishment an excellent illustration of the intermixture of fiscal, administrative, and

Alongside control over warfare stands federal control over the importation and exportation of goods. Benefits and harms may accrue to the people of the United States through these acts as well as through acts of war. Benefits have been invited by a policy of free trade in articles needed by domestic economy.[6] Harms to the domestic population, e.g., from opium or from diseased food products, have been combated by restrictive or prohibitive legislation. Injuries to the domestic economy, e.g., hurtful foreign competition with domestic goods, have been met by restrictive laws or by protective tariffs.

A parallel control is exercised by the federal government over immigration and naturalization.[7] For more than a century of our national life, the federal government pursued a policy of *laissez faire* as regards immigration; almost unlimited entry to this country was allowed to foreigners, and immigrants were readily admitted to citizenship. These policies were based on a felt need to fill up the vast open spaces of our West with people, especially with farmers from Europe. The first departure from these policies was represented by the Chinese Exclusion Acts, intended to protect American labor against the importation of cheap competitive labor from the Orient. Since the turn of the century, restrictions on immigration have multiplied enormously, so that now we have many restraints on both the *quality*, e.g., physical and mental health, occupation, moral character, etc., and *quantity* of immigrants, e.g., the quota system which fixes the number of persons of each nationality who can enter the United States. And naturalization is hedged about by many

regulative measures in governmental undertakings. See further on this point, sec. 7–17.

[6] Though this policy has sometimes been offset by the financial requirements of government, imports have been subjected to tariffs in order to raise revenue.

[7] Emigration and loss of citizenship are also subjects for possible federal attention. Emigration has received little if any notice; loss of citizenship is covered fully by federal laws dealing with nationality.

safeguards, calculated to prevent incompetent and undesirable persons from acquiring the status of citizens.

To a very limited extent, relations of governments to one another are covered by international law. This law professes to fix the patterns of behavior which states should follow in regard to one another and one another's nationals. However, the policies of international law are narrow and limited. International law is directed primarily to the policy of maintaining order between states; secondarily, it seems to be aimed to mitigate the harshness of war when peace is not kept. Moreover, there are no well-defined agencies for *making* international law, as there are for creating domestic law.[8] International law has developed chiefly through the voluntary adherence of independent states to common usages. These usages, by express or tacit acceptance, have taken on something of the general character of legal standards. In addition treaties can be constitutive of international law.[9] But there are no well-defined methods or agencies of *enforcement* to back up the standards of what is called international law. And the behavior patterns of international law are by no means complete and explicit. The result is that in practice the acts which any government will undertake and the policies it will pursue are, in the main, self-determined and not actually controlled by externally prescribed standards or policies.

Sec. 7–33. Problems. 1. In a note in the Michigan Law Review in 1934 appears the following statement of a problem:

[8] In this connection it is also worth noting that our Federal Constitution makes a treaty entered into by the federal government a part of the internal law of the United States. Art. III, Sec. 2. Such a treaty operates on persons and property in the United States essentially as federal statutes operate.

[9] At once the analogy to a contract between individuals comes to mind; this contract establishes obligatory lines of action for the parties who enter into it. But a treaty between states can do more. It can serve as the adoption of a constitution, and in this sense set up a frame of international government and determine policies and standards for the operation of that government.

"In April of this year a Minnesota physician, Dr. Clayton E. May treated for gunshot wounds a certain undesirable person, John Dillinger, very much in demand by the police. He further neglected to inform the police concerning his ministrations, and as a result, was tried in a federal court on a charge of harboring a fugitive wanted under a federal warrant, found guilty, and sentenced to serve two years in a penitentiary and to pay a fine of $1,000. Said a prominent English medical journal in commenting on the case '. . . colleagues in every country will applaud his action in not betraying a professional trust.' " [1]

After this statement of the problem, the note writer discusses it and concludes that there is no legal justification for the position taken by the English medical journal.[2]

How is this question related to our discussion of state policies toward organized groups? Do you agree with the note writer or with the English medical journal? Why?

2. A few years ago a group of employees of the Home Owners' Loan Corporation organized an association in the District of Columbia called Group Health Association, for the purpose of providing medical service on a prepaid insurance basis to its members and their families. This group undertook to employ licensed physicians to render the medical services which its agreement with its members called for. The activities of such voluntary health associations were strongly opposed by the American Medical Association and its subsidiary societies on the ground that the organization of these associations and their employment of doctors on salary were inimical to the best interests of the medical profession. In order to prevent the operations of Group Health Association, the American Medical Association and the Medical Society of the District of Columbia threatened any doctors who affiliated with, or served Group Health Association, with expulsion from membership. They also denied to doctors who

---

[1] Note, 226 THE LANCET 1183 (1934).
[2] 32 MICH. L. REV. 1164 (1934).

became affiliated with Group Health Association all privileges of consultation with members of the American Medical Association or the Medical Society, and finally they undertook through their control of hospitals of the District of Columbia to exclude all affiliated doctors and their patients from the use of such hospitals. The American Medical Association and the Medical Society were prosecuted and convicted for entering into a conspiracy to restrain trade. The conviction was sustained in the Supreme Court of the United States.[3]

The technical form of the charge and the specific arguments pro and con are not important for our purpose. How would you interpret this conviction in relation to our present subtopic?

Incidentally, it should be noted that the American Medical Association has completely reversed its position on this point and now promotes the organization of voluntary health associations as an antidote for the more feared "state medicine." What would be the significance of state medicine (a system in which the state employs doctors to furnish medical service to its population) in terms of the present subtopic?

3. The power of correction, vested by law in parents, is founded on their duty to maintain and educate their offspring. In support of that authority, they must have a "right to the exercise of such discipline as may be requisite for the discharge of their sacred trust." [4] And this power, allowed by law to the parent over the person of the child, "may be delegated to a tutor or instructor, the better to accomplish the purpose of education." [5]

"The better doctrine of the adjudged cases, therefore, is, that the teacher is, within reasonable bounds, the substitute for the parent, exercising his delegated authority. He is vested with the power to administer moderate correction, with a proper instrument, in cases of misconduct, which ought

[3] A. M. A. v. U. S., 317 U. S. 519 (1943).
[4] 2 KENT'S COMM.*203 (1896).
[5] Id. *205; 1 BL. COMM. *507 (1941).

to have some reference to the character of the offense, the sex, age, size, and physical strength of the pupil. When the teacher keeps within the circumscribed sphere of his authority, the degree of correction must be left to his discretion, as it is to that of the parent, under like circumstances. Within this limit, he has the authority to determine the gravity or heinousness of the offense, and to mete out to the offender the punishment which he thinks his conduct justly merits; and hence the parent or teacher is often said, *pro hac vice*, to exercise 'judicial functions.' " [6]

What does this judicial declaration suggest as to the basis for family discipline? How is the sphere of family discipline related to the sphere of law? How is the sphere of discipline in the schools limited by the law?

4. The State of Oregon passed a Compulsory Education Act which required every parent, guardian or other person having control of a child between the ages of 8 and 16 years to send him to the public school in the district where he resided, for the period during which the school was held for the current year. The validity of this act was challenged before the United States Supreme Court by the Society of Sisters and by a private school. The Supreme Court of the United States held the act invalid. It declared that the act constituted an unreasonable interference "with the liberty of parents and guardians to direct the upbringing . . . of children. . . ." The court also declared that: "The fundamental theory of liberty upon which all governments of this Union repose excludes any general power of the State to standardize its children by forcing them to accept instruction from public teachers only." [7]

What does this case signify in terms of competing institutional ends and areas of control? A statute which requires parents to send their children to *some* school until sixteen

---

[6] Boyd v. State, 88 Ala. 169 at 171 (1889).
[7] Pierce v. Society of Sisters, 268 U. S. 510 at 535 (1925).

years of age would be held constitutionally valid. What is the difference?

5. *United States v. Schwimmer.*[8] A fifty-year-old woman applied for naturalization as an American citizen. At the hearing on her application, and in the preliminary questionnaires, she indicated an unwillingness to bear arms in defense of this country. The Supreme Court affirmed the district court's denial of naturalization. Holmes, J., dissenting, said:

". . . if there is any principle of the Constitution that more imperatively calls for attachment than any other it is the principle of free thought—not free thought for those who agree with us but freedom for the thought we hate. I think we should adhere to that principle with regard to admission into, as well as to life within this country. And recurring to the opinion that bars this applicant's way, I would suggest that the Quakers have done their share to make this country what it is, that many citizens agree with the applicant's belief and that I had not supposed hitherto that we regretted our inability to expel them because they believe more than some of us do in the teachings of the Sermon on the Mount."

This decision and a similar decision in *United States v. MacIntosh*,[9] have been regarded as mere constructions of the intent of Congress. In *Girouard v. United States*,[10] both these cases were overruled and an interpretation essentially like that which Holmes urged was adopted.

Under the majority opinion of the *Schwimmer Case*, what policy is ascribed to Congress? Under Holmes' opinion, what policy is ascribed to Congress?

DETERMINANTS OF POLICIES

Sec. 7–34. More specifically about policy makers—the popular will. We have now listed a great variety of possible

---

[8] United States v. Schwimmer, 279 U. S. 644 (1929).
[9] 283 U. S. 605 (1931).
[10] 328 U. S. 61 (1946).

policies, and have considered the ways in which they may be interrelated and adjusted with one another. We have yet to deal with the processes through which these policies are formulated and determined. We have yet to consider more specifically who the policy makers are, how their choices are influenced and controlled, and where their policy notions come from. These questions remain for treatment in this final subtopic on the operation of our legal system.

All American governmental institutions rest on the fundamental assumption that "Governments are instituted among Men, deriving their just powers from the consent of the governed." [1] This assumption was part and parcel of social contract theories prevailing at the time when the federal government was founded. In terms of this fundamental assumption, the governed are entitled to fix the policies which government is to serve, and the methods and machinery through which these policies will be effectuated. [2] No one who had been brought up in the midst of the American tradition would ever think of questioning either of these propositions.

However, the popular will is, for the most part, inarticulate and unformulated; its practical effect on the operations of government is indirect and roundabout. The popular will

[1] Declaration of Independence, unanimously passed by the Congress of the thirteen United States of America, July 4, 1776.

[2] Indeed, the proceedings by which the federal government was established could well be viewed as the making of a popular compact. While the original naive conception of a popular compact has been discarded, the basic conception of popular sovereignty has not. This conception not only appears in the Declaration of Independence and the writings of various founding fathers, it lives on unchallenged and vigorous as ever; it is definitely announced in the Federal Constitution. The preamble to that instrument declares:

"We the People of the United States, in Order to form a more perfect Union, establish Justice, insure domestic Tranquillity, provide for the common defence, promote the general Welfare, and secure the Blessings of Liberty to ourselves and our Posterity, do ordain and establish this Constitution for the United States of America."

And the Tenth Amendment to the Constitution provides: "The powers not delegated to the United States by the Constitution, nor prohibited by it to the States, are reserved to the States respectively, or to the people."

can rarely be said to originate and carry through a policy determination of its own. Normally, the popular will is expressed through various agencies which profess to act as its representatives: the framers of constitutions, the legislatures, the courts, and other officials. To some extent, the popular will is expressed through the choice of officials who announce their advocacy of proposed programs. In some states, it can be expressed through the use of the initiative and referendum. In the main, however, the popular will is expressed only indirectly through measures formulated and proposed by official agencies, such as a constitutional convention or a legislature.

The limitations on the choice of policies which the people (popular will) may adopt by establishing constitutions or replacing or amending those it has, are theoretically negligible. If the people chooses, it can adopt any kind of government or any kind of policy whatever.[3] If unlimited power is to be found anywhere in our legal systems, analogous to the power of the British Parliament, this power is vested in the people. To be sure, such power is more a theory than a practical fact. The people is a rather inert body, as I have already pointed out. The people is governed by personal and social factors, which will be discussed in later sections. It is amenable to suggestions and advice; it is restrained, like every other agency of government, by traditional standards.[4]

Sec. 7–35. Framers of constitutions as policy makers. The framers of constitutions are obviously in a position to determine and formulate the policies to be pursued by the govern-

---

[3] This is definitely indicated by the preamble to the Constitution, which declares that it is adopted by the people of the United States, and by the Tenth Amendment, which reserves powers not given to the federal government, to the states and the people (see next preceding note). As Justice Holmes suggested in Gitlow v. New York (see sec. 7–25, problem 5) there is nothing in our Constitution to prevent the adoption of communism in this country if our people should want it.

[4] See also the discussion in sec. 7–45 of the question whether there are superhuman criteria of justice to guide policy makers.

ments which they establish. And, like the people, the framers are not subject to any immediate restraints on their choices. They are checked only by personal and social factors.[1]

To a substantial extent, the framers of our constitutions have laid out the policies for governmental agencies to pursue. For example, the framers of the Federal Constitution declare in the preamble thereof that the federal government is ordained and established "in order to form a more perfect Union, establish Justice, insure domestic Tranquility, provide for the common defence, promote the general Welfare, and secure the Blessings of Liberty to ourselves and to our Posterity." Again the framers of the Federal Constitution confer on Congress the power to "lay and collect Taxes, Duties, Imposts, and Excises, to pay the Debts and provide for the common Defence and general Welfare of the United States. . . ."[2] Such expressions of policy are explicit but they are very general. The government is intended to act for the general welfare, to provide for the common defense, and so on. Like other inventories of governmental policy heretofore mentioned, such formulations do not mean much as guides, unless they be broken down and stated in more specific terms.

However, explicit declarations of policy are not usually found in constitutions any more than in statutes. The framers are content to establish the principal organs of government and to define their powers. The ends for which these powers shall be used, the policies which the organs of government shall pursue, are not explicitly and specifically stated; they are left to implication from the powers given. Congress is given power to regulate interstate commerce. The purposes for which the power can be used are not defined. Is the use of this power limited to the protection and promotion of the flow of commerce? Can the power be used for the moral

---

[1] I refer here to the checks by human acts, ways, and institutions; the question whether there is a "higher law" beyond human control, which guides policy makers and others, is reserved for discussion in sec. 7–45.

[2] Art. I, Sec. 8, Cl. 1.

betterment of the community by preventing the shipment of lottery tickets across state lines? Can Congress use its control over commerce to improve working conditions and prevent child labor in industry? All these questions of policy in the use of the commerce power had to be answered, but all of the answers had to be found outside the specific language of the Constitution; and so of the purposes for which most of the powers conferred on the federal government by the Federal Constitution and on the state governments by their respective state constitutions. Powers are granted, but the purposes and policies for which the powers are to be used are left undefined.

Now while the framers of our constitutions have not been inclined to state the purposes for which powers might be used, they have taken great pains to prohibit their use for certain purposes. The framers have been concerned to prohibit acts of government which interfere with individual rights and liberties. These prohibitions of governmental action definitely limit the policies which government may pursue; they restrict the methods by which policies may be carried out. The federal government is expressly forbidden to abridge freedom of speech, of the press, and of assembly. Federal and state governments are forbidden to pass ex post facto laws and other retroactive legislation, and to deprive persons of life, liberty or property without due process of law. The state is forbidden to "pass any . . . law impairing the obligation of contracts," or to "make or enforce any law which shall abridge the privileges or immunities of citizens of the United States," or to "deny to any person within its jurisdiction the equal protection of the laws." The state and federal constitutions contain imposing arrays of provisions which guarantee jury trial in civil and criminal cases, which safeguard the individual against arbitrary arrests and searches, and which secure for his use the writ of habeas corpus. But the reasons for all these guarantees and prohibitions are not stated out. They are taken for granted. They are implied and not expressed. Why is the liberty of the individual given all these forms of protection? The Declaration of Independence and the early constitutions indicated that these liberties were regarded as natural endowments of the Creator, and required no justification other than that fact. This point of view has gradually changed. Today liberties of the individual are justified in terms of utility or policy. Even if we talk of them as natural rights, we try to find practical reasons for free speech, for the individual's right to hold property, for the guarantee of jury trial in criminal and civil cases, for the writ of habeas corpus, etc. Maybe these reasons or policies were implicit in earlier theories of natural rights and liberties. Maybe these reasons or policies are merely the invented rationalizations of our time. In any event, the need is strongly felt nowadays to invoke the policies behind the constitutional guarantees, as aids in applying and limiting them. This fact has put upon courts and theoretical writers, even more than upon legislatures, the burden of formulating and stating the policy considerations behind constitutional provisions, which the constitutions themselves do not express.

Sec. 7–36. Legislatures as policy makers. In actual fact, the legislatures (and I include the Congress of the United States) deal with policy matters more frequently and settle more policy questions than any of the other policy makers. They are, in practice, the chief agencies to determine the policies of government. They determine policies whenever they exercise any of their powers; when they enact statutes, when they create offices, when they impose taxes, and when they appropriate money. The legislatures act in these various ways with purposes in view, and to say that they determine policies is simply to say that they do have ends in view when they act.

But the legislatures must act within the constitutional framework. In this respect, these bodies are limited in their function as policy makers. They are checked by the express provisions of the constitutions, and by the policies of these instruments which are read into them by the courts. In this respect, the legislatures are in a different position from the people and the constitution maker. The latter are outside the constitutional framework, and free from constitutional limitations.[1] They might, for example, abolish private property, which the legislatures definitely could not do. The subjection of the legislatures' activity to constitutional limitations is what gives their policy making its peculiar character. How do these constitutional limitations affect the policy making of the legislatures?

The positive grants of power to legislate are usually so broad and general that they permit the legislative body to do almost anything that it chooses. In this regard, the grants of legislative power to the federal government are typical. What Congress can do in the exercise of its commerce power, its power to tax, its power to spend, its war powers, and its control over the currency, is almost unlimited. Under the decisions of the Supreme Court in the last fifteen years, there is practically no way to challenge the necessity for using any of these powers or the purpose for which any of them is used.*

The prohibitions of particular types of legislation and the guarantees of individual rights are more seriously limitative.

---

[1] The general idea here expressed is correct. I do not feel that it is necessary to clutter up the text with such qualifications as: 1, the proposition that even the popular will, as for example in amending a constitution, must follow the prescribed constitutional procedures for adopting an amendment; and 2, the proposition that even the framers of a state constitution cannot transcend the limitations of the Federal Constitution.

* (I.R.) See National Labor Relations Board v. Jones and Laughlin Steel Corporation, 301 U. S. 1 (1937); United States v. Darby, 312 U. S. 100 (1941); Steward Machine Company v. Davis, 301 U. S. 548 (1937); Helvering v. Davis, 301 U. S. 619 (1937).

Offhand, these prohibitions and guarantees might seem to stand in the way of any legislative regulation or control whatever. When the Federal Constitution (and likewise those of the states) makes such declarations as that Congress shall make no law abridging freedom of speech or the press, that no state shall pass a law impairing the obligation of contracts, and that no state shall deprive any person of life, liberty or property without due process of law, the declarations leave no room, if literally read, for legislative qualification or limitation. But our courts have definitely held from the beginning that these prohibitions and guarantees are not absolute. They do not stand in the way of some legislative regulation and limitation.

The character and amount of permissible legislative control varies with the subject matter.[2] As regards freedom of the mind and the guarantees of personal liberty, the Supreme Court and the state supreme courts have held the reins on legislation rather tight. They have stressed the importance of freedom of the mind and freedom of the person as the foundation for all our other rights and liberties. Any governmental interference in these areas has to be definitely justified. A law restricting liberty of mind or person must be predicated on actual social need. The presumption is in favor of liberty and against any type of restriction. The burden of proof is on the lawmaker (or on any one who relies upon such a law) to show that a real need exists. And the Supreme Court is prepared to examine the question of policy for itself. In short, the opportunity of the legislatures to introduce restrictive policies and measures in these areas is strictly limited.**

[2] The statements in this and the next succeeding paragraph are somewhat oversimplified, but they suffice for the purpose in hand. If anyone desires a more detailed and accurate conception of the law, he can obtain it by consulting the authorities cited in the next two notes addressed to the initiated reader.

** (I.R.) These views are indicated in the following cases: Schenck v. United States, 249 U. S. 47 (1919); Meyer v. Nebraska, 262 U. S. 390 (1923); Near v. Minnesota, 283 U. S. 697 (1931); Grosjean v. American

On the other hand, the legislatures enjoy a much wider latitude for policy determination in the economic sphere. Down to the advent of the New Deal, the so-called "conservative" majority of the Supreme Court was ready to treat all clauses of the Constitution alike. It took the position that liberty is the rule and restraint the exception in all spheres, whether economic or personal. It was ready to require that legislation controlling property and contract be sustained by adequate social reasons and to indulge a presumption in favor of liberty and against restriction of property rights and freedom of contract.[3] But the "liberal" minority of the Supreme Court (Holmes, Brandeis and Stone) insisted on a different presumption in this sphere. It wanted to presume that Congress or the legislature had acted with sufficient warrant and was justified in limiting individual economic interests. And this former minority view is the one which has prevailed with the majority of the New Deal Supreme Court. The effect of this view has been to place the burden of proof on those who challenge legislation in the economic sphere, and this burden is not easy to support. This means that the constitutional protection for economic interests has been largely taken away. The legislative policy makers are practically free to prefer what interests they choose, individual or social, in the economic sphere.***

Press Company, 297 U. S. 233 (1936); Cantwell v. Connecticut, 310 U. S. 296 (1940); Bridges v. California, 314 U. S. 252 (1941); Edwards v. California, 314 U. S. 160 (1941); Hill v. Texas, 316 U. S. 400 (1942); Adams v. United States, 317 U. S. 269 (1943); West Virginia State Board of Education v. Barnette, 319 U. S. 624 (1943); Murdock v. Pennsylvania, 319 U. S. 105 (1943); Martin v. Struthers, 319 U. S. 141 (1943); McNabb v. United States, 318 U. S. 332 (1943); Pollock v. Williams, 322 U. S. 4 (1944); Smith v. Allwright, 321 U. S. 649 (1944); Ashcraft v. Tennessee, 322 U. S. 143 (1944); Thomas v. Collins, 323 U. S. 516 (1945); McCollum v. Board of Education, 333 U. S. 203 (1948); Terminiello v. Chicago, 337 U. S. 1 (1949).

[3] See Adkins v. Children's Hospital, quoted above in sec. 7–21, problem 3.
*** (I.R.) These views are indicated by the following cases: West Coast Hotel Company v. Parrish, 300 U. S. 379 (1937); Railroad Commission of Texas v. Rowan and Nichols, 310 U. S. 573 (1940); Federal Power Com-

Sec. 7–37. Courts as policy makers. Courts are established for the immediate purpose of handling litigation. They are intended to apply legal provisions prescribed by the various formulating agencies above mentioned: the popular will, the framers of constitutions, and especially the legislatures. Such legal provisions include not only rules and principles of behavior for individuals and officials, they include also legal policies and methods. The courts are intended to effectuate policies and employ methods which have been predetermined by these formulating agencies; they are not expected to lay out policies by judicial fiat or to devise methods or machinery to carry them out. As Cardozo said, "When the legislature has spoken, and declared one interest superior to another, the judge must subordinate his personal or subjective estimate of value to the estimate thus declared. He may not nullify or pervert a statute because convinced that an erroneous axiology (here: judgment of policy) is reflected in its terms." [1]

This does not mean, however, that the courts have not had a large part in shaping legal policies and methods over the long pull. Most of the important policies of our legal system have had their first explicit formulation in judicial decisions. Legislation was relatively rare in the Anglo-American legal systems until the last few decades; both specific legal mandates and declarations of policies could be found only in the cases, and even today, many of the principal policies of the law of property, contract, and tort have to be sought for in the case law. For example, the whole of the doctrine of consideration and the policies behind it must be sought in judicial declarations. The same is true of the basic principles according to which compensation is awarded for tortious injuries,

mission v. Hope Natural Gas Company, 320 U. S. 591 (1944); Sage Stores Company v. Kansas, 323 U. S. 32 (1944); Carolene Products Company v. United States, 323 U. S. 18 (1944); and see generally ROTTSCHAEFER, THE CONSTITUTION AND SOCIO-ECONOMIC CHANGE (Cooley Lectures, 1948).
[1] THE GROWTH OF THE LAW 94–95 (1924).

e.g., the principle that liability must be based on fault; the principles regarding protection of the individual's reputation against defamation; and almost all the other policies of tort law. So that we are quite justified in saying that while the courts are bound to accept the policy determinations of the legislatures whenever these policy determinations are distinctly made, the courts themselves, through the slow processes by which litigation is settled in case after case, have built up and formulated many of the accepted notions of what our law is for and what our legal system is trying to achieve.[2] Indeed, these common law policy notions constitute a very considerable part of the items in our inventory of legal policies.

Moreover, in the processes of statutory interpretation, the courts are often required to embark on an exploration of the uncertain sea of policy. Not infrequently, legislative declarations of policy are absent or indistinct, as I have already said. Legislatures have not been prone to state explicitly what policies lie behind their acts. They have been inclined, on the whole, to limit themselves to more or less specific directions to individuals and officials. The courts are left to infer what the legislative objectives of these directions are. And when these objectives cannot be inferred with certainty, the courts are really called upon to declare a policy themselves. To be sure, the courts do not arbitrarily select this policy; they do not conjure a legal policy out of thin air. As Cardozo says in a later part of the passage above quoted, "Even when the legislature has not spoken, he (the judge) is to regulate his estimate of values by objective rather than subjective standards, by the thought and will of the community rather than by his own idiosyncrasies of

---

[2] In developing policies, courts regard themselves as bound by constitutional limitations, similar to those which apply to the legislatures. In addition, they recognize the binding force on their actions of such common law doctrines as the doctrine of precedent. See STONE, THE PROVINCE AND FUNCTION OF LAW 500 (1946).

conduct and belief." [3] In other words, even when the judge must supplement the policy determinations of legislation, he is limited by the ordinary canons of legislative interpretation and judicial lawmaking.

Lastly, and probably we must say most important of all, the courts under the American doctrine of judicial review are the final interpreters of the constitutions. In this capacity, they expound not only the specific provisions, but the policies and methods which are prescribed by these documents. The framers of the constitutions, like other Anglo-American legislators, have not usually stated the policies which their legislative declarations are intended to serve. They have left policies to implication. The consequence has been that the courts have filled in the policy factors which were lacking. A good example is the development which the clause regarding free speech and free press has received at the hands of the Supreme Court. The clause itself declares simply that Congress shall not pass any law abridging freedom of speech or of the press. The reasons for this provision are not stated. Justice Holmes, in various opinions, states what he regards as the policy reasons behind this clause: "that the ultimate good desired is better reached by free trade in ideas," "that the best test of truth is the power of thought to get itself accepted in the competition of the market," that these freedoms are not to be limited unless there is "a clear and present danger" of a speaker's bringing about substantive evils which the state has a right to prevent, and that "if there is any principle of the Constitution that more imperatively calls for attachment than any other, it is the principle of free thought. . . ." [4] These views ascribe to freedom of thought and expression a superlative importance and a preferred standing. They have been definitely adopted by the Supreme

---

[3] See note 1 above.

[4] See previous references to these views of Holmes in secs. 7–24, 7–27, problem 5, and 7–33, problem 5.

Court. They define the nature, the strength, and the limitations of the policy of free speech and free press. They operate just as effectively in the world of practical affairs as if they were written into the Constitution itself. And it goes almost without saying that a similar filling-in of policy notions has occurred in the interpretation of the commerce clause, the due process clauses, and all of the other important clauses of the Federal Constitution, not to speak of similar significant clauses of the state constitutions.

The practical bearing of this process of filling policy terms into the constitutions lies in its effect on the scope of governmental powers. The courts strike down as invalid legislative as well as other governmental action which runs contrary to the policies that they read into the constitutions. The courts' own policy in this regard may vary considerably. The courts' interpretive role may be performed in various ways; and the way they choose involves an important policy determination. Thus, for instance, the Supreme Court of the United States might originally have adopted a policy of favoring state's rights and local autonomy. Or, it could lean on the side of federal powers, as it actually did. Here was a policy determination of basic importance. Again, as regards the relation of government and individual, the courts can adopt widely differing policies.[5] The courts can regard themselves as bound to protect the individual in every way possible, as they have in effect done in regard to free speech and the guarantees of personal liberty. If the courts adopt this attitude and follow a policy of close supervision and scrutiny as regards governmental action, the scope of governmental powers is

[5] Compare the discussion here with that in the last two paragraphs of the next preceding section; see also the cases and other authorities there cited.

Also it is at the point where courts undertake to fill in policy notions that their answer to the question whether there is a superhuman criterion of justice becomes most significant. If the courts accept the postulate of a superhuman law which controls policy makers, the courts can invoke this law as a basis for limiting or striking down policy determinations by the legislature and others. See further discussion of this point in section 7–45.

necessarily narrowed. On the other hand, the courts can adopt a policy of deciding all questions of doubt in favor of governmental action, even where it impinges upon individual freedom. The practical effect of such a judicial attitude is to expand the powers of all the other agencies of government. It matters not whether the courts positively recognize the powers of these other agencies, or whether they simply permit the exercise of powers by a refusal to review cases where they are exercised. The practical importance of the supreme courts lies in their limitative function, their function as a restraint on the other organs of government. Their refusal to review governmental acts withdraws this limiting effect and serves as a license to other organs of government to expand the areas of their activities.

Recently we have witnessed a change in the Supreme Court's attitudes which has permitted the expansion of governmental powers along the lines just suggested. The Supreme Court has swung over to a policy of *laissez faire* in regard to the acts of other organs of government in our federal system.[6] This policy has been variously called a policy of judicial self-limitation, a *laissez-faire* policy, and a hands-off policy. However designated, this policy represents a reduction in the role of the Supreme Court as a check on the activities of other branches of government. The hands-off policy was a cardinal tenet of the Holmes constitutional philosophy. Its adoption by the "reconstituted Supreme

[6] The reasons for this hands-off policy cannot be better stated than in the words of Justice Holmes in his first opinion as a member of the Supreme Court:

"While the courts must exercise a judgment of their own, it by no means is true that every law is void which may seem to the judges who pass upon it excessive, unsuited to its ostensible end, or based upon conceptions of morality with which they disagree. Considerable latitude must be allowed for differences of view as well as for possible peculiar conditions which this Court can know but imperfectly, if at all. Otherwise a constitution, instead of embodying only relatively fundamental rules of right, as generally understood by all English-speaking communities, would become the partisan of a particular set of ethical or economic opinions, which by no means are held *'semper ubique et ab omnibus.'* " Otis v. Parker, 18 U. S. 606 at 608–609 (1903).

Court" furnishes the explanation of most of the changes in the meaning of the Federal Constitution which have occurred since 1937. The policy extends to the organs of the federal government and also to those of the states. It extends to legislative, executive, and administrative agencies alike. Only in regard to freedom of the mind and the personal guarantees has the opposed policy of close and strict interpretation of governmental powers been maintained. In the economic sphere, the hands-off policy prevails. Correlative to this hands-off policy of the Court, the powers of federal and state governments have expanded or been permitted to expand. Especially noteworthy has been the expansion of federal powers and functions; but the change has affected state powers significantly, too. The change has permitted a vastly increased governmental control over property, business, and all forms of economic activity.[7]

Sec. 7-38. Problems. 1. Consider the following decision, rendered in 1875, in which *Jessel*, M. R., a famous English judge, works out the solution of a policy problem:

"Now, it was said on the part of the Defendant, that such a contract as that which I have mentioned, a contract by which an inventor agrees to sell what he may invent, or acquire a patent for before he has invented it, is against public policy, and it was said to be against public policy, because it would discourage inventions; that if a man knows that he cannot obtain any pecuniary benefit from his invention, having already received the price for it, he will not invent, or if he does invent will keep it secret, and will not take out a patent. It must not be forgotten that you are not to extend arbitrarily those rules which say that a given contract is void as being against public policy, because if there is one thing which more than another public policy requires it is that men of full age and competent understanding shall have the utmost liberty of contracting, and that their contracts when entered into

[7] For the authorities on these various points, see the three notes for the Initiated Reader, attached to sec. 7-36.

freely and voluntarily shall be held sacred and shall be enforced by Courts of justice. Therefore, you have this paramount public policy to consider—that you are not lightly to interfere with this freedom of contract. Now, there is no doubt public policy may say that a contract to commit a crime, or a contract to give a reward to another to commit a crime, is necessarily void. The decisions have gone further, and contracts to commit an immoral offence, or to give money or reward to another to commit an immoral offence, or to induce another to do something against the general rules of morality, though far more indefinite than the previous class, have always been held to be void. . . . Does any one imagine that it is against public policy for an artist to sell the picture which he has never painted or designed, or for the sculptor to sell the statue, the subject of which is to be hereafter given to him, or for the author to sell the copyright of the book, the title of which is even as yet unknown, or, more than that, that a contributor to a periodical may agree that he will devote himself to the exclusive service of a certain periodical for a given period, for a given reward? These examples are, to my mind, entirely repugnant to the argument that there is any public policy in prohibiting such contracts. On the contrary, public policy is the other way. It encourages the poor, needy, and struggling author or artist. . . . This appears to me to apply as much to a patent invention as to any other subject which the intellect can produce. A man who is a needy and struggling inventor may well agree either for a present payment in money down, or for an annual payment, to put his intellectual gifts at the service of a purchaser. I see, therefore, not only no rule of public policy against it, but a rule of public policy for it, because it may enable such a man in comparative ease and affluence to devote his attention to scientific research, whereas, if such a contract were prohibited he would be compelled to apply himself to some menial or mechanical or lower calling, in order to gain a livelihood." [1]

What three primary policies enter into the court's thinking here? How would you characterize these three policies in

[1] Printing and Numerical Registering Company v. Sampson (1875) 19 L. R. Eq. 462 at 465–466.

terms of social interests? Which of them receives the court's nod? Why?

What is the practical bearing of this judge's statements that, "if there is one thing which more than another public policy requires it is that men of full age and competent understanding shall have the utmost liberty of contracting," and that "you are not lightly to interfere with this freedom of contract"?

What different choice is made by a legislature which fixes statutory minimum wages and maximum hours; or by a legislature which prescribes the terms and provisions which shall and shall not be written into a fire insurance policy or a life insurance policy?

2. In the following case, Mackay, J., of the Ontario High Court concluded that a particular kind of contractual clause was ineffective. Note the method which this judge followed in arriving at a principle of public policy to apply in the case before him. Where did he find this policy declared? In effect, who made the policy determination regarding race discrimination which Mackay, J., applied? [2]

"Application . . . for a declaration that a certain restrictive covenant is void. . . .

"*Mackay, J.:* The restrictive covenant which is the subject of this proceeding and which by the deed aforesaid the grantee assumes and agrees to exact from his assigns, reads as follows: 'Land not to be sold to Jews, or to persons of objectionable nationality.' Counsel for the applicant seeks the discharge and removal of this covenant on these alternative grounds: first, that it is void as against public policy; . . . The matter before me, so defined, appears to raise issues of first impression because a search of the case law of Great Britain and of Canada does not reveal any reported decision which would be of direct assistance in this proceeding. . . .

"The applicant's argument is founded on the legal principle, briefly stated in 7 Hals. (2nd ed.), pp. 153–4, that:

[2] Re Drummond Wren [1945] 4 D. L. R. 674.

'Any agreement which tends to be injurious to the public or against the public good is void as being contrary to public policy.' . . .

"It is a well-recognized rule that Courts may look at various Dominion and Provincial Acts and public law as an aid in determining principles relative to public policy: See *Walkerville Brewing Co. v. Mayrand*, [1929] 2 D. L. R., 63 O. L. R. 573.

"First and of profound significance is the recent San Francisco Charter, to which Canada was a signatory, and which the Dominion Parliament has now ratified. The preamble to this Charter reads in part as follows:

" 'We the peoples of the United Nations determined to save succeeding generations from the scourge of war, which twice in our lifetime has brought untold sorrow to mankind, and to reaffirm faith in fundamental human rights, in the dignity and worth of the human person, in the equal rights of men and women and of nations large and small . . . and for these ends to practice tolerance and live together in peace with one another as good neighbors. . . .'

"Under Articles 1 and 55 of this Charter, Canada is pledged to promote 'universal respect for, and observance of, human rights and fundamental freedoms for all without distinction as to race, sex, language, or religion.'

"In the Atlantic Charter to which Canada has subscribed, the principles of freedom from fear and freedom of worship are recognized.

"Section 1 of the *Racial Discrimination Act* provides:

" '1. No person shall,—

" '(a) publish or display or cause to be published or displayed; or

" '(b) permit to be published or displayed on lands or premises or in a newspaper, through a radio broadcasting station or by means of any other medium which he owns or controls, any notice, sign, symbol, emblem or other representation indicating discrimination or an intention to discriminate against any person or any class of persons for any purpose because of the race or creed of such person or class of persons.'

"The Provincial Legislature further has expressed itself in the *Insurance Act*, R. S. O. 1937, c. 256, s. 99, as follows:

'Any licensed insurer which discriminates unfairly between risks within Ontario because of the race or religion of the insured shall be guilty of an offence.'

"Moreover, under s. 6 of the Regulations passed pursuant to the *Community Halls Act,* now R. S. O. 1937, c. 284, it is provided that 'Every hall erected under this Act shall be available for any public gathering of an educational, fraternal, religious or social nature or for the discussion of any public question, and no organization shall be denied the use of the hall for religious, fraternal, or political reasons.'

"Proceeding from the general to the particular, the argument of the applicant is that the impugned covenant is void because it is injurious to the public good. This deduction is grounded on the fact that the covenant against sale to Jews or to persons of objectionable nationality prevents the particular piece of land from ever being acquired by the persons against whom the covenant is aimed, and that this prohibition is without regard to whether the land is put to residential, commercial, industrial or any other use. How far this is obnoxious to public policy can only be ascertained by projecting the coverage of the covenant with respect both to the classes of persons whom it may adversely affect, and to the lots or subdivisions of land to which it may be attached. So considered, the consequences of judicial approbation of such a covenant are portentous. If sale of a piece of land can be prohibited to Jews, it can equally be prohibited to Protestants, Catholics, or other groups or denominations. If the sale of one piece of land can be so prohibited, the sale of other pieces of land can likewise be prohibited. In my opinion, nothing could be more calculated to create or deepen divisions between existing religious and ethnic groups in this Province, or in this country, than the sanction of a method of land transfer which would permit the segregation and confinement of particular groups to particular business or residential areas, or conversely, would exclude particular groups from particular business or residential areas. The unlikelihood of such a policy as a legislative measure is evident from the contrary intention of the recently enacted *Racial Discrimination Act,* and the judicial branch of government must take full cognizance of such factors.

"Ontario, and Canada too, may well be termed a Province, and a country, of minorities in regard to the religious and ethnic groups which live therein. It appears to me to be a moral duty, at least, to lend aid to all forces of cohesion, and similarly to repel all fissiparous tendencies which would imperil national unity. The common law Courts have, by their actions over the years, obviated the need for rigid constitutional guarantees in our policy by their wise use of the doctrine of public policy as an active agent in the promotion of the public weal. While Courts and eminent Judges have, in view of the powers of our legislatures, warned against inventing new heads of public policy, I do not conceive that I would be breaking new ground were I to hold the restrictive covenant impugned in this proceeding to be void as against public policy. Rather would I be applying well-recognized principles of public policy to a set of facts requiring their invocation in the interest of the public good.

"That the restrictive covenant in this case is directed in the first place against Jews lends poignancy to the matter when one considers that anti-semitism has been a weapon in the hands of our recently-defeated enemies and the scourge of the world. But this feature of the case does not require innovation in legal principle to strike down the covenant; it merely makes it more appropriate to apply existing principles. . . .

"My conclusion therefore is that the covenant is void because offensive to the public policy of this jurisdiction. This conclusion is reinforced, if reinforcement is necessary, by the wide official acceptance of international policies and declarations frowning on the type of discrimination which the covenant would seem to perpetuate. . . .

"An order will therefore go declaring that the restrictive covenant attacked by the applicant is void and of no effect.

"Order declaring covenant void." [3]

---

[3] A similar result was reached by the Supreme Court of the United States in Hurd v. Hodge, 334 U. S. 24 (1948). The court based the result on a construction of the Civil Rights Act as well as on a public policy of the United States. See also Shelley v. Kraemer, 334 U. S. 1 (1948), where the court held that enforcement of such covenants by state courts was prohibited by the equal protection clause of the Fourteenth Amendment. See discussion of these cases in 46 MICH. L. REV. 978 (1948).

3. *Miller v. Schoene.*[4] By statute of Virginia, an administrative officer was authorized to order the destruction of red cedar trees as a means of preventing a disease called "cedar rust" which grows at one stage on cedar trees, and which infects, and injures apple trees at another stage. The cedars were valuable for ornament and for lumber. Apple-growing was one of the principal businesses of the state. The owner of some cedar trees, ordered to be destroyed, challenged the validity of the statute and the order made thereunder. The Supreme Court held that the statute and order were not invalid under the due process clause of the Fourteenth Amendment.

Stone, J., delivered the opinion of the Court. In part he said:

"On the evidence we may accept the conclusion of the Supreme Court of Appeals that the state was under the necessity of making a choice between the preservation of one class of property and that of the other wherever both existed in dangerous proximity. It would have been none the less a choice if, instead of enacting the present statute, the state, by doing nothing, had permitted serious injury to the apple orchards within its borders to go on unchecked. When forced to such a choice the state does not exceed its constitutional powers by deciding upon the destruction of one class of property in order to save another which, in the judgment of the legislature, is of greater value to the public. It will not do to say that the case is merely one of a conflict of two private interests and that the misfortune of apple growers may not be shifted to cedar owners by ordering the destruction of their property; for it is obvious that there may be, and that here there is, a preponderant public concern in the preservation of the one interest over the other."

Here the legislature makes the primary choice between competing policies; and then what follows? What is the role of the Supreme Court? How does it enter the picture?

---

[4] 276 U. S. 272 at 279 (1928).

4. *Hoff v. State of New York.*[5] Read again the report of this case as set out in section 5–13, problem 3.

What is the principal policy which the court works out here? Where does the court discover this policy? In Article I, Section 4, of the Constitution of New York? In the statutes referred to? Outside of either constitution or statute?

What bearing upon the decision of the case has the court's view that "Our constitutional guarantees of liberty are merely empty words unless a person imprisoned or detained against his will may challenge the legality of his imprisonment and detention"?

What is the role of the writ of habeas corpus in relation to this policy? What is the role of the action in the present case? What is the relevance of the judge's view that "The writ of habeas corpus is the process devised centuries ago for the protection of free men. It has been cherished by generations of free men who had learned by experience that it furnished the only reliable protection of their freedom."?

Sec. 7–39. Effects of policy-makers' attitudes. In our time, there has been much talk about the attitudes of the individual, and about the sum total of his attitudes, which is commonly called his "personality." This kind of talk has been a natural consequence of the current scientific interest in social psychology. The purport of this talk is that the actor's attitudes are determinative of everything he does, explain what he does and, if known, put one in a position to guess what he will do. In this connection, I am reminded of a popular story about the late laconic Calvin Coolidge. He had been to church and was asked what the sermon was about. He answered, "About sin." When further pressed to know what the preacher had said about this interesting subject, he answered tersely, "He was agin it." This last was enough to describe the preacher's general readiness to act by word

[5] 279 N. Y. 490 (1939).

or deed in opposition to sin; it gave a good idea of the kind of man he was and what to expect from him.

Analysis in terms of attitudes and personality has been especially common in discussions of the judicial process. It is urged that the judge's personality shapes and determines the ways in which he decides cases.[1] And, of course, the same type of analysis can be applied to the policy maker. His own attitudes can be viewed as prime determinants of the policies and methods as well as the specific patterns of behavior which he puts into the form of law. I have already referred to the importance of the attitudes of the Supreme Court and their effects on the determination of policy.[2] Other instances in which the attitudes of individual officials have counted in the determination of policy come readily to mind.[3] Chief Justice Marshall's views and attitudes played an enormous part in shaping our federal government and the role which it was to play. He believed firmly in the need to maintain a strong central government. He dominated the Supreme Court, and through its decisions made possible the widest exercise of federal powers and functions. One can hardly imagine what the present condition of this country would be if Roane or some other strong protagonist of state's rights had sat on the Supreme Court instead of Marshall. As Professor Ross has said, personal ascendancy is not yet a neglectable quantity "even in the rigid articulated mechanism of the 'legal state.' Despite its statutory framework, an office bulges when filled by the man of command, shrinks when occupied by mediocrity."[4] In our own recent history we have an outstanding instance of what Ross has in mind.

[1] See FRANK, LAW AND THE MODERN MIND (1930).

[2] See sec. 7–37, *ad fin.*

[3] Jefferson's views, and Jackson's likewise, strongly affected the course of American policy, and the attitudes and beliefs of various legislators have been equally influential.

[4] SOCIAL CONTROL 289 (1900). To much the same effect is Emerson's dictum, "An institution is the lengthened shadow of one man." (THE ESSAY ON SELF-RELIANCE 19 (1905).)

maker. All our lawmaking agencies derive almost all their ideas regarding policies and methods either from the legal tradition or from the suggestions of nonofficial individuals or writers of today.

Sec. 7–41. Group influence on policy makers. Just as the policy maker may borrow ideas from preceding policy makers and from individuals and writers, he may borrow from the usages of some other institutional group. Acting on the state's behalf, the policy maker makes the policy or standard of a nonlegal group a state policy. This process of borrowing standards often occurs in the case of practices of business and professional groups. The legal ways of dealing with commercial paper, for example, have for the most part been drawn from the usages of bankers and businessmen. The latter serve as sources of law, to use a conventional phrase, and thus a coincidence of standards results. Or the legal system may undertake to effectuate a policy which prevails in many churches and families—it may forbid dealings in intoxicants; it may pass a prohibition law. One of the most common instances in which our law has borrowed its policies and standards from other social institutions, such as the church and the family, has been the case of proper sex behavior. Here one finds many laws enforcing socially established standards of behavior, such as laws prohibiting sex intercourse between unmarried persons, penalizing acts contributing to the delinquency of children, forbidding the dissemination of obscene literature, and forbidding indecent exposure of the person.

An organized group, such as an association of farmers, workmen, manufacturers, professional men, or war veterans may do more than suggest policies to the policy maker or offer him ideas for adoption; it may exert a positive political pressure on the policy maker and exert a decisive control over the policies which the policy maker and other officials

pursue.[1] This can be done by democratic methods, as by putting representatives in the "seats of the mighty," or by exert-
ing political pressure on those who occupy such seats. Or it
can be done by methods which are illicit, as by bribery or
corrupt bargains. Either way the group's policy becomes the
policy of the state. The governmental machinery is made to
serve as an instrument for effecting the particular policies
of the dominant group. The latter can enact laws in its own
interest, apply and enforce existing laws in a self-serving
manner, or spend public funds for its own advantage. Usually
this type of domination is partial only; a group merely obtains
certain laws or other measures through its influence over the
legislature or other officials. Up to a certain point we look
upon the exertion of group influence as a normal phenomenon
in our democracy. In fact we rely upon the conflicting and
countervailing selfish interests of different groups to offset
and check one another through democratic processes. But
beyond a certain point, we regard the exertion of political
pressure and the exploitation of influence with governmental
agencies as a misuse of power for particular group advantage.
It is not easy to make the distinction in practice. For our
present purpose we need do no more than suggest that the
distinction can be made and that it is a matter of degree.

A more radical kind of group domination appears where
a military clique, or a popular mob, or a patriotic group
forcibly seizes political power by revolution.[2] We have had
only one such revolution in this country, that by which our
ties with Great Britain were severed. This kind of change
usually involves some important alterations of policies and
methods, and a sweeping displacement of top officials. But

---

[1] Of course individuals as such may do all these things; but usually individuals lead or organize groups and, through control of the latter, exercise
control over larger organized groups like the state.

[2] The slaveholding group of the southern states seized power therein at the
outset of the Civil War, and attempted to sever connections between the Con-
federate States and the United States; but this group was ultimately vanquished
by the power of the United States.

even the promoters of revolution do not usually attempt to destroy the going state and create another in its place.[3] Instead, they substitute new pilots who will steer the ship of state on a different course.

Sec. 7–42. Social and historical determinants—stability in state policies. The great mass of behavior patterns in any community, including methods of doing things and policy notions, are handed down from the past. They are passed along from generation to generation. In this sense, our ways and policies of today are fixed and determined by our forefathers. We have many of ours, for example our notions of the importance of liberty and personal security, from our colonial ancestors and their English forebears. Our ways and policy notions are explainable in terms of the evolution of the civilization in which we live.* They represent the experience of previous ages in regard to ways of living and the ends of various kinds of activity.

These traditional patterns of behavior and traditional notions of policy are built into each individual by training and education. They become part of the individual's habits of action and modes of thought. Aristotle, one of the greatest political thinkers of all time, accepted slavery as an institution,

---

[3] Occasionally a revolution has aimed to obliterate an existing state organization and to replace it with a new organization of its own. This was true of the Communist Revolution in Russia, which aimed to make a complete change and was successful in so doing. The first French Revolution also made, temporarily, an almost complete substitution. In this instance, however, the old state organization was restored after a time; later revolutionary changes of government in France have been of the character mentioned in the text.

* (I.R.) This fact was built up into a complete theory of legal development, by a "historical school" of jurists of the nineteenth century. According to their view law is nothing but "the jural form of the habits, usages and thoughts of a people" (Carter). "Throughout, it (law) is the product of silently working forces, not of the arbitrary will of a law giver" (Savigny). "Law is conceived as self-generative, evolving its rules in the form of customs without the interposition of conscious human agency or choice" (Dickinson). See critical discussion of this view by Dickinson, "The Law Behind Law," 29 Col. L. Rev. 113, 285 (1929) and items by Pound and Cardozo, cited therein; and extensive analysis of views of the "historical school" by Stone, Province and Function of Law 421 *et seq.* (1946).

and concluded that it was based on a sound policy. He maintained that:

"He who by nature is not his own but another's and yet a man, is by nature a slave. . . . But is there anyone thus intended by nature to be a slave, and for whom such a condition is expedient and right, or rather is not all slavery a violation of nature? There is no difficulty in answering this question, on the grounds both of reason and of fact. For that some should rule, and others be ruled, is a thing, not only necessary, but expedient; from the hour of their birth, some are marked for subjection, others for rule." He concluded that "some are by nature free, and others, slaves." [1]

Human slavery depends on a complex set of legal arrangements. Can anyone doubt that Aristotle's opinions of human slavery and the legal arrangements connected with it would have been different, if he had been brought up in the United States today?

What is true of individuals generally is, of course, true of the individuals who happen to become policy makers. It is true of the individuals collectively who constitute smaller groups, and true of the members of the all-inclusive group which we call a community or society. Behavior patterns of past generations become the behavior patterns of today. They represent habits and points of view common to the members of the community, and common to the present community and its predecessors.

When we put the contribution of today's lawmaker alongside this mass of traditional patterns of behavior and traditional notions of policy, his accomplishments appear relatively small. His creative role seems to be almost negligible. The great stream of behavior patterns, standards, and policies, flows by the lawmaker almost untouched and unchanged; his acts are like bursting bubbles on the surface of the stream.

[1] JOWETT, THE POLITICS OF ARISTOTLE 7–9 (1885).

He takes for granted most of his social heritage, and tacitly accepts it; even when he undertakes to make changes, he weaves his innovation out of old material. The traditional material which forms his cultural background embraces three elements which it will be useful for our purpose to differentiate: the folkways, the mores, and the legal traditions of the community.

The first of the traditional patterns of behavior are the *folkways*, to use the now familiar terminology of Sumner.[2] These patterns of behavior are habitual and common to a group of persons. As Sumner observes, folkways are habits for the individual and customs for the group. Examples of folkways are the practice of sleeping in beds, of sitting in chairs, of wearing buttons on coat sleeves, of having notches on men's coat collars, and so on.[3] These common modes of behavior grew up unplanned and unnoticed by those persons whose behavior conforms to them. Neither the lawmaker nor anyone else has anything to do with their origin.[4] Since they arise and are followed without intention and without thinking, they do not involve any policy factors.

The second traditional factor consists of what are called *mores*.[5] These develop out of the folkways.

"People are caught in the folkways before they know it. Whenever they become aware of the fact that they are 'in' the folkways, and criticize them and approve them, and continue to follow them, these folkways become 'mores.'

[2] See generally on the subject matter of this and the following paragraph, SUMNER, FOLKWAYS (1906).

[3] COOLEY, ANGELL, and CARR, INTRODUCTORY SOCIOLOGY 94 (1933).

[4] Lumley thus summarizes the doctrine of Sumner regarding the origin and nature of folkways: "People have similar individual needs and begin to satisfy them in similar ways in the same environment. This procedure makes folkways. The people did not *intend* to make folkways; they intended to satisfy their personal needs. But in doing this, they acted uniformly, repetitiously; they made mass action." (MEANS OF SOCIAL CONTROL 5, 6 (1925).

[5] "Mores" is the plural of a Latin word whose singular is *mos*, meaning custom.

The mores are those folkways which have been examined, judged useful and beneficial, and made into approved activity patterns." [6]

These differ from the folkways simply in the sense that individuals or groups discover a purpose or policy behind these ways, and accept this purpose or policy as the reason for following them. But, as with the folkways, one cannot point to any definite person or place of origin; their beginning is like that of ancient hymns and folksongs, cloaked by the veil of anonymity. The important feature of the mores is that they stand as guides for action. They are standards of behavior. And as the need for observance comes to be felt more strongly, these mores are adopted and backed up by various social institutions. At this point, our lawmaker may enter the picture. He may draw legal standards from the mores. The recent prohibition law stands as a good example of the fact that laws can be built on the ways of behavior (abstinence) which are regarded as right by a substantial part of the community, and be imposed on the rest of the community as the legally approved and sanctioned way of behavior. And the lawmaker may overrule the mores in part, as he did by the prohibition legislation which cut across the established ways of persons inclined to imbibe. For the most part, however, he does not disturb the mores. They are significant simply as aids in the job of social control, created and kept going by agencies entirely outside the legal system.

Finally, established law and legal ends constitute part of the traditional background of the policy maker. Here, I would include the constitutions, the statutes, the common law, established rules of method, and notions of what all these legal devices are for.[7] I would include also the works

---

[6] LUMLEY, MEANS OF SOCIAL CONTROL 6 (1925).

[7] As regards the nature and functions of the established legal context or background, see secs. 5-12, 5-16, 5-17, and 6-01 et seq.

of text writers and legal theorists. But someone may ask, are not the first mentioned items binding law, and not merely tradition? That they are binding cannot, of course, be denied, but that they are also part of the legal tradition is no less true. That they are binding simply means that they are a special part of the tradition to be accepted by Tom, Dick and Harry, and not disregarded as lightly as other traditional material may be. Our Constitution was adopted over a century and a half ago, and with a few changes is still operating. Many statutes have a like age, and normally, statutes continue to operate until changed. The common law is a continuous body of legal ideas, legal rules and legal methods, beginning in England and running down to today. The lawmaker of the present does not create or change any substantial part of his legal background; he accepts it and takes it for granted. It constitutes his stock of legal ideas.

When the lawmaker does undertake to create novel standards or strike out on new paths of policy, he cannot depart far from the traditional. Especially the judicial lawmaker hesitates to reach beyond the old material; his traditional methods require him to stick to hallowed principles and create as little as possible. And the legislative lawmaker is definitely a child of his day. He enacts standards and pursues ends which are already well known and commonly recognized. He reworks and clarifies traditional ideas. He introduces novelty in detail or manner of statement. He combines old elements in a new way. He borrows a novel idea from some thinker. But this modern Aristotle is himself limited by the notions of methods and policy of the community in which he lives. Neither he nor the legislator who follows him can raise himself far above the traditional ideas with which he has been indoctrinated.[8]

[8] But our appreciation of the import of the traditional factors in the shaping of policies and standards must not lead us to deny entirely the creative contributions of legislator and judge. These are most important, too. See chapters 4,

It is this traditional element, this legal lore, inert and built into members of the community, which gives stability to law, to legal institutions, to legal policies. Like habits generally, this built-in element is stable and hard to change. It represents the cumulative contributions of past generations to the ways and the ideals of the present. It adds certainty to your calculations and mine because we know how other people think and feel; and we know because we think and feel the same way as they do, having been trained in the same legal culture.[9]

Sec. 7–43. Change in state policies. Generally, policies are inherited, as we have just seen. But conditions change, and different policies become necessary. It is not only important to appreciate and formulate the policies that have been handed down from the past, it is important to see the need

5, and 6, and also the next section. On this point Justice Cardozo has well said: "Savigny's conception of law as something realized without struggle or aim or purpose, a process of silent growth, the fruition in life and manners of a people's history and genius, gives a picture incomplete and partial. It is true if we understand it to mean that the judge in shaping the rules of law must heed the *mores* of his day. It is one-sided and therefore false in so far as it implies that the *mores* of the day automatically shape rules which, full-grown and ready made, are handed to the judge. . . . The standards or patterns of utility and morals will be found by the judge in the life of the community. They will be found in the same way by the legislator. That does not mean, however, that the work of the one, any more than that of the other is a replica of nature's forms." NATURE OF THE JUDICIAL PROCESS 104–105 (1921).

And Dickinson adds that the judges "do not create the materials out of which the new rule is built, but they use them, select, reject, combine, emphasize, in short give form and life to them, as their personality and intellectual equipment dictate; and if this is not creative activity, no creative activity is performed by human beings." "The Law Behind Law," 29 COL. L. REV. 284 at 305 (1929).

For a full discussion of the point here made, see the items by Cardozo and Dickinson here cited as well as the items by Pound and Stone referred to in note * above.

[9] Of course, the legislator or judge may leave the existing order untouched because he does not think of the possibility of changing it; or he may leave it untouched because he regards stability as a desirable end. These two attitudes must not be confused. The intentional support of stability is involved in the recognition of social interests in peace and order, in security of acquisitions, and security of transactions.

for changes in them. This is normally the work of individual theorists and writers. Such men are the first to appreciate that certain policies need to be served and are not being served, or that existing standards do not serve the needs that they are intended to serve. They formulate new policies and measures to meet the needs of the day. They study past lore in order to learn what changes need to be made.

The state and other social institutions have special agencies to formulate, declare and effectuate their policies. One of the prime functions of these agencies is to make changes, when, as and if policy changes are needed. In the words of Cardozo, "Through one agency or another, either by statute or by decision, rules, however well established, must be revised when they are found after fair trial to be inconsistent in their workings with an attainment of the ends which law is meant to serve." [1] And I would add that these agencies are intended to act no less when it is necessary to change the ends which law has served in the past. To some extent, the changes in policies and methods are made without a full awareness of what is occurring. The policy maker passes a new statute, for example, to meet a specific need, and does not realize that he is departing from the policies of the past. The policy maker only realizes the direction he is following when some individual thinker becomes aware of the discrepancy between the traditional formulation of policy and the actual policies which are being pursued. Such a writer calls the discrepancy to the attention of the policy makers, and reformulates the policy of the time. But usually the function of the writer who studies policy changes is not merely to call attention to a change which has already come about. It is rather to call attention of policy makers to changes which need to be made in order to meet changed conditions. For example, the inequality of bargaining power in employer-

[1] THE GROWTH OF THE LAW 120 (1924).

employee relations was first talked about by theoretical writers and social reformers. It was thereafter recognized by many legislatures in social legislation, and lastly recognized by the judiciary which held a restraining hand on the policies that could be adopted under our constitutions.

It takes time for new policies to pass through this process of discovery, formulation, and adoption. There is always a strong tendency to adhere to the old. This is just another way of saying that habit and custom are strong. It is always hard to break their shackles. The leader in the policy field must overcome blind inertia and the tendency to adhere to what has always been done. Policy makers are not ready to accept forthwith suggested changes. There is always a space of time between someone's perception of a need and the recognition of this need by the policy makers of society. This period of delay is commonly called the cultural lag. Changes in law, like changes in all other forms of control in society, are subject to this lag. Law and legal policies always tend to fall behind the times.

However, policies are never completely stable. No list of policies is good for all time. Not only does any list of policies change with circumstances, but the emphasis on particular policies shifts as different social conditions develop. The history of our Western civilization shows striking changes in the policies professed by government. Four stages in the conscious thinking about the end of law are differentiated by Pound.[2]

Primitive government has acted chiefly to keep order. Its primary function has been the preservation of public peace. Its aim, explicit or implicit, has been to prevent open fighting among clans and other groups. In our attempts to regulate employee-employer relations, we are today in approximately this primitive stage of legal control. We have not yet reached

[2] INTRODUCTION TO PHILOSOPHY OF LAW 72 *et seq.* (1922).

the stage where other ends than the public order weigh heavily in the solution of conflict. In general, the victory is allowed to go to the side with the greater economic power— so long as violence does not occur.[3] Much the same observations can be made regarding efforts to regulate the field of international relations.[4] Conflicts in this sphere are not settled on the basis of fairness but on the basis of power and danger to the public peace. There is no effective superstate, and whatever check is exerted in the name of law is put forth chiefly to forestall open warfare between states.

At another stage in political development, peace and order are expanded to include the security of acquisitions and the security of transactions.[5] But even in this stage the state does not look far beyond considerations of stability and security. The general function of the state and its legal system may be summed up in terms of security, or of preservation of the *status quo*.

At a later stage, at least in the history of western European and Anglo-American legal systems, the emphasis shifts to the individual life, and particularly to individual liberty. The role of the law is conceived in a negative way. The function of the state is supposed to be to secure to each individual the maximum of liberty consistent with the like liberty of all. This was the period of history in which our American republic was born. This conception of state and legal function dictated many of the clauses of our constitutions; these instruments are replete with guarantees of individual liberty and security, all framed under the influence of the general idea that government is a necessary evil to be kept within fixed and narrow limits.

[3] Brandeis, J., dissenting in Duplex v. Deering, 254 U. S. 443 at 488 (1921), refers to this aspect of labor disputes, and suggests that it is possible "to substitute processes of justice for the more primitive method of trial by combat."

[4] See sec. 7–32.

[5] See secs. 7–08, 7–14, and 7–15.

Since the turn of the century our ideas of state policy have taken on a more social color. This does not mean that former conceptions of state objectives have been abandoned. It only means that they have been qualified and supplemented by a new stress on the general welfare. In the last century, the United States was predominantly rural and largely undeveloped. Goods were usually produced and consumed in the same locality; problems of transportation and marketing were relatively simple. The main objective of the government was to encourage the settlement and development of the country. Individual initiative could be relied upon to bring this about; the philosophy of liberty was an excellent philosophy for an age of discoverers and colonizers, as Pound has said. But the situation today is radically different and a different philosophy is required. Our country has become predominantly urban, highly industrialized, and overcrowded in major areas. Account has to be taken of the integrated processes of production, the complicated and extended lines of transportation, the delicate balance between markets and the supply of goods, and the effects of these complexities on the persons involved in them and on the community at large. There has been accordingly a shift of emphasis from problems of development to problems of evolving fair methods of producing goods and fair methods of distributing them. In putting more stress on these problems and in expressing this in the objectives which it attempts to achieve, the state today is simply responding to the conditions of our time.[6]

The policy maker must be always on the alert to make changes in our legal system as they are needed. History needs to be studied for what it can teach, but the hand of the past should not hold us to a helpless adherence to what is out-

---

[6] There are the questions, too, how far and how fast to go in substituting social effort for individual effort. Many lawyers, judges, and other solid thinkers believe that we have been moving too far too fast lately in the direction of socialization.

dated. Holmes has expressed this notion in the following felicitous language:

"The rational study of law is still to a large extent the study of history. History must be a part of the study, because without it we cannot know the precise scope of rules which it is our business to know. It is a part of the rational study, because it is the first step toward an enlightened scepticism, that is, toward a deliberate reconsideration of the worth of those rules. When you get the dragon out of his cave on to the plain and in the daylight, you can count his teeth and claws, and see just what is his strength. But to get him out is only the first step. The next is either to kill him, or to tame him and make him a useful animal. . . . It is revolting to have no better reason for a rule of law than that so it was laid down in the time of Henry IV. It is still more revolting if the grounds upon which it was laid down have vanished long since, and the rule simply persists from blind imitation of the past." [7]

But stability has its importance too. "The revision is a delicate task, not to be undertaken by gross or adventurous hands, lest certainty and order be unduly sacrificed. . . ." [8] It is always a nice question for the policy maker to decide whether the advantages of change outweigh the advantages of continuity. Change must not be made too rapidly and without consideration of consequences. Not always is change for the better. Just as there are some persons who are temperamentally inclined to assume that whatever is, is good, there are also those who are temperamentally inclined to assume that whatever is new, is better.

Sec. 7–44. Problems. 1. In an address to Congress, January 6, 1941, President Roosevelt spoke of the "basic things expected by our people of their political and economic systems." It goes without saying that Hitler would not have mentioned the same basic things on the same date. I quote

[7] "The Path of the Law," 10 HARV. L. REV. 457 at 469 (1897).
[8] CARDOZO, THE GROWTH OF THE LAW 120 (1924).

Roosevelt's remarks and ask that you explain how his remarks illustrate the general points made in section 7–40. What is the purpose of this inventory?

"The basic things expected by our people of their political and economic systems are simple. They are:
Equality of opportunity for youth and for others.
Jobs for those who can work.
Security for those who need it.
The ending of special privileges for the few.
The preservation of civil liberties for all.
The enjoyment of the fruits of scientific progress in a wider and constantly rising standard of living." [1]

2. Explain how group influence on the policy maker is illustrated by the discussion of the whaling customs in section 7–16, problem 4.

3. What do you make of the statement by Holmes that:

"The law, so far as it depends on learning, is indeed, as it has been called, the government of the living by the dead. To a very considerable extent no doubt it is inevitable that the living should be so governed. . . . But the present has a right to govern itself so far as it can; and it ought always to be remembered that historic continuity with the past is not a duty, it is only a necessity."? [2]

What does Holmes mean by the statement that "Continuity with the past is not a duty"? What does he mean by the suggestion that such continuity is a necessity?

4. Consider the following news item in relation to the traditional patterns of behavior mentioned in section 7–42: folkways and mores. Note particularly the word "custom" italicized in each of the first five paragraphs. Which of the two types of behavior patterns is meant by the word "custom" in each instance? The distinction turns particularly on the point at which a policy factor is appreciated.

[1] 87 CONG. REC. 46 (1941).
[2] Speech at a dinner in honor of Professor Longdell, June 25, 1895.

"*WHY PASS ON THE RIGHT.* The Conestoga wagon, the farmers' freight-hauling vehicle of the early days, is responsible for the present *custom* of vehicles passing on the right in the United States, according to the bureau of public roads.

"Before the extensive use of the Conestoga wagon it was the *custom* to pass vehicles on the left, following the earlier English rule.

"In England in the days when men traveled armed on horseback, it was the *custom* to pass to the left so that the sword or pistol arm would be on the side of the man passed. Later, in travel by coach or wagon, the driver sat on the right side to give his right arm free play in wielding the whip, and passing to the left he was better able to avoid entanglements with the wheels of passing vehicles. Traffic passes to the left to this day in England.

"On the continent—in France, Germany, and Italy—the postillion system of driving, by which the driver sat on the left wheel horse, existed in the early days for both coaches and wagons. To a man riding the left wheel horse passing to the right gives a better view of the passing vehicle. In these countries, passing to the right has always been the *custom*.

"In Italy, until the time of Mussolini, vehicles in the cities, where postillions were customary, passed to the right; in the country, where box wagons were much used vehicles passed to the left. Mussolini made passing *custom* uniform by decreeing that all should pass to the right.

"The drivers of the Conestoga wagons rode the left wheel horse. Passing to the right was more convenient in spite of the fact that it was the custom to pass to the left, as in England. Drivers riding the 'lazy board' of the Conestoga wagon—a board between the two left-side wheels that pulled out and could be ridden when driving from the side of the wagon—preferred passing to the right, and traffic was passed on that side.

"The deep wagon ruts in the singletrack roads made by the Conestoga wagon drivers were followed by other traffic." [3]

[3] *Ann Arbor Daily News*, Feb. 7, 1934.

5. During the latter part of the fifteenth century, between 1464 and 1470, Sir John Fortescue wrote a famous tract entitled *De Laudibus Legum Angliae*. Fortescue was for many years Chief Justice of England. He espoused the Lancastrian cause during the latter part of the Wars of the Roses and went into exile when the Lancastrian party was defeated. He wrote this tract for the benefit of Edward, Prince of Wales, eldest son of King Henry VI, during his exile in Barrois. In chapter 17 he says:

"The realm of England was first inhabited by the Britons; afterwards it was ruled and civilized under the government of the Romans; then the Britons prevailed again; next, it was possessed by the Saxons, who changed the name of Britain into England. After the Saxons, the Danes lorded it over us, and then the Saxons prevailed a second time; at last, the Normans came in, whose descendants retain the kingdom at this day: and during all that time, wherein those several nations and their kings prevailed, England has nevertheless been constantly governed by the same customs, as it is at present: which if they were not above all exception good, no doubt but some or other of those kings, from a principle of justice, in point of reason, or moved by inclination, would have made some alteration or quite abolished them, especially the Romans, who governed all the rest of the world in a manner by their own laws. Again, some of the aforesaid kings, who only got and kept possession of the Realm by the sword, were enabled by the same means to have destroyed the laws and introduced their own. Neither the laws of the Romans, which are cried up beyond all others for their antiquity; nor yet the laws of the Venetians, however famous in this respect, their Island being not inhabited so early as Britain; (neither was Rome itself at that time built;) nor, in short, are the laws of any other kingdom in the world so venerable for their antiquity. So that there is no pretence to say, or insinuate to the contrary, but that the laws and customs of England are not only *good*, but the *very best*." [4]

[4] DE LAUDIBUS LEGUM ANGLIAE, translated from the Latin by Francis Gregor, 50 *et seq.* (1874).

Do you think Fortescue's assumption that if the English customs "were not above all exception good" the English kings would have altered or abolished them, is a safe assumption?

Can you find an easy explanation for his view "that the laws and customs of England are not only *good,* but the *very best*"?

6. Does the family serve the same functions, socially speaking, in America at the present time as it did a century ago? Does it serve the same functions in an industrial society as in a primitive society? Various writers have observed that changes in family life resulting from the transition from home industry to the factory system have created new social problems. They have stressed the point that modern economic changes have largely destroyed the effectiveness of the family as a social disciplinary agency, and a great increase in juvenile delinquency has resulted.

How do these facts affect the social role of the state, the school, and law?

Sec. 7–45. Basic criteria for policy makers—nature and consequences. The foregoing sections of this chapter have been intended to describe various legal policies which find expression in all or part of our American legal systems and to explain how such policies are formulated and determined. Our account has shown, first, what the major policies have been, and now are; second, what human agencies make or contribute to policy determination; and third, what factors, such as habit, inertia, and mere lack of imagination, serve as limits on policy determination. This account of the process of policy determination—which I shall hereafter call the "empirical" theory [1]—is predominant in the judicial opinions

[1] The theory takes a variety of directions, each of which carries a different emphasis. The general method is the same in all. "Empirical" is the adjective which I have chosen to use. Other adjectives sometimes applied to the theory are: "scientific," "realistic," "pragmatic," and "positivistic." The adherents of the theory are prone to use the first two adjectives, scientific and realistic,

and legislative declarations of American policy makers today. It finds expression in the writings of Holmes, Pound, Wigmore, Llewellyn, and other leading thinkers. It adopts essentially the philosophical position of men like James and Dewey.[2]

The gist of the "empirical" theory is that our basic criteria of justice, our notions of policy, as well as our methods of resolving policy problems, are the work of human agencies. The theory holds that criteria of justice are derived from human experience. It avers that man, individually and collectively, standardizes his contacts with the world about him. According to this theory man systematizes his experiences in prescriptive terms (for direction and guidance) as well as in descriptive terms (for information);[3] he builds up goals and methods of action from his experiences, including his internal experiences, or feelings and felt needs. These goals and methods are merely grand inductions or generalizations which will organize his activities and dealings with the inanimate world and with his fellows. And, as these basic guides are created by man to serve his purposes, they are subject to revision and change by him as he finds that his needs or purposes change. Nevertheless, it is observable that man does not change these basic guides very often or very rapidly. They have a considerable degree of stability as a result of inertia and the fixity of man's habits. They are like buildings

as they carry rather favorable implications; those who are not friendly to the "empirical" theory are inclined to use the latter two adjectives, which have acquired in their hands a definitely unfavorable connotation.

[2] As a recent writer well says:

"The fundamental legal philosophy in America today is still pragmatism. Its best known instance is of course sociological jurisprudence as developed by Roscoe Pound. In a revolt against nineteenth century idealism Pound imported European ideas of the nature of law, fitted them to current pragmatic theories of philosophy, and with their aid gradually reworked the whole structure of American legal thought."

Cowan, "A Report on the Status of Philosophy of Law in the United States," 50 COL. L. REV. 1086 at 1092 (1950).

[3] See again the discussion of the important uses of language, directive and informative, in secs. 1–07 *et seq.*

which have been constructed and which for a long time endure unchanged. The buildings can be torn down and replaced by others when they cease to meet the needs of those who use them. So, the guides and criteria for proper action, built by man, are observed to be quite solid and lasting, and yet, they are also subject to be revised or discarded when they prove inadequate or cease to serve as satisfactory guides for man's activities.

But I would be leaving my account of the factors which enter into policy determination in an incomplete and one-sided form if I did not present another theory in regard to basic criteria of justice. This theory, which I shall call the "higher law" theory,[4] has always been represented in our American legal thinking. It declares that the "empirical" theory does not tell the whole story; in fact, it does not tell the most important part of the story about criteria of justice. The "higher law" theory postulates criteria which are outside human experience and are not created by man. This theory "has had a longer, continuous history than perhaps any other which still finds enlightened adherents in any field of thought."[5] It has been consistently maintained by Christian doctrine, and notably in the doctrine of the Roman Catholic Church, from St. Augustine and St. Thomas Aquinas to the modern neo-scholastics. The theory was accepted by the founders of our republic, who gave definite expression to it in the Declaration of Independence and the Preamble to the Constitution. In its secular form,

[4] Other names applied to the various forms which the "higher law" takes in the writings of its different adherents are "law of nature," "natural law," "moral law," and "Divine Law."

[5] Dickinson, "The Law Behind Law," 29 COL. L. REV. 113 at 114 (1929). Actually, the "higher law" theory takes various forms. But for our purposes only two are important: 1, the secular form or theory of natural law, and 2, the religious form, of which the best known type is neo-scholasticism. Other forms, illustrated in modern writing, such as the theories of Stammler, Kohler, and others, have had no marked influence on current American thinking, and are therefore not to be specifically discussed herein. For a discussion of them, see STONE, THE PROVINCE AND FUNCTION OF LAW (1946).

as a theory of "natural law," the theory can count among its supporters a substantial share of the best-known philosophers, moralists, and legal thinkers, from Plato and Aristotle, through Kant and Hegel, to writers of the present day.

A full exploration of these two theories and their implications would call for an extended voyage into the perilous seas of legal philosophy. In fact, a full exploration would furnish ample subject matter for a course for advanced students of our legal system. I am sure I am not justified in going far in the examination of these theories in this introductory survey; but I do think I am warranted in presenting here an abbreviated comparison of the two theories, together with their implications, because both theories figure prominently in American thinking about the fundamentals of law.* My statement will be aimed to explain problems and

* (I.R.) Suggestions for further reading on the matter of this section:
Cahn, E., The Sense of Injustice (1949).
Cohen, F., Ethical Systems and Legal Ideals (1933).
Cook, "Scientific Method and the Law," 13 A. B. A. J. 303 (1927).
Corwin, "The 'Higher Law' Background of American Constitutional Law," 42 Harv. L. Rev. 149, 365 (1928).
Cowan, "A Report on the Status of Philosophy of Law in the United States," 50 Col. L. Rev. 1086 (1950).
Dickinson, "The Law Behind Law," 29 Col. L. Rev. 113, 285 (1929).
Fuller, L., The Law in Quest of Itself (1940).
Haines, C., The Revival of Natural Law Concepts, Harvard Studies in Jurisprudence (1930).
Hall, J., Living Law in Democratic Society (1949).
Interpretations of Modern Legal Philosophies (Essays in Honor of Roscoe Pound) (1947).
Mermin, "The Study of Jurisprudence—A Letter to a Hostile Student," 49 Mich. L. Rev. 39 (1950).
My Philosophy of Law (By Sixteen American Scholars) (1941).
Patterson, "Pragmatism as a Philosophy of Law" (in The Philosopher of the Common Man) (1940).
Pound, R., Interpretations of Legal History, chapter VII, "An Engineering Interpretation" (1930).
Pound, R., Law and Morals (2nd ed., 1926).
Radin, "Natural Law and Natural Rights," 59 Yale L. J. 214 (1950).
Yntema, "The Implications of Legal Science," 10 N. Y. U. L. Q. Rev. 279 (1933).
See bibliography on this subject in Cowan, cited above; POUND, OUTLINE OF JURISPRUDENCE 48-59 (5th ed., 1943); and STONE, THE PROVINCE AND FUNCTION OF LAW 215 note (1946).
An exposition of Roman Catholic doctrine is furnished by FRIEDMANN,

positions without taking sides on the basic issues involved.[6] It will be as nearly objective as I know how to make it; though as an adherent of the "empirical" theory, I may manifest an unintentional bias for that theory. In any case I have no notion that the "empirical" theory is demonstrably right and the "higher law" theory can be shown to be wrong. When we get through this section of the text and the problems in the next section, I do not expect that anyone of you will have found occasion to change from the "higher law" view to the "empirical," or vice versa. At most I hope that some of you will have gotten clearer notions of the implications of the theory you adopt and that all of you will have acquired a tolerant attitude toward the theory you do not accept.[7]

The "higher law" theory holds that there are criteria of justice which lie beyond human reach. These criteria constitute "a system of independently existing and inherently valid law having its source wholly outside of government." [8] The

LEGAL THEORY, chapter 22 (2d ed., 1949) and LE BUFFE and HAYES, THE AMERICAN PHILOSOPHY OF LAW (1947).

One of the principal writers to reject the "higher law" view is Justice Holmes. See Collected Papers 310–316 (1920), an article entitled "Natural Law," first published in 32 HARV. L. REV. 40 (1918). A highly sympathetic statement of Holmes' philosophy and views is presented by LERNER, THE MIND AND FAITH OF JUSTICE HOLMES (1943). For a critical analysis of Holmes' views by a Catholic writer, see Ford, "The Fundamentals of Holmes' Juristic Philosophy," a paper included in an appendix to the work by Le Buffe and Hayes, above cited.

[6] It is with great diffidence that I attempt such a statement. A simple statement on this subject is not easy to prepare. It is apt to turn out to be oversimple and unsatisfactory to all parties. Indeed, I have tried hard to convince myself that it is unnecessary, and to find a rational basis for avoiding the task. I make the statement only because I have found that each time that I take up the matter of policy determination with a class, the discussion leads invariably into questions regarding "higher law" criteria of justice; to pass over this subject entirely, leaves many of the most earnest members of the class quite unsatisfied.

[7] Much of the writing in favor of each theory is polemical in character. This seems to me both unfortunate and unnecessary. Each theory can be stated in tenable form and each is entitled to respectful treatment by those who do not accept it.

[8] Dickinson, "The Law Behind Law," 29 COL. L. REV. 113 at 114 (1929).

"higher law" is ascribed to a superhuman source, to Nature or more specifically to man's nature, or to Divine Legislation. The "higher law" is absolute, immutable, and final. It requires no demonstration or proof, as it is self-evident, like the axioms of mathematics.[9] It is revealed to man by intuition or reason. The "higher law" stands, accordingly, like a super-constitution above human policy makers, as our Federal Constitution stands above the acts of federal and state officials.[10] It affords limitations on governmental actions. It is a barrier against unreasonable policies and methods. In addition, the "higher law" serves as source for legislative ideas and policies. It furnishes a positive basis from which to deduce or derive particular policies, such as the policy of protecting the individual's personality, from the intrinsic value of human life, and the policy of free contract, from the fundamental doctrine favoring individual self-assertion.[11] In the words of a recent writer, the functions of the "higher law" are "to guide, to criticize, and to measure the law as made by legislators and applied by judges so as to keep it in reasonable and just channels."[12]

Now with these two theories in mind, it will be worth while to compare them and their implications.

[9] Though the untrained and unenlightened may have unclear, imperfect or mistaken perceptions of the "higher law" as they may. of the axioms of mathematics.

[10] As a matter of fact, I think it is evident, from the various pronouncements of the founding fathers, that they believed they were embodying principles of the "higher law" in the constitutions which they framed, notably, in their declarations regarding popular sovereignty, the separation of powers, and the rights of the individual. (Bill of Rights, adopted in the form of the first eight amendments.)

[11] Perhaps it is fair to say that the two lines of theory, "higher law" and "empirical," lay emphasis on different aspects of the thinking process. The "higher law" theory puts greater stress on the deductive side of thinking; it is more concerned with what it can derive from its premises. The "empirical" theory is more concerned with the way it derives its premises and accordingly lays more stress on the inductive procedures. Of course, all thinking involves both generalization (induction) and the use of general premises (deduction); neither can really be ignored. I refer merely to the matter of focus of interest and corresponding emphasis.

[12] HAINES, REVIVAL OF NATURAL LAW CONCEPTS 306 (1930).

The "higher law" theory seems to enjoy a substantial advantage in its proffer of stable and permanent criteria. But this advantage, it is argued by the "empirical" theorist, is really illusory. Criteria of right, and of right governmental policy, have not in fact remained constant throughout human history. Not only does history show that laws and usages have varied and changed among mankind, but that such fundamental criteria as have been propounded by "higher law" theorists, have also varied and changed. Almost any practice which would be condemned today as violative of a "higher law," from polygamy and promiscuous sex relations to ruthless treatment of individuals and groups, has, at many times and stages in the history of mankind, been pursued as an approved policy.[13] The way the "higher law" theorist of today meets this difficulty is to say that the criteria which he now accepts have existed always and to treat the deviations from his criteria as aberrations.[14] He does not admit that his criteria are affected by what persons of any age, or by what "higher law" theorists before him, have accepted. This, for example, is what the advocate of "higher law" does when he speaks of human slavery as contrary to natural, i.e., "higher," law. But Aristotle, one of the most illustrious supporters of the "higher law" theory, did not so regard the institution of slavery, as I have already pointed out.[15] Slavery was universal in his day and he justified it as consonant with principles of natural law. No "higher law" theorist today would so define his criteria of justice as to permit slavery.[16] To the extent that the "higher law" theory takes the form of a

[13] SUMNER, FOLKWAYS (1906), chapters 6, 7, 8, 9, 10, and 15.

[14] Christian doctrine meets the problem of finding a stable and permanent "higher law" by deriving it from a single source, the Holy Scriptures. Christianity is said to be a part of the common law; it has strongly influenced American legal thinking. See POUND, THE SPIRIT OF THE COMMON LAW, chapter II: "Puritanism and the Law" (1921). Doctrines of the Jewish and other religions need not be considered here as they have not exerted immediate influence on notions of criteria of justice.

[15] See sec. 7–42 and note 1 thereto.

[16] See Chief Justice Marshall's opinion, quoted in sec. 7–46, problem 4.

natural law, its protagonists reach unanimous agreement only on two points, to wit, that there are fundamental criteria of justice, and that these criteria are beyond human control. In regard to the content of the criteria themselves the "higher law" theorists have never been able to agree.[17]

The "empirical" theory offers a ready account of variety and change in criteria of justice. These are relative, so it declares, to man's knowledge and his needs. General criteria, such as the welfare of the individual or the community or the group, are more or less emphasized at different times and places; and the specific forms of criteria of justice which are recognized, e.g., the individual and social interests which are protected, also vary with times and circumstances. In short, criteria of justice are relative and changing, not absolute and permanent. But, in opposition to this account, it is argued that the "empirical" theory abandons any real criteria in order to reach this logical result. Indeed, it is argued that the "empirical" theorist, when he derives his criteria from human sources, is faced with the dilemma of choosing criteria on a mere count of noses, or else of finding no criteria at all. What makes a policy or an act wrong according to the "empirical" theory? Is it the fact that the policy or act runs counter to a generally received opinion of the community? [18]

[17] After speaking of the long and fruitful history of the ideal of natural law, Felix Cohen says:

"It is not remarkable, then, that in so long and adventurous a history the doctrine of natural law should have been subject to widely divergent interpretations. In general, we may distinguish two main ingredients in this concept, ingredients which have been mixed in all proportions. There is first the notion of value. Natural law is primarily the law that ought to be. The second ingredient in the concept of natural law is the element of universality. Not only have these two elements been united in various ways, but occasionally one or the other has appeared alone in the natural law doctrine. It is with these extremes that our analysis of the theory can best begin." ETHICAL SYSTEMS AND LEGAL IDEALS 101–102 (1933).

[18] Theories of a social compact and of a general will once propounded as the bases for governmental authority, also served as intellectual devices through which to establish general or objective criteria of justice. Since the unreality of the supposed compact and general will have been made apparent, criteria resting on these bases have vanished from the practical scene.

Are criteria matters of majority opinion? Are they matters of the transitory opinions of rulers and policy makers? If so, what criteria does one have to oppose to the Nazi policy of exterminating Jews, or to the Soviet policy of utilizing slave labor? In fine, the "empirical" theory seems to be caught between a choice, on the one hand, of majority views in the world community or in smaller communities, and a choice, on the other hand, of the views of some governing minority, such as the officialdom of the time and place or an elite group such as the Fascist leadership which purports to know what is best for the community.

To these criticisms of his relativist views, the "empirical" theorist makes two answers. First, he says that variety of criteria and relativity of criteria cannot fairly be treated as a lack of any criteria at all; that, in fact, community criteria and opinions, and group criteria and opinions, do furnish real ideals; and that, though these ideals may manifest differences and variations, they also manifest a considerable degree of agreement among the communities of the world, or at least among those communities which we would call the civilized world. The acts of the Nazis and of the Soviet government are opposed by a real world opinion, and the spearhead of the opposition, the governments which led to the public condemnation and punishment of the Nazi crimes against humanity which now stand against the ruthless policies of Russia, are the British Commonwealth and the United States, in both of which the "empirical" theory of justice is now predominant. Second, the "empirical" theorist answers that if this welter of variant criteria is all that we have, we may as well admit the fact; that even the criteria which any "higher law" theorist proposes are but community or group ideals decorated with honorific adjectives; that what makes his criteria seem final, natural, and necessary to the "higher law" theorist is the fact that these are the criteria which he has been brought up with. Accordingly, so runs this answer, when we talk of a "higher law" as a basis for a policy, for a piece of legislation, or for a decision, "we are merely applying our own social standards and the *mores* of our own 'chosen' people and asserting for them the quality of universality and perfection." [19]

The obvious reply of the "higher law" theory to this last assertion is that the "higher law" and man's rational nature (not his experiences), are what fix in him the criteria he calls natural. Hence, English and American officials, in asserting human claims and rights against Nazi and Soviet tyrannies, are really expressing and responding to their perceptions of the "higher law." And so we wind up here in a sort of impasse: the one theory attributing basic criteria to human inductions, the other attributing them to a "higher law" implanted in man by Nature or the Divine Will.

Is there any solution to this impasse? I believe not. The two lines of theory start with different articles of faith and there is no way to settle the difference of basic beliefs. No theory undertakes to prove the soundness of all the premises on which it stands. As regards the "higher law" theory, the acceptance of certain premises on faith is obvious. [20] But I think it is sometimes assumed by those who accept the "empirical" theory—and assumed with a sort of smug complacence—that "empirical" theory takes nothing for granted. This, of course, is not true. The "empirical" theory, like the

---

[19] Corbin, "Rights and Duties," 33 YALE L. J. 501 at 504 (1924).

[20] Thus, a recent neo-scholastic writer says:

"Realism certainly makes a truthful point when it contends that it is essentially skeptical while scholasticism relies heavily upon faith. True it is that scholasticism has faith in traditional law, in man, in his power to reason, in his free will, and in the capacity of the judge to decide legal problems according to rules and principles. Scholasticism does not contend that man is free from prejudice or emotion; that he never acts instinctively. Far from it. But the scholastic jurist believes that it is within the nature of mankind generally to subordinate these emotional factors especially when the problem at hand is the determination of the rights and duties of individuals according to law." KENNEDY, in MY PHILOSOPHY OF LAW (By Sixteen American Scholars) 153 (1941).

"higher law" theory, postulates basic propositions on faith and without proof. For example, in the field of action it assumes that effective action is possible and worth while; that man is able to control men and things through his acts and standards. In the field of knowledge, it has faith in the efficacy of investigative procedures and of experiment and observation as tests for truth. Can one demonstrate that experiment is a better way of arriving at conclusions than intuition is? Perhaps many of us believe that it is, but this is only an assumption, though a basic one. It seems, therefore, that both "empirical" theory and "higher law" theory accept many propositions on faith and cannot avoid it. On this point the two theories are alike, not different. The difference, as regards their articles of faith, lies in the fact that the "higher law" theory accepts its articles of faith as final, whereas the "empirical" theory treats those things which are accepted on faith and those which are regarded, at any particular time, as proven, as subject to rejection and revision if experience at a later stage shows them to be untenable. Its unproven assumptions, as well as those which are proven, are only provisionally accepted.

Among the articles of faith common to the "higher law" theory and the "empirical" theory, as they are developed in this country, are the major tenets of our democratic creed. This creed constitutes a system of policy assumptions and beliefs. The most important are the assumptions regarding equality of men, regarding liberty of the individual, and regarding popular participation in the determination of governmental measures. Opposed to these assumptions can be constructed an equally complete and systematic group of premises, coupled with the aristocratic way of life. Such assumptions were part and parcel of Plato's political creed. Often, those of us who have had a democratic upbringing naively assume that no other political creed than ours can be entertained by any reasonable person. Quite the contrary is true. Our democratic beliefs are not only wines of recent vintage, but they have not been accepted as generally as the aristocratic kind. The aristocratic creed is, both, more ancient and more prevalent in practice, even today. I do not mean to challenge your faith in democracy. I share the same faith. I do mean to say that many persons, groups, and governments, in the course of history, have not shared our beliefs, and many even today do not share our "enlightened" point of view.

As is suggested in the last paragraph, the two major theories we are discussing are able to get together on the essentials of our democratic creed. This suggests a further important observation—the criteria of justice which are propounded by the adherents of the two theories are not too far apart. Regardless of how they are said to originate and regardless of whether they are viewed as final and absolute or as provisional and relative, the criteria which are offered are not very different and do not lead to widely divergent practical applications.[21] Both lines of theory find room for all the main individual and social interests which we have previously discussed. Only in two areas are the practical differences of any consequence. These are the areas of individual life and personality and of family relationships. Some "empirical" theorists might make a place for euthanasia and abortions, and for radical changes in legally approved sexual relationships. Practically all "empirical" theorists support sterilization, birth control, and liberal provisions for divorce. Certainly, all these measures and the policies they represent run counter to the basic tenets of Roman Catholics, the largest group in our American community which adheres to the thesis of a law above human law. According to these tenets, human life has a divine origin and marriage is a divine

[21] This fact is somewhat obscured by the tendency of adherents of both views to argue in an emotional and polemic fashion.

institution; and legislative policies along the lines mentioned are violative of the "higher law" and do not bind the consciences of individuals or officials.[22]

Part of the explanation of the fact that the two theories wind up in positions which are not too far apart is found in the fact that the two theories start with important common articles of faith; both take for granted the free will of actors, both take for granted that man can control his environment, both take for granted that human behavior can be guided by standards, by prescribed methods, and by idealized goals. But another part of the explanation of the similarity of the criteria propounded by the two theories inheres in the fact that the "higher law" theorist recognizes the validity of the "empirical" method in wide areas. He recognizes that there are fields in which his basic criteria are not involved. He recognizes the possibility of scientific study of human behavior in these areas and the propriety of applying the lessons of science therein. For example, the "higher law" theory would not purport to offer a solution of all problems regarding legal methods or legal machinery. It would not decide whether it is better to have written or oral pleadings in lawsuits, or whether it is better to provide for trial by jury or trial by judge. Furthermore, the "higher law" theory would recognize that there are areas in which its criteria would not determine what goals the policy maker may pursue. The "higher law" theory does not purport to cover all choices of the policy maker any more than human laws cover all choices of individuals and officials. In these uncovered areas, criteria of expediency apply, or, as I would prefer to say, "empirical" criteria.[23] So, in these areas, the policy maker

[22] Roman Catholic doctrine on this general subject is fully and explicitly stated in the ENCYCLICAL OF POPE PIUS XI "On Christian Marriage," Dec., 1930 (Paulist Press).

[23] Probably advocates of the two theories would not fix areas where "empirical" criteria apply in quite the same manner. It is even possible that I exaggerate the size of the area which neo-scholastics would concede to be

is guided at most by the kind of criteria which science can provide. In other words, both lines of theory come together in these areas where the "higher law" theory concedes that policy determinations are beyond its sway. Here, both lines of theory come together in recognizing that "empirical" criteria are applicable to policy determinations, and also in recognizing the privilege and discretion of human agencies freely to determine policies. Both lines of theory would agree, for example, that the human policy maker is competent to deal as he will with most problems in the fields of contract and property; that he may, in the light of human experience, expand or retract the area of free contract; that he may, on this basis, foster monopoly or restrict it; that he may, on the same basis, change the incidents of the ownership of property, and change the types of private property which are allowed and disallowed.[24] Indeed, I would say that these areas where the policy maker can look to experience and use his own judgment include most areas in which human law is applicable.

Both lines of theory recognize the possibility of actual policy determinations which deviate from the criteria which they propound. The "empirical" theory explains such deviations merely as typical divergencies of the actual from the ideal, found in all human affairs. The "higher law" theory condemns such deviations more emphatically, but nevertheless recognizes the possibility of "unjust" policy determina-

uncovered by "higher law." Perhaps, too, I do not put my points in just the way that neo-scholastics would put them. I cannot claim to have a complete understanding of their doctrine. However, I regard all of the possible reservations I have mentioned as beside my main point and believe that all "higher law" theorists would grant that point.

[24] The text states the present condition of both law and theory. It is worth noting, however, that every important legislative change in the fields of contract and property, made during the last century, has had to run the gauntlet of serious challenges. Statutes changing rights of inheritance, statutes restricting permissible uses of property, statutes fixing hours of labor and wages, statutes fixing prices of goods, have all been attacked (and sometimes successfully) as unconstitutional, or contrary to natural law, or both.

tions. From early Greek times down to the present day those who have maintained the "higher law" theory have recognized that human governments can make and enforce unjust laws. As an individual may violate the provisions of human and "higher law," governmental agencies can pursue policies such as Hitler's policy of destroying the Jews, which run counter to the "higher law." Sometimes the "higher law" theorist insists, with St. Augustine, that "a law that is not just, seems to be no law at all." [25] But St. Thomas Aquinas and the neo-scholastics do not deny that unjust laws can be and are made. The purport of their theory is, simply, that such laws ought not to be made.[26]

[25] At this point we can easily fall into what Cardozo calls mere "verbal disputations." NATURE OF THE JUDICIAL PROCESS 133 (1921). We can become involved in an equivocation about the definition of law. Two definitions are important for the present purpose. First is a definition which would include human laws and the "higher law" in one category, but which would give the "higher law" a superior status. In this sense, it would be said, in line with the dictum from St. Augustine, that human law which runs counter to the "higher law" is no law at all, just as we say in the United States that a statute which violates a constitutional provision is not law. In other words, within the hierarchy of legislation, one law is inferior to, and must give way to, another, in case of conflict between them. But, second, law may be used more narrowly to include only the standards, goals, and methods formulated and promulgated by human government. This is the sense in which I have used the term law up to the beginning of the present section, where we began our discussion of criteria of justice. In this sense, a law may be created by governmental agencies which is unjust and contrary to the criteria of justice postulated by the "higher law" theory or worked out by the "empirical" theory. Indeed, if we resolve to define law in this narrower sense, it is better to call these extrinsic criteria by the name of *morals*. In that case, I believe that not a few adherents of the "empirical" theory would be prepared to assert that there are principles of *morals* which are superior to human law and further that these principles are stable and permanent.

[26] St. Thomas Aquinas says:

"Laws framed by man are either just or unjust. If they be just, they have the power of binding in conscience, from the eternal law whence they are derived, according to Prov. viii. 15: *By Me kings reign, and lawgivers decree just things*. Now laws are said to be just, both from the end, when, to wit, they are ordained to the common good,—and from their author, that is to say, when the law that is made does not exceed the power of the lawgiver,—and from their form, when, to wit, burdens are laid on the subjects, according to an equality of proportion and with a view to the common good." *The Summa Theologica*, part II (first part). Literally Translated by Fathers of the English Dominican Province, Third Number, 69 (1927), as quoted in HALL'S READINGS IN JURISPRUDENCE 39 (1938).

Human sanctions to effectuate criteria of "higher law" or of "social justice" are not numerous or widely operative. Religious sanctions can be effective within the range where believers are affected. But legal sanctions are not ordinarily available for the very reason that the persons to be controlled are themselves in control of the legal system. The result is that neither the "higher law" theory nor the "empirical" theory undertakes to define very specifically what will happen by way of retribution or correction when, for example, the Nazis determine on a policy of exterminating Jews, or the Soviets on a policy of slave labor. The "higher law" theorist states consequences in terms of conscience; the policy maker violates the dictates of conscience when he acts, and persons supposed to be bound are not bound in conscience. And the "empirical" theorist offers nothing more definite by way of human sanctions to effectuate his criteria of "social justice"; he relies on public opinion of some sort. Obviously, public opinion does not interpose any serious practical barrier to measures which are pursued by a government entrenched in power and possessed of control over the agencies of propaganda and education that operate in the community. However, it is worth remembering that in the United States the Supreme Court is in a position to effectuate criteria of justice as it sees them. The Court can make its criteria effective against policy determinations and acts of other organs of our government. As Haines says: "The United States is practically alone in placing supercensors over its legislative chambers with often nothing more than the elusive rule of reason as a standard." [27] This means that the Supreme Court's policy notions supply the need for criteria of justice; it also means that the Court is able to effectuate its notions. Its policy notions represent collectively the criteria of an elite

---

[27] THE REVIVAL OF NATURAL LAW CONCEPTS 343 (1930); and as this writer says further: "The ultimate standard of what is reasonable or fair is the judicial conscience." *Ibid.* 344.

group. The Constitution itself was framed by an elite group of men at a time when belief in liberty and equality of individuals stood at the highest level in history. And unquestionably the criteria of justice which the Supreme Court reads into the Constitution are more exacting than most parts of our community would recognize. The fact that the Supreme Court is in a position to, and does, effectuate its criteria of justice serves in part to explain the relatively lesser interest in "higher law" in this country than in Europe. There has not been the strongly felt need here for a superhuman law to restrain human policy makers.[28]

The criteria propounded by the two lines of theory we are comparing are alike in another way; both lines of criteria are very general. Both lines fail to offer much in the way of direct guidance to the policy maker. For example, Bentham, who may be classified as an "empirical" theorist, lists four "subordinate" ends to be pursued by the legislator: subsistence, abundance, equality, and security for the individual; he offers the greatest happiness of the greatest number as an over-all criterion. Pound, a modern "empirical" theorist, lists individual and social interests essentially like those we have listed in our inventories in the earlier parts of this chapter, and then offers a general criterion of the "most efficacious social engineering," or, as he also says, a picture of giving effect to the maximum of human wants with the least sacrifice of other wants. The criteria offered by "higher law" theorists are essentially similar, though cast in different terms, and are likewise indefinite and general.[29] None of the programs offered by "empirical" or by "higher

[28] European countries have had recent bitter experience with dictators' acts and have not had any effective barriers to oppose against them.

[29] See, for example, the passage from St. Thomas Aquinas quoted in note 26 above. See, also, the discussion of Kohler's criteria by Pound, "Interpretations of Legal History," Chapter VII. Kohler talks in terms of maintaining existing values of civilization and creating new values. He says the goal of law is the "furthering of civilization through a forcible ordering of things."

law" theorists provides the policy maker with a simple guide for selecting policies to pursue, or a ready method for solving conflicts such as the conflict between the social interest in free speech and the social interest in the safety of the state. Both programs are so general that they leave opportunity for widely divergent interpretations and for disputes regarding applications.[30] Without an authoritative interpreter to tell the policy maker just what these criteria mean as applied to the specific policy determinations which he has to make, they cannot control his determinations in any direct sense.[31]

Nevertheless, the criteria of justice propounded by the two groups of theorists have real importance. They establish attitudes toward problems of policy determination. They adjure the policy maker to look beyond immediate ends, to goals which might not so readily be thought of. They call his attention to enduring, as against transitory, advantages. They involve a stress on, and a generalization of, the complex factors that enter into policy determination. In short, the invocation of a "higher law" and the reliance on "social justice" alike represent methods of dealing with legal problems in a wide perspective. And what is just as significant, both theories rest on a clear and definite faith in man's ability to shape his affairs according to ideals. Both involve a belief in the efficacy of man's efforts to control his relation-

[30] Indeed, it is a common observation in human affairs that the best principle can be misconstrued and used for an improper purpose. As Shakespeare says, "The devil can cite Scripture for his purpose." (*The Merchant of Venice*, Act I, Scene 1, line 9.) And we hardly need to be reminded of the pious-sounding doctrines which the Nazis cited to cover some of their worst misdeeds. Of course, in these cases, the citations were usually accompanied by actual misrepresentations of fact.

[31] Neo-scholastic doctrine does provide an authoritative interpreter to make interpretations so far as they involve the Word of God; final and infallible interpretive authority belongs to the head of the Roman Catholic Church. A comparable authority to interpret criteria of justice, so far as they are embodied in our Federal Constitution, can be said to belong to the Supreme Court. But the interpretations of these two agencies would only be recognized within limited spheres. There is no agency with universally accepted interpretive authority to construe the criteria of justice propounded by "higher law" theory or by "empirical" theory.

ships by standards. Both involve a faith in human progress.[32] The two theories may diverge from one another in their accounts of the origin and nature of our ideals. This divergence is important; and I see no way to erase it. But, practically, the difference is not as important and significant as the fact that both lines of theory stand together in postulating man's ability to shape his destiny according to his ideals of justice.

Sec. 7–46. Problems. 1. The Declaration of Independence (1776) begins with this sentence: "We hold these truths to be self-evident, that all men are created equal, that they are endowed by their Creator with certain unalienable Rights, that among these are Life, Liberty and the pursuit of Happiness."

How would an "empirical" theorist state essentially these same points?

[32] It may be argued that the "higher law" theory is not as progressive in tendency as the "empirical" theory inasmuch as the "higher law" theory postulates fixed and final criteria of justice. Of course, the "higher law" theory does not allow for change in its criteria, and this may mean that its criteria are not as adaptable as "empirical" criteria. But in fact, criteria of "higher law" are so general that they are adaptable to most changes of conditions. Thus, "higher law" theory has been invoked quite as often by those who advocated change to conform to ideals, as by those who opposed change and maintained that existing conditions were just what they ought to be. "Higher law" criteria have served again and again as revolutionary battle cries; that was their function when they were asserted at the beginning of our Republic against the pretensions and arbitrary acts of the British Government. And "higher law" theorists have been found quite as often in modern times among the advocates of social reform as "empirical" theorists. As one neo-scholastic writer says:

"It may surprise realist reformers to be informed that thirty years before the United States Supreme Court declared the Minimum Wage Law of the District of Columbia to be unconstitutional, Pope Leo XIII vehemently defended the right of the worker to a living wage in his famous encyclical, RERUM NOVARUM, and argued for such economic reform on the ground of natural law and natural justice. Incidentally, in this same encyclical will be found a plea for social and economic laws to improve the health, strength, housing, and factory conditions of wage earners, with particular regard to women and children—all proposed and defended in accordance with the law of God and the nature of man." KENNEDY in MY PHILOSOPHY OF LAW 159 (1941).

2. In his famous dissent in *Abrams v. United States*,[1] Holmes, J., expresses the following views on the subject of freedom of speech and opinion:

"Persecution for the expression of opinions seems to me perfectly logical. If you have no doubt of your premises or your power and want a certain result with all your heart you naturally express your wishes in law and sweep away all opposition. . . . But when men have realized that time has upset many fighting faiths, they may come to believe even more than they believe the very foundations of their own conduct that the ultimate good desired is better reached by free trade in ideas—that the best test of truth is the power of the thought to get itself accepted in the competition of the market, and that truth is the only ground upon which their wishes safely can be carried out. That at any rate is the theory of our Constitution. It is an experiment, as all life is an experiment. Every year if not every day we have to wager our salvation upon some prophecy based upon imperfect knowledge. While that experiment is part of our system I think that we should be eternally vigilant against attempts to check the expression of opinions that we loathe and believe to be fraught with death, unless they so imminently threaten immediate interference with the lawful and pressing purposes of the law that an immediate check is required to save the country."

What basic premise does Holmes adopt here? How far would you say he adopts it on faith? How far on the basis of experience?

Does he recognize the possibility of adopting another basic premise?

Does his position here accord with the "empirical" theory of the basis for criteria of justice?

3. *Loan Association v. Topeka*.[2]

Miller, J.:

"It must be conceded that there are such rights in every free government beyond the control of the State. A govern-

[1] 250 U. S. 616 at 630 (1919).
[2] 20 Wall. (U. S.) 655 at 662 (1874).

ment which recognized no such rights, which held the lives, the liberty, and the property of its citizens subject at all times to the absolute disposition and unlimited control of even the most democratic depository of power, is after all but a despotism. It is true it is a despotism of the many, of the majority, if you choose to call it so, but it is none the less a despotism. It may well be doubted if a man is to hold all that he is accustomed to call his own, all in which he has placed his happiness, and the security of which is essential to that happiness, under the unlimited dominion of others, whether it is not wiser that this power should be exercised by one man than by many.

"The theory of our governments, State and National, is opposed to the deposit of unlimited power anywhere. The executive, the legislative, and the judicial branches of the governments, are all of limited and defined powers.

"There are limitations on such power which grow out of the essential nature of all free governments. Implied reservations of individual rights, without which the social compact could not exist, and which are respected by all governments entitled to the name. No court, for instance, would hesitate to declare void a statute which enacted that A. and B. who were husband and wife to each other should be so no longer, but that A. should thereafter be the husband of C., and B. the wife of D. Or which should enact that the homestead now owned by A. should no longer be his, but should henceforth be the property of B."

On what does Miller, J., predicate the "higher law"?

4. *The Antelope.*[3] An American privateer harassing Spanish ships during the South American revolts against Spain seized slaves from Spanish and Portuguese vessels. The Supreme Court held that on the facts proved, all of the slaves should be disposed of according to United States law, except those shown to have been the property of Spanish claimants, which should be turned over to those claimant owners. As to the contention that these slaves should not

[3] 10 Wheat. (U. S.) 66 at 120–122 (1825).

be returned, since the slave trade was contrary to the law of nations, Marshall, C. J., said:

"The question, whether the slave trade is prohibited by the law of nations, has been seriously propounded, and both the affirmative and negative of the proposition have been maintained with equal earnestness.

"That it is contrary to the law of nature will scarcely be denied. That every man has a natural right to the fruits of his own labour, is generally admitted; and that no other person can rightfully deprive him of those fruits, and appropriate them against his will, seems to be the necessary result of this admission. But from the earliest times war has existed, and war confers rights in which all have acquiesced. Among the most enlightened nations of antiquity, one of these was, that the victor might enslave the vanquished. This, which was the usage of all, could not be pronounced repugnant to the law of nations, which is certainly to be tried by the test of general usage. That which has received the assent of all, must be the law of all.

"Slavery, then, has its origin in force; but as the world has agreed that it is a legitimate result of force, the state of things which is thus produced by general consent, cannot be pronounced unlawful.

"Throughout Christendom, this harsh rule has been exploded, and war is no longer considered as giving a right to enslave captives. But this triumph of humanity has not been universal. The parties to the modern law of nations do not propagate their principles by force; and Africa has not yet adopted them. Throughout the whole extent of that immense continent, so far as we know its history, it is still the law of nations that prisoners are slaves. Can those who have themselves renounced this law, be permitted to participate in its effects by purchasing the beings who are its victims?

"Whatever might be the answer of a moralist to this question, a jurist must search for its legal solution, in those principles of action which are sanctioned by the usages, the national acts, and the general assent, of that portion of the world of which he considers himself as a part, and to whose law the appeal is made. If we resort to this standard as the test of international law, the question, as has already been observed, is decided in favour of the legality of the trade. Both Europe and America embarked in it; and for nearly two centuries, it was carried on without opposition, and without censure. A jurist could not say, that a practice thus supported was illegal, and that those engaged in it might be punished, either personally, or by deprivation of property."

Here, Chief Justice Marshall distinguishes three kinds of law: the law of the United States, the law of nations, and natural law. How does he relate them to one another? Which law prevails when there is a conflict between natural law and either of the other types of law?

5. *State v. Malusky*.[4] On May 28, 1928, Joe Malusky entered a plea of guilty to a charge of engaging in the liquor traffic as a second offense. He was sentenced to serve a term of one year and six months in the state penitentiary. The statutes of North Dakota provided for an increased penalty upon conviction of a second offense involving moral turpitude. On appeal, Malusky contended that a violation of the state prohibitory act was not an offense involving moral turpitude. The Supreme Court of North Dakota, speaking through Nuessle, J., held that the violation of the prohibitory act was such an offense within the meaning of the statute. He said, in part:

"The fourth section of the act above quoted is that on which the appellant grounds this appeal. His first and chief contention is that the violation of the state prohibitory act, on account of which he was sentenced, though a felony, is not an offense involving moral turpitude.

"The term 'moral turpitude' is not new. It has been used in the law for centuries. It connotes something which is not clearly and certainly defined. See note in 43 Harvard L.

4 State v. Malusky, 59 N. D. 501 at 505–506 (1930).

Rev. p. 117. Generally it may be said that moral turpitude is evidenced by an act of baseness, vileness or depravity in the private and social duties which a man owes to his fellow man or to society in general. . . . Many cases may be found in the books dealing with the meaning of the term and attempting to apply it under varying facts and circumstances. Most of the cases seek to make a distinction between offenses mala prohibita and mala in se, and hold that only offenses mala in se involve moral turpitude. If this be the test it avails us little for the difficulty then is to discern the line between the two. History discloses that all offenses were at some time merely mala prohibita and as civilization advanced and social and moral ideals and standards changed they became one after another mala in se. Moral turpitude 'is a term which conforms to and is consonant with the state of public morals; hence it can never remain stationary.' Drazen v. New Haven Taxicab Co. 95 Conn. 500, 111 Atl. 861. At one time the wilful killing of another was not considered evil in itself, and this is so among some savage peoples today. At one time honor was vindicated and guilt and innocence determined by mortal combat between factions or individuals. Even now killing is justified in time of war. Larceny became an offense only as property rights were defined and society sought to benefit itself and protect the individual by penalizing the appropriation of property by those who could not justify such appropriation by the prescribed rules. Sexual crimes became such only as man progressed in civilization. At one time, not so greatly remote, prostitution was not regarded as immoral and in some countries is not even now banned by the law. However much every man may be answerable for his acts to his own conscience, society cannot permit each individual to say for it what is moral and what is immoral. To him who deliberately kills, murder is not immoral. To him who steals, larceny is not immoral. To him who lives only for the gratification of his appetites there is no immorality in doing so. Some standard must exist according to which the determination as to whether act or conduct is moral or immoral is to be made. That standard is public sentiment— the expression of the public conscience. It may be manifest, unwritten, and more or less nebulous, as legend, as tradition, as opinion, as custom, and finally crystallized, written as the law. Thus the standard is fixed by the consensus of opinion, the judgment of the majority. When the majority is slight there is, of course, greater opposition on the part of the minority to the standard. The majority may become the minority and the standard change. But so long as it is established, measurement must be made according to its terms. So we must say that those things which are discountenanced and regarded as evil and accordingly forbidden by society, are immoral and that the doing of them contrary to the sentiment of society thus expressed involves moral turpitude, and this regardless of the punishment imposed for their doing."

Reversed on other grounds.

How does Nuessle, J., establish a standard of moral turpitude? Does he reject "higher law" criteria of right and wrong?

6. In *Hoff v. State of New York*,[5] Lehman, J., said regarding the remedy of habeas corpus:

"Our constitutional guarantees of liberty are merely empty words unless a person imprisoned or detained against his will may challenge the legality of his imprisonment and detention. The writ of habeas corpus is the process devised centuries ago for the protection of free men. It has been cherished by generations of free men who had learned by experience that it furnished the only reliable protection of their freedom."

What assumption regarding the goals of our legal system does Lehman, J., make? Obviously a dictator (or an official acting on his orders) would not make the same assumption.

For what purpose does Lehman, J., have recourse to experience?

7. *Buck v. Bell.*[6] Mr. Justice Holmes delivered the opinion of the Court:

"This is a writ of error to review a judgment of the Supreme Court of Appeals of the State of Virginia, affirming

[5] 279 N. Y. 490 at 492 (1939), quoted at length in sec. 5–13, problem 3.
[6] 274 U. S. 200 at 205, 207 (1927).

a judgment of the Circuit Court of Amherst County, by which the defendant in error, the superintendent of the State Colony for Epileptics and Feeble Minded, was ordered to perform the operation of salpingectomy upon Carrie Buck, the plaintiff in error, for the purpose of making her sterile. 143 Va. 310. The case comes here upon the contention that the statute authorizing the judgment is void under the Fourteenth Amendment as denying to the plaintiff in error due process of law and the equal protection of the laws. . . .

"The attack is not upon the procedure but upon the substantive law. It seems to be contended that in no circumstances could such an order be justified. It certainly is contended that the order cannot be justified upon the existing grounds. The judgment finds the facts that have been recited and that Carrie Buck 'is the probable potential parent of socially inadequate offspring, likewise afflicted, that she may be sexually sterilized without detriment to her general health and that her welfare and that of society will be promoted by her sterilization,' and thereupon makes the order. In view of the general declarations of the legislature and the specific findings of the Court, obviously we cannot say as matter of law that the grounds do not exist, and if they exist they justify the result. We have seen more than once that the public welfare may call upon the best citizens for their lives. It would be strange if it could not call upon those who already sap the strength of the State for these lesser sacrifices, often not felt to be such by those concerned, in order to prevent our being swamped with incompetence. It is better for all the world, if instead of waiting to execute degenerate offspring for crime, or to let them starve for their imbecility, society can prevent those who are manifestly unfit from continuing their kind. The principle that sustains compulsory vaccination is broad enough to cover cutting the Fallopian tubes. *Jacobson v. Massachusetts*, 197 U. S. 11. Three generations of imbeciles are enough."

What does this opinion determine? Does it pass on the social desirability of sterilization? Does it decide the question whether sterilization is morally right?

Would a Roman Catholic judge be justified in issuing an order to sterilize a woman like Carrie Buck, pursuant to the provisions of a statute like the one involved here?*

8. At the conclusion of a record of his life, Henry L. Stimson appends an afterword which reads in part as follows:

"This book has recorded forty years spent largely in public life; from this record others may draw their own conclusions, but it seems not unreasonable that I should myself set down in a few words my own summing up. . . .

"No one can dispute the progress made by the man of today from the prehistoric man—mentally, morally, and spiritually. No one can dispute the humanitarian progress made more recently, since those times before the age of steam and electricity, when man's growth was limited by sheer starvation, and the law of Malthus was an immediate reality. . . .

"I have always believed that the long view of man's history will show that his destiny on earth is progress toward the good life, even though that progress is based on sacrifices and sufferings which taken by themselves seem to constitute a hideous mélange of evils.

"This is an act of faith. We must not let ourselves be engulfed in the passing waves which obscure the current of progress. The sinfulness and weakness of man are evident to anyone who lives in the active world. But men are also good and great, kind and wise. . . .

"I think the record of this book also shows my deep conviction that the people of the world and particularly our own American people are strong and sound in heart. We have been late in meeting danger, but not too late. We have been wrong but not basically wicked. And today with that

* (I.R.) As to conflicts between conscience and the human law, see Reynolds v. United States, 98 U. S. 145 (1878) (religious belief in polygamy); Jacobson v. Massachusetts, 197 U. S. 11 (1905) (religious belief opposed to vaccination); United States v. Schwimmer, 279 U. S. 644 (1929) (belief opposed to bearing arms); United States v. MacIntosh, 283 U. S. 605 (1931) (belief opposed to bearing arms); Hamilton v. Regents of University of California, 293 U. S. 245 (1934) (conscientious objection to military service).

strength and soundness of heart we can meet and master the future." [7]

What important articles of belief does this faithful public servant adopt?

How would his views take shape in criteria of justice? What would be his attitude toward improvement of the law?

9. Sir Austin Henry Layard quotes the following letter written by a Turkish Cadi to a friend of Layard's in response to "inquiries as to commerce, population and remains of antiquity of an ancient city, in which dwelt the head of the law:" [8]

"My illustrious Friend, and Joy of my Liver!

"The thing which you ask of me is both difficult and useless. Although I have passed all my days in this place, I have never counted the houses, nor inquired into the number of the inhabitants; and as to what one person loads on his mules and another stores away in the bottom of his ship, that is no business of mine. But, above all, as to the previous history of this city, God only knows the amount of dirt and confusion that the infidels may have eaten before the coming of the sword of Islam. . . . Listen, o my son! There is no wisdom equal unto the belief in God! He created the world, and shall we liken ourselves to him by seeking to penetrate into the mysteries of his creation? Shall we say, behold this star spinneth round that star, and this other star with a tail goeth and cometh in so many years! Let it go! He from whose hand it came will guide and direct it. . . . Thou art learned in the things I care not for, and as for that which thou hast seen, I defile it. Will much knowledge create thee a double belly, or wilt thou seek paradise with thine eyes? . . .

"The meek in spirit (El Fakir),
"Imaum Ali Zadi"

[7] STIMSON AND BUNDY, ON ACTIVE SERVICE IN PEACE AND WAR 671–672 (1948).

[8] NINEVEH AND BABYLON, A NARRATIVE OF A SECOND EXPEDITION TO ASSYRIA 1849–1851, 401–402 (1867).

What kind of position would you expect the Cadi to adopt toward changes and improvements in existing law?**

Compare his general attitude with Stimson's. What is the essential difference?

Sec. 7–47. General summary.[1] This completes our picture of the American legal system and its operation. The picture has been developed in terms of acts and standards for acts. In the first chapter, the role of language in the processes of legal control has been explained. In the second, the legal standards which serve as patterns for acts of the individual have been described, and we have seen how these standards are effectuated through acts and used in acts. In the third, legal standards for the guidance of official acts have been taken up and treated in a similar manner. In the fourth chapter, entitled Legislation, I have tried to show how standards are created by the legislature and by analogous subsidiary agencies; how these standards are stated; and when and where standards operate. In the fifth chapter, I have given an account of the processes by which legislative standards are interpreted; I have depicted the role of the judicial interpreter and the functions of rules of interpretation. In the sixth chapter I have offered an analysis of the procedures through which judges apply and make and unmake case law (precedents). And in the final chapter I have listed the recognized objectives or policies of American law; have described the modes in which governmental and other

---

** (I.R.) Compare what Pound says about the "give-it-up" philosophy, in Social Control Through Law 101 (1942); about belief in the futility of legislation, in The Spirit of the Common Law 46 (1931); and about juristic pessimism, in Interpretations of Legal History 66 (1930).

[1] The first paragraph of sec. 7–45 constitutes a resumé of the main points made in chapter 7. For this reason I dispense with the final section entitled "Summary" which I have appended at the conclusion of each of the other chapters. In its place I substitute a *general summary* to cover the entire work.

human agencies contribute to policy formulation; and have indicated how tradition and habit, and, according to one view, a "higher law" limit the determination and pursuit of policies.

From the beginning to the end of this portrayal, we have viewed the legal system as a going concern; we have examined the various uses that are made of standards and of prescribed methods to guide the behavior of individuals and officials; we have put stress on the instrumental character of the legal system and treated it as a mass of devices created by man to serve his needs.

TABLES

Table of Cases

General Index

[All references herein are to *section numbers*. The first figure in a section number indicates the chapter in which the section is to be found; the other figures, the position of the particular section in the chapter; thus section 6–10 is the tenth section in Chapter 6. This is primarily a *topical index. However, under the title Bibliography* will be found lists of recommended items for further reading.]

Offer and Acceptance. See Contracts.

Officials (O). See also Courts; Executive; Judge; Jury; Prosecutor; Significance of Official Acts; Social Interests; Standards for Official Acts.

effectuation of standards for individual through official acts, 2–29 to 2–42; 3–01 to 3–07.

use of standards for individual by officials, 2–45.

effectuation of standards for officials (O), 3–22 to 3–29.

need for effectuation against O—devices, 3–22; 3–24.

checks and balances—separation and integration of powers, 3–23.

control of inferior executives, 3–24.

control of chief executive, 3–25.

control of trial judge, 3–26; 3–29.

control of trial jury, 3–27; 3–29.

control of appellate judge, 3–28; 3–29, prob. 2.

use of standards for officials by various persons, 3–30 to 3–34.

use by executive officials, 3–30.

use by courts, 3–31; 3–34, prob. 1.

Order

significance of temporal order of acts, 2–27; 2–28.

peace and order. See Social Interests.

Overruling Precedents. See Common Law.

Party Presentation. See Actions.

Peace and Order. See Social Interests.

Penalties. See Individual Actor.

Permitted Acts

of individual, 2–05; 2–08; 2–13.

why legally defined, 2–05.

contractual permission, 2–05, n. 2.

relation to prohibited acts, 2–05; 2–05, n. **.

Persons, judicial control of persons and estates, 3–16.

Physical Acts. See also Verbal Acts.

distinguish control by force and by verbal acts, 1–09.

physical acts, 2–13; 2–13, n. 2; 304, n. 2.

Policies. See Law; Lawmaker; Legislation.

Popular Terms. See Interpretation of Legislation; Language.

Population, social control of, 7–22.

Powers

generally, 2–22; 3–02.

various meanings of, 2–22.

relation of powers and liabilities, 2–23.

effective acts and powers, 2–09 to 2–10; 2–22.

problems of classification and usage, 2–25.

powers of officials, 3–03; 3–05 to 3–21; 4–01 to 4–05; 4–28 to 4–34; 5–02; 5–16; 6–02; 6–03; 7–02 to 7–03; 7–34 to 7–38.